D0086355

Wetland Ecology

Principles and Conservation, Second edition.

Richly illustrated and packed with numerous examples, this unique global perspective introduces the fundamentals of wetland ecology from basic principles to advanced applications. Thoroughly revised and reorganized, this new two-color edition of this prize-winning textbook begins with underlying causal factors, before moving on to more advanced concepts that add depth and context.

- Examples carefully drawn from every major continent and wetland type give global context and help students see how their region fits into global patterns
- Many new illustrations and photographs increase the amount of natural history that supports the general principles
- A chapter on research methods provides useful guidance for the advanced student planning their own research
- Includes new chapters on wetland restoration and wetland services
- Clear chapter organization supports a wide variety of lecture plans, course objectives, and teaching styles

Paul A. Keddy, the first holder of the Schlieder Endowed Chair for Environmental Studies at Southeastern Louisiana University, has conducted wetland research as a professor of ecology for 35 years. He has published more than 100 scholarly papers on plant ecology and wetlands, as well as serving organizations such as the National Science Foundation, the National Science and Engineering Research Council of Canada, World Wildlife Fund, and The Nature Conservancy. His first edition of *Wetland Ecology: Principles and Conservation* won the Society of Wetland Scientists' Merit Award.

Wetland Ecology

Principles and Conservation

SECOND EDITION

PAUL A. KEDDY

CAMBRIDGE
UNIVERSITY PRESS

CAMBRIDGE
UNIVERSITY PRESS

University Printing House, Cambridge CB2 8BS, United Kingdom

One Liberty Plaza, 20th Floor, New York, NY 10006, USA

477 Williamstown Road, Port Melbourne, VIC 3207, Australia

314-321, 3rd Floor, Plot 3, Splendor Forum, Jasola District Centre, New Delhi - 110025, India

79 Anson Road, #06-04/06, Singapore 079906

Cambridge University Press is part of the University of Cambridge.

It furthers the University's mission by disseminating knowledge in the pursuit of education, learning and research at the highest international levels of excellence.

www.cambridge.org
Information on this title: www.cambridge.org/9780521739672

First published 2010
5th printing 2016

A catalogue record for this publication is available from the British Library

Library of Congress Cataloging in Publication data
Keddy, Paul A., 1953–
Wetland ecology : principles and conservation / Paul A. Keddy. – 2nd ed.
    p.   cm.
ISBN 978-0-521-51940-3 (Hardback)
ISBN 978-0-521-73967-2 (Pbk.)
1. Wetland ecology.   2. Wetland conservation.   I. Title.
QH541.5.M3K44 2000
577.68–dc22   2010009142

ISBN 978-0-521-51940-3 Hardback
ISBN 978-0-521-73967-2 Paperback

Additional resources for this publication at www.cambridge.org/9780521739672

Contents

The color plates are situated between pages 238 and 239

Preface to the second edition

Why a second edition? And how different is it from the first? These are two obvious questions that a writer must address. Overall, this is a major revision in form, but built around the same principles. Some chapters, such as Flooding and Fertility, are revised with new figures. Other chapters, including Services and functions and Restoration, are entirely new.

Having had ten years to observe reactions to the first edition, I now have a better understanding of how ecologists in general, and American students in particular, think about wetlands. I have therefore re-balanced and reorganized the book to better reflect these realities. At the same time, I have stuck to the view that a small number of general principles are needed to unify wetland ecology, and that a small set of causal factors are present in all wetlands, albeit in differing relative importance.

Over the book as a whole, I have reorganized the flow of ideas to place causal factors nearer the beginning, and in order of relative importance. Students, then, can start immediately with effects of flooding in Chapter 2 and fertility in Chapter 3. The more conceptually difficult material (such as zonation, biodiversity, and valuation of ecological services) has been moved to later in the book.

Each chapter begins with a few basic principles up front and early, usually accompanied by a few clear examples to illustrate the principle. The more difficult concepts are introduced later in each chapter. The inevitable exceptions also occur here – but only once the general principle is well established.

There is an entire new restoration chapter which draws upon practical examples from around the world, including the Everglades, coastal Louisiana, the Danube River, and the Yangtze River. As noted in the first edition, there is still an unfortunate tendency for wetland ecologists to work in geographical and taxonomic isolation, and this chapter tries to bring together a consistent worldwide perspective on restoration.

There is also a new chapter on research. I have moved certain topics to this chapter, in the view that an overview of tactics and strategies may be of most use to advanced students who are planning their own investigations.

Biodiversity conservation grows in importance with each passing year. I have rewritten the chapter on biodiversity to make the hierarchy of causation more clear. I have also introduced new information such as the IUCN *Red List* and principles for designing wetland reserve systems. I have also introduced wetland evaluation systems for land use planning.

I have removed examples and topics that time has taught were extraneous, and added in others, always trying to keep an international perspective, since wetland plants and animals do not recognize political borders. There are many new figures, including some drawn specifically for this book, as well as new photographs.

Names are always an issue. I have used common names for most groups where nomenclature is well established – particularly birds and mammals – but scientific names for plants and insects, owing to their diversity. In some cases, in appropriate context, I deviate from this rule. Since names continue to change (e.g. *Scirpus*, *Schoenoplectus*), I have resisted the temptation to make everything internally consistent. This sort of consistency introduces problems of its own – for example, if I were to change every incidence of *Scirpus* to *Schoenoplectus*, then students consulting the original papers could be misled. Hence, in most cases, I have used names that were current when the work was published.

One of the most basic principles of science is to have multiple working hypotheses. I have tried to include competing points of view in this book. I would like to think that we could encourage our students to accept that there are unknowns in science, and to respect differences of opinion as healthy, and as an opportunity for designing the research that will resolve the confusion.

Some people think the only way to read a book is to start at the beginning and plow through every word until the end, which might indeed seem challenging. This is not, in my opinion, the best option for using this book, or any book. Here are some others. (1) You could start by flipping through the book for just the color plates – they tell a story of their own. (2) Next you could choose a handful of black-and-white illustrations that catch your attention – each also tells a story. (3) You could read the first chapter for an overview of wetlands – the short story. (4) You could then read Chapters 2–8 that deal with causal factors in wetlands. (5) If you are a busy manager, you could consult Chapters 13 and 14 for restoration and conservation issues. (6) I would suggest that Chapters 9–12 be left for a second reading. They deal with more advanced topics that may be of more interest to graduate students and research scientists. (7) A very short course in wetlands and conservation would consist of Chapters 1 and 14 only. A longer course in wetlands and conservation would consist of Chapters 1–8 and 13–14. (8) Each chapter could also stand alone, so if there is a particular topic that you need to learn about – say nutrients or grazing – go directly to the chapter on that topic. (9) Finally, as I still have to remind my classes, there is an index. Use it. Some time has gone into selecting these topics. It is not just generated by a machine, but by human thought. Feel free to dive into a selected topic – say dams or coarse woody debris or amphibians or fire – and then work you way outward. Overall, the point is to make this book your own and use it in whatever way helps you grasp the material most quickly.

Although the volume of information on wetlands will always grow, I would like to think that the principles in this book are timeless, since wetlands themselves will always be organized by a few causal factors, leaving us with the task of documenting their consequences – for ecological processes, for surrounding landscapes, and for the wild species that live in wetlands.

PAUL KEDDY

Preface to the first edition

According to Bernard Shaw, writer of many a lengthy preface, the lesson intended by an author is hardly ever the lesson the world chooses to learn from his book. If Shaw is right (and who would risk disagreeing with him), why would anyone trouble to write a book? And why a book on wetlands?

In answer to the first question, the motivation of all writers includes a healthy dose of inspiration, frustration, and ego gratification. Events can conspire to feed these forces, with unfortunate consequences for both writers and the public. When Dr Birks first asked me to write this book, I therefore declined. In part, I was not convinced that a need existed.

Bringing a new book into the world requires the shouldering of parental obligations. (While one can keep one's rowdy children at home, a book is always on public display.) The world certainly has too many children, and only the most devoted reader, deep-pocketed publisher, or hardened bibliophile could believe that every author who is inclined towards writing should do so. The self-restraint that is a virtue in biological procreation, may be equally so for aspiring authors.

Events can, however, over-ride caution. Illness, like the threat of a hanging, tends to concentrate and clarify one's mind. Moreover, during the days chained to the wall before the hanging, one is inclined to dwell on shortcomings, particularly those of one's associates. But I digress. This is, after all, a preface to a book on wetlands.

The principal objective of this book is to try to provide some unity and coherence in the study of wetland ecology. To do so, I have organized this book into three sections. The first section (Chapters 1–3) emphasizes the properties of wetlands, or, in statistical terms, the dependent variables in our inquiry. The next section (Chapters 4–9) addresses the environmental factors that control these properties: in statistical terms, the independent variables. In these chapters, I freely range across wetland types and geographic regions. My self-assigned task is to illustrate the relationships among properties and environmental factors, whether they occur in an Amazonian floodplain, prairie pothole, boreal peatland or tidal marsh. The book may still tend to emphasize the types of wetlands with which I am most familiar, but this should not distract a reader from principles and scientific generalities. The final section (Chapters 10–12) illustrates some larger frameworks for studying the relationships between ecological properties and conservation biology. Assembly rules, functional groups, and restoration ecology receive particular attention.

The book has been prepared with several audiences in mind. It is intended as a text book for senior undergraduates, an introduction to key factors controlling wetlands for busy managers, and as general reading for any scientist intending to work in wet habitats. Further, the first chapter will, I hope, introduce the essential features of wetlands to a general reader; while superficial in places, it is less so than many popular treatises, and it will simultaneously remind more experienced readers about the salient features that make wetlands of particular interest to humanity. The main body of the book presents a general framework for the study of wetland communities. For practising wetland scientists I had an expanded purpose. The discipline of wetland ecology is currently Balkanized by habitat types, geographic regions, and study organisms. Many of the studies of particular wet habitats that I have read over the past decade have seemed blissfully unaware of nearly identical work in other habitats, wet or dry. By combining all wetland types within one book, I have tried to restore some conceptual unity to the discipline by emphasizing the essential processes that all wetlands share, and then by illustrating the ways in which some of them differ. Hence the part of the title referring to principles. I hope that specialists will be stimulated by seeing the parallel advances in habitat types and geographic regions other than their own, and that this enriched context will assist them with further progress within their own areas of specialization. In exchange, I trust they will forgive the inevitable oversights that annoy a specialist.

The final part of the title mentions conservation. Sound science is the essential foundation of good ecosystem management. Ecosystem management emphasizes ecological processes and their interconnections. This book takes exactly such a perspective: it begins with patterns present in wetlands, and then proceeds to the processes and interconnections that produce the patterns. The focus is upon communities and ecosystems themselves; implications for global biogeochemical cycles are mentioned from time to time, but they are not a primary focus. Rather, it is assumed that, in most cases, maintaining the normal processes within wetlands will ensure that their valued functions continue to occur. When, and if, it is necessary to manipulate wetlands in order to change some aspect of their global function, say, to increase wildlife production or to decrease methane production, this will always require knowledge of processes at the local community scale.

I first thought that such a book might be too personal a perspective on wetlands. Fields of enquiry are now so large that perhaps only multiauthored works are appropriate. However, my editor and advisor, Alan Crowden, has convinced me that many readers actually prefer a systematic and personal account of a field to a series of edited papers. Moreover, I have slowly convinced myself, too, that the existing literature is far too fragmented and diffuse and therefore confused. I have already written bluntly, perhaps too much so, of my views on symposium reports and festschrifts (Keddy 1991a, b, c). A number of recent symposium volumes on wetlands appear to be little more than expensive books with a haphazard collection of people giving a haphazard collection of papers with no unifying theme whatsoever except for the fact that all work in wet areas. Surely we can aspire to do better than this. While my own community oriented perspective undoubtedly has its limitations, it at least compensates with continuity and consistency.

I have tried to emphasize several research strategies. These include (i) greater emphasis upon measurable properties of ecosystems and (ii) the relative importance of different environmental factors that produce pattern. Far too many studies in wetlands consist, it seems, of little more than drawings of transects through wetlands or autecological studies of small groups of species living in wet places. Neither of these latter styles will inspire bright young scientists to enter the field. In fact, wetland community ecology is exciting, challenging, socially significant, and worthy of our best minds.

At first I was going to include a chapter on applications. But then my continued resistance to the forced distinction between theoretical and applied ecology intervened. Throughout this book there is an interplay between theory and application. In combining them we can achieve maximum impact upon knowledge with a minimal expenditure of effort. An appeal to efficiency itself ought to be sufficient, but we are now faced, in addition, with the rapid loss of the very ecosystems we study. We must hasten if we are to solve some of the growing problems with management of wetlands. Throughout the book there are practical examples that show that wetland ecologists have a great many useful things to say to environmental managers. Altered hydrology, eutrophication, loss of species – these are fundamental environmental issues and conceptual axes in the study of wetlands. There is therefore no single chapter on conservation alone because the entire book is about conservation.

Were it not for the inseparability of theory and application, this book might be considered schizophrenic. It is written with both the basic researcher and the resource manager in mind. I hope that both bright, young graduate students and cynical, overworked managers can benefit from consulting it. I have made abundant use of subheadings and figures so that parts that, at least on first reading, appear of secondary importance can easily be skipped. Each chapter will, I hope, be able to stand alone. Those needing an immediate short course, or feeling too harried to deal with an entire book, can obtain an overview of essentials with Chapters 1, 4, 5, and 12. Chapters 10 and 11 are the most speculative, and can be safely omitted from a first reading since they deal more with future possibilities than established phenomena.

Some of the limitations of the book are deliberate. I have placed an emphasis upon communities and on the factors than influence them. Although nutrient cycling is an important topic, I have not dealt with it extensively except under the heading of eutrophication. Similarly, systems models are already well covered in works such as Good *et al.* (1978), Mitsch and Gosselink (1986), and Patten (1990). Apart from eutrophication, I have left the topic of toxic contaminants to other better-qualified authors. There are also two fine compendia which already describe wetland types by region (Gore 1983; Whigham *et al.* 1992). I have not tried to duplicate their efforts. The logical structure of this book is built upon similarities in process rather than geography.

Finally (restrictions on travel are inclined to make one long-winded) this is not *just* a book on wetlands. I have tried to present not only an overview of wetland ecology, but to illustrate the general procedures with which one can dissect an ecological community to search for patterns and the mechanisms that may cause them. In this way, I hope to not only contribute to our understanding of wetlands, but to illustrate practices that will be of use in other vegetation types and ecological communities.

Since we began with Shaw, let us also close with him too. A successful book, according to Shaw, will impress the strong, intimidate the weak and tickle the connoisseur.

PAUL KEDDY

Acknowledgments

Let me start by acknowledging the many wetland ecologists whose work, cited or not, has produced the body of knowledge that allows such a book to be written. I hope I have faithfully transmitted the information and experience that they worked so hard to uncover. I have tried to give credit where it is due, but any voyage through a vast literature is bound to be personal; if you feel your work has not received the credit due, forgive me. Those who kindly contributed figures are acknowledged in the figure captions. Beyond this, I should mention some colleagues who cheerfully corresponded with me to help clarify issues. These included Barbara Bedford, Bruce Bury, Dan Campbell, Fangliang He, John Lopez, Reid Kreutsweiser, Ted Mosquin, Susan Newman, Michael Redmer, Stephen Richter, Clay Rubec, Fred Sklar, Rich Seigel, Orieta Hulea, Li Bo, Eugene Turner, Aline Waterkeyn, Doug Wilcox, and Robert Zampella. Beyond this Cathy Keddy has served dutifully in every task from chasing references to discussing content. The staff of the Carleton Place Public Library have also been cheerful in tracking down technical works from universities far afield.

Artists and photographers are often overlooked. I have tried to acknowledge them in captions wherever possible. Special thanks go to Howard Coneybeare, who produced the cover – a new version of the original line drawing used in the first edition – as well as Figure 2.18. I thank Rochelle Lawson for taking the plunge many years ago and preparing figures including 6.9, 6.11, 7.12, and 9.1. Thanks too to Betsy Brigham who prepared figures including 1.14, 2.19, 5.12, and 14.11. Finally, my son Ian and my spouse Cathy have spent many hours upgrading and refining older figures so they can inspire, educate, and delight a new generation of students. Perhaps a few younger readers will even consider the career path of biological illustration.

Chapter contents

1 Wetlands: an overview

All life contains water. From distant space, Earth appears as a mosaic of blue and green, blue for water, green for plants. This book is about the ecological communities that occur where green meets blue: wetlands. Wetlands are intimately associated with water. They are one of the most productive habitats on Earth, and they support many kinds of life. This book explores the general principles that control the distribution and composition of wetlands around the world. The cover (Figure 1.1, artwork by Howard Coneybeare) illustrates a typical temperate zone wetland. Common wetland plants shown include floating-leaved water lilies (*Nymphaea odorata*), emergent pickerelweed (*Pontederia cordata*), and shoreline reed canary grass (*Phalaris arundinacea*). The food web is largely composed of invertebrates that feed upon decaying plants. Near the top of the food web are vertebrates such as fish (yellow perch), reptiles (snapping turtle), and birds (great egret). The surrounding forests interact with the wetland. Amphibians, such as tree frogs, over-winter in the forest, while nutrients and runoff from the forest enter the wetland.

Wetlands have always influenced humans. Early civilizations first arose along the edges of rivers in the fertile soils of floodplains. Wetlands continue to produce many benefits for humans – along with fertile soils for agriculture, they provide food such as fish and waterbirds. Additionally, wetlands have other vital roles that are less obvious – they produce oxygen, store carbon, and process nitrogen. Of course, wetlands have also been a cause of human suffering, such as providing habitat for mosquitoes that carry malaria. And, for thousands of years, human cities in low areas have flooded during periods of high water. Philosophers and theologians may enquire how it is that one system can be both life-giving and death-dealing. Our more confined task as scientists is

- to explore the basic patterns that occur in wetlands,
- to uncover the causes of these patterns, and
- to guide society in wise coexistence with wetlands.

I intend to take you through these three steps in this book. Along the way, we will encounter not only hard science, but some entertaining natural history – fish that breathe air, mosses that drown trees, plants that eat insects, and frogs that climb trees. We shall also meet the world's largest wetlands, wetlands that perch on hillsides, wetlands that burn, and of course, wetlands that flood.

1.1   Definitions and distribution

Wetlands form at the interface of terrestrial and aquatic ecosystems and have features of both. While they may be highly variable in appearance and species composition, inundation by water is a shared characteristic that is, in turn, reflected in soil processes and adaptations of the biota. Thus wetlands are found where there is water, from saline coastal areas to continental interiors, but most are associated with fresh water.

FIGURE 1.1

1.1.1 Definition of wetlands

A wetland is an ecosystem that arises when inundation by water produces soils dominated by anaerobic processes, which, in turn, forces the biota, particularly rooted plants, to adapt to flooding.

   This broad definition includes everything from tropical mangrove swamps to subarctic peatlands. This single sentence of definition has a complex structure: there is a cause (inundation by water), a proximate effect (reduction of oxygen levels in the soil), and a secondary effect (the biota must tolerate both the direct effects of flooding and the secondary effects of anaerobic conditions). It is not the only definition, and maybe not even the best, but it shall get us started. Since many biologists and lawyers or agencies and organizations have attempted to define wetlands, we shall start with this simple idea. We shall explore other definitions in Section 1.8.1.

Since wetlands require water, the obvious place to begin is the distribution of water on Earth. Table 1.1 shows that a majority of the Earth's available water is in the oceans. A much smaller amount is present as fresh water. Heat from the sun drives a distillery, removing water vapor from the oceans and returning it to the land as precipitation. Some wetlands form along the edges of oceans; these tend to be mangrove swamps in equatorial regions and salt marshes at higher latitudes. A majority of wetlands are, however, freshwater ecosystems. They occur where rainwater accumulates on its way back to the ocean. Some people regard the distinction between freshwater and saltwater wetlands as critical, and you will often run into many documents that refer to "interior wetlands" and "coastal wetlands." Certainly salinity is very important in determining which kinds of plants and animals occur, but in this book we shall do our best to think about wetlands as one group of ecosystems.

Since life began in the oceans, most life, including freshwater life, has a chemical composition more like the ocean than fresh water (Table 1.2). Yet it appears that most life found in fresh water today did not originate in fresh water, but first adapted to land, and then adapted to fresh water. Fish, were, of course, an exception. The bodily fluids of freshwater aquatic animals still show a strong similarity to oceans. Indeed, many studies

Table 1.1 Mass of water in different forms on Earth

Form	Mass ($\times 10^{17}$ kg)
Chemically bound in rocks[a]	
Crystalline rocks	250 000
Sedimentary rocks	2100
Free water[b]	
Oceans	13 200
Ice caps and glaciers	292
Ground water to a depth of 4000 m	83.5
Freshwater lakes	1.25
Saline lakes and inland seas	1.04
Soil moisture	0.67
Atmospheric water vapor	0.13
Rivers	0.013

[a] Does not cycle.
[b] Part of hydrological cycle.
Source: From Clapham (1973).

Table 1.2 Concentrations of some common ions in animals, sea water, and fresh water (concentrations are given as mM/kg water)

Ions	Standard sea water	Fresh water (soft)	Fresh water (hard)	Crab (*Maia*) blood	Frog (*Rana esculenta*) blood	Crayfish (*Astacus fluviatilis*) blood (mM/l blood)	Rat (*Rattus rattus*) blood
Na^+	478.3	0.24	2.22	487.90	109	212	140
K^+	10.13	0.005	1.46	11.32	2.6	4.1	6.4
Ca^{2+}	10.48	0.067	3.98	13.61	2.1	15.8	3.4
Mg^{2+}	54.5	0.043	1.67	44.14	1.3	1.5	1.6
Cl^-	558.4	0.226	2.54	552.4	78	199	119
SO_4^{2-}	28.77	0.045	3.95	14.38	–	–	–
HCO_3^{2-}	–	–	2.02	–	26.6	15	24.3

Source: Modified from Wilson (1972).

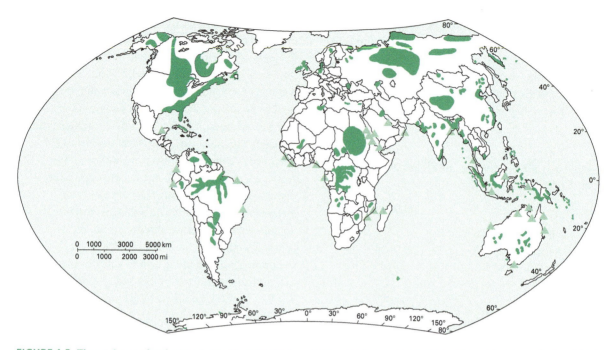

FIGURE 1.2 The major wetland areas on Earth. Mangrove swamps are shown as triangles. (Compiled from Dugan 1993 and Groombridge 1992.)

of ion balance in freshwater organisms show that fish, amphibians, and invertebrates attempt to maintain an inner ocean in spite of surrounding fresh water. They also show that, as with plants, access to oxygen becomes limiting once a site is flooded.

Wetlands have soil, so they are not truly aquatic like planktonic and pelagic communities. But they have standing water, so neither are they truly terrestrial. As a consequence, they are often overlooked. Terrestrial ecologists often assume they will be studied by limnologists, while limnologists may assume the reverse. We will therefore feel free to borrow from both terrestrial ecologists and limnologists in studying wetlands.

1.1.2 Distributions

Figure 1.2 presents an approximate distribution of global wetlands. Such a map has many limitations. It is difficult to map wetlands at the global scale for at least three reasons. Firstly, wetlands are frequently a relatively small proportion of the landscape. Secondly, they are distributed in small patches or strips throughout biomes, and therefore cannot be mapped at a scale suitable for reproducing in a textbook. Thirdly, they are very variable, and one biome can therefore contain a wide array of wetland types. Table 1.3 lists the largest wetland areas in the world. These set an important priority list for research and conservation.

1.2 Wetland classification

Now that we have a definition, and some idea of where wetlands occur, the next step is to sort them into similar types. Each type can be visualized as a

particular set of plant and animal associations that recur. This recurrence probably means that the same causal factors are at work. Unfortunately, the

Table 1.3 **The world's largest wetlands (areas rounded to the nearest 1000 km^2)**

Rank	Continent	Wetland	Description	Area (km^2)
1	Eurasia	West Siberian Lowland	Bogs, mires, fens	2 745 000
2	South America	Amazon River basin	Floodplain forest and savanna, marshes, mangal	1 738 000
3	North America	Hudson Bay Lowland	Bogs, fens, swamps, marshes	374 000
4	Africa	Congo River basin	Swamps, riverine forest, wet prairie	189 000
5	North America	Mackenzie River basin	Bogs, fens, swamps, marshes	166 000
6	South America	Pantanal	Savannas, grasslands, riverine forest	138 000
7	North America	Mississippi River basin	Bottomland hardwood forest, swamps, marshes	108 000
8	Africa	Lake Chad basin	Grass and shrub savanna, marshes	106 000
9	Africa	River Nile basin	Swamps, marshes	92 000
10	North America	Prairie potholes	Marshes, meadows	63 000
11	South America	Magellanic moorland	Bogs	44 000

Source: From Fraser and Keddy (2005).

terminology for describing wetlands varies both among human societies, and among their scientific communities. Thus one finds an abundance of words used to describe wetlands – bog, bayou, carr, fen, flark, hochmoore, lagg, marsh, mire, muskeg, swamp, pocosin, pothole, quagmire, savanna, slob, slough, swale, turlough, yazoo – in the English language alone. Many of these words can be traced back centuries to Old Norse, Old Teutonic, or Gaelic origins (Gorham 1953). Now add in other world languages, and the problem is compounded.

Given the global distribution, it is not surprising to find that abundant wetland classification schemes have been developed. They vary, for example, by geographic region, the intended use of the classification results, and the scale at which classification is undertaken. We will start with a simple classification system that distinguishes six wetland types largely on the basis of location and hydrology. After learning more about the environmental factors that control the development of wetlands and their communities, we will return to wetland definition and classification (Section 1.8).

1.2.1 The six basic types

To keep the terminology simple, we will begin with four types of wetland, and then add two to extend the list to six. One of the simplest classification systems recognizes only four types: swamps, marshes, fens, and bogs.

Swamp

A wetland that is dominated by trees that are rooted in hydric soils, but not in peat. Examples would include the tropical mangrove swamps (mangal) of Bangladesh and bottomland forests in floodplains of the Mississippi River valley in the United States (Figure 1.3).

Marsh

A wetland that is dominated by herbaceous plants that are usually emergent through water and rooted in hydric soils, but not in peat. Examples would include cattail (*Typha angustifolia*) marshes around the Great Lakes and reed (*Phragmites australis*) beds around the Baltic Sea (Figure 1.4).

FIGURE 1.3 Swamps. (*a*) Floodplain swamp (Ottawa River, Canada). (*b*) Mangrove swamp (Caroni wetland, Trinidad). (See also color plate.)

FIGURE 1.4 Marshes. (*a*) Riverine marsh (Ottawa River, Canada; courtesy B. Shipley). (*b*) Salt marsh (Petpeswick Inlet, Canada). (See also color plate.)

Bog

A wetland dominated by *Sphagnum* moss, sedges, ericaceous shrubs, or evergreen trees rooted in deep peat with a pH less than 5. Examples would include the blanket bogs which carpet mountainsides in northern Europe, and the vast peatland of the West Siberian Lowland in central Russia (Figure 1.5).

Fen

A wetland that is usually dominated by sedges and grasses rooted in shallow peat, often with considerable groundwater movement, and with pH greater than 6. Many occur on calcareous rocks, and most have brown mosses, in genera including *Scorpidium* or *Drepanocladus*. Examples can be found within the extensive peatlands of northern Canada and Russia, as well as in smaller seepage areas throughout the temperate zone (Figure 1.6).

Other wetland types could be added to these four. Two important ones are the following.

Wet meadow

A wetland dominated by herbaceous plants rooted in occasionally flooded soils. Temporary flooding excludes terrestrial plants and swamp plants, but drier growing seasons then produce plant communities typical of moist soils. Examples would include wet prairies along river floodplains, or herbaceous meadows on the shorelines of large lakes. These wetlands are produced by periodic flooding and may be overlooked if visited during a dry period (Figure 1.7).

Shallow water

A wetland community dominated by truly aquatic plants growing in and covered by at least 25 cm of water. Examples include the littoral zones of lakes, bays in rivers, and the more permanently flooded areas of prairie potholes (Figure 1.8).

Any attempt to sort the diversity of nature into only six categories will have its limitations. The Everglades, for example, have a peat substrate, moving water, and many reeds. So is it a fen or a marsh or wet prairie, a mixture of several of these, or something completely unique? Rather than worry further about this, we should probably admit that wetlands show great variation, and agree to not get stalled or diverted by debates over terminology. As Cowardin and Golet (1995) observe "no single system can accurately portray the diversity of wetland conditions world-wide. Some important ecological information inevitably will be lost through classification."

1.2.2 Some other classification systems

The system I present above has the advantage of simplicity and generality. You should be aware that there are more elaborate systems, and that these vary around the world. Each wetland classification system tries to summarize the major types of wetland vegetation, and then relate them to environmental conditions. Here are a few examples. We shall add several more near the end of the chapter.

A global summary

Figure 1.9 provides a summary that ties different classification systems into a unified whole. It begins with "water regime," from permanently waterlogged on the left to permanent shallow water on the right. Combining these three hydrological regimes with "nutrient supply," one obtains peatlands on the left, swamps in the middle, and lakes on the right. Further, the scheme then goes on to address the main plant forms that will occur. (One other system has been presented by Gopal *et al.* [1990] to summarize world wetland types. It again has two principal axes, hydrology and fertility, but it will be introduced at the end of Chapter 3 after these two factors have been explored in more depth.)

Hydrogeomorphic classifications

The location or setting of a wetland often has important consequences for duration of flooding and water quality. Hence, there are classification systems that emphasize the landscape setting of the wetland, such as the widely used Cowardin classification system (Table 1.4). Setting may be particularly

(a)

(b)

FIGURE 1.5 Bogs. (*a*) Lowland continental bog (Algonquin Park, Canada). (*b*) Upland coastal bog (Cape Breton Island, Canada). (See also color plate.)

(a)

(b)

FIGURE 1.6 Fens. (*a*) Patterned fen (northern Canada; courtesy C. Rubec). (*b*) Shoreline fen (Lake Ontario, Canada). (See also color plate.)

(a)

(b)

FIGURE 1.7 Wet meadows. (*a*) Sand spit (Long Point, Lake Ontario, Canada; courtesy A. Reznicek). (*b*) Gravel lakeshore (Tusket River, Canada; courtesy A. Payne). (See also color plate.)

FIGURE 1.8 Shallow water. (*a*) Bay (Lake Erie, Canada; courtesy A. Reznicek). (*b*) Pond (interdunal pools on Sable Island, Canada). (See also color plate.)

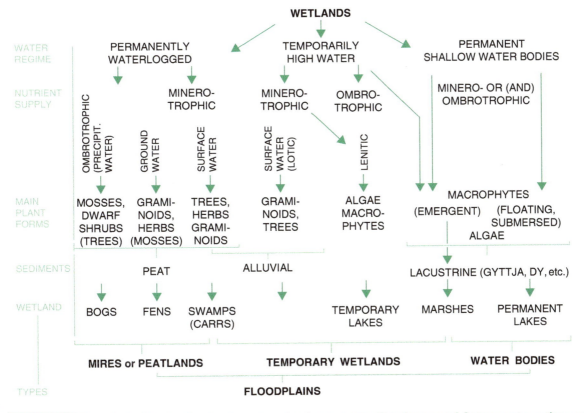

WETLANDS

WATER REGIME	PERMANENTLY WATERLOGGED	TEMPORARILY HIGH WATER	PERMANENT SHALLOW WATER BODIES

FIGURE 1.9 The principal kinds of wetlands can be related to two sets of environmental factors: water regime and nutrient supply (upper left). The term "water regime" refers to hydrological factors including depth and duration of flooding, while "nutrient supply" refers to chemical factors including available nitrogen, phosphorus, and calcium. (From Gopal *et al.* 1990.)

important for fens, since it affects so many aspects of hydrology and chemistry (Godwin *et al.* 2002). Many countries and regions have developed their own classification systems and procedures (e.g. Russia: Botch and Masing 1983; Zhulidov *et al.* 1997; China: Hou 1983; Lu 1995; Canada: Committee on Ecological Land Classification 1988).

A hydrological perspective

There are three main sources of water for wetlands – precipitation, groundwater, and water moving across the surface (Figure 1.10). Raised bogs are almost completely dependent upon the first, whereas floodplains are largely dependent upon the third. In practice, nutrient levels are often closely correlated with hydrology, since rainfall tends to be low in

nutrients, whereas water that flows across the surface or through the ground picks up dissolved nutrients and particulate matter. Wetlands can therefore be classified according to the relative proportions of these three water sources.

1.2.3 Combining classification systems

It is sometimes difficult to fit different classification systems together. Overall, you will likely need to use several classification systems at the same time. There may be international, national, state, and even local systems. Many of you will also inherit a situation in which you have multiple sets of information available, both in reports and on line. Let us walk through how the above information on

Table 1.4 Cowardin classification of wetlands and deepwater habitats

System	Subsystem	Class
Marine	Subtidal	Rock Bottom
		Unconsolidated Bottom
		Aquatic Bed
	Intertidal	Reef
		Aquatic Bed
		Reef
		Rocky Shore
		Unconsolidated Shore
Estuarine	Subtidal	Rock Bottom
		Unconsolidated Bottom
		Aquatic Bed
	Intertidal	Reef
		Aquatic Bed
		Reef
		Streambed
		Rocky Shore
		Unconsolidated Shore
		Emergent Wetland
		Scrub–Shrub Wetland
		Forested Wetland
Riverine	Tidal	Rock Bottom
		Unconsolidated Bottom
		Aquatic Bed
		Rocky Shore
		Unconsolidated Shore
	Lower Perennial	Emergent Wetland
		Rock Bottom
		Unconsolidated Bottom
		Aquatic Bed
		Rocky Shore
		Unconsolidated Shore
	Upper Perennial	Emergent Wetland
		Rock Bottom
		Unconsolidated Bottom
		Aquatic Bed
		Rocky Shore
	Intermittent	Unconsolidated Shore
		Streambed
Lacustrine	Limnetic	Rock Bottom
		Unconsolidated Bottom
	Littoral	Aquatic Bed
		Rock Bottom
		Unconsolidated Bottom
		Aquatic Bed
		Rocky Shore
		Unconsolidated Shore
		Emergent Wetland
Palustrine		Rock Bottom
		Unconsolidated Bottom
		Aquatic Bed
		Unconsolidated Shore
		Moss–Lichen Wetland
		Emergent Wetland
		Scrub–Shrub Wetland
		Forested Wetland

Source: From Cowardin *et al.* (1979).

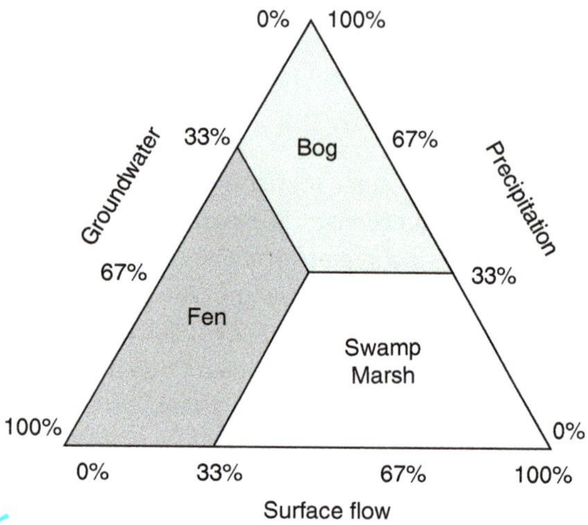

FIGURE 1.10 The principal kinds of wetlands can be related to water source: groundwater, precipitation, and surface flow. The relative importance of these sources varies among types of wetlands. (Modified from Brinson 1993a, b.)

classification might allow you to sort the work into useful categories.

- First, there is the identification of a site as wetland, and identification of its spatial boundaries. In the United States this is part of a formal process called "wetland delineation." Many parts of the world have similar procedures that result in maps of wetlands.
- Each wetland can be assigned to one the six basic types, or, perhaps, a combination of them.
- A hydrogeomorphic system puts the wetland into a landscape setting category.
- Depending upon where you work, there are likely to be one or more national or regional systems to apply, quite possibly using languages other than English. You may find yourself in a turlough, *várzea*, *igapó*, *corixos*, or Scirpo-Phragmitetum.
- There are likely to be particular species of interest, depending upon the agency employing you, and upon the type of project in which you are involved. This might be species that are uncommon in your region, indicator species, or species that are threatened at the global scale.

It is not, then, that one system is right and the other is wrong. Each provides useful information for certain purposes. To decide which is best for a particular project requires you to know the purpose of your work, including your audience, and the geographical and political region in which you will be working.

1.2.4 Plants, stress, and wetland types

In spite of all the variation in wetlands, there are still only a small number of causal factors. By looking at simple causes, we can reduce the difficulty of understanding the variation in types of wetlands. Figures 1.9 and 1.10 showed two ways of describing

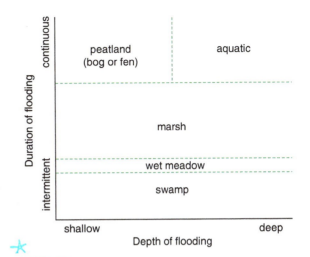

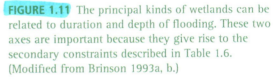

FIGURE 1.11 The principal kinds of wetlands can be related to duration and depth of flooding. These two axes are important because they give rise to the secondary constraints described in Table 1.6. (Modified from Brinson 1993a, b.)

these causes. Let us look at one more, which leads naturally to the idea of primary and secondary constraints. If we set aside other factors such as water chemistry or location, we can use just flood duration and depth as key factors (Figure 1.11). Even these two factors alone will produce five main wetland types. Fen and bog appear as peatland in the upper left, aquatic appears at the upper right, and marsh and swamp appear as broad zones across the bottom. Wet meadows may squeeze in between marsh and swamp depending upon the nature of water level changes.

This lays out the logic for the next few sections. First we will look at the main factor that causes a wetland: flooding. We will briefly examine effects of flooding on soils, plants, and animals. We will then look at some additional, or secondary, effects of flooding, and explore how these produce the different types of wetlands shown in Figures 1.3–1.8.

1.3   Wetland soils

Most soil types arise from chemical and microbial processes that occur in the presence of oxygen.

Wetlands are the exception – most lack oxygen – and therefore they have distinctive hydric soils. In this

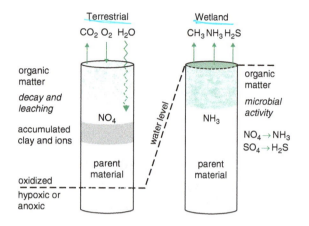

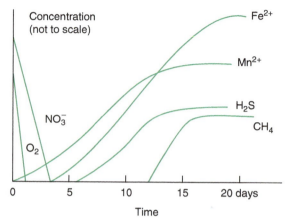

FIGURE 1.12 A typical terrestrial soil profile compared to a typical wetland soil profile. The principal differences arise largely out of the presence or absence of oxygen. Overall, wetland soils tend to store more organic matter, experience less leaching, and contain microorganisms that emit gases such as CH_3 (methane), NH_3 (ammonia), and H_2S (hydrogen sulfide).

section, we will discuss the effects of flooding on soil chemistry and the importance of wetland soils in global biogeochemical cycles.

1.3.1 Wetlands have reduced rather than oxidized soils

The general differences between terrestrial and wetland soils are shown in Figure 1.12. Oxidized soils have small amounts of organic matter near the surface, and major ions have been transported deeper into the soil column by leaching. Reduced soils in wetlands have larger amounts of organic matter, and instead of leaching, there is chemical transformation toward reduced elements. The presence of a distinctive soil type is therefore one defining characteristic of wetlands.

Since oxygen is so widely distributed in the atmosphere, wetlands provide one of the few places on Earth for microbial interactions that occur in reduced rather than oxidized conditions. Wetlands are therefore globally important for the chemical transformation of elements in the world's biogeochemical cycles.

FIGURE 1.13 The chemistry of a soil changes rapidly within days of being flooded. (From Brinkman and Van Diepen 1990 after Patrick and Reddy 1978.)

One cause of low oxygen (O_2) levels is the low rate of diffusion of oxygen in water, and hence in flooded soils. Oxygen and other gases diffuse about 10^3–10^4 times more rapidly in air than in water. Oxygen is soon depleted from flooded soils by the respiration of soil microorganisms and plant roots. The deficiency of oxygen is termed **hypoxia**, the absence of oxygen is termed **anoxia**. In the absence of oxygen, oxidation of organic matter ceases, and populations of microorganisms begin to change the ionic composition of the rooting zone (Ponnamperuma 1972, 1984; Faulkner and Richardson 1989; Marschner 1995).

1.3.2 The degree of reduction changes with time and depth

The effects of flooding on soil chemistry occur rapidly (Figure 1.13). Not only do O_2 and nitrate (NO_3^-) disappear in only a few days, gases such as methane (CH_4), hydrogen sulfide (H_2S) and ammonia (NH_3) begin to accumulate. As well, ions such as Fe_2^{2+} appear. Hence organisms living in wetland soils have at least three metabolic problems to contend with: not only is there a shortage of oxygen, but there are atypical concentrations of ions, and there are toxic gases.

The significance of these conditions requires a brief digression. Oxidized conditions are a consequence of life, and more precisely, of photosynthesis. The early atmosphere was anoxic (Day 1984; Levin 1992). The gradual accumulation of oxygen has been termed the "oxygen revolution." I have recently summarized the story of oxygen accumulation in another textbook (Keddy 2007, ch. 1). The main point here is that the hypoxic/anoxic conditions found in wetland soils represent a type of chemistry that was once common on earth. It is now mostly restricted to flooded sites.

The degree of hypoxia not only changes with time, but with depth. In many wetlands, one can identify three regions: standing water with dissolved oxygen, an upper oxidized layer of soil, and a deeper reduced layer of soil. As molecules are transformed in one layer, diffusion gradients arise to transport them to adjoining layers.

1.3.3 The processing of carbon, nitrogen, phosphorus, and sulfur

The chemical states of carbon, nitrogen, phosphorus, sulfur, iron, and other elements are affected by the state of oxidation in soils. Flooded soils are therefore critical in global biogeochemical cycles. Let us briefly consider changes in effects of flooding on four major elements: C, N, P, and S.

Carbon

Carbon arrives as organic matter, either from uplands, or from plants growing in the wetland. If oxygen is available, the organic matter is decomposed to carbon dioxide (CO_2), whereas if oxygen is scarce, it may be decomposed to methane (CH_4). This methane can diffuse into the atmosphere, where it becomes a powerful greenhouse gas. Some microorganisms, including Archea, intercept and consume methane. The organic matter that does not decay becomes stored in the soil in various forms including peat.

Nitrogen

Nitrogen arrives in wetlands in organic matter or in runoff as nitrate, NO_3^-. When the organic matter partially decays in the absence of oxygen, ammonia (NH_4) is produced, a process called ammonification. If oxygen is available (usually near the soil surface), this NH_4 is oxidized to NO_3^- by chemoautotrophic bacteria. This result is often a concentration gradient with nitrogen as NH_4 diffusing upward from deeper anoxic regions, while nitrogen in the form of NO_3^- diffuses downward. Other complex microbial transformations are superimposed. Most terrestrial ecosystems are sources of organic nitrogen and nitrate, whereas most wetlands are sinks, that is areas where nitrogen and other elements accumulate. Figure 1.14 shows the basic stages and locations

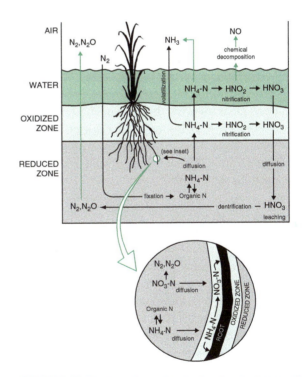

FIGURE 1.14 The transformation in the chemical state of nitrogen is driven by gradients of oxygen availability. These oxidation/reduction gradients occur at two scales. At the larger scale, oxidation decreases with water depth. At the small scale (inset) oxidation decreases with the distance from plant roots. (Illustration by B. Brigham.)

of nitrogen transformation, a topic to which we will return in the section on wetland services (Section 1.6).

Phosphorus

Nearly all of the phosphorus arrives in sediment and plant litter. Unlike nitrogen, there is no gaseous phase, and no valency changes occur during microbial processing. Wetlands again appear to act as sinks for phosphorus eroded from surrounding terrestrial ecosystems.

Sulfur

The sulfur cycle is more similar to the nitrogen cycle with multiple transformations by microorganisms. Sulfur arrives as organic debris, or in rainfall. If oxygen is available, the decomposition of organic matter can yield SO_4^{2-}. In the absence of oxygen, the product is H_2S. A concentration gradient can therefore arise, with the SO_4^{2-} diffusing downward to be transformed to H_2S by anaerobic bacteria, while H_2S diffuses upward to be oxidized. The H_2S can also diffuse into the atmosphere or react with organic matter. The diffusion of H_2S into the atmosphere explains the rotten egg smell sometimes noticed in wetlands. Most terrestrial ecosystems are sulfur sources, most wetlands appear to be sulfur sinks.

The above information illustrates how wetlands are important in maintaining the quality of flowing water. Some of the nutrients that arrive in wetlands remain stored in organic matter or sediment. Others are transformed to gases – in the case of nitrogen, to N_2, and in the case of sulfur, to H_2S. Artificially constructed wetlands are therefore sometimes used to treat nutrient-laden waters produced by human activities (Hammer 1989; Knight and Kadlec 2004). More background on the chemistry of flooded soils can be found in sources such Good *et al.* (1978), Ponnamperuma (1972, 1984), Mitsch and Gosselink (1986), Faulkner and Richardson (1989), Gopal (1990), Armentano and Verhoeven (1990), and Marschner (1995).

Finally, other factors can complicate the above processes, particularly the biota themselves. Here are two examples. Vascular plants can transport oxygen downward in their stems (Section 1.6), sometimes in sufficient quantities to oxidize the soil around their roots (Figure 1.14). This can obviously change the depth at which the above chemical transformations occur. It can also lead to deposits of metals like iron oxide in the rooting zone. Cyanobacteria, which are photosynthetic, can also fix atmosphere nitrogen, converting N_2 to protein, and therefore increasing nitrogen levels in a wetland. This is an important input of nitrogen for rice paddies.

1.4   Flood tolerance: the primary constraint

The presence of hydric plants, like hydric soils, is another attribute used to define wetlands. These plants, adapted to low levels of oxygen in the soil, provide the habitat template for all the animals, so we must spend some time with the plants first in order to understand the animals later.

1.4.1 Aerenchyma allows plants to cope with hypoxic soils

Since the roots of actively growing plants require oxygen to respire, there has been strong selective pressure to address the problems posed by hypoxia. Many plants have spongy tissue to allow air to reach buried roots. Others have metabolic adaptations to allow at least temporary growth in the absence of oxygen. Added detail can be found in Sculthorpe (1967), Hutchinson (1975), Kozlowski (1984a), and Crawford and Braendle (1996).

The principal adaptation to hypoxia has been the evolution of air spaces or lacunae, which may extend from the leaf parenchyma through the petiole into the stem and into the buried rhizome or root. These spaces are formed either from splits between cells, or by the disintegration of cells. The continuity of the air spaces though the plant were, according to Hutchinson (1975), illustrated by Barthelemy in 1874, who found that, when a leaf was placed under reduced pressure, air could be drawn upward from the rhizome. The system of lacunae is frequently called, in spite of Hutchinson's objections, aerenchyma. The transport of oxygen through aerenchyma is sufficiently efficient that roots may be able to oxidize their surroundings (Hook 1984; Moorhead and Reddy 1988) and even provide oxygen for the respiration of roots by neighboring plants (Bertness and Ellison 1987; Bertness 1991; Callaway and King 1996). The lacunae also provide a route for methane produced in the soil to escape into the atmosphere; genera including *Scheuzeria*, *Carex*, *Peltandra*, and *Typha* are known to transport methane (Cicerone and Ormland 1988). The presence of aerenchyma is one of the most obvious characteristics of wetland plants, being particularly well developed in marsh and aquatic plants.

How does air move through aerenchyma? The simplest and most obvious mechanism is diffusion. In addition to the passive diffusion of oxygen, there can be bulk flow of air through aerenchyma if an internal pressure gradient exists. Such bulk flow (also called convective through flow [Armstrong *et al.* 1991] or pressurized ventilation [Grosse *et al.* 1991]), has now been reported in wetland plants including *Phragmites australis*, *Carex gracilis*, and *Egeria elegans* (Armstrong *et al.* 1991) as well as *Hydrocleys nymphoides*, *Nelumbo nucifera*, *Victoria amazonica*, and *Alnus glutinosa* (Grosse *et al.* 1991). Typically, it was first documented by a German botanist in the late 1800s (Pfeffer 1897 in Grosse *et al.* 1991), but then overlooked for decades. In water lilies pressurized gases in young leaves flow down through the petiole into the rhizome. The air then moves back up the old petioles and escapes through the pores in older leaves (Figure 1.15). As much as 22 litres of air a day can enter a single floating leaf and flow to the rhizome (Dacey 1980; Dacey in Salisbury and Ross 1988, pp. 68–70). Most trees do not show obvious morphological features to withstand flooding, but

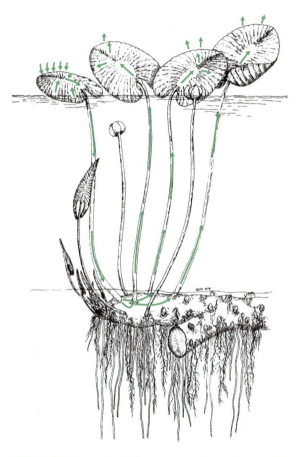

FIGURE 1.15 In water lilies, air enters through young leaves and exits through older leaves. Many other wetland plants have similar processes for transporting oxygen to rhizomes and roots. (From Dacey 1981.)

there is one conspicuous exception. Both major groups of woody plants, gymnosperms (e.g. *Taxodium*) and angiosperms (e.g. *Avicennia)*, produce above-ground extensions of their roots called pneumatophores (Figure 1.16) that may allow roots direct access to atmospheric gases. The wind flowing across dead stems of some reeds also generates another type of transport called venturi flow (Armstrong *et al.* 1992), in which case it appears that the dead stalks continue to function in conduction of oxygen. This may explain why some species are so resistant to prolonged flooding, and why mowing before flooding increases their sensitivity.

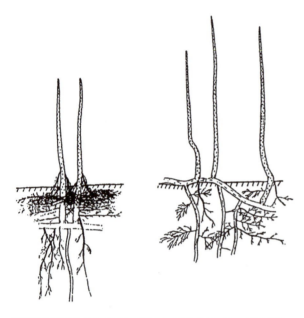

FIGURE 1.16 Pneumatophores, which grow vertically into the atmosphere from the roots of the mangrove, *Avicennia nitida*, may assist with aeration of those roots in flooded soils.

1.4.2 Metabolic adaptations in aquatic plants

In the absence of adaptations such as aerenchyma, wetland plants must cope using other means. They must deal simultaneously with the lack of oxygen and its many other consequences. Once flooded, the soil's oxygen is consumed, and toxic compounds such as ammonia, ethylene, hydrogen sulfide, acetone, and acetic acid are formed from the anaerobic decomposition of organic matter (Ponnamperuma 1984). From the plants' perspective, this "usually sets in motion a sequential and complicated series of metabolic disturbances" (Kozlowski and Pallardy 1984).

The first problem is survival. The second problem is to maintain growth in these unfavorable circumstances. One physiological mechanism may involve the capacity to avoid production of potentially toxic ethanol at the end of the glycolytic pathway. It has long been known, says Hutchinson (1975), that some water plants contain ethanol,

and that rhizomes of water plants such as *Nymphaea tuberosa*, *Sagittaria latifolia*, and *Typha latifolia* can live anaerobically for long periods of time. This remarkable tolerance of rhizomes to anaerobic conditions was demonstrated by Laing (1940, 1941) who grew rhizomes from genera including *Acorus*, *Nuphar*, *Peltandra*, and *Scirpus* in water through which nitrogen was bubbled. The rhizomes were able to respire anaerobically, producing ethanol in 3% or less of oxygen. Both *Peltandra* and *Typha* showed long persistence even in pure nitrogen. More recent work has expanded the list of species with growth apparently unimpeded by lack of oxygen (Spencer and Ksander 1997). Sulfides are also associated with anoxia, and it is possible that sulfides themselves could be having direct toxic effects upon roots, or interfering with the uptake of ammonium (Mendelssohn and McKee 1988).

1.4.3 Animals must also cope with hypoxia

In this chapter we are focusing upon plants, since they create the main wetland types and provide habitat for the wetland fauna. Yet note in passing that it is not only plants that are affected by hypoxia. Fish are too. When rivers flood, fish migrate into the floodplain to feed and reproduce; when the water recedes, fish can be trapped in shrinking pools. These pools quickly become hypoxic (Graham 1997; Matthews 1998). As they become warmer, oxygen levels fall. Algal mats begin to fill the water column; while providing some shelter for small fish, they increase hypoxia during hours of darkness. Oxygen levels become critical and direct mortality from hypoxia begins . . .

Some fish tolerate hypoxic conditions by gulping air. Air-breathing fish are thought to have evolved more than 400 million years ago, long before amphibians appeared (Graham 1997). There are 347 species in 49 families known to be air-breathing, and in nearly all, air-breathing is an adaptation to hypoxia. One well-known example is the lungfish (six species, including *Neoceratodus forsteri* in

Australia). Other examples are the bichar (*Polypterus* spp. in Africa), the gar (*Lepisosteus* spp. in North and Central America), and the bowfin (*Amia calva*), all of which are predators in shallow warm waters.

In addition to breathing air, some can walk away from the shrinking pool. The walking catfish (ten genera and ca. 75 species including *Clarias* spp.) are native to Asia and Africa, where they normally inhabit warm hypoxic water. When stranded, they can move across land, partly by wriggling, partly aided by their pectoral fins. When the Asian species was accidentally introduced to Florida in the 1960s, it spread to 20 counties in just ten years (Robins n.d.).

An alternative to walking away from a drying pool is to bury in the mud and wait for the next flood. Lungfish, which occur in South America, Africa, and Australia, will construct mucus-lined burrows and breathe through their modifed swim bladder until the site is re-flooded (Graham 1997). Fossil burrows containing lungfish have been found as far back as the Permian era. Some types of walking catfish can also walk on land, while others are known to dredge pools to make the water deeper.

Other fish also make burrows. Here is an historical account (Neill 1950) regarding the bowfin:

An Estivating Bowfin

On one occasion I was hunting squirrels in the Savannah River swamp near McBean, Richmond County, Georgia. While sitting quietly on a log, I was suddenly surprised to hear a thumping noise apparently emanating from the ground almost at my feet. Locating the sound, I dug into the ground to disclose, at a depth of about 4 inches, a roughly spherical chamber approximately 8 inches in diameter. In this chamber was a living bowfin, *Amia calva*. The fish was writhing about the chamber; the striking of its head against the chamber walls produced the sounds that had first attracted my attention. The surface soil was a hard, dried mud, but the walls of the chamber were soft and moist; they had been almost polished by the writhing of the fish. The river was nearly a quarter-mile distant, but the presence of yellowish silt on the nearby tree boles attested to previous flooding.

The situation immediately calls to mind the estivation of certain tropical lung-fishes. I suspect that *A. calva*, a species remarkably tenacious of life, could survive in a moist mud-chamber for considerable periods of time. (Wilfred T. Neill, Research Division, Ross Allen's Reptile Institute, Silver Springs, Florida)

Let us consider one more fish example – the Amazon River, which has more kinds of fish than any other river in the world. In one small floodplain lake in the Amazon, Junk (1984) found 120 fish species, of which 40 were regularly found under pronounced hypoxic conditions. Of these, ten could gulp oxygen from the air, and ten could use the lower lip like a gill. The adaptations of the others were unknown. Other fish avoid hypoxic conditions by diurnal migration from macrophyte stands during the day to open water at night. There are many biochemical means for tolerating anoxic conditions, at least for short periods (Kramer *et al.* 1978; Junk 1984; Junk *et al.* 1997). In the Amazon, many other animals avoid hypoxia by migrating into the river itself during dry periods; these include manatees, turtles, and invertebrates. Other animals survive the dry period with resting-structures such as eggs or turions; these include clams, sponges, and cladocerans.

Hypoxia is equally important in controlling the distribution of amphibians and reptiles (Goin and Goin 1971). Amphibians can exchange gases with the environment by means of gills, lungs, mucosa of the throat, or the skin; the relative importance of these pathways varies with habitat and species. Reptiles have a skin that is relatively impermeable to water; while this has allowed them to colonize land and diversify in terrestrial environments, it has reduced respiration through the skin, placing greater emphasis upon lungs for oxygen uptake. Among the reptiles, turtles seem especially adapted to tolerate hypoxia, and many of the aquatic turtles (e.g. in the genera *Trionyx* and *Sternothaerus*) can gain sufficient oxygen by pumping water in and out of the throat to allow long periods of submersion so long as the animal is not physically active. Most snakes, lizards, and even crocodiles are far less tolerant of anoxia (Table 1.5).

The rich diversity of insect life in wetlands provides for a great array of adaptations to hypoxia. One generalization is certainly possible. Many of the insects in wetlands survive hypoxic conditions by finding some way to retain or obtain access to the atmosphere (Merritt and Cummins 1984). The commonest adaptation is to have a tube to provide access to the atmosphere, although this is useful only in shallow water. Some beetle larvae have extended terminal spiracles, respiratory siphons, that provide access to the atmosphere. Some predatory beetles have truly aquatic larvae that breathe using gills, but they still return to the land for the pupal stage. Mosquito larvae and pupae float near the surface and use respiratory siphons to reach the atmosphere. For access to deeper water, bubbles of atmosphere can be carried. Diving beetles carry a bubble of air under the wing covers. Some aquatic bugs carry a film of oxygen on their ventral surface where it adheres to a dense coating of hydrophobic hairs. A few species of Diptera are known to pierce aquatc plants and withdraw air from the plant's aerenchyma. Gills, of course, are also found in many aquatic invertebrates, particularly in groups like the dragonflies and caddis flies, but gills require dissolved oxygen in the water. Insects that carry a film of air or bubble may in fact also be extracting oxygen from the water, since oxygen may diffuse from water into the film or bubble.

Table 1.5 **Tolerance of anoxia in various families of reptiles**

Order and family	No. species tested	Mean survival time (minutes)
Testudinata		
Chelydridae	1	1050
Testudinidae	14	945
Pelomedusidae	2	980
Kinosternidae	5	876
Trionychidae	1	546
Chelidae	2	465
Cheloniidae	2	120
Squamata		
Lacertilia		
Iguanidae	6	57
Gekkonidae	1	31
Anguinidae	1	29
Scincidae	4	25
Teiidae	1	22
Serpentes		
Viperidae	3	95
Boidae	3	59
Elapidae	1	33
Colubridae	22	42
Crocodilia		
Crocodylidae	1	33

Source: Data from Belkin (1963).

Overall, however, the more hypoxic the water, the more likely that the invertebrates are using atmospheric oxygen.

1.5 Secondary constraints produce different types of wetlands

We have seen that the primary constraint caused by flooding is reduced availability of oxygen. Now let us consider some additional consequences of flooding.

1.5.1 Secondary constraints in peatlands

Some wetlands are flooded more or less permanently, but the water table is near the soil surface

(Figure 1.11, upper left). Under these conditions decomposition is reduced but since there are no waves, flowing water, or tides to carry away debris, the organic matter accumulates. The setting of the wetland can control chemistry of the water. Of particular importance are elements that control the acidity of the water – such as calcium ions – and elements that control plant growth, such as nitrogen

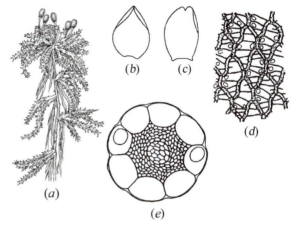

FIGURE 1.18 *Sphagnum* mosses often dominate peatlands. Their morphology and anatomy promote the storage of water and can raise the water table in these wetlands. Of particular significance are hyaline cells, which are dead at maturity and often have pores. (*a*) Shoot with attached sporophytes (*S. squarrosum*; from Kenrick and Crane 1997), (*b*) branch leaf, (*c*) stem leaf, (*d*) network of chlorophyllous cells in leaves surrounding the larger hyaline cells, (*e*) cross-section of stem showing hyaline cells in outer wall (*S. papillosum*; adapted from Scagel *et al.* 1996 and van Breeman 1995).

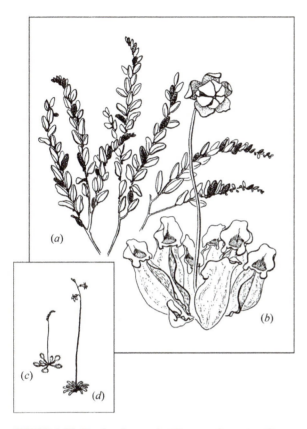

FIGURE 1.17 Peatlands are simultaneously wet and infertile and therefore the plants are often evergreen (e.g. *Chamaedaphne calyculata*, *a*). Others, like pitcher plants (*Sarracenia purpurea*, *b*), are carnivorous. Many other wetland and shoreline plants have the same adaptations, the sundew (*Drosera rotundifolia*, *c*) being carnivorous and water lobelia (*Lobelia dortmanna*, *d*) being evergreen.

and phosphorus. If the organic matter accumulates to a depth of about 10 cm, roots can become isolated from the mineral soils beneath the peat, and therefore become increasingly dependent upon dilute nutrients deposited in rainwater (Gorham 1957; Godwin 1981; van Breeman 1995). Therefore, in peatlands, the chemistry of the water – particularly acidity and nutrient status – become two critical factors (e.g. Gore 1983; Glaser *et al.* 1990; Vitt and Chee 1990).

Let us concentrate on nutrient status here. Adaptation to infertile conditions requires a variety of unusual plant traits (Figure 1.17). An obvious one is leathery and evergreen (sclerophyllous) leaves – which is peculiar because these types of leaves are also found in desert plants. A deciduous plant must continually replace the nitrogen and phosphorus lost in falling leaves – so evergreen leaves are generally thought to be an adaptation to cope with low soil fertility (Grime 1977, 1979; Chapin 1980; Vitousek 1982). Hence, evergreen shrubs (often in the Ericaceae) and evergreen trees (many in the Pinaceae) often dominate peatlands (Richardson 1991). A further consequence of sclerophyllous leaves is the fuel they provide for fires (Christensen *et al.* 1981).

Peatlands also exhibit a distinctive abundance of bryophytes. In bogs, one genus, *Sphagnum* (Figure 1.18), tends to be dominant, while in fens brown mosses such as *Scorpidium* or *Drepanocladus* are common (Vitt 1990; Vitt *et al.* 1995; Wheeler and Proctor 2000). Carnivorous plants are also found in peatlands, since the invertebrates trapped by the

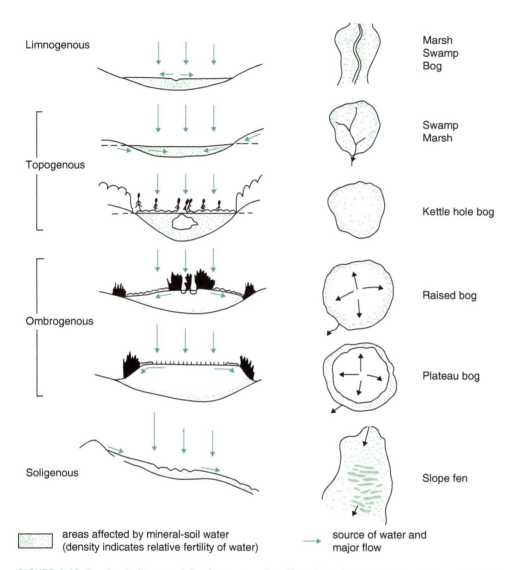

Limnogenous — Marsh / Swamp / Bog

Topogenous — Swamp / Marsh

— Kettle hole bog

Ombrogenous — Raised bog

— Plateau bog

Soligenous — Slope fen

☐ areas affected by mineral-soil water
(density indicates relative fertility of water)

→ source of water and major flow

FIGURE 1.19 Peatlands (bogs and fens) are strongly affected by their position in the landscape. This determines the relative importance of rainfall and groundwater, as well as nutrient levels and pH of the groundwater. (From Bridgham *et al.* 1996, from Damman 1986.)

plant provide an alternative source of nitrogen and phosphorus (Givnish 1988). Orchids are also often found in peatlands, particularly in fens, perhaps because their associate mycorrhizae assist with nutrient uptake. Many peatland plants are organized along gradients of peat depth and water chemistry (Slack *et al.* 1980; Glaser *et al.* 1990; Yabe and Onimaru 1997).

The chemical nature of groundwater is a critical factor determining the type of peatland (Bridgham *et al.* 1996; Wheeler and Proctor 2000; Godwin *et al.* 2002). Hence, the location within a landscape is critical. Four general categories can be recognized (Figure 1.19). Limnogenous peatlands occur beside lakes and rivers. Topogenous peatlands occupy depressions and valleys. Ombrogenous peatlands occur where peat has accumulated above the land surface. Soligenous peatlands occur on sloped land surfaces. Since the depth of peat affects the water chemistry, peat accumulation rates become an important controlling factor. As peat accumulates and absorbs water, the diminutive *Sphagnum* moss can even flood and kill forests, a process known as paludification (van Breeman 1995). Over time, peat can accumulate to a depth of many meters, gradually transforming the landscape (Dansereau and Segadas-Vianna 1952; Gorham 1953), a topic to which we will return in Section 7.2. Disturbances such as fire can reverse this process of peat accumulation (Kuhry 1994; White 1994).

1.5.2 Secondary constraints in aquatic wetlands

Standing water (Figure 1.11, upper right) produces a different type of environment. Here, in addition to low oxygen concentrations, the environmental factors are constant submergence, disturbance by waves, reduced availability of carbon dioxide, and the potential access to the atmosphere provided by floating leaves. The traits of aquatic plants therefore include well-developed aerenchyma, floating leaves, heavily dissected submersed leaves, and remarkably modified flowers (Figure 1.20). Aquatic plants have been the subject of two fine monographs (Sculthorpe 1967; Hutchinson 1975).

In aquatic wetlands, however, something more must be said about the problem of carbon acquisition, because this secondary constraint and its solutions are (almost) entirely restricted to aquatic macrophytes. Submersed aquatic plants are isolated from atmospheric supplies of carbon dioxide. In his monograph *Limnological Botany,* Hutchinson (1975) points out that the concentrations of carbon dioxide in water are similar to those in air, and even a little greater at low temperatures, placing aquatic plants in a rather different situation from respiring aquatic animals. If CO_2 concentrations in water are roughly equal to those in the atmosphere, "why should there be a problem at all?" Hutchinson answers that

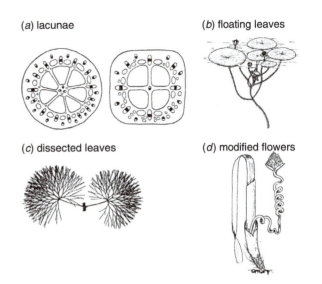

(*a*) lacunae (*b*) floating leaves

(*c*) dissected leaves (*d*) modified flowers

FIGURE 1.20 Four adaptations to standing water: (*a*) lacunae in stems and rhizomes (*Nymphaea* spp.), (*b*) floating leaves (*Brasenia schreberi*; Hellquist and Crow 1984), (*c*) dissected submerged leaves (*Camboba caroliniana*), (*d*) modified flowers that retract below water after pollination (*Enhalus acoroides*). (*a, c, d* from Sculthorpe 1967.)

"the assimilating plant is still at a disadvantage in the water, owing to the much lower coefficient of molecular diffusion in a liquid than that in a gaseous medium. Submerging a land plant in water ... may reduce its photosynthetic rate to a negligible value" (p. 145). There are at least three morphological or anatomical responses to increase access to dissolved CO_2: reduction in the waxy epidermis of leaves, reduced thickness of leaves, and most conspicuously, the elaboration of leaves to increase surface to volume ratios (Figure 1.20c). These are adaptations that would not be possible in terrestrial plants because of the need for support tissues, and because such changes would also greatly increase rates of water loss. The other main adaptation is a biochemical one, the uptake of bicarbonate ions rather than that of CO_2 directly. Hutchinson concludes that most higher aquatic plants have this capability. One set of exceptions, he says, includes *Lobelia dortmanna* and species of *Isoëtes*; we shall return to them shortly. Another exception appears to be the carnivorous *Utricularia purpurea* (Moeller 1978). In such cases carbon uptake is directly related to the concentration of CO_2 in the water. All of these exceptions appear to be restricted to infertile soft water lakes, perhaps in part because these lakes lack the diurnal depletion of CO_2 found in some eutrophic lakes (Moeller 1978).

Those unusual plants that are unable to extract bicarbonate from water appear to be able to absorb CO_2 from their roots rather than from their leaves. Consider the bizarre group of plants in the genus *Isoëtes*, an obscure group of herbaceous plants thought to be evolutionary relics related to fern-like plants such as *Lycopodium* and *Selaginella*. *Isoëtes* look rather like a small pincushion, and grow mostly in shallow water in oligotrophic lakes, although some species grow in temporary pools and a few are terrestrial. One member of this group, *Isoëtes andicola*, grows at high altitudes (usually >4000 m) in the Peruvian Andes, and the following account comes from work by Keeley *et al.* (1994). Over half this plant is composed of roots, and only the tips of the leaves emerge above ground and have chlorophyll (4% of total biomass). Most of the carbon for photosynthesis is obtained through the root system – from decaying peat rather than directly from the atmosphere.

In many oligotrophic lakes there is an entire group of plants called, because of their superficial resemblance to *Isoëtes*, "isoetids." These plants are apparently restricted to oligotrophic lakes where there are very low levels of inorganic carbon in the water. Some of these (e.g. *Lobelia dortmanna*) are also known to use their roots to take up CO_2 from sediments (Wium-Anderson 1971), and some have CAM (crassulacean acid metabolism) photosynthetic systems (Boston 1986; Boston and Adams 1986).

1.5.3 Secondary constraints in swamps

Sites that are deeply flooded for shorter periods of time (Figure 1.11, bottom) are generally covered in flood-tolerant trees, and these trees can be ranked in order of their flood tolerance (Kozlowski 1984b; Lugo *et al.* 1990). Hence, flood tolerance is the primary controlling factor in swamp forests, producing a pronounced change in tree species composition with elevation.

Since swamps are heavily forested, light becomes the important secondary factor. Low light levels inhibit the germination and growth of tree seedlings (Grubb 1977; Grime 1979). R. H. Jones *et al.* (1994) studied seedling regeneration over 4 years in four floodplain forests, cataloging over 10 000 seedlings – there was high mortality from shading during the first growing season. In all forests they examined, the composition of seedlings differed from the overstory trees, suggesting that composition would change if the adult trees died. They concluded that flooding, shading, and root competition were important environmental factors, but only in the years following establishment. The high rates of mortality and slow growth that they observed may be typical of densely shaded sites, but major disturbance did not occur during their study, so a period of rapid regeneration was not observed. Many tree species require gaps for their seedlings to establish (Grubb 1977; Pickett 1980; Duncan 1993). These gaps can be produced either by the death of individual trees, or when entire sections of forest are swept away by extreme floods or ice. The secondary constraint in this wetland type is therefore shading. Gap dynamics result. The processes of gap creation, seed dispersal to gaps, and establishment in gaps (Pickett and White 1985) therefore become prominent features of the ecology of swamp forests whether freshwater (Nanson and Beach 1977; Salo *et al.* 1986) or mangal (Lugo and Snedaker 1974).

1.5.4 Secondary constraints in marshes

Marshes arises in the region where the above three vegetation types intersect (Figure 1.11, center). Here, plants are exposed to three sets of environmental constraints. (1) Frequent inundation requires an ability to tolerate anoxia. (2) Frequent exposure to the atmosphere requires an ability to tolerate heavy

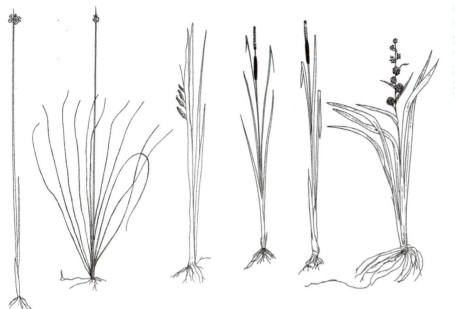

FIGURE 1.21 Although the size and shape of the photosynthetic shoots vary, nearly all marsh plants emerge each year from deeply buried rhizomes.

herbivory or fire. During longer dry periods, dense canopies can develop, so these plants must also be able to tolerate shade. (3) Finally, there is mechanical disturbance. When water levels are at intermediate levels, waves can break over the plants. In northern climates, waves can also grind ice onto the shore. Ice can also freeze onto the shoreline, and when water levels rise, large pieces of vegetation can be torn away. In short, all these different constraints require a very special type of plant. Marshes are the result. Unlike in swamps, woody shoots are not suitable: they would be burned by fire, ripped out by ice, or torn away by floods. The above-ground parts are therefore herbaceous. Rather like prairie plants, the herbaceous shoots arise from deeply buried rhizomes (Figure 1.21), these being horizontal stems that provide anchorage for shoots during light disturbance, storage during periods of unsuitable conditions, and regeneration after heavier disturbance (Archibold 1995). Many years ago Raunkaier (1937) recognized the importance of protecting meristems from damage. Most marsh

plants fall into his category of cryptophytes, plants that regenerate from buds, bulbs, or rhizomes that are completely buried in the substrate.

In cases of severe disturbance, even deeply buried rhizomes may be killed. This may occur when a site is deeply flooded for several years running. Managers have established that, in genera like *Typha*, the dead shoots can carry oxygen to rhizomes, but if the shoots have first been destroyed by fire or grazing, the rhizomes are far more sensitive to flooding (Kaminski *et al.* 1985). Intense grazing by mammals is well documented to destroy extensive stands of marsh plants (van der Valk and Davis 1978; Fritzell 1989). In addition to buried rhizomes, therefore, most of these species have long-lived seeds that persist buried in the soil (van der Valk and Davis 1978; Keddy and Reznicek 1986).

Since disturbance is intermittent, there are also periods when dense canopies may form and competition for light can become important. Deeply buried rhizome systems combined with dense arrays of shoots create strong interference with neighboring plants.

Table 1.6 **The primary constraint of flooding creates a series of secondary constraints that determine the ecological attributes of wetland communities**

Wetland type	Nature of flooding		Secondary constraints	Secondary characteristics	Key references to secondary constraints
	Mean level	Duration			
Aquatic	High	High (continuous)	Low CO_2 Low light Waves	Stress tolerance	Sculthorpe (1967) Hutchinson (1975)
Peatland	Low	High (continuous)	Infertility	Evergreenness Mycorrhizae Carnivory	Grime (1979) Chapin (1980) Givnish (1988)
Marsh	Medium	Medium (50% growing season)	Mechanical disturbance Grazing Fire	Buried rhizomes Annual shoots Seed banks	White (1979)
Swamp	Low (with seasonal highs)	Low (30% growing season)	Disturbance Shade	Gap colonization Shade tolerance	Pickett and White (1985) Grime (1979)

Large clones of *Typha* and *Phragmites* are able to dominate wetland communities to the detriment of other species with smaller growth forms and shorter shoots (Gaudet and Keddy 1988; Gopal and Goel 1993; Keddy *et al.* 1998). Further, many common genera of marsh plants appear to have the ability to interfere with neighbors through the production of toxins (Gopal and Goel 1993).

Most of the species that form dense stands in marshes belong to one evolutionary lineage of plants – the Monocotyledonae. Their distinctive anatomy appears to be closely associated with these conditions of recurring flooding and disturbance.

In summary, the main wetland types arise because of the distinctive combination of secondary factors that result from flooding (Table 1.6). Wet meadows are the only one of the basic six wetland types that do not appear as a distinctive region in Figure 1.11. From this perspective, wet meadows are probably best imagined as a particular kind of marsh, but one where drought is a frequent occurrence. Wet meadows are similar to marshes, except that most plants are smaller, and rather than persisting with deeply buried rhizomes, they appear more dependent upon frequent regeneration from reserves of buried seeds. Wet meadows may therefore represent an extreme type of marsh where rates of disturbance are so high, and the habitat so short-lived, that even reeds and grasses cannot establish dominance.

1.6 Wetlands provide valuable functions and services

Human societies are entirely dependent, both for their survival and well-being, upon the biosphere, the 20-km thick layer that provides all the necessities of life. We can evaluate the benefits provided by the biosphere, and wetlands in particular, to humans by measuring the many services it provides.

1.6.1 Ecological services: the de Groot approach

The overview by de Groot (1992) lists 37 services that natural environments perform for humans (Table 1.7). These range from the ozone layer's

---

Table 1.7 **Services that may be performed by natural environments including wetlands**

Regulation services

1. Protection against harmful cosmic influences
2. Regulation of the local and global energy balance
3. Regulation of the chemical composition of the atmosphere
4. Regulation of the chemical composition of the oceans
5. Regulation of the local and global climate (incl. the hydrological cycle)
6. Regulation of runoff and flood prevention (watershed protection)
7. Water catchment and groundwater recharge
8. Prevention of soil erosion and sediment control
9. Formation of topsoil and maintenance of soil fertility
10. Fixation of solar energy and biomass production
11. Storage and recycling of organic matter
12. Storage and recycling of nutrients
13. Storage and recycling of human waste
14. Regulation of biological control mechanisms
15. Maintenance of migration and nursery habitats
16. Maintenance of biological (and genetic) diversity

Carrier services: providing space and a suitable substrate for

1. Human habitation and (indigenous) settlements
2. Cultivation (crop growing, animal husbandry, aquaculture)
3. Energy conversion
4. Recreation and tourism
5. Nature protection

Production services

1. Oxygen
2. Water (for drinking, irrigation, industry, etc.)
3. Food and nutritious drinks
4. Genetic resources
5. Medicinal resources
6. Raw materials for clothing and household fabrics
7. Raw materials for building, construction, and industrial use
8. Biochemicals (other than fuel and medicines)
9. Fuel and energy
10. Fodder and fertilizer
11. Ornamental resources

Information services

1. Esthetic information
2. Spiritual and religious information
3. Historic information (heritage value)
4. Cultural and artistic inspiration
5. Scientific and educational information

Note: Services originally termed functions by de Groot.
Source: From de Groot (1992).

---

service of protecting humans from harmful cosmic influences to a landscape's service in artistic inspiration. Further, de Groot breaks these services down into four categories:

(i) *Regulation services* describe the capacity of ecosystems to regulate essential ecological processes and life support systems on Earth. Examples include regulation of the CO_2 and O_2 concentrations of the atmosphere.

(ii) *Carrier services* describe the space or suitable substrate needed for the conduct of human activities such as living, cultivation, and recreation. Examples include soil and rainfall for growing crops.

(iii) *Production services* describe the resources provided by nature, including food, raw materials for industrial use, and genetic raw material. Examples would include production of clean water for drinking and wood for building.

(iv) *Informational services* describe the role played by natural ecosystems in the maintenance of mental health by providing cognitive development, spiritual inspiration, and scientific appreciation of the world. Examples would include wilderness areas and historical landscapes.

1.6.2 Evaluating ecological services

Others have tried to work out dollar values for each service. Costanza *et al.* (1997a) tried to measure the value in dollars per hectare per year of 17 ecological services, including climate regulation, water supply and recreation, for 16 biomes. The total value of services performed by natural systems, $33 trillion, is roughly 1.8 times the global gross national product (GNP), itself an imperfect measure of human economic activity. Major services performed by wetlands included "disturbance regulation" at $4539 ha/yr, "water supply" at $3800 ha/yr, and "water treatment" at $4177 ha/yr. These numbers excluded estuaries, which themselves rated $21 100 ha/yr for "nutrient cycling."

The number of studies of economic value is steadily increasing. The World Wildlife Fund (also known as the World Wide Fund for Nature, WWF) undertook a review of 89 wetland evaluation studies (Schuyt and Brander 2004). To illustrate the types of services and their values, Table 1.8 shows the services provided by the Pantanal, one of the world's largest wetlands, and also with particularly high economic services (Seidl and Moraes 2000). You can see that flood control and water supply were the most important services in this wetland, followed by waste treatment, water regulation and cultural values. At the global scale, WWF concludes that the two most valuable services wetlands provide are (1) recreational opportunities and amenities (median value of $492 ha/yr) and (2) flood control and storm buffering (median value of $464 ha/yr). The most conservative estimate was that 63 million hectares of global wetlands provide services valued at $3.4 billion per year. This is conservative because the total area of wetlands, and the value per hectare, could both be larger. We will return to this study in Chapter 11.

The important point is that wetlands have enormous value, however you categorize the services

Table 1.8 Economic value of the Pantanal wetland (millions of 1994 US dollars per year)

Service	Value
Water supply	5322.58
Disturbance regulation	4703.61
Waste treatment	1359.64
Cultural	1144.49
Water regulation	1019.82
Nutrient recycling	498.21
Recreation	423.64
Habitat/refugia	285.04
Raw materials	202.03
Gas regulation	181.31
Erosion control	170.70
Food production	143.76
Climate regulation	120.50
Soil formation	60.22
Pollination	33.03
Biological control	30.39
Genetic resources	22.15
Total	15 721.12

Source: Adapted from Schuyt and Brander (2004) based on Seidl and Morases (2000).

that they perform. In Chapter 11 we will look at these services in more detail with particular emphasis upon production (including wildlife production), regulation of atmospheric carbon dioxide and methane levels, maintenance of the global nitrogen cycle, biodiversity, and recreation. When humans manipulate wetlands, whether by draining for agriculture, or flooding to increase certain species, many services are simultaneously changed, often with unknown consequences.

1.7   Causal factors in wetland ecology

As we have now seen, wetlands arise because there is water, but the particular kind of wetland, and the characteristics of its species or communities, will depend upon another set of environmental factors. The study of wetland ecology can therefore be approached as the study of these key environmental factors. If you know which factors predominate, you can predict the kind of wetland that will likely arise. Moreover, you will have a preliminary indication of which factors are important to the wild

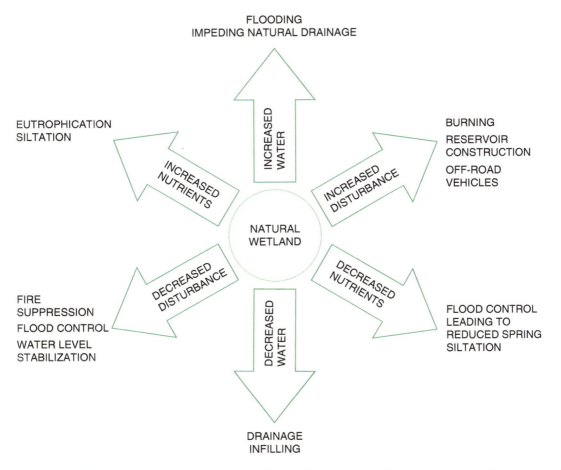

FIGURE 1.22 Three key factors (flooding, disturbance, and nutrients) control much of the variation in wetland communities. Hence, there is a chapter in this book for each of these key factors. If any one of these three factors is changed, the wetland will change in response.

creatures in that wetland. Take the Everglades as a well-known example. We shall look into the ecology of the Everglades in more detail later in the book. In terms of key factors, the Everglades are the result of extremely low nutrient levels, and seasonally varying water levels. Hence, the plants and animals that occur there must be able to tolerate these two key factors. And you can predict, with confidence, that if you increase nutrient levels, or change water levels, you will harm the species in that wetland. The key factor approach is therefore a very important way of thinking about wetlands. There are three principles that can guide our thinking about key factors.

1.7.1 Three principles

The first of the three principles, important in the study of key environmental factors that control wetland type and community composition, states that *a particular community or ecosystem is produced by multiple environmental factors acting simultaneously*. We can therefore picture any particular wetland (and that includes its species, communities, and services) as being a product of the pushing and pulling of opposing environmental factors (Figure 1.22). Any specific wetland you encounter has arisen as a temporary consequence of

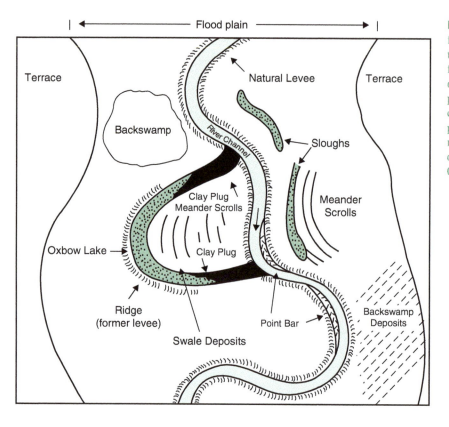

FIGURE 1.23 The wetlands in floodplains are the result of three principal processes: flooding, erosion, and deposition. These create a physical template that controls the composition and processes in wetlands along most rivers and in many deltas. (From Mitsch and Gosselink 1986.)

these multiple factors. It may be useful to consider this set of physical factors as a kind of *habitat template,* which both guides and constrains the biological communities and ecological processes that occur. Along most watercourses – the Mississippi River, the Danube River, the Amazon River, or the Yangtze River, for example – the movement of water, and particularly the movement of floodwaters, creates gravel bars, eroding banks, sand bars, oxbows, and deltas (Figure 1.23). Along such watercourses, the three most important factors in the habitat template may be (i) flooding, (ii) erosion, and (iii) deposition. These are not entirely independent, of course, but for the purposes of this book I have tried to tease them apart somewhat. There are therefore separate chapters for flooding, disturbance, and burial. Similarly, in small European peatlands, the most important factors in the habitat template may be (i) water availability, (ii) fertility, (iii) frequency of disturbances such as fire, and

(iv) intensity of grazing. Again, these are not independent of one another, but there are separate chapters on flooding, fertility, disturbance, and herbivory.

Each of these environmental factors has its own set of effects on a wetland. The second principle therefore states that *to understand and manage wetlands, scientists must determine the quantitative relationships between environmental factors and the properties of wetlands*. The study of each factor in the habitat template provides an opportunity to study such quantitative relationships. Examples might include (i) the production of fish as determined by floodplain area, (ii) the diversity of plants as controlled by fertility, or (iii) the composition of invertebrates produced by different rates of burial by sediment. These relationships summarize the state of human knowledge about the factors that create and control wetlands. The challenge for the scientist is to unravel these factors, discover their consequences for wetlands, and determine their relative importance. Throughout this book, I will try to share figures that show you key factors that control the properties of wetlands. The challenge for managers and conservationists is to first document these relationships, and then, if necessary, manipulate or regulate one or more of them to maintain or produce the desired characteristics of a wetland.

These challenges are made difficult by the many kinds of wetlands, and the many factors at work in them. The difficulty is compounded by a third principle: *the multiple factors that produce a community or ecosystem will change through time*. Wetlands are no different from other ecosystems, where disturbance from fire, storms, landslides, and floods controls the communities and species at a site. If humans change the factors acting on the wetland in Figure 1.22, say by decreasing spring flooding or increasing fertility, the balance of forces will shift and the wetland composition or function will begin to shift as well. The habitat template along watercourses in Figure 1.23 is constantly changing as moving water reshapes the environment. It is far too easy, and therefore far too common, for humans to study small fragments of this habitat complex (say one species or one vegetation type in one oxbow lake), losing track of the fact that the particular species and community types are but transitory occurrences at any location. To understand wetlands, and to manage them wisely, it is essential to appreciate their *multi*factorial and dynamic nature right from the start of our inquiry. Thus the introduction of these principles is early in the book.

All of the chapters that follow can be treated as elaborations on these principles, expanding the description of known relationships, and then discussing how these influence the study, conservation, and management of wetlands.

1.7.2 Six causal factors

By now you will appreciate how important it is for us to understand which environmental factors are dominant in each wetland we encounter. Yes, flooding is necessary, but so are other factors such as fertility and disturbance. The factors allocated separate chapters in this book are hydrology, fertility, disturbance, competition, herbivory, and burial, arranged (roughly) in declining order of importance. We can think of these as a kind of shopping list of factors that will operate to some degree in almost any wetland you encounter. (Note that ecologists may use slightly different words for referring to key factors – they are also called environmental filters, habitat templates, or causal factors, depending upon the situation.)

Other factors might be added. Four in particular should be mentioned at the start: salinity, positive interactions, time, and roads.

Salinity I have deliberately not added salinity in as a separate factor because this would immediately create a ghetto of sorts for saline wetlands, leading readers to overlook the many ways that saline wetlands are similar to freshwater wetlands. Often, however, you will see freshwater and saltwater wetlands (or interior wetlands and coastal wetlands) treated as if they were entirely different systems. If salinity had its own chapter, then peatlands might next have their own category, and would be a further loss of unity in the book. This sort of division of research by wetland type is something I actively sought to avoid. I do discuss salinity and its effects explicitly in Section 8.1. Further, there are also many excellent treatises on saline wetlands (e.g. Chapman 1974, 1977; Pomeroy and Wiegert 1981; Tomlinson 1986; Adam 1990; Silliman *et al.* 2009) which a single chapter could not duplicate.

Positive interactions Positive interactions could include floodplain trees providing food for fish, beavers creating ponds for frogs, and *Sphagnum* moss creating peat for orchids. While these may be locally important, I have not given them chapter status. This may appear to contradict my own work, since I have written about how textbooks ignore positive interactions (Keddy 1990a). There are fine reviews on mutualism (Boucher 1985; Smith and Douglas 1987). There is increasing evidence for positive interactions in wetlands (Bertness and Hacker 1994; Bertness and Yeh 1994; Bertness and Leonard 1997). But rather than combine such positive interactions in one chapter, I have sorted them by their main effects: fish and plants are discussed under flooding, alligator effects are discussed under disturbance, and peat accumulation under succession and burial.

Time Time is a critical factor that could have been included: entire lakes have come and gone over the 20 000 or so years since the last ice age, peat has accumulated for thousands of years as continental glaciers receded, beaver ponds come and go over centuries, and riparian wetlands are flooded each year. I have not included time as a separate factor, since time is often a surrogate for other causal factors that vary with time. Hence, time is rolled into each chapter: changes in hydrology during glaciation are introduced in hydrology, changes in

fertility with peat accumulation are discussed under fertility, fire cycles are discussed under disturbance, succession is discussed under zonation and burial, and so on.

Roads Roads do not fit neatly into any category, yet roads in particular, and paving in general, are causing major changes in wetlands. I have therefore added in this edition a new chapter called "other factors" that includes effects of roads (Section 8.2), coarse woody debris (Section 8.3), and some other factors that are important but that do not fall obviously into the main chapters.

I do not want you to think this is the only way to sort the many topics covered in this book. A book with separate chapters on salinity, positive interactions, and time could be written, and would undoubtedly have its merits. Those of you who wish to see time and positive interactions as separate chapters can consult my book *Plants and Vegetation* (Keddy 2007) to see wetlands viewed from this perspective.

1.8   More on definitions and classification of wetlands

Now, having a better understanding of the main types of wetlands, environmental conditions they have in common, and factors important in wetland creation and maintenance, let's return to our discussion of wetland definition and classification.

1.8.1 More on defining wetlands

We started with a single definition for a wetland in Section 1.1.1. Many other definitions, particularly longer ones, are possible. Some definitions are predominantly written by and for scientists, others by and for lawyers. We do not want to get tangled up in definitions – as Shakespeare observed, "How every fool can play upon the word." Yet many court cases that deal with wetlands can hinge upon definitions. So before we look at more definitions, we should

understand whether they are scientific or legal in their audience.

A scientific definition is a tool for the analysis of nature. The first definition described the domain of inquiry of wetland ecology. It also directed our attention to some processes in wetlands. But a tool should be retained only if it is useful. As our knowledge of a discipline grows, we may expect our definitions to slowly change too. There is an evolutionary process at work here: definitions help us investigate nature, and our investigation of nature helps definitions. Is a marine rocky intertidal zone a wetland? Are the contents of the leaf of a pitcher plant a wetland? How dry does a site have to become before it is no longer a wetland? These sorts of questions arise, and can confuse us. The definition above is quite satisfactory for beginning this book.

A legal definition is another matter. Although legal definitions can also evolve, the process is often much slower. Moreover, a clever lawyer can exploit any weakness in a definition, with the risk of serious social, economic, and environmental consequences. One can even have Supreme Court justices with no training in wetland ecology presuming to write definitions. Often these create more confusion than clarity.

The Ramsar Convention is an international treaty for wetland conservation. Adopted in 1971 in the city of Ramsar, in Iran, the "Convention on Wetlands of International Importance especially as Waterfowl Habitat" had 158 contracting parties by the end of 2008. Altogether, 1828 sites totaling some 168 million hectares have been designated. Participants accept the obligation to promote "as far as is possible the wise use of wetlands in their territory." Wise use is interpreted to mean the maintenance of the ecological character of wetlands (Navid 1988). The Convention uses a particularly broad definition of wetlands in Article 1:

... areas of marsh, fen, peatland or water, whether natural, permanent or temporary, with water that is static or flowing, fresh, brackish or salt, including areas of marine waters the depth of which at low tide does not exceed six meters.

Moreover, the area of coverage is broadened by Article 2, which provides that wetlands

... may incorporate riparian and coastal zones adjacent to the wetlands and islands or bodies of marine water deeper than six meters at low tide lying within the wetlands.

As a consequence, the Ramsar Convention includes rivers, coastal areas, and even coral reefs (Navid 1988). Although I have adopted a relatively broad coverage of wetland types in this book, coral reefs and rocky marine shorelines are excluded.

The Ramsar definition is short and all-inclusive. Not all are. The Committee on Characterization of Wetlands (1995) has prepared an entire book on this topic for the United States! One ventures into terrain

with "national delineation manuals," "interagency manuals," and "revised manuals" that arise as different agencies and government bodies struggle to legally define wetlands. Flawed definitions can easily allow a wetland to be destroyed by developers. The Committee on Characterization of Wetlands therefore developed a "reference definition" to stand outside of any single agency, policy or regulation. Their reference definition is:

A wetland is an ecosystem that depends on constant or recurrent, shallow inundation or saturation at or near the surface of the substrate. The minimum essential characteristics of a wetland are recurrent, sustained inundation or saturation at or near the surface and the presence of physical, chemical, and biological features reflective of recurrent, sustained inundation or saturation. Common diagnostic features of wetlands are hydric soils and hydrophytic vegetation. These features will be present except where specific physiochemical, biotic, or anthropogenic factors have removed them or prevented their development.

This longer definition still contains the essential elements of my shorter one: water, modified substrate, and distinct biota. We shall let Mitsch and Gosselink (1986, pp. 16–17) have the last word on this topic.

Because wetland characteristics grade continuously from aquatic to terrestrial, any definition is to some extent arbitrary. As a result, there is no single, universally recognized definition of what a wetland is. This lack has caused confusion and inconsistencies in the management, classification, and inventorying of wetland systems, but considering the diversity of types, sizes, location, and conditions of wetlands ... the inconsistency should be no surprise.

Enough on definitions. Applying a simple definition in a commonsense way allows us to begin. The Earth has about 5.6 million square kilometers of wetlands (Dugan 1993), an area equivalent to roughly ten times the size of France or nearly four times the size of Alaska. This book will emphasize what wetlands have in common. All the time, of course, we know that they will differ in detail – no two wetlands will ever be identical. Until the similarities are described, it is difficult to decide which differences are the important ones. This book therefore deliberately takes a top–down approach. We will begin with commonalities among wetlands at the global scale. Then, gradually, patterns can be dissected to uncover differences.

1.8.2 More on classification systems

We started with some simple classification concepts – six types of wetlands, controlled by their location, and hydrology. As soon as you try to apply a simple system, it becomes clear how complicated nature is. This is particularly so in tropical landscapes where there are large numbers of species, or at larger scales where climate, soil, and biota change, or in areas where topography produces many kinds of unusual circumstances. Hence, wetland classification systems can become rather larger and more complicated. Here are three examples.

Tropical Caribbean system

The challenge of any classification system is to simplify a complicated world. The Caribbean illustrates just how complicated it can be. In Cuba alone it is possible to define 27 classes, 53 orders, 80 alliances, and 186 plant associations, of which nearly one-quarter are wetlands. Cuba also has the largest wetland complex in the Caribbean; on the south coast near the Peninsula de Zapata there are some half-million hectares of mangroves and freshwater marshes. The diversity of wetlands across the Caribbean probably results from a combination of factors including the excess of rainfall over evapotranspiration, the varied topography, and the complex geology. The island of Puerto Rico, for example, has volcanic, plutonic, limestone, serpentine, sedimentary, and sandstone formations, and mountains exceeding 1000 m in the Cordillera Central, producing 164 soil types. Given the rich flora of the Caribbean, and the large number of endemic

species, a classification system using plant species names becomes too complex. Lugo *et al.* (1988) therefore recognize three main kinds of wetlands based upon geology and hydrology: riverine, basin, and fringe wetlands. Modifiers such as salinity, dominant life form, and nutrient status can then be superimposed. Adding three salinity levels (freshwater, oligohaline, and saline), three plant forms (herbaceous, scrub, and forest) and three nutrient levels (oligotrophic, eutrophic, and dystrophic) yields ($3 \times 3 \times 3 \times 3$) 81 basic wetland types, a system that is broad enough to include everything from mangal to montane seeps, yet simple enough to require only four main criteria for classification. The diversity of wetland types in Cuba, for example, is then reduced to 24.

African wetlands

Thompson and Hamilton (1983) use an even simpler system of our basic categories for describing the wide array of African wetlands. They recognize four main wetland types: (i) mangrove swamps and coastal peatlands, (ii) swamp forests, (iii) grass, sedge, and reed swamps, and, in uplands, (iv) flushes, cushion-bogs, and tussock sedge mires. Further subdivision can be based upon location (e.g. valley bogs) or dominant species (*Typha* marsh, *Papyrus* marsh). Compared with Lugo *et al.* (1988), formal rules and criteria may seem to be lacking, but this system none the less appears sufficient for a preliminary description of wetland types. (Note, however, that they use the word swamp more broadly than we do in this book; I recommend that we reserve the term swamp for only wooded wetlands: see Sections 1.2.1 and 1.5.3)

European phytosociology

Those reading the European literature will find that classification continues to finer and finer scales where each community type is ultimately given a separate name. For example, a *Phragmites communis* marsh in Poland would be placed in the Class Phragmitetea (R. Tx. et Prsg. 1942), Order Phragmitetalia eurosibirica (R. Tx. et Prsg. 1942),

Alliance Phragmition (Koch 1926), and Association Scirpo-Phragmitetum (Koch 1926) (vegetation type authors, not references, in parentheses). Palczynski (1984), for example, recognizes 7 classes, 10 orders, 14 alliances, and 37 associations in the Biebrza valley in Poland. Beeftink (1977) uses the same approach to classify salt marshes in northwestern Europe. I have not used such terminology in this book, but you can read more about it in sources such as Shimwell (1971) or Westhoff and van der Maarel (1973). At times, it seems that this creates confusion by distorting plant names and making work in wetlands obscure to all but a narrow group of experts. Perhaps local users, however, find it valuable, particularly in small reserves in human-dominated landscapes. In this book, I have tried to keep to simpler terminology. Thus the Scirpo–Phragmitetum Association would simply be called a *Scirpus–Phragmites* floodplain or *Scirpus–Phragmites* marsh, depending upon the circumstances.

1.8.3 Some confusions in terminology

Speaking of geographical and political regions, problems can easily arise. The word **swamp** causes much confusion between North Americans and Europeans. Inconsistent use of the word "swamp" causes problems even within England (Burnett 1964). The term "swamp" in British usage generally applies to wetlands in which the normal water level is above the soil surface, usually dominated by reeds (*Phragmites*), tall grasses, sedges, or rushes; the commonest kind being a "reed swamp." Similarly, in Africa, we saw that Thompson and Hamilton (1983) used the term swamp for grass-, sedge-, and reed-dominated herbaceous wetlands as well as for forested areas. In the definition used in this book (p. 7) herbaceous wetlands lacking peat are simply a kind of marsh; they may be further qualified with modifiers such as an "emergent marsh," "*Phragmites* marsh," "*Papyrus* marsh," or "lacustrine marsh" as the need arises.

Owing to the long history of interest in **peatlands**, there is a particularly diverse terminology here

(Gore 1983; Wheeler and Proctor 2000). In this book I use the world peatland inclusively, and avoid the word mire entirely. One might hope that the Russians would have sorted it out for us, having lived with peatlands for centuries, and having the world's largest, the West Siberian Lowland. Yet Zhulidov *et al.* (1997) tell us that until recently, there was not even a word for the general concept of "wetland." More than 30 local names (from *alasy* to *zaymischa*) existed and could be understood differently in different parts of the country. There is the further problem of translation from Russian to English.

Continuing with peatlands, the gradations between **bog** and **fen** also generate a great deal of terminology. The key factors appear to be the acidity of water, and the nutrient status of the water (Bridgham *et al.* 1996; Wheeler and Proctor 2000). These in turn control other characteristics such as rate of peat accumulation and plant species composition. Another set of terms emphasize the source of water, with bogs often being dependent upon rainfall (hence, **ombrotrophic**), while fens are connected to flowing groundwater (hence, **minerotrophic**). There are many more specialized terms. Where the groundwater has calcium as the dominant cation, fens with large numbers of plant species often arise, hence the utility of recognizing **calcareous fens** (Godwin *et al.* 2002). In cold climates, the flowing water though peatlands creates alternating ridges and pools at right angles to the direction of water flow (Figure 1.6*a*), producing **patterned fens** or string bogs (Foster *et al.* 1983; Mark *et al.* 1995). Around raised bogs, where water flowing off the bog meets mineral soils, a trough called a **lagg** is often found (Damman and Dowhan 1981; Godwin 1981). Overall, the proliferation of terms can be confusing to even the experts, in which case the simple distinctions between bog and fen, along with the categories shown in Figure 1.19, should suffice for most cases.

What to you call a wetland after people have built a wall around it? In the United States, these walls are often called levees, but levees also refer to natural features that arise along rivers. Hence, the term levee is misleading, unless you refer to "natural levee" and "artificial levee." The terms embankment or dyke might be better, with embankment implying an earthen structure and dyke implying a more elaborate one. An area surrounded by an embankment and drained does not seem to have a name in the United States, but is called a **polder** in Europe. Such terms must create nightmares for translators. Hence, as one example, one reads of polders (usually associated with the Netherlands) in Chinese landscapes. Although a Dutch word for a structure in China at first seems surprising, it actually is a step forward to consistency. I will use the term polder throughout this book.

These issues of terminology make it difficult for students and professionals alike. They make it difficult to communicate with other cultures. When it took a month to sail across the Atlantic, cultural differences in classification were perhaps inescapable. But in an era of international flights, e-mail, and global telephone linkages, not to mention books, scientific dialects are no longer acceptable. Let us hope that teachers will try to bequeath to their students one standard terminology. If we make the effort, perhaps we can all speak one language when in comes to wetlands. Hence, in this book, the narrow use of the word **swamp**, the broad use of the word **peatland**, and the consistent use of the term **polder**.

CONCLUSION

Let us conclude this chapter by reviewing the topics we have discussed so far, applied to one of the world's largest wetlands, the Pantanal. This wetland is an enormous savanna floodplain – 140 000 km^2, roughly the size of England – in central South America (Alho *et al.* 1988; Junk 1993; Alho 2005). Pantanal National Park protects part of the area.

The source of flooding is the Paraguay River, which flows southward through central South America, and eventually enters the ocean at Buenos Aires. The annual flood regime provided by the river is a critical factor. Much of the floodplain is seasonally flooded grassland where water levels can rise and fall many meters each year. The timing of the annual flood depends upon the rainfall upstream, which falls October through April, along with the lag until it reaches the Pantanal. Wildlife life cycles are closely tied to flood regimes. For example, consider fish. During the flood season fish move out of the river into the floodplains, while during dryer periods, the fish concentrate in pools where they become prey for birds. The birds use the fish to feed their young.

Depending on the depth and duration of flooding, different types of wetlands arise. These have local names in Portuguese (depressions are known as *corixos* and shallow water paths as *vazantes*. The rivers are lined with gallery forests and more elevated areas have semi-deciduous forests (Figure 1.24). As a consequence, aquatic and terrestrial vegetation (including cacti) are interspersed (Prance and Schaller 1982; Alho *et al.* 1988; Junk 1993). Much of the Pantanal, however, is marsh. One classification recognizes seven types of wetland vegetation, depending upon flooding regimes (Neiff 1986). Cattail swamps (Neiff's terminology), for example, are inundated only by occasional floods (5–10 years). The wetland can also be divided in to 11 geographical

FIGURE 1.24 Some scenes from the Pantanal. (*a*) vast area of seasonally inundated cerrado with forest islands, (*b*) gallery forest in foreground and semi-deciduous forest in background, (*c*) flooded savanna and gallery forest, (*d*) pond filled with *Eichhornia* and *Pontederia,* (*e*) sandy margin of Rio Negro showing *Vochysia divergens*, a tree characteristic of seasonally flooded areas, and (*f*) cattle grazing in a seasonally flooded savanna. (Courtesy G. Prance and J. Schaller.)

subregions – the Cáceres region, as one example, floods for up to 6 months out of the year, while others flood for lesser periods.

To put this in a regional context, a number of terrestrial vegetation types meet here: the cerrado biome of Central Brazil on the East, the semi-deciduous Amazonian forest to the northwest, and the chaco-like forest of Bolivia to the southwest. The wildlife is correspondingly rich, including jaguar, ocelot, giant anteater, giant otter, giant armadillo, crab-eating fox, pampas deer, and swamp deer, all threatened or endangered (Alho *et al.* 1988). There are 13 species of herons and egrets, 5 species of kingfishers, and 19 species of parrots. More than 540 species of fish have been recorded for the river systems as a whole.

The Pantanal provides many important services to the surrounding region (recall Table 1.8). Overall, the threats posed to this wetland, and the management problems that arise, typify the perils facing many of the world's wetlands.

Ranching Native populations of grazing animals have been slowly replaced by ranches. The subdivision of these ranches and intensification of grazing is even more detrimental to native plant communities.

Poaching The trade in animal hides continues. Just one 2500-kg shipment of hides contained 70 000 individual skins including jaguars, maned wolves, caimans, and snakes; the smugglers admitted that this shipment represented only 13% of all the skins (more than a half a million animals) that had been sent to Germany in the preceding 6 months (Alho *et al.* 1988). The added effects of removing large predators from this ecosystem are unknown.

Large-scale agriculture The native vegetation is being replaced with cropland, and the river thereby contaminated with herbicides, pesticides, and sediment. Alcohol distilleries for biomass fuels add to the contaminant load.

Deforestation This ongoing problem is being accelerated by illegal sawmills and fires set by ranchers.

Canalization The greatest threat may be the proposed Hidrovia Project (Bucher *et al.* 1993), a scheme that will use dredging and canals to create a 3440-km long waterway starting at Puerto Caceres in Brazil and ending at Nueva Palmira in Uruguay. The 1670 km of this project going straight through the heart of the Pantanal would be bound to cause major changes in hydrology and cause major changes throughout the flood zone.

A list like this can be depressing. This is why we need to understand key factors and causes and effects in wetlands. Without a general understanding, we end up only with a depressing list of threats, and no obvious course of action. This book provides an approach to addressing such problems. We begin with the simple question: where do wetlands occur and what types of wetland are present? We then ask which environmental factors produce each type of wetland. The most obvious causal factor is, of course, flooding, but secondary factors also produce the many different kinds of wetlands seen in a landscape. Once we understand the factors that produce the array of wetlands, and the different kinds of species in them, we are better able to predict the possible consequences of human actions. We can then make more intelligent assessments of which problems need to be solved first, and we can come up with a list of possible actions. In the final chapter we will explore the approaches that have been used to protect important wetlands.

Chapter contents

2 | Flooding

Water creates wetlands. The most important causal factor that we need to study is therefore water. The biological composition of the wetland, from its fish to its birds, from its plants to its insects, depends upon the way in which water moves through the wetland. Timing and rate of flow are critical.
In most landscapes there tend to be drier periods interrupted by pulses of flooding after rainfall or when snow melts. The more we study wetlands, the more we find that these cycles of flooding, also called flood pulses, are critical to understanding wetlands. There is an entire scientific discipline of hydrology, that addresses the occurrence, distribution, and movement of water (Ward and Trimble 2004; Brutsaert 2005).

Here we shall focus on flooding. The **amplitude** and **frequency** of water level fluctuations are probably the most important factors affecting the composition and function of wetlands. Water levels change over many timescales – the annual cycle of flooding is the most obvious, but there is also change from one year to the next. Let us begin, then, by considering these two sources of variation, flooding within and among years.

Within years Pictures of flooding (Figure 2.1) are a vivid reminder that flow rates change with the time of year in rivers around the world (Figure 2.2). High water periods or **pulses** (Middleton 2002) are natural and entirely predictable events. In the temperate zone pulses are produced each spring by the rapid melting of the accumulated precipitation of an entire winter. In tropical and subtropical rivers pulses are usually caused by rainy seasons such as monsoons. The size of pulses is often remarkable – the Amazon River, which carries approximately one-fifth of the Earth's total freshwater runoff, can change level by more than 10 m within a single year!

Among years There are also pronounced differences in water levels from one year to the next in most wetlands. This is caused by factors such as changes in rainfall patterns or timing of spring thaws. In the Great Lakes, historical records show that the yearly mean has ranged across several meters over a century

FIGURE 2.1 Flooding is a natural process in landscapes. When humans build cities in or adjacent to wetlands, flooding can be expected. This example shows Cedar Rapids in the United States in 2008 (*The Gazette*), but incidences of flood damage to cities go far back in history to early cities such as Nineveh mentioned in *The Epic of Gilgamesh* (Sanders 1972). (See also color plate.)

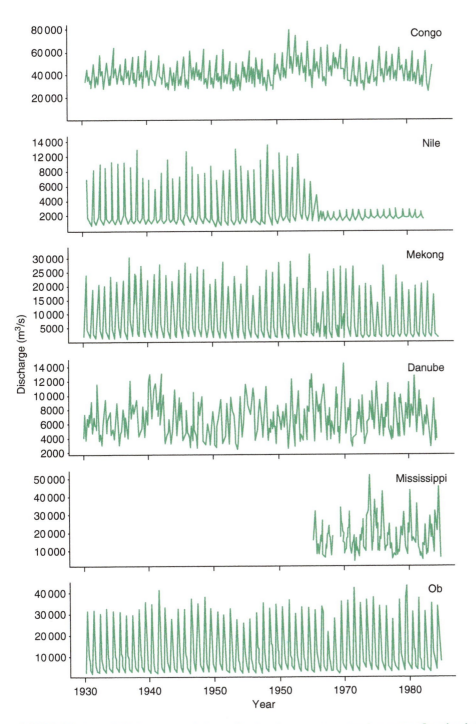

FIGURE 2.2 Annual high water periods, or flood pulses, create extensive areas of wetland along rivers. These rivers illustrate the variability of water level fluctuation patterns. The sampling stations are as follows: Congo (Kinshasa, Democratic Republic of the Congo), Nile (Aswan Dam, Egypt; note the effect of the dam on flood amplitude after 1965), Mekong (Mukdahan, Thailand), Danube (Ceatal Izmail, Romania), Mississippi (Vicksburg, U.S.A.), and Ob (Salekhard, Russia). (From Vörösmarty *et al*. 1996.)

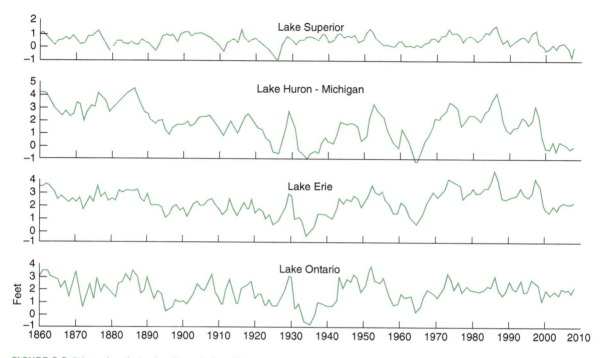

FIGURE 2.3 Water levels in the Great Lakes illustrate longer-term changes in water level. These changes too are part of natural processes that create wetlands. (From Environment Canada 1976 and Canadian Hydrographic Service 2009.)

(Figure 2.3). Cores that have been extracted from old sand deposits and dune systems in Lake Michigan track such water level changes back for more than 4000 years (Baedke and Thompson 2000; Johnston *et al.* 2007); peat deposits, shells, and pollen document early low-water stages in Lake Erie (Pengelly *et al.* 1997); old shorelines far inland document major changes in elevation and drainage since the departure of the ice sheets (Teller 2003). Such evidence, when compiled, shows that

wetlands – and entire lakes – have come and gone over the past 10 000 years (Figure 2.4).

In this chapter we shall look at some effects of water level fluctuations across a broad array of wetland types, and a broad array of plants and animals. We will also consider how human activities change these natural patterns, and examine attempts to predict the consequences for wetlands. But first a little bit of history.

2.1   Flooding and humans: an old story

Floods have been a part of human experience ever since the first settlements were built on floodplains. Stories of floods go back at least to the book of Genesis, which recounts how it rained 40 days and nights, how Noah built an ark which floated on the floodwaters, how "the waters prevailed exceedingly

upon the earth; and all the high hills, that were under the whole heaven were covered" (7:19).

Archeologists have found even earlier flood stories. In the 1830s, a young Englishman, Austen Henry Layard, spent some years excavating archeological sites in Mesopotamia (Sanders 1972).

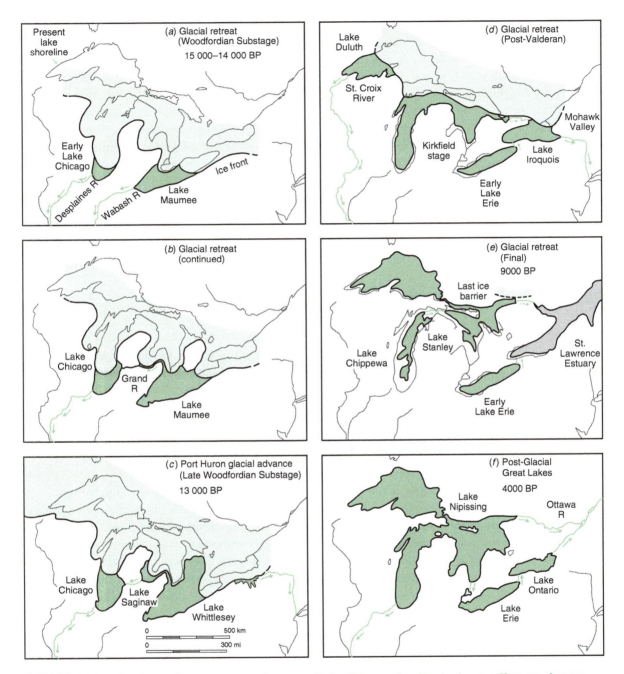

FIGURE 2.4 Water levels can change over even longer periods of time as the climate changes. Here are changes in the water levels of the Great Lakes over the past 20 000 years. (From Strahler 1971.)

One of the most significant discoveries was thousands of broken tablets from the palace of Nineveh. Nineveh, now in modern Iraq, was then an Assyrian city that fell in 612 BC to a combined army of Medes and Babylonians. The destruction was so complete that the city never rose again. Included in the ruins was the entire library of Assurbanipal "King of the World, King of Assyria." Over 25 000 broken tablets from this library were taken to the British Museum. When deciphered, they revealed a story now known as *The Epic of Gilgamesh*. One section of this epic narrates how there was a flood. "The rider of the storm sent down the rain ... a black cloud came from the horizon; it thundered within where Adad,

lord of the storm, was riding ... For six days and nights the winds blew, torrent and tempest and flood overwhelmed the world ..." (pp. 110–11). This epic also has a boat full of survivors who come to rest on a mountain and who release a dove to search for land.

In *The Epic of Gilgamesh*, as now, floods are depicted as tragedies. Says the epic, "Would that famine had wasted the world rather than the flood. Would that pestilence had wasted mankind rather than the flood." (p. 112). This attitude is similar to the accounts of flooding presented by reporters today. One of the objectives of this chapter is to tell the rest of the story and put floods in their proper ecological context.

2.2   Some biological consequences of flooding

Water level fluctuations affect wildlife by creating and maintaining different wetland habitat types. In addition, nearly all species of animals are sensitive to both the depth of water and the timing of floods. Let us look at a few examples.

2.2.1 Wading birds in the Everglades

The Everglades are famous for their great variety of wading birds including great egrets, white ibis (Figure 2.5a), wood storks, and roseate spoonbills. Annual low-water periods force small fish to concentrate in the remaining few wet areas, where they become prey for wading birds (Brosnan *et al.* 2007). Nesting is timed to coincide with these low-water periods. Wood storks, for example, are very dependent upon high concentrations of small fish for feeding their nestlings. Gradual and consistent declining water levels throughout the nesting period appear to be critical for such birds to raise their young.

2.2.2 Frogs in temporary ponds

Many species of frogs and salamanders breed in temporary ponds, also known as vernal pools. In the

north, these ponds are filled by melting snow. Further south, they may be filled by winter rain. Adult frogs and salamanders often live in adjoining forest areas. As soon as standing water becomes available they must move to the ponds, mate, and lay eggs. The juveniles must then grow rapidly and reach maturity before the water dries up (Pechmann *et al.* 1989; Rowe and Dunson 1995). It is a race against time.

One example is the Mississippi gopher frog (Figure 2.5b). Adult gopher frogs spend most of their life in the longleaf pine forests, often living in burrows constructed by gopher tortoises or mammals or even crayfish. They breed in small isolated ponds. The timing and frequency of winter rain is critical; normally rain fills the ponds around December. The ponds dry out during the summer – in nearly half the years, the pond dries before young can emerge (Richter *et al.* 2001, 2003).

Other environmental factors also need to be considered in maintaining habitat for gopher frogs. The ponds must dry up completely, because this kills fish which would otherwise eat the tadpoles. During dry periods, the surrounding longleaf pine forests must burn to maintain habitat for adults. The timing of rain, drought, and fire are all

FIGURE 2.5 Many wetland organisms are dependent upon annual flood pulses. Animals discussed here include (a) white ibis (U.S. Fish and Wildlife Service), (b) Mississippi gopher frog (courtesy M. Redmer), (c) dragonfly (courtesy C. Rubec), and (d) tambaqui (courtesy M. Goulding). Plants discussed here include (e) furbish lousewort (bottom left; U.S. Fish and Wildlife Service) and (f) Plymouth gentian. (See also color plate.)

important. Real estate development, reduced water tables, roads, logging, fire suppression, and fish stocking have all taken their toll on this habitat. Although the Mississippi gopher frog once occurred along the gulf coastal plain from Louisiana to Alabama, there is now only a single population of about 100 individuals (Richter and Seigel 2002).

2.2.3 Birds in salt marshes and deltas

In deltaic marshes, even small pulses of fresh water can change salinity. The Camargue in southern France is one of Europe's largest deltas, and is bracketed by two branches of the Rhone River. The Rhone carries fresh water from the north southward to the Mediterranean Sea and into an area with hot dry summers and moisture deficits. The Camargue is well known for its population of flamingoes. Flamingoes (there are six species in the world) are filter feeders and depend upon populations of aquatic invertebrates such as fairy shrimp, which they separate from the mud with their distinctive bills. The greater flamingo (the species in the Camargue) feeds largely on macroinvertebrates; the composition and abundance of the macroinvertebrates is strongly affected by hydroperiod and salinity (Waterkeyn *et al.* 2008). Rice fields, canals, and other human alterations to hydrology can therefore have a significant effect upon food supplies; we will return to this topic later (Section 8.1.5).

Tidal cycles also affect water levels and salinity. Humans may manipulate both through the construction of ditches and impoundments. The costs and benefits of these structures are controversial. Certainly, they can have major effects on birds. Consider an example from salt marshes on the east coast of North America. One study compared three flooding regimes – typical salt marsh, impounded marsh, and areas that had been partially flooded by plugging drainage ditches (Burger *et al.* 1982). The impoundments had more than five times as many birds as the natural tidal marshes and had many red-winged blackbirds, gulls, terns, shorebirds, and waterfowl. Salt marsh species, such as clapper rails,

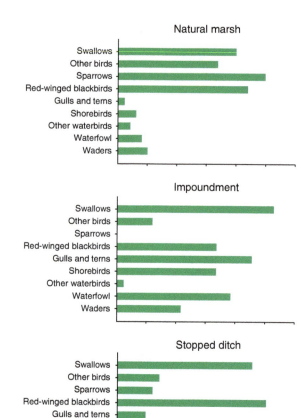

FIGURE 2.6 The composition of birds changes with salinity and flooding. Compare these three different kinds of coastal marsh: natural salt marsh, impounded marsh, and marsh with stopped ditches. (From data in Burger *et al.* 1982.)

seaside sparrows, and sharp-tailed sparrows, were, however, absent from impoundments (Figure 2.6). Thus changes in the water level regime not only changed the abundance of birds, they also caused dramatic shifts in composition.

2.2.4 Fish in floodplains

Fish (Figure 2.5d) behavior and life cycles are also closely tied to periods of inundation. In her monograph on tropical fish, Lowe-McConnell (1975) says "In both Africa and South America where much of the land is very flat peneplain, the rivers inundate immense areas, on a scale unknown in temperate regions. Submerged seasonally and drying out for part of each year, these floodplains are interspersed with creeks, pools and swamps, some of which retain water throughout the year." (p. 90) Although rains occur in the summer, flood peaks occur well after the rains have started; the delay depends upon the origin of the main floodwater and the time taken to travel downstream. As the rising water floods up channels and creeks, it releases fish imprisoned within ponds and swampy areas. Still higher levels then create a vast sheet of water. This water is enriched in nutrients from decaying organic matter, including the droppings of grazing animals, perhaps first baked by sun or fire. "This leads to an explosive growth of bacteria, algae and zooplankton, which in turn supports a rich fauna of aquatic insects and other invertebrates. The aquatic vegetation, both rooted and floating, grows very rapidly." (p. 92) Many fish then migrate upstream and move laterally onto the floodplain to spawn. The eggs hatch within a few days, so the young appear when food is plentiful. The high-water period allows feeding, growing, and fattening. Once water levels fall, the fish move back into the main river. Some fish are killed by being stranded in drying pools. Even ungulates such as peccaries (*Tayassu pecari*) have been observed visiting floodplains to feed upon fish trapped by falling water (Fragoso 1998). This same general sequence of events occurs in rivers throughout the tropics including Africa, South America, and Asia (Figure 2.7).

2.2.5 Macroinvertebrates

Vernal pools which are filled by rainfall or by melting snow, and which then progressively dry during the summer, also provide habitat for many insects. The insect fauna changes with the duration of standing water, often termed hydroperiod. Hydroperiod affects nearly all the species in the pond, including plants, amphibians, and fish. Insects (Figure 2.5c) often receive less attention. Insects process a large proportion of the biomass in wetlands (Chapter 1), they provide food for species ranging from minnows to flamingoes, and they can also be predators that feed upon amphibian larvae. It was with the latter interest that Tarr *et al.* (2005) used dip nets to sample the predatory macroinvertebrates that occupied vernal, intermediate, and permanent ponds – a gradient from short to long hydroperiod.

Short hydroperiod wetlands (those lasting less than 4 months after spring thaw and drying in May–July) were generally small (ca. 0.05 ha), were covered by a forest canopy, supported shrubs, and contained logs and leaf litter. The long hydroperiod wetlands were larger (ca. 2.5 ha) and had well-developed aquatic plant assemblages including *Sparganium* spp. and *Potamogeton* spp. A total of 6202 aquatic invertebrates representing 47 genera were collected, with a mean of more than 10 genera per wetland. The most widespread genus was predatory diving beetles (*Acilius* spp.) while the most abundant genus was backswimmers (*Notonecta* spp.). Overall, the diving beetles dominated the short hydroperiod wetlands, while backswimmers became more dominant with increased duration of flooding (Figure 2.8).

Invertebrates are generally more common in permanent ponds and marshes, with hundreds or thousands of individuals in a single square meter. These invertebrates provide food for many wetland species including fish, amphibians, and waterbirds. To illustrate their abundance and composition, Table 2.1 shows invertebrate communities in wetlands managed for migrating waterfowl. Note that most invertebrates occur on the bottom, with relatively few in the water column. Where abundance significantly differs with depth, more invertebrates occur in shallow rather than deep water.

2.2.6 Rare plants in wet meadows

Many rare plants also depend upon fluctuating water levels. The endangered furbish lousewort (*Pedicularis furbishiae*) (Figure 2.5e) occurs on the banks of the

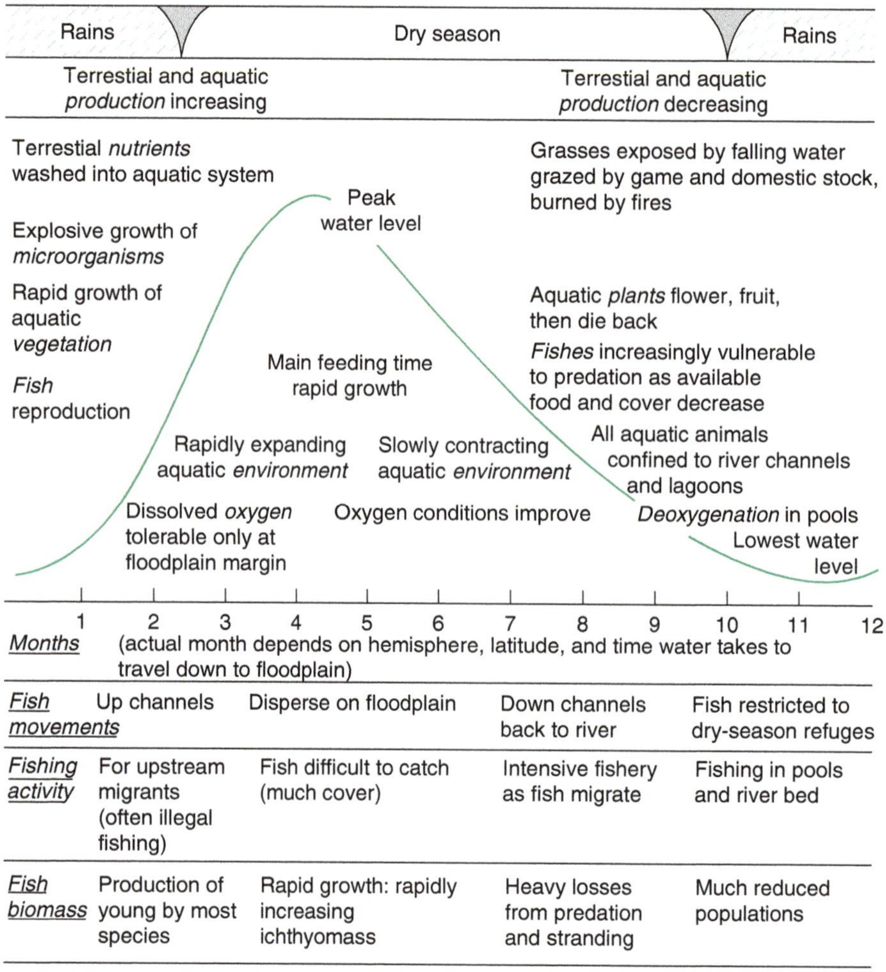

FIGURE 2.7 The life cycles of floodplain fish are closely tied to annual flooding. (From Lowe-McConnell 1975.)

St. John River that flows along the Canada–United States border. The lousewort establishes in areas that are disturbed by ice scour and slumping of the soil associated with spring flood pulses (Menges and Gawler 1986). These types of shorelines may support entire associations of rare plants. The Plymouth gentian (*Sabatia kennedyana*) (Figure 2.5*f*) grows in seasonally flooded wet meadows along the Tusket River in Nova Scotia. This is the only river north of Cape Cod with rich wet meadows supporting significant Atlantic coastal plain species (including both pink coreopsis and Plymouth gentian) that are considered rare, threatened, or endangered in Canada

(Keddy and Wisheu 1989). Some of the flood periods result from melting snow in the spring, but others are caused by occasional severe storms. One thunderstorm in summer 1983 raised water levels 75 cm over two days, completely submerging the wet meadows. In drought years extensive areas of river and lake bottom are exposed. The number of plant species on shorelines is correlated with watershed area across 37 lakes (Hill and Keddy 1992). The mechanism appears to be this: the larger the watershed area, the larger the amplitude of water level fluctuations, the broader the wet meadows, and hence the more species of plants.

Table 2.1 **Abundances of the most common macroinvertebrates in relation to water depth (shallow vs. deep) in freshwater marshes**

		Density (number/m^2)			
		Benthos samples		Water column samples	
Invertebrate taxa		Shallow	Deep	Shallow	Deep
Class Crustacea	Amphipoda	760	531	1	0
	Cladocera	3581	4775	172[a]	19
	Copepoda	1955	1520	–	–
	Eucopepoda	–	–	25[a]	3
Class Gastropoda	Basommatophora (Physidae)	1061	1061	<1	1
Class Insecta	Coleoptera (Dystiscidae)	1061	1061	1	<1
	Diptera (Chironomidae)	3682[a]	796	3[a]	1
	Hemiptera (Corixidae)	1061	1061	2[a]	1
Class Oligochaeta		3797	5128	2	2

[a] Means significantly different between depths.
Source: After Riley and Bookhout (1990).

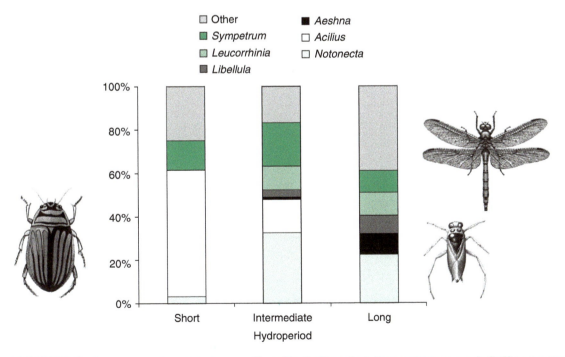

FIGURE 2.8 Predatory macroinvertebrates are affected by hydroperiod, from temporary ponds (left) to permanent ponds (right). *Acilius* (left) are diving beetles, *Notonecta* (bottom, right) are backswimmers, and the other genera are dragonflies (top, right). (After Tarr *et al.* 2005; images from Clegg 1986.)

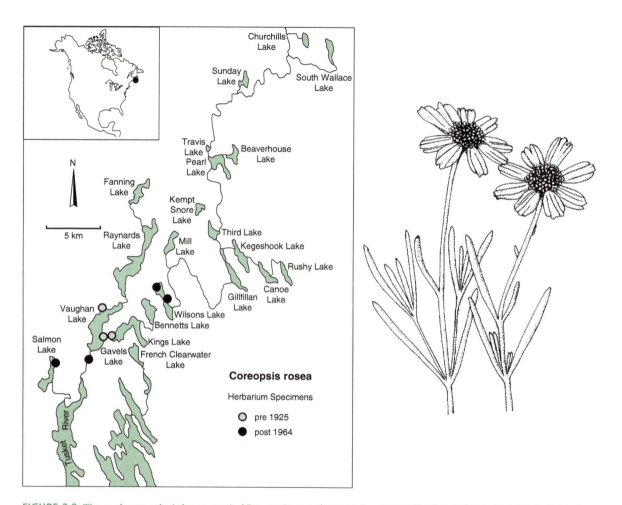

FIGURE 2.9 The endangered pink coreopsis (*Coreopsis rosea*) grows in seasonally flooded wet meadows along the Tusket River, Nova Scotia. The lightly shaded circles show sites from which the species disappeared after the construction of a hydroelectric generating station in 1925. (After Keddy 1985.)

Dams have a negative effect on such plants. Both pink coreopsis and Plymouth gentian once occurred more widely in the lower lakes of the Tusket River watershed (there are pre-1925 specimens from early botanical exploration), but they no longer occur there (Figure 2.9). All three of these lakes were converted to reservoirs for the Tusket Falls generating station in 1925. Pink coreopsis now survives only in those lakes where water level fluctuations are unaffected by reservoirs.

2.3   A survey of water level fluctuations

We have discussed some of the effects of water level fluctuations. Now we will take a closer look at these fluctuations in the different sources of water than can be associated with wetlands.

2.3.1 Rivers

Large fluctuations in water levels are certainly the rule. We have already encountered 10-m changes

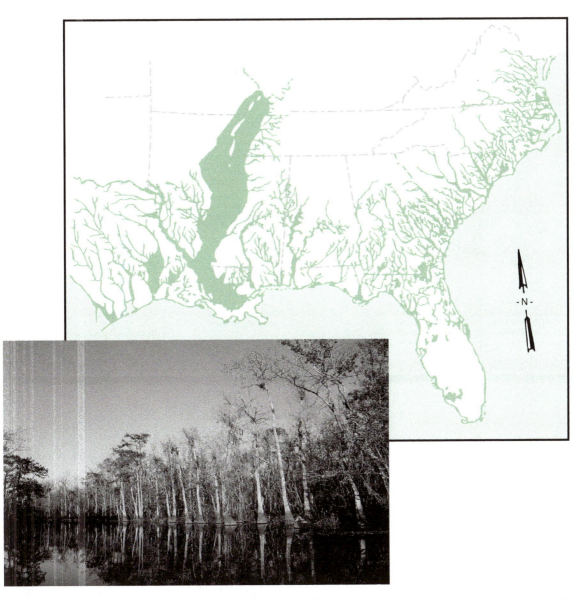

FIGURE 2.10 Spring floods produce the extensive bottomland forests that accompany many large rivers, such as those of the southeastern United States of America. (Map from Mitsch and Gosselink 1986.) (See also color plate.)

in the water levels in the Amazon, and seen the seasonal variation in flow of major rivers (Figure 2.2). These seasonal floods produce the extensive bottomland forests that occur along rivers in Europe (Palczynski 1984; Grubb 1987), central North America (Robertson *et al.* 1978), the Amazon River basin (Duncan 1993), and Africa (Denny 1985; Petr 1986).

Figure 2.10 illustrates the original extent of such floodplain forests in southeastern North America. Floodplain forests often intergrade with other wetland types. For example, in eastern Africa, the Upper Nile swamps at the headwaters of the Nile are enormous – some $16\,000\,km^2$ of permanent swamp, $15\,000\,km^2$ of seasonal swamp, and a further $70\,000\,km^2$ of seasonal

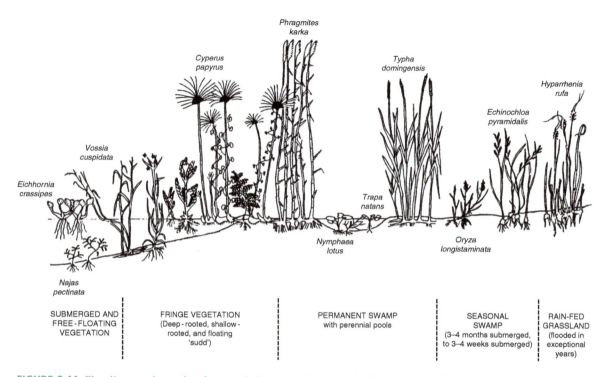

FIGURE 2.11 Flooding produces the characteristic vegetation types in the extensive Upper Nile swamps. (From Thompson 1985.)

floodplain (Denny 1993b). Seven different vegetation types arise (Figure 2.11). The wettest areas (left) have aquatic plants, while the driest (right) have seasonally flooded grasslands. Downstream, the river has cut a floodplain, where the moisture gradient goes from open water (left) to palm and acacia trees on the second terrace (Figure 2.12). Although the species names change, similar types of zonation occur in river systems throughout the world.

Dams and reservoirs are so widespread today that it is often difficult to imagine the enormous expanses of swamp forests and herbaceous wet meadows that once accompanied free-flowing rivers. One of the few free-flowing rivers remaining in Europe is the Torne River in Sweden, and it has wide expanses of herbaceous wetland between the forested floodplain and normal summer water levels (Figure 2.13). Vast wet meadows are also found along undammed rivers in northern North America (Figure 2.14).

These wet meadows along rivers (and, of course, other herbaceous vegetation types such as alvars, wet prairies, and marshes) occur because something removes the trees and keeps them from invading the shoreline. This factor is spring flooding, which in high-latitude rivers is accompanied by large ice floes.

Hence, the critical question for research or management appears to be this: what is the minimum amount of flooding needed to kill trees? This will set the lower limit of the forest and the upper limit of the wet meadow. The answer depends upon the particular tree species, but very few can tolerate permanent flooding (Kozlowski 1984b). Silver maple (*Acer saccharinum*) is one tree species that is widespread in floodplains of northeastern North America. In a study conducted in the Ottawa River on the flood tolerance, and hence lower limits of silver maple, the best predictor of the occurrence of trees combined two hydrological variables: the timing of the end of

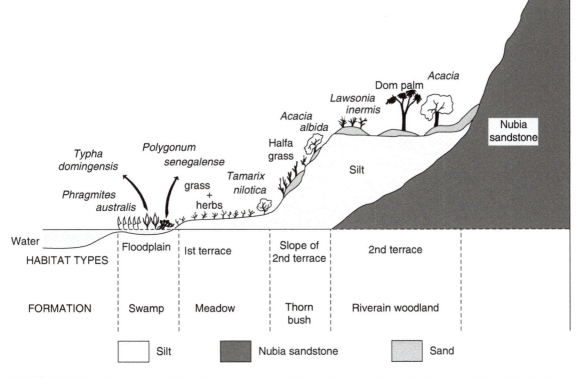

FIGURE 2.12 Flooding, along with sediment erosion and deposition, produces the characteristic vegetation types of the Lower Nile floodplain. (From Springuel 1990.)

the first flood and the beginning of the second flood. The probability of finding a wooded as opposed to herbaceous wetland is a function of these two factors (Figure 2.15). The duration of the first flood is critical. The period of 70 days flooding corresponds to roughly one-third of the average growing season at this latitude. Farther south, woody species such as *Acer saccharum* and *Fraxinus pennsylvanica* can tolerate 100 and 160 days of flooding (Robertson *et al.* 1978). Timing of the second flood is probably important for the following reason: if a second flood follows closely on the first, it represents simply a prolongation of the unfavorable conditions. If, on the other hand, there is a significant gap between floods, there is a period of more favorable conditions; the longer this favorable period, the greater the opportunity for plants to recover enough to withstand a second adverse period. Different

predictive models may be needed for different parts of the world, particularly where differences in climate may interact with tolerances to flooding (e.g. Poiana and Johnson 1993; Johnson 1994).

2.3.2 Lakes

Flooding and drying cycles seem typical of many water bodies, ranging from the smallest beaver ponds to some of the largest lakes. Changes in vegetation with falling water level have been frequently observed. The American naturalist and philosopher Thoreau was a keen observer of nature. In 1854 he wrote:

This rise and fall of Walden [Pond] at long intervals serves this use at least; the water standing at this great height for a year or more though it makes it difficult to walk around it, kills the shrubs and

FIGURE 2.13 Annual spring floods create a broad wet meadow along the unregulated Torne River in Sweden. (Courtesy C. Nilsson.)

FIGURE 2.14 Extensive wet meadows are produced by spring flooding along northern rivers that flow into Hudson Bay. (Courtesy M. Oldham.)

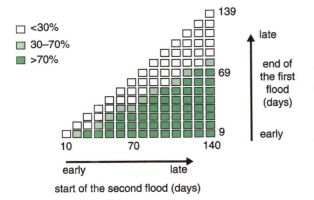

FIGURE 2.15 The probability of finding woody as opposed to herbaceous plants in a wetland can be predicted by knowing when the first flood ends and when the second flood (if any) begins. (From Toner and Keddy 1997.)

trees which have sprung up about its edge since the last rise ... and, falling again, leaves an unobstructed shore; for, unlike many ponds and all water which are subject to a daily tide, its shore is cleanest when the water is lowest ... By this fluctuation the pond asserts its title to a shore, and thus the shore is shorn, and the trees cannot hold it by right of possession. (H. D. Thoreau 1854)

Beginning our survey with large lakes, Raup (1975) studied the vegetation of the Athabasca–Great Slave Lake region of northwestern Canada during the period 1926 to 1935. He too emphasized the importance of water level fluctuations in producing wet meadow communities and made observations on shoreline succession.

Water levels in the Great Lakes fluctuate over decades and centuries (Figure 2.4). These changes in water level cause dramatic changes in shoreline vegetation (Keddy and Reznicek 1986; Reznicek and Catling 1989). Rich wet meadows, fens, and wet prairies (recall Figures 1.6 and 1.7) are maintained by periodic flooding that kills woody plants. Many of the common genera in these habitats (e.g. *Carex, Cyperus, Juncus, Polygonum*) are known to produce persistent seed banks. In similar marsh vegetation types, seed densities are typically 3000 seeds/m², although in one wet meadow, they exceeded 38 000/m². Low-water periods allow these seeds to germinate (Figure 2.16). Such dynamic changes in water level and vegetation maintain a rich flora of some 450 plant species. The short-term effects of high water levels can be deleterious; Farney and Bookhout (1982) observed declines in waterfowl nesting, as well as drastic declines in muskrats. However, these long-term fluctuations are necessary to maintain the full array of wetland communities and their associated wildlife (Prince and D'Itri 1985; Reznicek and Catling 1989; Smith *et al.* 1991).

Over the last 15 000 years and the retreat of the Wisconsinan ice sheet, the Great Lakes have changed dramatically in area, distribution, and drainage (Figure 2.4). Lake Agassiz, Lake Algonquin, Lake Minesing, Lake Chicago, Lake Tonawanda, Lake Warren, and the Champlain Sea have come and gone (Karrow and Calkin 1985). Figure 2.4 does not show Lake Agassiz, a 350 000-km² body of meltwater that covered much of southern Manitoba and western Ontario about 10 000 BP. This lake was partly created by an ice dam on its eastern outlet. When this ice dam melted, Lake Agassiz drained along the Laurentide ice margin, entered Lake Superior and then discharged through the North Bay outlet of the Great Lakes (Figure 2.4e). Calculations of discharge rates yield values of 200 000 m³/s, which, to put it in context, is 13 times the mean discharge of the Mississippi River at New Orleans today (Teller 1988). At this rate it could have taken only 2 years for the water level of Lake Agassiz to fall 12 m.

On the other side of the world, changes in the water levels of African lakes are caused by the seasons as well as long-term changes in rainfall. The rise in water levels is often rapid from the influx of floodwaters, whereas the subsidence is slower, resulting from evaporation and reduced runoff (Talling 1992). In Lake Chilwa, changes in water elevation of 2.5 m were recorded over one decade. Lake Victoria has a fluctuation in amplitude of about 1.5 m each year (Denny 1993b). As in the Great Lakes of North America, the levels of Lake Victoria have also changed with climate. Before 12 500 BP, Lake

FIGURE 2.16 During a low water year in Lake Erie there was dense regeneration of *Scirpus* and *Sagittaria* plants in Metzger Marsh. (Courtesy D. Wilcox.) (See also color plate.)

Victoria had low levels and lacked an outlet, probably being surrounded by swamps and savanna. There were also periods with much higher water levels, probably within the past 10 000 years, whose presence is documented by old beaches encircling the lake at 3, 12, and 18 m above current levels (Kendall 1969).

Equally dramatic changes occur in small ponds and lakes (Mandossian and McIntosh 1960; Salisbury 1970; Keddy and Reznicek 1982; Schneider 1994). During low-water periods, rich shoreline floras may emerge from reserves of buried seeds (Figure 2.17). Intervening high-water periods kill woody plants. Hence, there is a common process underlying the maintenance of wet meadows along rivers (Figures 2.13, 2.14), those of the Great Lakes (Figures 1.6, 1.7), and those of the smaller lakes and even vernal pools.

2.3.3 Beaver ponds

Beavers construct dams that obstruct water flow, thereby flooding the forest and creating small ponds (Figure 2.18). Before the arrival of Europeans, the beaver population of North America was estimated to be 60 to 400 million, with a range stretching from arctic tundra to the deserts of northern Mexico.

Beavers convert small watercourses to open ponds (Figure 2.19, phases 1–3). Dams may fail during floods, or holes may be punched in them by mammals such as otters, and then wet meadows develop from buried seeds (Figure 2.19, phase 4). Although nearly 40 species of plants are known from beaver pond seed banks, Table 2.2 shows that a few genera of monocotyledons are most common. Dam breaking and repair cycles produce short-lived periods of low water alternating with wet meadows. Hence, the long-term process of converting forest to wetland (phases 1 and 2) can end in a rapidly alternating state between pond and wet meadow (phases 3 and 4).

There is also a longer-term cycle. Abandonment of the dam will result in a short-lived mud flat and then a beaver meadow. Eventually, the forest will

FIGURE 2.17 During low-water periods a rich wet meadow flora emerges from buried seeds on the shoreline of Matchedash Lake, Ontario. Typical high water levels are indicated by the tall grasses at left; the canoe marks the summer water level in a low year. (From Keddy and Reznicek 1982.)

reinvade. This longer cycle of beaver ponds alternating with swamp forest probably has a frequency of centuries rather than decades. It may take that long for food trees to re-establish, at which point the process of damming begins again.

Much of North America is recovering from a period of low beaver activity – populations were very low at the turn of the century as a result of heavy trapping. They then expanded rapidly after 1940. As a typical example, in Voyageurs National Park in northern Minnesota, aerial photographs from 1940 through 1986 show an increase in pond sites from 71 to 835 (Johnston and Naiman 1990). During the first half of the period (1940 to 1961) ponds were created at the rate of 25/yr but later (from 1961 to 1986) the rate declined to 10/yr.

Beaver ponds provide important habitat for amphibians, mammals, and birds. In one sample of 70 wetlands with beaver activity, a total of 106 species of spring birds was found, with 9 to 39 species per wetland (Grover and Baldassarre 1995). Larger wetlands had more species, as did wetlands with active beaver colonies. Active ponds had more open water, more standing dead trees, more flooded emergents, and a higher habitat diversity index. There were 19 obligate wetland species in active ponds compared with 12 in inactive ones, and there were 18 facultative wetland species that used cavities in the standing dead trees. Beaver ponds provided habitat for more than half of the regional avifauna.

Beavers are only one of many organisms that create, modify, or maintain natural habitats, a type of organism we could call an ecosystem engineer (Jones *et al.* 1994). In wetlands, other examples would be alligators excavating wallows (Section 4.3.5) or *Sphagnum* mosses building peat bogs (Section 7.1.6).

FIGURE 2.18 Beavers can produce water level fluctuations by building dams that periodically break or are abandoned. (Courtesy Friends of Algonquin Park.)

FIGURE 2.19 The beaver pond cycle going from forest with stream (1), to new pond with dead trees (2), to established pond with aquatic plants (3). When the food supply diminishes, indicated by the presence of conifers, the dam fails and a beaver meadow forms (4). Eventually, forest succession can reverse the process. (Illustration by B. Brigham.)

2.3.4 Potholes and related wet depressions

Some wetlands with seasonal flooding are not connected to large rivers or lakes, being dependent instead upon local sources of water such as rain and snow. These include a wide array of wetland types with local names including potholes, vernal pools, and playas. Let us survey them, roughly north to south.

Prairie potholes were formed by the glaciers that covered and then retreated from the continent of North America, leaving behind millions of depressions across over half a million square kilometers of prairie stretching from Alberta south eastward to Iowa. These depressions are filled by melting snow and, depending upon depth, the water table, and summer rainfall, they range from ephemeral to permanent wetlands. An early explorer

on an expedition under General Sully against the "hostile Sioux" wrote in 1870: "The entire face of the country is covered with these shallow lakes, ponds and puddles ..." (in Kantrud *et al.* 1989). More than 20 million ducks representing 12 common species breed in this region. Common species are mallard, blue-winged teal, northern pintail, northern shoveler, and American widgeon (Batt *et al.* 1989). The dominant herbivores are muskrats and waterfowl (Murkin 1989).

Pothole vegetation includes wet prairie, wet meadows, marshes, and submersed aquatics, controlled by three main environmental gradients: water regime, salinity, and disturbance (Walker and

Table 2.2 **The ten most common species that germinated from the mud in a series of beaver ponds in Canada**

Species	Number of seedlings
Juncus effusus	388
Leersia oryzoides	355
Scirpus cyperinus	224
Juncus brevicaudatus	155
Ludwiga palustris	89
Hypericum boreale	87
Unknown dicot	66
Elocharis obtusa	57
Galium palustre	56
Hypericum majus	49

Source: From Le Page and Keddy (1998).

Wehrhahn 1971; Shay and Shay 1986; Adams 1988). The first is flooded for a few weeks each spring, whereas the last is permanently flooded except during severe drought (Kantrud *et al.* 1989). Buried seeds allow plant species to survive inhospitable periods and then re-emerge after prolonged flooding or drought (van der Valk and Davis 1978; van der Valk 1981). Dominant plants include *Phragmites communis, Typha latifolia,* and *Scirpus* spp. (Shay and Shay 1986). The major water input is from melting snow, while the major loss is from evaporation. Since below-ground flow is relatively slow (0.025–2.5 m/yr), the ponds are hydrologically isolated from one another in the short term (Winter and Rosenberry 1995). Potholes also vary in salinity, ranging from fresh (<500 μS/cm) through brackish (500 to 15 000 μS/cm) to saline (>45 000 μS/cm) and values exceeding 10 000 μS/cm are common (LaBaugh 1989). One classification scheme for potholes has the four vegetation zones mentioned above combined with three other features: low prairie immediately adjacent to the wetland, fens where groundwater seeps into the pothole, and an "alkali zone" with saline water (Figure 2.20). There are four hydrological types: ephemeral, intermittent, semi-permanent, and permanent (Woo *et al.* 1993).

Half of these potholes have already been drained and ploughed. Further risks arise from a gradual decline in the water table. In the Nebraska sand hills, for example, irrigation from wells is increasing in extent; by 1985 there were over 70 000 irrigation wells registered, with an estimated volume of water removal approaching 10^8 m^3/yr (Novacek 1989). Wet meadows are most at risk.

Playas occur further to the south in North America, in the arid high plains, in large circular depressions filled during the spring rainy season (Bolen *et al.* 1989; Smith 2003). Some 22 000 playas occur in Texas and New Mexico. The dominant species are perennial grasses. The dominant environmental factors are elevation and unpredictable wet–dry cycles, with fire and grazing thought to be of secondary importance. Playas were once used as wallows by herds of bison and antelope in a manner reminiscent of the African megafauna. Seed banks again allow plants to tolerate fluctuating water levels (Haukos and Smith 1993, 1994).

Vernal pools can be found further west, in an area extending from southern Oregon though central California into northern Baja California, Mexico (Bauder 1989). Winter rains fill small depressions for periods of 3 to 5 months, producing pools ranging from 20 to 250 m^2 in area and up to 30 cm deep. These pools have a unique flora termed vernal pool ephemerals, many of which are annuals endemic to the California floristic province. This flora is absent when water stands for more than 6 months.

In some semidesert regions of Russia, shallow undrained basins are called firths, padinas, or saladas depending upon the depth and duration of flooding (Zhulidov *et al.* 1997). Many of these are found in the loess deposits northeast of the Black Sea. Firths are shallow (2–4 m) undrained basins which maintain lush meadow vegetation during summer droughts. Padinas, shallower than firths, but 0.2–5 km in diameter, are filled by melting snow, whereas saladas are associated with salt domes and contain saline water. In the adjoining steppe zone, reed thickets (plavni) form in continuously flooded lowlands, particularly those associated with river deltas (Zhulidov *et al.* 1997).

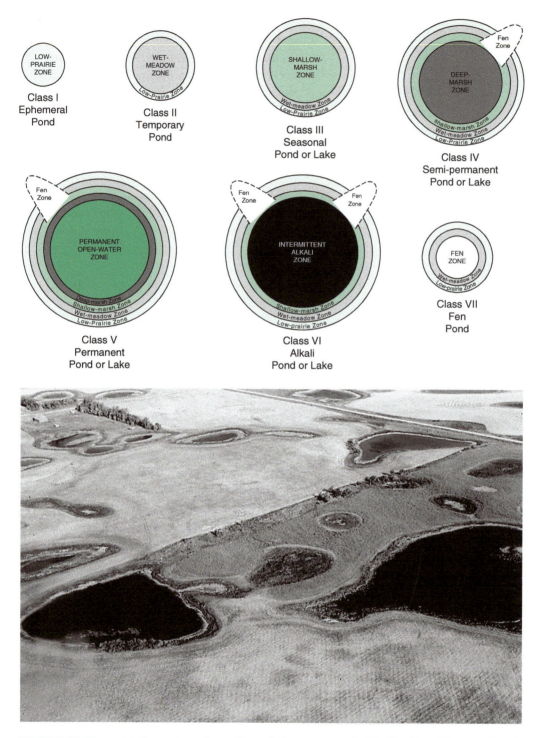

FIGURE 2.20 The vegetation patterns in prairie potholes are controlled by flooding. Here is a classification system showing vegetation zones for seven types of prairie potholes (from Stewart and Kantrud 1971 in van der Valk 1989) and an aerial view of potholes of differing classes near Minnedosa, Manitoba (Courtesy C. Rubec). (See also color plate.)

Wet savannas

Depressions can also support a wide array of wet savannas and prairies, particularly in the subtropics and tropics. Although these could be added as yet another wetland type, they share many of the characteristics of wet meadows, having species that tolerate only short periods of flooding and having high plant diversity. In cases where the soil remains waterlogged, fen species may also occur. Three examples follow: the North American gulf coast savannas, the Orinoco River savannas, and the Cape Peninsula of southwest Africa.

In flat coastal plain areas of southeastern North America, there are large areas of longleaf pine (*Pinus palustris*), often interspersed with savannas and wet depressions. These infertile wet depressions support an array of unusual wetland types with extremely rich floras. Sedges in the genus *Rhynchospora* and species of pitcher plants in the genus *Sarracenia* are characteristic (Peet and Allard 1993; Christensen 1999). Water level fluctuations, infertile soils, and fire are three of the main natural factors responsible for this high diversity. These wetlands also provide habitat for many amphibian species including the Mississippi gopher frog (Figure 2.5*b*).

Savannas extend southward along the Gulf of Mexico and Caribbean Sea into northern South America. One vast savanna (>500 000 km²) stretches between the Andes Mountains in the west and the Guyana Highlands in the east, being drained by the Orinoco River. In Venezuela, Huber (1982) has described how savannas develop on white sand soils "characterized by marked fluctuations in the water content ... Shortly after the beginning of the rainy season these soils readily become water-saturated in consequence of the first heavy rainfalls; for the rest of the rainy season, the water accumulates above the soil for a short time after each rainfall, then it eventually drains away superficially towards the small creeks and rivulets" (p. 224). These infertile seasonally wet savannas support a great variety of plant species. Some like the Eriocaulaceae, Xyridaceae, and Haemodoraceae extend north along the Gulf Coast. A few grasses occur, but they "never form a dense cover" (p. 236).

Of course, similar types of habitats occur elsewhere in the world. The arid Cape Peninsula in southwest Africa has some of the highest levels of plant diversity and endemism recorded in the world (Cowling *et al.* 1996a, b). There is high topographical heterogeneity, long and steep rainfall gradients, a variety of infertile soils, and frequent fire. The predominant vegetation is a fire-prone shrubland called fynbos containing thousands of species of southern hemisphere plant groups (including distinctive families like the Restionaceae and Proteaceae); but where rainfall and topography permit, wetlands occur. Seasonally waterlogged sites have distinctive floras (Table 2.3).

The above are only selected examples. Short-lived pools are widespread, and will vary with the source of the water, the type of substrate, and the length of the growing season. When seen during the dry season, it may be hard to appreciate that they are a wetland vegetation type, yet during the wet season, the importance of water becomes self-evident.

2.3.5 Peatlands

Some of the world's largest wetlands are peatlands (Fraser and Keddy 2005). In order for peat to accumulate, primary production must consistently exceed decomposition. For this to occur, water levels must be relatively stable. Otherwise, decomposition and fire during low-water periods would remove the peat. To illustrate, in one series of wetlands in Japan, valley fens (with significant peat accumulation) had some of the lowest changes in summer water level (SD < 10 cm) whereas marshes showed some of the highest fluctuations (SD > 20 cm) (Yabe and Onimaru 1997).

When the peat is thin, groundwater is the key source of moisture. The calcium content of the groundwater controls acidity, while the nitrogen and phosphorus concentrations control fertility. These two gradients produce much of the variation in fen vegetation (Bridgham *et al.* 1996; Godwin

Table 2.3 **Seasonally flooded and/or waterlogged soils in South Africa support an extremely rich flora with families of plants including the Restionaceae, Proteaceae, and Ericaceae; the fynbos flora alone has more than 7000 plant species and seven endemic plant families**

Vegetation	Environment	Common species
Upland fynbos	Shallow seasonally waterlogged sands	*Thamnocortus nutans, Chrondropetalum ebracteatum, Ursinia nudicaulis, Restio bifidus, Ehrharta setacea, Watsonia borbonica, Penae mucronata, Cliffortia rusciflolia, Erica hispidula, Chondropetalum mucronatum*
Wet fynbos	Shallow seasonally waterlogged sands on sandstone at low altitudes	*Ischyrolepis cincinnata, Tertaria cuspidata, Elegia filacea, Thamnochortus lucens, Cliffortia subsetacea, Erica imbricata, Leucadendron laureolam, Pentaschistis curvifolia, Restio quinquefarius, R. bifurcus*
Wetlands	Seepage sites with shallow–medium depth sandy soils with high organic matter over sandstone bedrock	*Penaea mucronata, Berzelia abrotanoides, Platycaulos compressus, Leucadendron laureolam, B. lanuginosa, Pentaschistis curvifolia, Osmitopsis astericoides, Watsonia tabularis, Psoralea pinnata, Restio quinquefarius*

Source: Modified from Cowling *et al.* (1996b).

et al. 2002). As peat accumulates, the influence of groundwater chemistry declines. Hence, peat accumulation can change groundwater controlled fens to ombrotrophic (rainwater controlled) bogs. In cores, this transition can be recognized by changes in the nature of the peat, particularly the appearance of *Sphagnum*. Many peat sequences therefore begin with sedge peat and end with sphagnum peat (Tallis 1983; Kuhry *et al.* 1993). As peat accumulates, the water table can slowly rise. Peatlands can therefore bury previously forested land, grassland, or even bare rock, a process known as **paludification** (van Breeman 1995). In some cases paludification may be attributed to changes in the climate, but in other cases it seems to be driven simply by local factors that control rates of growth and decomposition (Walker 1970; Frenzel 1983). If the water regime of a site is changed by humans, say by removing the tree cover and reducing evapotranspiration, peat accumulation may be triggered.

As peat accumulates, a raised bog with a dome-like shape may form, producing ombrogenous raised bogs, as shown in Figure 1.19. Here, the underlying topography has less impact upon vegetation. Slowly but steadily, as peat accumulates, there is a shift away from control by local hydrological factors toward control by climatic factors (Foster and Glaser 1986).

Melting spring snow can modify this process. In regions where snow accumulates and then melts rapidly in the spring, the flush of oxygenated water can increase rates of oxidation and produce mineral-rich water flows above the anaerobic zone; this maintains fens. In such circumstances, raised bogs become restricted to areas with minimal water flow such as water divides.

In ombrotrophic bogs, the water table is determined by the balance between inputs from rain and losses through evaporation and seepage. To give some feel for the variation in water levels that is possible, during a dry summer at Wicken Fen in England, the water table dropped as much as 48 cm below the peat surface, although declines of 4 to 20 cm were more typical (Ingram 1983). A dry summer in Finland caused the water table of a bog to drop some 25 cm (Kurimo 1984). In Labrador, Canada, pools on the surface of raised bogs may entirely dry out, forming a mud bottom that cracks from desiccation (Foster and Glaser 1986).

Each species will respond to changes in water level. By way of illustration, consider the effects of low water on one bog species, *Carex exilis*, a widespread sedge of eastern North America. In coastal areas it occupies ombrotrophic bogs, whereas inland it occupies soligenous fens. After a series of transplants and greenhouse experiments, Santelmann (1991) concluded that the water table is the critical factor. *Carex exilis* occurs in those peatlands where the water table remains close to the surface, and it is absent from mid-continental bogs, because the water

table normally drops 20 cm or more below the moss surface.

Overall, the hydrology of peatlands differs largely from that of other wetlands with respect to the amplitude of fluctuations, frequency of fluctuations, source of water, and mineral content of the water. The ombrotrophic bog, with its somewhat more stable water table, dependent upon local precipitation, may therefore be regarded as being nearly the exact opposite of the many examples of forested floodplain where distant rainfall causes the water levels to fluctuate by many meters.

2.4 General relationships between wetlands and water level fluctuations

In Chapter 1 you saw the six principal types of wetlands: bog, fen, swamp, wet meadow, marsh, and aquatic ecosystems. The last four of these represent a sequence of vegetation types associated with increasing duration of flooding. From the perspective of wetland classification, these are distinctive types of wetlands. From the perspective of flooding, they are merely four regions in a continuum of communities that are ever-changing, short-lived responses to water levels. Let us reintroduce these four wetland types as they relate to flood pulses.

2.4.1 Swamps

The highest elevations in wetlands are only occasionally flooded by the highest flood pulses. This is the zone of woody plants – called swamps, bottomland forests, riparian forests, or floodplain forests. At higher elevations (landward), they grade into upland forests; at the other end (waterward), they are killed by prolonged flooding and replaced by more flood-tolerant herbaceous plants. Large areas of the world fall between these two extremes: flooded enough to exclude terrestrial plants, but not enough to kill trees (Lugo *et al.* 1990). Extensive areas of floodplains along rivers are dominated by riparian forests (e.g. Junk 1983; Denny 1985; Sharitz and

Mitsch 1993; Messina and Connor 1998). Only a few types of trees can withstand permanent flooding (Kozlowski 1984b). Table 2.4 shows some typical survival times for trees exposed to permanent flooding.

2.4.2 Wet meadows

At somewhat lower elevations, where the duration of flooding is sufficient to kill woody plants, swamps are often replaced by wet meadows. Wet meadows usually support more plant species than any other vegetation type. In the absence of periodic flooding, this zone is invaded and dominated by woody plants. Occasional flooding, however, kills the woody plants and allows regeneration of wet meadow plants from buried seeds (Keddy and Reznicek 1986; Schneider 1994). The plants here tend to rapidly establish from buried seeds, producing wet meadows that persist until woody plants reinvade the site, or another flood peak occurs. Two other factors are often associated with the formation of wet meadows. Scouring by ice and waves can prevent reinvasion by woody plants (e.g. Raup 1975; Keddy 1989b). Infertile soils may delay reinvasion by woody plants. This may be why infertile wet meadows tend to have particularly rich floras (Moore *et al.* 1989).

Table 2.4 Relative survival time under inundation of some flood-tolerant trees

Species	Survival time (yr)
Quercus lyrata	3
Q. nuttalii	3
Q. phellos	2
Q. nigra	2
Q. palustris	2
Q. macrocarpa	2
Acer saccharinum	2
A. rubrum	2
Diospyros virginiana	2
Fraxinus pennsylvanica	2
Gleditsia triacanthos	2
Populus deltoides	2
Carya aquatica	2
Salix interior	2
Cephalanthus occidentalis	2
Nyssa aquatica	2
Taxodium distichum	2
Celtis laevigata	2
Quercus falcata	1
Acer negundo	0.5
Crataegus mollis	0.5
Platanus occidentalis	0.5
Pinus contorta	0.3

Source: From Crawford (1982).

2.4.3 Marshes

Marshes are flooded for longer periods of time than wet meadows. Wet meadows may be inundated only during flood peaks, whereas marsh vegetation is flooded for most of the growing season. As a consequence, marsh plants have traits for flood tolerance such as aerenchyma (recall Figure 1.15). While marsh species can tolerate flooding, most still require occasional dry periods to regenerate from seeds (van der Valk and Davis 1976, 1978; Smith and Kadlec 1983). Thus, while both marshes and wet meadows are produced by flooding, the duration of flooding and its timing differs between them.

2.4.4 Aquatic communities

At the lowest elevations flooding is more or less continuous; the species here are not dependent upon water level fluctuations for their regeneration. Chapter 1 listed a number of features that allow aquatic plants to tolerate prolonged flooding. These included the presence of aerenchyma to transmit oxygen to the roots, reinforced floating leaves, dissected leaves, and greatly modified flowers (Figure 1.20). Many of the studies on this zone are found in the limnology literature (e.g. Sculthorpe 1967; Hutchinson 1975; Wetzel 1975).

If we look at shoreline wetlands as dynamic features that result from flood pulses, there are two important lessons. (1) The greater the long-term amplitude of water level fluctuations in a landscape, the greater the area of wetland. (2) The relative abundance of these four wetland types in a landscape will depend upon the frequency and duration of flooding. Overall, in the absence of water level fluctuations, we can predict that wet meadows and marshes either shrink or disappear entirely (Figure 2.9).

2.5   Reservoirs, dams, and floodplains

Humans are far more effective at constructing dams than are beavers. The world is now covered with reservoirs created by *Homo sapiens*. As a result, natural water level fluctuations are being disrupted around the globe. Alteration of hydrology is believed to be one of the three major causes of damage to aquatic animals; in the United States of America alone, there are now more than 75 000 large dams (higher than 8 m) and 2.5 million small ones (Richter *et al.* 1997). The giant Three Gorges Dam has recently been built on the Yangtze River in China (Figure 2.21); it will flood more than 1000 km^2

FIGURE 2.21 Dams built by humans, such as the Three Gorges Dam recently constructed on the Yangtze River, increasingly disrupt natural flood pulses in the world's great rivers. (Courtesy ChinaFotoPress/Li Ming.) (See also color plate.)

(Wu *et al.* 2004) while changes in sediment transport will affect areas far downstream along the coast to Shanghai. Many more dams are being proposed for other large rivers.

The nature of the alteration to natural flood patterns will depend upon the purpose of each dam. The effects will also differ between the reservoir upstream from the dam and the river downstream. The list of negative impacts from the construction of dams includes destruction by flooding, mercury contamination, release of greenhouse gases (CO_2, CH_4), and damage to migratory fish species (Rosenburg *et al.* 1995). A nearly universal effect of dams is the reduction in spring flooding and a consequent reduction in wetland area in the remaining floodplain, along with conversion of wet meadows to swamps.

There are four main effects of dams upon hydrology (Klimas 1988).

Water levels stabilized The near-permanent inundation or saturation of substrates that were formerly periodically exposed.

Shifted flood timing Flooding can be delayed by months, sometimes until well into the growing season of vegetation.

Increased flooding Embankments and artificial levees act like linear dams and increase flood peaks by constraining the flow of water onto adjacent floodplains.

Decreased flooding By holding back runoff during normal flood periods, the duration and area of flooding are reduced.

2.5.1 Upstream effects: the reservoir

The pattern of fluctuations in a reservoir depends upon its purpose. The frequency of water level fluctuations may decrease if the reservoir is intended to stabilize water levels for recreation or shipping. Or, the frequency of fluctuations may increase if the reservoir is being used to provide pulses of water for daily peaks in power demand. Similarly, the amplitude may be reduced if the dam stores water during low-water periods, or it may be increased if the dam is used to

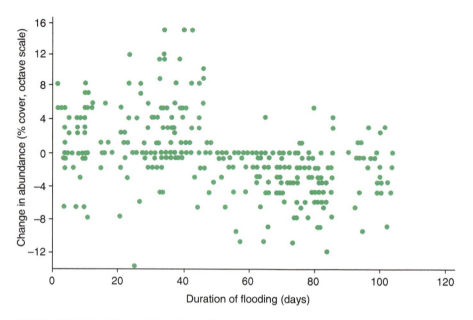

FIGURE 2.22 The effects of duration of flooding on the change in abundance of plants in a northern European reservoir. (From Nilsson and Keddy 1988.)

regulate water levels in headstock ponds for power generation. Every reservoir may be considered to have its own water level personality, determined in part by the purpose of its construction, and in part by the personalities of the people who maintain it.

Consider one extreme example: the Gardiken Reservoir in northern Sweden covers an area of 84 km^2 (Nilsson 1981). Water levels may fall as much as 20 m, exposing approximately 56 km^2 of shoreline. This reservoir is of particular interest because it represents some sort of biological limit to how much one can alter water levels in wetlands, since the water levels are almost exactly the reverse of natural cycles. It is lowest in spring (in order to provide storage for melting snow) and it is highest in the autumn. It is then progressively lowered during the winter in order to generate hydroelectric power, which, in Sweden, is needed most during the winter. You might predict that reversing the entire water level cycle would have dramatic effects upon vegetation. You would be right. Most of the reservoir shore is barren, except for a 1–2 m-wide strip of sparse vegetation close to the high water level. That is, this combination of conditions is so extreme that no plants can tolerate the conditions

over most of the reservoir. If the duration of flooding was around 60 days, the vegetation remained more or less unchanged. If the duration of flooding was less than this, the abundance of plants increased, and if it was greater than this, the abundance of plants decreased (Figure 2.22). Hence, 60 days was the threshold that managers needed to consider to maintain shoreline plants. Studies in Norway indicate that as amplitude increases, plants can grow at lower elevations (Rørslett 1984, 1985).

2.5.2 Downstream effects: altered hydrology

The impacts downstream from the reservoir may affect an even larger area of landscape than the reservoir itself. Downstream from the dam, water levels are usually stabilized, particularly if the dam has been constructed to hold back spring flow and release water later in the year. By reducing spring floods, dams eliminate immense areas of wetland in a watershed. Almost every watershed in the world has been altered by the construction of dams. Hence, there has been a global trend to reduce river pulses during spring runoff (Dynesius and Nilsson 1994).

This also means that any remaining rivers without dams have high conservation value.

Some of the severe negative consequences of altered hydrology are shown by the Peace–Athabasca delta in Alberta, Canada (Gill 1973; Rosenberg and Barton 1986; Rosenberg et al. 1995). It is part of the larger Mackenzie River system, discharging into the Arctic Ocean. The Peace–Athabasca delta is "probably the most important northern delta in North America for nesting and is used by hundreds of thousands of birds" (Rosenberg and Barton 1986). The delta consists of $39\,000\,km^2$ of wetlands formed where the Peace River flows into Lake Athabasca (Figure 2.23).

In 1968 the Bennett Dam was completed 1200 km upstream on the Peace River. One effect was the end of the annual June pulse of floodwaters (Figure 2.23, bottom). This led to rapid changes in the vegetation of the delta, with many of the herbaceous wetlands becoming woody vegetation (Figure 2.24). The rate of change was remarkable: within two years (by 1970) the total area of the nine largest water bodies had decreased by 28%, and the numerous perched lakes and ponds of the delta were drying up at the rate of 12% per year. Large grasses and willows spread rapidly. Because of its importance, the problems of the delta were studied by the Peace–Athabasca Delta Implementation Committee (1987), which recommended constructing weirs to hold back floodwaters and re-create flood pulses. Although this could not repair all the damage caused by the Bennett Dam, it made the best of a bad situation.

The Peace–Athabasca situation can be considered a well-studied example of what is now a global problem: dam building and wetland destruction *downstream*. Similar changes can be expected wherever dams are built. A few more examples follow. The Akosombo Dam on the Volta River in Ghana created "Lake Volta" with a surface area of some $8500\,km^2$ and annual drawdowns of some 3 m (Petr 1986). The dam has stabilized river flow leading to increased plant growth on the river banks, the increased population of a plant-associated snail, and the spread of schistosomiasis. Alteration of vegetation downstream from dams has been observed in many other watersheds, including the Colorado

River in Arizona (Turner and Karpiscak 1980), the Milk River in Alberta and Montana (Bradley and Smith 1986), the Platte River in Nebraska (Johnson 1994), the Kissimmee River in Florida (Toth 1993), and streams in the Sierra Nevada (Harris et al. 1987). As with the Peace River, floodplains are being invaded by woody vegetation.

When riparian forests are surrounded by arid prairies rather than forested landscapes, the effects of reduced spring floods may be more severe. Poplar forests in river valleys are "thriving oases for wildlife" amidst the dry plains of western North America (Rood and Mahoney 1990). These riparian forests may support a variety of trees, shrubs, and smaller plants absent from the surrounding landscape (Johnson et al. 1976): "As the poplars die, so dies the whole riparian forest. Wildlife habitat is lost, the forest canopy is lost, and the forest understorey dies." Reduced water levels may directly stress the older trees, but more importantly, the dams reduce erosion and the movement of sediment, thereby eliminating sites for poplar seedlings to establish. These changes are occurring throughout arid areas of North America (Patten 1998) and, most likely, other arid areas as well.

2.5.3 Dikes are another kind of dam

Dams are not the only way that humans manipulate water level fluctuations in floodplains. Increasingly, rivers are contained within walls to prevent local flooding, particularly in heavily populated areas. Consider just three examples. The Vistula, which drains more than half of Poland, is more than 1000 km long, yet "has side walls on almost its whole length" (Kajak 1993). The Mississippi River is similarly constrained (Figure 2.25). There are also walls along sections of two of the largest rivers in the world, the Ganges and the Brahmaputra, with extensions planned (Pearce 1991). These sorts of walls destroy wetlands. Nearly every delta and floodplain in the world is experiencing these effects.

There is an additional indirect effect of building dams and dikes: the lands temporarily protected from spring flooding are frequently converted to agriculture or urban uses. Because this change is so

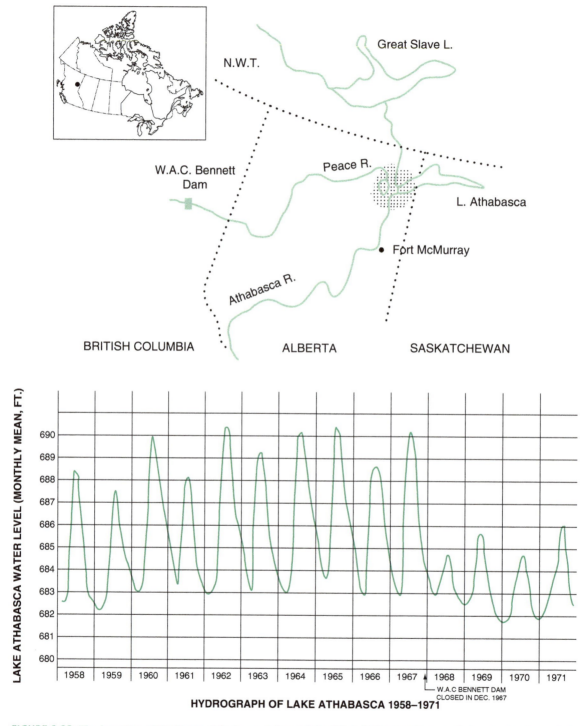

FIGURE 2.23 The location of the Peace–Athabasca delta and the W. A. C. Bennett Dam and changes in the hydrology of Lake Athabasca once the dam was completed. (After Peace–Athabasca Delta Project Group 1972.)

Succession on exposed lake bottom

Succession on meadows

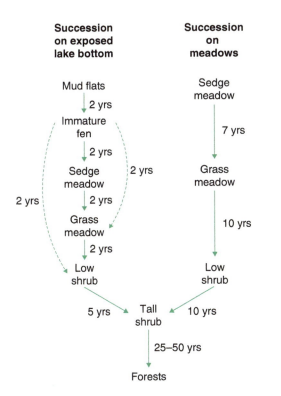

FIGURE 2.24 Changes in the vegetation in the Peace–Athabasca delta after the W. A. C. Bennett Dam (Figure 2.23) reduced spring flooding. (After Peace–Athabasca Delta Project Group 1972.)

obvious and dramatic, it is sometimes easy to overlook the primary effect of dams, levees, embankments, and dikes – the loss of wetland area and conversion of meadows to swamps or upland. Dams, dikes, and agriculture are a devastating combination for alluvial wetlands. In the Mississippi River floodplain, for example, there were originally an estimated 8.5–9.5 million hectares of wetland forest; by the 1990s, only some 2 million remained (Figure 2.26). When large floods do breach one of these walls, massive flooding and loss of life can result (Barry 1997).

Overall, humans seem to have a fascination with changing natural hydrology, and allowing the return of natural water levels is therefore often one of the simplest yet most powerful ways of restoring a wetland.

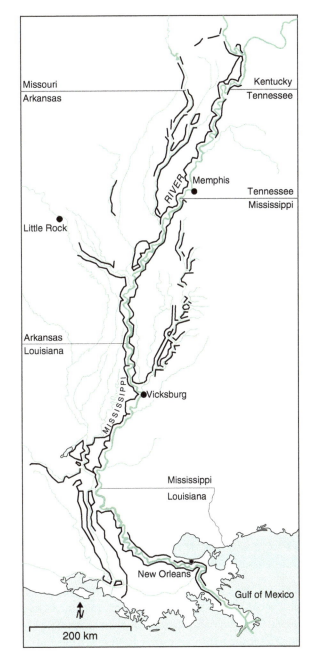

FIGURE 2.25 Rivers are increasingly constrained within walls and dikes. This causes extensive losses of floodplain wetlands, and occasional catastrophe when a big flood breaches the wall. Here are the walls built along the lower Mississippi River as of 1986. (From U.S. Army Corps of Engineers 2004.)

2.6 Predicting consequences for wetlands

Having looked at the causes of water level fluctuations and their effect upon wetland species and habitats, we now turn to examining the potential consequences for wetland ecosystems.

2.6.1 Stabilized water levels reduce plant diversity and marsh area

We have seen how many wild species require fluctuating water levels. We could summarize the observations in this way. (1) The greater the long-term amplitude of water level fluctuations in a landscape, the more extensive the area of wetland will be. (2) The relative abundance of wetland types in a landscape will depend upon the frequency and duration of flooding. Figure 2.27 shows what happens when humans reduce flood peaks and augment low-water periods. Natural water level fluctuations (top) result in a shoreline with broad wet meadows and marshes. The bottom portion shows a stabilized shoreline where the woody plants reach the aquatic zone. Increasingly, shorelines like the lower illustration are becoming typical of watersheds. Broad wet meadows such as we saw in Figure 1.7 are becoming increasingly uncommon, with a consequent loss of habitat for the many kinds of plants and animals that occupy meadows and marshes.

2.6.2 A model for predicting how flooding increases wetland area

It is one thing to describe changes in vegetation that occur after a dam is constructed. In some cases, this is the proverbial situation of closing the barn door after the horse has escaped. What we need to be able to do is predict the severity of the changes that will occur before a project is built so that we can fully establish the consequences beforehand. We know the general pattern – illustrated by the Peace River wetlands – that dams reduce flooding, that reduced flooding causes wetlands to shrink, and that herbaceous wetlands are invaded by woody species.

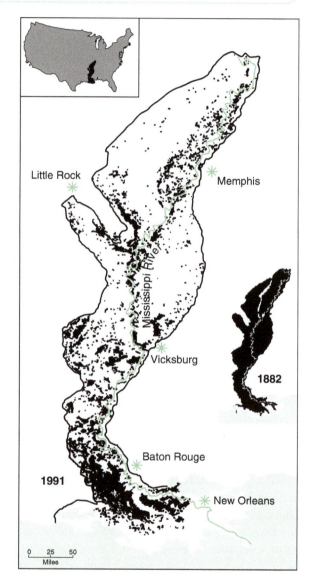

FIGURE 2.26 The remaining bottomland forests of the Mississippi floodplain. Once a river is constrained by dams and dikes, the floodplain is often cleared for agriculture. This can obscure the more widespread but less obvious effects of reduced spring flooding, such as encroachment by terrestrial species, conversion of wet meadow to woody plants, and changes in function and biological diversity. (From Llewellyn *et al.* 1996.)

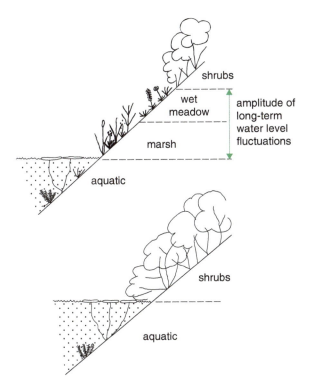

FIGURE 2.27 Stabilizing water levels compresses wetlands from four zones (top) to two zones (bottom). (From Keddy 1991a, b.)

Better predictive models are needed.

One tool, logistic regression, which was used to construct Figure 2.15, may hold considerable promise. This approach attempts to predict the occurrence of woody plants from basic water level patterns.

Another tool uses simple relationships between flooding and vegetation to predict changes in wetland area. This model was developed and tested for the Great Lakes. The Great Lakes contain a rich array of wetland types, including wet meadows, marshes, shoreline fens, and swamps that provide important habitat for fish, waterfowl, and rare plant species (Smith *et al.* 1991). Large areas of these wetlands have been drained. Humans have also reduced the amplitude of water level fluctuations. There is often pressure to control them further to simplify shipping and satisfy cottage owners. The problem was this: how much wetland loss would be caused by further reducing flood peaks?

The model looked at two critical points, the upper and the lower limit of herbaceous wetlands on a shoreline. First consider the upper limit, the landward edge of wet meadows. To model the landward edge of the wet meadow, it was necessary to consider the die-back and recolonization by woody plants. It was first assumed that the die-back of woody plants was caused by the highest water levels during a year. It was next assumed that after dying back, the woody plants reinvade toward the lake. After a lag time (to account for seed dispersal and sapling establishment), the shoreline is reforested using a simple exponential model. This allowed predictions of the lower limit of woody plants from projected water levels. The top line in Figure 2.28 shows occasional periods of death, a lag, and then slow reinvasion. The lag time in this model was 18 years; lag times of 20 or 15 years made little difference.

Now consider the lower limit. The model assumes that the lower boundary of the marsh is set by the yearly low water level, with marshes arising the same year from buried seeds. When the water rises, wetland plants die back over several years. The bottom line in Figure 2.28 shows wetlands forming as lake levels fall, and then decreasing as water levels rise. Lag times of 4 or 2 years as opposed to 3 made little difference. Overall, the lower limit of the wetland tracks much more closely the low water level.

The area between these two lines is then the extent of wet meadow and marsh as a function of time. When the model is applied to water levels between 1910 and 1985, it shows great areas of wetland that occurred during the low water period of the mid-1930s and the mid-1960s.

What about the future? This same model was then used for different future scenarios for water level regulation. If further reductions in amplitude occurred, the model predicted losses approximating 30% of the wetlands in Lake Ontario alone. This approach is particularly valuable because it emphasizes how wetlands are dynamic features that change in response to water levels. Indeed, if larger amplitudes were re-established by changing existing water control structures, even larger areas of wetland might

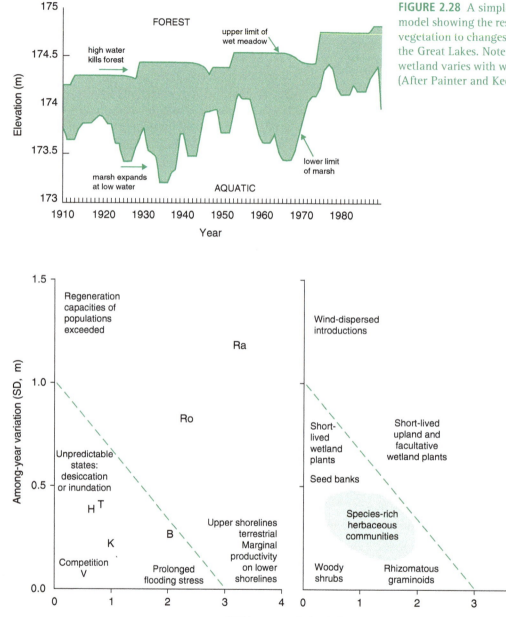

FIGURE 2.28 A simple simulation model showing the response of wetland vegetation to changes in water levels in the Great Lakes. Note that the area of wetland varies with water level history. (After Painter and Keddy 1992.)

FIGURE 2.29 The effects of water level variation upon shoreline vegetation. The stippled area contains lakes whose hydrological regimes produce rich floras, while hypo- and hypervariable zones represent impoverished systems. Rich floras with many rare species occur in unregulated lakes with high catchment areas such as Kejimkujik (K) and Bennetts (B), both lakes with immediate water level fluctuations (within years and among years). In contrast, hypovariable lakes such as unregulated lakes with small catchment areas and head ponds (e.g. V, Vaughan) lose many species through competitive exclusion by shrubs. Hypervariable lakes such as storage reservoirs (above the dashed line, e.g. Ro, Rossignol and Ra, Raynard) lose species and are subject to invasion by exotic species. The stippled area is therefore the desirable management target. Increased catchment area can push lakes into the region of high richness, but reservoir construction can push lakes into the hypervariable state. (From Hill *et al.* 1998.)

be produced. More elaborate models using GIS data and different types of embayments confirm this story, and extend it to increased habitat availability for waterbirds such as yellow and king rails (Wilcox and Xie 2007). Since similar processes likely occur in most large lakes, natural water level fluctuations are probably critical for wetlands in many of the world's large lakes, providing a powerful tool for restoring wetlands and maintaining biological diversity (Keddy and Fraser 2000).

2.6.3 A summary model: frequency and intensity of flooding

We have seen that two of the most important components of flooding are frequency and amplitude (intensity). These could be assigned to orthogonal axes and the space would represent all possible pair-wise flood combinations. Imagine then plotting biological properties such as plant diversity or numbers of rare species. We could use data from the many reservoirs or wetlands of the world in order to explore patterns. Unfortunately, the required data are scattered through an enormous number of studies that describe individual cases. As a first step in this direction, Figure 2.29 shows a plot for a few lakes, and identifies a probable region of high plant species richness. This is based upon a set of lakes in eastern North America, and there is currently no way to know how well we can extrapolate beyond this geographic region or to other properties. This chapter thus ends with a lament. Here we have possibly the two most important environmental factors influencing wetlands, yet we lack the data to predict the changes in wetlands along these axes. We have our work cut out for us.

CONCLUSION

Fluctuations in water level (e.g. spring flood pulses) are essential for maintaining the diversity and abundance of wildlife species in wetlands. We have seen examples including wading birds, frogs, fish, and rare plants. Species composition and functions of wetlands are determined largely by the frequency and amplitude of flooding. This variation in water level occurs not just within a year but also from year to year. Swamps, wet meadows, marshes, and aquatic ecosystems represent a sequence of vegetation types associated with increasing duration of flooding – four regions in a continuum of communities that are ever-changing, short-lived responses to water levels. Under natural conditions, large water level fluctuations are typical of rivers, the Amazon having an annual fluctuation of 10 m. Among lakes, yearly fluctuations of a few meters generally occur. Plant species richness in lakes is greatest when water level fluctuations are intermediate in magnitude. Low-water periods are important for species that persist as seeds buried in the sediment. High-water periods drown woody vegetation and allow marsh and wet meadow expansion. In peatlands, by contrast, water levels must be relatively stable in order for peat to accumulate.

Stabilization of water levels for uses such as recreation, power generation, transportation, or flood control results in reduced wetland area and lower species diversity. Maintaining natural hydrology is an essential part of wetland conservation and management. Yet dams continue to proliferate, with major new projects in areas including the Amazon River in South America, the Yangtze River in Asia, the Congo River in Africa, and the Tigris and Euphrates Rivers in the Middle East. Although our knowledge about the importance of flood pulses is growing, it seems that wise application of this knowledge is required.

Chapter contents

3 Fertility

A few resources control the production of living organisms. All living organisms are built mainly from six elements – CHNOPS (carbon, hydrogen, nitrogen, oxygen, phosphorus, sulfur). If any of these basic elements is in short supply, growth and reproduction will be slowed. Generally, it seems that the two most important elements are nitrogen and phosphorus – for both plants and animals. Hence, we can use the availability of nitrogen and phosphorus as one way to judge how suitable a habitat is for living creatures. The general word we use to describe this suitability is **fertility**. Let us start with plants.

3.1   Fertility and plants

Fertility controls primary productivity (biomass), with nitrogen and phosphorus supplies often limiting plant growth. Sites with low levels of these nutrients are termed infertile. While biomass is directly correlated with fertility, species richness is inversely correlated with fertility. The importance of particular nutrients can be determined through field experiments in which they are supplemented and the effects on plants documented.

3.1.1 Nitrogen and phosphorus often limit plant and animal growth

The availability of nitrogen and phosphorus determines how fast plants can grow. More fertile areas have, among other things, bigger plants, faster-growing plants, more biomass, and hence more production to support more animals. You can easily do the simple experiment of adding nutrients to plots in a marsh, and find, not surprisingly, that the plants get bigger. So what more, you might ask, do we need to know? Surprisingly, there are many unknowns, and many problems arise out of unexpected consequences of fertility. A most obvious example is the case of the Everglades, where millions of dollars are being spent trying to keep nutrients from entering the wetlands. There are often times when having more plant growth is not a good thing. So here are some questions that we need to answer.

- What levels of nitrogen and phosphorus produce fastest growth?
- Are some wetlands already saturated with nutrients?
- Which is more important, nitrogen or phosphorus?
- How does fertility affect species composition?
- Why do infertile habitats support so many species?
- Why does high fertility often cause rare species to disappear?

These questions indicate that not all wetlands respond to fertilization, and when they do, sometimes the consequences are unexpected or undesirable. At the same time, the nutrient levels of many wetlands are being pushed higher by nutrient laden waters from farms and cities, and even by nutrients in precipitation.

3.1.2 Fertility increases biomass

Since wetlands are known to be areas with rapid plant growth, it seems reasonable to assume that nitrogen and phosphorus are often relatively available. This is likely because water runs downhill, steadily transporting nutrients out of upland areas and into wetlands.

As a simple experimental example of responses to fertility, we subjected plots of coastal Louisiana to three treatments that increased fertility: added sediment, added fertilizer, and added sediment and fertilizer. Biomass increased with all three experimental treatments (Figure 3.1). This result is not surprising, first because we know that fertilizer generally makes plants grow better. Moreover, the wetlands in this experiment were currently not

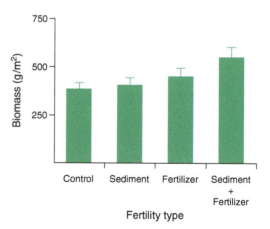

FIGURE 3.1 The short-term effects of increased fertility upon biomass of an oligohaline coastal marsh in Louisiana (mean $\pm$ 1 SE, $n = 96$, $p < 0.001$). (From Keddy *et al.* 2007.)

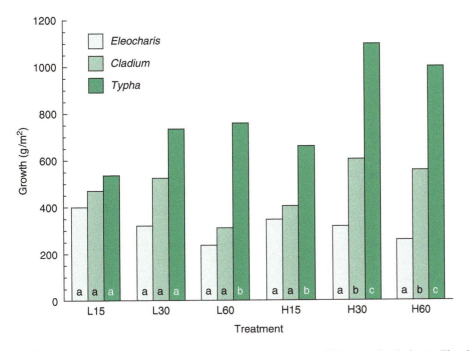

FIGURE 3.2 The effects of added phosphorus on the growth of three wetland plants, *Eleocharis interstincta*, *Cladium jamaicense*, and *Typha domingensis*. L = low nutrients (P = 50 µg/l, NO$_3$ = 10 µg/l), H = high nutrients (P = 100 µg/l, NO$_3$ = 1000 µg/l), each at water depths of 15, 30, and 60 cm. Histograms with the same letter indicate that the species are not significantly different from one another within the treatment. (From Newman *et al.* 1996.)

receiving annual spring flooding from the Mississippi River, and so were cut off from normal nutrient supplies.

Figure 3.1 showed that biomass increases with fertilization, but what of the individual species that make up the biomass? Let us switch examples to another study, one that will also be useful later in the book. Wetlands in the Everglades are naturally dominated by sedges including *Eleocharis interstincta* and *Cladium jamaicense*. These two species, and cattails (*Typha domingensis*), were experimentally subjected to two different nutrient levels. Take some time to explore Figure 3.2. First, note that all three species had similar growth – in shallow water at low nutrients. And, second, as you would expect, adding nutrients generally increased plant growth. But there were also differences among the species and treatments (Figure 3.2). First, consider the effects of fertilization. *Eleocharis* did not grow faster when fertilized. *Cladium* grew

only slightly faster. But *Typha* responded the most of all. Hence, on a relative basis, cattails were most affected by fertilization. *Typha* also grew better in the deeper water than the shallow water. Hence, more flooding and more nutrients leads to more cattails. This example typifies what has been found in many other studies – species that naturally occupy infertile areas show limited response to fertilization, it is invasive species that are best able to use the added nutrients to increase growth rates.

What about animals? Although the term fertility is normally associated with plants, there is good evidence that it may be usefully extended to other organisms such as animals and fungi, where rates of growth are also dependent upon the availability of resources. Most plant tissues have relatively low (<5%) nitrogen content, which greatly reduces their value to herbivores. We will see in Section 3.4, and in the later chapter on herbivory (Chapter 6), just how few nutrients are available in plant tissues, and the extreme effort animals require to extract those nutrients. But we should introduce the concept here while we are still thinking generally about fertility. In order to gain precious nutrients, animals may feed selectively on newly growing shoots, or on seeds, or on the cambium of trees, in order to obtain slightly higher levels of key resources. They may have multiple chambered stomachs where microorganisms assist in breaking down plant tissues. They may even eat their own excrement to extract nutrients that the digestive system missed the first time through – a practice known as coprophagy. Coprophagy illustrates the extremes to which animals must go to obtain nutrition from plants. Beavers are a well-known example.

Hence, if fertilization increases the levels of N and P in plant tissues, we might expect it to increase the value of the plants to herbivores. Now return to Figure 3.1, and consider what happens in the presence of herbivores. In this experiment, half of the plots were surrounded by fence to keep out grazing animals, while half of the plots were open to grazing. To keep the figure simple, I have not shown the complexities of grazing effects. But they are simple to explain. Nutrients increase plant biomass – if there are no grazing animals present. In plots exposed to grazing, the newly growing plants were eaten so rapidly (mainly by nutria) that there was no change in biomass (Keddy *et al.* 2007, 2009a). Hence, in the absence of herbivores, fertilizing made more plant material; in the presence of herbivores, fertilizing apparently made more herbivores.

3.1.3 Sites lacking N and P can be called infertile or stressed

The opposite of a fertile site is an infertile site. Some wetlands, including bogs, wet pine savannas, pocosins, and parts of the Everglades, are extremely infertile. Such infertile sites can also be referred to as stressed sites. Any environmental factor that constrains plant productivity is generally termed a

stress (e.g. Grime 1977, 1979; Levitt 1980; Larcher 1995). Animal ecologists have used the word adversity to describe the same kind of constraints (Southwood 1977, 1988). Hence, we would say that plots on the left of Figure 3.1 were the most stressed of the four treatments.

Although nitrogen and phosphorus are the key elements to consider, they are of course, not the only elements that can limit plant and animal growth. For plants, other resources include potassium and magnesium, as well as carbon dioxide. In flooded sites, resources like soil oxygen can limit growth; in others (but rarely wetlands), scarcity of water has similar effects. Factors such as high salinity or low temperatures can also reduce growth rates, and therefore are also considered to affect fertility.

3.1.4 Nutrients often control primary production

The resources required by living organisms can be deduced from their chemical composition. Most, as noted, are composed of just the elements, C, H, N, O, P, and S. Table 3.1 shows the basic elemental composition of different species of wetland plants. Since plants have to accumulate the elements in this table, here is more good evidence that nitrogen and phosphorus are important. But which one is key? Here there are conflicting opinions.

Table 3.1 **Major nutrients in wetland plants**

Element	Temperate species (%)[a]	Tropical species (%)[b]
N	2.26	1.99
P	0.25	0.19
S	0.41	–
Ca	1.34	0.88
Mg	0.29	0.29
K	2.61	3.10
Na	0.51	0.36

[a] From Boyd (1978), $n = 28$–35.
[b] From Junk (1983), $n = 75$.

The fundamental importance of nitrogen is illustrated by occurrence of an amino group (–NH₂) in every amino acid. Every protein requires that critical molecule of nitrogen.

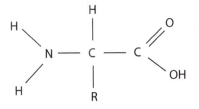

The need for nitrogen is inescapable.

Some ecologists believe that nitrogen is the one key resource limiting terrestrial plant communities (Vitousek 1982; Tilman 1986; Berendse and Aerts 1987). However, such generalizations may be inappropriate for wetlands. Freshwater ecologists studying phytoplankton have concluded that phosphorus is the critical limiting nutrient (e.g. Vallentyne 1974; Schindler 1977; Smith 1982; Rigler and Peters 1995). This is why such an effort is made to remove phosphorus from sewage. So, if we seek the key nutrient controlling plant production in wetlands, would it be best to start with the terrestrial view and study nitrogen, or to start with the aquatic view and study phosphorus? There is no easy answer.

Even in lakes, where phosphorus is the essential nutrient controlling algal biomass, it seems that nitrogen does play an important role by modifying the relationship between algal biomass and phosphorus (Smith 1982). Further, as the ratio of nitrogen to phosphorus increases, cyanophytes (blue–green algae) are replaced by other phytoplankton (Schindler 1977; Smith 1983). Thus N : P ratios can control both amounts and composition of phytoplankton.

You might ask if it matters. Here is one illustration that it does. The Everglades are receiving a steady input of both nitrogen and phosphorus from sugar cane plantations, and, as a consequence, the plants are changing, with apparently negative consequences for many other species including wading birds like the wood stork. If you were in charge of Everglades conservation,

would you put your money into controlling phosphorus or nitrogen (or both)? We will look at this situation more closely in Chapter 13, but meanwhile, the case of the Everglades illustrates just why we need to separate the effects of nitrogen and phosphorus in wetlands.

3.1.5 Is it N or P? Experimental assessments of nutrient limitation

One way to assess the relative importance of elements in controlling plant growth in wetlands is to supplement the nutrients in field experiments.

Let us start with an early study of fertilization in species-rich dune slacks (a type of wet meadow) where Willis (1963) added N, P, K, and NPK fertilizer to different plots. The dominant species were *Agrostis stolonifera, Anagallis tenella, Bellis perennis*, and three species of *Carex*. The plots receiving complete nutrients (NPK) produced three times as much biomass. The greatest deficiencies, concluded Willis, were for nitrogen and to a lesser degree, phosphorus. He then transplanted pieces of turf to the greenhouse and submitted them to different fertilization treatments. The results were similar to the field trials. He concluded "the sparse growth and open character of the vegetation of the Burrows are brought about mainly by the low levels of nitrogen and phosphorus in the sand ..." This work also showed how the changes in biomass were accompanied by changes in the species composition. The field plots that received complete nutrients had fewer plant species and were dominated by grasses. Willis also observed that sedges and rushes appeared to be particularly successful in areas of phosphorus deficiency. Hence, just as N : P ratios change the kind of phytoplankton in lakes, N : P ratios may control which particular plant group dominates a wetland.

Another fertilization study was carried out in three types of bogs in southern England (Hayati and Proctor 1991). A native species of sedge, *Carex echinata*, was planted in pots of peat from each site, and then different fertilizers were applied in factorial design.

Table 3.2 **Limiting factors in seven habitat types, as determined by biomass response in fertilization experiments**

Habitat	N	P	K	N + P	N + K	P + K
Wet grassland	3	0	2	0	4	0
Wet heath	0	3	0	0	0	0
Rich fen	7	5	0	0	0	0
Poor fen	2	1	0	0	0	0
Litter fen	1	2	0	1	0	0
Bog	1	3	1	0	0	0
Dune slack	5	2	0	2	0	0
Total (45 cases)	19	16	3	3	4	0

Note: Figures indicate number of cases in which the element was shown to be limiting.
Source: From Verhoeven *et al.* (1996).

There were three main effects: due to N, to P, and to between-site differences. Nitrogen was more limiting in the peat from wet heathlands, whereas P was more limiting in the peat from the blanket bog. There was a minor effect of K, suggesting that it was present in adequate supply everywhere except in the blanket bog.

While growing plants in pots provides simple experimental design, it is always open to the criticism that it does not necessarily show the importance of nutrients under more natural field conditions. But it is often convenient. Studies using sediment collected from different waterways and put into pots suggested that N rather than P usually limited plant growth (Barko and Smart 1978, 1979; Smart and Barko 1978). And the work illustrated in Figure 3.2 was also done in pots, albeit rather large ones.

The number of fertilization studies grows steadily. By 1996, Verhoeven *et al.* could review no fewer than 45 studies of fertilization in seven types of herbaceous wetlands. The result? There was an almost even split between nitrogen-limited sites and

phosphorus-limited sites (Table 3.2). Co-limitation, that is, a response only to combined fertilizations, was rare. Wet heathlands all had growth limited by phosphorus, whereas fens and dune slacks could be limited by either nitrogen or phosphorus. The wet grasslands were the most complicated, with cases of N, K, and N+K limitation. Regrettably, there was no category for floodplain.

The concentration of nutrients in plant tissues tells us something about the availability of nutrients and simultaneously tells us about the value of the plants to herbivores. The same set of 45 studies was explored for tissue nutrient concentrations (Verhoeven *et al.* 1996). The typical N : P ratio in control sites was 15 : 1. Their conclusion? "[T]he N : P ratio of above-ground biomass at the end of the growing season (August) provides a reliable indicator of the degree to which each of these elements has been limiting plant growth …". They conclude that N : P ratios greater than 16 indicate phosphorus limitation, while N : P ratios less than 14 indicate nitrogen limitation.

3.2   Infertile wetlands are constrained by low nutrient levels

Fertility levels in wetlands range between two extremes. At the high extreme, there are large floodplains and deltaic swamps, such as those of the

Mississippi, Rhine, or Amazon, where the eroded nutrients from an entire watershed are deposited. These areas have high nutrient levels and rapid plant

Table 3.3 Ionic composition (ppm) of rainwater and of runoff from rocks of different geological origin

Site/rock type	Ca^{2+}	Mg^{2+}	Na^+	K^+	HCO_3^-	SO_4^{2-}	Cl^-
Rainwater							
Newfoundland	0.8	–	5.2	0.3	–	2.2	8.9
Wisconsin	1.2	–	0.5	0.2	–	2.9	0.2
Minnesota	1.0	–	0.2	0.2	–	1.4	0.1
Northern Sweden	1.2	0.2	0.4	0.3	–	2.5	0.7
Central Sweden	0.6	0.1	0.3	0.2	–	2.6	0.5
Guyana	0.8	0.3	1.5	0.2	–	1.3	2.9
Runoff water							
Nova Scotia							
Granite	1.0	0.5	5.2	0.4	[a]	5.9	7.7
Quartzite and slate	2.1	0.4	3.0	0.6	1.8	5.2	4.9
Carboniferous strata	3.0	0.6	3.6	0.5	6.1	5.3	5.4
Bohemia							
Phyllite	5.7	2.4	5.4	2.1	35.1	3.1	4.9
Granite	7.7	2.3	6.9	3.7	40.3	9.2	4.2
Mica schist	9.3	3.8	8.0	3.1	48.3	9.5	5.4
Basalt	68.8	19.8	21.3	11.0	326.7	27.2	5.7
Cretaceous rocks	133.4	31.9	20.7	16.4	404.8	167.0	17.3

[a] Not detected.

Source: From Gore (1983), after Gorham (1961).

growth and enormous production of wetland animals. Because of their economic importance, these fertile wetlands often receive much attention from ecologists.

Other areas are near the low extreme, and are inherently infertile, particularly those that occur on infertile substrates and are largely dependent upon rainfall for nutrients. Rainwater has very low nutrient levels relative to groundwater, although nutrient levels do increase as water flows downstream (Table 3.3). Examples of infertile areas include:

- Depressions in rocks such as granite or gneiss, which erode slowly, and consequently provide few minerals of use to plants (e.g. Guyana Highlands of South America).
- Sand plains left by retreating continental ice sheets after the ice age (e.g. sand plains of central Wisconsin).
- Old shorelines of lakes that no longer exist because of changes in climate (e.g. shorelines of glacial Lake Algonquin along Lake Huron).
- Peatlands, where accumulated peat stores nutrients, and prevents plant roots from reaching mineral soil (e.g. West Siberian Lowland).
- Old soils where recurring fire and heavy rain have depleted soil nutrients (e.g. Gulf Coastal Plain of the United States).
- Other areas where rain is the primary source of water (e.g. Everglades).
- Local features such as sand spits produced by coastal erosion and deposition (e.g. Long Point on Lake Erie).

These infertile areas are significant for several reasons. First, they develop distinctive types of wetlands such as peat bogs, wet meadows, or wet savannas. Second, they are very sensitive to any increase in nutrient availability. Third, they

FIGURE 3.3 Many wetlands have low fertility. Examples include peat bogs (*a*, Algonquin Provincial Park, Ontario), the Everglades (*b*), shorelines in sand plains (*c*, Axe Lake, Ontario; courtesy M. Sharp) and wet savannas with old soils (*d*, Buttercup Flats, De Soto National Forest, Mississippi). (See also color plate.)

have strong gradients in plant composition related to soil nutrient levels. Since human activity tends to increase nutrients flowing into wetlands – from human sewage, from erosion, and even from pollution falling in the rain – all these types of wetlands are at particular risk from added nutrients. We shall look at four examples here: peatlands, the Everglades, sand plains, and wet savannas.

3.2.1 Peatlands

We saw in Chapter 1 that infertility is a defining characteristic of peatlands (Figure 3.3*a*). Recall that is the result of low rates of decomposition – vital nutrients like nitrogen and phosphorus remain stored in organic molecules. Hence, small amounts of groundwater can significantly affect nutrient availability, and the kinds of plant and animals that occur (Bridgham *et al.* 1996; Godwin *et al.* 2002). When the peat layer is thin, plants can obtain nutrients from groundwater and soil, but as peat depth grows, this source of nutrients is shut off. Eventually, only the nutrients in rainfall (and of course, from small amounts of decay) are available for plants. The result is that many plants have evergreen leaves to conserve nutrients. Others are carnivorous plants that obtain nitrogen and phosphorus from the bodies of insects and other small invertebrates. You saw three examples in Figure 1.17. Hence fertility gradients are very important in controlling the species composition of peatlands.

Among the dominant plants involved in building peatlands are mosses in the genus *Sphagnum* (Figure 1.18). There may be more carbon stored in *Sphagnum*, dead and alive, than in any other genus of plant (Clymo and Hayward 1982). When groundwater is available, more genera of mosses are found, particularly so when the groundwater is calcareous – examples include the genera *Scorpidium*, *Drepanocladus*, *Brachythecium*, and *Calliergonella* (Malmer 1986; Vitt 1990, 1994). It appears that calcium gradients are most important for controlling moss composition, with a clear shift away from *Spagnum* mosses above a pH of 5. Nitrogen and phosphorus gradients are more important for vascular plant composition. It is probably best to treat these as two independent gradients – calcium controlling the pH, nitrogen and phosphorus controlling fertility (Bridgham *et al.* 1996; Wheeler and Proctor 2000). Hence, the composition of fens is strongly affected by the chemical composition of the bedrock.

3.2.2 The Everglades

The Everglades, too, were once a vast rain-fed wetland, with extremely low nutrient levels (Figure 3.3*b*). This region of North America is very flat, and a slow but steady flow of water flow from north to south produced a distinctive sedge-dominated vegetation type adapted to wet infertile conditions (Loveless 1959; Davis and Ogden 1994; Sklar *et al.* 2005). Phosphorus concentrations across most of the Everglades were likely as low as 4 to 10 pg/l and loading rates averaged less than 0.1 g P/m^2 per year.

The distinctive communities of the Everglades are a response to these infertile conditions. Saw grass (*Cladium jamaicense*) is particularly common. Pools of shallow water have carnivorous plants in the genus *Utricularia*. Cyanophytes, which you recall, can fix atmospheric nitrogen, are prominent in the pools, and are the basis for a

food web which eventually supports wood storks and flamingoes.

3.2.3 Sand plains and shorelines

Some parts of the world have enormous sand plains (Figure 3.3*c*), most often the result of outwash from receding glaciers. Since sand contains few nutrients, and since it is easily leached, sand plains have distinctive vegetation. Small lakes often form on sand plains, with distinctive wet meadow communities. The figure shows a small lakeshore on the sand plain left by glacial Lake Algonquin. Another well-known example is the New Jersey Pine Barrens (Forman 1998; Zampella *et al.* 2006; Figure 14.17). Sand plains tend to have dry ridges alternating with wet valleys. Even in sand plains best known for dune systems, small wetlands may form in the swales between dunes.

3.2.4 Wet savannas

Those readers in the north temperate zone tend to take young landscapes for granted – most northern areas were buried in ice within the last 50 000 years. Other areas of the world, however, have not been glaciated, and may contain soils that have been exposed to weathering for millions of years. On the Gulf Coastal Plain of North America, soils tend to be very infertile. Recurring fire is an important cause: when plant tissues burn, the nitrogen is often returned to the atmosphere (a process termed volatilization), while phosphorus remains in the ash, often being leached by rainfall. Hence, these soils become increasingly deficient in key elements for plant growth. At the same time, however, their flat surfaces often restrict runoff, so large wet savannas (Figure 3.3*d*) can form (White *et al.* 1998; Christensen 1999). These savannas are dominated by grasses and sedges, but also include many species of orchids and carnivorous plants. Carnivorous plants are so abundant that these are sometimes known as pitcher plant savannas.

3.3   Other issues related to fertility

Having considered fertility and plants from the perspectives of primary productivity and low nutrient levels in wetlands we will now explore other adaptations of plants to differing degrees of fertility and the effects of gradients.

3.3.1   Infertile habitats have unique species

Plants in infertile wetlands have to be able to tolerate chronic shortages of nitrogen and phosphorus. Infertility is a major force affecting plant evolution, and plants found in infertile conditions share a set of traits such as slow growth, evergreen foliage, the uncoupling of growth from nutrient uptake, investment in anti-herbivore defenses, and the occurrence of mycorrhizae (Grime 1977, 1979).

Figure 1.17 introduced some plants from infertile wetlands. Let us explore this topic a little more. The evolution of carnivory is one of the most dramatic consequences of infertile conditions. Carnivorous plants obtain nitrogen and phosphorus from other sources than the soil (Givnish 1988). The Venus fly-trap is one of the best-known examples (Figure 3.4a). Many other plants are evergreen; these include herbaceous genera such as *Lobelia*, *Eriocaulon*, *Xyris*, and *Scirpus* as well as many trees and ericaceous shrubs (Richardson 1981; Richardson and Gibbons 1993). It is believed that evergreenness allows nutrient investment in leaves to be amortized over longer time periods.

Some evergreen species even use CAM photosynthesis, during which carbon is stored at night for later use during daylight (Boston 1986; Boston and Adams 1986). CAM is thought to be associated with deserts – hence, its presence in some wetland plants such as *Isoëtes* is unexpected. A few plants have symbiotic sources of nutrients – the widespread *Myrica gale* of bogs and lakeshores has root nodules in which nitrogen fixation occurs (Bond 1963). Many wild orchids are mycorrhizal

(see Section 3.3.5) and occur in relatively infertile wetlands – the white spikes of eastern prairie fringed orchid (*Platanthera leucophaea*) are an increasingly rare sight, as the species is threatened or endangered throughout its range (Figure 3.4b).

In general, wetland managers will often find that infertile wetlands have rare species and relatively low rates of growth. Hence they are inordinately sensitive to factors like sedimentation from logging and disturbance from all-terrain vehicles or cattle.

(a)   (b)

2 cm   6 cm

FIGURE 3.4 Infertile wetlands often provide habitat for unusual plant species. (*a*) The Venus fly-trap (*Dionaea muscipula*; from Pietropaolo and Pietropaolo 1986), restricted to a few coastal bogs in the Carolinas. (*b*) The eastern prairie fringed orchid (*Platanthera leucophaea*; from Reddoch and Reddoch 1997), threatened or endangered throughout its range in North America.

3.3.2 Fertile habitats often have fast-growing species

In highly productive habitats, nutrients are, by definition, not limiting to growth. In such circumstances, light soon becomes limiting. Plants tend to be tall and fast-growing. Canopies are rapidly produced in the spring using reserves from buried rhizomes (Figure 3.5). Competition for light has been a factor in plant communities since the first terrestrial plants began to form erect shoots and shade one another. Thus, in herbaceous vegetation,

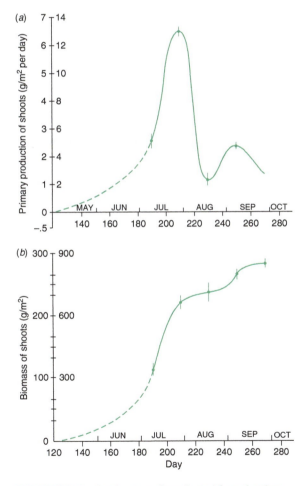

(a)

Primary production of shoots (g/m² per day)

(b)

Biomass of shoots (g/m²)

Day

FIGURE 3.5 On fertile sites, there is rapid production of shoots in the spring, as shown by (a) primary production and (b) biomass as a function of time of year. (After Auclair *et al.* 1976b.)

tall shoots, broad canopies, and deeply rooted rhizomes for support all can be regarded as traits that arose out of intense competition for light (e.g. Grime 1979; Givnish 1982).

Dense stands of plants with tall shoots arising from deeply buried rhizomes occur around the world. Three examples are papyrus (*Cyperus papyrus*) along the Nile, reeds (*Phragmites australis*) along the Baltic Sea in Europe, and cattails (*Typha* spp.) in the Mississippi River delta. Most of these plants are in one evolutionary lineage, the Monocotyledonae, with the vast majority being in the Cyperaceae (e.g. *Carex, Scirpus, Eleocharis, Cyperus, Rhynchospora, Cladium)* or the Poaceae *(Calamagrostis, Glyceria, Oryza, Phragmites, Phalaris, Panicum)*. Other families include the Typhaceae (*Typha* spp.), Sparganiaceae (*Sparganium* spp.), and Juncaceae (*Juncus* spp.)

While these areas may have high primary production, plant diversity is often low. Large clones of *Typha* and *Phragmites* are able to dominate wetland communities to the detriment of other species with smaller growth forms and shorter shoots (Gaudet and Keddy 1988; Moore *et al.* 1989). Since many species of waterfowl require open areas of water, and a mixture of different vegetation types for feeding, dense stands composed of a single species are often undesirable for wildlife as well. Wildlife managers strive for "hemi-marshes" that have a 50 : 50 mix of emergent vegetation and open water, as well as other sources of plant diversity such as shrub borders (Verry 1989). High fertility increases the rates at which the plants grow and refill gaps. Hence, managers often have to resort to artificially changing water levels, or burning, or even using heavy equipment, to retain the desired mixture of habitat types. We will return to this topic in Section 3.5.

3.3.3 Fertility gradients organize wetlands at different scales

Differences in fertility can explain many of the patterns one sees in wetlands. Within watersheds, for example, the headwaters may have small sandy-bottomed streams, while the river mouth may have deep alluvial sediments. Within one lake, shores exposed to waves will have coarse infertile substrates, whereas shores in sheltered bays will have rich accumulations of silt, clay, and organic matter.

To illustrate the differences caused by soil fertility gradients, wetland plants can be grown in sediments collected from different habitats. For example, Smart and Barko (1978) grew four different marsh plants in different types of sediment. They found that the growth rates of these plants (*Spartina alterniflora, S. foliosa, S. patens*, and *Distichlis spicata*) were an order of magnitude higher on clay than on sand, with intermediate growth on silty clay. Similar kinds of experiments have shown that growth on fine substrates is much higher than growth on coarse ones for a wide range of wetland plants including submersed aquatics (Denny 1972), emergents (Barko and Smart 1978), and species on seasonally flooded shores (Sharp and Keddy 1985; Wilson and Keddy 1985).

One way to visualize the many effects of fertility is through multivariate analysis. One first collects information on a large number of plots, and then uses one of several multivariate methods to explore how measured nutrient levels are related to biological factors (Shimwell 1971; Digby and Kempton 1987). Figure 3.6 shows a typical result – the interrelationships of soil nutrients, biomass, and primary productivity in a riparian wetland. In this case, biomass and productivity are positively correlated with nitrogen ($r = 0.38, 0.39$) but negatively correlated with phosphorus ($r = -0.29, -0.23$).

It is difficult to know how far one can generalize from these sorts of studies. In a nearby *Carex*-dominated ecosystem, there were no significant correlations between production and either N or P (Auclair *et al.* 1976b). It appears that generalizations are difficult to achieve! Perhaps the relationships between fertility and biological factors such as biomass depend upon the scale at which you look. If you sample a small homogeneous area, patterns may not be detectable at all. If you sample a large heterogeneous area, patterns may be clear. To illustrate this scale effect, I have assembled a set of tables (Table 3.4)

showing correlations between nutrients and biological factors at five different scales, from the large scale down to the small scale. Let us begin at the large scale.

The upper panel (Table 3.4a) shows correlations among major nutrients in a series of wetland types representative of eastern North America, ranging from highly fertile sites (e.g. *Typha* marshes and floodplains) to highly infertile sand or gravel shorelines where insectivorous genera such as *Drosera* and *Utricularia* were common. At this scale, all major nutrients are positively correlated, so one can reasonably talk about fertility gradients without distinguishing among the major nutrients. Both organic matter and the silt and clay content are also positively correlated with these nutrient levels. This makes sense, since nutrients can attach to organic matter or clay particles.

At the intermediate scale, Table 3.4b shows correlations among major nutrients within a single lake. This gradient results from wave action and ice scour (Chapter 4). Again, major nutrients are positively correlated. Similar patterns occur within a single watershed (Table 3.4c).

Moving to smaller scales at the bottom of the table, at the most local scale, this pattern begins to disappear. Table 3.4e shows correlations among nutrients within one vegetation type – the *Carex* meadow mentioned above. Note that nitrogen is still positively correlated with soil organic matter, but phosphorus is negatively correlated with nitrogen. Similar results occur in the more heterogeneous *Scirpus–Equisetum* wetland (Table 3.4d). In neither of these latter habitats is N significantly correlated with P.

Hence, at landscape scales, natural fertility gradients appear to be a general feature of wetlands. At local scales, these patterns may be harder to detect.

3.3.4 Fertility gradients and the composition of peatlands

We have seen that peatlands are generally infertile, and that fens are strongly affected by the chemistry of the groundwater. Let us look at a few more examples.

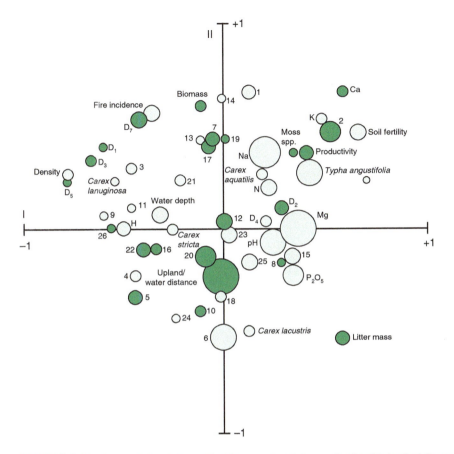

FIGURE 3.6 The interrelationships of fertility, productivity, and other biological features in a riparian wetland in eastern Canada. The multivariate method is factor analysis. The first and second components are shown on the horizontal and vertical axes, respectively. Factor loadings on the third component are represented by circle diameters (light = negative, dark = positive). D_1–D_7 are species diversity indices. Other variables include: 1, soil organic matter; 2, soil $(Ca + Mg)/(K + Na)$; 3, days elapsed after 1 May; 4, tussock incidence; 5, distance to upland; 6, distance to water; 7, biomass; 8, average stem height; 9, *Equisetum fluviatile*; 10, *Onoclea sensibilis*; 11, *Thelypteris palustris*; 12, *Potentilla palustris*; 13, *Viola pallens*; 14, *Hypericum virginicum*; 15, *Galium palustre*; 16, *Lysimachia thyrsiflora*; 17, *Lythrum salicaria*; 18, *Cicuta bulbifera*; 19, *Utricularia vulgaris*; 20, *Impatiens capensis*; 21, *Lycopus uniflorus*; 22, *Campanula aparinoides*; 23, *Carex diandra*; 24, *Calamagrostis canadensis*; 25, *Sparganium eurycarpum*; 26, *Sagittaria latifolia*. (From Auclair *et al.* 1976a.)

In central North America, Glaser *et al.* (1990) studied a large peatland that included fens and a raised bog. This site had a strong chemical gradient. For example, the rich fens had a pH above 7 and Ca concentrations ranged from 20 to 45 mg/l. In contrast, the raised bog had a pH below 4 and a Ca concentration below 1.1 mg/l. The number of plant species tended to increase with rising pH and Ca concentrations. In the foothills of the Rocky Mountains, Slack *et al.* (1980) described peatlands having pools of water alternating with raised ridges, a patterned peatland such as you saw in Figure 1.6*a*. The distribution of plant species was closely related to water level, with the wetter areas tending to be dominated by the moss *Scorpidium scorpioides* and the sedge *Carex limosa*.

Table 3.4 **Fertility gradients in wetlands from large scale (top) to small scale (bottom). Note that patterns fade as the scale becomes smaller**

(a) *Marshes in northeastern North America*

	% organic	P	N	K	Mg	pH
Standing crop	0.77	0.76	0.66	0.58	0.67	−0.28
% organic	1.00	0.77	0.57	0.50	0.51	−0.47
P		1.00	0.72	0.56	0.66	−0.13
N			1.00	0.53	0.63	−0.02
K				1.00	0.70	−0.28
Mg					1.00	−0.14

Source: From Gaudet (1993), Table 1.2.

(b) *The shores of a temperate zone lake*

	Mg	% organic	P	K	pH
Standing crop					
Mg	1.00	0.52	0.86	0.73	0.22
% organic		1.00	0.51	0.48	0.16
P			1.00	0.64	0.20
K				1.00	0.09
pH					1.00

Source: From Keddy (1984).

(c) *One wetland complex in the Ottawa River watershed*

	% organic	P	N	K	Mg	pH
Standing crop	0.74	0.80	0.69	0.76	0.69	−0.45
% organic	1.00	0.80	0.61	0.66	0.62	−0.61
P		1.00	0.62	0.82	0.59	−0.46
N			1.00	0.68	0.53	−0.18
K				1.00	0.64	−0.35
Mg					1.00	−0.72

Source: From Gaudet (1993), Table 1.4.

(d) *One vegetation zone of the St. Lawrence River*

	Standing crop	% organic	P	N	K	Mg	pH
Standing crop	1.00		0.34	−0.29	0.38	0.49	0.17	0.21
% organic		1.00	−0.27	0.37	0.75	0.59	0.18
P			1.00	−0.01	−0.48	0.33	−0.55
N				1.00	0.39	0.32	0.14
K					1.00	0.43	0.38
Mg						1.00	0.12
pH							1.00

Source: From Auclair *et al.* (1976a), Table 1.

Table 3.4 (*cont.*)

(e) Carex *meadows, St. Lawrence River*

	Standing crop	% organic	P	N	K	Mg	pH
Standing crop	1.00	0.13	−0.02	−0.02	−0.22	−0.23	−0.11
% organic		1.00	−0.39	0.30	0.52	0.17	−0.14
P			1.00	−0.26	0.18	−0.21	0.03
N				1.00	0.24	0.26	0.04
K					1.00	0.16	−0.01
Mg						1.00	0.52
pH							1.00

Source: From Auclair *et al.* (1976b), Table 1.

In European peatlands, similar patterns and gradients are evident, although distance from the sea often becomes an added factor, particularly in controlling Na, Mg, and Cl concentrations (Malmer 1986; Wheeler and Proctor 2000). One large wetland occurs in the floodplain of the Biebrza River in northeast Poland (Wassen *et al.* 1990). The larger part consisted of fens with species such as *Carex lasiocarpa* and *C. chordorrhiza* but floodplain marshes occurred further downstream and along river margins dominated by *Glyceria* (Palczynski 1984). Shrubs such as *Betula humilis* occurred on drier sites. Parts of the valley are mowed and grazed by either cattle or elk. Flood frequency and soil nutrients were apparently the primary factors controlling species composition. The number of plant species was greatest (33 species/10 m^2) in those fens receiving only groundwater and having low productivity (ca. 1 kg/m^2); the typical sedge was *Carex limosa*. The number of plant species was lowest in the fertile *Glyceria maxima* floodplains (13 species/10 m^2) where productivity was highest (ca. 6 kg/m^2).

A survey of 45 fens in New York State documented the importance of groundwater characteristics in controlling species composition (Godwin *et al.* 2002). In particular, this study documented the importance of setting in the landscape: geology, connection to watercourses, and wetland area were all important factors affecting composition. The pore water of isolated fens was significantly more enriched that the pore water of fens connected to surface water. Hence, it would appear that fens are particularly sensitive to changes occurring in the surrounding landscape.

Peatlands also occur in the southern hemisphere. The Magellanic moorland comprises some 44 000 km^2 distributed along the southwestern edge of South America, from Tierra del Fuego north to about 45° S (Arroyo *et al.* 2005). These peatlands tend to be embedded within a matrix of southern temperate forest. There is a strong gradient in rainfall and wind speed, declining inland from west to east. In the drier east, ombrotrophic blanket bogs are most common, and *Sphagnum* is dominant. In the wet and exposed western regions, cushion-forming plants are more common than *Sphagnum*. This region has a flora with an evolutionary history rooted in the old continent of Gondwana; hence the species and families are often unfamiliar to those with experience in the northern temperate zone – typical wetland dominants include *Astelia* (Bromeliaceae), *Donatia* (Donatiaceae), and *Gaimardia* (Centrolepidaceae). In spite of the fact that the names and evolutionary origins are different, gradients of moisture supply, nutrients, and location remain important factors controlling peat depth and species composition.

3.3.5 Mycorrhizae can supplement nutrient availability

Fungi associated with plant roots are called mycorrhizae. They assist in taking up nutrients, particularly phosphorus, from infertile soils (e.g. Read *et al.* 1976; Smith and Douglas 1987; Marschner 1995). The orchids are one group that are well known for having mycorrhizae (recall Figure 3.4*b*). In general, we can say that mycorrhizae are widespread across the plant kingdom. For example, in coniferous forest, more than 90% of the species are infected. We also know that mycorrhizae are particularly important for phosphorus uptake. Yet, in spite of their general importance, mycorrhizae are not so prevalent in wetlands (e.g. Anderson *et al.* 1984; Peat and Fitter 1993; Cornwell *et al.* 2001). This may be another consequence of hypoxic soils – most fungi require oxygen to grow. We may speculate, therefore, that soil nutrient gradients – particularly phosphorus gradients – are even more important in wetlands than in terrestrial habitats.

In one survey across many species and moisture levels, mycorrhizal infection declined with flooding from 27% infection in dry areas to less than 1% in wet areas (Rickerl *et al.* 1994). *Carex atherodes* and *Juncus tenuis* had no mycorrhizae. *Scirpus fluviatilis* had no mycorrhizae in wet sites, but was slightly colonized in dry areas.

Or consider the enormous sedge genus, Cyperaceae, which often occupies infertile habitats – an example is the vast areas of saw grass (*Cladium jamaicense*) in the Everglades. Sedges are apparently not commonly mycorrhizal (Peat and Fitter 1993). In the sedge genus *Carex* there seem to be three groups, one group that is not mycorrhizal, one group that is consistently mycorrizal, and one group where status is closely dependent upon local conditions (Miller *et al.* 2001). In fens, all the dominant monocots appear to be non-mycorrhizal, although the subdominant dicots are mycorrhizal (Cornwell *et al.* 2001).

There are other exceptions – the aquatic plant *Lobelia dortmanna* is mycorrhizal. This may be related to the release of oxygen by *Lobelia* roots, which can create local aerobic pockets (Pedersen *et al.* 1995).

Bogs also appear to be exceptions. Overall, there are three main types of mycorrhizal association (endomycorrhizae, ectomycorrhizae, and ericoid mycorrhizae), each associated with different soil types (Read *et al.* 1985; Lewis 1987). In bogs, the ericoid association is predominant. In this mycorrhizal association, ascomycete fungi are affiliated with ericaceous plants. The fine individual hyphae, ramifying near the soil surface, appear to capture nitrogen (Read *et al.* 1985; Lewis 1987). Ericoid mycorrhizae apparently provide lower rates of nitrogen uptake than other mycorrhizae, thereby supporting correspondingly low plant growth rates (Woodward and Kelly 1997).

In general, then, it appears that the anoxic conditions in wetlands reduce the presence and abundance of most mycorrhizae. This limits nutrient uptake, particularly phosphorus uptake. But there are also conspicuous exceptions.

3.4   Animals and fertility

The very concept of fertility is usually seen to be an issue only for plant ecologists. It is not. Although many studies focus on plants as a source of energy for animals, it is possible that plants are equally important as a nitrogen source (White 1993). Animals must get their nitrogen from plants in the form of ready-made amino acids. Because nitrogen is in such short supply, plants are very economical in their use of nitrogen. Table 3.1 suggested an average nitrogen content of around 2%, less than half that of animal tissues. Even when plants are grown under fertile conditions, nitrogen content is rather similar and very low – between 0.5% and 2% (Figure 3.7). At very best, by concentrating on seeds, pollen, or cambium, animals may be able to harvest a food source that is about 5% nitrogen dry weight (White 1993). This has

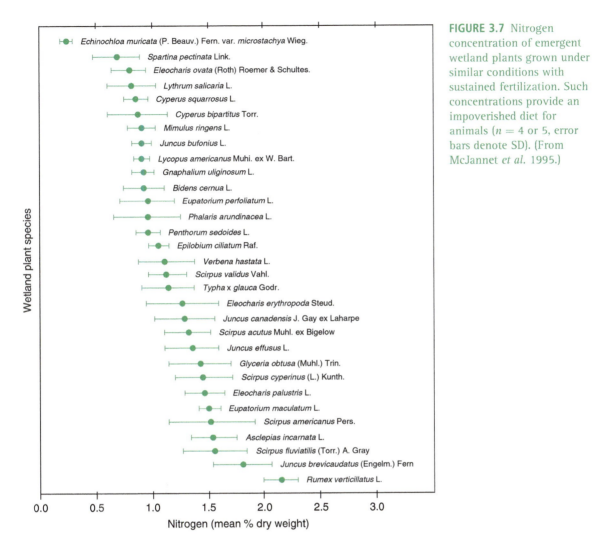

FIGURE 3.7 Nitrogen concentration of emergent wetland plants grown under similar conditions with sustained fertilization. Such concentrations provide an impoverished diet for animals ($n = 4$ or 5, error bars denote SD). (From McJannet *et al.* 1995.)

led some to suggest that nitrogen, not energy, is the limiting resource for animal communities. White provides extensive documentation of nitrogen limitation in the animal kingdom. Animals may therefore be more sensitive to soil fertility gradients than we might at first assume.

We already know that plants, although bathed in atmospheric nitrogen, are often desperately short of nitrogen. It now appears that the situation may be even worse for animals. White therefore suggests that animals have been strongly selected to counter these environmental shortages. He identifies six basic strategies:

(i) synchronizing life cycles with availability of food with higher nitrogen content;
(ii) selecting those tissues with higher N content;
(iii) eating quickly and digesting more efficiently;
(iv) supplementing plant food with animal protein;
(v) territoriality and social behavior;
(vi) enlisting the help of microorganisms.

Many examples of (i) to (v) can be seen throughout the animal kingdom. We could reinterpret a majority of dietary studies around the theme of extracting nitrogen from an impoverished environment. White's book is replete with examples. This is useful to consider before beginning the chapter on herbivores – wetlands may look green, but much of the green tissue may be of little value to herbivores.

Point (vi) may be worth a brief digression. Over the past decades, plant ecologists have increasingly studied the role of mycorrhizae in plant nutrient budgets. Now White reminds us that animals too have associations with microorganisms to cope with chronic nutrient limitations. For example, microorganisms provide a large part of the nitrogenous food of ruminants (Janis 1996). Instead of excreting urea in urine, ruminants will often transport urea back to the rumen. Some nitrogen-fixing microorganisms live in animal guts. Perhaps the use of microorganisms to escape nitrogen limitation is an important evolutionary parallel in plants and animals.

3.5   Eutrophication: too much of a good thing

We have already discussed the effects of nutrient levels on fertility. What happens when eutrophication occurs and why?

3.5.1   Human activity often increases nutrient levels in wetlands

A major consequence of industrialized civilization has been the erosion of soils and heavy fertilization of agricultural ecosystems. As a consequence, nitrates and phosphates have increased in rainwater and runoff (Figure 3.8). Moreover, much of the nitrogen used in agriculture has not been obtained from natural sources, but extracted from the atmosphere industrially using the Haber process. This process was only developed in the early 1900s, but it has radically altered the global nitrogen cycle by vastly increasing the amount of biologically available nitrogen in the biosphere (Pimental et al. 1973; Freedman 1995). To put the Haber process in context, the amount of industrially fixed nitrogen applied to crops during the period 1980 to 1990 more than equaled all industrial fertilizer applied previously in human history (Vitousek et al. 1997).

Wetlands are places where such nutrients tend to accumulate. Overall, there seem to be four general consequences. First, in marshes and wet meadows, fertilization alleviates nutrient limitation, and causes an increase in biomass, thereby reducing the number of species present. Small plants, carnivorous plants, and evergreen plants are particularly likely to disappear. Second, those plants receiving the nutrients may become more palatable to herbivores, increasing herbivore populations. Third, in shallow water, increased populations of floating algae can kill aquatic macrophytes. Fourth, when the algae and macrophytes decay, oxygen is consumed, leading to hypoxic conditions that kill fish.

The study of nutrients in lakes helps us understand impacts on wetlands, which often fringe lakes. Eutrophication has had major negative effects upon fish production in the Great Lakes (Christie 1974; Vallentyne 1974). Decreasing N:P ratios can also cause nitrogen-fixing cyanobacteria to replace other

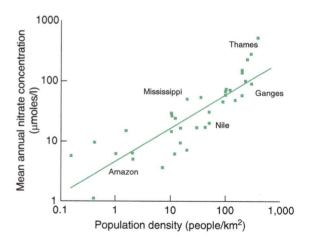

FIGURE 3.8 Nitrate concentration of water in 42 major rivers plotted against population density in the surrounding region. (From World Resources Institute 1992.)

species of planktonic algae (Schindler 1977; Smith 1983). So let us look more closely at the process of eutrophication in lakes.

3.5.2 Runoff carries nutrients into lakes, rivers, and wetlands

So far we have treated fertility as an independent variable, and we have asked about its effects on wetlands. Now let us move back one step in causation, and treat fertility as the dependent variable. Let us ask what factors determine the levels of nutrients arriving in a wetland. There is a large scientific literature on this topic because the negative effects of eutrophication upon water quality have been a matter of great concern for decades (e.g. Vallentyne 1974; Rigler and Peters 1995), and because the effects of eutrophication on wetlands like the Everglades are increasingly obvious (Newman *et al.* 1998; Sklar *et al.* 2005).

Since the Great Lakes, North America, are among the largest bodies of fresh water in the world and have been well studied, let us use them as the main example (International Joint Commission 1980). Phosphorus is the major nutrient of interest, owing to the fact that these studies were carried out with an emphasis upon phytoplankton and fish production. Table 3.5 shows that the major sources of phosphorus in the Great Lakes arise from sources including urban areas, land use (mostly rural), and atmospheric deposition. Let us consider urban and rural runoff first, leaving atmospheric deposition for Section 3.5.3.

Urban areas can be considered to be point sources, unlike rural areas which are diffuse sources of nutrients. Point sources have high inputs per hectare from small areas, whereas diffuse sources have low inputs per hectare but from much larger areas. To help us think clearly, we can use forested areas as a natural reference point. They have the lowest levels of P loading, less than a kilogram per hectare per year, often much less (0.02 to 0.67 kg/ha per year). Urban areas may contribute much more phosphorus, from 0.1 to 4.1 kg/ha per year. Areas under construction have an even higher load as a consequence of soil erosion (see also Guy 1973 and Chapter 7). Apart from erosion during construction, sewage is an obvious factor in urban areas. Runoff into storm sewers is also important: the latter contains high concentrations of nutrients from lawns and pet feces. Such urban nutrient sources are rather straightforward – one needs proper sewage treatment, and effective treatment of runoff from storm sewers. These can be dealt with technologically (wastewater treatment) or culturally (by encouraging citizens to reduce lawn area, use less fertilizer, or reduce the numbers of outdoor pets).

Rural land use is very variable. Runoff contributes from 0.1 to 9.1 kg P/ha per year. The amount of phosphorus in stream water has been related to a variety of predictors that describe land use. The lowest levels, as you might expect, are for areas

Table 3.5 Major sources of phosphorus (metric tonnes) in the Great Lakes

Source	Lake Superior	Lake Michigan	Lake Huron	Lake Erie	Lake Ontario
Municipal sewage	268	2298	515	6828	2815
Industrial	135	279	122	347	102
Land use	2238	1891	2442	8445	3581
Atmospheric	1566	1682	1129	774	488
Upstream lakes	–	–	657	1070	4769
Total	4207	6150	4857	17 464	11 755

Source: After International Joint Commission (1980).

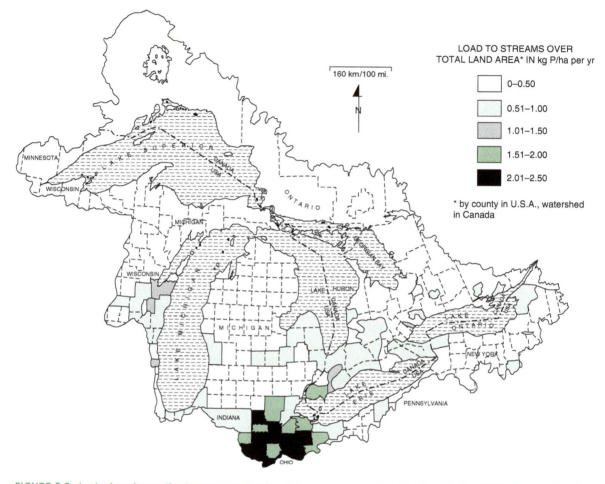

FIGURE 3.9 Agricultural contributions to nutrient levels in streams entering the Great Lakes. (After International Joint Commission 1980.)

under forest. The best predictor for high phosphorus is the amount of the watershed in row crops (International Joint Commission 1980). In lakes with agricultural watersheds (Lake Michigan, Lake Huron, Lake Erie) two-thirds of the diffuse load of nutrients was attributable to runoff from cropland (Figure 3.9). In watersheds without agriculture, forestry becomes a more important source of nutrient loading to lakes. In an artificially deforested watershed, dissolved nitrogen jumped from ca. 1.0 to >40 kg/ha of nitrate, and from ca. 33 to >300 kg/ha of particulates (Bormann and Likens 1981). Sediment yield is also affected by the nature of forestry practices, with

a commercial clearcut yielding turbidity values between 10 and 10^2 times larger than a cut conducted to protect water values (Lee 1980). Road construction is one of the greatest impacts of forestry upon water quality (Forman and Alexander 1998). Agriculture and forestry can therefore be modified to greatly reduce diffuse nutrient loading.

The Great Lakes can be considered the classic example for the study of nutrient inputs from watersheds. Now let us consider a few more examples. Much further south, in Tampa Bay, the largest open-water estuary in Florida, over 2 million people live in the adjoining watershed, contributing nitrogen, phosphorus, and suspended solids (Greening 1995). Shading by algae has damaged seagrass (*Thalassia testudinum*) beds. Nitrogen was emphasized in this study, with over half of the nitrogen loading attributable to diffuse sources including residential runoff (13%), rangelands (14%), and intensive agriculture (6%). A further one-fourth came from atmospheric deposition. Thus, a full three-fourths of the nitrogen load came from non-point sources. Although this study represented a different geographical region, and a different major nutrient, the importance of rural land use was again emphasized.

In the nearby watershed of Lake Okeechobee, dairy farms are the major source of phosphorus loading, followed by cattle ranching (Rosen *et al.* 1995). Land management activities have been undertaken to reduce phosphorus loading; these included fencing cows away from streams, maintaining vegetation strips adjacent to streams, constructing cattle crossings over streams, and recycling dairy barn wash water. In some cases, there have been cash payments to buy out dairies, with restrictive deeds on the property to prevent future use as a dairy. Changing the use of land is quite a different technical problem from constructing urban sewage treatment plants, but as the above studies show, it is equally important for the reduction of eutrophication of wetlands.

We should briefly mention two other examples of downstream effects from nutrients produced by intensive agriculture, the Everglades and the Gulf of Mexico. Upstream land use is a major cause of eutrophication in the Everglades. When changes in land management upstream were unable to reduce nutrient levels sufficiently, managers built enormous treatment ponds, where, it is hoped, agricultural runoff can be treated much like point sources of pollution (Newman *et al.* 1998; Sklar *et al.* 2005). It is, however, not yet proven that plants in treatment ponds can sufficiently reduce nutrient levels, and the costs involved may require managers to consider purchase and decommissioning the sugar cane fields. The Gulf of Mexico is surprisingly similar. Here

nutrients generated far upstream, as far north as the cropland south of Lake Erie in Figure 3.9, are transported south by the Mississippi River, where they generate large populations of phytoplankton along the coast. When the phytoplankton die, they sink in the water and decay, producing a large hypoxic zone (known popularly as "the dead zone") which damages marine fisheries (Mitsch *et al.* 2001; Turner and Rabelais 2003). Such examples invite you to consider how nutrients link humans to wetlands – the sugar you consume in your diet is responsible for gradual destruction of the Everglades, while the corn that is used to produce beef is damaging fish production in the Gulf of Mexico.

You will often hear that wetlands are nutrient sinks which trap nitrogen and phosphorus, reducing the eutrophication of downstream aquatic ecosystems (Richardson 1985). Is this true, and what might its effects be upon the wetlands? Comparative studies of phosphorus retention capacity among 20 sites showed, however, that it was extremely variable, with a phosphorus absorption index ranging from 163 in swamp forests to a mere 8 in pocosin peats (Richardson 1985). Richardson then compared four different sites that had received high loadings of phosphorus-laden wastewater. The abandoned old field continued to remove 96% of the added phosphorus in spite of a loading three times as high as the three wetlands (Figure 3.10). "Collectively, these data indicate that high initial rates of phosphorus removal will be followed by large exports of phosphorus within a few years" (p. 1426).

The design of artificially constructed wetlands for removing nutrients from wastewater (Hammer 1989, Kadlec and Knight 2004) is a topic we will consider further in Section 11.3.5. If there is an emerging consensus, however, it is the view that it is better to manage landscapes carefully to reduce the nutrients that are released, rather than to try to remove the nutrients once they have entered surface water. The fact that nutrients are increasingly falling in rain and snow only serves to emphasis the need to address the problem at its source.

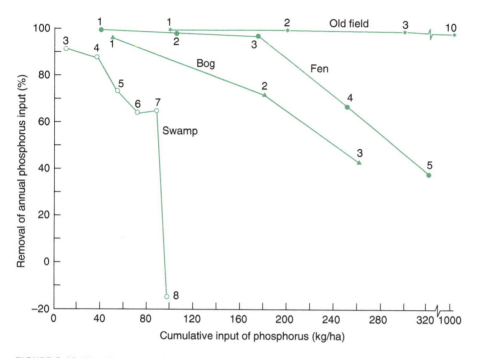

FIGURE 3.10 The change in phosphorus removal efficiency of four habitats – a fen, a white cedar swamp forest, a blanket bog, and an abandoned old field – as a function of cumulative phosphorus inputs. The numbers along each line indicate the number of years of phosphorus addition. (From Richardson 1985.)

3.5.3 Precipitation also is a source of nutrients

Although sewage and runoff are the major sources of nutrient inputs to some wetlands, nutrients carried by precipitation also fertilize landscapes (see line 4 in Table 3.5). Much of this comes from human sources, but even before humans began generating pollution, dust storms in deserts contributed nutrients to the atmosphere. The dust was transported long distances and fell in rain (Jickells *et al.* 1998). The large areas of the Earth that are covered with loess or wind-deposited soil testify to the enormous amounts of dust that move through the atmosphere. In addition to these sources, the burning of fossil fuel, and to a lesser extent, biomass, now adds both nitrogen and sulfur to rainfall (Vitousek *et al.* 1997). Over the last century, the concentration of nitrogen-containing compounds in rainwater has steadily increased. Germany now

receives in the order of 25 kg N/ha each year in rainfall (Ellenberg 1989). This is enough to produce significant changes in vegetation. More recently, pollution control measures may be having some positive effect. In the United States, over the period of 1980–92, SO_4^{2-} concentrations fell at 42 of 58 monitoring sites in the country (Lynch *et al.* 1995). Less than a fifth of these sites showed significant declines in NO_3^-, however.

There are good reasons for expecting atmospheric pollution levels to continue increasing, given the growth of the world's population and the burning of coal and oil. To put the problem in context, long pollution records can be obtained from ice cores taken from glaciers (Figure 3.11). These data suggests that any short-term reductions of nutrients in precipitation still leave us well above pre-industrial deposition rates. The scattered peaks of sulfate deposition can be traced back to volcanic eruptions such as Lab (1783) and Tambora (1815).

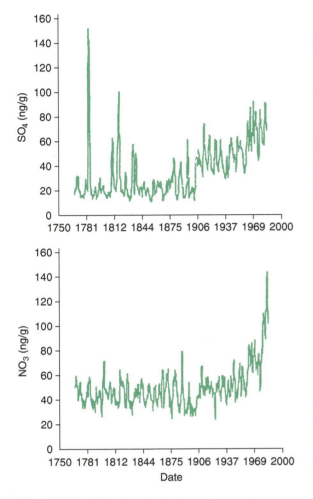

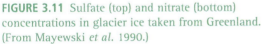

FIGURE 3.11 Sulfate (top) and nitrate (bottom) concentrations in glacier ice taken from Greenland. (From Mayewski *et al.* 1990.)

The ratio of nutrients in rainfall has also been changing. Pre-industrial concentrations of nitrate were roughly twice those of sulfate; in contrast, at the turn of the nineteenth century, they were nearly equivalent. Recent surges in nitrate emission have again caused nitrate levels to exceed sulfate (Mayewski *et al.* 1990). Hence, the changes associated with eutrophication seem likely to continue as both runoff and rainfall are contaminated by high levels of elements including nitrogen and phosphorus.

3.5.4 Eutrophication reduces diversity in wet meadows and marshes

In general, higher nutrient levels lead to higher amounts of biomass. Higher amounts of nutrients, combined with higher biomass, almost without exception cause the composition of wetlands to change, and plant diversity to decrease. It is important to understand the pattern: that increased nutrient levels reduce plant diversity, particularly affecting uncommon types of species. Since managers are faced with these sorts of nearly irreversible changes, it is also important to understand the mechanism that causes these changes. Many arise out of the effects of fertility upon competition, which we shall explore in more detail in Chapter 5. But let us have a quick introduction here.

Experimental fertilization provides one tool for studying effects of eutrophication. Figure 3.12 shows the results from a study where 12 experimentally created wetland habitats were generated under both low and high fertility. High fertility levels led to much higher levels of biomass (left, dark histograms), irrespective of the habitat types. Simultaneously, high fertility levels led to reduced numbers of plant species (right, dark histograms). The general explanation is that fertilization increases competition, particularly for light, as we shall see in Chapter 5.

We shall see field data from wetlands in eastern North America show similar patterns (Section 9.4). We will see more about this problem in the Everglades in (Section 13.2.2). Fertilization in salt marshes also results in dramatic changes in zonation (Section 10.3.7).

3.5.5 Eutrophication can lead to die-offs of aquatic plants

The effects of eutrophication on aquatic wetland communities are studied rather less than effects on phytoplankton and fish. It often appears that eutrophication is associated with declines in the abundance of macrophytes. This at first

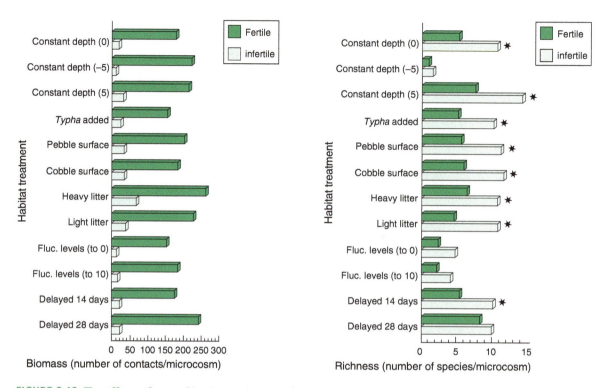

FIGURE 3.12 The effects of eutrophication on biomass (left, all differences significant) and number of species (right, * indicates significant differences) in 12 artificially created wetland habitats. (From Wisheu *et al.* 1990.)

appears counterintuitive. It certainly is the opposite of what we see in marshes and wet meadows. The presumed explanation is that increased fertility leads to increased phytoplankton biomass. The plankton then absorb light and shade out macrophytes (Phillips *et al.* 1978; Moss 1983; Pieczynska 1986; Osborne and Polunin 1986). Figure 3.13 presents a hypothesis that relates the decline in macrophytes to eutrophication. In estuaries, eutrophication appears instead to stimulate macroalgae, which, through shading or anoxia induced by decomposition, eliminate macrophytes such as *Zostera marilla* (Valida *et al.* 1992).

In order to understand the effects of eutrophication, it is necessary to know whether aquatic plants are able to use nutrients in the water column as opposed to the substrate.

Carignan and Kalff (1980) used radioactive phosphorus to compare sediment vs. the water column as sources of phosphorus in nine common aquatic plants, and found that the majority of nutrients are removed from the sediments (Table 3.6). Even under hypertrophic conditions, the sediment contributed nearly three-fourths of the phosphorus taken up during growth. This has two important implications. First, from the point of view of this chapter, aquatic plants are not that different from other wetland plants. We can talk about fertility gradients in the substrate even among aquatic plants. Second, macrophytes may be visualized as pumps that remove nutrients from sediments and return them to open water (Barko and Smart 1980). This may affect attempts to manage wetlands for reduced nutrient levels.

Table 3.6 Uptake of phosphorus from sediments by nine macrophyte species

Species	Percentage uptake from sediments
Myriophyllum alterniflorum	104.4
Potamogeton zosteriformis	107.4
Potamogeton foliosus	98.6
Callitriche hermaphroditica	94.2
Elodea canadensis	99.0
Najas flexilis	100.8
Myriophyllum spicatum	99.4
Heteranthera dubia	95.2
Vallisneria americana	103.1

Source: After Carignan and Kalff (1980).

3.5.6 Eutrophication is reducing diversity in European vegetation

Western Europe, with its high human population density and long history of human use, may be a useful general model. As noted above, nitrogen levels in rainfall have become very high. Ellenberg (1985, 1988) predicts that species normally found at low fertility will gradually disappear from the European landscape. Ellenberg has ranked species according to the nitrogen levels at which they normally occur, thereby identifying the subset of plants that require infertile habitats. These are species at risk. Because eutrophication is occurring across the entire landscape, a significant proportion of the European flora is at risk (Figure 3.14).

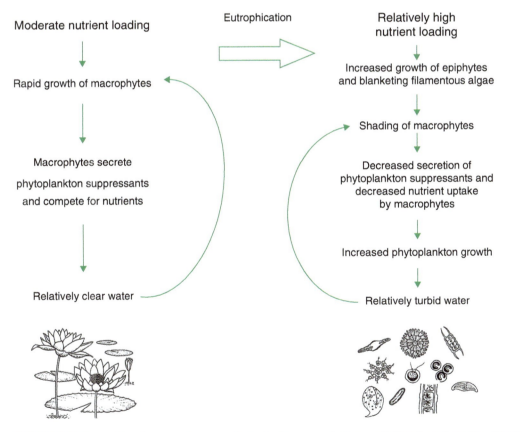

FIGURE 3.13 Eutrophication may increase phytoplankton populations and thereby reduce the abundance of aquatic macrophytes. (After Phillips *et al.* 1978.)

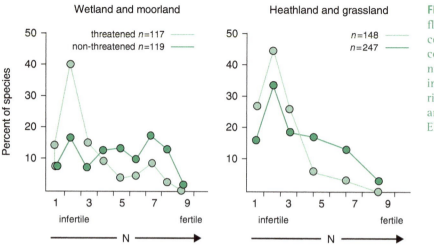

FIGURE 3.14 The threatened flora of Europe (light line) is concentrated in nutrient-poor conditions. Note that the nitrogen level of the sites increases from left (infertile) to right (fertile). (From Wisheu and Keddy 1992 after Ellenberg 1985.)

Let us look more specifically at heathlands, a kind of peatland. In western Europe, species diversity has declined, and evergreen *Erica tetralix* heaths have been replaced by the grass *Molinia caerulea* (Aerts and Berendse 1988; Sansen and Koedam 1996). A nitrogen deposition rate above 10–15 kg N/ha per year is sufficient to accelerate this change – present rates in Flanders exceed 40 kg N/ha per year! Sod cutting may help reverse this process, and retain species rich peatlands, with more deeply cut and regularly flooded sites allowing the growth and persistence of pioneer species such as *Drosera intermedia* and *Rhynchospora fusca*. Eventually, however, *M. caerulea* achieves dominance, and at current nitrogen deposition rates, Sansen and Koedam (1996) believe that sod cutting frequencies will have to be increased from 50-year to 10-year intervals. Verhoeven *et al.* (1996) point out that if mowing removes nitrogen faster than it is deposited, it may be possible to retain a species composition more typical of pristine areas.

The experimental application of nitrogen fertilizer for agricultural purposes also illustrates the potential changes in vegetation with atmospheric deposition. In the moors of Somerset, UK, which are wet grasslands on lowland peat, experimental applications of nitrogen fertilizer at levels greater than, or equal to 25 kg/ha produced striking changes in the vegetation (Mountford *et al.* 1993). After only 4 years, sedges such as *Carex nigra* and rushes were replaced by widespread agricultural grasses such as *Holcus lanatus* and *Lolium perenne*. While there was an upward trend in species richness in control plots, richness declined in high nitrogen treatments.

To take a global perspective, nitrogen deposition maps for Earth (Townsend *et al.* 1996) show that high rates of deposition already occur in western Europe and eastern North America, and that there are early signs of a third area in eastern Asia. The examples in this chapter show that dealing with eutrophication and the problems posed by species requiring infertile habitats will be a long-term problem facing both scientists and managers.

3.6   Calcium interacts with fertility in peatlands

Thus far in this chapter we have concentrated on nitrogen and phosphorus. This is justified because of their abundance in plants and animals. They are not, of course, the only elements that affect wetlands.

Others important elements include magnesium, potassium, iron, and calcium. Calcium stands out since it is closely related to the acidity of groundwater (Bridgham *et al.* 1996; Wheeler and Proctor 2000).

The difference between acidic sites and calcareous sites has long been known to affect plant growth and plant distributions, with those species restricted to calcium-rich soils being known as **calciphilous** (Weaver and Clements 1938). The principal factor controlling calcium concentrations is the parent material. Peatlands on limestone or marble, for example, have higher concentrations of calcium in the groundwater. Calcium concentrations reduce acidity of the groundwater. This is not the sole affect. Under alkaline conditions, Ca^{2+} will bind with P to form calcium phosphates, lowering the amount of P available to plants (Bridgham *et al.* 1996). This process may explain the phosphorus deficiency of some European peatlands.

Plants can further modify the water chemistry of a site. *Sphagnum* mosses are thought to acidify water (Bridgham *et al.* 1996; Verhoeven and Liefveld 1997). The litter of most plants is deficient in calcium, which can further acidify the substrate (Fitter and Hay 2002). Oxidation by roots and aerenchyma also affect the soil chemistry (Section 1.3).

Overall, calcium concentrations, in association with pH, have a large effect on the type of wetland

that arises. These two factors are particularly important for the distinction between bogs and fens (Figure 3.15). Fertility, principally nitrogen and phosphorus availability, is then another independent factor. If we treat pH and calcium as one acidity gradient (since they are correlated), acidity co-varies with fertility to produce the major vegetation types of peatlands (Figure 3.16).

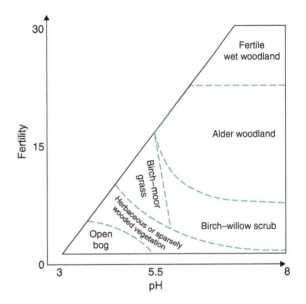

FIGURE 3.16 Fertility and pH control the vegetation types in British peatlands. (From Wheeler and Proctor 2000.)

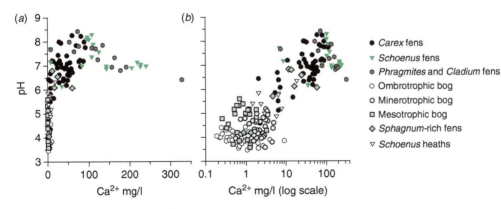

FIGURE 3.15 The relationships between pH, calcium concentration, and vegetation type for 193 water samples from peatlands in Britain and Ireland plotted using (*a*) arithmetic and (*b*) logarithmic scales for calcium. (From Wheeler and Proctor 2000.)

3.7   Fertility and hydrology explain a great deal about wetlands

The wetland classifications introduced in Chapter 1 assumed that hydrology and fertility were the two controlling factors in wetlands. Now that you know more about fertility, let us look at one final scheme, Figure 3.17, that combines fertility on the horizontal axis (from infertile to fertile) with hydrology on the vertical axis (duration of waterlogging superimposed upon water level changes). Four wetland types are then produced from left to right: bogs, fens, marshes, and swamps. The figure further discriminates between infertile fens and fertile fens. The addition of salinity as a factor produces both salt flats at the upper left and salt marshes at the lower right. Superimposed upon these is the zone of peat formation, showing the interaction between fertility and waterlogging. Finally, the region which woody plants can occupy is stippled. Many of the factors discussed so far are therefore neatly combined into one figure. Note too that there is a region between the peat formation and tree formation zone, showing that in some hydrological regimes, open meadows may be formed where the soils have limited amounts of peat, but are still too wet for trees to occur. Other factors such as peat production and the phase transition between woody and herbaceous species are also illustrated.

The diagram in Figure 3.17 raises other challenging questions to consider. Where, for example would carnivorous plants occur? Is there a region where particular kinds of disturbance are most severe? Where might gap colonization predominate? Where would the most methane be produced? Where might above-ground competition give way to below-ground competition? Where would grazing be the most intense? Which areas would have the most wading birds? And how will wetlands change if eutrophication continues? Some answers appear obvious; others are not. A diagram such as this one challenges ecologists to put the pieces together into meaningful patterns.

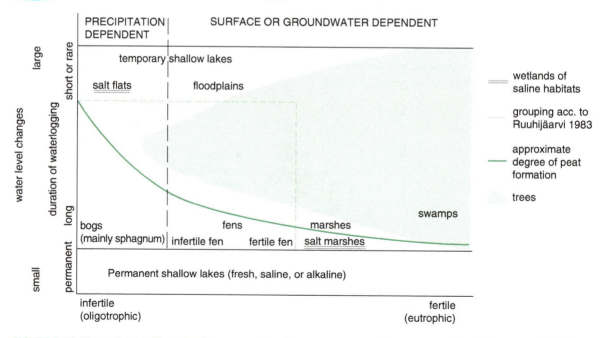

FIGURE 3.17 The major world wetland types can be related to two causal factors: water level changes and fertility. (From Gopal *et al.* 1990.)

Plants and animals are CHNOPS organisms, being composed primarily of these elements. Among them, nitrogen and phosphorus are particularly important since supplies often limit the growth and reproduction of both plants and animals. The importance of particular nutrients can be determined through field experiments in which they are supplemented and the effects on plants documented. While biomass is directly correlated with fertility, species richness is inversely correlated with fertility. Infertile sites such as sand plains, depressions in weather-resistant bedrock, and peatlands, where nutrients are in short supply, are typically rich in plant species and may harbor species adapted to such conditions. Variation in fertility can account for wetland patterns at multiple scales. In peatlands, fertility co-varies with a calcium–acidity gradient to produce the vegetation array observed. In some wetlands mycorrhizae increase nutrient availability. Eutrophication of wetlands as a result of excess nitrogen from human activities reduces wetland species diversity and can result in aquatic plant die-off. Infertile wetlands are particularly at risk. Together, fertility and hydrology explain a great deal about wetland composition, function, and distribution.

Chapter contents

4 Disturbance

In the last chapter we saw that fertility controls the rate of production of biomass. Disturbance removes that biomass (Figure 4.1). Common examples of disturbance include fire, ice scour, and storms. The effects of herbivores are also classified as disturbance, although we will deal with herbivory in a later chapter. At the level of the plant, disturbance is any process that removes foliage, meristems, or other tissues. Disturbance is an all-pervasive process in nature (e.g. Sousa 1984; Pickett and White 1985; Botkin 1990). Recall that Figure 3.1 showed how fertility increased the biomass in a coastal marsh; Figure 4.2 shows the same experiment – but now four types of disturbance have been added. You can see that the amount of biomass in this marsh depends upon both fertility and disturbance.

But **disturbance** is a dangerous word. It is dangerous because many people assume they understand it when they do not. Let us define disturbance more precisely as *a short-lived event that removes biomass and thereby causes a measurable change in the properties of an ecological community.*[1] Hence, the word disturbance should be reserved for events that

have three key elements: they are short-lived, they reduce biomass, and they cause a measurable change in properties of the system. If you are looking for a more general word that does not imply biomass removal, the word "perturbation" or even "event" is a good substitute. An event may not be a disturbance if it has no measurable effects.

This definition needs further clarification. What is short-lived? We use the life spans of the dominant organisms, as suggested by Southwood (1977). By short-lived, we mean an event with *duration much shorter than the lifespan of the dominant species in the community*. According to this definition, a fire or severe drought would generally be a disturbance. But not climate change and not eutrophication. By insisting upon measurable change we further require that you identify at least one property (e.g. biomass, diversity, species composition) and show that it has changed. No change, no disturbance (see Cairns 1980). This definition fits well with other work including Grime's (1977, 1979) work on plant communities, and Southwood's (1977, 1988) approach to measuring time relative to lifespans.

Although change in biomass is the predominant point, disturbances may change more than biomass.

FIGURE 4.1 Fire removes biomass from wetlands during droughts. It also alters fertility by volatilizing nitrogen and recycling phosphorus. If the fire is sufficiently intense to burn the organic soil, pools of water can form in the depressions. (Courtesy C. Rubec.) (See also color plate.)

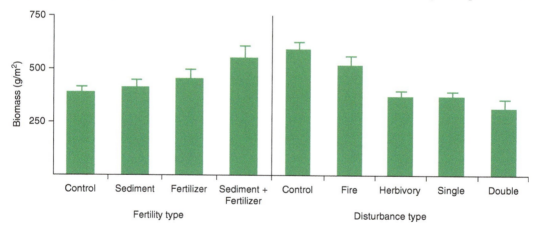

FIGURE 4.2 Biomass increases with fertility (left) and biomass decreases with disturbance (right). The disturbances are fire (annual burning), herbivory (mainly grazing by nutria), and a single or double application of herbicide. (From Keddy *et al.* 2007.)

[1] I have slightly narrowed usage of the term relative to the first edition.

Fire, for example, may also burn peat, creating new water-filled depressions. Waves may also remove silt and clay, producing coarse-textured infertile substrates. Ice can drag boulders to create furrows. Trees blown down by hurricanes can leave mounds of earth with an adjoining depression.

4.1 Disturbance has four properties

Having defined disturbance, it is important that we understand its four properties before we can move on to consider its effects.

4.1.1 Duration

Duration refers to how long an event lasts. A fire may last only a few minutes as the fire front passes. Burial by litter can kill salt marsh plants in as little as 8 weeks (Bertness and Ellison 1987). Flooding for 3 years may be required to kill most emergent wetland plants in freshwater marshes (Figure 4.3).

4.1.2 Intensity

Intensity refers to the severity of the effects of an event. A simple measure of intensity is the proportion of biomass at a site that is killed or removed. The more biomass removed, the more intense the disturbance. A grazing moose could remove 10% of the biomass at one site; a severe frost might kill half of the foliage; fire could remove all the above-ground biomass. Some events, such as ice scour and hurricanes, do more than remove biomass, and therefore have even higher intensity. A factor that disturbs one type of organism (say, plants) might not disturb another (say, wading birds), so the change in abundance of several groups might be measured simultaneously.

4.1.3 Frequency

Different types of events recur with different frequencies. Floods often happen on a yearly basis. Fires may occur once a decade, only after sufficient fuel has accumulated. Hurricanes may strike a section of coast a few times in a century. Water levels in the Great Lakes may reach extremes only once a century. In general, the greater the intensity of disturbance the lower the frequency.

4.1.4 Area

Different events affect different sized areas of landscape – a fallen tree may affect square meters, a fire may affect tens of hectares, while a hurricane may affect thousands of square kilometers.

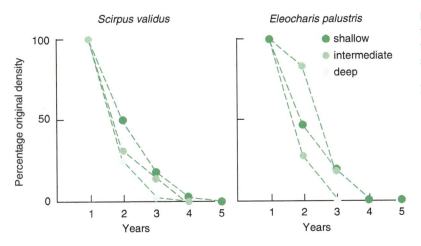

FIGURE 4.3 The effects of flooding to three different water depths on the survival of two emergent plant species. (From Keddy and Reznicek 1986, data from Harris and Marshall 1963.)

4.2 Disturbance triggers regeneration from buried propagules

When biomass is removed, resources such as light become more available. If the biomass is burned, the ashes will contain phosphorus. Buried reserves of viable seeds, often called **seed banks**, allow plants to rapidly recolonize disturbed patches and exploit the light and nutrients there. Seed densities in excess of 1000 seeds per square meter are common in both prairie marshes and freshwater coastal marshes, and densities in excess of $10\,000/m^2$ are common in wet meadows (Table 4.1). These high densities of buried seeds provide evidence of the importance of recurring disturbance and regeneration in wetlands. The importance of seed banks for regeneration is particularly well established in prairie wetlands (van der Valk and Davis 1976, 1978) and lakeshore wetlands (Keddy and Reznicek 1982, 1986).

For many marsh and wet meadow species, regeneration in gaps provides the only opportunity for establishment from seed. Buried seeds appear to detect these natural disturbances in three ways: increased fluctuations in soil temperature,

Table 4.1 Densities of buried seeds found in a selection of wet meadows and marshes

Wetland habitat	Seedlings/m²	Reference
Prairie marshes		
Typha spp.	2682	1
Scirpus acutus	6536	1
S. maritimus	2194	1
Phragmites australis	2398	1
Distichlis spicata	850	1
Open water	70	1
Open water	3549	2
Scirpus validus	7246	2
Sparganium eurycarpum	2175	2
Typha × *glauca*	5447	2
Scirpus fluviatilis	2247	2
Carex spp.	3254	2
Open water	2900	3
Typha × *glauca*	3016	3
Wet meadow	826	3
Scirpus fluviatilis	319	3
Fresh or brackish coastal marshes		
Typha latifolia	14 768	4
Former hayfield	7232	4
Myrica gale	4496	4
Streambank	11 295	5
Mixed annuals	6405	5
Ambrosia spp.	9810	5
Typha spp.	13 670	5
Zizania spp.	12 955	5
Sagittaria lancifolia	2564	6
Spartina	32 826	6
Wet meadows in lakes or ponds		
Lakeshore, 75 cm water	38 259	7
Waterline of lake	1862	8
30 cm below waterline	7543	8
60 cm below waterline	19 798	8
90 cm below waterline	18 696	8
120 cm below waterline	7467	8
150 cm below waterline	5168	8
Small lake, shoreline	8511	9
Small pond, sandy	22 500	10
Small pond, organic	9200	10
Beaver pond, Canadian shield	2324	11

References: 1, Smith and Kadlec 1983 2, van der Valk and Davis 1978; 3, van der Valk and Davis 1976; 4, Moore and Wein 1985; 5, Leck and Graveline 1979; 6, Baldwin and Mendelssohn 1998a; 7, Nicholson and Keddy 1983; 8, Keddy and Reznicek 1982; 9, Wisheu and Keddy 1991; 10, Schneider 1994; 11, Le Page and Keddy 1998.

increased quantity of light, and changes in the quality of light (Grime 1979). Thus, most plants adapted to exploit natural disturbances are stimulated to germinate by a combination of high light levels and fluctuating temperatures (Grime *et al.* 1981).

The intensity of the disturbance will determine the importance of buried seeds. If the disturbance does not kill below-ground biomass, the plants may rapidly regenerate from rhizomes. In one study of oligohaline coastal *Spartina* marshes, three levels of disturbance were created: controls, non-lethal disturbance, and lethal disturbance. The most intense disturbance resulted in vegetation with the largest number of species (Figure 4.4). In saline environments, seed densities are often lower: $50/m^2$ (Hartman 1988) to $500/m^2$ (Bertness and Ellison 1987) and a majority of the recolonization of the wetland results from expansion by neighboring plants. Periodic flooding with fresh water may, however, provide the opportunity for some salt marsh species to establish from buried seeds

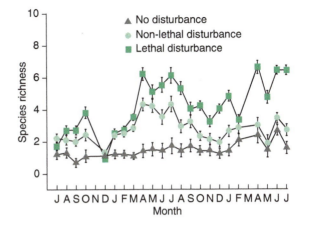

FIGURE 4.4 Effects of three levels of disturbance on the number of plant species in an oligohaline *Spartina* marsh in Louisiana (0.5 × 0.5 m quadrats, ±SE). (From Baldwin and Mendelssohn 1998a.)

(Zedler and Beare 1986). Hence, a short period of rainfall or a freshwater pulse may have a long-term impact on species composition. We will return to this topic in Section 4.5.

4.3 Examples of disturbance controlling the composition of wetlands

Disturbance can be caused by a number of natural or man-made phenomena, from erosion and ice through to mowing and logging.

4.3.1 Erosion along rivers creates as well as destroys wetlands

In the lower reaches of watersheds, and in deltas, rivers flow though valleys filled with alluvial sediments (recall Figure 1.23). These alluvial sediments often have extensive floodplain forests (swamps) and to a lesser degree, marshes. The alluvial sediments are continually reworked by the river, and these cycles of erosion and deposition produce a wide array of wetland vegetation types.

One of the most dramatic examples comes from the Peruvian Amazon, where 26.6% of the modern

lowland forest shows characteristics of recent erosion and deposition, and fully 12% of the Peruvian lowland forest is in successional stages along rivers (Figure 4.5). During one 13-year period the mean lateral erosion rate of meander bends was 12 m/yr. The total area of newly created land available for primary succession was $12\ km^2$, representing nearly 4% of the present floodplain area. The new substrates are first colonized by herbaceous plants (species of *Tessaria*, *Cyperus*, *Ipomoea*, and *Panicum*), then small trees (species of *Cecropia*, *Ficus*, and *Cedrela*) gradually form a closed canopy, and eventually these became mixed with later successional trees. Altogether there is a pioneer flora of 125 plant species (Kalliola *et al.* 1991). Salo *et al.* (1986) conclude:

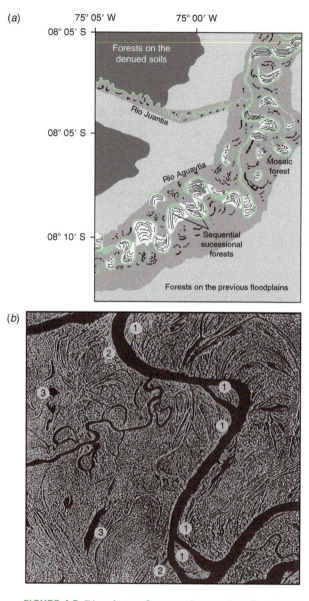

FIGURE 4.5 Disturbance from erosion continually creates new bands of vegetation in many floodplains. (*a*) Map of the meander system of the Ucayali R. at Pucallpa, Peru. (*b*) Landsat multispectral scanner image downstream from (*a*) showing 1–vegetation colonization, 2–eroding forests, 3–oxbow lakes. (From Salo *et al.* 1986.)

According to the repetitive nature of river dynamics, the migration of the river channel course creates a mosaic of successional forests within the present meander plain. The mosaic forest is composed of patches of differentially aged sequential successional forest and patches of forests originating from a succession on the sites of former oxbow lakes. The annual floods further modify the mosaic pattern.

Similar processes have been decribed in In New Zealand alluvial forests, where the presence of two conifers in the Podocarpaceae (*Dacrycarpus dacrydioides* and *D. cupressinum*) is the result of recurring disturbance on the floodplain. In northwestern North America *Populus balsamifera* establishes on newly deposited sediments (Nanson and Beach 1977) while in the Mississippi River delta it is *Salix nigra* (Johnson *et al.* 1985). Similar processes have been described in the Okavango delta of Africa (Ellery *et al.* 1993) and in floodplains along the River Murray in Australia (Roberts and Ludwig 1991).

Overall, there is good evidence that continual disturbance and reworking of alluvial sediments produce much of the plant and habitat diversity in floodplains, and partly account for the very high plant species diversity of tropical floodplain forests.

4.3.2 Fire creates a mosaic of vegetation types in the Everglades

It may be difficult to imagine a fire ripping through a stand of water lilies, but many kinds of wetlands do indeed burn during dry years. Fire in prairie potholes has already been mentioned. Fire frequency, along with hydrology, determines the kind of wetland found across much of the southeastern United States (Table 4.2). Fire is also regarded as a major control of plant diversity in boreal circumpolar peatlands (Wein 1983), pocosin peatlands (Christensen *et al.* 1981), and the Everglades (Loveless 1959).

Fire becomes important during prolonged periods of drought. Low-intensity fires can simply remove existing above-ground biomass, shift composition from woody to herbaceous wetlands, and increase plant diversity (Christensen *et al.* 1981;

Table 4.2 **Flooding and fire regimes in the many kinds of non-alluvial wetland communities found in the southeastern United States (Figure 3.3 shows one example); note how changing the soil, hydroperiod, or fire frequency produces a vast array of different types of wetlands**

Community	Canopy dominants	Soil organic matter	Hydroperiod/ water source	Fire frequency
Forested wetlands in basins				
pond cypress pond forest	*Taxodium ascendens*	mineral to organic	6–12 months rainfall	infrequent, 20–50 years
swamp tupelo pond forest	*Nyssa biflora*	organic to peat	6–12 months rainfall	rare, one fire per century
cypress dome	*Taxodium ascendens*	peat	6–9 months rainfall	20+ years
basin swamp forest	*Nyssa biflora, Acer rubrum, Liquidambar styraciflua*	organic	6–9 months groundwater	infrequent, 20–50 years
Wetland complexes (from forested to open water) in basins				
limestone pond complex (karst ponds)		mineral	deep groundwater	1–10 years/ yellow sand, 36–60 years/ white sand
coastal plain small depression pond		mineral	variable	dependent on surrounding forests
coastal plain lakeshore complex		mineral	variable	rare, one fire per century
Okefenokee swamp wetland mosaic		mineral–peat	variable	infrequent, 20–50 years
Woodlands and savannas on flat coastal terraces				
slash pine flatwoods	*Pinus serotina*	mineral	<3 months groundwater	3–10 years
wet longleaf pine flatwoods	*Pinus palustris*	mineral	<3 months groundwater	3–10 years
wet longleaf pine–slash pine flatwoods	*Pinus palustris, Pinus serotina*	mineral	<3 months groundwater	3–10 years
longleaf pine savanna	*Pinus palustris*	mineral	3–6 months groundwater	1–5 years
coastal plain pitcher plant flat	Many graminoid and herbaceous species and *Sarracenia* spp.	mineral	6 months groundwater	1–5 years
Woodlands and savannas in basins				
pond cypress savanna	*Taxodium ascendens*	mineral	6–9 months rainfall	20+ years
pond pine woodland	*Pinus serotina, Cyrilla racemiflora*	shallow organic and peat	6–9 months rainfall	10–20 years

Table 4.2 (*cont.*)

Community	Canopy dominants	Soil organic matter	Hydroperiod/ water source	Fire frequency
Evergreen shrub wetlands				
low pocosin	*Pinus serotina, Cyrilla racemiflora, Zenobia pulverulenta*	deep peat, >0.5 m	6–9 months rainfall	15–30 years
high pocosin	*Pinus serotina, Cyrilla racemiflora, Lyonia lucida*	shallow peat, <0.5 m	6–9 months rainfall	15–30 years
small depression pocosin	*Pinus serotina, Cyrilla racemiflora, Lyonia lucida*	shallow peat, <0.5 m	6–9 months rainfall	15–30 years

Source: After Sutter and Kral (1994).

Thompson and Shay 1988). More intense fires, however, can burn the organic soil of wetlands and create new openings with very different species composition, even open water (Loveless 1959; Vogl 1969). Since we have been told that "The importance of fire and its influence on the vegetation of the Everglades can hardly be over-emphasized" (Loveless 1959), let us begin with this example.

Although the landscape of south Florida is flat, the Everglades have many different vegetation types "from open water sloughs with sparse macrophytes to sedge and grass-dominated freshwater marshes, open pine stands and dense broad-leaved evergreen forest" (White 1994). This variation arises principally because of minor differences in elevation and hence water supply. Superimposed upon this are natural disturbances, principally fires, but also floods, droughts, storms, and freezing temperatures. These disturbances tend to be short-lived, but the communities recover from them slowly because the Everglades have very low nutrient levels. Hence, there is a basic asymmetry: disturbance is fast, recovery is slow. Occasional disturbances can generate a mosaic in which each patch of vegetation represents a different degree of recovery from the last disturbance. The rates of recovery will

depend upon the amount of vegetation (if any) that persists through the disturbance, the influx of new propagules from adjoining areas, and the productivity of the site. As peat accumulates, there is a succession from open water sloughs to forested tree islands (Figure 4.6). Light fires will create patches in the vegetation; more severe fires consume peat, reduce the relative elevation, and return the site to an earlier successional stage.

During the past 20 years, approximately 25% of wet prairie and slough has been replaced by stands of saw grass, probably as a consequence of reduced flooding and decreased fire frequency. Wet prairies and sloughs have higher plant diversity, and are major sites of periphyton production and important habitats for crustaceans and fish. Drainage and fire control therefore have not only changed the vegetation, but the capacity of the area to produce and support other organisms. Restoration of the Everglades will require restoration of flooding and fire as natural disturbances, a topic to which we will return in Chapter 13.

Extensive deltas may be created largely by sediment from rivers, and shaped by flooding, but fire may also shape their composition. Jean and Bouchard (1991) believe that fires set by aboriginal inhabitants prevented woody plants such as alders

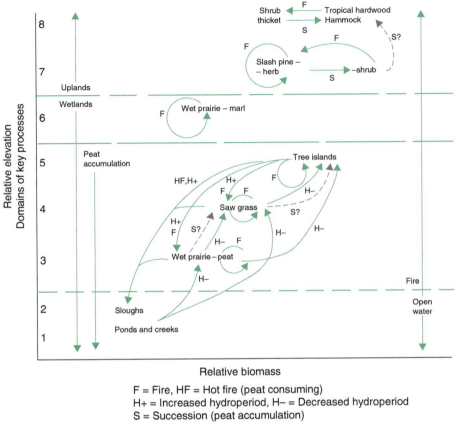

F = Fire, HF = Hot fire (peat consuming)
H+ = Increased hydroperiod, H− = Decreased hydroperiod
S = Succession (peat accumulation)
S? Uncertain succession

FIGURE 4.6 Plant communities of the central freshwater Everglades are strongly affected by fire. In the absence of fire, wooded tree islands can form. Light fires change plant composition, while more severe fires consume peat and can create new shallow water sloughs. (From White 1994.)

from invading wet meadows along the St. Lawrence River in eastern North America. Fire also appears to control litter accumulation and plant diversity in *Carex*-dominated wetlands along the St. Lawrence River (Figure 4.7). Farther north, in the Peace–Athabasca delta, fire reduced the density of the dominant species, and increased the number of dicotyledons that germinated (Figure 4.8).

Peatlands are particularly useful for the study of fire because, under certain circumstances, charcoal layers and macrofossils record both the fire history and the vegetation responses to the fire. *Sphagnum*-dominated peatlands are probably the most abundant peatland type in western boreal North America. Many

have charcoal layers as a consequence of past fires (Kuhry 1994). The study of cores taken from the peat indicates that there has been a fire approximately every 1150 years. While this may be a surprisingly high rate of fire frequency for a wetland, it is still an order of magnitude less frequent than estimates of fire frequency in coniferous forests in western boreal Canada (e.g. Ritchie 1987).

Of course, fire frequency depends in part upon climate. During the hypsithermal, a period of warmer and drier climate about 7000 years ago, fire frequencies in peatlands appear to have been twice a high as in the past 2500 years. These fires not only burned the vegetation, but they also burned

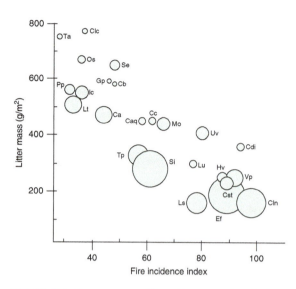

FIGURE 4.7 The amount of litter (litter mass) and plant species diversity are related to fire incidence index in a riverine wetland (letters refer to species, circle diameter indicates the diversity of the vegetation in which each occurs). (After Auclair *et al.* 1976b.)

the superficial peat deposits. In spite of this, the cores suggest that the effect of peat surface fires on vegetation was short-lived. This is apparently also the case in contemporary reports of peat fires. An interesting natural history story complements these findings; *Sphagnum* can apparently regenerate from stems at depths 30 cm into the peat deposit (estimated to be 25–60 years old) (Clymo and Duckett 1986).

What might the relationship between fire and peat accumulation be? Kuhry (1994) estimated fire frequency as the number of macroscopic charcoal layers per 1000 years, and peat accumulation rates were determined from radiocarbon dating. There was a negative relationship between peat accumulation rates and fire frequency (Figure 4.9). It appears, then, that the flush of nutrient-rich ash released by burning (and the presumed higher plant growth rates) does not compensate for the loss of peat consumed by the fire. Thus, fires retard the growth of peatlands. This has consequences for the study of global warming because peatlands are an important

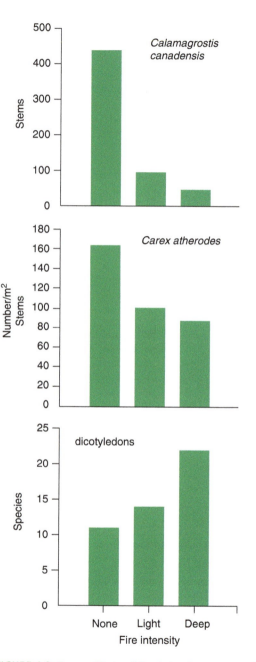

FIGURE 4.8 Some effects of fire intensity upon wetland plants in the Peace–Athabasca delta. (From data in Hogenbirk and Wein 1991.)

reservoir for carbon storage. An increase in temperature would presumably lead to higher frequencies of burning, which, in turn, would lead to further releases of stored carbon in the peatlands (Gorham 1991; Hogg *et al.* 1992) and lower rates of formation of peatlands.

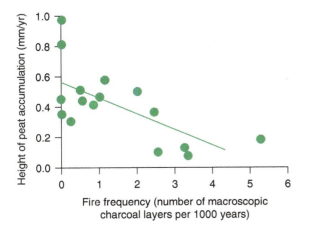

FIGURE 4.9 Peat accumulation is related to fire frequency in peatlands of western boreal Canada. (From Kuhry 1994.)

The effects of severe fires in British peatlands were observed in 1976. The period between May 1975 and August 1976 was the driest in England since at least 1727. In the North York Moors National Park 62 uncontrolled fires burned in the summer of 1976 (Maltby *et al.* 1990). Some of the most severe fires affected 11 km^2 where fire burned deeply into blanket peats and largely removed the areas of thinner peat. Further disturbance was caused by wind and rain erosion, and freeze–thaw processes. The post-fire vegetation was dominated by bryophytes, at first with *Ceratodon purpureus* and after a decade with *Polytrichum* spp. Perhaps, they suggest, bryophyte-dominated patches reflect past fires.

As fire changes the vegetation, it also affects the animals found in wetlands. One study found more birds on a burned shoreline than on an adjacent unburned area (Table 4.3). In another study of fire, experimental 0.10-ha plots were burned in water fowl impoundments (Laubhan 1995). The type of vegetation depended upon when the site was burned. Sites burned in the spring had greater cover of

Table 4.3 Resident birds on unburned and burned portions of a shoreline wetland near the Florida/Georgia border. The numbers represent totals obtained from 63 sampling trips in 1971

Species	Control	Burned
Common egret (*Casmerodius albus*)	5	22[a]
Bobwhite (*Colinus virginianus*)	14	1
Cardinal (*Richmondena cardinalis*)	2	14[a]
Common crow (*Corvus brachyrhynchos*)	0	10[a]
Common gallinule (*Gallinula chloropus*)	8	25[a]
Great blue heron (*Ardea herodias*)	0	8*
Little blue heron (*Florida caerulea*)	7	32[a]
Mockingbird (*Mimus polyglottos*)	0	6
Common grackle (*Quiscalus quiscula*)	0	15[a]
Red-winged blackbird (*Agelaius phoeniceus*)	66	150
Snowy egret (*Leucophyx thula*)	0	7
Total	102	290

[a] Paired *t*-tests for repeated samples, but no replication of treatments.
Source: From Vogl (1973).

annual plants and produced many seeds whereas sites burned in summer were more than three-fourths bare ground. Hence, spring burns can create favorable conditions for waterfowl by stimulating seed production, whereas summer burns produce mud flats favorable to migrating shorebirds. Burning is also used to enhance marsh vegetation for muskrats (Smith and Kadlec 1985a). Since much of the effort to manipulate marshes for wildlife is by creating patches, we will return to this topic below (Section 4.4)

4.3.3 Ice causes intense disturbance at many scales

Anyone who has seen enormous great cakes of ice grind against the shoreline during spring flooding will be impressed by the power of ice scour to modify vegetation. In salt marshes or large lakes, one can often find meter-square pieces of marsh, with 20 or more centimeters of substrate, chopped out of the ground and moved aside. In floodplains, trees may have scars near eye level that mark where ice cakes hit them during the spring.

The effects of ice begin with freezing along the shoreline forming an "ice foot" (Geiss 1985). Sediment can become incorporated into this ice foot. There is also the constant grinding as ice freezes to the shore and shifts as water levels rise and fall. Movement of spring ice can create ridges and a distinctive undulating topography along shorelines (e.g. Bliss and Gold 1994). The power of ice to create such ridges is vividly illustrated by a single ice push occurrence in Lake Ontario in March 1986, which piled ice to a height of 2.5 m and moved boulders greater than 200 kg (Gilbert and Glew 1986). Entire sections of shoreline can be torn out of place when ice is lifted by rising water levels (Figure 4.10). Many northern rivers have a conspicuous trim line where ice has cut a sharp lower boundary to the riparian forest, allowing herbaceous wetland to expand (Gill 1973); you can see this in Figures 2.13 and 2.14. Ice can also create dams and change

local flood regimes and water flow patterns (Prowse and Culp 2003).

One way to measure how ice damage varies with elevation is to put wooden pegs into a wetland in the autumn, and measure the amount of damage accumulated over different periods of time. Figure 4.11 shows a typical vertical profile of ice damage on shores, with and without exposure to waves. Organic content and silt/clay content are also negatively correlated with ice damage (Table 4.4). Frequently, woody plants grow closer to the water on shores protected from ice damage (Keddy 1983). A substitute for such direct measurements is to determine the water levels during the period when a shoreline is frozen (Rørslett 1985).

Given the importance of ice scour on shorelines, it seems that there is much more that could be done with such simple techniques. For example, entire beds of pegs of different sizes could be used to map both the intensity and area of winter disturbance. These could be compared to known water levels during the winter. Both could be tested for their ability to predict vegetation patterns.

4.3.4 Waves create disturbance gradients

Waves are events of very short duration and high frequency. But the cumulative effects of chronic exposure to waves are complex. In his study of British lakeshores, Pearsall (1920) summarizes both direct effects (e.g. biomass removal from plants, uprooting, seed dispersal) and indirect effects (e.g. erosion of nutrients, sorting of substrates, litter transport). Exposure to different amounts of wave energy can create very different types of wetland communities.

Information on wave effects goes back at least as long as people have sailed. Storms destroyed much of the Spanish Armada, thereby changing European history. They also badly damaged artificial channel ports constructed for the Normandy landings in the Second World War, almost changing European

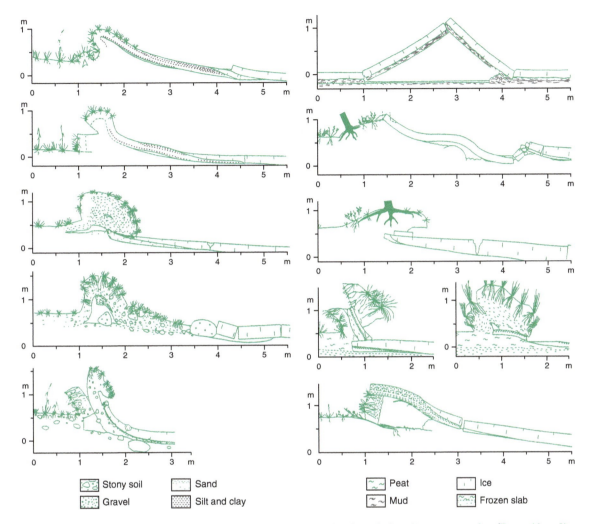

FIGURE 4.10 Ice can have a major impact upon shoreline wetlands and shoreline topography. (From Alestalio and Haikio 1979.)

history again (Blizard 1993). It is therefore natural that much of the work on waves can be found in manuals published by military agencies including the U.S. Army Corps of Engineers (e.g. U.S. Army Coastal Engineering Research Center 1977). Their equations have been recently adapted for use by aquatic ecologists (e.g. Keddy 1982, 1983; Weisner 1990). Overall the principle is simple: the amount of wave energy arriving at a shoreline increases with distance to the opposite shore (fetch) and with the number of directions from which waves can arrive. Using data on fetch and wind directions, one can rank areas of shoreline in terms of relative degrees of wave energy that they experience. Such exposure gradients change the proportion of silt and clay in sediments, and, in turn, the zonation patterns of shoreline species. Moderate exposure to waves seems to expand the areas of wet meadows and marshes, while high levels of exposure produce open sand or gravel shorelines.

Chronic wave exposure removes fine particles and leaves coarser substrates. Soil texture is known to have major effects upon germination (Harper *et al.*

Table 4.4 **Scouring by ice can reduce the silt and clay content of the soil (an indirect measure of fertility), reduce the organic content of the soil, and increase the area of habitat without shrubs, as shown by these data from a temperate zone lakeshore. Ice scour was measured by over-winter damage to wooden pegs in $n = 121$ quadrats**

	Silt and clay	Organic content	Shrub-free area
Ice scour	-0.37^a	-0.47	0.31

[a] Correlation coefficients, $p < 0.001$.
Source: After Wisheu and Keddy (1989b).

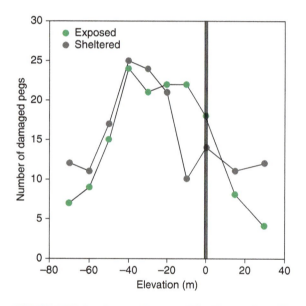

FIGURE 4.11 Ice damage (measured by the number of ice-damaged pegs) as a function of elevation on two contrasting shorelines. The vertical line shows typical late summer water levels. (Unpublished data in which 25 1.25-cm diameter wooden pegs, each 20 cm long, were pounded 10 cm into the ground in the summer of 1980 and damage was assessed the following spring. The study site is described in Keddy 1981.)

1965; Oomes and Elberse 1976; Vivian-Smith 1997). Given the conspicuous gradients in soil texture on shorelines, and the importance of regeneration from buried seeds (Salisbury 1970; Leck *et al.* 1989), we might anticipate that germination of marsh plants will be significantly affected by exposure. When seeds of ten shoreline plants were sown along a soil texture gradient, germination was generally highest in the fine susbstrate (Keddy and Constabel 1986).

Waves can also amplify the effects of ice and kill plants directly. When we planted 840 wetland plants on seven sections of lakeshore (Wilson and Keddy 1988), fewer than one-third (265) were still alive the following year. Some species were particularly sensitive; *Viola lanceolata* and *Drosera intermedia* were both nearly all dead. The remaining species had rates of mortality from 32% to 91% depending upon the exposure of the site to waves. Since the effects of waves and ice may vary from year to year, depending, say, upon the timing of ice breakup and the direction of winds at that time, these factors together can impose a great deal of disturbance that, while predictable in the long run, is local and patchy on a year-to-year basis.

4.3.5 Animals create many types of disturbance in wetlands

Animals eat plants and thereby remove biomass. An entire chapter on grazing follows this one in Chapter 6. The general conclusion from that chapter is that grazing can have major effects on wetlands, but the area of habitat affected is often rather small. There are exceptions – extreme damage can occur over large areas occasionally, when large populations of muskrats feed in prairie marshes, or large populations of geese feed in coastal marshes.

Animals have other effects beyond grazing, however. We have already noted the effects of beavers on wetlands (Section 2.3.3). Another animal that makes ponds, albeit much smaller ponds, is the alligator (Figure 4.12). During winter dry periods, gator holes may be the only ponds remaining in a wetland (Loveless 1959; Craighead 1968). The alligator maintains ponds by pulling loose plants and dragging them out of the pool. Thicker muck is either pushed or carried to the edges of the pond.

Gator holes were once a predominant feature of southern wetlands, and are still evident in the

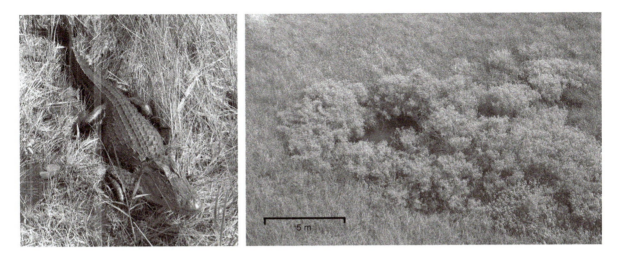

FIGURE 4.12 A gator hole in the Everglades along with its creator and occupant (not to scale). The alligator excavates a hole, which supports aquatic plants and animals, and the earth mound around the edge of the hole develops its own characteristic plant community. Large expanses of wetland can be dotted by such holes and mounds. (See also color plate.)

Everglades. Craighead reminds us that alligators were once much more common, that "in the first two decades of this century every inland pond, lake and river held its quota of alligators." He suggests a density approaching one alligator per acre in some regions. The naturalist William Bartram, who traveled the St. John's River in 1774–6, described alligators massed around his boat. He reported (Bartram 1791) that, when camping on beaches, it was necessary to keep a large fire burning all night for protection.

Gator holes are "reservoirs for an amazing biological assemblage." Within them live "diatoms, algae, ferns, flowering plants, protozoans, crustaceans, amphibians, reptiles and fish" (Craighead 1968). The productivity of these ponds is enhanced by uneaten food. Larger animals, such as hogs and deer, are killed by drowning but may be left for several days for ripening. The aquatic flora includes widespread genera such as *Myriophyllum, Utricularia, Potamogeton, Nymphoides*, and *Najas*. The shallow water near the banks has marsh genera such as *Peltandra, Pontederia*, and *Sagittaria*. Connecting the gator holes are well-developed trail systems. These trails may be eroded by heavy gators into troughs that are 15 cm deep and 60 cm wide. Up to

this point, we have considered alligators to be a cause of disturbance; alligators may also simultaneously reduce the rates of disturbance by other animals like nutria (Keddy *et al.* 2009).

Animals and physical factors may both have impacts on wetlands. Prairie potholes (Section 2.3.4) are affected by four major kinds of disturbance, all of which can shift the type of wetland vegetation that occurs (van der Valk and Davis 1976, 1978). First, water may act as a disturbance. If there is too little water, the pond becomes a mud flat and many of the marsh plants die (Figure 4.13, upper left). If there is too much standing water, and they are submerged for several years, many marsh plants will also die (Figure 4.13, lower right). In either case, the return of more typical water levels allows regeneration of the plants from buried seeds, the "marsh seed bank" in the center of the figure. Muskrats also feed on wetland plants, and since they will dig up plants to eat the rhizomes too, their effects can be severe. If muskrat populations become dense enough, they can strip the vegetation from a wetland, producing what is known as an "eat out." Fire can also burn through potholes during periods of drought. Hence, the

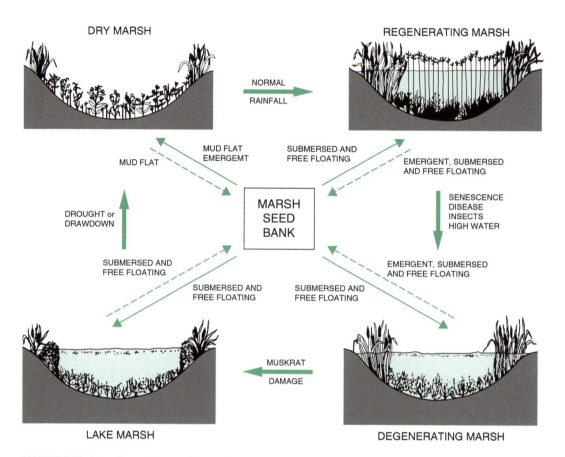

FIGURE 4.13 Disturbance by muskrats and drought can shift prairie potholes from one ecological state to another. (After van der Valk and Davis 1978.)

vegetation in a prairie pothole depends upon how long ago a disturbance occurred, whether the disturbance destroyed only the shoots or the rhizomes as well, and how long the vegetation has had to recover.

4.3.6 Traditional disturbances include mowing and peat-cutting

In Europe there is a long cultural history of mowing wetlands (Elveland 1978, 1979; Elveland and Sjoberg 1982; Müller *et al.* 1992). At some sites with a long history of mowing or grazing, distinctive plants and animals occur as a consequence of the continual removal of biomass. Mowing is common elsewhere,

too. In China, reeds are collected for paper-making. In Iraq reeds are used for making homes. Many small farms in North America used to depend upon collection of "marsh hay" for feeding animals. When mowing ceases, stands of a few large marsh plants such as *Phragmites* or *Typha* may replace meadows that have high plant diversity.

Peat-cutting (Figure 4.14) could be considered a more extreme kind of mowing, in that the substrate is removed to be burned as a fuel. Disturbance by past peat-cutting is thought to be an important factor generating plant diversity in European peatlands. For example, there were nineteenth-century peat cuttings in the Norfolk Broadland where 50–70 cm of peat had been removed, down to the underlying

FIGURE 4.14 Peat is a traditional source of fuel in many northern regions, and peat-cutting is a source of disturbance in peatlands. This stereograph shows cutting and carting turf at a bog near Kiltoom, County Roscommon, Ireland. (Courtesy Library of Congress, P&P.)

clay (Giller and Wheeler 1986). These became ponds ("turf ponds") which now have unusual vegetation types including species-rich fens. To maintain such rich fen communities, continued peat-cutting may be a necessary management tool. This is consistent with the suggestion that peat-cutting will be necessary in much of western Europe in order to remove nutrients accumulating from atmospheric deposition (Sansen and Koedam 1996). Modern peat-cutting for the horticultural industry creates much larger disturbances, with the result that restoration becomes more complicated (Campbell and Rochefort 2003; Cobbaert *et al.* 2004).

Prairie potholes are also affected by mowing. Walker and Wehrhahn (1971) studied the environmental factors controlling prairie wetlands in Saskatchewan, Canada, and concluded that the most important environmental factor was disturbance ("grazing, mowing and natural disturbance"). This result occurred in spite of their original intention to avoid disturbed sites. Species such as *Eleocharis palustris, Glyceria grandis,*

Alopecurus aequalis, and *Beckmannia syzigachne* occurred in disturbed areas.

4.3.7 Logging is a widespread disturbance in forested wetlands

Logging certainly removes biomass from a forest and is therefore a disturbance. The removal of trees from wetlands continues around the world, from people hand-harvesting mangrove firewood in the Ganges delta, to enormous skidders hauling second-growth cypress logs out of the Mississippi River delta. Some wetlands are protected to varying degrees by legislation requiring sustainable logging. Others are not. The removal of the biomass itself may have relatively small effects, compared to secondary effects, which include ruts from skidders and the construction of roads and canals to transport logs or logging equipment. There is no space here to discuss properly the status of the world's wetland forests, and the degree to which they are, or are not, being logged in a sustainable manner. There is

FIGURE 4.15 A two-drum pull boat working in a canal that was cut into a cypress swamp in Louisiana (date unknown). (From Williams 1989.)

enormous variation in types of logging and degrees of sustainability. Canada allows logging of peatlands in the boreal forest. The alluvial forests of the Congo remain at great risk. The military dictatorship in Burma is depleting that country's forests rapidly. Overall, we can say that the ultimate criterion for evaluating logging disturbance has to be sustainability – that is, whether the forest will regenerate. Since the seedlings of wetland trees are sensitive to flooding, minor changes in hydrology can have a big impact on whether seedlings can re-establish.

Let us look at one historical example – cypress swamps (Norgress 1947; Mancil 1980; Williams 1989; Conner and Buford 1998; Keddy *et al.* 2007) – which typifies the logging history of wetlands, and which illustrates how the negative effects can linger and interfere with regrowth. Large areas of the American south were once covered in cypress forest, or cypress mixed with species of tupelo (recall Figure 2.10). The Timber Act of 1876 allowed the sale of large tracts of swamp for 25 to 50 cents per acre. Huge tracts were purchased by wealthy timber barons. Teams of loggers felled the enormous trees and steam-powered pull boats used cables and winches to drag the fallen trees to the open water.

Canals for pull boats were excavated at 3048 m intervals, allowing entire forests to be stripped systematically (Figure 4.15). The repeated skidding of logs along a track scoured a mud- and water-filled ditch 1.8–2.4 m deep. In some places, logs were winched into canals from one point, in which case the pull boat runs radiate outward like spokes of a wheel. Logging activity peaked in the early 1900s, and a few decades later the forests were exhausted and the mills began to close. In summarizing the impact of the industry on the local economy, J. H. Foster of the U.S. Forest Service said the lumber industry:

… obtained their lands at low prices and have made fortunes from the increase in the value of the timber. The industry does not develop the country permanently and the earnings are seldom invested where they are of any benefit to the community. (Norgress 1947, p. 1051).

More than 100 years later you can still see both parallel and wheel-shaped markings in the wetlands north of New Orleans (Figure 4.16). As a result, not only were the trees removed, but the hydrology was permanently changed, which may have made these swamps more susceptible to saltwater pulses from

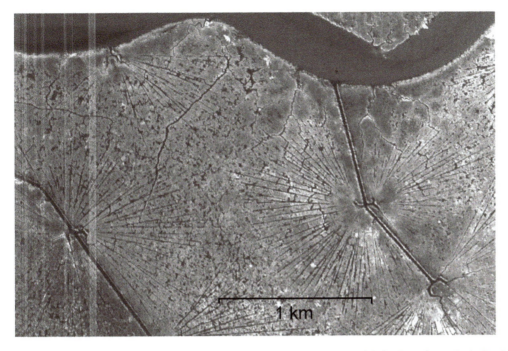

FIGURE 4.16 Aerial view of the wetlands between Lake Maurepas and Lake Pontchartrain in Louisiana. These marshes were once cypress swamps. The parallel and wheel-shaped markings are mud- and water-filled ditches made by pull boats dragging trees through the swamp during logging operations in the early twentieth century.

hurricanes, and less able to respond to rising sea levels. Large areas with failed regeneration have become anthropogenic marshes. The degree to which coastal swamps can be re-established requires that we consider not only past logging history, but the effects of levees, of sediment deposition, and of rising sea levels.

4.3.8 Hurricanes impose a predicable series of events

Humans tend to view hurricanes and other major storms as catastrophes. From the point of view of a wetland, however, a hurricane is simply a major but infrequent disturbance. Storm tracks show that major storms produced by warm ocean water are a regular occurrence in coastal areas (Figure 4.17). Humans have short memories, and often do not see the recurring element of hurricanes, even when

warned that they are inevitable. Wetlands, and the species in them, have, however, been affected by hurricanes for tens of thousands if not millions of years. The main effects of a hurricane are predictable (e.g. Conner *et al.* 1989; Loope *et al.* 1994; Turner *et al.* 2006):

- felling of trees (wind)
- saltwater pulses (storm surge)
- freshwater pulses (rain)
- sediment redistribution (waves).

This sequence of events is more or less predictable.

Felling of trees When the storm comes on shore, the strong winds fell trees, creating tree-fall mounds and gaps for regeneration. There is good evidence that trees native to gulf coast forests such as longleaf pine and bald cypress are less damaged by strong winds than species that have been

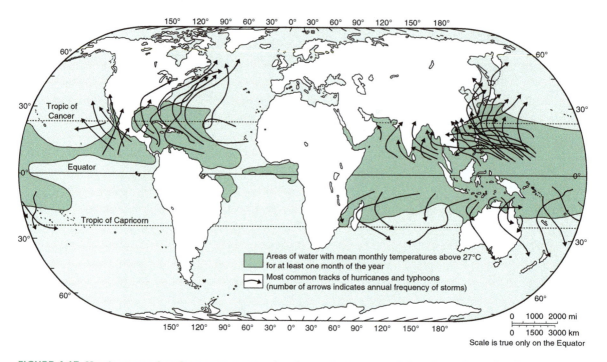

FIGURE 4.17 Hurricanes and typhoons are a natural and recurring source of disturbance in wetlands. (From *Encyclopedia Britannica* 1991.)

produced by human modification of these landscapes. It is possible that the dead trees stimulate increased fire in the wake of hurricanes (Myers and van Lear 1998).

Saltwater pulses Strong winds push a wall of seawater inland. This causes flooding, and it raises the salinity of the wetlands that are inundated. This wall of seawater carries seeds and woody debris across different kinds of wetlands. When it recedes, salinity levels are elevated and salt-sensitive species like bald cypress may die as a consequence.

Freshwater pulses Heavy rainfall also accompanies hurricanes, raising local river levels, and diluting the salt water. Hence, it is by no means obvious that the combination of a saltwater pulse followed by heavy rain will necessarily change local salinity levels.

Sediment redistribution The waves generated by the winds can churn up sections of marsh, releasing sediment, and then redistribute the sediment (Liu and Fearn 2000; Turner *et al.* 2006). At larger timescales, hurricanes are implicated in both destroying and building coastal wetlands. River deltas normally go through cycles of building aggradation and degradation over some thousands of years (Boyd and Penland 1988, Coleman *et al.* 1998) (Figure 4.18). Often, the last trace of an ancient delta is a chain of offshore sand islands. The process may not be smooth. Major floods may build sections of new delta; major hurricanes may destroy sections of degrading deltas. The process may therefore be more like a series of steps.

The effects of hurricanes can be compared to those of fire. Both are natural processes that have affected wetlands for millennia. Both are viewed by humans as catastrophes. Both, however, are essential for

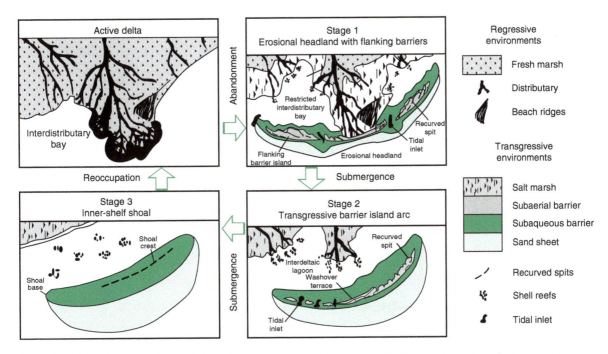

FIGURE 4.18 Deltas grow as sediment accumulates at the mouth of a river, but once the river changes course, the delta gradually deteriorates into islands and offshore shoals. Storms and hurricanes play a significant role in reshaping the sediment. (From Penland *et al.* 1988.)

producing the natural array of wetland types and natural distribution of plants and animal species. Perhaps the best advice we can give humans is not to build their homes in areas that flood regularly or burn regularly.

4.3.9 Frosts can convert mangrove swamp to salt marshes

Cold can also kill plant tissues and change wetlands. One important transition point in coastal wetlands is the temperature threshold at which mangroves can, or cannot, survive. At this threshold, herbaceous wetlands become wooded wetlands. This transition point occurs at about 32° North latitude and 40° South latitude (Stuart *et al.* 2007). Pulses of cold weather kill mangroves. For example, in the 1980s, cold winter weather killed mangrove forests (*Avicennia germinans*) in Florida, and it is estimated that 30 years will be required for recovery (Stevens

et al. 2006). Similar events occurred in Louisiana. Hence, frost sets the latitudinal limits of mangal (Figure 4.19).

A warmer climate with rising sea levels might allow mangroves to expand northward into what are now cypress marshes, as well as possibly changing cypress swamps into mangrove swamps. However, this scenario requires several cautions. If an increase in mean temperature is accompanied by an increase in variation in temperature, it is possible that cold pulses flowing from the north will remain sufficiently frequent to kill mangroves. Other factors associated with warmer climates include rising sea levels, increased hurricane frequency, and increased salinity from evapotranspiration. Overall, however, models suggest that if global temperatures rise, the area of mangroves in areas like Florida is likely to increase with time, probably at the expense of freshwater wetlands (Doyle *et al.* 2003).

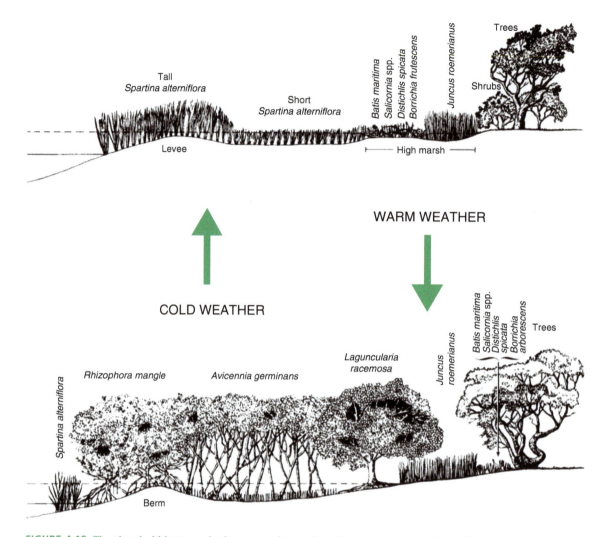

FIGURE 4.19 The threshold between herbaceous salt marsh and mangrove swamp is set by the frequency of periods of freezing weather. The top panel shows northern Florida and the bottom panel shows southern Florida. (Adapted from Montague and Wiegert 1990.)

4.4   Disturbances can create gap dynamics

In some situations, disturbance occurs as discrete patches (Sousa 1984; Pickett and White 1985). In such circumstances, one can measure the rate at which new patches are formed, and the rate at which they are colonized. Much of the research on patch dynamics focuses on forests, where storms can create patches ranging from the size of a single fallen tree to entire stands blown down (Urban and Shugart 1992). There are fewer studies of patch dynamics in wetlands, yet we might reasonably expect this

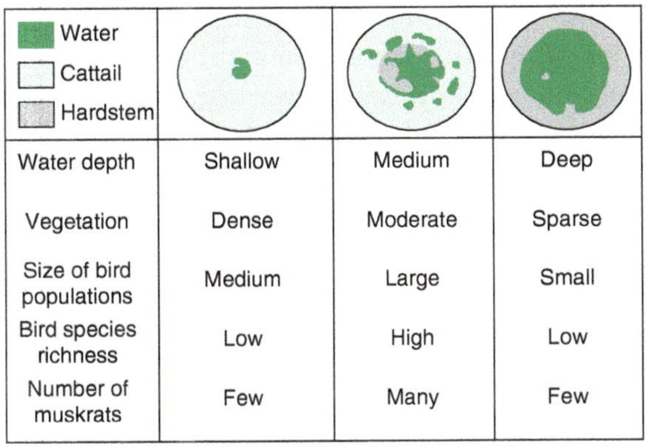

■ Water □ Cattail ▨ Hardstem			
Water depth	Shallow	Medium	Deep
Vegetation	Dense	Moderate	Sparse
Size of bird populations	Medium	Large	Small
Bird species richness	Low	High	Low
Number of muskrats	Few	Many	Few

FIGURE 4.20 Gaps in the vegetation create habitat interspersion in freshwater marshes and control the suitability of the marsh for ducks, muskrats, and other species. (After Weller 1994a.)

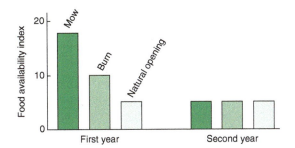

FIGURE 4.21 Burning and mowing can change the abundance of invertebrates in marshes. (From Ball and Nudds 1989.)

process to be important. Examples might include patches burned by fire, eaten by muskrats, cut out by ice cakes, killed by floating mats of litter, or buried by alluvial deposits. We will look at examples from fresh and salt marshes.

4.4.1 Patch creation and management of freshwater marshes

Waterfowl prefer patches in marshes. Patches can be formed by flooding, fire, or herbivores (e.g. Weller 1978, 1994a; van der Valk 1981; Ball and Nudds 1989). Figure 4.3 showed that as little as 3 years of flooding can kill stands of emergent plants and create a new patch type. Recurring disturbances can create a mosaic of different vegetation types; the simplest example may be dense stands of cattails interspersed with patches of open water (Figure 4.20). Experimental studies have shown that breeding ducks select a 1 : 1 ratio of these two patch types (e.g. Kaminski and Prince 1981).

Since many shallow-water marshes are slowly dominated by cattails, mosaics can often require deliberate human manipulation (Verry 1989). A variety of mowing implements from machetes to

50-hp tractors have been used to cut cattail stands (Kaminski *et al.* 1985). While cutting temporarily reduces shoot density, the main factor limiting regrowth is the duration of flooding after the mowing. A depth of 40 cm of water in the spring can prevent regrowth (Kaminski *et al.* 1985). In another mowing study, circular patches of 0.02, 0.09, and 0.15 ha were either cut or burned into cattail stands along Lake St Clair in Canada (Ball and Nudds 1989). Food availability for waterfowl was estimated by sampling the aquatic invertebrates. Mowed patches had higher invertebrate availability than burned patches (Figure 4.21), but there was no detectable effect of patch size. They conclude that, if the objective is to increase food supplies for ducks, mowing is superior to burning; not only does it produce more invertebrates, but the clearings last longer.

Fire and mowing were also manipulated in a 3500-ha brackish marsh in California, where over 100 000 dabbling ducks may over-winter (Szalay and Resh 1997). The dominant plant here is the grass *Distichlis spicata*; stands of this plant were either subjected to hand mowing or burning in late summer, and then flooded. Since flooding immediately after burning or mowing can eliminate *Distichlis* (Smith and Kadlec 1985b), the experimental flooding was delayed until some weeks after mowing. During the following winter, invertebrate biomass was sampled. The dominant macroinvertebrates were a *Chironomus* larva (Diptera) and a water boatman, *Trichocorixa* (Hemiptera). Copepods were the dominant microinvertebrate. Burning increased the abundance of *Chironomus* and *Trichocorixa* by roughly a factor of ten relative to controls, but mowing did not have significant effects. Invertebrate populations are thus sensitive to perturbations such as fire and mowing, and the timing, area, and intensity of disturbance can affect their relative abundance.

4.4.2 Salt marshes: recolonization of bare patches is mainly by rhizomes

In the typical zonation of salt marshes in eastern North America two species are dominant, *Juncus gerardi* higher on the shore and *Spartina patens* lower on the shore. Bare space is often generated when dense mats of litter are deposited by tides. The litter is mainly leaves of *S. alterniflora*. If covered for more than 8 weeks, marsh plants are generally killed (Bertness and Ellison 1987). The resulting bare patches are recolonized in several ways. Some species arrive as seeds (e.g. *Salicornia europea*). Some species arrive as runners from adjoining plants (e.g. *Distichlis spicata*). Eventually the patches are reinvaded by *J. gerardi* and *S. patens*. There is thus a continual process of patch creation and patch recolonization (Bertness 1991). Unlike in freshwater marshes, seed banks appear to play only a minor role in the re-establishment of vegetation; instead, vegetative expansion from adjoining plants predominates (Bertness and Ellison 1987; Hartman 1988; Allison 1995).

To explore these dynamics, Bertness made artificial bare patches of three sizes ranging from 0.06 to 1 m². He then transplanted seedlings and tillers of four species into these patches and recorded their survival (Figure 4.22). He reports that larger patches (left) had higher salinity than the surrounding vegetation, and that survivorship therefore increased as patch size/salinity decreased. Transplants into existing vegetation (as shown by the column C for controls)

also had very low survival in spite of low salinity in the surrounding vegetation, showing that competition from existing vegetation also prevents the establishment of transplants (see Chapter 5). Apparently competition is temporarily reduced in gaps and the important factors then become relative colonization rates and relative tolerances to salinity. The relative amounts of *Salicornia europea*, *Distichlis spicata*, and *Juncus gerardi* or *Spartina patens* therefore depend upon the frequency of disturbance in these marshes.

In more southern areas, particularly those with Mediterranean-type rainfall patterns (wet winters, dry summers), salinity may play an important role in creating large patches of new marsh. During dry years, hypersaline conditions develop; marsh species such as *Spartina foliosa* and *Typha domingensis* cannot tolerate these conditions and are slowly replaced by salt-tolerant species such as *Salicornia virginica*. This process is reversed during abnormally wet years, when higher stream flows and longer rainfalls flush accumulated salt from the soil. This creates a low-salinity gap in which seedlings can germinate and establish. If the gap is short (3–6 weeks), only halophytic species such as *S. foliosa* can establish, but if it is extended, brackish and freshwater marsh species can establish as well. The duration and intensity of the next hypersaline period will then determine which of these species survive. There is thus a constant cycling through different vegetation types driven by changes in moisture supply (Figure 4.23).

On the topic of saline wetlands, you could think about the effects of frost on mangroves as generating a similar type of patch dynamics. Rather than there being a single point that defines the northern limit of mangroves, we may think of the zone receiving frost as a region in which mangroves suffer recurring death and recolonization, thereby driving changes in the composition of other shoreline species.

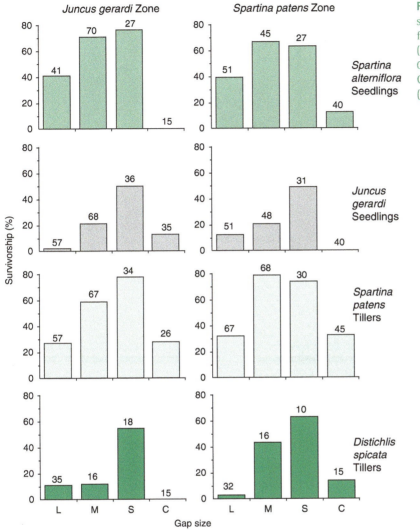

FIGURE 4.22 The effects of the size of gaps upon the survival of four transplanted marsh plants (L = large, 1 m^2; M = medium, 0.5 m^2; S = small, 0.25 m^2; C = control, dense vegetation). (From Bertness 1991.)

4.5 Measuring the effects of disturbance in future studies

It is often difficult to compare studies of disturbance because there are so many kinds of disturbance. If we are going to understand better the effects of disturbance on plant communities as a whole and wetlands in particular, we must more precisely define, and then measure, the relative effects of disturbance upon community properties. One way disturbance could be measured consistently is to measure relative change in species composition. There is a wide range of measures of similarity between samples (Legendre and Legendre 1983). Using a standard measure of ecological similarity, one could define a range of disturbance intensities from 0 (the community is the same before and after

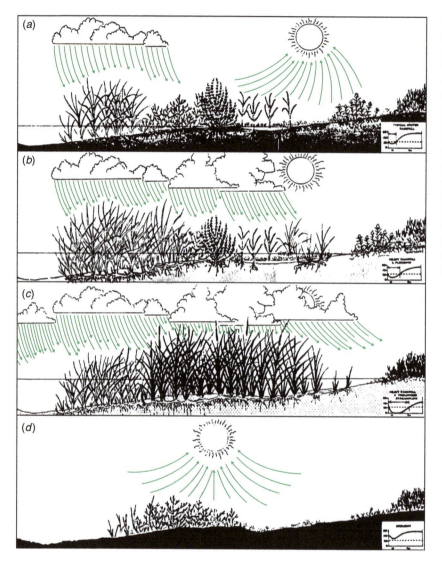

FIGURE 4.23 Cyclical changes of salt marsh vegetation in arid climates. (*a*) Typical situation where brief periods of low salinity allow salt marsh species to germinate and establish. (*b*) Floods reduce salinity and allow expansion of *Spartina foliosa*. (c) Prolonged flooding illuminates salt marsh vegetation and allows brackish marsh species to establish. (*d*) Periods without rainfall or flooding create hypersaline conditions which kill all but a few highly salt-tolerant species such as *Salicornia virginica*. (From Zedler and Beare 1986.)

the event) to 1 (the community is completely different after the event). Figure 4.3 showed that the deeper the flooding of a wetland, the more rapid the decline in abundance of two emergent plants. If we were measuring the degree of similarity each year, it is obvious that the dissimilarity through time increases most rapidly with the deepest flooding (that is, most intense disturbance). We would observe similar effects if, instead of using composition, we used biomass of these plant species as our measure.

In addition to measuring disturbance consistently, it would also be useful to determine how the effects of disturbance vary among different types of habitats or among different groups of species. Here is an example that did both. Moore (1998) artificially created bare patches in five different riverine wetland habitats ranging from exposed sandy shorelines to sheltered organic bays. At each of the five sites, 1-m² bare plots were created and the vegetation in them repeatedly compared with undisturbed controls over two growing seasons. There were two questions: (i) did the effects of disturbance change among the five wetland types and (ii) did the effects of disturbance vary with the way in which the plants were assessed: species, guilds, and communities? Suprisingly, a single growing season was sufficient for community-level properties such as biomass, richness, and evenness to return to control levels. The dominants removed at each site tended to remain depressed for the first growing season, although by the second year effects were negligible. At the guild level, recovery was also rapid, although there were minor changes, such as a modest increase in facultative annuals. The species level of organization tended to be the most sensitive to disturbance. Overall, it appeared that removing above-ground biomass had a marginal effect on this vegetation type; this may not be a great surprise, given the dynamic nature of riverine wetlands.

The measurement of disturbance effects is often complicated by changes in wetlands that occur while the study is ongoing. Moore tested whether removal effects varied among five wetland vegetation types by measuring the magnitude of removal effects for each ecological property and for each wetland site standardized to account for initial differences and changes with time. Returning to the beginning of this chapter, recall that for an event to qualify as a disturbance, there has to be some change in properties. Hence, we need to ask: (1) what is the effect of an event like drought or biomass removal, (2) is it significantly different from zero, and (3) how does it vary among sites or species? Moore's measure of removal effects for each variable was

$$Z = (x_0 \times y_t)/(x_t \times y_0)$$

where x_0 is the mean value for the property in the control sites during the pre-treatment survey, x_t is the mean value in the control sites during the post-treatment survey, y_0 is the mean value measured in the disturbance treatment during the pre-treatment survey, and y_t is the mean value measured in the disturbance treatment during the post-treatment survey (see Ravera 1989). The value is thus independent of initial levels of the properties, and is independent of ongoing temporal trends in the community. A Z value of 1.0 indicates no treatment effects, while values above or below 1 indicate

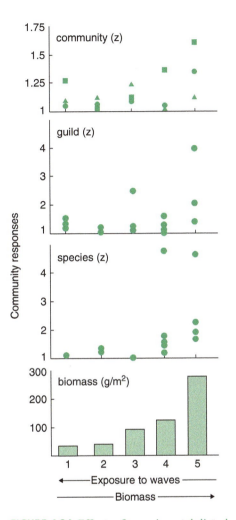

FIGURE 4.24 Effects of experimental disturbance (the removal of all biomass) upon several properties of five different wetland communities. The community gradient is arranged from exposed sites (left) to sheltered bays (right), which produces the biomass gradient shown in the bottom panel. Z is used to measure the amount of change from controls 1 year after the disturbance; the greater Z, the greater the departure from control values. The top panel combines three response variables: cover ▲, richness ■, and evenness ●. After 1 year (shown) the effects were significant at the species and guild level, but not at the community level; after 2 years, the effects were non-significant. (After Moore 1998.)

increase or decrease. Hence, it should be possible to compare effects of disturbance quantitatively for a wide array of properties of wetlands and types of species. In the case of Moore's study, the experimental disturbance had the greatest effects in sheltered bays (Figure 4.24). Perhaps this is because these are the wetland communities where disturbance was normally most infrequent.

CONCLUSION

Disturbance is a short-lived event that removes biomass, causing a measurable change in the properties of an ecological community. We have seen that disturbance can have major effects upon wetlands and at many scales. Droughts, fires, floods, ice, logging, and winds are but a few of the factors that can quickly change the type of wetland community in a landscape. At smaller scales, when small patches are disturbed, disturbance increases the heterogeneity of the habitat, and sets up a system where patches are being created and recovering from disturbance. Species may then disperse among those patches. Managers can deliberately make disturbances that vary in duration, intensity, frequency, or area to create desired kinds of habitats.

One way to further summarize this chapter and combine the many types of disturbance in nature is to select two of the four measurable properties, intensity and area, as in Figure 4.25. At the upper left are disturbances that are generally of low intensity in small patches, such as grazing. Ice scour is a disturbance that still may occur in small patches, but with much higher intensity. Atmospheric deposition of pollutants (not shown) may produce

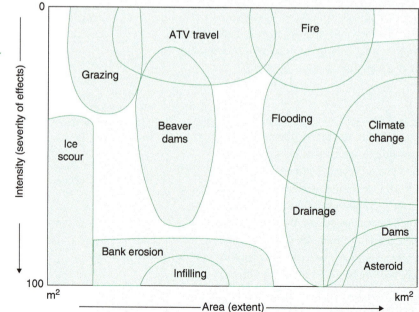

FIGURE 4.25 Intensity and area plotted for an array of natural disturbances in wetlands.

only small changes in composition, but these may cover very large areas. Finally, there are events like the construction of hydroelectric dams which have high intensity and affect large areas.

These kinds of disturbances play an important role in determining the area and species composition of wetlands. They also interact with other factors including fertility, competition, and herbivory. Hence they are important, and often overlooked, factors that affect vast areas of wetland. They also provide, when used wisely, important tools for managing and restoring wetlands to achieve specific conservation objectives, such as maintaining habitat for rare species of wildlife.

Chapter contents

5 Competition

Up to this point in the book we have largely focused on the physical factors that control the structure and function of wetland communities: flooding, fertility, and disturbance. It is now time to consider biological factors. We begin here with **competition**. We will define competition as *the negative effects that one organism has upon another by consuming, or controlling access to, a resource that is limited in availability.* That is, it is an interaction in which both organisms experience a negative effect. Competition is widespread and important, although its importance depends upon the species or the habitat being considered. As just one of many possible examples consider the effects of competition upon common marsh plants (Figure 5.1). The effects of competition were measured by moving six species of plants into two sets of conditions: clearings (no competition) and intact vegetation (competition). In every case, the plants in clearings grew significantly better than the plants with neighbors. The difference in the height of each pair of histograms gives one measure of how important competition was for that species – in this case, *Pontederia cordata* seemed to be the weakest competitor, since it showed the greatest reduction in vegetated plots.

The basis of competition is lack of resources. All living organisms require a rather limited number of elements to make up their bodies (Table 5.1). Some organisms will accumulate these resources at the expense of others, thereby reducing growth, survival, or reproduction of their neighbors. An experiment like that in Figure 5.1 does not tell us which resource(s) were the cause of the competition, merely that it occurred. In plant communities, light is a particularly common source of competition; for animals, it is often food.

Competition is a biological force that relentlessly drives wetland communities toward dominance by a few kinds of species. In particular, wetland plant communities rapidly become dominated by a few species, usually those best able to exploit light. Consider a few examples. Marshes often become dominated by large leafy rhizomatous species in genera such as *Typha*, *Phragmites*, and *Schoenoplectus*. Wet meadows become dominated by tall rhizomatous grasses such as *Calamagrostis canadensis* or *Phalaris arundinacea,* or by shrubs. Aquatic communities become dominated by floating-leaved species in genera such as *Nymphaea* and *Nelumbo*. Even swamps are often dominated by a few tree species – *Acer saccharinum* or *Taxodium distichum*. And then there are the invasive species which often spread precisely because of their strong competitive abilites. Aquatic communities are at particular risk from free-floating exotics such as water hyacinth (*Eichhornia crassipes*), giant salvinia

(*Salvinia molesta*), or water lettuce (*Pistia stratiotes*); all other wetland types are at risk for invasives that produce dense canopies. The growing list of woody invasives such as melaleuca (*Melaleuca quinquenervia*) shows how canopy-forming species can rapidly transform habitats (Section 13.5) and tend to produce monocultures across a wide array of habitats.

The objective of this chapter is to provide some principles to understand how competition structures wetland communities, how natural forces tend to generate plant diversity, and how many human interventions decrease plant diversity.

Table 5.1 Major elements required by living organisms and their functions

Element	Function
C	Structure; energy storage in lipids and carbohydrates
H	Structure; energy storage in lipids and carbohydrates
N	Structure of proteins and nucleic acids
O	Structure; aerobic respiration for energy release
P	Structure of nucleic acids and skeletons; energy transfer within cells
S	Structure of proteins

Source: After Morowitz (1968).

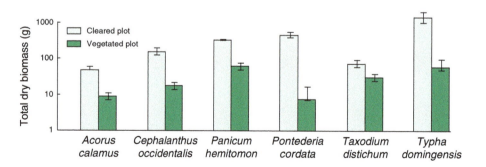

FIGURE 5.1 Competition has negative effects on plant growth, as illustrated by the difference in growth of six marsh plants when transplanted into cleared or vegetated plots in an coastal marsh. (Adapted from Geho *et al.* 2007.)

5.1   Some examples of competition in wetlands

Before we delve into the details of the principles behind competition it will be helpful to consider a few specific examples and the experiments that have been used to study them.

5.1.1 Experiments are needed to detect competition

You cannot demonstrate that competition is occurring simply by making one-time observations of a wetland. Experiments are necessary. Hence, we have less evidence on the importance of competition than we do for physical factors. The design of experiments to detect competition and measure its impacts is a challenging topic that you will need to read about elsewhere (Underwood 1986; Keddy 2001). Here we will simply look at some examples that illustrate the types of experiments that have been done and what they tell us about the effects of competition in wetlands.

The basic approach to measuring competition is simple in principle – remove a species and measure whether any of the remaining species benefit – say with higher growth rates, higher survival rates, or more offspring. These kinds of experiments have been done. We will look at four groups that have been studied: plants, amphibians, fish, and birds.

5.1.2 Competition among plants

In Figure 5.1 you saw an experiment which looked at the effects of all neighboring plants combined. Often, experiments instead look at each pair of plants in isolation. Let us look at one such experiment conducted along the coast of southeastern North America. Selected plants were removed from wetlands, and then remaining species were monitored to see if any of them benefited from the removal. The study included both low marsh and high marsh. In the high marsh, *Spartina patens* was

removed, and in the low marsh, both *S. alterniflora* and *S. patens* were removed. The upper left panel in Figure 5.2 shows how to interpret such studies. Only one species, *Fimbristylis spadiceae*, showed a significant response to the removal of its neighbors! Apparently, competition was a weak force in this wetland.

The above study may have made a mistake by trying to look at too many species at once. Let us therefore look at a study involving fewer species, and more types of experimentation, but still in coastal marshes. In one part of this study, species were transplanted into situations with and without neighbors, and their performance was monitored. Performance was significantly lower when the plants had neighbors (Figure 5.3), showing that neighbors indeed had negative effects. The negative effects were much more dramatic than those in Figure 5.2. In general, competition severely reduced performance. Competition was important in both marsh zones (top *Juncus gerardi* zone, bottom *Spartina patens* zone). The one exception, *J. gerardi*, performed well even when transplanted into locations already occupied by other species, suggesting that *J. gerardi* is competitively dominant to both *S. patens* and *D. spicata*. This idea of competitive dominants and subordinates is one we to which we will return shortly.

Many invasive species are floating aquatics, including *Eichhornia crassipes* (water hyacinth), *Salvinia molesta* (giant salvinia), and *Pistia stratiotes* (water lettuce). The effects of floating-leaved aquatics are of particular interest because the competition has to be asymmetric – that is, a floating plants can shade a submersed one, but the reverse cannot occur (Keddy 1976). Consider the invasive *Hydrocharis morsus-ranae* (frog bit), which is spreading rapidly over ponds on my own property. To test for effects of competition from this species, Catling *et al.* (1988) anchored 70 circular 1-m² floating hoops in each of two study sites in eastern North America.

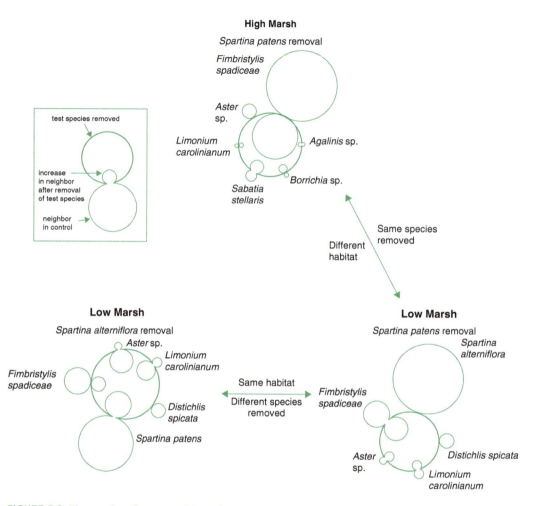

FIGURE 5.2 The results of a competitive release experiment among pairs of plants in a coastal wetland. Circle size is a measure of abundance either before or after the removals, as shown in the panel on the upper left. In this example, only the response of *Fimbristylis* was statistically significant. (From Keddy 1989 after Silander and Antonovics 1982.)

In half of the hoops, the frog bit was removed; in the other half it was added, to produce a cover of 65%. After just one growing season, the aquatic macrophytes in the removal plots had 72% cover, while those in the plots with frog bit had only 4% cover. The species that declined significantly included *Elodea canadensis, Myriophyllum heterophyllym, Potamogeton pusillus, P. nodosus, P. zosteriformis, Sparganium eurycarpum,* and *Utricularia vulgaris.*

5.1.3 Competition among larval amphibians

Many amphibians breed in temporary ponds in the spring. Do they compete with one another? There have been many studies, and the general answer is yes. In one study in North America, Wilbur (1972) examined pools containing three species of mole salamanders (*Ambystoma* spp.) along with a larger amphibian community including tiger salamanders,

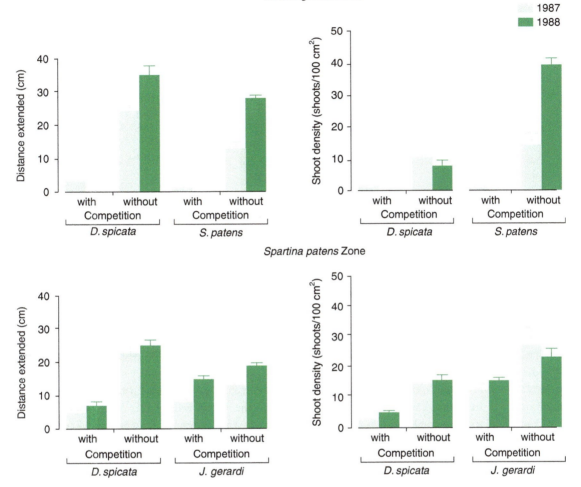

FIGURE 5.3 Effects of competition on three salt marsh plants, *Distichlis spicata*, *Spartina patens*, and *Juncus gerardi*, in two different vegetation zones. Plant growth was measured using distance extended (left) and shoot density (right) in plots with and without neighbors. (From Bertness 1991.)

American toads, gray tree frogs, and wood frogs. Cages were inoculated with different numbers and kinds of amphibian eggs. The cages had one, two, or three species. At the end of the summer, performance was measured three ways: survivorship, body weight, and length of time of the larval period for all survivors. There was intense interspecific competition (Figure 5.4). For example, *A. laterale* (left) had body weights reduced by nearly two-thirds when 32 neighbors were added. Further, there was asymmetry; *A. laterale* (left) was far more sensitive

to *A. tremblayi* than *A. tremblayi* (right) was to *A. laterale*.

5.1.4 Competition among fish in lakeshore marshes

Sunfishes are a group of spiny-rayed freshwater fishes that dominate the fish faunas of small lakes over much of central North America. In Michigan, for example, there are seven to ten species, five of which are in the genus *Lepomis*. There are three principal

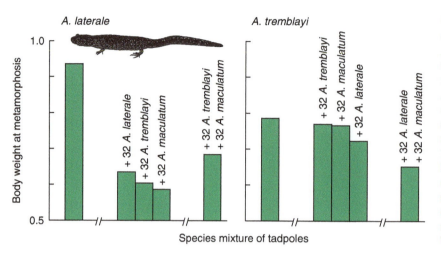

FIGURE 5.4 Effects of competition on salamanders *Ambystoma laterale* (blue-spotted salamander, 12 cm long, from Conant and Collins 1998), *A. maculatum*, and *A. tremblayi*, as measured by body weight at metamorphosis. The control animals lived in pens containing 32 individuals, while the others had experimental additions of either more of the same species, or more of two other salamander species. (Data and nomenclature from Wilbur 1972.)

habitat types: emergent vegetation, open water, and near the bottom. The pumpkinseed (*L. gibbosus*) feeds near the substrate whereas the bluegill (*L. macrochirus*) is found higher in the water column, with further separation among species based upon food size. The green sunfish (*L. cyanellus*) is restricted to the shallow and vegetated inshore habitats (Werner 1984; Wootton 1990). In one set of studies different mixtures of these three sunfish species were introduced into small experimental ponds (e.g. Werner and Hall 1976, 1979). When alone, each species occupied the emergent vegetation zone, where larger prey are found. When green sunfish were present, however, the bluegill and pumpkinseed were forced into the other habitats, to the open water or near the sediment.

5.1.5 Competition among birds in marshes

Birds are a very obvious form of life in most wetlands. It seems natural to ask whether the kinds of birds you see, and where you see them, is influenced by competition. Let us be clear that the focus here is on competition between species. We know, of course, that *within* a species, male birds compete with one another for access to females; indeed Darwin addressed this issue more than 100 years ago.

Here, however, we want you to know whether competition between species can influence the kinds of birds that you might see in a particular wetland.

The yellow-headed blackbird and red-winged blackbird are easy to identify by their yellow heads, or red wing patches, respectively. They conveniently perch in clear sight. Both species prefer to build nests in deeper water where cattails are emergent. Perhaps the deeper water offers some protection against nest predators, ranging from snakes to feral cats. The yellow-heads seize the deep-water sites, even chasing out red-wings that have already arrived. The red-winged blackbirds are then displaced into shallower water or even upland sites around the pond (Miller 1968). Hence, we have a clear case of competition, with the yellow-headed blackbird dominant over the red-winged blackbird.

Of course these are just two species, and as Rigler (1982) reminds us (Section 12.3) if there are 100 species of birds in a wetland, there will be nearly 5000 possible competitive interactions between pairs of bird species. (Actually 4950, if you ignore the interaction of each species with itself.) Although you will frequently see the above two species of blackbirds included in ecology books, they may be misleading – are they typical of the other 4949 interactions that might be occurring? To answer this question, we have to consider more species.

Looking for other birds that nest in or near cattail marshes, grackles, another kind of blackbird, have little effect on red-winged blackbirds, and red-wings in turn have only minor effects on grackles (Wiens 1965). Marsh wrens, however, are fierce competitors, breaking eggs and killing the nestlings of blackbirds (Bump 1986; Leonard and Picman 1986). What about other waterbirds, like herons and ducks? Experimental evidence is harder to obtain. Some biologists suggest that the present differences in their diets or leg lengths or nest locations shows that there was strong competition in the past. This argument, known as "the ghost of competition past" is speculative (Connell 1980; Jackson 1981).

Overall, then, the kind of birds we see in particular wetlands seems likely to be largely the result of the available habitats and food sources (Weller 1999). True, there are a few remarkable exceptions – such as the yellow-headed blackbirds displacing the red-winged blackbirds, and marsh wrens smashing the eggs of both blackbirds. But these examples may be noteworthy precisely because they are so atypical. The surprising truth may be that since birds are so dependent upon habitat, it is competition among plants that has the biggest effects on birds, since it is competition among plants that does indeed influence habitat.

5.2   Competition is often one-sided

Many textbooks leave the impression that competition occurs between pairs of species that are nearly equal in competitive ability. Anyone who watches sports will realize that the occurrence of nearly equal competitive abilities between two teams is infrequent – how many tied games do you see? More often, there is a clear winner and a clear loser. The greater the difference between the winner and the loser, the more one-sided the competition. Of course, if the interaction is one-sided enough, the loser may not even be there any longer. One-sided competition is usually called asymmetric competition. The greater the difference between the performance of the two species, the greater the asymmetry (Keddy 2001). We generally refer to the loser as the subordinate species, and the winner as the dominant species.

Consider the fish study above. It illustrates asymmetric competition, with the green sunfish winning. There is an important and often overlooked consequence of asymmetric competition – species are not always found in their preferred habitat. The green sunfish remained in the preferred habitat because it was the dominant species. The other two species were forced by the green sunfish to occupy suboptimal habitat. To put it in other words, these fish all shared

a preference for emergent vegetation. The fact that they occupied different habitats was actually the result of competitive displacement of subordinate species by the dominant species. This is nearly identical to the situation with the blackbirds.

Now consider some plant examples. Both Bertness (1991) and Catling *et al.* (1988) found strong asymmetric interactions. *Juncus gerardi* was dominant over the other salt marsh species. The floating plant *Hydrocharis morsus-ranae* could shade submersed plants until few were left.

To what extent might such asymmetry be a general property of plant competitive interactions? In order to determine if something is common, you need lots of examples. In this case, we need many experiments that have measured competition. Think again about a sports example. What is the average degree of asymmetry in a particular sport? If all the teams were nearly equal, the average asymmetry would be small, nearing zero except for random events like dropped balls or dishonest referees. In real ecosystems we almost never have enough studies to judge just how asymmetric competition tends to be. Not nearly enough studies have been made on asymmetry in large numbers of species interactions. There is one exception, an experiment in which seedlings of

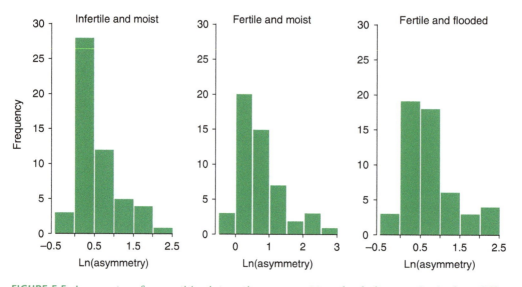

FIGURE 5.5 Asymmetry of competitive interactions among 20 wetland plant species in three different wetland environments. (Courtesy B. Shipley, after data in Keddy *et al.* 1994.)

17 freshwater marsh and wet meadow plants were grown in pairs with three other species, yielding 51 competitive interactions. A measure of asymmetry was calculated for each of these pairs plus pairs (3) of the other species. The interactions were strongly asymmetric (Figure 5.5). Moreover, the degree of asymmetry changed with environment, being greatest under fertile and flooded conditions resulted in greater asymmetry than did the unfertilized, moist condition.

5.3 Competition for light produces competitive hierarchies

If competition among plants is asymmetric – and most examples show it is – then strong competitors will tend to dominate landscapes. Weak competitors will be less common, and may indeed be absent entirely if they have already been displaced by the dominant competitor. But by looking at the landscape, we would never guess that these species were absent solely because of their weak competitive abilities. In fact, if competition is generally asymmetric, a most interesting question emerges: why are there so many species in wetlands? Why do we not find just the same few strong competitors in nearly every situation?

This question also has management and conservation implications. Is it possible that rare species are often weak competitors? How do weak competitors survive at all? What if humans make interactions more asymmetric by fertilizing wetlands? What types of conditions might provide refuge for weak competitors? We will return to these themes later in the chapter, and later in the book. Let us continue with this topic by looking at the tendency of a few species to indeed dominate marshes. As noted in Chapter 1, large areas of the world's wetlands are dominated by large leafy species with deeply buried rhizomes: think of *Phragmites australis*, *Typha latifolia*, *Calamagrostis canadensis*, or *Cyperus papyrus*. And then there are genera like *Schoenoplectus*, *Carex*, *Rhynchospora*, *Phalaris*, *Vossia* .... All have species with dense canopies that can produce nearly solid single species stands (also called monospecific stands). Think of the number of problems produced by invasion of wetlands by *Phragmites* and *Typha* alone. Is there are general principle we can find?

Let us begin with an observation by Sculthorpe, who is of historic significance because he wrote an important monograph on aquatic plants (1967). When he talks about reed swamps, he says:

Although … compositional changes may occur, it is apparent that numerous … plants tend to form extensive pure stands. These species assert their status early and attain a seasonal or permanent predominance. Of the numerous factors responsible, rates of vegetative reproduction and antagonism between species of similar or different life form are perhaps the most important. Vigorous vegetative spread, by means of rhizomes, stolons, and tubers, is a typical attribute of several reed-swamp dominants, notably species of *Carex, Glyceria, Phalaris, Phragmites, Schoenoplectus [Scirpus]*, and *Vossia*. In a favourable site one species may gain an early initiative and increase much faster than any competitor … most mature reed-swamps are so dense that they resist infiltration by larger free-floating rosettes and severely reduce the amount of light reaching the water, thus indirectly inhibiting the growth of invading submerged species. (pp. 426–7)

Note the two processes Sculthorpe emphasizes (1) rates of vegetative reproduction and (2) antagonism, by which he means competition. We could rephrase this as a hypothesis: that many wetlands are occupied by competitive dominants with rapid rates of vegetative spread and dense canopies. The presence of dense canopies suggests that competition is for light, and the dominant species is the one best able to shade its competitors.

One way to asses this would be to grow plants underneath such canopies to measure how much their growth is reduced by shading. This experiment has been done, although in pots rather than under field conditions. The experiment involved first creating artificial wetlands dominated by a single species. Seven species were used to create such conditions. The experiment included species that form dense canopies (e.g. *Typha angustifolia*), species that occupy gaps in wetlands (e.g. *Penthorum sedoides*), and an invasive species that is spreading in wetlands (*Lythrum salicaria*). After 3 years, 48 other

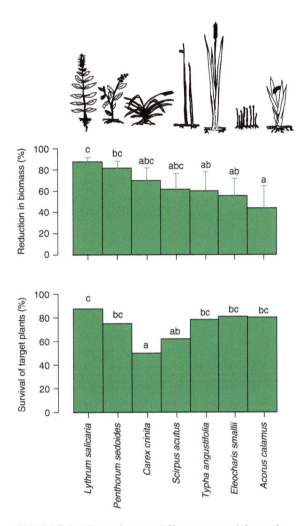

FIGURE 5.6 Effect of seven different perennial marsh plants (illustrated at top, named at bottom) upon the growth (biomass) and survival of 48 other (target) wetland plant species. Note that they are ordered by their ability to suppress other wetland species. The relatively small effects of *Typha angustifolia* likely result from the small size of the pots, which may have limited above-ground competition. (From Keddy *et al.* 1998.)

species of wetland plants were introduced to these monocultures and allowed to grow for 4 months. The effects on the performance of these 48 species was calculated as the standardized difference between their weight when grown alone, and their weight when grown under a canopy. Overall, the monocultures reduced growth and survival by more than one-half

(Figure 5.6). This indicates for a broad array of wetland plants (48 species in this case) that the presence of a canopy has significant negative effects on their growth.

Pot experiments do have their limitations. A better, although more difficult experiment, would involve transplanting native species into an actual marsh, putting some in clearings (that is, without competition) and putting others into intact vegetation. That, of course, is what was done to produce Figure 5.1. The intact vegetation was not a monoculture, but it was dominated by two clonal species with dense canopies (*Schoenoplectus americanus* 28% cover and *S. robustus* 10% cover, along with *Sagittaria lancifolia* 8% cover). Now for more background: this was part of a larger study in which 16 species were introduced

to cleared and vegetated plots. There were other factors studied in this experiment, including the effects of added sediment and the effects of herbivores (Geho *et al.* 2007). The data used to illustrate effects of competition came from plots that were protected from herbivores. *Taxodium distichum* and *Typha domingensis* are shown for comparison, because of their ecological importance in these habitats; both were most affected by grazing, which obscured the effects of competition shown in the figure. This is a reminder that although competition may be an important factor in wetlands, it is rarely the only factor. The effects of competition must always be interpreted knowing that other factors – in this case grazing – are also present.

5.4   Dominant plants are often larger than subordinate plants

Are there some general ways to recognize plants that are competitive dominants in wetlands? We have Sculthorpe's opinion, while other plant ecologists (Grime 1979; Givnish 1982; Keddy 2001) agree that height is one of the important characteristics of dominant plants. One way to assess this is to measure the competitive ability of a large number of species, and measure some of their life history traits such as height, and ask if the two are related. Gaudet and Keddy (1988) did exactly this – they measured relative competitive performance of 44 freshwater wetland plants from a wide array of habitats. They estimated relative competitive performance by measuring the relative ability of each of these

44 species to suppress a common indicator species, the invasive *Lythrum salicaria*. The more the test plants were able to reduce the growth of *L. salicaria*, the better competitors they were judged to be. Gaudet and Keddy then looked for plant traits that could predict this ability. Both height and above-ground biomass were good predictors of competitive performance (Figure 5.7). In this experiment, species including *Typha latifolia* and *Phalaris arundinacea* both had high competitive ability. We may thus conclude that competition may be very important in wetlands, that species often tend to have unequal competitive abilities, and that many wetlands are dominated by species with dense canopies.

5.5   Escape in space: competition in patches

Perhaps some weak competitors indeed survive by finding patches where the dominant plant does not occur, like the clearings created in the experiment shown in Figure 5.1. Others have already thought about this. More than 50 years ago Skellam (1951) showed that weak competitors can indeed survive – as long as they can disperse better than strong

competitors. The argument goes like this (Pielou 1975). Imagine two competing species that reproduce once a year. Let A be the stronger competitor and B the weaker competitor. Wherever they coexist, A invariably wins. Therefore, the only habitat in which B can reproduce includes those sites in which it occurs alone (Figure 5.8). Assume that the landscape

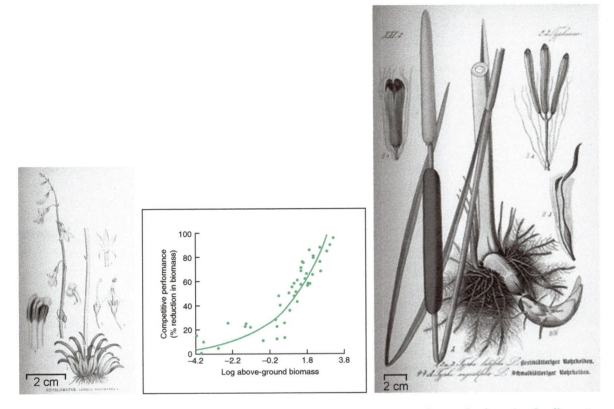

FIGURE 5.7 Competitive performance increased with plant size across an array of 44 wetland species. Small rosette species (e.g. *Lobelia dortmanna*) occur on the left side of the figure, while large leafy species (e.g. *Typha latifolia*) occur on the right. Competitive performance was measured as the percent reduction in biomass of a common test species. (After Gaudet and Keddy 1988.) (See also color plate.)

has N sites, or patches of habitat, and that at equilibrium the expected proportion of sites with a single A individual at the end of the growing season is Q. This means that NQ of the sites are dominated by species A. Therefore, only $N(1 - Q)$ remain for B to occupy. If we call this remaining portion of sites (those that allow B to survive) q, then q must be greater than zero for the competitive subordinate to survive in that landscape. We want to know how much better dispersal of B must be for this to occur.

Therefore, let F and f be the number of seeds produced by species A and B, respectively. For species B to persist, f/F must be great enough to ensure that $q > 0$. It can be shown that, for this to occur, f/F must exceed $-Q/(1 - Q) \ln(1 - Q)$. Provided this condition is met, species B will continue to occur in the landscape in spite of its weak competitive ability. There may be many cases where the types of disturbance we saw in Chapter 4 provide circumstances for this kind of process to operate.

5.6 Escape in time: competition and disturbance

There is an another alternative to dispersing to a disturbed patch. The alternative is to wait for a disturbance to make a patch where the plant already occurs. If disturbances occur often enough, which we have seen is often the case, it may indeed be best to sit and wait for the competitive dominant to be

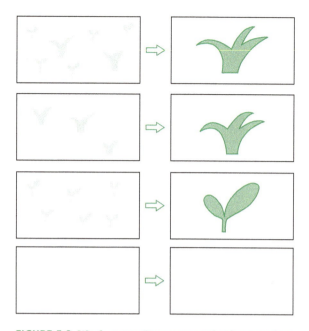

FIGURE 5.8 Weak competitors can survive by escaping to habitat patches that are not occupied by stronger species. Four possible combinations of seedlings are shown on the left, and the outcome of adults is given on the right. (From Pielou 1975 after Skellam 1951.)

killed. Many species seem to have adopted this strategy. We saw in Table 4.1 that many marsh plants have enormous numbers of buried seeds. Since these seeds can remain dormant for many years, if not decades, they need only wait – and soon a fire, flood, or grazer will create the conditions for them to germinate. If you look closely at many seed bank species, they have small seeds that seem to lack any dispersal agent. They simply fall in place and wait

for disturbance to create a clear patch. Some species may also wait for disturbance as adults – small fragments of rhizome may persist under a competitive dominant, and quickly produce new shoots after a disturbance. Indeed, plants may persist for years as small fragments of rhizome. When the competitive dominants die, they rapidly produce vigorous shoots and flowers.

There is an important exception. Most species of trees do not have seed banks. They appear to depend almost exclusively upon dispersal in space. It is not clear why this should be the case, but it seems to be true for a broad array of tree species around the world. Many trees produce wind-dispersed seeds; the cottonwood trees that establish along river banks are a good example. Other wetland trees produce seeds that float and are carried by floods to new sites; cypress and tupelo are two examples. Some trees in the Amazon produce hard fruits that are dispersed by fish.

The lack of tree seeds in soil is important for managing many wetland types. It means that when managers lower water levels or burn wetlands to stimulate germination from buried seeds, it is largely herbaceous plants that establish. Invasion by woody plants takes longer, and requires living woody plants nearby as a seed source. This delays their establishment. Of course, given the importance of competition for light, woody plants will usually eventually dominate wetlands – unless another fire or flood or drought kills the woody plants and allows marshes to re-establish.

5.7   Gradients provide another way of escaping in space

So far we have established that wetlands have intense competition, at least among the plants. Hence, many species found in wetlands have to avoid competition by finding temporary gaps in the vegetation. This may involve dispersal to a newly created gap, but can also involve dispersal forward in time to a future disturbance. Disturbance is such an all pervasive

force in wetlands that there is always likely to be a patch somewhere that is not yet occupied by dominant competitors. It is less clear to what extent these generalizations apply to animals, partly because there is an insufficient number of experiments. However, the little evidence available suggests that animals are often affected by competition, and may be displaced by competition to habitats that are suboptimal. Examples of this include both fish (Werner and Hall 1976, 1979) and blackbirds (Miller 1968).

There is one other possible escape from competition. It is possible that certain habitats have inherently low levels of competition, and that these habitats provide refuges from competitive dominants. Perhaps there are certain conditions that continually kill competitive dominants, allowing weaker competitors to survive. Since competitive dominants often have large leafy canopies, we may propose that habitats that make it difficult to produce or maintain such canopies are prime candidates. Since producing large shoots requires rapid growth and available nutrients, habitats that are chronically low in nutrients may be less likely to support such species. At very least, the rate at which competitive dominants cover the landscape should be reduced. Similarly, chronic disturbance may continually remove shoots, and once the below-ground organs die form lack of energy from shoots, it may take a very long time indeed for the dominants to re-establish. Candidate factors include waves (which break off shoots), ice (which grinds off meristems or uproots rhizomes), and fire (which removes shoots). A combination of low nutrients and recurring disturbance might be expected to be the worst of both worlds for dominant plants: not only are the shoots continually disrupted, but the resources to replace them are in short supply.

A series of experiments has been carried out to test whether competition does change in the predicted way along such gradients. Before showing the results, we need to note that plants present experiments with a particular problem: they grow and compete in two entirely different habitats, above and below ground. There is little reason to believe that competition among roots for nitrogen and phosphorus will obey the same rules as competition among shoots for light. Hence, we have to deal with above- and below-ground competition as separate factors. There are two possible extremes: above- and below-ground competition show the

same patterns along gradients, or above- and below-ground competition show the opposite patterns along gradients. There are theoretical grounds for thinking that each might be the case (Grime 1979; Tilman 1982), but rather than indulge in theoretical arguments, the task is to design an experiment.

Experiments that test for gradients of competition must by their very nature be large, because the same experiment has to be repeated at multiple locations. If you don't include a large number of possible habitats, you can't test for a competition gradient. Hence, there are many fewer examples. Most come from work done along shorelines, where wetlands are spread out along a gradient running from infertile sandy shores to fertile densely vegetated bays. What might the patterns in competition be along such a gradient? To answer this question, one can transplant one or more species into a series of habitats along this gradient, each habitat having both cleared and uncleared plots. After a period of time, all the plants are harvested. We will call these plants grown in test plots "phytometers" (*sensu* Clements 1935) since we are using them to measure the level of competition at each site in a standard manner. If there is no difference between the growth of the phytometer in the cleared plot and the vegetated plot, there is no competition at that location. Think for example of Figure 5.1 again – if there was no difference between the cleared plots and vegetated plots, there would be no evidence for competition. The greater the difference between the two, the more intense the competition. The results of several experiments arranged along gradients indicated that the effects of competition increased with fertility and biomass (Wilson and Keddy 1986a, b). Moreover, it appeared that the plants were sorted along the gradient according to their relative competitive ability.

There is at least one complication to the above pattern – plants have to compete with one another in two different environments at the same time: above ground and below ground. That is, there can be shoot competition, or root competition, or some combination of the two. How might these two kinds of competition change along such a gradient? Since there has been only one large experiment to date, I will describe it in more detail. Two species were used as phytometers, *Carex crinita* and *Lythrum salicaria*. The habitat was a gradient of biomass found in a sand shoreline system along the Ottawa River. At one end were open sand shorelines with small numbers of stress-tolerant plants. And the other end of the gradient there was a sheltered bay that was densely vegetated with canopy-forming species. At 60 different locations, competition intensity was measured and separated into above-ground and below-ground competition. Total competition intensity increased with increasing biomass (Figure 5.9, top), and this was solely the result of an increase in above-ground competition intensity (Figure 5.9, middle). Below-ground competition intensity was constant along the gradient (Figure 5.9, bottom).

If biomass gradients indicate the presence of competition gradients, we can make a prediction: the competitive ability of a species will predict where it is found in a wetland. If so, where are the weak competitors found in nature? To answer this question, Gaudet and Keddy (1995) first measured the relative competitive ability of 44 wetland plant species (recall Figure 5.7), and, independently, measured their position along several different gradients. Sites with higher biomass had stronger competitors (Figure 5.10a). Stronger competitors were more common in sites with more organic soils (Figure 5.10b). Stronger competitors also occurred in sites having higher levels of nitrogen or phosphorous (Figure 5.10c, d). Stronger competitors were also positively associated with levels of the lesser nutrients, magnesium and potassium (Figure 5.10e, f). In general, then, habitats with low biomass and small plants – sandy shores, wet meadows, shoreline fens, pannes, some kinds of wet prairies – have species with relatively low competitive ability.

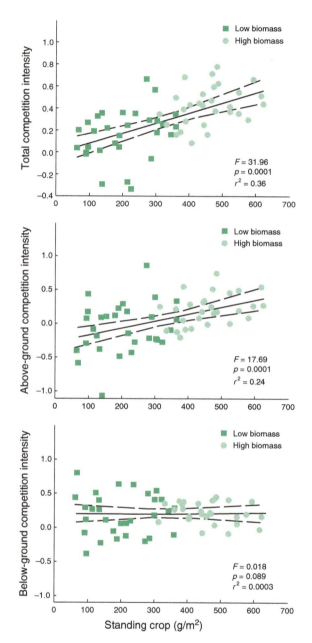

FIGURE 5.9 Competition intensity increased with standing crop in a set of 60 experimental plots representing a gradient from open sandy shoreline to densely vegetated marsh. Most of this was the result of changes in above-ground competition (middle panel). Below-ground competition (bottom) did not change along this gradient. (From Twolan-Strutt and Keddy 1996.)

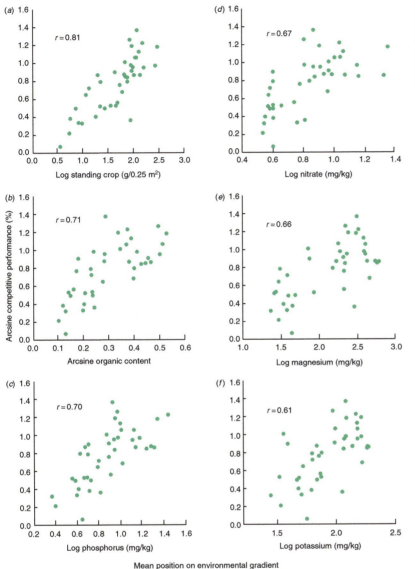

FIGURE 5.10 Competitive performance of 40 wetland plants was correlated with their field distributions along six different field gradients. (From Gaudet and Keddy 1995.)

5.8   Competition gradients produce centrifugal organization

We have therefore established that competition occurs in wetlands. Some wetlands are dominated by large leafy competitive dominants that produce high biomass communities – cattail or papyrus marshes being obvious examples. Other sites that are infertile and disturbed have low biomass, which is associated with lower competition intensity, and provide a refuge for species that are weaker competitors. We can combine these observations into a centrifugal model (Figure 5.11). This model combines many biomass gradients, and therefore many kinds of wetland gradients, into

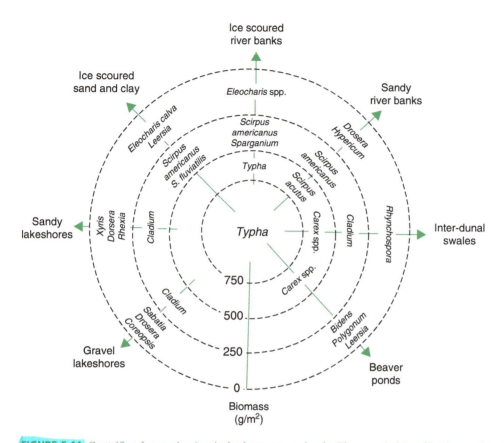

FIGURE 5.11 Centrifugal organization in herbaceous wetlands. The core habitat (fertile, undisturbed) has high biomass (ca. 1000 g/m²) and is dominated by large canopy-forming species such as *Typha*. The low-biomass peripheral sites have many different kinds of environmental constraints and kinds of species. (After Moore *et al.* 1989.)

one diagram. Let's take a closer look at some of its implications.

5.8.1 The centrifugal model links high competition with low diversity

From the perspective of the centrifugal model, there are a few types of core habitats and a very large number of peripheral habitats. The core habitat is typically dominated by one of a few largely leafy rhizomatous species – Figure 5.11 shows *Typha*, but other genera such as *Phragmites*, *Phalaris*, *Scirpus*, *Calamagrostis*, and *Papyrus* are typical core species.

Arrayed around the core habitat are many different kinds of low-biomass communities. Low-biomass

sites can be produced by many different kinds of environmental factors. Some peripheral sites may have low phosphorus levels. Some peripheral sites may have low nitrogen levels. Some may have low nitrogen and phosphorus levels combined. All three of the foregoing situations could occur with high or low soil calcium. And all these nutrient combinations could occur in sites that are burned, or washed by waves, or scoured by ice. Some unusual low-biomass habitats may even be the result of forces that no longer occur, such as continental glaciers, post-glacial rivers, or ancient lakes. There are so many kinds of peripheral habitats that it is hard to generalize about them. We can say that they have low biomass and unusual species. Beyond that, one needs to look closely to discover the cause of the low biomass and the particular kind of species that occur.

5.8.2 Rare species are most often found in peripheral habitats

An important prediction of the centrifugal organization model is that rare species will be restricted to peripheral habitats. Since the number of rare and endangered species in the world continues to grow, we may need to place a particular emphasis upon management for peripheral habitats.

Peripheral habitats often have distinctive, and unusual, plant species. The particular species depend upon where you happen to live or travel. Here are a few examples that are included in this book. An infertile wet meadow near Georgian Bay (Figure 3.3c) may have *Rhexia virginica* and *Drosera intermedia*. An infertile low-biomass habitat in the Everglades (Figure 3.3b) may have *Cladium jamaicense* and *Utricularia vulgaris*. An eroded shoreline along a river may have *Pedicularis furbishii* (Figure 2.5e). An infertile wet meadow in Nova Scotia may have *Coreopsis rosea* and *Sabatia kennedyana* (Figure 1.7b). An infertile low-biomass panne on the edge of Lake Ontario (Figures 1.6b, 1.7a) may have *Parnassia glauca*, *Lobelia kalmii*, or *Physostegia virginiana*. An infertile wet prairie may have *Platanthera leucophaea* (Figure 3.4b). An infertile depression along the Gulf Coast of North America (Figure 3.3d) may have several species of *Sarracenia* and *Pinguicula*. Infertile coastal bogs in the Carolinas may have *Dionaea muscipula* (Figure 3.4a). These are only a few examples, and you could find many more. The point is that there are many kinds of peripheral habitats and many kinds of unusual species that can occur where conditions limit the accumulation of biomass and prevent the invasion by clonal canopy-forming species.

We can draw a few general conclusions:

- Any landscape will have far more peripheral habitats than core habitats.
- The peripheral habitats in a landscape contain most of the biological diversity.
- The core habitats will tend to be dominated by a few species.
- Any factor that increases fertility, or decreases disturbance, will tend to force more habitats into the core type of habitat.

5.8.3 Peripheral habitats are at risk

We saw in Chapter 3 that fertility has an important role in controlling the habitats and species in wetlands. Humans are increasing the nutrient levels in wetlands, a process known as eutrophication. We saw that eutrophication produces changes in individual plant communities, as documented in early work on the fertilization of interdunal communities (Section 3.1.5) and in experimental communities (Section 3.5.4). Modern humans have many ways to increase the fertility of wetlands: human sewage, sewage from all the animals being raised to feed people, drift and runoff from fertilized fields, mining phosphorus rocks, removing nitrogen from the atmosphere, and even burning coal and oil. We have already seen that increased levels of nutrients in rainfall are threatening rare plants and their habitats in Europe (recall Section 3.5.6). From the perspective of the centrifugal model, these are processes that push peripheral habitats toward the core, increasing plant biomass, and decreasing plant diversity. Overall, peripheral habitats as a group are at risk from eutrophication.

We saw in Chapter 4 that disturbance is a natural process in landscapes. Humans are reducing the natural disturbance regimes that used to create wild places. Natural fires are largely suppressed, although they are usually replaced by much hotter conflagrations that have far more severe consequences. We have seen this repeatedly in western North America, particularly California. Roads and cities are natural fire breaks that prevent fires from naturally spreading across landscapes. Large herds of wild grazing animals are increasingly rare; and some types of herbivores are now extinct. No longer are large wet prairies in central North

America grazed by millions of bison, or burned by lightning-caused fires. Increasingly, wet meadows exist as small fragments surrounded by human-dominated landscapes.

There is growing evidence from North American wetlands that wet meadows are being replaced by competitive dominants such as *Typha × glauca*. Once established, *Typha × glauca*, like other dominants (Grime 1979) produces a dense canopy and thick deposits of litter. The causes of this change are unclear – hypotheses include changes in hydrology (more stable water levels), changes in fertility (higher nutrient levels), changes in herbivory (lower grazing intensity), changes in disturbance (fire suppression), and genetic changes (hybridization with *T. angustifolia*) (e.g. Newman *et al.* 1998; Boers *et al.* 2007; Wilcox *et al.* 2008). Note that almost every category of causal factors – hydrology, fertility, disturbance, herbivory, and competition – is implicated. It may well be that all these factors together are producing the change, causing a continent wide shift to one vegetation type.

While we will return to this issue in Chapter 9, the principle is clear. Increased fertility, or decreased natural disturbance, leads to higher biomass. Small plants are replaced by large canopy-forming species, and diverse communities are replaced by simpler ones. Overall, peripheral habitats slowly become more like core habitats, leading to an overall decrease in the diversity of wetland vegetation types (Figure 5.12). Small plants from orchids and carnivorous plants (Figure 3.4) to evergreen rosette

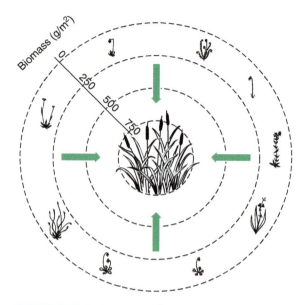

FIGURE 5.12 By increasing fertility and reducing natural disturbance, humans push wetlands from species-rich peripheral habitats to densely vegetated core habitats (dark arrows). In this figure, the core species is in the genus *Typha*. The peripheral species (from top, clockwise) are in the genera *Drosera*, *Utricularia*, *Rhexia*, *Sagittaria*, *Drosera*, *Parnassia*, *Eleocharis*, *Sabatia*, and *Pinguicula*. Many species in peripheral habitats are at increasing risk from human changes to the landscape.

species (Figure 1.17*d*) are increasingly at risk. Without careful management of wetlands, the future will belong to large clonal plants, and most wetlands will have core habitats with dense shade and large accumulations of litter.

5.9 Rare animals are found in peripheral habitats: the case history of the bog turtle

Thus far we have discussed plants, since they make it relatively easy to do large experiments, and because they provide the habitat for animals. We have moved from the basic principles of competition along gradients to the concept of peripheral habitats with many kinds of weak competitors.

It is a bit of a leap, but let us conclude with looking at how competition among plants can affect a vertebrate species. If there are animals that are restricted to peripheral habitats, then the invasion of these habitats by large leafy competitors may indeed illustrate how plant competition can affect animal

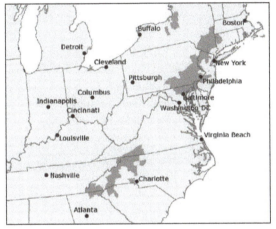

FIGURE 5.13 Animals may also depend upon peripheral habitats. The bog turtle (*Clemmys muhlenbergii*), North America's smallest turtle (9 cm, 115 g), occurs in wet meadows. (Photo courtesy R. G. Tucker, Jr., U.S. Fish and Wildlife Service; map, U.S. Fish and Wildlife Service.) (See also color plate.)

populations. Here is one possible example. Let me be clear that it is just one example. There are likely many more such species around the world. Our example will be the diminutive bog turtle, which most of you have probably never seen. Yet this turtle is being put at risk by plant competition. Here is the story.

The bog turtle is the smallest turtle in North America, with adults generally less than 10 cm long (Figure 5.13). It ranges from New York in the north to Georgia in the south, and has protected status in many states because its population is declining. Since it lays only a few eggs a year, populations can only grow slowly. This turtle lives in wet meadows and fens. Here is how the New York Natural Heritage Program (2008) describes its habitat:

In New York, bog turtles occur in open-canopy wet meadows, sedge meadows, and calcareous fens. The known habitat in the Lake Plain region of the state includes large fens that may include various species of sedges, such as slender sedge (*Carex lasiocarpa*), bog buckbean (*Menyanthes trifoliata*), mosses (*Sphagnum* spp.), pitcher plants (*Sarracenia* sp.), scattered trees, and scattered shrubs. In the Hudson River Valley, bog turtle habitats may be isolated from other wetlands or they may exist as part of larger wetland complexes. These wetlands are often fed by groundwater and the vegetation always includes various species of sedges. Other vegetation that is frequently found in southern New York bog turtle sites includes shrubby cinquefoil (*Potentilla fruticosa*), grass-of-parnassus (*Parnassia glauca*), mosses (*Sphagnum* spp.), horsetail (*Equisetum* sp.), scattered trees such as red maple (*Acer rubrum*), red cedar (*Juniperus virginianus*), and tamarack (*Larix laricina*), and scattered shrubs such as willows (*Salix* spp.), dogwood (*Cornus* spp.), and alder (*Alnus* spp.).

Another habitat description (McMillan 2006) says:

... bog turtles are most likely to occupy sunny meadows with soft, wet soils and low-growing vegetation ... For nesting, they seek the sunlight of an open canopy and hummocks, where *Carex stricta* or other sedge species and sphagnum moss offer slightly raised, drier habitat. These higher areas are critical because bog turtles nest within their core habitat, rather than travelling upland like most other turtle species .... Restored habitat must also include soggy soils. Here the turtles spend most of their time, half-buried in muck. The same near-steady water temperatures that cool turtles on hot days keep them warm on colder days ... And when it's time to hibernate in late September, a bog turtle moves to the base of a shrub or other sheltered area, where seeping groundwater ensures a constant temperature until it emerges into the warmth of May.

In 1997 the Endangered Species Act designated the bog turtle's status as "threatened." Although this turtle is also harmed by factors like the pet trade and by roadkill, a key problem is the loss of habitat. Wet meadows, as we have seen in Chapters 1–4, depend upon natural disturbances, such as water level fluctuations of large lakes. In the absence of disturbance, they become dominated by shrubs and trees. Note that the first habitat description even mentions *Parnassia glauca*, which is the wet meadow species in Figure 1.7*a*. As we have seen above, wet meadows are being invaded by large clonal plants such as *Phalaris arundincaea*, *Lythrum salicaria*, and *Phragmites australis*. Hence, the long-term survival of bog turtles means maintaining natural disturbance regimes, and possibly using fire or grazing to prevent dominance by competitively dominant plant species (McMillan 2006; Smith 2006).

Many other wet meadow species are likely to benefit from such management, including box turtles, spotted turtles, wood turtles, Baltimore checkerspot butterflies, bog buckmoths, sedge wrens, and several rare sedges and orchids (McMillan 2006).

CONCLUSION

Competition for resources is an important biological process in wetlands and can be measured only with experiments. It is known to be important for many kinds of plants, and controls their distribution in time and space. Its importance for animals is less well understood, although there are occasional cases where it seems to be very important, including certain salamanders and certain birds.

It may be that many kinds of animals are affected indirectly by competition among plants rather than directly by competition with other animals. There are two important examples. First, animals that are restricted to peripheral habitats are negatively affected when those habitats are turned into core habitats with dense vegetation and closed canopies. Second, animals that require wet meadows and marshes are negatively affected when these habitats become wooded. Although we have not looked in depth at competition from woody plants in this chapter, it is apparent from many of the examples in Chapters 2 and 4 that in the absence of recurring flooding or disturbance, many kinds of herbaceous wetlands will become forested wetlands, with consequent changes in the plants and animals.

Competition is often one-sided, or asymmetric, where competing species have different competitive abilities. Strong plant competitors with rapid rates of vegetative spread and dense canopies will tend to dominate in habitats with ideal conditions. Weak, subordinate species may survive by dispersing to or growing into patches unoccupied by the dominant species as a result of the disturbance processes described in Chapter 4. They also may be displaced to less desirable locations (peripheral habitats) where the dominant species is unable to establish. Such gradients in competition are the basis for the centrifugal model of plant community organization in which the central core habitat is occupied by large leafy competitive dominants. As one moves away from these conditions and resource limitations increasingly affect growth, biomass declines as does competition. Peripheral habitats at the gradient ends, where competition is lowest, typically support distinctive and rare plant and animal species and protection of these habitats is critical for maintaining species diversity.

The ultimate challenge of wetland management is to maintain examples of all the different types of wetlands that occur in nature, and to ensure that they retain their natural biological diversity. Hence, it is important to understand how fertility, disturbance, and competition interact to produce different kinds of wetland habitats. Some types of wetlands are easy to create – small impoundments with cattails and painted turtles and red-winged blackbirds. Other types of wetlands are hard to maintain and even harder to create. As a consequence, entire suites of species are disappearing from our landscape. Gopher frogs. Bog turtles. Wood storks. Snail kites. Although there are often other issues like hunting or road mortality, too often there is one single cause: insufficient habitat. The task of the wetland manager is to retain this diversity, and to re-create the habitats that these species need. In order to maintain the full range of wetland types, and their full diversity of species, we need to appreciate how competition organizes wetlands.

Chapter contents

6 Herbivory

Many kinds of animals eat plants, so it might be reasonable to expect animals to have a significant effect on wetlands. Yet when we visit wetlands, we find that many are green and covered in plants, which could mean that herbivores are relatively unimportant. So just what is the story?

In general, we will see that plants are actually rather well defended from animals. There are two particular ways by which this occurs. First, the plants may have chemical defenses that deter herbivores from eating the plant, or interfere with their ability to digest the plants. Further, many plants have such low nutrient levels in their tissues that they provide a very poor food source and are thereby avoided.

We shall also see that there is evidence that predators may keep the populations of herbivores from becoming large enough to remove the plants from wetlands. The absence of natural predators may, in fact, be what has caused those exceptional cases where herbivores have turned the marsh into mud flats.

Herbivory interacts with other factors. Some processes add biological material to wetlands, and other processes remove it. The former include photosynthesis, growth, and reproduction; the latter include fire, decomposition, and herbivory. Processes that remove biomass are generally considered to be disturbances (Chapter 4). Disturbances can be considered either abiotic (flooding, fire, ice scour, landslides) or biotic (herbivory, burrowing, trampling). In some ways these disturbances are similar; in other ways they are different. They are similar in that standing crop is temporarily reduced, and light penetration is increased; they are different in that herbivory has the potential to be far more selective than other disturbances.

6.1   Some herbivores have large impacts on wetlands

Overall, there are only a few known cases where animals remove most of the vegetation and turn the wetland into mud. We shall begin with these few obvious examples. In many other cases, the effects of animals are much less obvious. The animals are apparently removing certain kinds of plants preferentially, but not affecting the dominant ones.

6.1.1 Effects of muskrats on freshwater wetlands

Small mammals such as muskrats have long been studied because of their importance to the fur industry. Fritzell (1989) and Murkin (1989) have reviewed some aspects of muskrat grazing in prairie wetlands, while O'Neil (1949) and Lowery (1974) have described their impacts on coastal wetlands. Muskrats not only consume large amounts of fresh plant material, but the amount of cattail destroyed and not consumed may be two to three times that. Around their lodges, muskrats may remove 75% of the above-ground standing crop in areas 4–5 m in diameter. In his classic book on muskrats, O'Neil describes how "The marsh is denuded of all vegetation by a complete eat-out and the peaty floor is usually broken to a depth of as much as

20 inches" (p. 70). Small fenced areas called exclosures (Figure 6.1) illustrate how completely the plants can be removed by grazing animals.

By destroying patches of vegetation, muskrats can greatly influence the composition of wetlands. When muskrats destroy mature vegetation, the marsh plants can regenerate from buried seeds, or from buried fragments of rhizome. Cycles in muskrat populations are therefore somewhat like cycles of rainfall, in that both drive changes in plant composition (Figure 4.13). Together, they control the composition of many small wetlands.

Grazing can also interact with fire. Smith and Kadlec (1985a) found that grazing intensity was particularly high in burned areas, where it ranged from 48% for *Typha* to 9% for *Scirpus maritimus*. It may be that plants shoots that are newly emerging after a burn have higher nutrient levels in their tissues. Burning has been used historically to manage marshes for muskrat production (O'Neil 1949); however, it should not be used as a tool without clear objectives and awareness of the potential impacts on other wetland species. In coastal marshes, peat production may be necessary to adjust to rising sea levels. In other wetlands, such as the Everglades (recall Section 4.3.2), fires that

FIGURE 6.1 Sometimes grazing animals, such as nutria, can almost eliminate wetlands plants – as illustrated by this experimental fenced plot (exclosure) in a Louisiana marsh. (Courtesy Louisiana Department of Wildlife and Fisheries.) (See also color plate.)

burn peat can change the wetland from wet prairie or marsh to shallow water.

6.1.2 Effects of snow geese on boreal salt marshes

The effects of foraging by lesser snow geese on coastal wetlands have also been extensively studied (e.g. Jefferies 1988a; Bazely and Jefferies 1989; Belanger and Bedard 1994). There is growing evidence of serious impacts – of the approximately 55 000 ha of salt marsh along the coasts of Hudson Bay and James Bay, one-third is considered "destroyed" and another third "nearly devastated" with the geese now moving to feed on the remaining third (Abraham and Keddy 2005). The impacts of goose feeding can even be seen on satellite photographs (Figure 6.2) There are several reasons why goose populations have increased to this level, including increased food during migration, and reduced hunting pressure.

Exclosure experiments allow scientists to measure the severity of grazing. In one set of small experimental plots (Table 6.1) Jefferies (1988a) found that effects depend upon the type of feeding activity,

grazing on above-ground tissues only, or grubbing, which includes consuming rhizomes as well. Grazed plots were nearly identical to control plots; in contrast, grubbing for rhizomes significantly reduced the number of shoots of both graminoid and dicotyledonous species.

The geese can have an effect on long-term vegetation changes along the coast. Typically, low marsh consists of *Puccinellia–Carex* swards, which slowly change to *Calamagrostis–Festuca* swards as elevation increases from isostatic uplift. Geese can delay this process by heavy grazing, but when small exclosures (0.5 × 0.5 m) were built, the normal succession occurred and there was eventual dominance by *Calamagrostis deschampsoides* and *Festuca rubra* (Hik *et al.* 1992).

6.1.3 Effects of nutria on marshes

The nutria or coypu (*Myocastor coypus*) is a large (up to 10 kg) South American rodent that has been introduced to both North America and Europe. Typical of the problems in wetland terminology, this animal is called coypu in the European literature (Moss 1983, 1984) and nutria in the American

Table 6.1 **Effects of herbivory (grazing and grubbing) by geese on wetlands along the coast of Hudson Bay – small-scale details for Figure 6.2. The data give the total number of shoots of graminoid plants and dicotyledonous plants in plots on intertidal flats (plots were 10 × 10 cm, n = 10, SE in parentheses)**

	Graminoid plants		Dicotyledonous plants	
	June	August	June	August
Ungrubbed plots				
Grazed plots	45.5 (5.0)	45.0 (7.5)	4.0 (2.0)	4.8 (1.8)
Exclosed plots	45.5 (5.0)	45.8 (7.8)	4.0 (2.0)	4.1 (1.7)
Grubbed plots	7.0 (1.0)	15.0 (5.2)	2.2 (0.7)	1.0 (0.8)

Source: From Jefferies (1988a).

FIGURE 6.2 Geese are grazing coastal wetlands along the shore of Hudson Bay so intensely that some areas of marsh have been converted to mud flats, as shown in this July 18 satellite image of the Knife River delta in Manitoba, Canada. The mud flats are indicated by the bright strip of land. (U.S. Geological Survey 1996.) (See also color plate.)

(Atwood 1950; Lowery 1974). Whichever name you use, Lowery (1974, p. 29) describes them as "huge, ungainly, stupid looking rodents" that have a devastating impact upon native vegetation.

In England, nutria were introduced to fur farms about 1929. Of course, some escaped, and then multiplied to an estimated 200 000 animals by the 1960s. Moss (1984) observes that coypus "are extremely destructive grazers, uprooting reed and other swamp [marsh] plants to eat the rhizomes," and attributes the loss of fringing reed marshes to herbivory by *M. coypus*.

In North America, fur farmers similarly introduced nutria in the 1930s. Again they escaped, and by the 1950s there were an estimated 20 million of these rodents "chewing away at the foundations of our wetlands" (Lowery 1974, p. 30). At the same time the number of muskrats declined.

Table 6.2 **The effects of grazing by *Myocastor coypus* on deltaic wetlands as illustrated by four 40 × 50 m exclosures and paired control areas**

Species	I Exclosure	I Control	II Exclosure	II Control	III Exclosure	III Control	IV Exclosure	IV Control
Amaranthus tamariscina	–	–	–	–	16	–	–	–
Alternanthera philoxeroides	12	–	–	–	14	–	6	–
Justicia ovata	27	19	31	11	62	40	24	35
Leersia oryzoides	2	–	3	–	51	7	87	27
Paspalum distichum	–	–	–	–	3	3	5	–
Polygonum punctatum	14	1	2	–	52	1	33	12
Sagittaria latifolia	95	1	128	–	82	59	73	22
Sagittaria platyphylla	18	1	11	–	18	4	52	5
Scirpus americanus	–	–	–	–	4	1	9	–
Scirpus validus	1	–	–	–	5	–	6	2
Spartina alterniflora	–	–	–	–	1	–	6	–
Typha domingensis	9	–	–	–	–	–	–	–
Total cover	178	22	175	11	308	115	301	103
Total species	8	4	5	1	11	7	10	6

Note: Numbers are cover value sums for 30 plots.
Source: Shaffer *et al.* (1992).

Fenced exclosure experiments have been used to study the impacts of nutria – Figure 6.1 shows the impacts of nutria. But what are the details? Table 6.2 shows that, relative to controls, exclosure plots had much higher cover and more plant species. Plants that were preferred food of *M. coypus* (e.g. *Sagittaria platyphylla*, *S. latifolia*) dominated exclosures, while species presumably less preferred (*Justicia ovata*, *Leersia oryzoides*) dominated the control sites.

Grazing can also change the distribution of species. Although *S. latifolia* is a relatively flood-tolerant species, it was restricted to higher elevations, which Shaffer *et al.* (1992) attribute to the grazing by *M. coypus* at lower elevations. Shipley *et al.* (1991b) similarly found that damage (in this case from muskrats) to emergents such as *Acorus calamus* was much greater at lower elevations in riverine marshes. More recent work in Louisiana by Taylor and Grace (1995), using smaller exclosures, showed that the biomass of dominant plant species

such as *Panicum virgatum*, *Spartina patens*, and *S. alterniflora* increased if *M. coypus* was excluded, but they were unable to detect changes in the number of species.

The secondary effects of herbivory may be even more dramatic. We have seen three examples now of herbivores that not only eat foliage, but actually dig up and destroy rhizomes. Plants can replace damaged leaves from below ground, but once the rhizomes are destroyed, the plant dies. Moreover, the positive effects of the rhizomes on stabilizing the wetland soil are lost. Once the plants are damaged or gone, the productivity declines, and so there is less accumulation of peat. Hence, grazing animals can actually change the rate at which wetlands respond to sedimentation and changes in sea level. Even partial defoliation can be harmful, since shoots transport oxygen to rhizomes (Section 1.4). Hence, grazing can increase the sensitivity of plants to other environmental factors, particularly flooding.

6.2   Wildlife diets document which animals eat which plants

It has long been observed by naturalists that animals feed on wetland plants. Most of us will have seen one or more examples: a beaver lodge made of willow trees, a muskrat house made of *Typha* and *Sparganium*, a moose munching on water lilies at sunset, or a duck feeding on *Potamogeton*. Wildlife biologists have investigated this in two principal ways: they have observed feeding by wild animals, and they have studied feces to reconstruct diets. They have then tabulated the biological utilization of wetland plants for the use of managers.

To illustrate, Table 6.3 shows the kinds of plants consumed by snapping turtles (like the one on the cover), while Table 6.4 shows plants consumed by waterbirds. Let us consider four other examples in more depth.

Table 6.3 The contents of the stomachs of 22 snapping turtles

Food item	Number of stomachs	Percent of samples
Plants		
Potamogeton sp.	15	68.2
Algae	8	36.4
Polygonum sp.	6	27.3
Lemna sp.	4	18.2
Other	9	40.9
Fish		
Carp (*Cyprinus carpio*)	16	72.8
Pike (*Esox lucius*)	6	27.3
Bass (*Micropterus* sp.)	4	18.2
Perch (*Perca flavescens*)	4	18.2
Mollusks		
Snail (*Physa, Planorbula, Gyraulus*)	21	95.4
Other	4	18.2
Insects	11	50.0
Birds	5	22.7
Turtles	1	4.5

Source: From Hammer (1969).

Table 6.4 Plant species identified in the gizzards of 1102 birds of 15 species of waterfowl in 58 locations in the eastern United States and Canada (abundance was measured by volumetric percentage)

Scientific name	Common name	Abundance
Potamogeton spp.	pondweeds	13.29
Polygonum spp.	smartweeds	6.69
Zizania aquatica	wild rice	5.10
Scirpus spp.	bulrushes	4.90
Najas flexilis	northern naiad	4.32
Lemna, Spirodela, etc.	duckweeds	2.97
Vallisneria spiralis	wild celery	2.49
Leersia, chiefly *L. oryzoides*	cutgrass	2.02
Setaria spp.	bristlegrasses	1.62
Echinochloa, chiefly *E. crusgalli*	wild millet	1.59
Sparganium spp.	bur-reeds	1.33
Carex spp.	sedges	1.21
Sagittaria spp.	arrowheads	1.00
Brasenia schreberi	watershield	0.95
Nymphaea spp.	water lilies	0.77
Ceratophyllum demersum	coontail	0.77
Bidens spp.	beggar's ticks	0.65
Cyperus spp.	sedges	0.57
Pontederia cordata	pickerel weed	0.48
Zea mays	corn	2.30
Fagopyrum esculentum	buckwheat	1.40
Sorghum vulgare	sorghum	0.51
Algae (microscopic)	algae	0.87
Characeae	algae	1.87
Miscellaneous		14.69
Total		74.36
Invertebrates		25.64

Source: Adapted from Crowder and Bristow (1988).

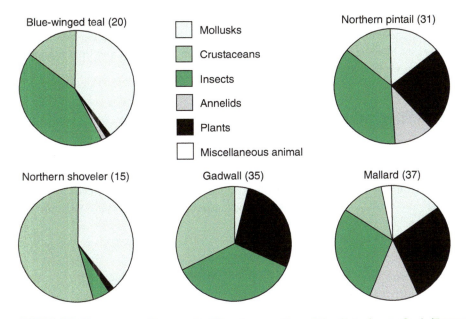

FIGURE 6.3 Plants can make up a significant proportion of the diet of waterfowl. (From van der Valk and Davis 1978.)

Waterbirds consume both plants and invertebrates. Egg-laying females and young tend to emphasize invertebrates in their diets, presumably because of the higher food quality of animal protein. Even so, Figure 6.3 shows that some species such as the northern pintail and gadwall consume plants directly as one-fourth of their diet, while Table 6.4 shows the importance of plants in waterbird diets as a whole. Most such studies focus on the food quality of plants for waterfowl, however. Whether the waterbirds, in turn, affect the plants is much less explored.

Many fish are also dependent upon wetland plants. A striking example is the fish that feed upon fruits and seeds in floodplain forests (Goulding 1980). The Amazon basin has some of the largest areas of flooded forest in the world – some 70 000 km². Some trees are flooded to depths of 15 meters and for up to 10 months of the year. Plant germination and growth appear to be restricted to the few months when the floodplain is drained. Up to 3000 species of fish may inhabit this region. Of the more than 1300 described

to date, about 80% are either catfishes or characins (Figures 2.5d, 9.1). The latter group has radiated extensively in the Amazon lowlands, and includes carnivores, frugivores, detritivores, and planktivores. Goulding closes by suggesting that this is very important for human welfare too – some 75% of the commercial catch may originate in flooded forests.

Perhaps the most remarkable conclusion, however, is that most animals eat not the plants themselves, but rather feed on other animals that feed on decaying plants. Study after study over the past 50 years has demonstrated the same startling result: a vast majority of plant biomass goes directly into the decomposer food web, where it is processed by small invertebrates and microorganisms. This generalization ranges from arid tropical grasslands (Desmukh 1986) to temperate salt marshes (Adam 1990), although aquatic algae are an apparent exception (Cyr and Pace 1993). Further, fire often removes a substantial portion of biomass not consumed by decomposers; in tall grass areas like the Serengeti plains, more than half of the plant biomass is burned (Desmukh 1986). Therefore, while it is easy for us to observe plants that have been grazed by animals, we should remember that scenes like Figures 6.1 and 6.2 are rare – overall, grazing animals process less than 10% of the biomass in the vegetation. The rest decays and then supports a decay-based food web.

6.3　Impacts of some other herbivores on wetlands

Having dealt with some of the most extreme examples in Section 6.1, let us now move on to explore some of the more typical examples of herbivory that occur in wetlands.

6.3.1　Snails in salt marshes

The periwinkle snail (*Littoraria irrorata*) often feeds on salt marsh cordgrass (*Spartina alterniflora*). Snail densities can reach hundreds per square meter. To measure effects of snail grazing, Silliman and Zieman (2001) constructed 1-m^2 cages in a Virginia salt marsh, and created three levels of snail density: zero, ambient, and three times ambient. They also manipulated fertility by adding nitrogen as ammonium chloride. Figure 6.4 shows that as snail density increased from left to right, the production of cordgrass fells from 274 to 97 g/m^2. When nitrogen was added, the snail removal had an ever greater effect, cordgrass growth falling from 1490 to 281 g/m^2. The reduction in growth was not just the result of tissue being consumed by the snails. It appears that the rasping by the snail radulae causes and maintains wounds, leading to the death of stems and leaves, and thereby suppressing plant growth. Hence, the effect of snails is not only grazing, but defoliation and diversion of plant tissue to the detritus food web. Silliman and Zieman suggest that this effect of snails be called "top down control."

What controls the abundance of snails in natural marshes? Snails are eaten by predators including crabs and turtles – a topic to which we return in Section 6.6.2. Snails are also thought to have important impacts on freshwater wetlands, and their impacts on aquatic plants may in turn be controlled by fish that eat snails (Brönmark 1985, 1990; Carpenter and Lodge 1986; Sheldon 1987, 1990).

6.3.2　Large mammals in African grasslands

Large herbivores like the hippopotamus affect wetlands by grazing, and by excavating depressions

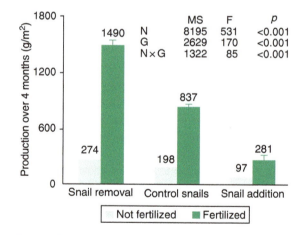

FIGURE 6.4 Snail grazing has significant impacts on salt marsh cordgrass (*Spartina alterniflora*). Note that the middle histogram was the control containing the naturally occurring snail populations. When fertilizer was added (dark histograms), plant production increased, but the negative effects of grazing remained. Both main effects and the interaction term are significant, $p < 0.001$. (After Silliman and Zieman 2001.)

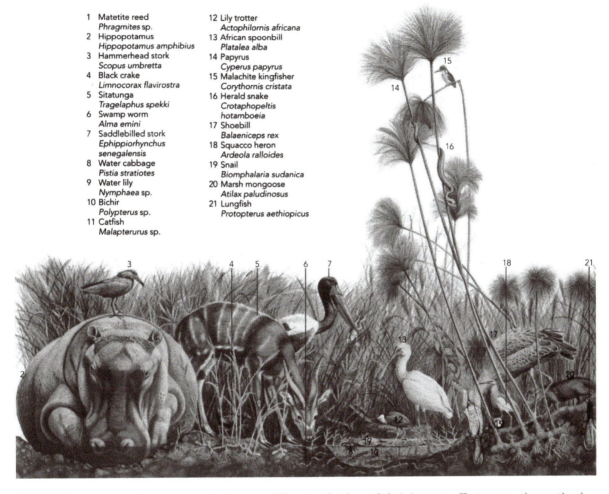

1 Matetite reed
   Phragmites sp.
2 Hippopotamus
   Hippopotamus amphibius
3 Hammerhead stork
   Scopus umbretta
4 Black crake
   Limnocorax flavirostra
5 Sitatunga
   Tragelaphus spekki
6 Swamp worm
   Alma emini
7 Saddlebilled stork
   Ephippiorhynchus senegalensis
8 Water cabbage
   Pistia stratiotes
9 Water lily
   Nymphaea sp.
10 Bichir
   Polypterus sp.
11 Catfish
   Malapterurus sp.

12 Lily trotter
   Actophilornis africana
13 African spoonbill
   Platalea alba
14 Papyrus
   Cyperus papyrus
15 Malachite kingfisher
   Corythornis cristata
16 Herald snake
   Crotaphopeltis hotamboeia
17 Shoebill
   Balaeniceps rex
18 Squacco heron
   Ardeola ralloides
19 Snail
   Biomphalaria sudanica
20 Marsh mongoose
   Atilax paludinosus
21 Lungfish
   Protopterus aethiopicus

FIGURE 6.5 Large herbivores remain important in African wetlands, and their impacts affect many other wetland species. (From Dugan 2005.) (See also color plate.)

(Figure 6.5). There are, however, many other herbivores that use wetlands only seasonally. It is easy for us to focus on only those herbivores that are permanent residents of wetlands. To keep a broader perspective, let us consider the temporary use of wetlands by large African mammals (Western 1975; Sinclair and Fryxell 1985). Recall (Chapter 1) that many of the large ungulates on the African plains graze in wetlands during the dry season, and then use the surrounding grasslands in the wet season.

As consequence, each vegetation type receives a period free from herbivory, and as well, by using the combined productivity of this range of habitats, many more animals can be supported (Sinclair and Fryxell 1985). The ungulate populations in Africa are large and diverse; for example, Sinclair (1983) points out that one family, the Bovidae (in the order Artiodactyla), containing the buffalo and antelope, has as many species (78) as the most diverse rodent family, the Muridae. Some of these bovids are adapted to wetlands, such as the kob and lechwe. Ungulates, as a whole, have four main habitats: forest, savanna, desert, and wetland (Sinclair 1983); and the wetlands range from forested swamp to *Papyrus* marshes to seasonally flooded wetlands (Thompson and Hamilton 1983; Howard-Williams and Thompson 1985; Denny 1993a, b). Most large mammals use these wetlands at some time of year (Table 6.5), and distance from water is a good predictor of biomass of herbivores (Figure 6.6), but the shortage of water has placed constant selective pressure upon herbivores. There have been two main evolutionary responses. Independence from water requires a shift from herbivory on grasses to browsing upon shrubs; browsers are less dependent upon water and wetlands. Further, reproduction is timed to coincide with the rainy season when the habitat is as productive as possible; this is found in species such the elephant, white rhinoceros, zebra, hippopotamus, warthog, buffalo, giraffe, and kudu. The importance of seasonal surges in production is illustrated by an exception to the above rule (Sinclair 1983). "Lechwe live on riverine floodplains that are seasonally flooded . . . Optimum food conditions occur when water is at the lowest level exposing the greatest area of floodplain, and it is then that the peak of births occur." Such studies should remind us that many animals that are not normally considered "wetland" animals may benefit from the wetlands in a landscape.

6.3.3 Slugs and sheep in peatlands

In contrast to the African plains, the peatlands of the British Isles have vast herds of slugs and sheep. Overall, there are more than 1 million ha of moorland in Britain (Miller and Watson 1983). The principal habitat gradients are soil moisture, soil nutrient supply, and sheep grazing intensity. These areas have been extensively modified by humans. The original oak forests were cleared during Roman and medieval times, and eventually replaced by scrub and grassland following the use of the mountains for grazing. The density of the main vertebrate herbivores is estimated as 50 sheep, 65 red grouse, 10 red deer, and 16 mountain hare per km^2 in the highlands of Scotland. Even so, less than 10% of the primary production of *Calluna vulgaris* (heather) is actually consumed by herbivores (Miller and Watson 1983).

Consider the example of moorland in Snowdonia, northern Wales. Here there is a mosaic of vegetation types including grassland, *Eriophorum* mire, and heath (Perkins 1978). Slug species such as *Agriolimax reticulatus* and *Arion intermedius* can reach densities exceeding 10/m^2. They consume approximately 1 g/m^2 per month (Lutman 1978). Sheep are the dominant vertebrate herbivore, with densities from 5 to 19 animals per hectare (Brasher and Perkins 1978). The sheep show a preference for grassland areas (*Agrostis–Festuca* swards) and reject sedges, rushes, and herbs, many of which are typical of wetter sites. Red grouse are often studied because of their hunting value. They feed primarily upon *C. vulgaris* shoots, but eat only a negligible proportion of the primary production on their territories (Miller and Watson 1978). The principal effects of grouse arise from the human practice of burning moorlands to improve the habitat for grouse hunting. This changes plant species composition, stimulating the growth of *Calluna* in particular, and may have deleterious effects upon the development of wet blanket bog (Rawes and Heal 1978). Further, the burning leads to volatilization of nitrogen and leaching of potassium from the remaining ash (Miller and Watson 1983).

An exclosure experiment in the Pennines, northern England, showed that after 7 years of excluding sheep, biomass increased by 50%, and the number of plant species declined from 93 to 67 (Rawes and Heal 1978). These patterns typified drier areas; grazing on the blanket bog itself is so low that the sheep appear to have "little noticeable effect." Comparison with a bog that was grazed continually for many years suggests that grazing reduces the shrub *C. vulgaris* and increases *Eriophorum vaginatum*.

Table 6.5 Seasonal habitat changes in the large herbivores of the Rukwa Valley, Tanzania; habitats used for the greatest duration are italicized

Animal species	Time of year											
	Jan	Feb	Mar	April	May	June	July	Aug	Sept	Oct	Nov	Dec
Elephant		Acacia and escarpment woodlands					*Floodplain*					Woodlands
Buffalo	Woodlands – *Lakeshore and delta grasslands*						*Floodplain*					Woodlands
Hippopotamus	*Fringe river and delta grasslands*				Wander widely along drainage						*River fringe*	
Puku				Delta and lakeshore grassland all year								
Topi	Perimeter grassland		*Lakeshore and delta grassland*				Vossia *pasture*			Acacia woodland		
Zebra	Acacia woodland		Perimeter grassland	Acacia parkland						Acacia woodland		
Bohor Reedbuck				*Floodplain grassland*			*Floodplain grassland*					
Eland	Dry perimeter plains				*Delta grasslands and* Vossia *pasture*					Acacia woodland		
Giraffe and Impala					Acacia grassland							
Warthog				Acacia grassland and forest edge		Woodlands						
Waterbuck, Duiker, Baushbuck, and Steinbuck												

Source: After Vesey-FitzGerald (1960).

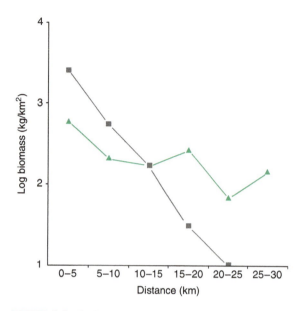

FIGURE 6.6 The biomass of herbivores varies with distance from water during the dry season in Kenya. Water-independent browsers (triangles) are less affected than water-dependent grazers (squares). (From Western 1975, in Sinclair 1983.)

6.3.4 Rhinoceros in tropical floodplains

Although large herbivores like rhinoceros are becoming rare, their potential impacts upon vegetation need to be considered, if only because their effects will be lost if the species becomes extinct. We may think of rhinoceros as representing some of the large numbers of enormous animals that once occurred in our landscapes, but which were killed off by aboriginal hunters (Section 6.4.4).

Asian lowland forests contain several large herbivores including the Asiatic elephant, greater one-horned rhinoceros, and Javan rhinoceros. Tree diversity is relatively low, but large browser biomass is almost as high as the highest values reported from Africa (Dinerstein 1992). More than 300 of the greater one-horned rhinoceros (*Rhinoceros unicornis*) occur in Royal Chitwan National Park in Nepal. Two tree species are dominant, *Litsea monopetala* (Lauraceae) and *Mallotus philippinensis*

(Euphorbiaceae). All of the understory *Litsea* showed signs of moderate to heavy browsing and trampling by rhinoceros. Exclosure experiments showed that *Litsea* growth was enhanced when it was free from browsing for 3 years.

Rhinoceros also distribute the seeds of floodplain trees such as *Trewia nudiflora*, which produces a hard green fruit. Dung piles in floodplain grasslands appear to be important colonization sites. Thirty-seven other plant species have been recorded from rhinoceros latrines and the flora as a whole includes 77 fleshy-fruited species that are dispersed by vertebrates (Dinerstein 1991). At the time of these studies, the rhinoceros population was recovering from heavy poaching, so natural population levels would be expected to have greater impact.

6.3.5 Effects of cattle on the flooding Pampa

Unlike African grasslands, Pampean grasslands in South America developed under low intensities of natural herbivores (Facelli *et al.* 1989). Cattle and horses were introduced by the Spanish settlers in the 1500s, and in the mid-1800s, fences were built, so that herbivory was further intensified. As agriculture replaced ranching, natural grasslands were ploughed, except for areas subjected to regular flooding, the flooding Pampa. Such trends are similar to those found in the Pantanal (see conclusion, Chapter 1) and the North American prairies. The Pampas of Argentina cover some 750 000 km²; the main wetland area is in the Salado basin, a flat area approximately 60 000 km² with mild winters and warm summers. Facelli *et al.* (1989) compared a 1-ha plot that had been grazed steadily at a stocking rate of roughly one head per 2 ha with a 1-ha plot from which cattle had been excluded for 9 years. Grazing had major effects on species composition. The ungrazed site had cover that was 95% monocotyledons, particularly large tussock grasses; *Paspalum dilatatum* and *Stipa bavioensis* dominated. The tall grasses form a dense canopy which probably shades out shorter species.

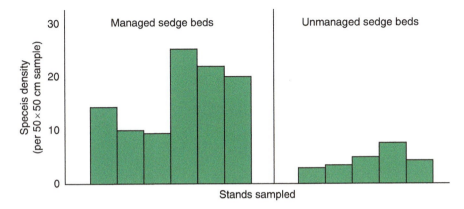

FIGURE 6.7 Mowing by humans can change the number of plant species (as measured by species density) in English sedge beds. (After Wheeler and Giller 1982.)

In contrast, the grazed community was almost 60% dicotyledonous species, many of which were exotic, such as *Mentha pullegium*.

6.3.6 Humans as herbivores: mowing

Humans sometimes harvest wetland vegetation to feed livestock, to gather thatching for roofs, or even to construct boats. Although such activities are often considered quaint by urban scientists, they are considered important in Europe, for example, because mowing and the product – thatched roofs – are needed to maintain traditional landscapes. Mowing as traditionally practiced often increases the number of plant species found in wetlands. Managed sedge beds (composed largely of *Cladium mariscus*) had lower biomass, less litter, and more species than unmanaged beds (Figure 6.7). As well, bryophytes were largely restricted to managed beds. The effects of mowing on reed beds (composed largely of *Phragmites communis*) were much less noticeable. Mowing and grazing are not necessarily equivalent – in European salt marshes, grazed areas had more more species than mowed areas (Figure 6.8).

When traditional mowing ceases, changes occur. In wet meadows along the Oste valley in northwestern Germany, the cessation of mowing allowed valued marsh marigold meadows (e.g. *Caltha*

palustris, Senecio aquaticus) to develop into stands of reeds and tall forbs (e.g. *Glyceria maxima, Phalaris arundinacea, Urtica dioica*). These latter species produce dense shade and thick accumulations of litter, which reduce diversity in plant communities. Overall, the number of plant species declined from ca. 30 species to ca. 10 species (Müller *et al.* 1992). Mowing twice a year restored typical plant diversity within 3–5 years. The wet grasslands scattered along slow-flowing rivers in Belgium also have a history of mowing (Dumortier *et al.* 1996). Mowing effects were measured in an experiment that varied the timing (one of 6 months, June to November) and number of harvests (one or two harvests, July and October). Overall 63 plant species were recorded. Harvesting once or twice increased the number of plant species, while the number declined with time in the unmowed control plots. Different mowing times likely select for different species composition. The most important plant traits for predicting responses to mowing appear to be germination characteristics and the degree of rhizome production. Rhizomatous species are most damaged by midsummer harvesting, since summer is when their shoots would normally translocate energy back to roots and rhizomes; consequently, rhizomatous plants are favored by late fall harvesting.

Although many other landscapes such as North American wet meadows do not have a long tradition

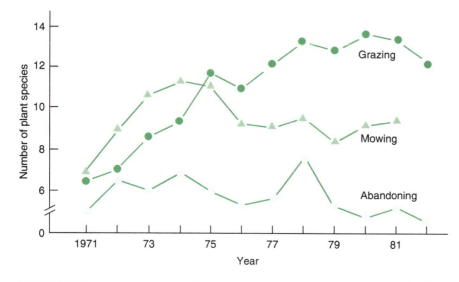

FIGURE 6.8 Species richness plotted against time in European salt marshes with three contrasting types of management ($n = 5$, 2×2 m^2 quadrats). (After Bakker 1985.)

of mowing, the increasing dominance of wetlands by large clonal plants such as *Phragmites australis* and *Phalaris arundinacea* is becoming more of a management problem (Keddy 1990a; Kercher *et al.* 2004; Zedler and Kercher 2004). (Of course, historians will remind us that removing "marsh hay" from wetlands was a time-honored tradition in early European settlement of North America.) On one hand, we could argue that there are some valuable lessons to be learned from wetland management in Europe, and a remarkable lack of respect of the literature on this topic is found in many North American articles.

On the other hand, before we start using mowing elsewhere, it is essential to appreciate that many of the wetlands in western Europe have been produced by, or at least shaped by, mowing or grazing, for hundreds if not thousands of years. Their problems arise when traditional gazing and mowing regimes cease. Other vegetation types, however, may not have a history of mowing or herbivory, particularly the infertile peatlands and alluvial wetlands in less populated regions of the Earth. The floras in such regions may be stress tolerators (*sensu* Grime 1977, 1979) and mowing or herbivory could have negative effects upon them.

6.4   Plants have defenses to protect them against herbivores

In order to protect themselves against the impacts of herbivores, plants have evolved many different tactics for defense. In this section we will cover some of the common strategies employed by wetland plants.

6.4.1   Morphological defenses

Spines, thorns, and prickles deter herbivores (e.g. Crawley 1983; Marquis 1991; Raven *et al.* 1992).

If many such plants were present in wetlands, it would be relatively convincing evidence that herbivores are important in wetlands. Yet, in spite of the many plants that bear large spines, few occur in wetlands. Figure 6.9 shows a few selected examples of devices thought to protect wetland plants from herbivores.

Where anti-herbivore traits are present, evidence suggests that herbivory is less important under water than above it. *Pontederia cordata*, which is shown on

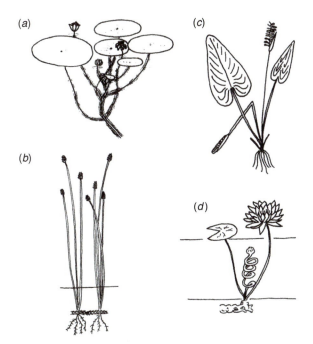

FIGURE 6.9 Some traits that confer resistance to herbivory: (*a*) gelatinous coating on stems and foliage (*Brasenia schreberi*; from Hellquist and Crow 1984), (*b*) buried rhizomes (*Eleocharis palustris*), (*c*) peduncle that bends to submerge fruits (*Pontederia cordata*), (*d*) peduncle that coils to pull fruits into the water (*Nymphaea odorata*).

the cover of this book, has showy flower stalks, but once the flowers are pollinated, the stem bends to hide the stalk under the water (Figure 6.9*c*). Similarly, *Nymphaea odorata* has conspicuous flowers on the surface of many northern lakes and slow-moving rivers, but once the flowers are pollinated, the peduncles coil like a spring, pulling the fruits down to the bottom of the lake (Figure 6.9*d*).

6.4.2 Chemical defenses

Chemical traits are less visible than morphological ones, but may be equally important in deterring herbivory. While some plant compounds have obvious roles to play in photosynthesis, growth, and reproduction, others do not. These latter **secondary**

metabolites were once thought to be just waste products. It has now become clear that many of these compounds play active and important roles in defending plants against herbivores (Marquis 1991). There are three main groups of anti-herbivore compounds: terpenes, phenolics, and nitrogen-containing secondary products (e.g. Taiz and Zeiger 1991). There is only limited information on anti-herbivore defense compounds in wetland plants in standard references such as Rosenthal and Berenbaum (1991). This could be a consequence of either one of two causes: the actual rarity of defense compounds in wetlands (a phenomenon of real ecological interest) or the lack of study of wetland plants by chemists (a phenomenon of interest only to those who study the behavior and sociology of scientists). There are passing references to glucosinolates (Louda and Mole 1991), coumarins (Berenbaum 1991), and possibly iridoid glycosides (Bowers 1991) in protecting wetland plants from herbivorous invertebrates. Coumarins have been found in more than 70 plant families, and these include important wetland families such as the Cupressaceae, Araceae, Cyperaceae, Poaceae, and Juncaceae (Berenbaum 1991).

In contrast with these sources, McClure (1970) documents a prominent role for secondary metabolites in aquatic plants. Going from wet to dry, he found that flavonoids are predominant in free-floating species, phenols and flavonoids are found in submerged and emergent taxa, and alkaloids predominate among rooted floating-leaved species (e.g. the Nymphaeaceae). In contrast, terpenoids are apparently more common in plants of waterlogged soils and seasonally flooded areas (e.g. Cyperaceae, Poaceae, Acanthaceae). Ostrofsky and Zettler (1986) examined 15 species of aquatic plants including *Cabomba caroliniana*, *Vallisneria americana*, and nine species of *Potamogeton* to assay for alkaloids, finding between 0.13 and 0.56 mg/g dry weight, values that are "low, but certainly within a range which is pharmacologically active, and consistent with a potential role as herbivore deterrents." The actual kind of alkaloid varied greatly among

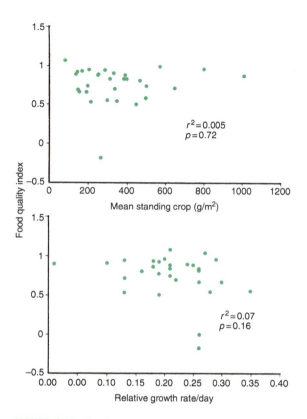

FIGURE 6.10 The food quality of 30 kinds of wetland plants is correlated neither with the biomass of the habitat (top) nor with the relative growth rate of the species (bottom). (After McCanny *et al.* 1990.)

to reduce impacts of herbivores, and whether the production of defense compounds varies among habitats. McCanny *et al.* (1990) evaluated the anti-herbivore defenses in 42 wetland plant species, and then tested whether anti-herbivore defenses were increased in infertile habitats where the costs of grazing to plants should be greater (Coley 1983). First they extracted secondary metabolites from the test plants, and added them into the diet of an insect herbivore. The larvae showed reductions in growth of up to 50%, thereby showing some evidence of anti-herbivore compounds. There was no difference in toxicity of forbs and graminoids. The food quality index (as measured by the performance of the insect herbivore) was then plotted against the fertility of the habitat typical of each plant species. There was no relationship between the food quality index and soil fertility, plant biomass (Figure 6.10, top), or plant relative growth rates (Figure 6.10, bottom).

In conclusion, while there is some evidence that morphological traits or secondary plant metabolites play a role in defense against herbivores, the evidence is far from conclusive. The study of effects of grazing upon existing communities requires evidence outside the comparative realm.

species, with the *Potamogeton* species being no more similar to each other than to other genera. Gopal and Goel (1993) list other examples such as fatty acids, allomones, mustard oils, and steroids, but in general the role of such secondary metabolites is still poorly documented and even more poorly understood. The compounds may provide defense against herbivores, but there may be other functions such as antimicrobial activity and allelopathic interactions with competing neighbors including planktonic algae.

Simply screening for the presence of possible defense compounds in wetland plants, while helpful, still leaves important unanswered questions. We need to know whether these compounds are actually able

6.4.3 Nitrogen content is the key to understanding food quality

Nitrogen is thought to be the most important factor determining food value of plants (Lodge 1991; White 1993). We have also already seen that nitrogen content of aquatic plants is frequently well below 5% (Table 3.1), and Lodge (1991) shows that emergent, floating, and submersed macrophytes, as well as algae, all have similar nitrogen contents, usually of 2% to 3% (with extremes from 1% to at least 5%). These are very low values for supporting grazing animals. Hence, it may be that the strongest defense wetland plants have against herbivores is the low quality of the food they provide.

To illustrate the importance of nitrogen content to herbivores tissues, White (1993) describes attempts to control *Salvinia molesta*, an aquatic fern from Brazil which has become a serious weed in many tropical regions. Initial attempts to import and establish insects from Brazil to control it in Australia and Papua New Guinea had variable success; at concentrations of nitrogen of 1% or less dry weight, the imported pyralid moth could not establish. "However, increasing the level of nitrogen in the fern to only 1.3% dry weight by simply adding urea fertilizer to the water can cause an to explosive increase in the abundance of the moth and severe damage to the plants" (p. 77). The species of weevil introduced from Brazil to Australia to combat *Salvinia* was also limited by nitrogen availability. In contrast, when Lodge (1991) studied herbivory preferences of the crayfish *Orconectes rusticus* among 14 submersed macrophytes, he found clear preferences for certain species, but he was unable to detect statistically significant differences in nitrogen content among the plants.

Simple comparisons of plant tissue may conceal real differences in nitrogen content if herbivores are consuming only selected tissues. In general, herbivores show a preference for reproductive structures, particularly seeds, and newly growing shoots. We have already noted above that muskrats are attracted to feed on new shoots in burned areas. Sinclair (1983) and White (1993) have described many examples of herbivores preferentially selecting new growth. Beavers not only favor certain species, as we shall see below, but they consume mainly the young bark and cambium, which has much higher nutrient content than the actual wood. White adds the example of green turtles (*Chelonia mydas*), marine herbivores that feed on the aquatic vascular plant called seagrass (*Thalassia testudinum*). These turtles maintain areas of cropped seagrass and feed upon the flush growth in the cropped area, ignoring adjacent stands of tall seagrass. Beavers can be seen doing the same – once some larger trees have been felled, the new saplings that regenerate can provide a steady source of younger and more edible trees.

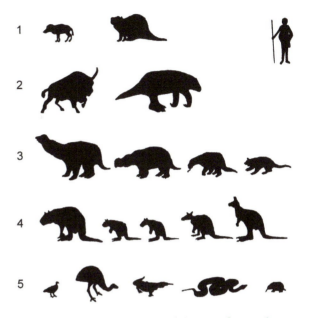

FIGURE 6.11 Some examples of the megafaunas that became extinct at the time humans arrived in North America (top) and Australia (bottom). North America: 1, *Platygonus, Castoroides*; 2, *Bison latifrons, Nothrotheriops*. Australia: 3, *Diprotodon optatum, Zygomaturus trilobus, Euowenia grata, Thylacoleo carnifex*; 4, *Procoptodon goliah, Sthenurus maddocki, Sthenurus atlas, Protemnodon brehus, Macropus ferragus*; 5, *Progura gallinacea, Genyornis newtoni, Megalania prisca, Wonambi naracoortensis, Zaglossus ramsayi*. A human is shown for scale. (Adapted from Martin and Klein 1984.)

6.4.4 Herbivores of the past: missing pieces

There is a further complication. As we try to put the puzzle of herbivory together, we find there are important missing pieces. The presence of anti-herbivore defenses tells us that herbivores affected evolution, but it in no way demonstrates the active occurrence of herbivory in present-day communities. This point is by no means trivial or pedantic. We know that, in relatively recent times, only about 10 000 years BP, both North America and Australia lost entire megafaunas (Figure 6.11). It has been argued that many plants possess adaptations to dispersal by large mammals that are now extinct

(Janzen and Martin 1982). It seems equally plausible that plants could have adaptations to protect themselves from herbivores that no longer play a role in determining wetland community structure. Further into the past, in the late Mesozoic, we also find herbivorous dinosaurs, and some of these are thought to have been semi-aquatic. The effects of herbivory on wetlands may thus extend back hundreds of millions of years.

Take, for example, the giant beaver (Kurtén and Anderson 1980; Parmalee and Graham 2002). This species reminds us that near the end of the last ice age, North American wetlands had beavers the size of black bears felling trees, while herds of millions of bison, horses, and camels waded through wetlands. Only Africa remains (Figure 6.5) to illustrate how many other parts of the world might have been. Elsewhere, near the end of the last ice age, a majority of these animals became extinct. The precise cause is still argued, but it is most likely the result of over-hunting by newly arrived predators – human beings.

Bones of *Castoroides ohioensis* have been found from Florida to Alaska, although the largest concentrations are south of the Great Lakes, hence the name. The giant beaver could have weighed 200 kg (compared to 30 kg for a modern beaver). Their teeth were up to 15 cm long. Experts disagree whether the giant beaver felled trees; some authorities suggest that the animal likely fed more like a modern muskrat. However, one Ohio fossil site appeared to have a lodge constructed from saplings about 7.5 cm in diameter. And a relatively well-preserved beaver pond, locked in permafrost on Ellesmere Island in the Canadian Arctic, has gnawed sticks. Perhaps the early painting of the animal (Figure 6.12) was correct after all.

The great beaver is here to make a point. Reading a book like the *Pleistocene Mammals of North America* (Kurtén and Anderson 1980) one is struck by the recurrence of two themes: wetland habitats and extinct species. An entirely haphazard selection of important fossil sites include former "shallow vegetation-choked water" in Texas (p. 35), "ponds or stream channels" in California (p. 53), and "pond

FIGURE 6.12 Giant beavers (*Castoroides ohioensis*), up to 2.5 m long and weighing 60–100 kg, were once widespread in North America, but became extinct after the last ice age. Note the black bear for scale. (Painting by O. M. Highley, from Tinkle 1939.)

and marsh habitat" in Florida (p. 57). Of course, there were many other habitats, including caves and grasslands, but the large number of fossil sites that were once wetlands matters to those of us who study wetlands. And the wetland fauna – now vanished – including glyptodonts (a creature that looked like a turtle but was a mammal), the giant beaver mentioned above, megathere ground sloths (some weighing more than 3 tons), equine horses and zebras, and giant tortoises (*Geochelone* spp.). The bones of these species are mixed with familiar species that we find in wetlands today – including marsh rice rats, muskrats, beavers, and moose. One is left with the disturbing impression that not only has the fauna changed, but key processes such as herbivory and disturbance may now be a mere shadow of their former extent and intensity.

So, let us end with a series of questions raised by such missing species. We concluded that herbivores can occasionally destroy their food supply, as in the case of the muskrat "eat-outs" described by O'Neil (1949). We also concluded that such events appear to be infrequent. (And, in any case, it is decomposers that process a majority of the plant material in wetlands.)

Now to the questions. Are such "eat-outs" a natural consequence of population dynamics of herbivores? Are they just a natural part of the vegetation cycle of wetlands, as in Figure 4.13? Or should we view them as something dysfunctional? Perhaps eat-outs are evidence of a missing predator that once controlled the herbivore. Does, say, the absence of large alligators, or absence of timber wolves, allow more eat-outs than in the past? Or is the reverse true, were eat-outs actually more common, even typical, back when North America had more big herbivores? Are most wetlands now in a state that by historical standards would be under-grazed? Were there other species that depended upon disturbance from large herbivores? If so, are they in decline or even extinct from lack of habitat? Perhaps the effects of introduced grazers, like nutria in Louisiana, actually produce the sort of heavily grazed wetlands that may have been common in the past. Should we also suggest that it was normal to have streams and rivers blocked not only by many more beaver dams, but by larger dams built by larger beavers?

Not all scientific questions have easy answers, so I leave you to think about what, if anything, examples such as the extinct giant beaver tell us about the significance of grazing in wetlands today.

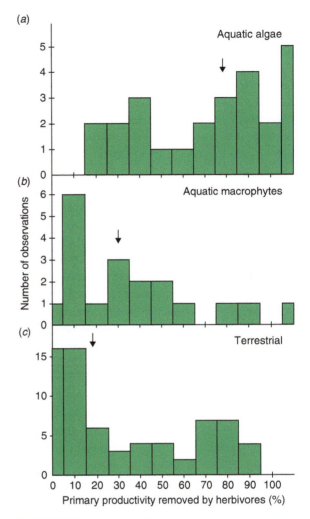

FIGURE 6.13 Frequency distributions of the proportion of annual net primary productivity removed by herbivores for (*a*) aquatic algae (phytoplankton, $n = 17$, and reef periphyton, $n = 8$); (*b*) submerged ($n = 5$) and emergent ($n = 14$) vascular plants; and (*c*) terrestrial plants ($n = 67$). Arrows indicate median values (aquatic algae, 79%; aquatic macrophytes, 30%; terrestrial plants, 18%). (From Cyr and Pace 1993.)

6.5 General patterns in herbivory

One of the most fundamental properties of grazing is the proportion of the primary productivity that is consumed. This proportion can be considered a measure of the "importance" of herbivory in a particular habitat. Cyr and Pace (1993) compiled estimates of this property for a wide array of aquatic and terrestrial habitats: the producers were phytoplankton ($n = 17$), reef periphyton ($n = 8$), submerged macrophytes ($n = 5$), emergent macrophytes ($n = 14$), and terrestrial plants ($n = 67$). Figure 6.13 shows the importance of herbivory when these are lumped into three groups: aquatic algae, aquatic macrophytes, and terrestrial plants. A striking result from this figure is that aquatic macrophytes are much more like terrestrial plants than aquatic algae. This echoes earlier themes in fertility, where we were challenged to decide whether wetland plants were limited by phosphorus (as with algae) or by nitrogen (as with many terrestrial plants), finding that both phosphorus and nitrogen could be important depending upon the type of wetland. The median proportion of productivity removed by herbivores of aquatic macrophytes is some 30% (compared to 79% for algae and 18% for terrestrial plants). Plotting the rate of removal by herbivores against primary productivity (Figure 6.14, top) gives a linear relationship with a slope not different from 1, suggesting herbivores remove the same proportion of primary productivity across a wide range of fertility levels. The top of Figure 6.14 also shows that consumption rates are apparently an order of magnitude lower in macrophytes (triangles) than algae (circles).

In the rest of their analyses, Cyr and Pace regrettably combine algae and macrophytes into one "aquatic" category for comparisons with terrestrial plants. However, certain general conclusions about herbivores in wetlands can be extracted. Figure 6.14 (bottom) plots the biomass of herbivores against net primary productivity in all habitats. The two triangles at the upper left are submerged macrophyte beds where herbivore biomass was strikingly high. (The circle at the lower left is a terrestrial tundra site.) Excluding the two outlying triangles, herbivore biomass increases significantly with productivity, and, also excluding the outlying circle, there is no significant difference between the lines for aquatic and terrestrial habitats. Therefore, for a given level of net primary productivity, herbivores reach similar average biomass in aquatic and terrestrial ecosystems. Important questions about wetlands remain unanswered, and Figure 6.13 suggests that much could be learned by treating wetlands as a

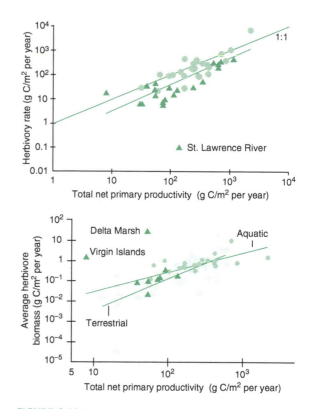

FIGURE 6.14 Rate of grazing (top) and herbivore biomass production (bottom) both increase with net primary productivity (algae, dark circles; macrophytes, triangles; terrestrial, light circles). (From Cyr and Pace 1993.)

separate category in future work of this sort. This criticism aside, Cyr and Pace have provided an important introduction to the study of herbivory in wetlands.

Lodge (1991) reviewed some 25 experiments that measured herbivory in wetlands, covering examples from invertebrates grazing upon submersed macrophytes to mammals and birds grazing upon emergent macrophytes (see also Brinson *et al.* 1981). Herbivore impact, estimated by the difference in biomass between grazed and ungrazed plots, ranged from 0% to 100%, with many values in the 30% to 60% range. He concludes that many herbivores can therefore have a substantial effect upon macrophytes.

6.6   Three pieces of relevant theory

In this chapter we have looked at a number of examples of herbivory and plant defense; now we will think about some of the theoretical models that underlie the impacts of herbivory.

6.6.1 Selective grazing can increase or decrease diversity

Herbivores can either increase or decrease plant diversity. In this chapter, we have seen examples of both. It is important that you have a general understanding of why it can go either way. One key issue is how selective the herbivore is. There are good biological reasons for expecting very selective herbivory, for the animal to prefer certain plants and certain tissues because of higher palatability or higher nutrient content.

Beavers (*Castor canadensis*) are a good example. One can walk through the forest and easily see both the stumps of the trees that they ate, and the remaining trees that they left. Hence, beaver diets have inspired a good bit of study. Typically, one counts and measures all the trees eaten and samples the trees left (Table 6.6). One can then measure whether the beavers preferred certain species or sizes by using different measures of electivity. In one example from Massachusetts, for example, Jenkins (1975) concluded:

They preferred trees of certain genera, they preferred trees of certain diameters and their diameter preferences varied with genus. Specifically, the Blue Heron Cove beavers favored birch, selected against pine, and cut about the same proportion of oak and maple at each site as were available at that site.

Hence, at that site, beaver were shifting the forest from birch to pine. Preferences changed within and among years (Jenkins 1979) and with distance from water (Jenkins 1980). Overall, beaver diets depended upon the selection of trees available to them, the size of those trees, and the time of year.

Now imagine the following circumstances. Picture a plant community, say a forest, having a mixture of species, some common and some uncommon. Now introduce a herbivore. What will happen? The answer is that we don't know unless we specify the feeding habits of the herbivore. Consider two extremes.

- At one extreme, the herbivore feeds upon the rarer species in the landscape. In this case, adding herbivores will actually reduce diversity.
- At the other extreme, the herbivore feeds solely upon the common species and avoids the uncommon species. In this case, adding herbivores will increase diversity.

Of course, the herbivore, if it had no preferences, would feed on the species in direct proportion to their occurrence in nature. In this case, the effects would be small, and largely determined by the species' relative degrees of resistance to the damage of

Table 6.6 The trees eaten (yes) or not eaten (no) by beaver in three size classes at one site in a tract of forest surrounding a beaver pond in Massachusetts

Diameter (cm)	Birch (*Betula*) yes	no	Maple (*Acer*) yes	no	Oak (*Quercus*) yes	no	Pine (*Pinus*) yes	no
2.5–6.2	0	0	10	4	0	0	0	1
6.3–11.3	11	7	0	9	1	2	0	1
>11.3	11	14	0	12	1	7	0	5

Source: From Jenkins (1975).

herbivory. Yodzis (1986) provides a mathematical exploration of these situations. Such investigations illustrate that the effects of introducing exotic herbivores, or reintroducing extirpated herbivores, may be difficult to predict.

Returning to the beavers in Table 6.6, by favoring birch in their diet, they were selectively removing it from the landscape. There are many consequences.

Diversity From the perspective of the forest and landscape, birch was the most common species, and pine was less common. In this plot, beavers would tend to increase tree diversity by removing the commonest species selectively. If we applied specific measures of diversity to these plots, we could quantify just how much diversity changed.

Composition In addition to changing diversity, beavers were shifting the forest composition toward conifers. On my own property, the valleys are filled with conifers – pine, spruce, fir, and cedar, along with freshly cut hardwood stumps – suggesting that the beavers are continuing to remove the deciduous trees and leaving the conifers, thereby creating conifer-dominated woodlands.

Other effects There are other secondary effects, since the type of breeding birds and number of forest floor plants will likely change with the tree species, particularly the dominance of conifers. This is a reminder that when beavers are called "ecosystem engineers," they are not only making wetlands, but are changing the forests around the pond.

Beavers also illustrate – with trees – how mowing can change herbaceous vegetation. In one sense, mowing can be thought of as simulating a relatively unselective herbivore. Mowing actually is somewhat selective – it tends to preferentially remove larger species with dense canopies, thereby allowing smaller species such as rosette forms to persist. Hence, as we have seen in European wet meadows, it is generally found that mowing increases biological diversity.

6.6.2 Bottom–up or top–down? The overlooked potential for biological control of herbivores

There is one other issue about herbivores that demands careful thought. There are two very different ways of thinking about plants and herbivores, and it is by no means clear which view is correct. I have written this chapter in a way that sidesteps the problem because of the uncertainties. But this does not mean you can ignore the topic, because it may have important implications for managing wetlands. From one perspective, call it the **top–down** view, the composition of wetlands is controlled by species at the top of food webs, that is by predators, who control herbivores, and hence control vegetation. From another perspective, called the **bottom–up** view, the composition of wetlands is largely driven by plant–environment interactions, and herbivores and predators merely feed on surplus material. Both are possible (e.g. Hunter and Price 1992; Power 1992). To offer one specific example, do plants determine the abundance of alligators (bottom–up) or do alligators determine the abundance of plants (top–down) (Figure 6.15)?

At the very least, we can be certain that there is some bottom–up control, for the very simple reason that, without plants, the consumers disappear (Hunter and Price 1992). It is therefore quite reasonable to start off with the assumption that the vegetation in wetlands controls wildlife, both through habitat and food. But, as for the second issue, whether the consumers also influence or control the producers, this turns out to be much less clear-cut. Resurrecting Hairston et al. (1960) we can naively observe that most wetlands are green – since the plants are not eradicated by herbivores, something else must be controlling herbivore abundance. So far, it seems plausible. But then, as White (1993) argues, a good deal of this green matter has such low nitrogen content that it hardly qualifies as food anyway, and the growing literature on secondary metabolites (Rosenthal and Berenbaum 1991) suggests that much

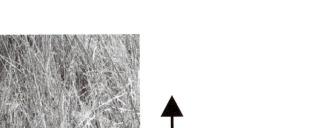

FIGURE 6.15 Does the amount of vegetation control the abundance of nutria, and hence the number of alligators? Or does the number of alligators control the abundance of nutria, and hence the amount of vegetation? The first is termed bottom–up control, and the second is termed top–down control. It is by no means clear which is the correct view, or whether both are happening simultaneously. (See also color plate.)

visually apparent green food is well protected from herbivores. Therefore, the issue of whether herbivores control the abundance of plants, and the composition of wetlands, is open for evaluation.

Second, apparently clear-cut dichotomies like this, while attractive, often turn out to be misleading (Dayton 1979; Mayr 1982; Keddy 1989a). It is possible that both operate simultaneously, that neither operates except for rare exceptions, or that other factors such as habitat productivity (Oksanen 1990), habitat heterogeneity (Hunter and Price 1992), or omnivory (Power 1992) may override the apparent dichotomy.

You should be aware that there could be even more possibilities, three at least, and the kind of grazing system found depends upon the primary productivity of a site, including the supply of soil resources to plants (Oksanen *et al.* 1981). According to this model, herbivore pressure should be most severe in relatively unproductive environments. As primary productivity increases, the impact of herbivory should decline because the growing abundance of the herbivores allows predators to survive and regulate herbivore populations. In very productive systems, herbivory again becomes important owing to the occurrence of predators upon the predators, which releases the herbivores from regulation. (Oksanen *et al.* 1981) present a model, building upon work by Fretwell (1977) that shows how such transitions in herbivore–plant relationships might occur, and they present some data that are qualitatively consistent with these kinds of changes. There are, in fact, many possible complex feedbacks, such as animals increasing the rates of nitrogen cycling, fertilizing plants with their waste products, and even altering competition between plants and soil microbes for nitrogen (McNaughton *et al.* 1988). Hence, generalizations about interactions between herbivores and plants, while highly desirable, await further experimental testing of such models.

Does it matter? Let us illustrate two cases where it might. First, we have the example in Figure 6.4 where grazing by snails may control the amount of vegetation in coastal marshes. Where these salt

marshes are declining, it is possible that the snails are causing the decline – and that the snails have increased in abundance because humans have killed the crabs that would normally control the snails (Silliman and Zieman 2001). Similarly, there is clear evidence that nutria are causing enormous damage to coastal wetlands (Figure 6.1). But alligators are a major predator on nutria, and it may be that nutria damage is increasing because humans have been preferentially killing the large alligators that would otherwise control the nutria populations (Keddy *et al.* 2009). Hence, while the issue of top–down or bottom–up might appear to be theoretical, those who ignore the possibility of top–down control may be blinding themselves to important possibilities for biological control of herbivores. Perhaps areas where coastal marshes are declining need more crabs and more alligators.

6.6.3 Simple models show how populations can both grow and crash

The effects of grazing upon vegetation, and the response of herbivores to vegetation, can both be explored with simple mathematical models. One of the simplest models adapts the logistic equation, which is widely used by ecologists to describe the growth of animal populations (Wilson and Bossert 1971). The logistic model assumes that, when there are few organisms and abundant resources, growth is (almost) exponential, but that, as population size increases, and resources become scarce, the population growth slows and reaches a level known as the carrying capacity, K. This can be used equally to describe plant populations (Noy-Meir 1975; Starfield and Bleloch 1991) as:

$$\frac{dP}{dt} = gP\frac{(K - P)}{K}$$

where P is the amount of plant material (e.g. biomass/unit area), g is the growth rate, and K is the maximum amount of plant material that a unit area can support. Another way of thinking about this that is more similar to familiar animal population models is to

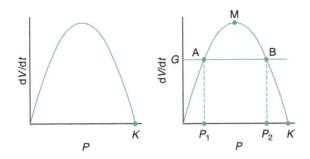

FIGURE 6.16 A simple model for herbivore–plant interactions. The vegetation growth rate dP/dt is plotted against plant biomass P for the logistic model: (left) no grazing and (right) constant grazing pressure G. (After Starfield and Bleloch 1991.)

consider P to be the number of plant cells and K the carrying capacity of plant cells for a particular area of landscape.

To explore the behavior of vegetation without herbivores, we can plot growth rate (dP/dt) against biomass (P), which produces an inverted parabola (Figure 6.16, left). The growth rate of the population of plant cells therefore at first increases as more and more cells are available for photosynthesis, and then slowly declines as the resources available to each cell become restricted. The botanical logic behind this seems to make sense: when plant biomass is low, each new cell will improve the photosynthetic capacity of the vegetation, but as biomass increases, more and more cells will be needed to provide structural support for photosynthetic cells, and others will be shaded so that photosynthesis is below the maximum potential. If we compare short turf, for example, with young forest, the number of plant cells allocated to support tissues (trunks, branches, and stems) becomes a considerable proportion of the biomass in a forest. Further, the lower leaves on the trees are shaded by the upper leaves. Yet another way to think of this is the compounding effects of competition for resources such as light and nutrients; growth ceases when resources become severely constrained. In any case, when the mean photosynthetic yield of all cells just balances their mean respiratory demands, growth will come to

a halt; the level K on the horizontal axis will have been reached. Halfway between 0 and K the growth rate is at a maximum. This is the familiar pattern of logistic growth; the novelty lies solely in applying it to plant biomass. The level of biomass K will depend upon environmental factors such as flood duration, growing season and soil fertility. In the absence of herbivores, all vegetation will tend toward point K.

Now, add in a constant grazing pressure from a herbivore. Assuming that the herbivores remove a fixed amount of biomass per unit time, designated G, the equation becomes:

$$\frac{dP}{dt} = gP\frac{(K-P)}{K} - G.$$

Since the grazing rate is set to be independent of biomass, we can plot G as a horizontal line across the parabolic model of plant growth (Figure 6.16, right). There is no need to solve the differential equation to learn a good deal about the behavior of such a herbivory system; a good deal can be deduced simply from the structure of the equations and the resulting graph (Starfield and Bleloch 1991). Returning to the growth of vegetation, it is apparent that the growth rate is positive only between points A and B, where the growth parabola lies above the herbivory rate, and biomass therefore accumulates. On either side of this range, the herbivory rate exceeds the growth rate. At points A and B, growth just matches herbivory.

The next step is to examine stability by considering what kinds of changes might occur through a period of time. Let's consider point B, where the corresponding amount of plant biomass is indicated as P_2. If growing conditions improve, pushing the amount of biomass to the right, the growth rate will fall below the herbivory rate, and the vegetation will decline back to level P_2. If, on the other hand, drought or flooding were to reduce biomass below P_2, then simultaneously, the difference between the herbivory rate and the growth rate increases, so that biomass accumulates, pushing the system back toward point P_2. Since the system returns to point B when it is lightly perturbed, this is called a stable equilibrium point.

Point A, in contrast, is unstable, because the same procedure shows that, if the system is perturbed, it slides even further away from point A. If it is perturbed to the left of P_1, say, by a drought, then growth rates fall further and further below the herbivory rate until the plants disappear; the system slides to the bottom left and collapses. Conversely, if there is a surge of growth above P_1, then the vegetation temporarily escapes from herbivory, and continues to move to the right, because as biomass increases, the difference between herbivory rate and growth rate increases as well. Eventually the entire system slides over to point P_2. In this simple system, then, the only stable point is one where plant biomass is P_2. Over a broad range of biomass levels, this model herbivory system will return to this point after perturbation.

These dynamics can be deduced slowly from the structure of the equations. If, further, the growth rate of plants were actually measured to establish the maximum growth rate (point M), then one can see that if the herbivory rate were increased above this level M (equivalent to sliding the horizontal line above the parabola) the animals would graze faster than the vegetation grew, which is an unstable situation.

Other models could be used to describe herbivore–plant interactions, by, for example, allowing for growth rates to fluctuate in response to rainfall or flooding, or using a different model for plant growth (Starfield and Bleloch 1991). Others have addressed the interactions between plants competing for light (Givnish 1982) and their responses to added herbivory pressure (Oksanen 1990). If grazing pressure is not constant, but varies with plant biomass, then a variety of outcomes is possible, depending upon the functional responses of the herbivore (Yodzis 1989).

CONCLUSION

The food quality of plant species for herbivores is determined by their nitrogen content, nitrogen being a limiting factor for plant and animal growth (Chapter 3). To reduce biomass loss, plants may be equipped with morphological (gelatinous tissue coating, buried rhizomes, peduncle movement to immerse fruits) or chemical (terpenes, phenolics, and nitrogen-containing secondary products) defenses to deter herbivores. Herbivores can either increase or decrease plant diversity, depending on the intensity of grazing and the species consumed.

To what extent are grazing animals, just like flooding or fire, able to control the composition and functions of wetland communities? When you look out across a vast green wetland you may think the effects of herbivores are small; when you look at mud flats with small vegetated cages (Figure 6.1), you may think the effects of herbivores are enormous. Overall, it seems that properly designed exclosure experiments are too few and far between to draw any firm conclusions. The evidence to date suggests that in most cases herbivores are far less important than flooding, fertility, or competition are in creating the types of wetland communities we see. In general, it appears that the plants in wetlands determine the abundance of the herbivores (bottom–up control) rather than vice versa (top–down control). But, there may be important exceptions, such as snails, beavers, and snow geese. Wetland ecologists thus face two tasks in their future work: the first to determine what generalizations about herbivores are possible, and the second is to discover the noteworthy exceptions.

Since some kinds of herbivores are increasing in abundance – from nutria and snow geese (which we have discussed here) to white-tailed deer and carp (which you will have to read about on your own) – it is likely that the impacts of grazing upon wetlands will be a topic you will often have to consider.

Chapter contents

7 | Burial

Our fear of being buried alive is illustrated by its frequent occurrence in our literature, from Sophocles' (ca. 495–406 BC) play *Antigone*, in which King Creon condemns Antigone to entombment "in a hollowed cave living," to Edgar Allen Poe's (1809–1849) macabre stories such as "The premature burial." Yet being buried alive is a common, one might even say routine, occurrence for many plants and benthic animals found in wetlands.

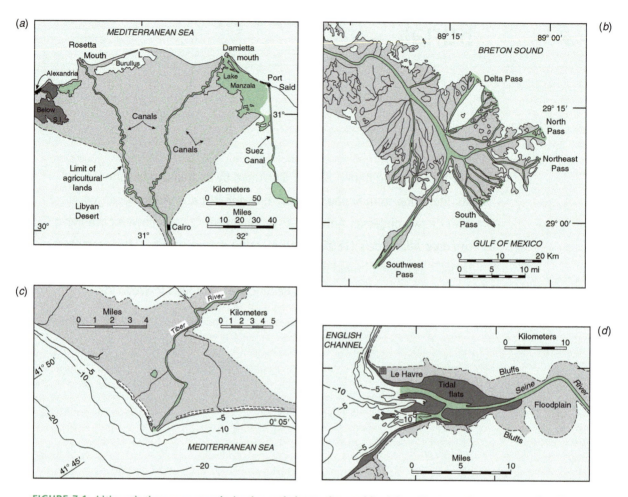

FIGURE 7.1 Although they vary greatly in size and shape, the world's deltas illustrate the amounts of sediment that are transported and deposited by rivers. Here are four examples: (*a*) Nile, (*b*) Mississippi, (*c*) Tiber, (*d*) Seine. (From Strahler 1971.)

Constant burial is one way in which wetlands differ from most terrestrial ecosystems. Many of the other factors that affect wetlands occur in terrestrial communities: disturbance, competition, and herbivory, for example. Terrestrial communities are rarely subject to burial, an exception being catastrophic events such as volcanic eruptions or landslides (e.g. del Moral *et al.* 1995; Grishin *et al.* 1996) or chronic deposition of wind-deposited sand (e.g. Maun and Lapierre 1986; Brown 1997). Such events may be dramatic and conspicuous, but they are also infrequent enough that they are rarely

significant factors. Most books on terrestrial ecology would not have a chapter on burial. In contrast, rivers continually erode the land's surface and carry sediments that are deposited in wetlands as water movement slows (Figure 7.1). It is estimated that the world's rivers deliver in the order of 10^{10} tons of sediment per year to their deltas (Figure 7.2). Burial is clearly a routine experience for riparian wetlands.

The amount of sediment varies among rivers (Figure 7.3). In your own travels, you may have seen rivers that are nearly clear and rivers that seem muddy because of the amount of sediment

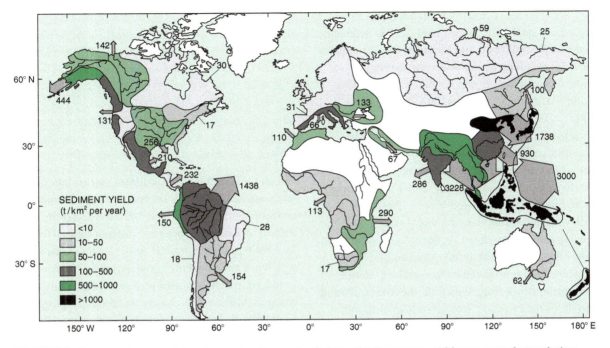

FIGURE 7.2 The annual suspended sediment load in major drainage basins; arrow width corresponds to relative discharge, numbers give average annual input in millions of tons. (From Milliman and Meade 1983.)

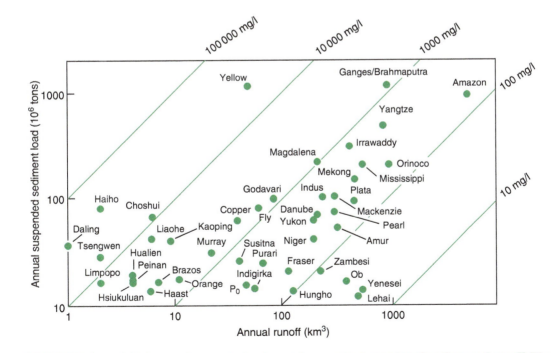

FIGURE 7.3 Annual discharge of suspended sediment from major rivers plotted against total runoff. Diagonal lines show equivalent sediment concentrations. (From Milliman and Meade 1983.)

they are carrying. The Ganges/Brahmaputra River apparently carries the largest load of river sediment in the world (Milliman and Meade 1983). It produces the delta that largely comprises the nation of Bangladesh, as well as the Sundarbans, one of the world's largest mangrove swamps (Section 8.5, Figure 8.18). Asian rivers, in general, are among the most prodigious producers of sediment. Taiwan, for example, an island of 36 000 km^2 (roughly half the size of Ireland or the same as Indiana), produces nearly as much sediment as the entire coterminous United States (Milliman and Meade 1983). The Yellow, Ganges/Brahmaputra, and Amazon have the highest annual suspended sediment loads in the world (Figure 7.3, top). In the Amazon River, the suspended particles include "fine-grained marine and volcanic rock fragments from the Andes, silt and clay from the intensely weathered lowlands and organic particles" (Richey *et al.* 1986). On the coast of China's Jiangsu province, sediment from the Yellow River has accretion rates exceeding 40 cm/yr (Lu 1995). These rivers are building coastal wetlands.

Of course, reading about the sediment moving down rivers is different from actually seeing it. Some sediment is transported as particles suspended in the water column. But larger particles bounce along the bed of the river, a process both witnessed and vividly described by a salvage operator named James Eads who, in the mid-1800s, lowered himself to the bottom of the Mississippi River in a self-made diving bell. Here is what he saw:

The sand was drifting like a dense snowstorm at the bottom … At sixty-five feet below the surface I found the bed of the river, for at least three feet in depth, a moving mass and so unstable that, in endeavoring to find a footing on it beneath my bell, my feet penetrated through it until I could feel, although standing erect, the sand rushing past my hands, driven by a current apparently as rapid as that on the surface. (Quoted in Barry 1997, p. 26)

Not all burial results from sediment carried into wetlands. Some burial is the result of organic matter produced within the wetland itself. It is therefore helpful to distinguish between **autogenic** burial (burial by locally produced organic matter such as occurs in peat bogs) and **allogenic** burial (burial by externally produced materials carried by water, as Eads saw for himself). Much of this chapter will focus on allogenic burial, if only because rates of burial are generally much higher in this category. Also, the process of autogenic burial has already been introduced earlier in this book (Section 1.5.1). Both can cause changes in plant and animal communities, but with autogenic burial, this may occur on timescales of 10^3 to 10^4 years, whereas allogenic burial typically requires 10^0 to 10^2 years. The terms autogenic and allogenic are easy to confuse in my experience; try to remember that auto (originally from the Greek *autos*) means self (as in *auto*graph or *auto*mobile). There are other names – Brinson (1993a, b) uses the terms "biogenic accumulation" and "fluvial deposition."

Let us continue this topic by looking more closely at rates of burial.

7.1 Exploring rates of burial

We have seen that there are two principal sources of material that bury wetlands: sediment carried in from other locations (allogenic), and organic matter produced locally (autogenic). Either can dominate, depending on location. Deltas, for example, are buried largely by sediment carried from upstream. Peat bogs are buried largely by organic matter produced by the plants. Generally speaking, burial in deltas is much faster.

7.1.1 A brief introduction: rates of burial are usually only millimeters per year

One way to measure rates of burial is to examine cores taken from wetlands. Here are some examples for you to consider, generally arranged from low to high. Deposition rates of 0.1 to 0.7 mm/yr have been found in interdunal ponds (Wilcox and Simonin 1987). In boreal and subarctic peatlands peat accumulates at rates from 0.2 to 0.8 mm/yr (Gorham 1991). Burial rates of wetlands in the English landscape are slightly higher, in the order of 0.2 to 2 mm/yr, with a majority in the lower range (e.g. Walker 1970). Higher rates of 3–6 mm/yr appear to be more typical of salt marshes (Niering and Warren 1980; Stevenson *et al.* 1986; Orson *et al.* 1990) and mangrove swamps (Ellison and Farnsworth 1996). Burial rates of 10 to 20 mm/yr occurred in the eutrophic Norfolk Broadlands (Moss 1984), while even higher rates occur in deltas. Cores record 20 mm/yr for the Atchafalaya River in Louisiana (Boesch *et al.* 1994), while other information sources document up to 51 mm/yr in the Yangtze delta (Yang *et al.* 2003) and the Ganges/ Brahmaputra delta (Allison 1998).

Often, large amounts of sediment arrive in a single pulse. Floods and storms can deposit 10 or more cm of sediment in a single year (e.g. Robinson 1973; Zedler and Onuf 1984; Rybicki and Carter 1986; Lui and Fearn 2000; Turner 2006). Historical records show too that the arrival of humans in a landscape will often lead to a pulse of sedimentation. For example, annual rates of deposition in a floodplain in eastern North America were below 0.1 mm prior to this century, but then accelerated by about a factor of ten to approximately 1 cm/yr with increasing human populations (Rozan *et al.* 1994). In rapidly eroding watersheds of Asia, deposition rates can exceed 40 cm/yr (Lu 1995). Sediment accumulation can be very rapid in deltaic areas. Continuing with east Asia, the Yellow River is second only to the Ganges/ Brahmaputra in sediment load (Figure 7.3). More than 30% of its sediment discharge occurs during August floods. In contrast, January accounts for less than 1% of the total. With this volume of sediment arriving, the shoreline has been moving outward into the ocean at about 1.5 km/yr (Schubel *et al.* 1986).

Once the sediment is deposited it may not stay in one location. In deltas, rivers frequently change location and sediment is eroded and moved. Historical records emphasize the dynamic nature of these deposits. Conveniently, the historical duration of Chinese civilization gives us historical records that would be unavailable elsewhere. For example, in 1128 the Yellow River suddenly shifted its course southward, and from 1128 to 1855 the river mouth moved eastward by 90 km, adding an area of some 15 700 km^2. In 1855, the Yellow River again shifted northward. As river inputs decreased in southern areas, waves eroded these older deposits. About 1400 km^2 of land has now been reclaimed by the sea (Chung 1982). Now that dams are trapping sediment, the delta is shrinking. The edge of the Yellow River delta has been moving inland at 20 to 30 m annually and tidal land has sunk at rates of 5 to 10 cm/yr over the past 50 years (Chung 1982).

Although large floods are the major source of sediment, hurricanes can also deposit sediment in deltas. Sediment cores taken out of deltas record such events. At the mouth of the Pearl River on the Gulf of Mexico, cores reveal an accumulation of 8.5 m of material over a period of some 6000 years (Figure 7.4). Much of the material is organic, combining peat produced in the estuary with organic debris carried downstream. Layers of inorganic material show where hurricanes hit the marsh. In the Pearl River, Hurricane Camille (1969) left a layer of clay; in nearby Mississippi, closer to the eye of the hurricane, there is a layer of sand. At least nine distinct layers of clay or silt appear to mark the impacts of hurricanes within the last 4000 years – roughly a hurricane adding sediment to the marsh once every 400–500 years. The reworking of sediment by storms is an important process in producing typical coastal wetlands (Figure 7.5). For a longer-term view of sediment redistribution in deltas, revisit Figure 4.18.

7.1.2 Sediment loads increase with rainfall and deforestation

In general, the amount of sediment in rivers, and therefore the amount of burial downstream, is

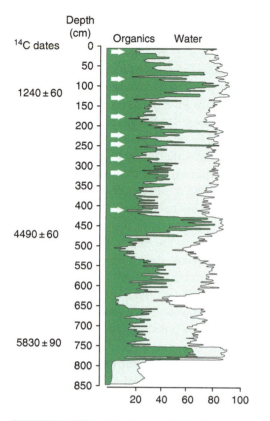

FIGURE 7.4 This sediment core from the mouth of the Pearl River on the Gulf of Mexico shows how more than 8 m of material accumulated over about 6000 years. Periods of organic accumulation from peat (organics) were interrupted by pulses of storm-deposited material (white arrows) attributable to hurricanes. (From Liu and Fearn 2000.)

determined by rainfall and vegetation cover. Cultivated watersheds have sediment loading rates orders of magnitude higher than forested watersheds (Figure 7.6). This is consistent with the results of studies on eutrophication (Section 3.5.2) where the clay content of the soil and amount of land in row crops are the best predictors of phosphorus loadings to watercourses. Although larger rivers can be expected to carry larger volumes of sediment, rainfall and human disturbance to vegetation can play equally important roles in determining sedimentation rates in watersheds.

Rainfall and vegetation cover can be broken down into a number of subcategories for making predictive models. In one such model (Howarth et al. 1991) soil erosion was predicted with an equation containing the following elements: area of the land type, a soil erodibility factor, a topographic factor, vegetation cover, agricultural practices, and rainfall erosivity. Each of these terms can then be estimated from technical manuals (Haith and Shoemaker 1987; Howarth et al. 1991). For example, rainfall erosivity (RE_t) includes assessments of storm energy and intensity, modified for dormant periods as opposed to the growing season. The specific parameters will, of course, vary with climate, soil type, and other features of the landscape. For those having limited patience with such models, the patterns are simple. In terms of time, most sediment is produced during short periods of intense rainfall. In terms of space, most sediment comes from areas of easily eroded soil on steep slopes where the natural vegetation is continually perturbed by humans.

7.1.3 Sediment produces a diverse array of wetland types

Let us move to a tropical example of burial by sediment. The entire Amazon basin is a vast display of kinds of wetlands produced by different amounts of sedimentation (Figure 7.7). Sedimentation in the west, the near-Andes area, is extremely high, reaching levels of almost 1000 tons/km^2 per year, leaving 100-m thick deposits downslope. Floodplains in the eastern Brazilian lowlands are greatly influenced by sea levels. The main valley of the Amazon River has seen both periods of erosion during low sea levels, and deposition during periods of higher water. These rising (and falling) sea levels appear to have substantially influenced the entire development of the Amazon basin.

Some 80 000 years BP, during the Glacial Maximum, sea levels may have fallen more than 100 m below recent levels (Irion et al. 1995), initiating a period of erosion that deepened the Amazon by some 20–25 m (Müller et al. 1995). After 15 000 BP, sea

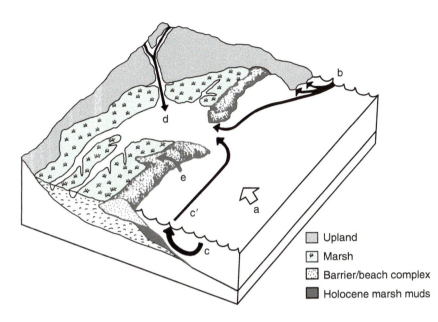

FIGURE 7.5 There are many sources of sediment in coastal marshes: (a) resuspension of offshore shelf or lagoonal muds with landward transport during storms; (b) erosion of headlands or abandoned deltas with transport to marsh via longshore currents; (c) wave cutting of marsh muds exposed in lower shore face with transport to the marsh via longshore currents (c′); (d) riverine input; and (e) overwash redistribution. (From Michener *et al.* 1997.)

Legend:
- Upland
- Marsh
- Barrier/beach complex
- Holocene marsh muds

levels rose about 2 cm per year and the Amazon valley was drowned because sedimentation rates were not high enough to balance rates of rising seas levels (Irion *et al.* 1995). During this period, a large freshwater lake about 1500 km long and up to 100 km wide may have extended from the mouth of the Amazon inland to about 65° W. The maximum size of this lake appears to have been reached around 6000 years BP. Sediment cores recovered from the deep-sea fan of the Amazon in the Atlantic Ocean suggest that, during this time, large quantities of continental detritus no longer reached the sea, being deposited instead in the sediment trap created by this lake. As sediments were deposited here, ridges, swales, and levees would have formed in the middle Amazon area. Superimposed upon these large-scale processes are the ongoing processes of erosion and deposition producing large meander complexes and the shallow lakes known as *várzeas* (Salo *et al.* 1986; Junk and Piedade 1997).

7.1.4 Sediment loads decrease when dams are constructed

The deposition of new sediments is an essential part of the formation of coastal wetlands and deltas. Large dams have another enormous effect on wetlands: they form huge settling basins which store the sediment that would otherwise have traveled downstream to build coastal wetlands. The suspended load in the Mississippi River decreased by about one half from 1963 to 1982 (Boesch *et al.* 1994). Over and over again, it appears that the results are clear and obvious: build large dams on a river, and watch the coastal wetlands disappear. It has happened over and over again in human history. Even so, it is remarkable how many people do not appreciate that land is being lost in Louisiana simply because large dams upstream are trapping sediment. And the Three Gorges Dam in China is now starting the same process, with wetlands being lost at the mouth of the river as the sediment inexorably fills the reservoir behind the dam. The southern Yellow River delta has already sunk at rates of 5–10 cm/yr over the past 50 years (Chung 1982). Of course, at large timescales, eventually the dams will fill with sediment and become wetlands; when, inevitably, the dam breaks, the wetland will erode, and the sediment will move downstream. The disappearance of coastal wetlands due to dams is therefore a temporary effect from the point of view of a geologist. However, humans who have built their homes in coastal wetlands, or who depend upon fish

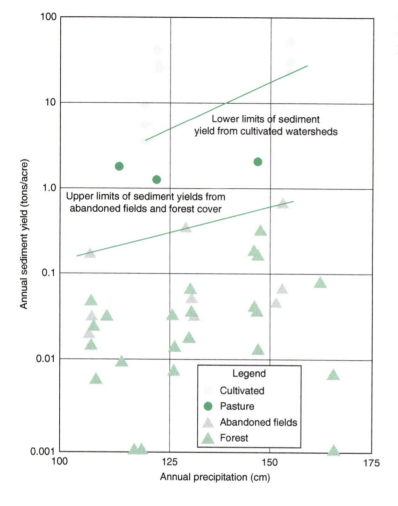

FIGURE 7.6 The annual sediment yield of a watershed is affected by annual precipitation and land use. (After Judson 1968.)

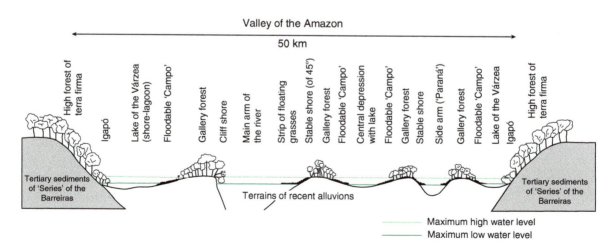

FIGURE 7.7 Much of the diversity of wetland types in the Amazon basin arises from different depths of sediment and from the erosion and redeposition of the sediment. (From Sioli 1964.)

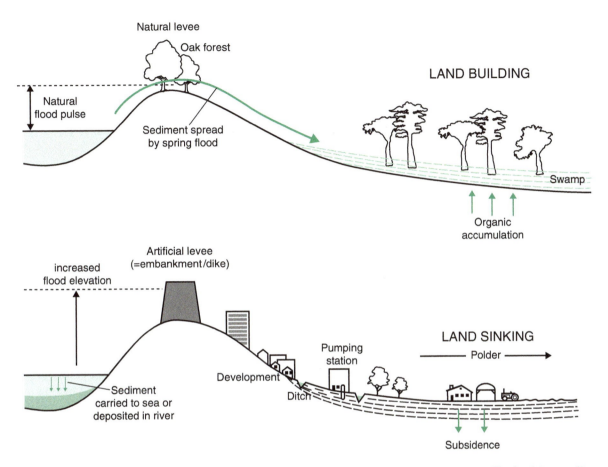

FIGURE 7.8 Recurring spring floods produce natural levees along many natural watercourses. The land is actually higher near the river, and vast wetlands occur at lower elevations, where they are sustained by annual flooding and sediment deposition (top). When humans build artificial levees, they shut off the process of annual flooding. Not only does the process of burial (deposition) stop, but decomposition often leads to further subsidence in the land surface (bottom). Hence, in the long run, artificial levees make flooding increasingly dangerous.

growing in coastal wetlands, cannot afford to take such a long-term view.

7.1.5 Sediment deposition is prevented by artificial levees

There are levees and then there are levees. The first, which we might call "natural levees," are built by the river itself. The second, which we might better call "dikes" or "embankments," are much taller and are built by humans to control flooding. For some reason, we continue to use one word to describe two very different features.

We need to understand the difference.

Natural levees are built by the river itself as it deposits new layers of sediment along its banks. It is these annual deposits of new soil, in part, that make floodplains ideal for plant growth. Since the sediments settle out of the water when the river begins to spill over its banks, the *deepest* layers of sediment are actually deposited *closest* to the river. In this peculiar way, the river builds a wall of sediment, known as a levee, along each side of the watercourse (Figure 7.8, top). Thus, when you want high land, you generally walk toward, not away from, the river. Since the levees are the highest and driest regions of the floodplain, the river often flows through the highest rather than the lowest land. Behind the natural levee walls, drainage into the river is impeded, and extensive swamps can form where water ponds. Streams may even develop on the floodplain parallel to the main river and flow for miles until they are able to traverse the natural levee and connect with the river. During floods the river will occasionally cut through the levee and deposit new layers of sediment in fan-shaped deposits of sediment known as crevasse splays (Saucier 1963; Davis 2000).

Humans who settle in such landscapes usually want to be able to prevent flooding in the spring. In the case of the Mississippi River, the story of human-built levees goes back to New Orleans (which was founded on a natural levee) which by 1726 had built artificial levees 1.2–1.8 meters (4–6 feet) in height to provided protection for the city. Levees were gradually extended upstream and downstream from New Orleans, and then to the opposite bank. As the levees grew in length and height, the water was confined to narrower areas, and so naturally, the water began to rise higher. Some engineers thought that the added rate of flow would scour the river deeper and thereby compensate for the narrowing of the floodplain. But there were unintended consequences – the desired scouring did not occur and building one set of levees merely forced the construction of longer and higher levees. Moreover, when the soil became drier, rates of decomposition increased, so the ground actually began to fall (Figure 7.8, bottom). In some areas of the world, drained land has subsided by many meters.

Returning to the Mississippi, by 1812 there were more than 250 km (150 miles) of levee on each side of the river. In 1858 the total of the two sides exceeded 1600 km (Barry 1997). In some cases these levees rose to a height of nearly 12 meters. Today 3635 km of levee have been built to corral the Mississippi waters – 2652 km along the Mississippi itself and 983 km along the banks of the Red and Arkansas Rivers and in the Atchafalaya basin

(recall Figure 2.25). While the levees along the Mississippi are a well-known example, they are also rather new. The construction of levees for flood control and irrigation has been a prominent feature of human development in deltas around the world, particularly those of Asia, Mesopotamia, and Europe, where they may date back not just hundreds, but thousands of years.

7.1.6 Autogenic burial is usually rather slow

Autogenic burial means burial by locally produced organic matter. We have already seen (Chapter 1) how peat, composed largely of *Sphagnum*, may accumulate and in doing so cause changes in the water table. Further, as peat accumulates, plants become increasingly isolated from the mineral substrate, so that distributions are controlled both by water levels and nutrient gradients produced by the peat itself (Chapter 3). The general outline of how *Sphagnum* buries the underlying substrates has been understood for at least a century (Gorham 1953, 1957; Gore 1983; Zobel 1988), and Figure 7.9 shows how the underlying substrate becomes blanketed in peat, with small depressions becoming forested, and larger depressions going through a longer period ringed by floating bog vegetation. Eventually, the peat accumulates to such a depth that the vegetation is little affected by the underlying topography, and instead becomes largely controlled by climate (Foster and Glaser 1986; Zobel 1988). If, however, the topography has sufficient relief, runoff can then continue to control the peatland, with areas of comparatively rapid drainage remaining as fens, and those isolated from moving water developing into ombrotrophic raised bogs. Some idea of the time required for the transformations in Figure 7.9 is available, since many areas now dominated by peatlands were deglaciated less than 10 000 years ago.

Radiocarbon dating and intensive study of individual bogs give a deeper understanding of

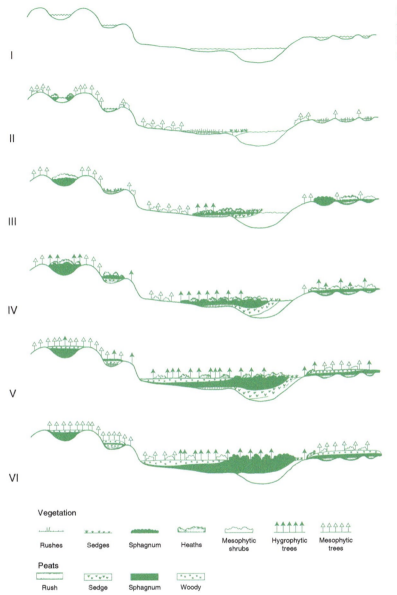

FIGURE 7.9 The development over time of peatlands on landscapes on the Precambrian shield. (From Dansereau and Segadas-Vianna 1952.)

I

II

III

IV

V

VI

Vegetation

Rushes	Sedges	Sphagnum	Heaths	Mesophytic shrubs	Hygrophytic trees	Mesophytic trees

Peats

Rush	Sedge	Sphagnum	Woody

how a landscape becomes buried in peat. One can recognize three hypotheses that might explain how large ombrotrophic bogs form. There could be initiation of peat accumulation across a broad area, with steady accumulation of peat but no lateral expansion, in which case the area of the bog would remain unchanged but the depth would increase steadily through time. Another possibility is that peat could begin to accumulate at a number of individual sites followed by expansion and fusion of the separate peat islands into one large bog. Peat might also begin to accumulate at one site and gradually increase both in depth and area. This process has been explored in the Hammarmossen bog in the Bergslagen region of central Sweden; this bog developed on a broad flat outwash plain and has been

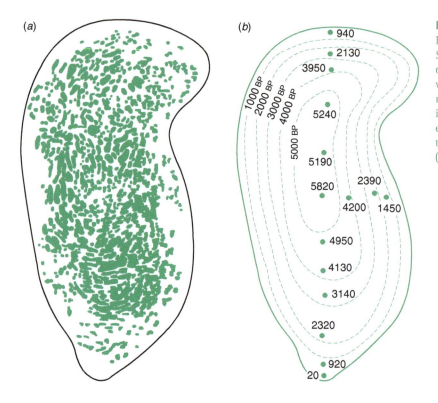

(a)　*(b)*

940
2130
3950
1000 BP
2000 BP
3000 BP
4000 BP
5000 BP
5240
5190
5820　2390
4200　1450
4950
4130
3140
2320
920
20

FIGURE 7.10 A top view of the Hammarmossen bog in central Sweden, showing (*a*) the distribution and size of open-water pools, and (*b*) basal radiocarbon dates with interpolated isochrones for bog expansion. The peat is 4 m thick at the center of the bog. (From Foster and Wright 1990.)

well studied by European scientists. To discriminate among the three models for bog formation, Foster and Wright (1990) took peat cores from a series of locations in this bog and obtained radiocarbon dates from the bottom of each core near the mineral soil. Figure 7.10 shows the general outline of this bog, with the open-water pools covering its surface; the adjoining sketch gives contours of bog age as determined by radiocarbon dating. The bog began forming some 6000 years BP, with growth initiated near the center under what is now the deepest peat. It seems clear that in this case, the bog has not only grown upward by peat accumulation (the peat depth near the middle is some 4 m, for a rate of accumulation of 0.67 mm per year), but it has also expanded laterally at a rate of some 200 m per 1000 years.

The careful dating of pools also allowed Foster and Wright to study the process by which pools form on the surface of raised bogs. They conclude that "pool development is the result of biological processes

under hydrological control." Pools apparently begin as small hollows on the relatively steep slopes covered by shallow peat. As the peat accumulates, these turn into pools. Presumably the rate of peat accumulation in the hollows is less than that of the adjoining ridges, so that over time the peat rises around the depression. At the same time, the water table rises. The plants near the center of the depression are gradually killed and replaced by open water. Adjoining pools may coalesce to produce larger pools.

Peat cores taken from five peatlands in boreal Canada were also examined to study processes of peat formation (Kuhry *et al.* 1993). All five cores were initially dominated by wetland plants such as *Typha* and *Carex*. These were replaced by fen mosses, leading to inferred pH of about 6.0 and a water table at 5–15 cm below the vegetation surface. Subsequently, *Sphagnum*-dominated peatlands developed at each site, in which case pH levels apparently fell to 4.0–4.5. This transition from fen

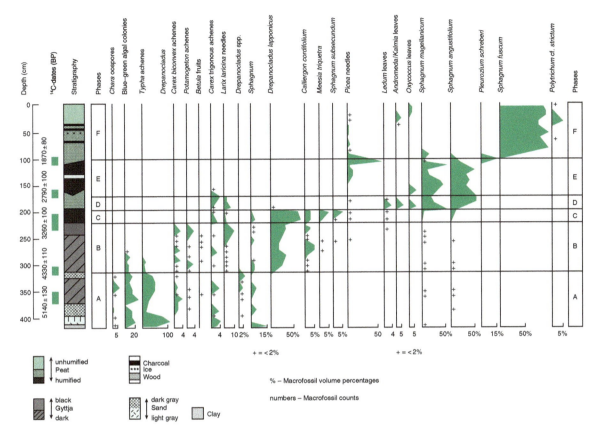

FIGURE 7.11 The vegetation history of a site in boreal Saskatchewan reconstructed from macrofossils. Note the vegetation zones A–F, beginning (A) with *Typha* and *Carex* and ending (F) with *Sphagnum fuscum*. Further, note the comparatively rapid transition from fen (*Drepanocladus*: B, C) to bog (*Sphagnum*: D, E, F). (From Kuhry *et al.* 1993.)

to bog was rapid (Figure 7.11). The overall sequence from marsh to fertile fen to infertile fen to *Sphagnum* bog took place over >2000 years in southern sites, but <1500 years in northern sites.

7.2   Burial changes the species composition of wetlands

We have learned how burial can occur in wetlands and how rates can differ, but what effects does it have on wetland ecosystems? Let's begin by considering how it changes the species found in wetlands.

7.2.1 Evidence from plant traits

We could start the biological consideration of burial by examining the morphology of wetland plants.

Many wetland plants have well-developed rhizomes and pointed shoots (Figure 7.12). Examples include genera such as *Carex, Juncus, Phragmites, Scirpus,* and *Typha*. Pointed shoots and underground storage structures are considered to be adaptations for penetrating accumulations of leaf litter (Grime 1979), and it is likely that the same traits also are adaptations for penetrating accumulations of sediment. Sediment deposition will often be

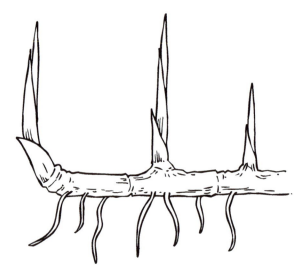

FIGURE 7.12 Rhizomes and pointed shoots allow buried plants to re-emerge.

correlated with litter deposition. Litter also influences the species composition of a wide array of plant communities (Sections 6.3.6, 9.4). Litter contributes, of course, to peat formation. If deep enough, it can kill patches of plants (Section 4.4.2). And large amounts of big litter or coarse woody debris also may be deposited (Section 8.3) in wetlands.

In contrast to plants with large shoots, small evergreen rosette plants are intolerant of burial, and this may in part be why they are largely restricted to eroding shorelines (Pearsall 1920) or to infertile conditions with low primary productivity. At a larger scale, this may also explain, in part, why such plants are often restricted to oligotrophic lakes. Eutrophic lakes and bays with high sedimentation rates are generally occupied by larger rhizomatous plants. So are many coastal wetlands. While we can explain such patterns in part by differences in relative competitive abilities (Chapter 5), differing tolerances to burial may also play a role.

7.2.2 Evidence from experimental studies

Experimental studies show that burial can change the composition of plant communities. Here are three examples; many more could be cited.

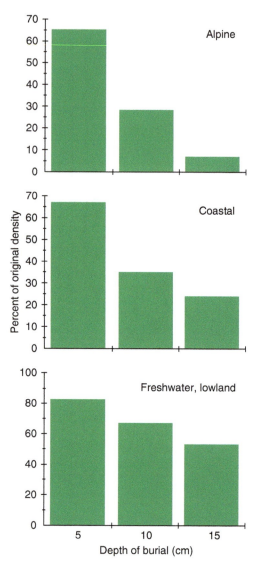

FIGURE 7.13 Effects of burial (measured as percent of original shoot density) plotted against depth of burial in three wetland vegetation types. (From data in van der Valk *et al.* 1983.)

In one study, three wetland types were experimentally buried: alpine, freshwater lowland, and coastal (van der Valk *et al.* 1983). In general, the alpine wetlands were most sensitive to burial (Figure 7.13). This was likely because many of plants were short species with slow growth rates (e.g. *Oxycoccus microcarpus*, *Parnassia palustris*). The freshwater lowland wetlands, in contrast, had taller species (e.g. *Eleocharis palustris*, *Equisetum fluviatile*). After a further year of growth, the coastal wetlands showed most recovery and the alpine wetlands the least. In general, regeneration from buried seeds was marginal; most recovery was from buried rhizomes.

In a second study, salt marsh vegetation near San Francisco was covered with 10 cm of sediment dug out of nearby tidal channels (Allison 1995). Overall, vegetation cover returned to control values after only 2 years. Species such as *Salicornia virginica* and *Distichlis spicata* recovered quickly. Other species such as *Frankenia grandifolia* and *Jaumea carnosa* recovered only when the burial occurred early in the growing season. In general, plots were revegetated by ingrowth from adjoining plants, or else from buried rhizomes. There was very little seedling establishment. Recovery was relatively rapid because the buried areas were only 1-m^2 circular plots; since most recovery was from adjoining areas, larger areas of spoil or sediment would presumably take much longer to recover.

Individual species have also been studied. *Valisneria* is a widespread aquatic plant. The tubers and rhizomes provide reserves for shoots to re-emerge after burial, and also provide food for waterbirds. Yet as little as 20 cm of sediment killed more than half the tubers (Figure 7.14). Burial by sand was more damaging than burial by silty clay; only 15 cm of sand caused as much mortality as 20 cm of silty clay. Rybicki and Carter (1986) conclude that, since *Valisneria* tubers normally grow under 10 cm of sediment, storms carrying as little as 10 cm more can damage stands of aquatic plants.

These selected studies emphasize an important point in the ecology of burial. The effects of burial on a particular wetland or species are likely to depend upon the depth of burial and the degree to which burial is a common feature of the habitat. Deltaic wetlands are regularly buried by allogenic sediment, so it would not be surprising if they were relatively resilient to small annual accretions of

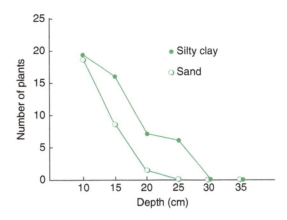

FIGURE 7.14 The number of viable *Valisneria* plants decreases with depth of burial. (From data in Rybicki and Carter 1986.)

sediment. The effects would obviously be different if the plants were buried more deeply. The deeper the burial, the more likely that the plant composition will change, since deeper burial will increase mortality, will change elevation, and will require re-establishment from seeds dispersed with the sediment.

To put such studies in context, let us look at one extreme case of burial from the Mississippi River delta. In 1849, levees near Bonnet Carré were broken by a breach nearly a full mile wide. The river poured into the landscape and laid down a deposit of sediment that covered 91 km^2 (35 square miles) (Saucier 1963). The total volume was calculated at 142 million m^3 (5 billion cubic feet). We can put this into more familiar terms. If we assume generously that one large truck load of sediment is 7.6 m^3, and if we hired full trucks to arrive at the rate of one per minute, dumping 24 hours per day and 7 days per week (some half a million trips per year), it would still take more than 35 years to spread this much sediment. Note that an event like this is not necessarily uncommon in coastal wetlands, and that it would include the full range of burial effects. Near the breach, the 2 m of sediment would have likely killed all the herbaceous plants. Further away from the breach, the burial would decline, until at the fringes of the deposit, less than 1 cm would have been typical, and the primary effect may have been the augmented

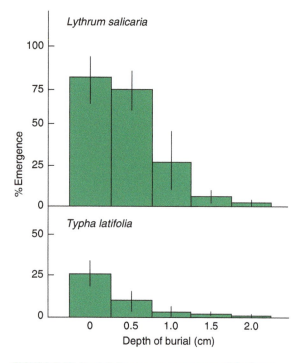

FIGURE 7.15 Burial decreases emergence of *Lythrum salicaria* and *Typha latifolia*. (F. Terillon and P. A. Keddy unpublished data.)

Table 7.1 **Effects of contaminated meltwater upon percent germination of five wetland plant species (*n* = 5 replicates of 36 seeds each)**

Species	Snowmelt concentration (%)		
	0	20	100
Aster umbellatus	5.8	2.0	0
Dulichium arundinaceum	11.6	3.4	0
Scirpus cyperinus	14.2	10.2	0
Typha latifolia	13.2	7.2	1.0
Lythrum salicaria	30.0	19.2	9.0

Source: From Isabelle *et al.* (1987).

fertility. Each flood and the sediment, then, can create a wide array of effects from outright death to just increased fertility. The details depend upon the type of plants present at the start, the depth of burial, and the type of seeds present in the sediment.

7.2.3 Seedlings are particularly sensitive to burial

Seedlings are likely to be much more sensitive to burial. A survey of 25 wetland plant species revealed germination was frequently above 80% in the light but many of the same species had 0% germination in darkness (Shipley *et al.* 1989). One could therefore assume that relatively small amounts of sediment would therefore prevent many species from even germinating. Even 1 cm of sediment is sufficient to reduce emergence by more that 50%; 2 cm of burial reduces emergence to negligible levels (Figure 7.15).

Similar results are reported by Galinato and van der Valk (1986) and Dittmar and Neely (1999). Therefore, even small amounts of sediment can change the species composition of wetlands. Not only does germination of individual species decline, but diversity as a whole decreases significantly with depth (Jurik *et al.* 1994). Species with larger seeds are less sensitive to burial (Jurik *et al.* 1994).

There is a confounding factor in such work. Sediment may also contain a variety of toxic substances, particularly if the sediments originate in agricultural fields or urban areas (e.g. Reynoldson and Zarull 1993). The foregoing studies by Jurik *et al.* (1994) used sediment collected from a sediment trap in a ditch draining several soy bean and corn fields. This has the advantage of being a relatively natural treatment, since these sorts of habitats are a major source of sediment for wetland ecosystems. However, these sediments may also have contained herbicides or fungicides which could affect germination quite independently of burial. Sediments washed from urban areas are likely to contain contaminants, particularly salts from road de-icing (Field *et al.* 1974; Scott and Wylie 1980). In cold climates, contaminated snow is routinely dumped directly into rivers, or else allowed to melt in vacant lots which drain directly into storm sewers. To test for effects of such contaminants upon the establishment of wetland plants, Isabelle *et al.* (1987) watered pots containing standard seed mixtures of five wetland plant species with meltwater from snow removed from urban streets. Both the biomass and richness of the experimental plant communities were reduced by increasing concentrations of snowmelt (Table 7.1). Meltwater alone significantly reduced germination. The only two species growing at high concentrations were *Typha latifolia* and *Lythrum salicaria*, two widespread plant species that are common in ditches and roadside wetlands.

7.3   Burial has impacts on many animal species

Sedimentation is regarded as one of the three leading threats to freshwater aquatic ecosystems, the other two threats being exotic species and impoundments (Richter *et al.* 1997). As a consequence of these threats, Richter *et al.* observe that there is "a quiet crisis taking place beneath the surface of the world's rivers and lakes," conservative estimates suggesting, for example, 20% of the world's freshwater fishes are extinct or in serious decline. Aquatic organisms seem to be disproportionately at risk of extinction; in the United States of America, for example, between 14% and 18% of terrestrial vertebrates are considered to be at risk, whereas the figures for aquatic life are two to four times higher (some 35% for amphibians and fishes, 65% for crayfish, and 67% for unionid mussels). The primary cause of the altered sediment loads is agricultural non-point pollution, a factor already seen to be a major cause of increases in nutrient levels in wetlands (Section 3.5.2). Road construction is another major source of sediment in watersheds (Section 8.2).

Burial by sediment has two main consequences for wetland animals. First, aquatic invertebrates and fish eggs are smothered by fine layers of silt and clay (e.g. Cordone and Kelley 1961; Ryan 1991; Waters 1995). Second, aquatic plants can be stimulated by the nutrients in the sediment, and when these plants decompose under the ice during the winter, they can reduce oxygen to levels where aquatic life is killed (e.g. Vallentyne 1974; Wetzel 1975). Lemly (1982) studied the effects of both nutrient loading and sedimentation upon aquatic insects in an Appalachian mountain stream (Figure 7.16). The Plecoptera, Trichoptera, and Ephemeroptera

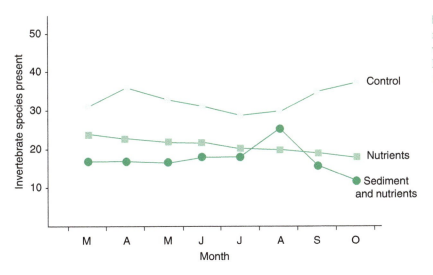

FIGURE 7.16 Changes in the number of invertebrate species with nutrient and sediment loading to a stream. (After Lemly 1982.)

all declined in richness, density, and biomass with increased sedimentation. Many of the insects collected had their respiratory structures clogged with soil particles. Moreover, fine sand and organic silt adhered to their body surfaces. The groups most sensitive to sedimentation were the filter feeding Trichoptera and Diptera. Sediment loading appeared to be more detrimental than simple eutrophication. Other effects of sediment may be more indirect; in aquatic communities, suspended clay may shift competitive dominance from cladocerans to rotifers by interfering with feeding by the cladocerans (Kirk and Gilbert 1990).

Sediment yields for forested watersheds typically are 3–12 tons/km^2 per year. This leaps to ca. 300 for a clearcut watershed and to ca. 3600 for clearcutting followed by farming and pastures; a construction site yielded ca. 49 000 tons/km^2 per year (Bormann and Likens 1981, Table 2–4). These changes are also evident in Figure 7.6, and appear to have been a consequence of human activity for millennia (e.g. Hughes and Thirgood 1982; Binford *et al.* 1987); even Plato complains, in his *Dialogues*, that humans have caused extensive soil erosion in Attica.

In the study above by Lemly (1982), logging, residential construction, and grazing were the sources of inorganic silt, and cattle were the source of nutrients. In the case of streams, the effects of deforestation are even more serious because there are two further consequences. First, the water becomes warmer, thereby reducing concentrations

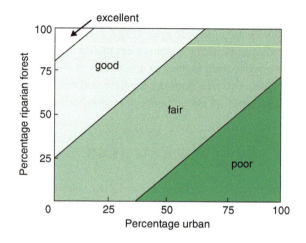

FIGURE 7.17 Biotic integrity of streams can be predicted from two watershed properties: percentage of land that is urban and percentage of riparian forest remaining. (After Steedman 1988.)

of dissolved oxygen for fish and invertebrates. Second, tree leaves are the base for stream food webs. For all these reasons, the amount of riparian forest is considered to be an important predictor of the biotic integrity of streams (Figure 7.17). As the amount of urban land use in a watershed increases, increased amounts of riparian forest are needed to compensate. As Figure 7.17 shows, excellent biotic integrity values are only possible if riparian forest exceeds 75% and urban land use is less than 20%. We will return to this topic in the next chapter, when we address the impacts upon wetlands of roads in particular, and adjacent land use in general.

7.4   Sedimentation, sediment cores, and plant succession

Nearly every introductory textbook in ecology uses the example of hydrosere succession, or pond succession, to illustrate how ecological systems change progressively through time. We will set aside this topic, and the possible connections between wetland zonation and ecological succession, for Chapter 10. But since we are exploring burial,

we should emphasize the importance of sediment cores taken from wetlands (e.g. Figure 7.4), and the information that can be gained through the examination of pollen and macrofossils in sediment cores (e.g. Figure 7.11). These cores document long-term changes in vegetation that can counter too much short-term thinking. Once one has a set of such cores, one can try to put together a larger narrative about how landscapes have changed through time. Here is one example. Walker (1970) studied sedimentation rates in a set of 20 sediment cores from across England, trying to reconstruct changes in wetland vegetation type through time. Although the accumulation of sediment was associated with a gradual change from open water to floating-leaved plants to reeds to bog, the sequence of changes in vegetation was not so constrained as one might expect. In all, he recorded 71 vegetation transitions. Of these, 17% showed reversal of this sequence, most short-lived, which he attributes to local changes in lake level, temperature, or trophic status of the lake water. In a second stage he extracted 159 transitions and concluded: "The most impressive feature of these data is the variety of transitions which have

been recorded and which must reflect the flexibility of the succession." For example, "significant numbers of transitions to bog take place directly from reed swamp, fen and swamp carr." Many of these vegetation types or seral stages last 1000 years or longer.

Such data do suggest we should be cautious in drawing too many conclusions about plant succession and sediment accumulation, unless we simultaneously consider factors that can counter succession, including fire, flooding, erosion, burial, or changing climate (Walker 1970; Yu et al. 1996). The persistence of individual vegetation types for 1000 years or longer emphasizes that ecological communities may possess some resilience when faced with either allogenic or autogenic forces of change.

7.5 Ecological thresholds: burial, coastlines, and sea level

Burial, like fire, has two apparently contradictory effects. In the short term, it may cause immediate death. It damages many plant and animal individuals and species. And it may extinguish wetlands by filling them with sediment. In the long term, however, sedimentation may create new habitat for the same organisms that were killed. This is particularly important in coastal areas, where newly deposited sediment builds enormous deltas (Figure 7.18). So rather than one general rule about burial in wetlands, the impacts of burial depend upon the species, the location, and the timescale. Let us look at the longer timescale issues here.

Sedimentation becomes vital to wetlands when sea levels are rising, since if the total of allogenic and autogenic burial does not keep up with sea level, the land will disappear. Global sea levels have risen at 1.8 mm/yr for the past century (Figure 7.19). Thus, any wetland in which accretion is less than this rate will disappear under water (Nuttle et al. 1997). This is already happening along the Louisiana coast, where rates of loss are given at something like 65 km^2 of

wetlands per year (Boesch et al. 1994). A simple explanation for the situation in Louisiana, the many hectares of vanishing wetlands, is that the sum of allogenic and autogenic burial is less than the rate of sea level rise. Hence, factors that increased burial would seem to be beneficial. There would not, you think, be much room for debate about the future of coastal ecosystems. The objectives should be clear: increase rates of burial.

In practice there are problems. There are other factors that also must be considered. An important one is the subsidence of sediments deposited in previous years. Humans perturb the process of sedimentation in multiple ways, from logging cypress swamps to building levees to digging coastal navigation canals to using boats that generate shoreline-eroding wakes. All of these factors, and more, have to be put together to decide whether a wetland is rising fast enough to keep up with sea level. Overall, the principal factor seems to be reduced sediment input, largely as a result of artificial levees (Boesch et al. 1994), but there

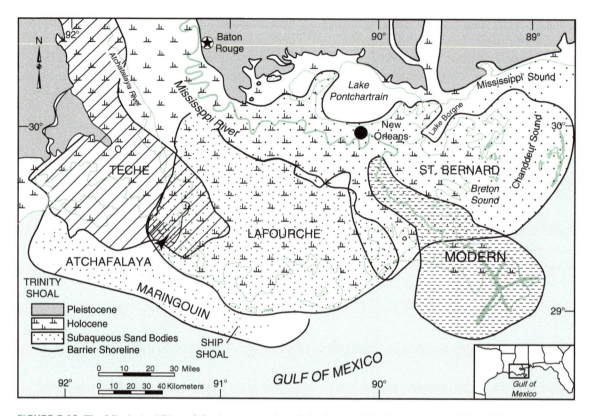

FIGURE 7.18 The Mississippi River delta is a composite of six distinct delta lobes produced by different courses of the Mississippi River over the past 7000 years. If the delta is to grow, rates of sedimentation must exceed the combined effects of subsidence and sea level rise. (From Boesch *et al.* 1994.)

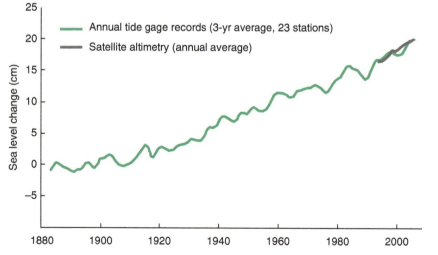

FIGURE 7.19 Global sea levels, averaged over many locations, have risen at 1.8 mm/yr for the past century. (Douglas 1997; adapted from R.A. Rohde at www.globalwarmingart.com.)

are also other important factors including construction of canals (Turner 1997) and grazing by nutria (Wilsey *et al.* 1991; Grace and Ford 1996; Keddy *et al.* 2009a). And then, of course, there is the difficulty of measuring the rates at which sea levels rise and fall, particularly when glaciers far away can produce enormous volumes of water over short periods. The most difficult issue is that the rate of burial may just about balance the rate at which sea level is rising. If the forces are almost equally balanced, then rather minor factors or rather small differences in process rates might decide whether land is lost or gained. That is what makes work with thresholds (popularly termed "tipping points") (Gladwell 2002) so tricky: the consequences may be enormous (for example, the loss of millions of hectares of coastal wetlands), but the threshold (or tipping point) may result from what appear to be minor issues.

More generally a **threshold** arises when a small change in a causal factor produces an unexpectedly large change in the response factor. A familiar example (and one that greatly affects wetlands) is temperature: at just above 4 °C, there is fluid water; at just below 4 °C, there is ice. Beyond the region of the threshold, significant changes in temperature have much less impact. Another familiar example is flooding – when there is just enough water to fill soil pores, the soils shifts from oxidized to reducing, two very different ecological states. Another example comes from peatlands. When just enough peat accumulates that plant roots cannot reach mineral soil beneath the peat, the wetland changes rapidly from a fen to a bog.

Now let us consider examples that are important for coastal management. First, if global carbon dioxide levels increase, it is likely that rates of photosynthesis will also increase. At the same time, rising temperatures will cause glaciers to melt and sea levels to rise. You can read opinions that since coastal plants will grow faster, coastal marshes will keep up with rising sea levels. The problem is that such simplistic opinions ignore rates of decomposition. Rising temperatures will also likely increase rates of decomposition. As you saw in Chapter 1, the world's largest peatlands occur not in areas where production is high, but in colder areas where decomposition is slow. There is a threshold where rates of accumulation just balance rates of rising sea level – pass this point, and the coastal wetland disappears. To continue with this example, if there is added production from higher photosynthesis, the added production may simply be consumed by herbivores. Higher plant growth rates might simply make more nutria. And, if the coastal wetlands have top–down control, alligators, by feeding on nutria, might reduce nutria populations just enough to tip the balance toward accretion of new land from autogenic accumulation. Or not. In a finely balanced system, such effects are not improbable, but they are difficult to measure. Enormous populations of microorganisms and invertebrates consume a lot of litter that could become peat. Millions of nutria can eat a lot of organic matter too. The resulting balance is critical, and it would be easy for coastal wetland to slip over the threshold.

Now an exception. Lest you assume that you can assume this of all coastal wetlands, you should be aware of exceptions. Along the Hudson Bay lowlands of Canada, extensive areas of salt marsh occur on a shoreline that is rising some 1.5 cm/yr (Glooschenko 1980) due to post-glacial rebound (also termed isostatic rebound). The marshes here are similar in composition to those of Alaska and northern Europe (e.g. *Puccinellia phryganodes*, *Triglochin maritimum*) but as the land rises, salinity falls, and freshwater marsh species (e.g. *Carex palacea*, *Typha latifolia*) invade. Further inland are extensive bogs and fens interspersed with raised beach ridges. These wetlands are all very young, not because of newly deposited sediment, but because deglaciation occurred only some 8000 years ago, and new marshes continually form as land rises from beneath the sea. Emerging coastlines with salt marsh vegetation are also found in other areas including Alaska, Scandinavia, Australia, and South Africa (Stevenson *et al.* 1986) as well as around the Great Lakes (Baedke and Thompson 2000; Johnston *et al.* 2007).

In summary, over larger timescales of centuries and millennia, then, the balance among erosion, sedimentation, subsidence, and emergence produces much of the physiographic diversity of coastal wetlands (Figure 7.5). These changes can be slow and gradual, or, if a threshold is involved, rapid. Beware of simplistic generalizations about cause and effect. And plan for the worst.

7.6   So is sediment bad or good?

Sometimes the books about wetlands appear to contradict themselves. In some books you can read that wetlands are important for their role as filters that prevent suspended solids from entering watercourses. One assumes, therefore, that these solids must be accumulating in the wetlands. Indeed, if sediment is accumulating, then it is only a matter of time until that wetland disappears – coastal wetlands being an exception of sorts. Too often this simple issue of logic is ignored. For example, Hutchinson's (1975) treatise on limnological botany has only one relevant index reference "rate of accumulation, supposed effect" which refers to Pearsall's views in the 1920s. Another even longer compendium (Sharitz and Gibbons 1989), 1265 pages dealing with wetlands and wildlife (roughly twice the length of Hutchinson), has not a single main reference to sedimentation effects. The single subreference (Richardson 1989) occurs in a section titled "wetlands as filters" and refers to a series of studies that document the effects of wetlands as filters of suspended solids. One can only look at images like Figure 7.1 and wonder.

Much of the literature on sediment, and most if not all of the models, implicitly assume that sediment is undesirable. This is reasonable for heavily populated watersheds where humans have greatly increased rates of erosion by stripping forests and ploughing fields (e.g. Figure 7.6). This assumption, however, still has to be put into perspective. Certainly, abnormally high levels of sediment are undesirable for vegetation types such as fens, or fish species such as salmon and trout. At the same time, fresh alluvial sediments are necessary for building deltas, the establishment of tree species on floodplains, and therefore for all the plant and animal species that require alluvial forests. It is therefore necessary to think carefully about the timescales and the location. The rates of sediment deposition that would destroy small fens and wet prairies in the upper watersheds of rivers could be necessary for the deltaic wetlands farther downstream.

Sediment carried by rivers is deposited in wetlands as water movement slows and thus burial is a common event in riparian wetlands. Rates of allogenic burial (by material carried into wetlands) are generally more rapid than rates of autogenic burial (resulting from organic material produced in wetlands). Both the amount of rainfall and the degree of vegetation cover that occur in a watershed affect the amount of burial that occurs in wetlands. Many wetland plants are adapted to burial, having pointed shoots and spreading by rhizomes. Experimental studies of burial have shown that the amount and type of sediment affects both plants and community composition and that seedlings and filter-feeding animals are particularly sensitive. While burial may cause the immediate death of wetland organisms, it also can create new habitat for them. In assessing the costs and benefits of burial, species, location, and timescale must be taken into account. The role of sediment in wetlands, and its management, is likely to grow with importance in the coming years, as dams continue to alter sediment supply rates, and changing climate causes sea level to rise.

Chapter contents

8 Other factors

We have so far explored the six most important factors that control wetlands. If you understand these six factors, and how they affect wetland composition and functions, you have done well. Hydrology is certainly the most important, with fertility next. In spite of this you would be surprised at the number of books published on wetlands that do not even have entries for words like "nutrients" or "fertility" in the index! It is important that we put our knowledge of wetlands into the big picture – first things first.

At the same time, there are other factors that do not fit neatly into any of these six categories. As with a statistical analysis, we have extracted six main effects, but sources of variance remain. We can either ignore the rest of the variation, or consider some of the sources. The goal of this chapter is to examine a few "other factors." Although their occurrence in this chapter means that they are regarded as being generally less important than the preceding six factors, there are local conditions where these "other factors" may become very important indeed.

8.1   Salinity

The ocean is a vast pool of saline water which has enormous effects on coastal wetlands, and produces distinctive types of wetlands (Figure 8.1). Salinity is normally measured as the conductance of water, and expressed in parts per thousand, with normal oceans having ca. 35 ppt. The major dissolved elements are sodium, chloride, sulfur, and magnesium. Higher salinity areas occur where freshwater inputs are low and evaporation is high (e.g. Mediterranean Sea, 38 ppt) while lower salinity areas occur where freshwater inputs are high and the climate is cooler (e.g. Baltic Sea, as little as 1 ppt).

Some people will be shocked to see salinity listed here, as merely another factor. You could, as I said in Chapter 1, divide the entire world of wetlands into freshwater wetlands and saltwater wetlands, or interior and coastal wetlands. Indeed, some books restrict themselves to only freshwater or only saline wetlands. From one perspective, this is quite reasonable. But it creates problems, too. It tends to make us overlook the many processes that freshwater and saltwater wetlands share. It also breaks scientists into groups that sometimes hardly seem to talk to one another. In this book

FIGURE 8.1 Salinity changes the species composition of wetlands from mangrove swamp (left, Florida Keys, USA; courtesy G. Ludwing, U.S. Fish and Wildlife Service) to salt marsh (bottom right, El Yali, Chile; courtesy M. Bertness) to oligohaline marsh (top right, Gulf of Mexico, Louisiana). (See also color plate.)

I wish to to emphasize how all wetlands share many common features, species, processes, and problems. All wetlands experience flooding, all wetlands are affected by fertility, all wetlands are affected by disturbance, and so on. There is much we can learn from emphasizing commonality. We can think of saltwater wetlands as freshwater wetlands with another causal factor imposed.

So how does this new causal factor affect the group of wetlands we call coastal wetlands? There are two main ways. First, salinity is harmful to many species, even many species that normally occur in wetlands. Second, salinity changes the pool of species that can form a habitat. Let us look at them in turn, first using plants, and then expanding to macroinvertebrates.

8.1.1 Salinity depresses the growth of many species

The negative effects of salinity arise because of the added stress that salinity puts on plants. It requires added energy, and often specialized mechanisms, to deal with the salinity. Hence, plant growth rates are depressed (Pezeshki *et al.* 1987a, b; McKee and Mendelssohn 1989). Figure 8.2 shows the responses of four marsh species to five different salinity regimes over 3 months. The salinity regimes used were (1) 0 g/l salinity, (2) final salinity of 6 g/l reached in 6 weeks, (3) final salinity of 6 g/l reached in 3 days, (4) final salinity of 12 g/l reached in 3 weeks, (5) final salinity of 12 g/l reached in 3 days (Howard and Mendelssohn 1999). In all cases, higher salinity reduced growth. Seedlings are sensitive to

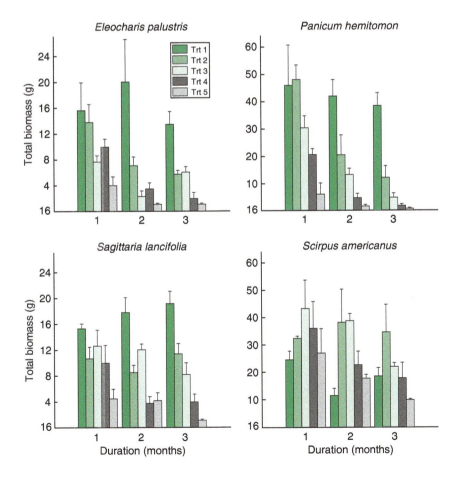

FIGURE 8.2 The effects of salinity upon plant growth. Four common coastal species show decreased growth with increased exposure to salinity. The five salinity treatments simulate pulses such as might be caused by storms. (1) 0 g/l salinity, (2) final salinity of 6 g/l reached in 6 weeks, (3) final salinity of 6 g/l reached in 3 days, (4) final salinity of 12 g/l reached in 3 weeks, (5) final salinity of 12 g/l reached in 3 days. (From Howard and Mendelssohn 1999.)

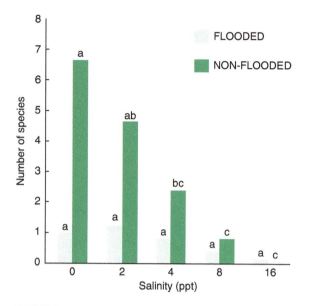

FIGURE 8.3 The number of species of marsh plant emerging from soil samples taken in Louisiana and exposed to flooded and non-flooded treatments over five salinities. Flooding reduces germination (as you would expect from Chapter 2). Salinity also reduces germination, until at 16 ppt, flooded and non-flooded samples have negligible emergence. (From Baldwin *et al.* 1996.)

salinity as well. When marsh soils are exposed to saline water, the number of species germinating decreases with increasing salinity (Figure 8.3)

The most likely cause of depressed growth is the difficulty of obtaining water. The plants may be flooded daily at high tide, but they may still not have access to soil water. Normally, water uptake occurs because evapotranspiration creates osmotic gradients within plant tissues. The water deficit is transmitted down the plant through the xylem, thereby causing water to diffuse into roots (Salisbury and Ross 1988; Canny 1998). The greater the salinity, the stronger this osmotic gradient must be to extract water from the soil. One can measure these water deficits in photosynthetic tissues using a pressure bomb (Scholander *et al.* 1965), which yields readings of xylem tension in megapascals. Plants growing in salt water have a much more negative tension in their xylem (Figure 8.4), reflecting the difficulty in withdrawing water from saline solutions. In addition, there are likely physiological stresses from the ionic composition of the water, and ionic accumulations in the plant tissues (Howard and Mendelssohn 1999). A more detailed exploration of the consequences of salinity can be found in standard reference works (e.g. Chapman 1974; Tomlinson 1986; Adam 1990).

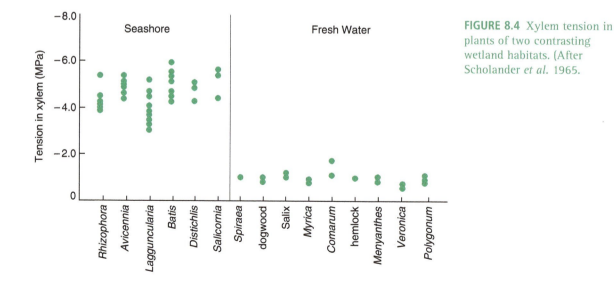

FIGURE 8.4 Xylem tension in plants of two contrasting wetland habitats. (After Scholander *et al.* 1965.

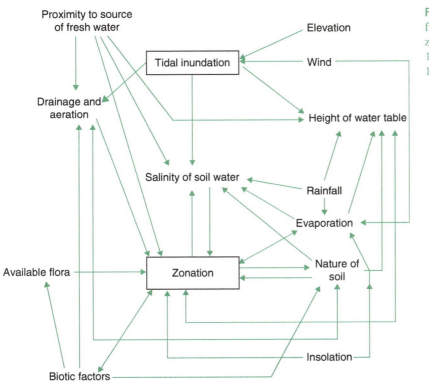

FIGURE 8.5 Environmental factors influencing salt marsh zonation. (Modified from Adam 1990 and Clarke and Hannon 1969.)

Of course, salinity is just one of many factors affecting coastal wetlands. You have already seen examples of fertility and disturbance and burial affecting coastal wetlands too. These produce a complex network of cause and effect (Figure 8.5). One other important factor is climate – cool periods with lots of rain can reduce salinity, whereas hot periods of drought can increase it. Indeed, evaporation from shallow pools can create salinity higher than the ocean – hypersaline conditions. Hence, as Figure 4.23 showed, wetland plants may germinate only during cool wet periods where salinity remains low enough for seedlings to establish.

Overall, you can think of salinity as an added cost that a plant has to bear to grow in a coastal environment. The added cost may become critical when the plants are already struggling to cope with other forces like grazing and hypoxia. Here is one example which tested for possible interactions of

salinity with two factors discussed earlier in the book, flooding and herbivory. Grace and Ford (1996) focused upon a common marsh plant, *Sagittaria lancifolia*. Pieces of turf containing this species were exposed to factorial combinations of salinity, flooding, and simulated herbivory. Here is the critical point – none of these factors alone significantly affected the test plants (Figure 8.6) – but all three factors combined produced negative effects on the plants. Hence, if one did only the work in the first four histograms – each factor alone – one could conclude that salinity, flooding, and herbivory were unimportant. But the last two histograms tell a rather different story. When these three factors are combined (hsf: herbivory + salinity + flood), plant size falls significantly. If fertilizer is added to this combination to try to compensate for the damage (hsff: herbivory + salinity + flood + fertilizer), there is no benefit. Of course, plants in Louisiana coastal marshes are exposed to herbivory, salinity,

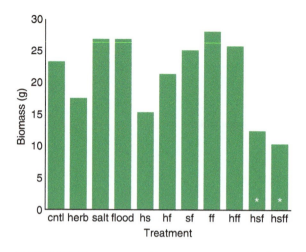

FIGURE 8.6 The response of one common marsh plant, *Sagittaria lancifolia*, to simulated herbivory (herb), salinity (salt), and flooding (flood). Although the effect of each factor or each pair of factors is insignificant relative to controls (cntl), when all three factors are combined (hsf: herbivory + salinity + flooding), plant size falls significantly. If fertilizer is added to this combination to try to compensate for the damage (hsff: herbivory + salinity + flooding + fertilizer), there is no benefit. (From Grace and Ford 1996.)

and flooding simultaneously. This illustrates how multiple factors interact to produce coastal wetlands, and demonstrates the general principle of multiple interacting factors emphasized in Chapter 1.

8.1.2 Salinity reduces the size of the species pool

Saline environments appear to pose a nearly insurmountable obstacle to plant adaptation. The other primary consequence of high salinity is reduced plant diversity. When wetland plants are exposed to increasing salinity, they eventually die. Only a small proportion are able to tolerate the salinity of the ocean (Figure 8.7).

In tropical areas, woody plants can occupy saline wetlands, producing intertidal forests (Tomlinson 1986); the tree species are referred to as mangroves, whereas the vegetation is called mangal. Tomlinson reports that there are only 9 major genera of

mangroves and some 34 species in the world, with 11 minor genera contributing a further 20 species. Including the associates of mangroves, this list can be extended by a further 60 species. To put these figures into perspective, some 90 woody plant species have been found in a single 500-m^2 transect in a tropical riparian floodplain of central America (Meave *et al.* 1991) – that is, one small section of freshwater forest has the same number of species as all of the world's mangal flora. A few more examples – there are some 200 genera and 2600 species in the palm family, but only four are commonly found in mangal (Tomlinson 1986, pp. 30, 295). The family Myrsinaceae has over 1000 species in about 30 genera distributed throughout the tropics and subtropics, but only four species occur in mangal (p. 284). The question as to why so few plants have evolved salt tolerance remains an open one. We may nevertheless conclude that one of the major effects of salinity is to reduce the number of plant species present.

This means that coastal wetlands can look very different, since they have species that are different from interior wetlands. When only a few species dominate a coastal wetland, say in the case of the grass *Spartina alterniflora*, the study of coastal wetlands can easily become the study of that single species. Similary, when the coastal wetland is dominated by mangroves, wetland ecology can easily be confused with the study of mangrove ecology. In these cases, it is easy to become so wrapped up in the ecology of *Spartina*, or mangroves, that one loses track of the fact that the wetland is still behaving in many other ways like a typical wetland. There are hypoxic soils. Water levels change. Nutrients affect plant distributions. Organisms compete for critical resources. Disturbance causes abrupt changes in composition. And so on.

8.1.3 Salinity is a critical gradient for subdividing estuaries

It is frequently convenient to divide coastal wetlands into four categories depending on the salinity: fresh, intermediate, brackish, and saline. Although these

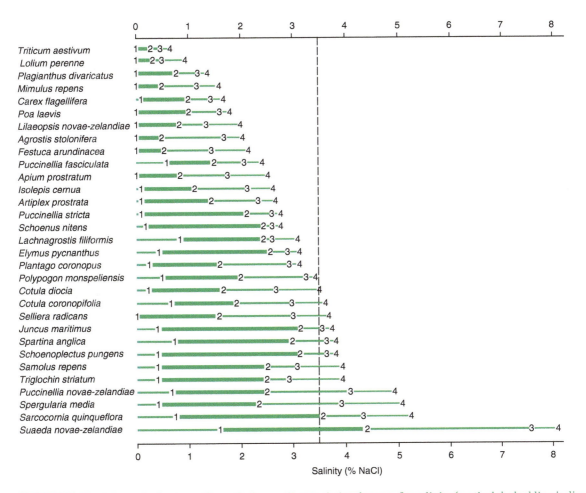

FIGURE 8.7 Coastal marsh plants can be ranked according to their tolerance for salinity (vertical dashed line indicates ocean salinity). (From Partridge and Wilson 1987.)

are designated based on salinity levels, they can often be readily identified by the plant species present (Table 8.1). The fauna changes in response to the salinity and in response to the kinds of plants present.

8.1.4 Salinity is often a short-lived pulse

Although it is convenient to talk about a site from the perspective of a mean salinity (e.g. brackish or intermediate, Table 8.1), in most estuaries, higher salinity arrives in pulses when storms drive salt water inland. When Hurricane Katrina hit the Louisiana

coast in 2005, the water in Lake Pontchartrain, which normally oscillates around 2 ppt (1.5 to 2.5), leaped to nearly 4 ppt for a little over a day (Figure 8.8). This was salt water pushed inland. Note, too, that in the wake of the storm, salinity dropped to oscillate at under 2 ppt (1.5 to 2), presumably as a consequence of fresh water arriving in rainfall. Hence, one hurricane can first increase salinity, and then decrease it. The disturbance caused by the hurricane may therefore be followed by a period of more rapid establishment and growth.

Salt water pulses affect estuaries over a wide range of time scales. Figure 8.8 showed a pulse from one

Table 8.1 **Common plant species (ranked 1 = most abundant to 5 = least abundant), total number of plant species, and area of coastal marsh types in Louisiana**

	Marsh type (salinity, ppt)			
	Saline >15	Brackish 6–15	Intermediate 2–6	Fresh <2
Spartina alterniflora	1	4		
Distichlis spicata	2	2		
Juncus roemerianus	3	5		
Spartina patens	4	1	1	5
Batis maritima	5			
Scirpus olneyi (Schoenoplectus americanus)		3		
Phragmites communis (P. australis)			2	
Sagittaria lancifolia			3	2
Bacopa monnieri			4	
Eleocharis sp.			5	3
Panicum hemitomon				1
Alternanthera philoxeroides				4
Total no. species	17	40	54	93
Area (ha)	323 344	479 957	263 855	494 526

Source: After Chabreck (1972).

hurricane. In the Baltic Sea, which has extremely low salinity levels of ca. 1 ppt (depending, of course, upon location), rivers are the source of fresh water, while saline water enters from the North Sea through the Danish Straits (Helsinki Commission 2003). The wetlands on the coast of the Baltic therefore include many fresh and intermediate species that are not normally encountered in estuaries (Figure 8.9). Occasional low pressure systems allow salt water to flow much more rapidly into the Baltic – 1913, 1921, 1951, 1976, 1993, and 1994 – each had major salinity pulses. These pulses tend to counterbalance the accumulation of freshwater inputs from rivers and raise salinity levels. Pulses also carry oxygen-rich water into the Baltic, which is an important issue for fisheries of the region.

In summary, the major effects of salinity on coastal wetlands are (1) the reduction in plant growth rates and (2) the reduction in the pool of species. The fact that there are fewer species often amplifies the importance of single species such as *Spartina alterniflora* in coastal marshes or *Rhizophora mangle* in coastal swamps. The salinity is determined by the balance between freshwater inputs from rivers and saltwater inputs from the ocean, which can fluctuate at many scales depending upon tides, currents, and storms.

8.1.5 Animals are similarly affected by salinity and salinity pulses

Animals repond in similar ways to the plants. Let us use macroinvertebrates as an example. The number of species of aquatic invertebrates, particularly those in the Insecta, normally increases with increased flood duration, since it allows groups with longer larval stages to reproduce successfully. If the water is saline, however, it lowers the number of species,

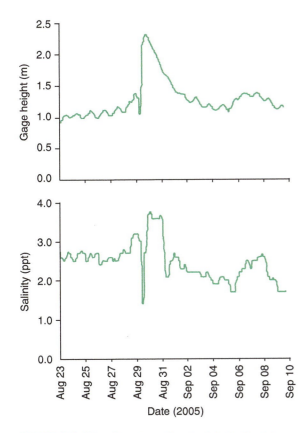

FIGURE 8.8 When Hurricane Katrina hit the Louisiana coast (August 30, 2005), it produced a pronounced pulse in water levels and salinity, here illustrated by a monitoring station at Pass Manchac (measured by U.S. Geological Survey 301748090200900). (After Keddy *et al.* 2007.)

just as with plants, often leading to dominance by a few salt-tolerant genera. Hence, the volume and duration of freshwater input is critical.

The Camargue in southern France is one of Europe's largest deltas, and is bracketed by two branches of the Rhone River. The Rhone carries fresh water from the north southward to the Mediterranean coast, into an area with hot dry summers and moisture deficits. Many of the species that occur here, from reeds to flamingoes, are tolerant of brackish conditions. Thus the delta in general, and the Camargue in particular, are very

susceptible to changes in salinity, which can change with freshwater flows from upstream that vary with precipitation, or due to local human impacts of canals and drainage for rice cultivation.

The Camargue is well-known for its populations of waterbirds, including flamingoes (Figure 8.10). Many waterbirds feed on macroinvertebrates. Hence, the factors controlling the composition and abundance of aquatic macroinvertebrates are of broad interest. Many of the wetlands fill with water during the winter, and then dry out during the summer, being flooded for from 5 to 9 months. One study examined a set of 30 such temporary wetlands (Waterkeyn *et al.* 2008). Most macroinvertebrates were identified to genus, except the Diptera, which were identified to family level.

A total of 19 zooplankton taxa and 49 macro-invertebrate taxa were identified. We will look only at the macroinvetebrates. The mean number of macroinvertebrate taxa in a wetland was 14. The number of taxa declined with increasing salinity (Figure 8.11). The rarer species were restricted to the fresher ponds. Some dragonflies appeared to be able to tolerate salinities up to 22–25 mS/cm, but overall they too declined with increasing salinity. A few Coleoptera (such as *Berosus* sp.) and some Hemiptera (such as *Sigara* sp.) were also tolerant of salinity. The snail *Potamopyrgus antipodarum*, originally native to New Zealand, is spreading worldwide (Alonso and Castro-Diez 2008) – note its presence, too, in the more saline conditions.

During the heavy autumn rains, fish can enter the wetlands. Fish have a negative effect on the invertebrates. One of the most common fish is *Gambusia affinis* (the mosquitofish) which has been introduced worldwide for mosquito control; it should be no surprise that a fish feeding on invertebrate larvae can cause changes in macroinvertebrate composition, but it is a reminder that controlling mosquitoes with predator fish may have unexpected effects on other non-insects, some of which may be predators themselves.

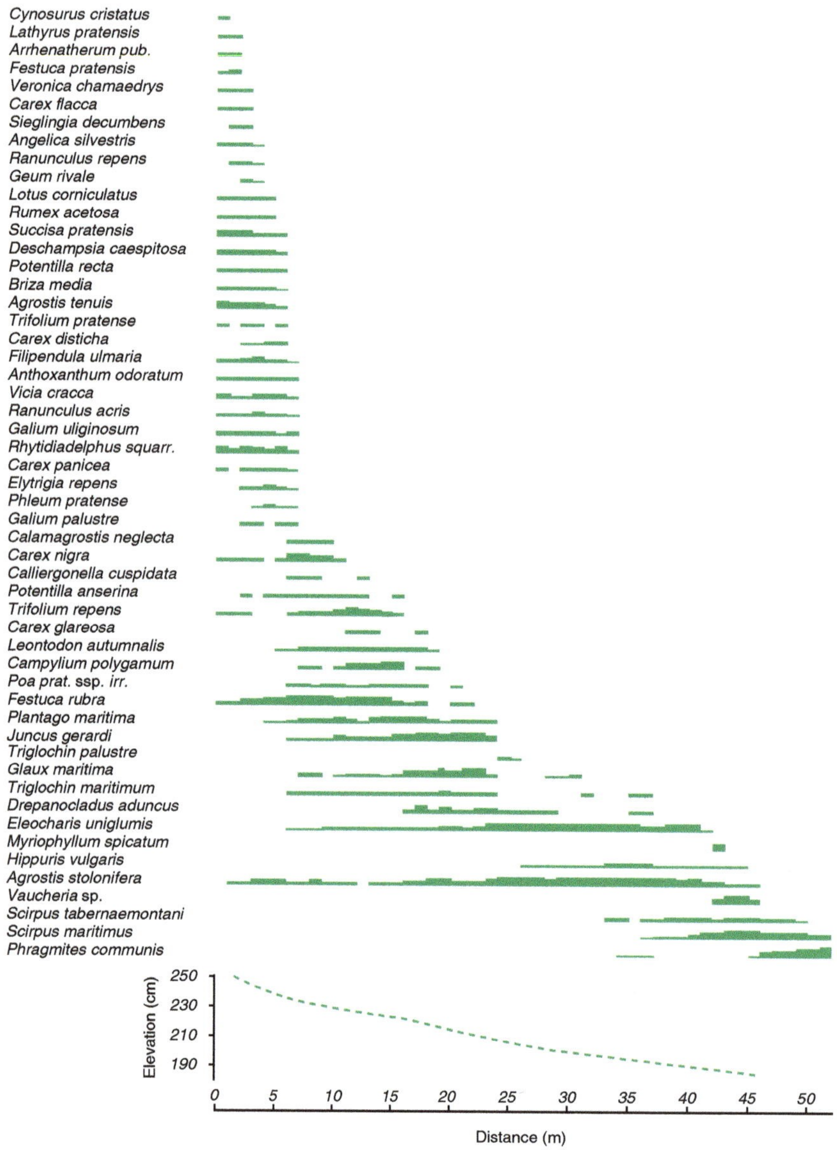

FIGURE 8.9 Zonation of wetland plants on a section of the Baltic coast. Note that the deeper water has *Phragmites communis*, and that *Spartina* is not present, illustrating the relatively fresh conditions in the Baltic Sea. (From Tyler 1971.)

8.2 Roads

Roads and networks of roads now cover large portions of Earth and generally have a profound and negative effect upon wild species and habitats (Forman and Alexander 1998; Trombulak and Frissell 2000; Forman *et al.* 2002). In this section we will not only consider the obvious effects of roadkill, but also a wide array of indirect effects such as altered drainage and fire regimes.

FIGURE 8.10 The flamingoes of the Camargue wetland on the Mediterranean coast depend upon invertebrates for food. (Courtesy A. Waterkeyn.) (See also color plate.)

8.2.1 Roads are everywhere and still expanding

Roads are now so all pervasive that conservation planners now map "road-less areas" as small fragments of landscape worthy of conservation – simply because of the absence of road effects.

Some statistics (Brown 2001). The area of the United States devoted to roads and parking lots covers an estimated 16 million hectares (61 000 square miles). For every five cars added to the U.S. fleet, an area the size of a football field is covered with asphalt. The United States is losing 650 000 hectares of wild land per year to development. Land that is paved is land lost for wildlife. Moreover, land that is paved drains rapidly into sewers and rivers, increasing local flood peaks.

8.2.2 The direct effect: roads kill animals

One of the obvious effects of roads is clear and direct: the toll taken in animal deaths. Anyone who has paid attention to dead animals on roads will notice the carnage, not only large animals like armadillos and porcupines, but many smaller animals including toads, frogs, salamanders, snakes, and turtles. The mortality rate is so high that the absence of such carcasses on a stretch of road may be a reliable indication that the local populations have been exterminated. To give you a sense of the scale, on one warm spring night I returned from the theater to find my lane carpeted in migrating frogs. We stopped, and individually removed them so we could get home – 101 frogs on that small stretch

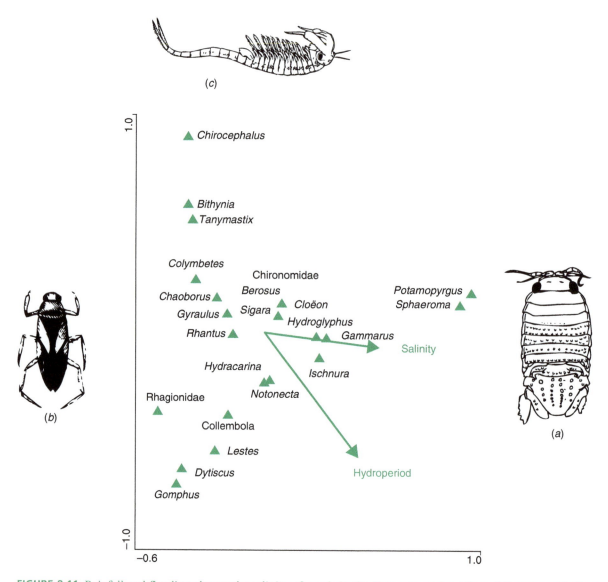

FIGURE 8.11 Rainfall and flooding change the salinity of ponds in the Camargue and produce different populations of invertebrates. The most saline ponds have *Sphaeroma* (*a*) and an introduced snail (*Potamopyrgus antipodarum*), whereas dragonflies and backswimmers (*b*, *Notonecta*) occur at intermediate salinities, and fairy shrimp (*c*, *Chirocephalus*) typify fresh water ponds. (After Waterkeyn *et al.* 2008.)

of road. Imagine if we had simply driven through them, as too many people do.

Here are just four examples that illustrate the rates of death on roads. Snake mortality levels 0.188 per km were found in one set of 15 North American studies (Jochimsen 2006). A study in India found 73 reptiles (representing 24 species, mainly snakes) and 311 amphibians (mainly ranids, rhacophorids, and caecilians); the reptile mortality level was 0.43 per km (Vijayakumar *et al.* 2001). An Australian survey found mortality rates of 0.3 per km per week. There were 529 carcasses of 53 vertebrate species including mammals (bandicoot, brushtail possum), birds (noisy miner, Australian magpie), and lizards (eastern bluetongue lizard, bearded dragon) – smaller animals like frogs were thought to be underrepresented in this sample because of issues with visibility and rapid decay. Wider roads provide greater obstacles, and multiple lanes of traffic may be impassible to slow-moving species – Aresco (2004) found that 95% of 343 turtles were killed as they first entered the highway adjacent to the shoulder, and the remaining 5% were killed in the first two traffic lanes, with mortality rates estimated at 1294 per km per year.

8.2.3 Indirect effects may be more important than roadkill

On top of the effects of direct mortality are indirect effects (Trombulak and Frissell 2000; Forman *et al.* 2002). Probably the most important is their interference with natural drainage patterns. They are a source of sediment, particularly during construction, but often for many years thereafter. Salt that is put on northern roads seeps into adjoining wetlands. Roads provide access for hunting and poaching and perhaps off-road vehicles. They provide a route for invasive species. Roads often attract other development such as housing estates

or logging. Hence, the extent of the road network near a wetland, is a strong negative predictor of the number of species likely to be found (Figure 8.12).

Roads at a distance from a wetland can still have many effects, but they may be more subtle and require careful analysis for detection. Houlahan *et al.* (2006) studied 74 small wetlands and tried to measure the effects of different land uses upon them. Wetland area and presence of streams had a pronounced positive effect while roads and houses had pronounced negative effects (Figure 8.13). The effects extended as far as 250–400 m from roads. The presence of forests also has a strong positive effect.

Large areas of paved land do not allow water to infiltrate the soil, leading to rapid surges of water immediately after rain, and then longer periods that are comparatively dry. Runoff from paved areas can cumulatively lead to lower water tables that result in losses of small streams and springs.

To put the effects of paving in context, consider how much has been written on coastal wetland loss in Louisiana. Yet in North America as a whole, the loss of land to urban development is proceeding at a rate 100 times faster than the loss of the Louisiana coast.

8.3 Logs and coarse woody debris

There are numerous historical accounts of logs and fallen trees (coarse woody debris) clogging rivers. At one time, river banks may have been littered with this kind of debris, with effects upon everything from rates of soil erosion to fish feeding. So few of us have seen a natural river with natural logjams that it is easy to forget the effects they once had.

One early description of debris in rivers comes from the Freeman and Custis expedition that traveled 990 km (615 miles) up the Red River in 1806 (Flores 1984; MacRoberts *et al.* 1997). This expedition was a lesser-known twin to the famous Lewis and Clark expedition up the Missouri. Freeman and Custis

reported that the Red River was entirely blocked by a series of gigantic logjams that began just north of modern-day Natchitoches and continued for approximately 160 km to the vicinity of present-day Shreveport (Figure 8.14). Freeman describes each in turn (since he is compiling a detailed report, and since each must be bypassed "with great exertion") but let us combine the accounts for an overall picture of this feature.

It consists of the trunks of large trees, lying in all directions, and damming up the river for its whole width, from the bottom, to about three feet higher than the surface of the water. (Flores 1984, p. 127).

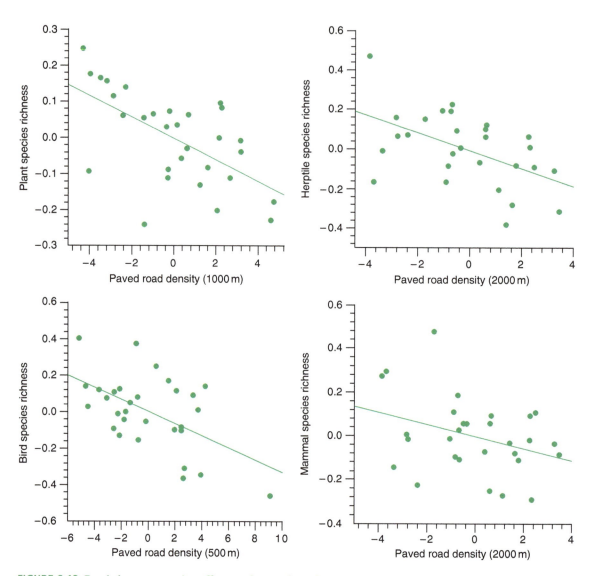

FIGURE 8.12 Roads have a negative effect on the number of species of plants, herptiles, birds, and mammals in wetlands. Residuals of the species richness–area regression are plotted against residuals of the paved road density–area regression. (From Findlay and Houlahan 1997.)

The logjams were so solid that "bushes and weeds" and even trees covered the surface, while "the men could walk over it in any direction." It took Freeman and Custis "fourteen days of incessant fatigue, toil and danger, doubt and uncertainty" to pass through the Great Raft. The logs blocked commercial boat passage, and it eventually took some 50 years and federal funds to clear it, a task finished finally in the 1870s.

A similar mass of trees blocked the Atchafalaya River in the early 1800s, extending for some 65 km (Reuss 1998). Some witnesses claim that humans and even horses could pass over the river on this debris. Once a cut upstream was made by Shreve in 1831, the source of logs declined and the raft stopped growing. Despite repeated attempts to burn or otherwise clear the raft after 1831, it re-formed. Finally, with the

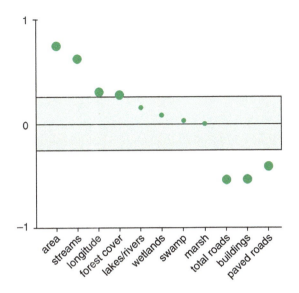

FIGURE 8.13 The effects of different environmental factors upon the number of plant species in a wetland. The vertical axis is the standardized regression coefficient, the gray zone represents non-significance. The horizontal axis lists environmental factors that were measured. Wetland area and presence of streams had a pronounced positive effect (upper left) while the total length of two-lane roads, the number of buildings, and total length of paved roads had a pronounced negative effect. Longitude and forest cover had weak positive effects ($n = 58$). (After Houlahan *et al.* 2006.)

services of a snagboat, the last of the raft was removed in 1860.

These are but two examples. A more quantitative picture emerges from Bayou Teche in 1847, where, over a distance of 32 km, 1455 logs were taken from the bed of the bayou, and 961 stumps and snags removed. Nearby, 1887 snags and logs were removed from Bayou Lafourche (Reuss 1998, p. 34).

It would be interesting to study early explorers' descriptions for a better account of woody debris

distribution. Consider a few examples. Iberville's trip from the Mississippi River to Lake Maurepas in 1699 was delayed because the watercourse was clogged with roots and logs (McWilliams 1981, p. 6). He also describes rivers "carrying along many trees" (p. 54). Weddle (1991) reports that Iberville found distributaries choked with drift logs (p. 61) and "choked by sandbars and uprooted trees" (p. 148).

Coarse woody debris is known to be very important to a wide array of forest species (Harmon *et al.* 1986), providing everything from germination sites for tree seedlings to hiding places for amphibians. In contrast, the importance of coarse woody debris for providing wildlife habitat in rivers and wetlands is too often underestimated. It not only provides shelter, but modifies sediment deposition patterns, creating pools that are used by many aquatic species (Bilby and Ward 1991; Francis and Schindler 2006). For fish, coarse woody debris provides at least three positive effects: it provides shelter that decreases predation risk, it provides visual isolation that reduces contact between fish, and it provides refuge from the current that minimizes energy expenditures (Crook and Robertson 1999). Logs on shorelines can provide shelter and basking sites for many kinds of turtles (Figure 8.15). As the human population increases on shorelines, the amount of coarse woody debris declines (Francis and Schindler 2006).

Large piles of dead wood may once have provided a matrix that armored coastal barrier islands, oyster reefs, and wetlands. Human activities have reduced the supply of driftwood. Many of the proposals for coastal restoration that are intended to armor shorelines may simply be an expensive and non-renewable replacement for a natural product that once played a similar role.

8.4 Stream type

We have already seen many examples of how a surrounding landscape affects a wetland. The proximity of roads has negative effects, while the proximity of forests has a positive effect. We have even seen that the presence of a stream has a measurable positive effect on the number of plants

FIGURE 8.14 Enormous amounts of woody debris were once a natural feature of water courses and shorelines. The Great Raft dammed the Red River and flooded the surrounding area. (Photo by R. B. Talfor, courtesy Noel Memorial Library Archives, Louisiana State University, Shreveport.)

in a wetland. The type of watercourse is therefore likely to be an important factor. Using slope and geomorphology as the main variables, the Rosgen system (Figure 8.16, top) sorts rivers in nine types from Aa + (very steep) though to G (gentle). There are obvious changes in the type of channel configuration along this gradient, with braided streams and meanders on the right. Other factors such as entrenchment, sinuosity, and width to depth ratio also change with slope. Combining eight of these slope categories (A to G) with six classes of bed material (1 (rock) to (6) silt and clay), produces a matrix of 48 possible types of stream. Only a small subset of these, mainly in groups C, DA, and E have large associated wetlands (Figure 8.16, bottom). Thus, simple factors that you can see on maps, like type of substrate and slope, will tell you a good deal about the types of wetlands likely to be found in a landscape. The slope of the river bank

is obviously one of the most important factors that will determine whether the wetland is a narrow strip of riparian vegetation or a broad wetland. The type of watercourse also has a great deal of impact on burial, which we explored earlier (Chapter 7).

Although we can think of the Rosgen system as a template that produces different wetland vegetation types, there is also a feedback loop where the vegetation itself controls the river. In classes C, DA, and E, the vegetation can have a strong impact on width to depth ratios.

Wetland ecologists are often expected to be knowledgeable about riparian habitats, particularly where the adjoining wetlands control rates of bank erosion and wildlife habitat. The Rosgen system provides a way to view wetlands from the landscape scale, and from the point of view of freshwater organisms like fish.

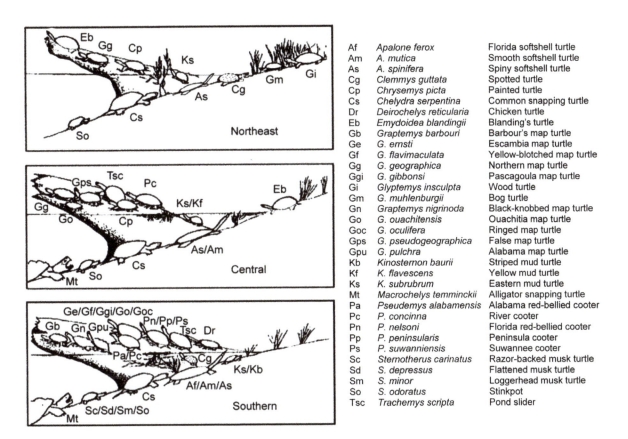

Af	*Apalone ferox*	Florida softshell turtle
Am	*A. mutica*	Smooth softshell turtle
As	*A. spinifera*	Spiny softshell turtle
Cg	*Clemmys guttata*	Spotted turtle
Cp	*Chrysemys picta*	Painted turtle
Cs	*Chelydra serpentina*	Common snapping turtle
Dr	*Deirochelys reticularia*	Chicken turtle
Eb	*Emydoidea blandingii*	Blanding's turtle
Gb	*Graptemys barbouri*	Barbour's map turtle
Ge	*G. ernsti*	Escambia map turtle
Gf	*G. flavimaculata*	Yellow-blotched map turtle
Gg	*G. geographica*	Northern map turtle
Ggi	*G. gibbonsi*	Pascagoula map turtle
Gi	*Glyptemys insculpta*	Wood turtle
Gm	*G. muhlenburgii*	Bog turtle
Gn	*Graptemys nigrinoda*	Black-knobbed map turtle
Go	*G. ouachitensis*	Ouachitia map turtle
Goc	*G. oculifera*	Ringed map turtle
Gps	*G. pseudogeographica*	False map turtle
Gpu	*G. pulchra*	Alabama map turtle
Kb	*Kinosternon baurii*	Striped mud turtle
Kf	*K. flavescens*	Yellow mud turtle
Ks	*K. subrubrum*	Eastern mud turtle
Mt	*Macrochelys temminckii*	Alligator snapping turtle
Pa	*Pseudemys alabamensis*	Alabama red-bellied cooter
Pc	*P. concinna*	River cooter
Pn	*P. nelsoni*	Florida red-bellied cooter
Pp	*P. peninsularis*	Peninsula cooter
Ps	*P. suwanniensis*	Suwannee cooter
Sc	*Sternotherus carinatus*	Razor-backed musk turtle
Sd	*S. depressus*	Flattened musk turtle
Sm	*S. minor*	Loggerhead musk turtle
So	*S. odoratus*	Stinkpot
Tsc	*Trachemys scripta*	Pond slider

FIGURE 8.15 Coarse woody debris provides important basking sites for turtles (species shown for North American regions), as well as habitat for many other animal species. (Adapted from Bury 1979.)

8.5 Human population density is becoming a key factor

Human population density continues to increase – there are twice as many people in the world as when I was born. The human population continues to grow. The rate of growth will depend upon factors like the number of children in a family, access to birth control, religious belief, age of reproduction, and quality of medical care. There are many scenarios (Figure 8.17) but all probable ones show continued growth. According to many calculations, we have already passed the sustainable level for humans, measured as the annual rate of return of natural resources. That is, we humans are now consuming more each year than the Earth produces. We maintain levels above this by eating into the world's ecological capital – old forests, fish stocks, soil, and fossil fuels to give four examples. This is only a temporary solution – it is like living on savings. Once the savings are gone, there is nothing. There are groups promoting zero population growth, and even population reduction. Densely populated countries like China already impose a policy of one child per family, but without other nations following this example, it is hard to envisage a future without severe problems. Since humans manipulate landscapes – whether it is grazing cattle on floodplains, cutting mangroves for fuel, or building enormous dams and levees, the fate of wetlands is closely tied to human populations.

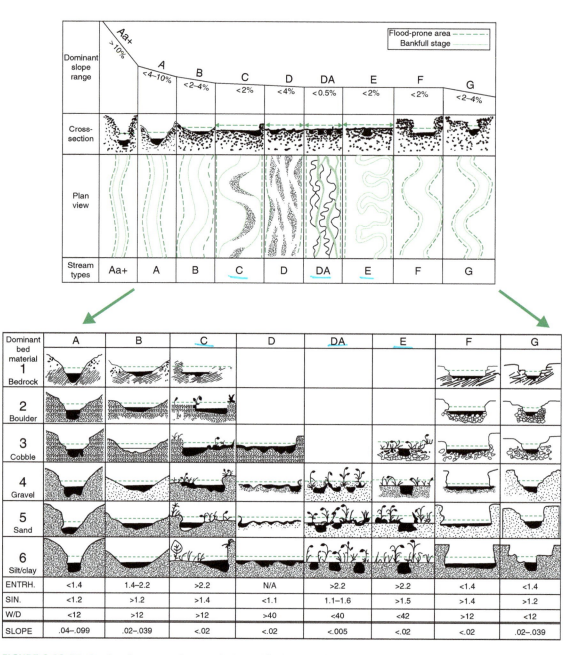

FIGURE 8.16 Wetlands often occur in association with rivers and streams. Nine types can be recognized based upon geomorphology and relief (Aa+ to G). (From Rosgen 1994.)

As humans increasingly dominate landscapes, their activities become an overriding effect. This is not to say that the six main factors (hydrology, fertility, disturbance, competition, herbivory, and burial) are unimportant, but that each of these is itself driven by human activity. Wetland managers may be trying to manipulate one or more of these factors, but human population density is the real driver.

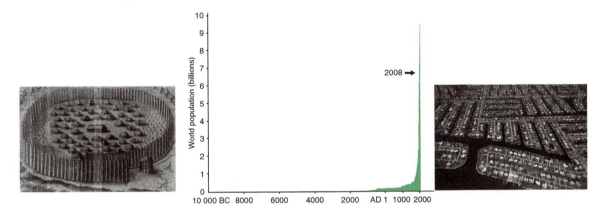

FIGURE 8.17 The size of the human population is an important causal factor that drives many other environmental factors including levee construction, drainage for agriculture, and road construction. Actual population shown as of December 31, 2008 and projected estimates shown to 2050. (Based on data from the U.S. Census Bureau.)

As an example of this, let us turn to one of the world's most densely populated regions, the delta of the mighty Ganges River in Bangladesh. The Ganges River, one of India's best-known rivers, has built a delta with sediment carried downstream from glaciers in the Himalayas. It intersects with a second river, the Brahmaputra, which drains the Tibetan plateau.

Most of Bangladesh is one large delta. It is home to more than 150 million people – about 25 times the population of Louisiana. Yet the land area is almost identical to Louisiana, making it one of the most densely populated countries in the world. A human population of this size is bound to have negative effects on the landscape under the best of conditions. Since most of the area is delta, about one-third of the country floods each year during the rainy season.

The original delta was fringed with enormous mangrove swamps. The original state of the delta was likely similar to the Sundarbans, which are said to be the largest remaining piece of estuarine mangrove forest in the world (Figure 8.18). This area is probably best known for its population of Bengal tigers. Part of the Sundarbans occurs in the Indian state of West Bengal, where it is called Sundarbans National Park (ca. 1300 km^2) while in Bangladesh there are three separate wildlife sanctuaries totaling *ca.* 139 700 ha. The birds include storks, ibis, herons, ducks, and

eagles. There are also freshwater crocodiles and dolphins. So important is this area for wildlife conservation that it is also designated as a UNESCO World Heritage Site and a Ramsar site.

Much of the natural coastal vegetation has been altered by logging and agriculture. The delta was once a vast magrove swamp of some 20 000 km^2, complete with animals like Bengal tigers. First settled around 1770, this former mangrove swamp now has a population in excess of 4 million people. The forests were logged, and the land converted to farmland for crops like rice. Saltwater intrusion is causing reduced agricultural production and affecting drinking water supplies. As the land has increased in salinity, rice farmers have converted to shrimp production. The combination of an increasing population with a shrinking land mass seems to be a recipe for distaster.

The current situation along the coast was described in an interview reported in the *Guardian Weekly* (McDougall 2008), with Gita Pandhar, a 25-year-old woman:

When I was young, this was all rice-fields and herds of cows. It was beautiful, a wonderful place to grow up, in isolation away from the mainland. The farmland my grandfather first

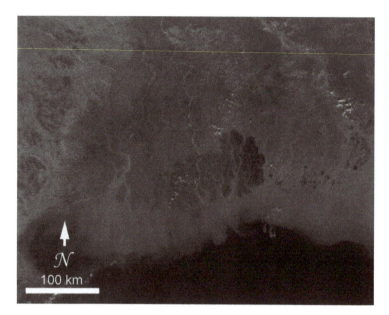

FIGURE 8.18 The Sundarbans, the world's largest mangrove swamp, occur largely in one of the most densely populated areas in the world, Bangladesh. Note the abrupt boundary where the wetland is not protected from exploitation, and note the sediment plumes coming out of the Ganges River. (From Earth Observing System, NASA.) (See also color plate.)

tended is now poisoned with salt. All the arable land has been replaced by swamp. We used to burn dung as fuel, but there is nowhere to graze and now we have to cut the last of the wood here to cook with.

The flood problems in this delta are often reported in connection with global warming, but many factors have to be considered. Deforestation of the Himalayas may have increased flooding and the load of silt. Dams upsteam in India have changed the hydrology of the rivers. Levees, when built, interfere with sedimentation, and trap water during heavy rains. Human population density is very high, and lack of planning allows people to live in highly flood-prone areas. Melting glaciers do appear to have increased runoff, at least temporarily, though once the ice has melted, river flows may then decrease. Overall, flood records show that the height of the average spring flood is decreasing, while simultaneously the occasional flood peaks are increasing (that is, decreased mean with increased variance). Of course, all of these issues may be secondary to the most basic fact that deltas are unstable landscapes. River courses in deltas naturally shift during flood pulses and

hurricanes, eroding some areas while building new areas.

Typically, structural solutions are being implemented. Hundreds of kilometers of embankment are being strengthened, accompanied by drainage sluices to allow better drainage from the impounded areas (Agrawala *et al.* 2003). Drainage is being improved, with new bridges and culverts on rural roads. Mangroves are being replanted. New proposed expenditures are in the billions of dollars for projects ranging from hurricane shelters to river "erosion control." Here is how the OECD study summarized the situation:

The huge sediment loads brought by these Himalayan rivers, coupled with a negligible flow gradient add to drainage congestion problems and exacerbate the extent of flooding. The low coastal topography contributes to coastal inundation and saline intrusion inland. Bangladesh also lies in a very active cyclone corridor that transects the Bay of Bengal. The societal exposure to such risks is further enhanced by its very high population and population density, with close to 800 persons per square kilometer in vulnerable areas such as the coastal zones. (p. 49)

In 2007, Cyclone Sidr hit Bangladesh and killed over 3000 people. To what do we attribute this? Natural deltaic processes? Overpopulation? Lack of land use planning? Deforestation in the mountains? Dams upstream? Global warming? Rising sea levels? Increasingly, the task of managing wetlands will be difficult to separate from managing human societies.

CONCLUSION

Both the type of wetland, and the composition of the species, are a consequence of many environmental factors acting simultaneously (Section 1.7). Some of these factors are likely more important than others. In Chapters 1 to 8, we have looked systematically at these causal factors, starting with those that are generally most important. Of course, there are factors beyond those discussed here (Section 1.7.2). We might profitably add sections on mutualism, or calcium, or warfare, or heavy metals, or exotic species, or off-road vehicles, as six examples. Each of these may be important in certain locations. We have to stop somewhere. We could also observe that human population growth is an overriding factor that controls many of the factors we have discussed here. Having now covered the essential factors that are generally important around the world, you have the background to explore any specific wetland you encounter. Often your work may involve deciding which factors are currently most important in influencing a wetland, and which are having positive or negative effects. Starting with hydrology, fertility, and disturbance will usually be helpful. You now have a shopping list.

We could say that the general purpose of wetland ecology is to determine which causal factors determine which consequences. We are now going to change focus and begin to explore just what kinds of biological consequences arise from these causal factors. That is, we are going to move from factors that cause events to factors that are consequences of events. Another way of describing this is a change from independent variables to dependent variables. The consequences, or the dependent variables, include diversity, productivity, and ecosystem services.

Chapter contents

9 Diversity

A fundamental property of any ecosystem or habitat is the number of species it contains. Some wetlands contain large numbers of species; some contain few. Within a single wetland, there is similar variation, with some habitats being species rich and other species poor. Such patterns in diversity have long been of keen interest to ecologists (e.g. Williams 1964; Pielou 1975; May 1986; Huston 1994; Gaston 2000) and conservation biologists (Ehrlich and Ehrlich 1981; World Conservation Monitoring Centre 1992). The long-term goal of such work is to determine how many species occur in different parts of the world, and to uncover the factors that predict how many we will find in specified conditions. Since there are good reasons to fear that up to one-fourth of the world's species could disappear in the coming century, it is important to manage wild places, including wetlands, to maximize the number of native species found globally. When species are at risk of extinction – be they quill worts or tigers – managers must create and protect enough habitat to allow their populations to recover. Hence, the study and understanding of diversity occupies a central position in wetland ecology. The objective of this chapter is to survey the number wetland species found in major groups of organisms and then introduce you to some of the critical environmental factors that control them. Often only a couple of factors will determine whether a wetland supports many species or only a few.

9.1   Introduction to diversity in wetlands

Let us begin with the world as a whole. How many species of different types of wetland organisms are there? One source of comparative data is a survey of freshwater animal diversity (Lévêque *et al.* 2005) that used both published sources and museum collections (Table 9.1). The overall conclusion is that some 100 000 animal species require freshwater habitats. Of these, some 50 000 are insects; there are 21 000 vertebrate species, 10 000 crustacean species, and 5000 mollusk species. Among the vertebrates, amphibians occur solely in fresh water, with ca. 5500 species. To this list of freshwater species one would need to add species using coastal wetlands for a global total. Let us look at the diversity of three groups by way of illustration.

9.1.1 Wetlands have many species of fish

The Amazon River has more species of fish (ca. 2000) than any other river in the world, with particularly large numbers of species of characoids and siluroids (Figure 9.1). The former group includes the fruit-eating fish in the genus *Colossoma* (Figure 2.5*d*) that forage in forests during high-water periods.
It also includes the carnivorous piranha. The latter group includes the many species of catfish that forage in deeper water. South America as a whole has some 5000 species (Lévêque *et al.* 2005).
The next most important rivers for fish biodiversity are the Congo and the Mekong Rivers, the latter having the world's largest freshwater fish, the Mekong giant catfish.

9.1.2 Wetlands have many species of waterbirds

Wetlands often have spectacular numbers of birds. If we begin with about 9000 species of birds in the world, and then take a conservative estimate – that

Table 9.1 **The species of freshwater organisms provides a pool from which wetland communities are assembled according to biogeography, physical factors, and biological interactions. There are two sources of uncertainty in these numbers: the total number of species in the groups, and, more seriously, the number of species that occur in wetlands. Note that marine species in coastal marshes are not included**

Phylum	Number of freshwater species	Comments
Porifera	197	
Cnidaria	30	
Nemertea	12	
Platyhelminthes	500	
Gastrotricha	250	
Rotifera	1 817	
Nematoda	3 000	
Annelida	>1000	
Bryozoa	70–75	
Mollusca	5 000	
Arthropoda	>65 000	
Branchiopoda	>813	Particularly vernal pools
Ostracoda	3 000	Mostly benthic
Copepoda	2 085	Mostly planktonic
Malacostraca	4 165	Mostly marine
Arachnida	5 000	
Insecta	>50 000	Mainly Diptera and Trichoptera
Chordata	>21 000	
Teleostomi	13 400	
Amphibia	5 504	All but absent from marine
Reptilia	250	
Aves	1 800	
Mammalia	100	

Source: Adapted from Lévêque *et al.* (2005).

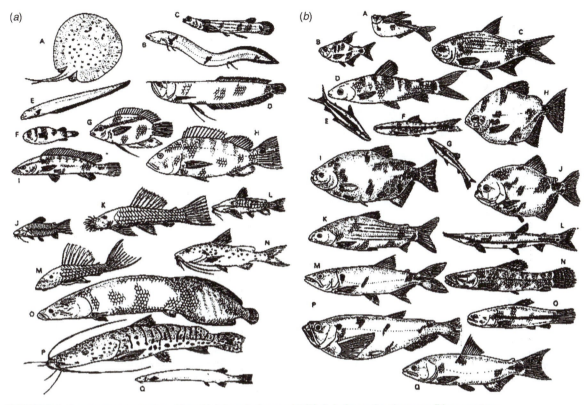

FIGURE 9.1 Some representative siluroid (*a*) and characoid (*b*) fish from the Amazon River system. (From Lowe-McConnell 1975.)

20% are wetland dependent – we arrive at an estimate that some 1800 birds may be wetland dependent. Wading birds are one obvious group, as are ducks and kingfishers (Lévêque *et al.* 2005). The Ramsar Convention (The Convention on Wetlands of International Importance; see Section 14.4.3) defines "waterfowl" as species of birds that are "ecologically dependent upon wetlands" and it uses the term "waterbird" as being synonymons with "waterfowl" for the purposes of the application of the Convention (Delany and Scott 2006). According to the fourth edition of *Waterbird Population Estimates* (Delany and Scott 2006), there are 878 waterbird species in 33 families occurring in 2305 biogeographic populations. The largest number of waterbird populations (815) is found in Asia, followed by the Neotropics (554)

and Africa (542). Fewer waterbird populations are found in Oceania (390), North America (384), and Europe (351) (global total does not equal regional population sum because populations are often distributed over more than one region). Data on species trends are not available for about 20% of these populations. About 1% of the populations are extinct, while about one-fourth show a decreasing trend. Oceania is an exception, with 7% extinct, and only 12% decreasing – but Oceania also lacks data on 57% of the species.

At the local scale, the number of birds encountered will often depend upon the amount of forested wetland. In North American wetlands, higher numbers of species occur in riparian forests, swamps, and shrub-dominated wetlands (Figure 9.2).

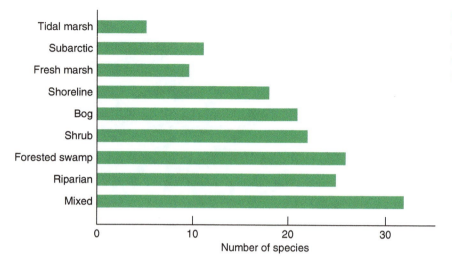

FIGURE 9.2 Median number of species of birds occupying different wetland vegetation types in North America. (After Adamus 1992.)

9.1.3 Most mammals use wetlands occasionally

Only about 100 mammal species have an obligate dependence on wetlands (Lévêque *et al.* 2005), with common examples including nutria, muskrats, beavers, and otters. Some are among the smallest mammals – there are four water-dependent shrews (genus *Sorex*) in North America and ten species in Europe and Asia. Some are also among the largest mammals – the hippopotamus (*Hippopotamus amphibius*) occurs only in Africa as does the pygmy hippopotamus (*Hexaprotodon liberiensis*). There are also semi-aquatic ungulates, the sitatunga (*Tragelaphus spekei*) in Africa, the marsh deer (*Blastocerus dichotomus*) in South America, and the water buffalo (*Bubalus bubalis*) in Asia. The unusual mammal, the duck-billed platypus, an aquatic but

egg-laying species, occurs only in Australia. Many other mammals use wetlands seasonally. More than 120 species of mammals have been recorded from the Pantanal (South America) and the Okavango delta (Africa) (Junk *et al.* 2006). The Sundarbans, part of the Ganges/Brahmaputra River delta, are said to be the largest piece of estuarine mangrove forest in the world. This area is probably best known, however, for supporting the world's largest remaining population of Bengal tigers (Junk *et al.* 2006). The Mississippi River wetlands provide important habitat for large carnivores including the panther and Louisiana black bear (Keddy *et al.* 2009b). In many savanna areas, wetlands provide places of refuge for large herds of mammals during periods of drought (Sinclair 1983; Sinclair and Fryxell 1985). Including these species would considerably lengthen the list of wetland-dependent mammals.

9.2   Four general rules govern the number of species in wetlands

There are some broad general rules that we can build upon – rules that might have been called laws if ecology was as old as physics. Four general rules summarize nearly 200 years of research on the topic (Williams 1964; Pielou 1975; Huston 1994; Rosenzweig 1995). Later in this chapter I will add a few more that are more recent.

9.2.1 The number of species decreases with increasing latitude

The number of species at low latitudes greatly exceeds the number at higher latitudes. This pattern became obvious during the 1800s as global explorers including Wallace, von Humboldt, and even Darwin

FIGURE 1.3 Swamps. (*a*) Floodplain swamp (Ottawa River, Canada). (*b*) Mangrove swamp (Caroni wetland, Trinidad).

(a)

(b)

FIGURE 1.4 Marshes. (*a*) Riverine marsh (Ottawa River, Canada; courtesy B. Shipley). (*b*) Salt marsh (Petpeswick Inlet, Canada).

(a)

(b)

FIGURE 1.5 Bogs. (*a*) Lowland continental bog (Algonquin Park, Canada). (*b*) Upland coastal bog (Cape Breton Island, Canada).

FIGURE 1.6 Fens. (*a*) Patterned fen (northern Canada; courtesy C. Rubec). (*b*) Shoreline fen (Lake Ontario, Canada).

FIGURE 1.7 Wet meadows. (*a*) Sand spit (Long Point, Lake Ontario, Canada; courtesy A. Reznicek).
(*b*) Gravel lakeshore (Tusket River, Canada; courtesy A. Payne).

FIGURE 1.8 Shallow water. (*a*) Bay (Lake Erie, Canada; courtesy A. Reznicek). (*b*) Pond (interdunal pools on Sable Island, Canada).

FIGURE 2.1 Flooding is a natural process in landscapes. When humans build cities in or adjacent to wetlands, flooding can be expected. This example shows Cedar Rapids in the United States in 2008 (*The Gazette*), but incidences of flood damage to cities go far back in history to early cities such as Nineveh mentioned in *The Epic of Gilgamesh* (Sanders 1972).

FIGURE 2.5 Many wetland organisms are dependent upon annual flood pulses. Animals discussed here include (*a*) white ibis (U.S. Fish and Wildlife Service), (*b*) Mississippi gopher frog (courtesy M. Redmer), (*c*) dragonfly (courtesy C. Rubec), and (*d*) tambaqui (courtesy M. Goulding). Plants discussed here include (*e*) furbish lousewort (bottom left; U.S. Fish and Wildlife Service) and (*f*) Plymouth gentian.

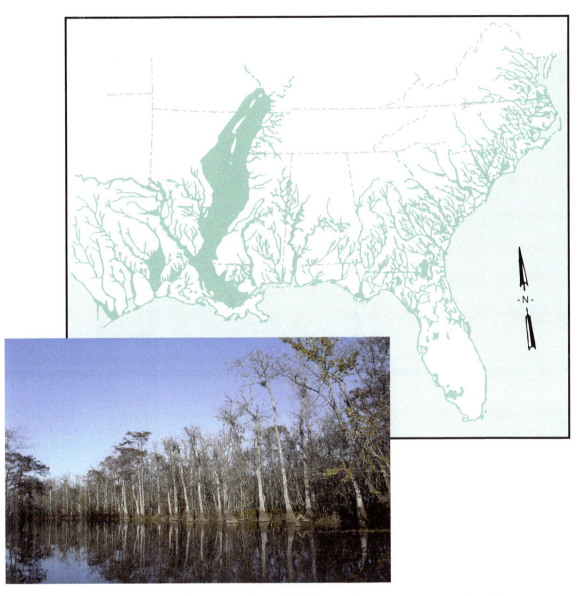

FIGURE 2.10 Spring floods produce the extensive bottomland forests that accompany many large rivers, such as those of the southeastern United States of America. (Map from Mitsch and Gosselink 1986.)

FIGURE 2.16 During a low water year in Lake Erie there was dense regeneration of *Scirpus* and *Sagittaria* plants in Metzger Marsh. (Courtesy D. Wilcox.)

FIGURE 2.21 Dams built by humans, such as the Three Gorges Dam recently constructed on the Yangtze River, increasingly disrupt natural flood pulses in the world's great rivers. (Courtesy ChinaFotoPress/Li Ming.)

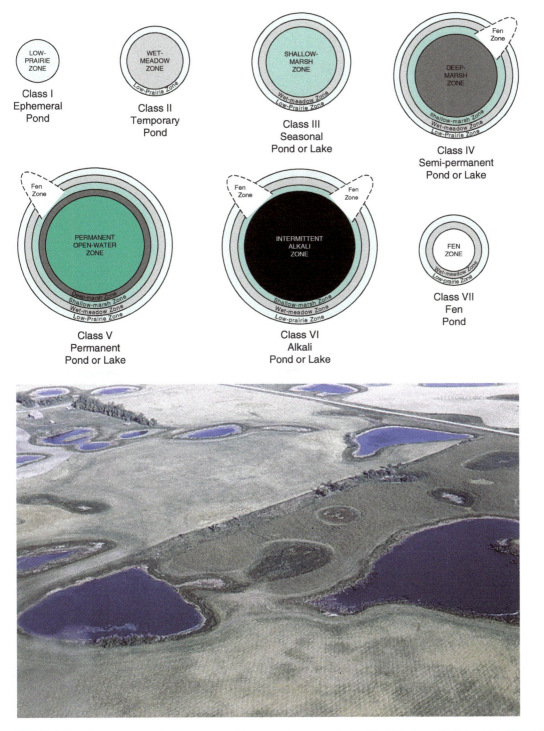

FIGURE 2.20 The vegetation patterns in prairie potholes are controlled by flooding. Here is a classification system showing vegetation zones for seven types of prairie potholes (from Stewart and Kantrud 1971 in van der Valk 1989) and an aerial view of potholes of differing classes near Minnedosa, Manitoba (Courtesy C. Rubec).

FIGURE 3.3 Many wetlands have low fertility. Examples include peat bogs (*a*, Algonquin Provincial Park, Ontario), the Everglades (*b*), shorelines in sand plains (*c*, Axe Lake, Ontario; courtesy M. Sharp), and wet savannas with old soils (*d*, Buttercup Flats, De Soto National Forest, Mississippi).

FIGURE 4.1 Fire removes biomass from wetlands during droughts. It also alters fertility by volatilizing nitrogen and recycling phosphorus. If the fire is sufficiently intense to burn the organic soil, pools of water can form in the depressions. (Courtesy C. Rubec.)

FIGURE 4.12 A gator hole in the Everglades along with its creator and occupant (not to scale). The alligator excavates a hole, which supports aquatic plants and animals, and the earth mound around the edge of the hole develops its own characteristic plant community. Large expanses of wetland can be dotted by such holes and mounds.

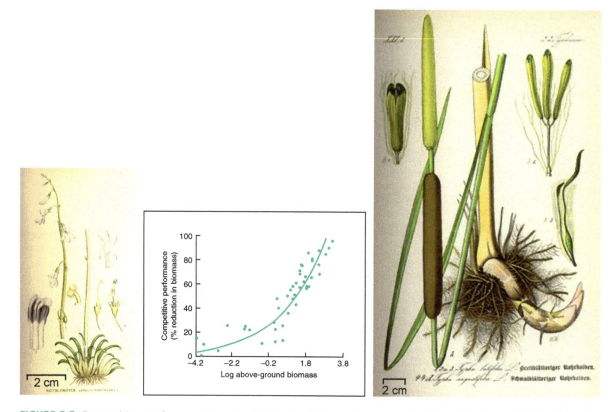

FIGURE 5.7 Competitive performance increased with plant size across an array of 44 wetland species. Small rosette species (e.g. *Lobelia dortmanna*) occur on the left side of the figure, while large leafy species (e.g. *Typha latifolia*) occur on the right. Competitive performance was measured as the percent reduction in biomass of a common test species. (After Gaudet and Keddy 1988.)

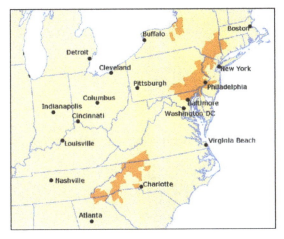

FIGURE 5.13 Animals may also depend upon peripheral habitats. The bog turtle (*Clemmys muhlenbergii*), North America's smallest turtle (9 cm, 115 g), occurs in wet meadows. (Photo courtesy R.G. Tucker, Jr., U.S. Fish and Wildlife Service; map, U.S. Fish and Wildlife Service.)

FIGURE 6.1 Sometimes grazing animals, such as nutria, can almost eliminate wetlands plants – as illustrated by this experimental fenced plot (exclosure) in a Louisiana marsh. (Courtesy Louisiana Department of Wildlife and Fisheries.)

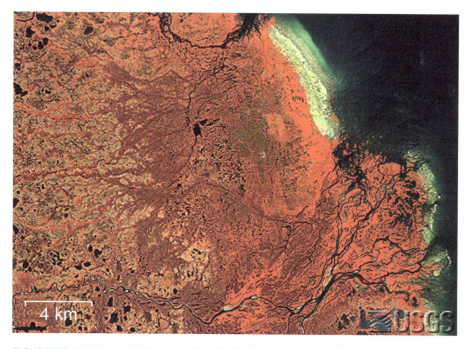

4 km

FIGURE 6.2 Geese are grazing coastal wetlands along the shore of Hudson Bay so intensely that some areas of marsh have been converted to mud flats, as shown in this July 18 satellite image of the Knife River delta in Manitoba, Canada. The mud flats are indicated by the bright strip of land. (U.S. Geological Survey 1996.)

1 Matetite reed
  Phragmites sp.
2 Hippopotamus
  Hippopotamus amphibius
3 Hammerhead stork
  Scopus umbretta
4 Black crake
  Limnocorax flavirostra
5 Sitatunga
  Tragelaphus spekki
6 Swamp worm
  Alma emini
7 Saddlebilled stork
  Ephippiorhynchus senegalensis
8 Water cabbage
  Pistia stratiotes
9 Water lily
  Nymphaea sp.
10 Bichir
   Polypterus sp.
11 Catfish
   Malapterurus sp.

12 Lily trotter
   Actophilornis africana
13 African spoonbill
   Platalea alba
14 Papyrus
   Cyperus papyrus
15 Malachite kingfisher
   Corythornis cristata
16 Herald snake
   Crotaphopeltis hotamboeia
17 Shoebill
   Balaeniceps rex
18 Squacco heron
   Ardeola ralloides
19 Snail
   Biomphalaria sudanica
20 Marsh mongoose
   Atilax paludinosus
21 Lungfish
   Protopterus aethiopicus

FIGURE 6.5 Large herbivores remain important in African wetlands, and their impacts affect many other wetland species. (From Dugan 2005.)

FIGURE 6.15 Does the amount of vegetation control the abundance of nutria, and hence the number of alligators? Or does the number of alligators control the abundance of nutria, and hence the amount of vegetation? The first is termed bottom–up control, and the second is termed top–down control. It is by no means clear which is the correct view, or whether both are happening simultaneously.

FIGURE 8.1 Salinity changes the species composition of wetlands from mangrove swamp (left, Florida Keys, USA; courtesy G. Ludwing, U.S. Fish and Wildlife Service) to salt marsh (bottom right, El Yali, Chile; courtesy M. Bertness) to oligohaline marsh (top right, Gulf of Mexico, Louisiana).

FIGURE 8.10 The flamingoes of the Camargue wetland on the Mediterranean coast depend upon invertebrates for food. (Courtesy A. Waterkeyn.)

FIGURE 8.18 The Sundarbans, the world's largest mangrove swamp, occur largely in one of the most densely populated areas in the world, Bangladesh. Note the abrupt boundary where the wetland is not protected from exploitation, and note the sediment plumes coming out of the Ganges River. (From Earth Observing System, NASA.)

FIGURE 9.4 Differences in elevation produce much of the diversity found in wetlands, as illustrated by this example of zonation.

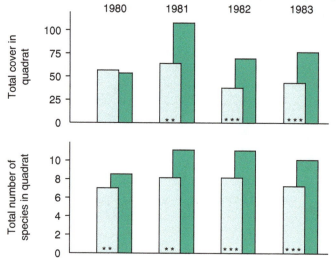

FIGURE 10.7 Shrubs occupy higher elevations in many wetlands (top). Experimentally removing the shrubs increases the cover and number of species of herbaceous wetland plants (bottom). (From Keddy 1989b.)

FIGURE 11.6 Coal was produced in vast wetlands such as this Carboniferous coal swamp. (© The Field Museum, #GE085637c.) When coal is burned, the stored carbon returns to the atmosphere as carbon dioxide. Stored nutrients such as nitrogen are also released.

FIGURE 13.2 Four stages of restoration in one of the author's wetlands: former wetland dried out by drainage ditches (upper left), replacing old beaver dam and filling ditches with earth (upper right), first year (lower left), second year (lower right). The wetland is now a breeding site for wood frogs, leopard frogs, mink frogs, spring peepers, American toads, gray tree frogs, green frogs, and bullfrogs.

1 Everglade kite,
  Rostrhamus sociabilis
2 Pileated woodpecker,
  Phloeceastes pileatus
3 Prothonotary warbler,
  Protonotaria citrea
4 Rough green snake,
  Opheodrys aestivus
5 Limpikin,
  Aramus guarauna
6 Raccoon, *Procyon lotor*
7 Flamingo,
  Phoenicopterus ruber
8 Mississippi alligator,
  Alligator mississippiensis
9 Roseate spoonbill,
  Ajaia ajaja
10 Eastern fox squirrel,
   Sciurus niger
11 Snail,
   Isognomon melina alata
12 Green tree frog,
   Hyla cinerea
13 Green anolis,
   Anolis carolinensis
14 Zebra butterfly,
   Heliconius charitonius
15 Purple gallinule,
   Porphyrula martinica
16 Snail, *Pomacea flagellata*
17 Swamp rabbit,
   Sylvilagus sp.
18 Oxeye tarpon,
   Megalops cyprinoides
19 Cottonmouth moccasin,
   Ancistrodon piscivorus

FIGURE 13.3 A scene from the Everglades. The Comprehensive Everglades Restoration Plan aims to protect and restore the conditions that maintain the native biota of the Everglades. (From Dugan 2005.)

FIGURE 13.4 Enormous canals have altered the natural hydrology of the Everglades, and provided a conduit for nutrient enriched water to enter the wetlands.

FIGURE 13.5 Removing artificial levees will also restore wetlands. (left) Prior to dike removal. (right) After removing some 6 km of dikes, natural flood regimes were restored and in 2004 the Danube River flowed freely over Tataru Island. (Courtesy World Wildlife Fund.)

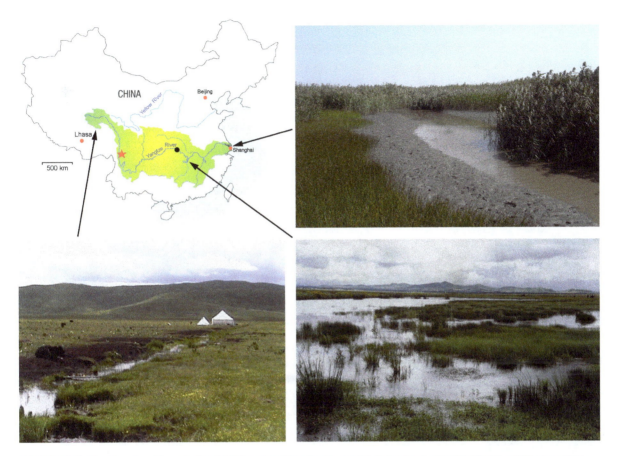

FIGURE 13.8 The Yangtze River is the third longest river in the world. It begins in the highlands of Tibet, amidst some of the world's largest high-altitude peatlands (Ruoergai peatland, bottom left; courtesy Wetlands International). Here it also flows through mountains which comprise one of the world's biodiversity hotspots, the mountains of Southwest China (star, top left). Further east it passes through large lakes such as Dongting Lake (lower right; from www.hbj.hunan.gov.cn/dongT1/default.aspx). Where it enters the sea there are large deltaic wetlands (top right; courtesy M. Zhijun). The world's largest dam, the Three Gorges Dam (Fig. 2.21), is indicated by the black dot (top left).

FIGURE 13.10 The Caernarvon Diversion structure on the Mississippi River allows floodwaters to pass through an artificial levee and enter the wetlands of Breton Sound in the distance. (Courtesy J. Day.)

4 cm

FIGURE 13.12 Invasive aquatic plants, like water hyacinth (*Eichhornia crassipes*, bottom; courtesy Center for Aquatic and Invasive Plants, University of Florida), are notorious for their ability to invade and to dominate wet places (top; W. Durden, U.S. Department of Agriculture, Agricultural Research Service). They can reduce both biological diversity and ecological services. Such invasives pose a significant risk to restored wetlands as well as to natural wetlands.

FIGURE 14.1 The Mesopotamian marshes (top; © Nature Iraq) have been affected by humans for thousands of years, most recently by drainage, dam construction, and warfare (bottom; from Lawler 2005). *Phragmites* reeds are the mainstay of marsh culture, being used as housing material, woven into mats, and fed to water buffalo.

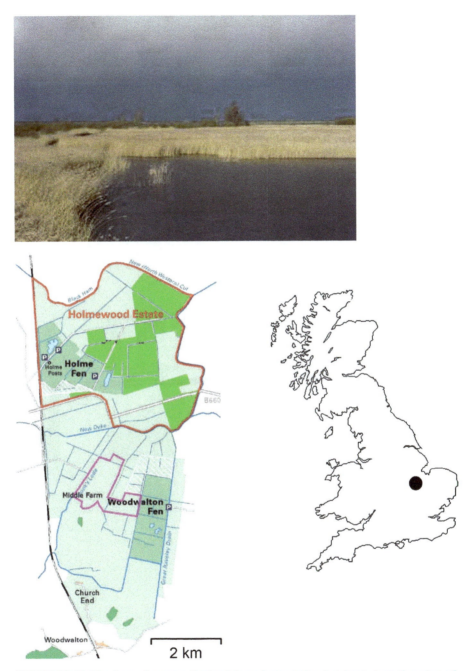

FIGURE 14.13 The fens of eastern England have been drained at least since the reign of Charles I in the early 1600s. Over 99% have been lost. The Great Fen Project plans to restore 3000 hectares around two core remnants, Holme Fen and Woodwalton Fen (top). (Courtesy The Wildlife Trust, Cambridge.)

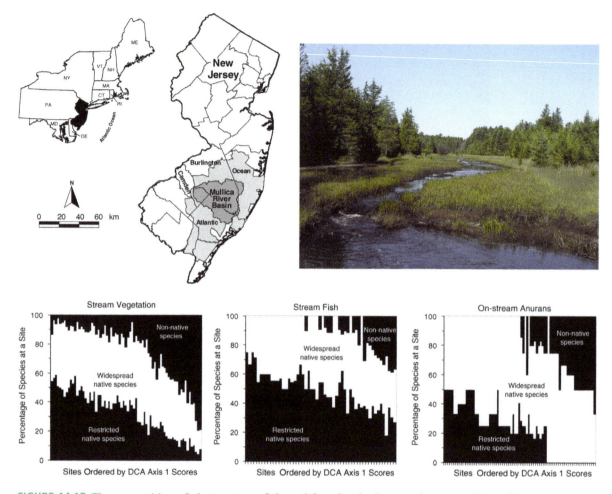

FIGURE 14.17 The composition of plants, stream fish, and frogs/toads changes along a gradient of human impact. These 88 sites from the Mullica River basin in New Jersey are ordered by scores obtained from detrended correspondence analysis (DCA) from least impacted by humans (left) to most impacted by humans (right). (From Zampella *et al.* 2006; photo of Tulpehocken Creek courtesy J. F. Bunnell.)

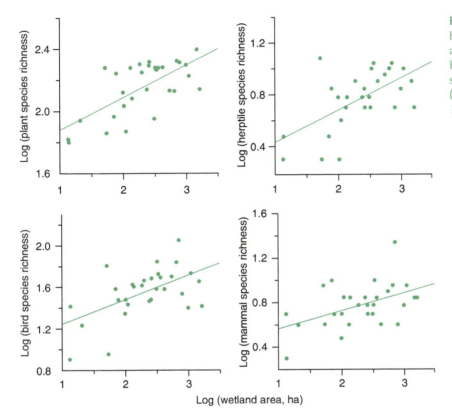

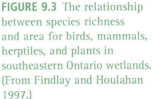

FIGURE 9.3 The relationship between species richness and area for birds, mammals, herptiles, and plants in southeastern Ontario wetlands. (From Findlay and Houlahan 1997.)

reported on the immense number of new species observed in equatorial regions (Edmonds 1997). While the causes of this latitudinal pattern remain unclear (Rosenzweig 1995; Gaston 2000), it is widespread and well documented, although there may be exceptions within certain restricted groups of species or habitats.

Tropical wetlands therefore have more species than temperate wetlands. The Amazon, for example, has more than 1000 species of flood-tolerant trees, whereas the Mississippi River wetlands have about 100 and the peatlands of northern Canada have about ten (Junk *et al.* 2006). Similar patterns occur with most other groups of organisms.

9.2.2 The number of species increases with area

The relationship between species and area sampled can be quantified as

$$S = c\,A^z$$

where S is the number of species, A is the area, and c and z are constants. This exponential relationship is conveniently turned into a linear one by taking logarithms of both sides:

$$\log S = \log c + z \log A,$$

in which case the constant (log c) represents the intercept of the line and the slope is given by z. This relationship was first quantified using plant species in England (Arrhenius 1921; Williams 1964) and has now been documented for many kinds of plant and animal species (Connor and McCoy 1979; Rosenzweig 1995). In a similar way, the number of species found usually decreases with the isolation of the location (Darlington 1957; MacArthur and Wilson 1967).

This pattern has been shown in wetlands for major groups including plants, reptiles and amphibians, birds, and mammals (Figure 9.3). Similarly, the

Table 9.2 The slope (z) of the species–area relationship $S = cA^z$ for various biota

Biota	z
Aquatic plants in Adirondack lakes	0.225
Aquatic plants in Danish ponds	0.289
(two districts)	0.266
Fish in Ontario lakes	0.20
Fish in Wisconsin lakes	0.29
Fish in New York lakes	0.24
Mollusks	0.23
Various studies ($n = 90$)	0.31

Source: After Weiher and Boylen (1994).

number of fish is related to lake size (Gaston 2000). This has important implications for the design of protected areas – generally, the larger the area protected, the more species the area will support. This is one reason that it is important to protect the world's largest wetlands (Table 1.3).

Weiher and Boylen (1994) compared an array of published studies from aquatic habitats using the standard regression model $S = cA^z$ (Table 9.2). All slopes fell between 0.20 (fish in Ontario lakes) and 0.29 (aquatic plants in Danish ponds), and were generally lower than those of 90 other studies reviewed by Connor and McCoy (1979). Weiher and Boylen suggest that the lower slopes in lakes may be a result of smaller species pools for freshwater organisms. This first estimate of ca. 0.25 is a useful reference point for other studies.

9.2.3 The number of species increases with topographical variation

In any given area of landscape, the greater the range of elevation, the more different kinds of species there will be. That is, mountainous areas have more species than flat areas. Thus the Andes have more species than any other region in the world. Wetlands tend to be flat, except in the notable cases

of blanket bogs and seepage areas on hillsides. If topography generates diversity, why would wetlands have many species? Is this a contradiction? Perhaps – but flooding creates many subtly different moisture regimes, and each moisture regime also has a characteristic set of species (Figure 9.4). Indeed, studies of zoned communities in the next chapter will show how even minor changes in water affect the distribution of species. A few centimeters of water in a floodplain may simply be the equivalent of many meters of elevation on a mountainside (Nilsson and Wilson 1991). Figures 2.11 and 2.12 also illustrate how many species can occupy a small area of wetland by occupying slightly different water levels.

9.2.4 A few species dominate most samples

In any sample, a few species are common, and many are uncommon. The pattern is obvious to anyone who has spent time looking for wild creatures. At first one finds many new species, but once the common species have been identified, much more time is required to find each new species. Even sorting a grab sample of mud from the bottom of a pond will reveal this phenomenon. In spite of the fact that this pattern is found nearly everywhere, its causes are not yet understood. However, it is a useful general rule. A common way of showing this pattern is the rank–abundance drawing, in which one orders species left to right in order of abundance, and then shows the abundance of each species on the vertical axis. There are many measures of abundance – biomass, number of individuals, cover, frequency, or some combination of these that we might call simply importance. The steeper the curve, the more a few species dominate the sample. Figure 9.5 shows 14 examples of such curves – note that the steepest curve is from a cattail marsh where there are only five species present. Contrast this with the curve immediately to the right from freshwater tidal wetlands – although again there are a few dominant species, there are many more less-common ones.

FIGURE 9.4 Differences in elevation produce much of the diversity found in wetlands, as illustrated by this example of zonation. (See also color plate.)

This pattern of dominance occurs across many scales. At the largest scale it is known as the canonical pattern (Preston 1962a, b; Pielou 1975; May 1981, 1986). At the local scale it is known as the "law of frequency" (Raunkiaer 1908; McGeoch and Gaston 2002; Clark *et al.* 2008). Within a single sample the pattern is generally illustrated with a ranked abundance list or dominance–diversity curve shown above (Peet 1974).

There is no perfect way to describe the dominance and diversity patterns in a group of species. Here are some options. You can simply list all the species – but that ignores the fact that some are much more common than others. You can simply count the number of species – the number you get is often called species richness – but this number says nothing about what kinds of species you found. (There are a confusing number of names for this property, including species richness, species density, and alpha diversity. Where possible I have used species richness but be aware that other sources may not.) You can prepare a dominance–diversity curve – but some audiences will have trouble interpreting it. You can fit lines to the dominance–diversity curves and describe the equations (e.g. Wilson *et al.* 1996), which is a good deal of work and certainly beyond most audiences. You can calculate a single number called diversity that summarizes the relative abundances of all the species. Formulae for calculating two of these diversity indices are shown below.

The formula for Simpson's diversity index is:

$$C = \sum_{i=1}^{S} (p_i)^2$$

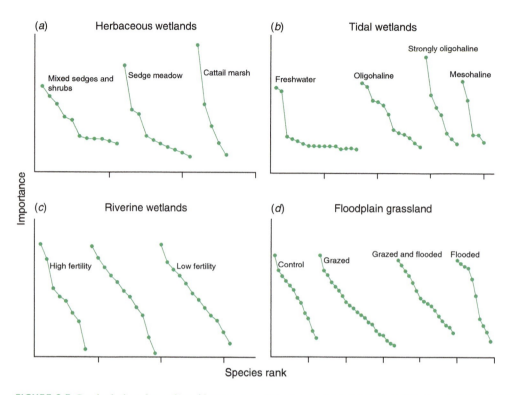

FIGURE 9.5 Ranked abundance lists (dominance–diversity curves) for four different wetlands: (*a*) herbaceous (after Gosselink and Turner 1978), (*b*) tidal (after Latham *et al.* 1994), (*c*) riverine (after Weiher and Keddy 1995), and (*d*) floodplain grassland (after Chaneton and Facelli 1991).

The formula for the Shannon–Weaver (Shannon–Wiener) diversity index is:

$$H' = - \sum_{i=1}^{S} (p_i)(\ln p_i)$$

where C and H' are index numbers, s is the total number of species in the sample, and p_i is the proportion of all individuals in the sample that belong to species i.

While it is nice to have a single number (and it is often used, see for example Figures 3.6 and 4.7), a single number also hides much of the information.

As I said, there is no perfect solution. You can read more about measuring diversity elsewhere (e.g. Peet 1974; Pielou 1975). In this book, I have tended to prefer the simplest data – number of species, or species richness (the terms are interchangeable), but have included some data on diversity for completeness.

In spite of the problems with measuring diversity, we are left with a useful general rule – nearly everywhere you go, a few species monopolize the habitat. Dominance is the rule and hence a majority of species are relatively uncommon or even rare.

9.3 Selected examples

The preceding section introduced four general principles. Now let us take a closer look at how they apply in selected groups of

species and selected locations. We will also look for other rules that apply to specific groups or locations.

9.3.1 Factors affecting the number of species of fish

At large geographic scales, climate, salinity and area are predominant factors. "Of the 20,000 recent fish species known to science, over 40 per cent live in freshwaters, and the majority of these live ... within the tropics..." (Lowe-McConnell 1975, p. 4). The three rivers with the largest fish faunas are the Amazon, Congo, and Mekong Rivers. Each has large areas of wetland. In rivers, the number of fish species is closely related to the area of the river basin (World Conservation Monitoring Centre 1992). A similar but weaker relationship is found with lake area (Barbour and Brown 1974; Gaston 2000).

In African rivers, river basin area predicts the number of fish species according to the following formula (Welcomme 1979, 1986):

$$S = 0.449A^{0.434}.$$

The Niger River, has, for example, 160 species (the above equation predicts 190). This relationship does not apply to other continents, since similar-sized rivers in South America (e.g. Parana, Orinoco Rivers) have about 370 species and in Asia, the Mekong has some 600.

Returning to the Amazon, something more needs to be said about this fish fauna, the largest in the world. Lowe-McConnell (1987) notes that many of its 1000 tributaries have yet to be surveyed. The majority of the described species are characoids and siluroids. The characoids are mostly laterally compressed, silvery, open-water fish that are active by day. They have undergone spectacular adaptive radiation, include both the fruit-eating *Colossoma* and carnivorous piranha, and are probably "one of the most diverse groups of living vertebrates" (Lowe-McConnell 1975, p. 38). The siluroids ("catfish"), by contrast, are mostly bottom-living and nocturnal. They include piscivores, planktivores, and even parasites. Apart from the characoids and siluroids, the other notable group are the gymnotoids, the nocturnal electrogenic fish. They use electric signals to sense the environment and communicate with each other, and the electric eel, in addition, uses electricity to defend itself and capture prey.

Perhaps the most unusual group is the fruit-eating characoids, which live in flooded forests and feed upon fruits and seeds (Goulding 1980). This group vividly illustrates the theme of Chapter 2 – that water levels change greatly with season and year. Many of these species, such as *Colossoma*, are commercially important; this species comprised nearly half the 31 000 t landed at Manaus in 1976. It is captured throughout the year with gill nets in flooded forest.

At more local scales, but still within the Amazon, up to 50 species can occur in one water body, although only a subset of these will be common, for as with most other groups, a few species dominate each sample (Lowe-McConnell 1987). There is also turnover along habitat gradients; the fast-flowing Andean streams have a specialized fauna of algal-grazing catfish, whereas the estuarine reaches have largely marine species. Lowe-McConnell also suggests that an added component of diversity can be attributed to the use of forest foods, since this increases both the volume and array of food relative to rivers in which plankton are the main source of primary production.

Leaving the Amazon, and the tropics, for temperate zone lakes, Table 9.3 shows that even at the relatively local scale of 18 small lakes, species richness increases in with lake area. Beyond this, the table shows that fish species richness in the summer was significantly related to lake pH ($r = 0.70$) and vegetation structure ($r = 0.69$). Within smaller bog pond lakes, vegetation diversity accounted for more than half of the variation in the summer ($r = 0.84$), but the patterns disappeared during the winter. In larger lakes with cetrachids, winter oxygen and depth were the best predictors ($r = 0.59$), and in the small bog ponds with cyprinids, substrate type and vegetation together were the only significant predictors of the number of fish species.

Table 9.3 **Factors predicting species richness of fish in Wisconsin lakes**

Independent variable	Summer $y = a + bx$				Winter $y = a + bx$			
	r		a	b	r		a	b
All lakes ($n = 18$)								
1. Log (lake area)	0.69	*	1.86	3.50	−0.08	NS	3.14	−0.26
2. Log (maximum depth)	−0.47	*	8.25	−5.50	0.04	NS	2.69	0.34
3. Log (connectedness + 1)	0.60	*	3.58	1.96	−0.30	NS	3.64	−0.67
4. Log (alkalinity)	0.66	*	1.58	3.87	−0.02	NS	2.94	−0.09
5. Log (conductivity)	0.60	*	−7.70	7.20	−0.06	NS	3.82	−0.52
6. pH	0.70	*	−9.98	2.39	0.14	NS	0.58	0.34
7. Log (total dissolved solids)	0.42	NS	−0.58	3.95	−0.07	NS	3.59	−0.45
8. Log (winter oxygen + 1)	−0.42	NS	7.48	−2.83	0.02	NS	2.78	0.11
9. Substrate diversity	−0.08	NS	6.48	−0.66	−0.27	NS	4.04	−1.48
10. Vegetation diversity	0.69	*	2.66	3.93	0.00	NS	2.83	0.00
11. Depth diversity	−0.12	NS	7.33	−1.61	0.19	NS	1.36	1.72
12. Depth and substrate	0.08	NS	4.92	0.72	−0.02	NS	2.98	−0.10
13. Depth and vegetation	0.58	*	−0.47	4.22	0.07	NS	2.30	0.35
14. Substrate and vegetation	0.50	*	0.73	3.67	−0.16	NS	3.98	−0.81
15. Depth, substrate, and vegetation	0.57	*	−2.16	4.25	−0.08	NS	3.58	−0.39

Notes: Correlation coefficients (r, $* = p \leq 0.05$) and linear regressions for summer and winter species richness (y) vs. each of 15 environmental factors (x). Multiple regressions most closely predicting species richness are as follows: summer richness = 3.75 + 4.56 log area − 3.84 substrate diversity ($r^2 = 0.67$, $p \leq 0.05$); winter richness = −3.15 + 1.14 pH − 1.30 log (connectedness + 1) ($r^2 = 0.24$, $p > 0.05$).
Source: From Tonn and Magnuson (1982).

9.3.2 Factors affecting the number of insects

Determining the number of species of aquatic invertebrates in a wetland is an identification challenge (or perhaps nightmare), since some aquatic larvae can be identified only to genus or order. And, remember, the insects comprise only one small group of aquatic invertebrates. About 2% of insects have aquatic stages, for a total of 50 000 freshwater species worldwide. The dominant groups include the Diptera (flies, more than 20 000 species), Trichoptera (caddis flies, more than 10 000 species), Coleoptera (beetles, more than 6000 species), and Odonata (dragonflies and damselflies, 5500 species). Hence,

diversity is sometimes measured only as the number of genera, which, of course, significantly underestimates the species diversity. Recall, as but one example, that Tarr *et al.* (2005) collected a total of 6202 aquatic invertebrates, which represented 47 genera, with a mean of more than 10 genera per wetland – and these were only large and predatory species. Thus the number of genera of invertebrates in a wetland is usually much greater than the number of species of amphibians, birds, or fish. This is one reason that the invertebrates are poorly known.

Hydroperiod as a key factor. In a set of 42 wetlands in New Hampshire (Tarr *et al.* 2005), the number of genera increased with the length of the hydroperiod

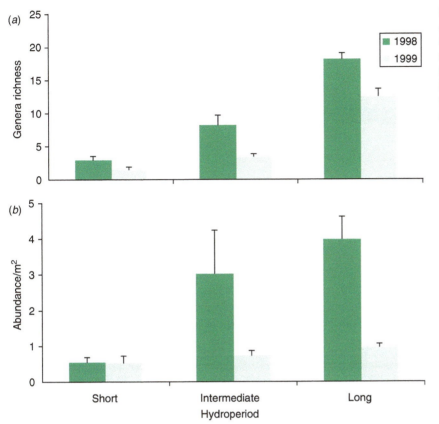

FIGURE 9.6 The number of genera (*a*) and the overall abundance of predatory macroinvertebrates (*b*) increases with hydroperiod, from emphemeral ponds (left) to permanent ponds (right). (After Tarr *et al.* 2005.)

(Figure 9.6). Short hydroperiod wetlands had few genera and relatively low abundance of those genera; the dominant genus was *Acilius*, predatory diving beetles. Other groups like *Notonecta* and *Libellula* were largely restricted to and dominated the long hydroperiod wetlands.

The presence of predatory fish species did not significantly influence invertebrate genera richness but did significantly reduce the abundance of invertebrates in the permanent wetlands. The fish also were associated with distinctive invertebrate communities. *Libellula*, *Leucorrhinia*, and *Notonecta* were more likely to occur in wetlands without predatory fish. *Buena*, *Basiaeshna*, and *Hydaticus* were more likely to occur in wetlands with predatory fish. Since the presence of fish has a major impact upon amphibians and invertebrates, one should be cautious about introducing fish to ponds that do not have them. (The many "helpful" people who want to stock goldfish in ponds seem remarkably unaware of the impacts on frogs and invertebrates, or about what will happen if these fish escape into a nearby lake or river, where they can grow to 33 cm in length.)

In coastal areas, hydroperiod is often connected to salinity, particularly in warmer climates where water in pools evaporates and can lead to hypersaline conditions. In the Camargue, the south-flowing Rhone River supplies fresh water to coastal wetlands. The major factors affecting the composition of invertebrates are therefore salinity and hydroperiod (Figure 8.11).

As an aside, students and teachers may find keeping an aquarium with invertebrates to be an enjoyable and educational experience. The diversity of life history types and species that can be found in

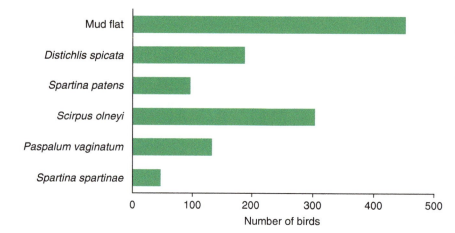

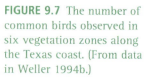

FIGURE 9.7 The number of common birds observed in six vegetation zones along the Texas coast. (From data in Weller 1994b.)

even a small sample of pond mud is remarkable, and the aquarium does not require a great deal of care. Clegg, author of a popular guide to pond life (Clegg 1986) notes that building small ponds is suitable for private gardeners and for schools. Britain, for example, has 44 species of damselflies and dragonflies, and since they can usually be identified with binoculars, they provide a sport equivalent in interest to birdwatching. At one time, wetland managers had to manage wetlands mainly for hunting and fishing. The goal was easy to count: number of ducks, number of pelts, number of fish. The large and growing group of non-consumptive users has shifted the emphasis toward other species including birds and amphibians, and to wildlife viewing rather than killing. The European experience, and the proliferation of field guides to groups like dragonflies (Clegg 1986, Mead 2003) suggests that wetland managers will soon not only have to maintain wetlands for ducks, or for birds and amphibians, but also for other species such as dragonflies and diving beetles. If citizen scientists can be used to monitor species such as dragonflies, the data may provide very sensitive indicators of changes occurring in wetlands.

9.3.3 Factors affecting the number of species of waterbirds

As with fish, amphibians, and reptiles, the bird fauna of the tropics is richer than that of other regions,

with some 85% of all species or subspecies being tropical (Darlington 1957). The number of waterbird populations also varies by geographic region with Asia having almost twice as many as each of the other five regions (Africa, Europe, Oceania, Neotropics, North America; see Section 9.1.2) of the world (Delany and Scott 2006).

At the much smaller scale, the number of birds changes with the type of wetland. Along the coast, salinity is always likely to be an important consideration. Many birds use coastal marshes during migration, and the number of bird species changes among the vegetation types, *Scirpus olneyi* marshes having more species and individuals than other vegetation zones (Figure 9.7). Largely unvegetated mud flats, however, had both the highest number of individuals and species of birds; this is the favored location for shorebirds to forage for invertebrates. This might lead us to suspect that the total number of bird species in a wetland will correspond rather well with the number of vegetation types. This seems to be generally true if the vegetation types also differ in physical structure, less so if the changes are merely in plant species composition. Further, the physical structure appears to have both a vertical and horizontal component. The vertical component refers to structural complexity of the plants, more structural complexity usually generating increased bird diversity (e.g. MacArthur and MacArthur 1961; Huston 1994), in which case

FIGURE 9.8 Although Eskimo curlew were abundant in 1870, it is highly unlikely that anyone reading this book will see one. After market hunters had exterminated the passenger pigeon, they moved on to the Eskimo curlew. (Illustration by T. M. Shortt, from Bodsworth 1963.)

forested wetlands will generally have more species of birds than herbaceous wetlands. Census reports of breeding birds confirm this: forested riparian wetlands have a median of 25 bird species whereas freshwater marshes have only 9.5 (Adamus 1992). The horizontal component of structural diversity refers to the patchiness of habitat. Wetlands with patches of vegetation interspersed with patches of open water are most desirable for waterfowl (e.g. Weller 1978; Kaminski and Prince 1981; Ball and Nudds 1989). The breeding bird census data from Adamus illustrate this horizontal component; vegetation types reported as "mixed" had a median of 32 bird species, the highest number of species reported (Figure 9.2).

Waterbird populations change with time owing to a combination of factors including precipitation, breeding habitat, over-wintering habitat, and hunting pressure. There is as yet no consensus on the relative importance of these factors. Certainly, the cases of outright extinction can often be attributed to the primary force of over-hunting combined with secondary effects of habitat destruction. Two examples:

The *Labrador duck* once nested in the Canadian Maritimes, and was even painted by artists like Audubon; the last individual was shot on Grand Manan Island, New Brunswick, in April 1871. "The most plausible explanation of its passing seems to be that the already small numbers were singly unable to withstand persecution by man, particularly on its restricted breeding grounds" (Godfrey 1966, p. 74).

The *Eskimo curlew* (Figure 9.8) once numbered in the millions, nesting in northern Canadian wetlands and wintering in South American coastal marshes. After the extinction of the passenger pigeons, sport and market hunters turned to shooting curlews, which were highly valued for their taste. Between 1870 and 1890, they were all but exterminated. "Migrating in flocks, often large ones, numbers could often be killed with a single shotgun blast. Sometimes the confused and decimated flocks returned to the decoys only to receive another barrage ..." (Godfrey 1966, p. 145). Curlews "were marketed in all eastern cities, and it was not unusual for twenty-five or thirty hunters to bring in as many as 2,000 curlews in a single day" (Johnsgard 1980). Combined with this onslaught was the clearing of North American prairies used during the migration northward. One of the last known Eskimo curlews was shot on Montauk Point on Long Island on September 16, 1932 by Robert Cushman Murphy. A few were seen reliably near Galveston in the 1960s, and one was killed on Barbados in 1964. They are now assumed to be extinct, although occasional reports of sightings persist. The death in Barbados in 1964? Remarkably, in spite of their toll, these archaic hunting practices continue in Barbados. Tens of thousands of shorebirds are shot each year on artificial lakes using lures, caged birds, and amplified bird calls.

9.3.4 Factors affecting the number of species of amphibians

There are 5504 species of amphibians in the world, all of them restricted to fresh water. This includes 4837 Anura (frogs and toads), 502 Caudata (newts and salamanders), and 165 Gymnophiona (caecilians) (Lévêque et al. 2005). Since amphibians have moist, permeable skin, and eggs and larvae that are sensitive to desiccation, environmental factors related to moisture should be important predictors of abundance (Darlington 1957) and, at least at large geographical scales, the number of amphibians is strongly related to temperature (Arnold 1972; Gaston 2000). For example, compare two North American studies – 22 ponds having 25 species of amphibians (Snodgrass et al. 2000) and 36 ponds having 14 species (Werner et al. 2007) – with one reserve in Ecuador combining floodplain and forest which had 75 species of amphibians (Pearman 1997). Other studies have found that species composition

and richness change with precipitation, soil moisture, altitude, and forest structure (Guyer and Bailey 1993; Pearman 1997). Overall, there are several generalizations that emerge.

Larger areas generally support more species (Findlay and Houlahan 1997), although in one set of small ponds on the coastal plain (most less than 10 ha) this pattern did not occur and hydrology was more important (Snodgrass et al. 2000). The latter authors also showed that the smallest ponds can have species not found in other ponds.

Longer periods of standing water will often increase diversity (Pechmann et al. 1989; Snodgrass et al. 2000; Werner et al. 2007), so long as predation by fish does not become a factor (Wilbur 1984). Fish populations have a negative effect on the number of species found (Snodgrass et al. 2000) as they can eat the eggs, young, and adults. If the fish are eliminated, the number of amphibian species starts to increase again (Werner et al. 2007). Predatory insects like diving beetles may also be more common in permanent water bodies (Tarr et al. 2005). For some species, short periods of standing water ensure that fish do not occur, but then there is the risk of death by desiccation before emergence – recall the example of the gopher frog.

Forest cover in the surrounding landscape has strong positive effects (Findlay and Houlahan 1997). One of the important reasons for this relationship is the number of amphibian species, from mole salamanders to tree frogs, that over-winter under logs or in trees. In Ecuador, both the richness of amphibians, and the proportion of *Eleutherodactylus* frogs (those that produce young adults from eggs) declined near pastures (Pearman 1997). Forest cover of a pond itself is likely to reduce amphibian diversity (Werner et al. 2007). Recall that the index of biotic integrity for streams is also positively correlated with forest cover (recall Figure 7.17). Recall too from Section 8.2 that roads and urbanization have a strong negative effect on amphibians.

9.3.5 Factors affecting the number of species of mussels

Riparian wetlands often contain clear streams with gravel and sand bottoms. These can provide habitat for invertebrates including freshwater mussels. There are estimated to be 840 species of freshwater mussels in the world (Graf and Cummings 2007) with the largest numbers in the Nearctic (302 species) and the Neotropics (172 species). Many are at risk from changes to the freshwater environment. The list of endangered species in the United States, for example, had 62 species of mussels in 2008. Different species of mussels use different sizes of streams and different substrate types, from mud through to gravel. Hence the flow rates and sedimentation rates are critical. Both of these are strongly affected by wetlands. Since mussels disperse by attaching to fish during their glochidial life stage, the presence of a healthy population of the host fish species is also necessary.

Consider one example. The Louisiana pearlshell (*Margaritiferi hembeli*), about 10 cm long, is known from only 24 populations in Rapides and Grant Parishes of Louisiana where it occupies sand and gravel bottoms in flowing water. In some habitats, they reach densities of 300/m^2, and an age of 75 years (Johnson and Brown 1998). It is considered "threatened" by the U.S. Fish and Wildlife Service (1989) and "critically endangered" by the IUCN (Bogan 1996). The host species, brown madtom (*Noturus phaeus*), is widespread. The principal factors that damage mussel populations are changes in water quality, particularly increases in sedimentation. The Louisiana pearlshell populations occur in Kisatchie National Forest, where they are at risk from sedimentation associated with both logging and grazing. Nearby mining is also producing sediment. Beavers can also negatively affect mussels by impounding streams. The growing use of all-terrain vehicles is a further threat to these species, both from the direct impacts of being crushed by vehicles driving through shallow water, and from the

resulting erosion. This one species illustrates how careful management of riparian zones will be critical for the long-term survival of many mussel species, and adds to the list of species negatively affected by roads.

9.3.6 Factors affecting the number of species of plants in freshwater wetlands

Latitude has unexpected patterns. Since it is well documented that the number of species in most groups of organisms including fish, amphibians, birds, and mammals increases with decreasing latitude (Gaston 2000), we would expect the same pattern in plants. In terrestrial plants, this is indeed what we find. For example the average 0.1-ha plot of lowland neotropical forests has from 53 to 265 species, whereas equivalent areas of temperate forest have some 20 to 26 plant species (Grubb 1987; Gentry 1988). Similarly, while Costa Rica has a flora of some 8000 to 10 000 species, the Carolinas, which are four times as large, have a vascular flora of only 3360 (Radford *et al.* 1968). Against this background, Crow (1993) reports a contradictory observation: such patterns do not occur in aquatic plants, and if anything, the flora is richer in the temperate zone. Since this result is quite remarkable, a few more details are necessary. Crow compared the floras of a number of different types of wetlands using published and original data for tropical and temperate regions. New England had 89 species of aquatic plants, and the Carolinas 65, whereas Costa Rica had only 38 and Panama just 35. In the sedge family (Cyperaceae), the same patterns occur: northeastern North America 217 species, the Carolinas 231 and Central America a mere 94. The middle Amazon, by comparison, has only 37 species of Cyperaceae (Junk and Piedade 1994).

The same sort of unexpected diversity trends arise on a habitat-by-habitat basis. Consider marshes first. Palo Verde National Park in Costa Rica, a large marsh situated along Rio Tempisque, had a flora of 66 species; in contrast, a single marsh of about 1 hectare (2 acres) on the shores of the Great Lakes had a wetland flora of 128 species (Stuckey 1975) and a mere 1800 m² of longleaf pine savanna in the southeastern United States can have 140 species (Peet and Allard 1993). Temporary aquatic habitats in the Guanacaste Province of Costa Rica yielded a flora of 32 species, compared to 42 for vernal pools in southern California. In the recently glaciated peatlands of North America, studies of individual sites yield floras of some 100 species, whereas in the Cordillera de Talamanca only 20 species were found. The same trend occurs in coastal habitats: New Hampshire salt marshes have a vascular flora of 81 species, whereas mangrove habitats in the Caribbean have fewer than three species each. Admittedly, not all the data are strictly comparable, but Crow's compilation suggests that something is fundamentally different about global patterns of species richness in wetland plants.

As noted earlier, elevation is very important, since it controls, among other things, the duration of flooding. This is why topographical variation is so closely related to diversity – the greater the range of elevation, the more kinds of habitats. You can see this on a single shoreline, where the number and kind of species changes with elevation (Figure 9.9). Flooding reduces the number of species at lower elevations, while shrubs reduce the number of species at higher elevations (Figure 2.27). Hence, there is a corridor of diversity in the seasonally flooded zone.

Superimposed upon elevation gradients, small scale microtopographical heterogeneity is an important source of species richness – even a modest hummock (Vivian-Smith 1997) or tussocks of sedge (Werner and Zedler 1997) are emerging as important sources for species richness. A tussock of one species like *Carex stricta* can provide habitat for many other species depending upon the time of year (Figure 9.10). Tree islands in wet savannas and peatlands similarly support many kinds of plant and animals species (Sklar and van der Valk 2002),

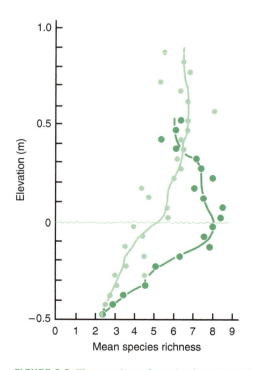

FIGURE 9.9 The number of species (species richness) increases with elevation in a shoreline wetland, although the pattern differs between an exposed shore (light circles) and a sheltered shore (dark circles). (From Keddy 1984.)

thereby increasing the number of species in a wetland. Topographic variation should therefore being included in wetlands under restoration (Keddy and Fraser 2002; Bruland and Richardson 2005).

Disturbance and fertility effects are superimposed on patterns produced by topography. Disturbance and fertility operate by controlling the amount of biomass on a site. Biomass itself is an important predictor of plant diversity. Sites with high biomass often have dense canopies and dense accumulations of litter. As but one example of the negative effects of biomass, Auclair *et al.* (1976a) collected measures of diversity in plots from a riverine marsh, and found diversity was highest where soil nutrients and biomass were low (Figure 9.11).

(a) March

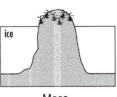

ice

Moss

(b) May

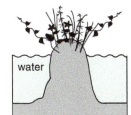

water

Carex stricta
Lycopus uniflorus
Polygonum sagittatum
Galium trifidum
Bidens coronata

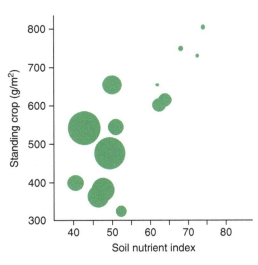

FIGURE 9.11 Plant diversity in a freshwater marsh is higher in locations with lower soil nutrients and lower biomass (standing crop). The circle diameter is proportional to diversity calculated using the Shannon–Weaver index. (After Auclair et al. 1976a.)

(c) July

Carex stricta
Lycopus uniflorus
Bidens coronata
Polygonum sagittatum
Galium trifidum
Lysimachia thyrsiflora
Sagittaria latifolia
Bidens cernuus
Pilea pumila

(d) September

Carex stricta
Lycopus uniflorus
Lemna minor
Pilea pumila
Galium trifidum
Scutellaria lateriflora
Aster sp.
Equisetum arvense
Mentha arvensis

FIGURE 9.10 Even a single tussock of sedge can provide habitat for many other plant species over a growing season. (From Peach and Zedler 2006.)

9.3.7 Factors affecting the number of plant species in peatlands

Overall, plant diversity in peatlands tends to increase with calcium and nutrients in the groundwater (Wheeler and Proctor 2000). Bryophytes appear to be particularly sensitive to calcium levels, while vascular plants are more affected by nutrients. Such gradients are closely connected to landscape setting (Godwin et al. 2002). At the larger scales, plant diversity generally increases with topographic heterogeneity, growing season, and proximity to the ocean. Local factors such as grazing or mowing may also change the number of species.

As the first example, consider patterns in a set of 65 raised bogs from across eastern North America (Glaser 1992). There were 81 species in total, with from 13 to 50 in individual bogs. Bogs in the southern continental region (north of the Great Lakes) contained fewer than 20 species, whereas bogs in the maritime region had from 32 to 50 species. The most important factors controlling richness were precipitation ($R^2 = 0.605$) and growing season ($R^2 = 0.570$), each of which accounted singly for more than 50% of the variation in species richness among bogs. In another series of bogs, fens, and conifer swamps in boreal Canada (Jeglum and He 1995), plant diversity increased significantly with pH, calcium, and nitrogen. Similar results are reported from Alberta (Vitt and Chee 1990) and Minnesota (Figure 9.12). Overall, fens at high latitudes with

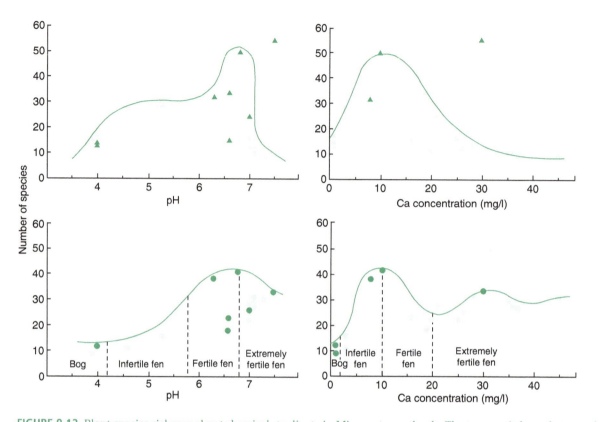

FIGURE 9.12 Plant species richness along chemical gradients in Minnesota peatlands. The top row is bryophytes and the bottom is vascular plants (dark symbols = forested, light symbols = non-forested). (From Glaser *et al.* 1990.)

low temperatures, high microhabitat diversity, and pH about 6.5 have the highest bryophyte and vascular plant diversity (Vitt *et al.* 1995).

Since one of the defining characteristics of peatlands is the abundance of bryophytes, this component of the vegetation can be examined independently of the others. A study of 96 peatlands of continental western Canada found 110 bryophyte species representing three groups: 64 mosses, 26 hepatics, and 20 sphagnums. The number of bryophytes increased with latitude ($R^2 = 0.088$) and decreased with mean annual temperature ($R^2 = 0.145$) (Vitt *et al.* 1995). None of the surface water variables was correlated with richness, and by far the most important factor was the number of microhabitats ($R^2 = 0.455$) as measured by hummocks, pools, and tree bases.

To explore the effects of proximity to the coast, Gignac and Vitt (1990) studied 27 peatlands, from the coastal islands of British Columbia to the interior of Alberta. *Sphagnum fuscum* was the most widespread species, and appeared to be little affected by climate and surface water chemistry. Of the 18 bryophyte species found, seven were limited to oceanic areas (e.g. *S. pacificum*). Some, such as *S. lindbergii*, occurred largely in oceanic sites, but extended inland in infertile fens.

Let us consider one more example, a large wetland complex (>2500 km^2) on the edge of the Tibetan plateau at the headwaters of the Yellow River. This, the largest wetland area in China, is a mixture of peatlands and marshes (Tsuyuzaki *et al.* 1990). Here 135 plant species comprised eight major vegetation types. At the lower elevations, frequently flooded, the dominant species were sedges (*Carex enervis, C. meyeriana*) along with *Equisetum limosum* and *Potentilla anserina*. Dryer areas were dominated by *Ranunculus pedicularis, Polygonum sphaerostachyum*, and *Trollium ranunculoides*. The mean number of species per quadrat increased along this gradient from 3.5 to 10, illustrating the impact of flooding in restricting particularly the number of forbs. Further west in Tibet, grazing by yaks, sheep, goats, and horses is a common use of wetlands; the mean number of species declined from 8 to 4/m^2 with increased grazing intensity (Tsuyuzaki and Tsujii 1990).

9.3.8 Factors affecting the number of species of plants in intertidal environments

In Chapter 8, we saw how few plant species could tolerate saline conditions. As a consequence, gradients of salinity are an important factor controlling plant diversity in coastal wetlands, with lower salinity corresponding to higher numbers of species.

The first example comes from the Guadalquivir River delta, some 1500 km^2 in the southwest of Spain on the shore of the Mediterranean (García *et al.* 1993). The total flora for the site comprised just 87 plant species, including widespread perennial herbaceous genera such as *Scirpus, Juncus, Phragmites, Cynodon, Polygonum*, and *Senecio*, some of these genera suggesting near freshwater conditions; at higher elevations, there were many more annuals with scattered stands of chenopoid shrubs. Species richness in 0.25-m^2 quadrats ranged from 2 to 26. All of the high-richness quadrats occurred at low salinity. Half of the variation in richness could be accounted for by salinity alone; in contrast, biomass of the quadrats could explain only one-fourth of the variation.

Now consider plant diversity along the coast of the Gulf of Mexico. Gough *et al.* (1994) studied the plant diversity in 36 marsh communities.

Most of these plant species were perennial, including widespread genera such as *Aster, Eleocharis, Scirpus*, and *Spartina*. The best predictor of plant richness was elevation – it alone accounted for 52% of the variation in the number of plant species (Figure 9.13*a*). At the lowest elevations, there was only slightly above one species per square meter, while at high elevations, the number approached nine. Species richness also decreased with salinity (Figure 9.13*b*) and biomass (Figure 9.13*c*), but increased with soil organic matter (Figure 9.13*d*). Overall, a multiple regression analysis incorporating elevation, salinity, soil organic matter and biomass accounted for 82% of the variation in species richness.

9.3.9 Factors affecting the number of woody plants in swamps

In terrestrial ecosystems, tree diversity decreases with latitude and aridity, but increases with topographic and geological variation (Gentry 1988; Latham and Ricklefs 1993; Specht and Specht 1993; Austin *et al.* 1996). As we have already seen in Chapters 2 and 8, flooding and salinity strictly constrain the growth of woody plants. Keogh *et al.* (1998) collected a data set consisting of more than 250 plots from forested habitats. In tropical areas, terrestrial forests had >120 species per plot, whereas freshwater wetlands averaged only 31 species per plot. Temperate climates, peat substrates, and salinity all further reduced the number of species of trees found (Figure 9.14). Some combinations of constraints, such as northern temperate climate and salinity (salt marsh), were incapable of supporting any trees at all. The additive effects of local environmental constraints are probably the most important factors controlling tree species richness in wetlands. Each constraint appears to reduce the number of species by some two-thirds, with salinity exerting a much stronger effect than peat, cold, or flooding.

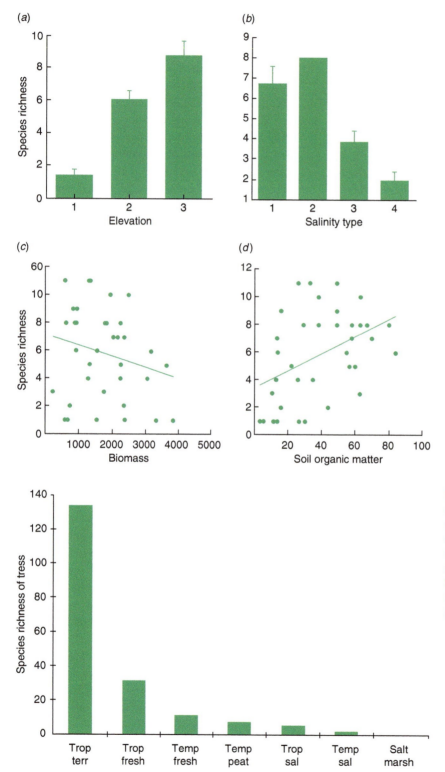

FIGURE 9.13 Plant species richness patterns in Gulf coast wetlands: effects of (a) elevation, (b) salinity, (c) biomass, and (d) soil organic matter. (From Gough et al. 1994.)

FIGURE 9.14 The species richness of trees in five types of forested wetlands compared to tropical terrestrial forests (left) and salt marshes (right); $n = 257$, Kruskall–Wallis ANOVA, five categories, $p < 0.0001$. (From Keogh et al. 1998.)

9.4   Some theory: a general model for herbaceous plant communities

A relatively small number of environmental factors can often successfully predict the numbers of species occupying a wetland. For fish the most important factors are pH, oxygen levels, and vegetation structure. For plants, the factors are elevation, salinity, and fertility. The primary goals in studies of biological diversity are to first uncover these factors controlling species richness, and then to rank them in order of importance. Once such lists are available for a wide array of habitat types and organisms, the task of comparison can begin.

Since many wetland managers have to manage vegetation, we should look in more depth at factors influencing plant biomass and plant diversity. Let us begin this story with Grime's (1973) observation in British grasslands that habitats with intermediate levels of biomass appeared to have the largest numbers of plant species. He postulated that there is a general relationship in vegetation between species richness and standing crop, of the form shown in Figure 9.15. Moreover, he postulated that at one end of the gradient, species richness is low because of high levels of stress or disturbance, whereas at the other end, species richness is low because of dominance by a few strong competitors.

This pattern was first documented in wetlands in English fens subjected to different types of management (Figure 9.16a). These fens were located in the Norfolk Broadland, some 3300 ha of fen along watercourses draining into the sea at Great Yarmouth. This work raised the promising possibility that one could develop a general predictive model that would relate species richness to biomass. In the next extension, Wisheu and Keddy (1989a) tested whether this "intermediate diversity" model applied to wetlands on another continent, and further tested whether the pattern was the same in four different vegetation types. A somewhat similar pattern emerged (Figure 9.16b), but the

coefficients of the regression lines also varied among the four habitats. Thus, while the overall shape of the relationship had broad generality, the specific shape was apparently less consistent. The absence of high-biomass sites was thought to be responsible for failure to detect a decrease in species richness at high biomass; Figure 9.16c shows that when high-biomass sites were added, the typical Grime-type curve emerged.

The level of biomass associated with high species richness is of particular interest. Does it vary among vegetation types? That is, even if the shape of the curves vary somewhat, does the region of high diversity always occur at similar biomass levels? Table 9.4 compares a series of published studies; the results are similar enough to hold promise, but not as consistent or tidy as one might hope. Perhaps a much larger data set with many more quadrats is necessary.

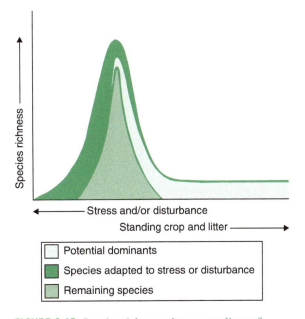

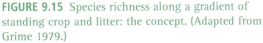

FIGURE 9.15 Species richness along a gradient of standing crop and litter: the concept. (Adapted from Grime 1979.)

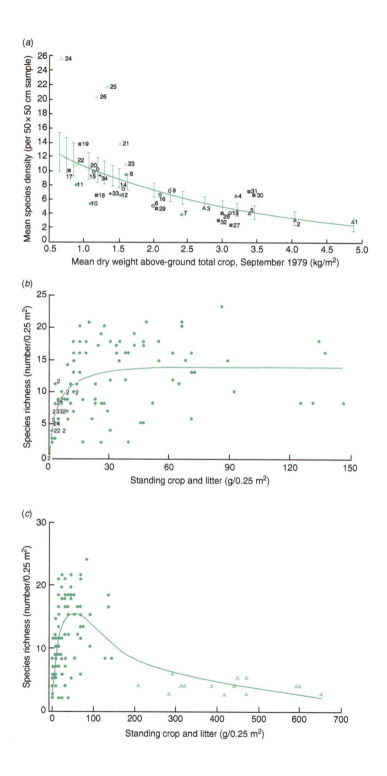

FIGURE 9.16 Plant species richness along gradients of standing crop and litter: (*a*) fens (From Wheeler and Giller 1982), (*b*) lakeshores in Nova Scotia (From Wisheu and Keddy 1989a), and (*c*) lakeshores in Nova Scotia (dots) and high biomass *Typha* marshes in Ontario (triangles) (From Wisheu and Keddy 1989a).

Table 9.4 **Standing crop and litter values associated with maximum species richness in an array of wetlands. Note that standing crop and litter are expressed as g/m^2 and not g/0.25 m^2. Maximum richness occurs at approximately 500 g/m^2 in terrestrial vegetation**

Site	Habitat type	Standing crop and litter (g/m^2) at maximum species richness
Wilsons Lake, NS, Canada	Occasionally flooded gravel lakeshore	200
	Occasionally flooded boulder lakeshore	140
	Frequently flooded gravel lakeshore	260
	Frequently flooded boulder lakeshore	80
Eastern Canada	Marshes and wet meadows	60–400
Axe Lake, ON, Canada	Lakeshore	50–300
Ottawa River, ON, Canada	Riverine wetland	300
Green Swamp, NC, USA	Pine–wiregrass savannas	280
Gelderse Vallei, the Netherlands	Reed swamp, grassland, road verges	400–500
Westbroekse Zodden, the Netherlands	Fens	400–500
	Wet grassland	425
Norfolk Broadland, UK	Herbaceous fen	1500
Northeast Europe	Chalk grasslands	150–350

Source: From Wisheu and Keddy (1989a).

Data from more than 400 quadrats in Eastern North America (Figure 9.17*a*) show that wetlands with biomass in the range of 50 g/0.25m^2 had the highest diversity across a wide range of wetland sites. Figure 9.17*b* shows, moreover, that if rare species alone are considered, the vast majority of nationally rare wetland species occur in the very low standing crop habitats, less than 100 g/0.25 m^2. Similar patterns are found in fens – across 86 herbaceous fens, the number of species ranged from 2 to 50 in 0.25-m^2 quadrats, and standing crop and litter ranged from 80 to >2900 g/m^2. The plot of species richness against biomass was very similar to that in Figure 9.15, heavily skewed to the left with maximum species richness around 1000 g/m^2 (Wheeler and Shaw 1991). The highest biomass and lowest species richness occurred in sites dominated by *Phragmites australis*, and sites with high biomass had few if any rare species. Wheeler and Shaw conclude: "Maintenance of low-growing swards of herbaceous fen vegetation is particularly important for the conservation of many rare fen species."
At this large scale (wetlands representing a broad range of habitats) the pattern is clear and consistent. Of course, the particular rare species that occur at low biomass change from one region to the next.

How do tropical wetlands fit this pattern? Rejmankova *et al.* (1995) sampled marshes from floodplains and depressions in northern Belize; these marshes are usually mostly flooded all year long, but are occasionally disturbed by fire and desiccation. In general, plant diversity was remarkably low, with a mean of some five plant species in 5 × 5 m quadrats. Plant species richness still reaches a maximum at intermediate levels of biomass in *Typha domingensis* marshes (Figure 9.18). Further, if one adds in high biomass reference sites from the Everglades (indicated with *), the decline in species richness at high biomass levels becomes evident. Thus, a similar pattern to temperate zone marshes emerges, with two

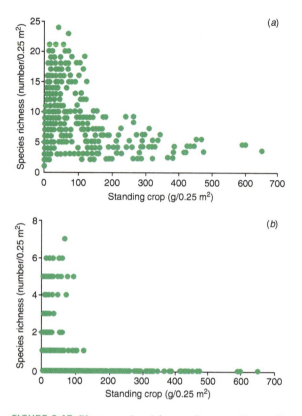

FIGURE 9.17 Plant species richness along gradients of standing crop (*a*) for 401 0.25-m² quadrats in eastern North America; (*b*) same quadrats but nationally rare species only. (From Moore *et al.* 1989.)

key exceptions: overall species richness is strikingly lower, and the region of highest species richness is shifted to the right. Similarly, large clonal perennials such as *Eleocharis mutata* and *Typha domingensis* form extensive nearly pure stands in floodplain marshes along the Rio Tempisque in Costa Rica (Crow 1993). This tendency for dominance by a few such species is, suggests Crow, one possible explanation for the low diversity of herbaceous wetland plants in the tropics.

There remains a great deal of scatter around the lines in Figure 9.17. There are at least three ways to try to reduce variance and increase precision. First, one could try to reduce the residual variance by adding in a second predictor variable besides biomass. If biomass is a crude measure of productivity, then disturbance might be an appropriate second factor to use. There is no easy way to measure disturbance, but Shipley *et al.* (1991a) used the proportion of species that were functional annuals as a surrogate, in which case the proportion of flora being perennials becomes an inverse surrogate of disturbance. Using both biomass and the proportion of plants that are perennial it was possible to predict plant species richness with greater success (Figure 9.19).

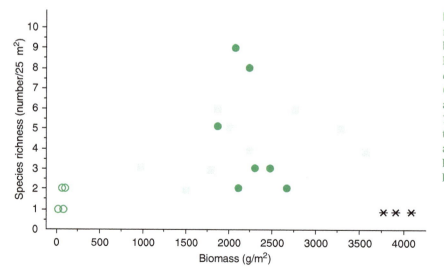

FIGURE 9.18 Plant species richness plotted against biomass for marshes in Belize. Circles are *Eleocharis cellulosa*, squares are *Cladium jamaicense*, and dots are *Typha domingensis*. *Typha domingensis* stands in the Everglades (asterisks) are added for comparison. Plots are 5 × 5 m². (From Rejmankova *et al.* 1995.)

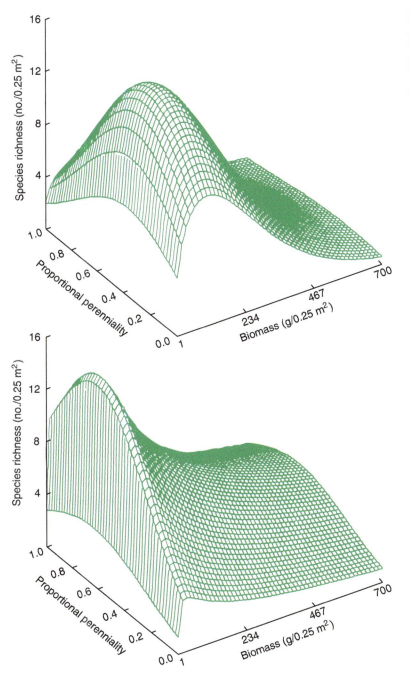

FIGURE 9.19 Plant species richness as a function of both biomass and the proportion of species that are perennial for two geographic locations, Quebec (top) and Ontario (bottom). (From Shipley *et al.* 1991a.)

Seventy-five percent of the variance could be accounted for in a set of 48 quadrats from Quebec, and 45% of the variation in a larger data set of 224 quadrats from southern Ontario.

A second approach to greater precision would be to try reducing unexplained variation by dividing the data into smaller units. Instead of comparing across many vegetation types, one might look for better

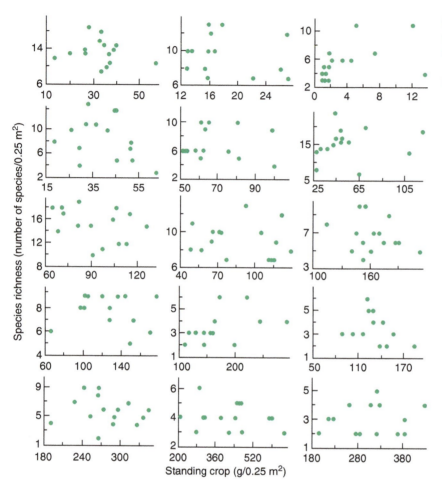

FIGURE 9.20 Plant species richness as a function of standing crop within 15 vegetation types. (From Moore and Keddy 1989.)

relationships within single vegetation types. In many cases this would also shorten the biomass gradient because long biomass gradients are usually the result of comparison across many vegetation types. If the data are divided this way, the intermediate biomass model cannot be detected at all (Figure 9.20). Apparently the factors and processes that produce the intermediate diversity pattern occur only in large-scale comparisons across vegetation types.

A third approach to greater precision requires reconsidering the statistical methods. In his original work, Grime (1973) proposed that the relationship applies to *potential* species diversity. A significant problem with this verbal formulation is that "potential diversity" cannot be measured. Most workers have used curve-fitting techniques

which assume that all observed data points have equal weighting. However, taking the original wording precisely, Grime proposed that there is an outer envelope or upper limit to species richness. It was only the outer limit of the relationship he drew in Figure 9.15. There is a growing set of tools called quantile regression which is useful for studying the edges of data sets (Cade *et al.* 1999; Cade and Noon 2003), a procedure that prescribes envelopes within which data points will lie. Figure 9.21 uses a hand-drawn line to delineate the species richness envelope. This technique is now being used to re-explore patterns in wetland data sets (e.g. Schröder *et al.* 2005). Moving our attention from patterns in means to patterns in edges changes the type of questions we might ask. Instead of trying to

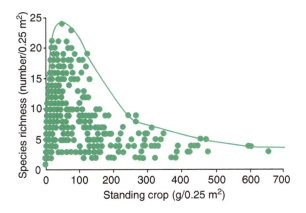

FIGURE 9.21 A boundary line or envelope marks the upper limit of species richness in herbaceous wetlands. (After Moore *et al.* 1989, in Wisheu *et al.* 1990.)

account for scatter around the line, as Shipley *et al.* (1991a) attempted to do, if one begins with an edge, the challenge is to explain why many sample units fall below the line.

Saline marshes may be on exception to this model, at least at relatively small scales. The patterns in Figure 9.13 seemed to demonstrate that physical factors were more important than biomass. If one excludes certain extreme environments – lowest elevations, saline and brackish marshes – a much stronger relationship between species richness and biomass emerges, one accounting for 34% of the variance. Even so, the pattern is simply one of decreasing species richness with increasing biomass, with no evidence of a curvilinear component. The explanation given by Gough *et al.* (1994) is that physical factors control potential richness by controlling the pool of species available (that is, the set having the appropriate physiological tolerance limits: Figure 8.7) and this control may be

so strong that it overrides most other processes. Hence, we will next have to look more closely at the topic of species pools (Section 9.5).

Experiments may also help to clarify causal relationships. Hacker and Bertness (1999) extended these descriptive studies of salt marshes by setting up competition experiments in several zones in a New England salt marsh. In this system, plant species number is low in the high and low intertidal and high in the middle intertidal. They established plots with and without plant neighbors, finding that competition was more important in the high intertidal while physical factors were most important in the low intertidal. In the middle zone, direct positive interactions apparently influenced species richness – three of the four species died (*Atriplex patula, Iva frutescens,* and *Solidago sempervirens* but not *Limonium nashii*) without neighbors but had minimal mortality with neighbors. These positive effects were due to one particular facilitator species, *Juncus gerardi,* which ameliorated the soil conditions that develop in its absence. It shaded the soil, decreasing evaporation and resulting salt accumulation, and oxygenated the soil with its aerenchyma. They concluded that the higher species richness in the middle intertidal is dependent on three co-occurring conditions – the absence of a competitive dominant, less harsh physical conditions than the lower intertidal, and the presence of a facilitator species. Hence, the model first described by Grime may apply rather well to the vertical gradient encountered along coastlines. Moreover, positive interactions may increase plant diversity in such stressed habitats (Hacker and Gaines 1997). The entire topic of zonation on shorelines will be the focus of the next chapter.

9.5   More theory: the dynamics of species pools

We have looked at many different scales in this chapter, from large global-scale relationships to patterns in single wetlands. It is important to realize that the patterns one finds will depend upon the scale

of a study. Thus, the intermediate biomass model of Section 9.4 concentrated on predicting the number of species in small areas or small pieces of habitat. But when planning parks and nature reserves, there is less interest in the number of species per sample unit, the focus being the total number of species protected in a reserve system.

This distinction among the number of species in a sample unit, the number in one park, and the number in a pool, is important for both theoretical and applied purposes. As we increase the size of each sample unit (e.g. quadrat), or as we increase the number of such units, more species will be encountered. The relationship has been well documented, and is generally asymptotic – that is to say, the number of new species encountered declines with sampling effort until, in theory, all of the species have been encountered and tallied (e.g. Pielou 1975). The asymptote is a good estimate of the number of species in the habitat type. In practice, if sample units become large enough, or numerous enough, new habitats are encountered, in which case the number of species tends to continue increasing with the sampling effort. Further, as the scale of sampling is expanded, the controlling processes are likely to change, with local processes such as competition being eclipsed by processes such as landscape history or speciation (Ricklefs 1987). It is therefore important to specify in advance exactly what habitat type or geographic locale is being inventoried. The word **pool** then describes the complete list of species for that habitat, park, or geographic locale.

Eriksson (1993) has provided a simple model to help explore the relationships between community richness (the number of species in a local community), and the number in the pool. Let the number of species in a particular community, S, be a function of local colonization and extinction, just as the number of species in the pool, N, is a function of speciation and extinction. The local colonization rate is then proportional to the number of species in the species pool, N, minus the number of species already present in the community, S – that is, the number of potential colonizers left in the pool. The local extinction rate, however, is a function only of the number of species already present. Adding in two proportionality constants for the rates of colonization, c, and extinction, e, S changes with time (t) as follows:

$$\frac{dS}{dt} = c(N - S) - eS,$$

and at equilibrium the value of S is

$$S^* = N(c/c + e).$$

This simple expression yields some predictions. First, if the local extinction rate, e, is very low, then S^* will be close to N; that is, the local community will contain most of the species in the pool. Second, if the rates of colonization and extinction are equal, that is $c = e$, then $S^* = 1/2N$; the local community will have one half of the species in the pool. Third, if extinction rates are much higher than colonization rates, the community will be species poor and yet the number of invading species per unit time will be relatively high. One simple explanation, then, for communities having many species is the existence of a large species pool; that is to say, S is large because N is large. Eriksson calls this the species pool hypothesis. Depending upon the values of e and c, however, a variety of other scenarios can be postulated.

In many cases, ecologists have data not on the entire community, but only on the number of species in a series of samples from that community, such as the number of species in a set of quadrats, traps, nets, or transects. The total number of species encountered in the sampling therefore becomes a working estimate of the pool; the greater the sampling effort, the more reasonable the assumption becomes. Describing all these possible sample types as a "sample unit" for the sake of linguistic convenience, we can ask what relationships might exist between the number and composition of sample units and the species pool. In the extremely unlikely case where all sample units are identical in composition, then the species richness of any one sample unit will be the same as the pool. The greater the compositional difference between each pair of sample units, the greater pool

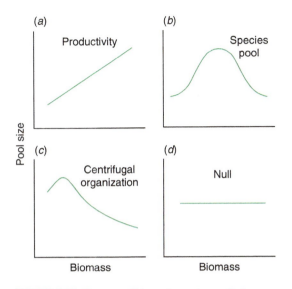

FIGURE 9.22 Four possible patterns in pool size along a biomass gradient. (After Wisheu and Keddy 1996.)

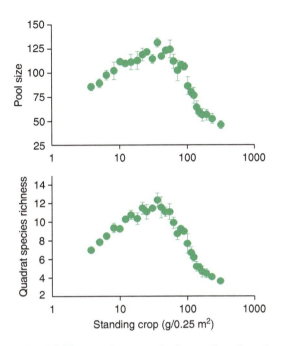

FIGURE 9.23 Actual patterns in the number of species at two scales: pool size (top) and species richness plots (bottom). (After Wisheu and Keddy 1996.)

size will be relative to the number of sample units. We have already seen (Section 9.4) how species richness (or number of species per sample unit) varies along biomass gradients. Suppose we now take the same gradient, but ask instead how pool size varies along it.

Several relationships between pool size and environmental conditions might be postulated. From one point of view (e.g. Connell and Orias 1964), pool size may be highest in high-biomass wetlands because these have the most energy to allocate among species (Figure 9.22a). Alternatively, pool size may simply mirror species richness (Figure 9.22b), high pool diversity occurring where the number of species in plots (also called species density or alpha diversity) is also high (e.g. Preston 1962a, b; Taylor et al. 1990; Eriksson 1993). Although this latter hypothesis may perhaps seem the most likely, particularly based upon what we know about global diversity patterns, it is founded upon the assumption that the degree of similarity among quadrats does not differ along gradients. If the average difference between quadrats is greater in low-biomass

conditions, then the pool size curve will be shifted to lower biomass habitats (Figure 9.22c). This would likely be the case with centrifugal organization (Keddy 1990a). Wisheu and Keddy (1996) tabulated data for 640 quadrats from shoreline marshes across eastern North America, plotting both species richness and pool size against biomass (Figure 9.23). Both reached maxima in similar habitats with approximately 50 g/0.25 m². The number of species in plots was a nearly constant percentage of pool diversity, irrespective of the biomass of the sites examined.

The ecological processes that cause this pattern in pool size remain unclear. We cannot even say with certainty which mode of causation operates. Is the pool pattern (produced by large-scale evolutionary processes) causing the well-known intermediate diversity pattern? Or is the alpha diversity pattern (produced by local ecological processes such as stress, disturbance, and competition)

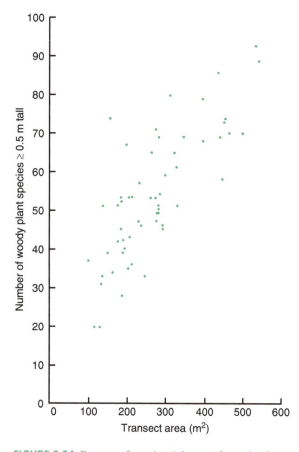

FIGURE 9.24 Pattern of species richness of woody plants occurring in tropical riparian forests – species richness increases with sampling scale and with no sign of an asymptote. (From Meave *et al.* 1991.)

causing the pool pattern? These sorts of basic questions have important consequences for the way in which we both design and manage nature reserve systems.

Comparable data for other wetlands are not available, so we do not know how general the patterns in Figure 9.23 are. Pool sizes in tropical bottomland forests must be remarkable, since Meave *et al.* (1991) found that the number of plant species continued to climb linearly as quadrat size approached 500 m^2 (Figure 9.24). Such tropical riparian floodplain forests may be extremely important centers for the protection of biological diversity (Salo *et al.* 1986; Meave and Kellman 1994). This stands in sharp contrast with Crow's (1993) observations on the restricted size of species pools in aquatic vascular plants. Riparian corridors in general appear to have high numbers of plant species and may support a significant proportion of the entire flora of an area; Nilsson and Jansson (1995) found that just four free-flowing rivers supported 366 plant species, or 18% of the entire Swedish flora of vascular plants. Meave and Kellman (1994) report 292 plant species from a mere 1.6 ha, and suggest that riparian corridors may have provided reservoirs of diversity for rainforest plants during periods of drier climate.

9.6   Conservation of biological diversity

There is a very important, and still frequently misunderstood, connection between local species diversity and pool size. Conserving "biodiversity," which is an important conservation goal (e.g. World Conservation Monitoring Centre 1992; Reid *et al.* 1993; Noss 1995), requires us to think about the full species pool for an area. At the largest scale, our challenge is to maintain the species pool of the entire planet or at least of a region, a topic to be more

fully addressed in Chapter 14. But most managers must focus on maintaining or increasing diversity at only one location. It is entirely possible that our attempts to increase local diversity can actually reduce biodiversity, that is, reduce the species pool. To understand this apparent paradox, consider the following two examples.

Altering the hydrology of salt marshes with dikes increased the number of birds found (Figure 2.6) and it doubled bird species richness. This might at first appear to be a worthy contribution to conservation of biological diversity. The added birds in impoundments, however, were generally birds that occurred in other freshwater wetlands, whereas the birds in the natural salt marshes were more specialized species such as clapper rails and sharp-tailed sparrows. Impounding a salt marsh may simply increase numbers of common birds and decrease uncommon ones. From the global perspective, diversity is decreased.

A similar management outcome can be seen when infertile wetlands (Figure 3.3) become more fertile. As a specific example, consider the New Jersey Pine Barrens, where there are many rare plants, in part because the habitats are very infertile. This infertility means that carnivorous plants are particularly well represented in the flora. Human activities often increase the fertility of sites. Sites that are thus enriched support nearly three times the number of species as pristine sites (Table 9.5). Enrichment therefore increases local diversity, but this increase is almost entirely accounted for by the invasion of exotic species better adapted to higher nutrient levels. Infertile sites, in contrast, have floras that are 88% composed of native species, 12% of which

Table 9.5 Species occurring at pristine and enriched coastal plain sites in the New Jersey Pine Barrens

	Number of species	Percent carnivorous	Percent non-native
Pristine sites	26	12	12
Enriched sites	72[a]	0	96

[a] Actual count was 73. One species was unidentifiable as to being native or non-native.
Source: From Wisheu and Keddy (1992), after Ehrenfeld (1983).

are carnivorous. Again, the local increase in diversity occurs because common species are added at the expense of uncommon ones.

The general rule, then, is that if increasing local diversity is achieved by increasing populations of globally common species, or decreasing globally rare ones, the local management is being counterproductive. Measuring species richness or diversity is no substitute for thinking. Management for maintaining "biodiversity" only makes sense if one takes a global perspective as the context for evaluating local actions.

CONCLUSION

Often our first step in the study of a wetland is to determine which species occur there. There are often good data on birds and amphibians, with poorer data on invertebrates and plants. Partly this is because there are so many more kinds of invertebrates and plants. There are some general rules that allow us to judge how many species an area is likely to have: I have shown you four of them. In addition, there are other rules that apply more specifically to individual groups. Amphibians, as we saw, are positively affected by adjoining forest, and negatively affected by adjoining roads. Plant diversity tends to be higher in infertile habitats with low biomass.

Overall, the task of protecting species requires us to set aside large areas with large species pools and minimize the detrimental effects of humans upon them. We now have good maps of which parts of the world have the most species – the world's biological hotspots (Myers *et al.* 2000). We also know that each of these needs to have large protected areas with well-designed buffer zones (Noss and

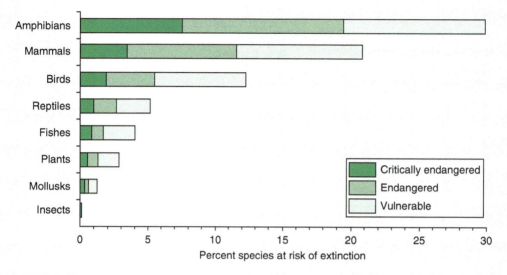

FIGURE 9.25 At the global scale, many species have become so rare that they face extinction. The IUCN *Red List* documents species at risk of extinction in three categories: critically endangered (extremely high risk), endangered (very high risk), or vulnerable (high risk). Note that more than one in four amphibians is vulnerable (IUCN 2008).

Cooperrider 1994; Noss 1995). This is an important priority for reversing the processes that are driving species to extinction.

With regard to future research, it would be useful to understand better why diversity varies in the way it does. A vast majority of the examples discussed in this chapter used descriptive approaches, experimental studies being much less common. I have described a few experiments elsewhere in this book (e.g. Figures 3.12, 4.4, 5.9). These illustrate the potential of properly designed field experiments to inform us of factors controlling species richness, but they also illustrate the limitations of experimentation. Most existing experimental studies suffer from two restrictions. The first is their small scale, usually small quadrats or microcosms, although much larger-scale experiments are possible. The second is their dependent variable, often the abundance of a few selected species, in which case overall consequences for diversity cannot be ascertained. The study of diversity requires a wise mixture of descriptive and experimental studies.

Overall, we can conclude that we have some encouraging general principles about factors like area, heterogeneity, and fertility and their effects on diversity. Still, there is a need for humility – humans need to approach wetland management with caution, given the real risk of making things worse rather than better. The mistaken assumption that increasing local diversity must be good (even when it decreases global diversity) is a perfect example of widespread misapplication of theory in management.

Overall, we are in an era when diversity is declining, certainly at the global scale (Wilson 1993) and often at the local scale as well. The number of species at risk of extinction, as documented by the *Red List* maintained by the IUCN, is high (Figure 9.25) and continues to rise alarmingly. It is doubtful that anyone will ever see an Eskimo curlew again. Hence, there seems to be a great need to apply wisely our existing information on diversity in wetlands.

Chapter contents

10 Zonation: shorelines as a prism

Given the remarkable diversity of wetland types and the complexities of their processes and composition that we have seen in the first nine chapters, how might we begin systematic scientific study? This is an important issue not only for those of us concerned with wetland ecology, but also for practitioners of ecology in general. Where and how do we start? One is reminded of the old Buddhist story about the blind scholars and the elephant. Asked to describe the elephant, the first scholar, touching the massive side, states "It is like a wall." The second scholar, holding the tail, says "No, it is like a piece of rope." The third, holding the trunk, insists "You're both wrong. It is a kind of snake." And so on. We constantly risk that scholarly understanding of the phenomenon will be distorted by our starting point, or by our own limited frames of reference. Yet, we must start somewhere. Wetlands provide one feature that may assist us in scientific study: they are often arranged along gradients.

10.1   The search for fundamental principles

Anyone who has visited a wetland is likely to have been struck by the power of gradients to produce rapid changes in composition. Whether it is a northern lakeshore, a tree island in the Everglades, a delta on the coast of Louisiana, or a tropical floodplain, minor changes in water depth often produce profound changes in the types of plants and animals that we see. These rapid changes in composition often produce visible bands of different ecological communities, or what is often called **zonation**. These provide a powerful tool for understanding wetlands. They also provide an

opportunity for people working in wetlands to contribute to the larger field of ecology. Gradients function like prisms. Prisms take ordinary light and spread it out into a spectrum for scientific study; a gradient does the same for a complicated ecological community. This spectrum provides us with a pattern we can study. Such patterns are necessary for initiation of scientific inquiry, and zonation provides ready-made patterns. There is a long-established habit of describing wetlands by sketching zonation patterns (Figure 10.1) and as the sketches remind us, zonation patterns

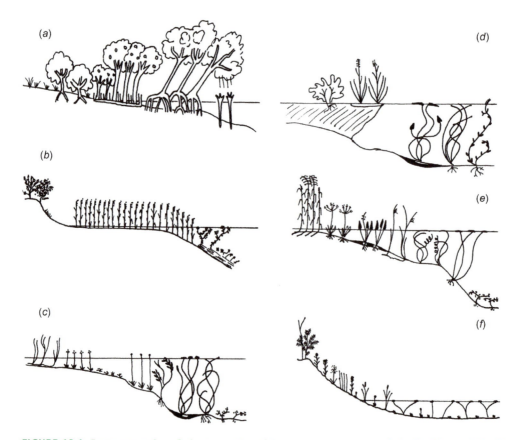

FIGURE 10.1 Some examples of plant zonation: (*a*) a mangrove swamp of the Caribbean (after Bacon 1978); (*b*) the eastern shore of Lake Kisajno, northeastern Poland, a typical small-lake phytolittoral (after Bernatowicz and Zachwieja 1966); (*c*) a sandy shoreline (after Dansereau 1959); (*d*) a bog (after Dansereau 1959); (*e*) the St. Lawrence River (after Dansereau 1959); (*f*) Wilson's Lake, Nova Scotia (after Wisheu and Keddy 1989b).

summarize much of the spatial variation in wetlands. Further, many of our conceptual models in ecology are built around gradients and the distribution of species along them. The oft-repeated admonition by my Ph.D. supervisor, Chris Pielou, was that ecologists should stop trying to find imaginary homogeneous habitats and use the gradients that nature has provided. For all of these reasons, much of my own wetland work has involved the study of gradients.

Wetland zonation can be thought of as a natural experiment (*sensu* Diamond 1983) where nature has set up a pattern of variation for us to investigate. Most zonation patterns summarize the consequences of differences in water level, from floodplains in Brazil (e.g. Junk 1986) to temperate zone peatlands in Asia (e.g. Yabe and Onimaru 1997) and from salt marshes in Spain (e.g. Garcia *et al.* 1993) to lakeshores in Africa (Denny 1993b). A wetland spread out along a shoreline is not only like a spectrum, it may also be compared to a cadaver neatly spread out and already partly dissected in order to help a struggling medical student. Like medical students, we may find it useful to begin where nature has given a helping hand rather than leaping immediately into unattended surgery.

10.2 Shorelines provide a model system for the study of wetlands

Vegetation on shorelines is closely connected with water levels (e.g. Pearsall 1920; Gorham 1957; Hutchinson 1975). The result is conspicuous zonation. The large rivers and lakes of the world provide extensive areas of such shoreline habitat (Table 10.1). It is natural that our first reaction to zonation is to pull out a field note book and make a sketch of it. Recall the six sketches of zonation patterns from studies in different parts of the world in Figure 10.1. One gains the impression that some wetland ecologists still think that once a sketch of plants has been made, the scientific work is done. In truth, it has barely begun. Primary production, for example, varies among these zones reaching a maximum in shallow water emergent macrophytes (Figure 10.2). The distribution of animals is, in turn, related to the zonation of wetland plants (Figure 10.3).

Zonation of animals in wetlands has received less attention perhaps because animals are less visible and more mobile. But we might expect similar sorts of patterns with them, if only because flooding can directly change food supplies, or indirectly change the habitat by changing the vegetation. For example, Price (1980) has documented zonation patterns of 11 species of foraminifera in salt marshes. Arnold and Frytzell (1990) found that flooding was an important factor in predicting the distribution of mink, with a strong tendency for them to select large semi-permanent and permanent wetlands with high water levels and irregular shorelines. The distribution of breeding birds also shows zonation, with species showing marked preference for certain vegetation zones in both freshwater marshes (Prince *et al.* 1992; Prince and Flegel 1995) and salt marshes (Weller 1994b).

Each gradient may appear to have its own zonation pattern, depending upon the species that are present. Hence, it may first be useful to review the big picture – to recall that there are typically four wetland types along a gradient of water level and elevation (recall Figure 2.27). Highest on the shore are wooded wetlands. These are only flooded for short periods of time each year and are dominated by trees and shrubs. At lower elevations with more flooding, woody plants give way to wet meadows. Although wet meadows are flooded for much of the year, they are uncovered for several months in each growing season, and so are occupied by plants that show only minimal modification to cope with flooding. As flooding increases further, wet meadows give way to

Table 10.1 **Large rivers and lakes that provide extensive areas of shoreline with zoned plant and animal communities**

	Country	Average annual discharge at mouth (m^3/s)
Ten largest rivers of the world		
Amazon	Brazil, Peru	180 000
Congo	Angola, Democratic Republic of the Congo	42 000
Yangtze Kiang	China	35 000
Orinoco	Venezuela	28 000
Brahmaputra	Bangladesh	20 000
Yenisei	Russia	19 600
Rio de la Plata	Argentina, Uruguay	19 500
Mississippi–Missouri	U.S.A.	17 545
Lena	Russia	16 400
Mekong	Burma, Cambodia, China, Laos, Thailand, Vietnam	15 900

		Surface area (km^2)
Ten largest lakes of the world		
Caspian Sea	Russia, Kazakhstan, Turkmenistan, Iran	371 000
Lake Superior	Canada, U.S.A.	83 300
Lake Victoria	Kenya, Tanzania, Uganda	68 800
Aral Sea	Kazakhstan, Uzbekistan	66 458
Lake Huron	Canada, U.S.A.	59 570
Lake Michigan	U.S.A.	57 016
Lake Tanganyika	Burundi, Tanzania, Democratic Republic of the Congo, Zambia	34 000
Great Bear Lake	Canada	31 792
Lake Baikal	Russia	31 500
Lake Nyasa	Malawi, Mozambique, Tanzania	30 500

Source: After Czaya (1983).

emergent marsh, with plants that grow under flooded conditions; these sites may only be uncovered for a short time during drought periods, and as a result, plants show increasing morphological adaptation to flooding. Linear leaves and aerenchyma become conspicuous. Below this, plants occur that are truly aquatic, many with floating leaves.

Even peatlands, which sometimes seem to operate differently from marshes and swamps, are zoned in a similar manner. Both bryophytes and vascular plants change along elevation gradients (Vitt and Slack 1975, 1984), with the bryophytes being more sensitive to the water table than most vascular plants (Bubier 1995; Bridgham *et al.* 1996). Pools of water have herbaceous aquatic plants, and shallow depressions support emergent sedges. At higher elevations, shrubs become increasingly dominant (Dansereau and Segadas-Vianna 1952; Gorham 1953; Glaser *et al.* 1990; Bubier 1995).

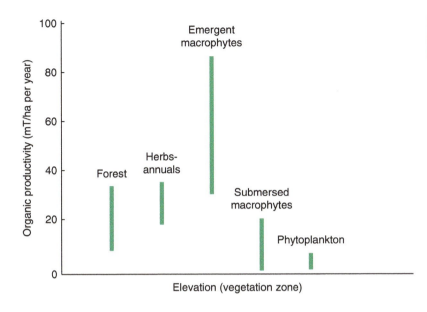

FIGURE 10.2 Changes in primary production with water level. (After Wetzel 1989.)

10.3   Possible mechanisms of zonation

We have recognized the importance of zonation to the study of wetland ecology; now we will move on to explore some the possible processes behind it.

10.3.1 Ecological succession

Many interpretations of zonation emphasize that plant communities in Figure 10.1 appear to follow a temporal trend, that is, they appear to repeat the sequence of events that would occur as a wetland gradually filled in with detritus and turned into land. "Zonation, therefore, is taken to be the spatial equivalent of succession in time, even in the absence of direct evidence of change" (Hutchinson 1975, p. 497.) This view that zonation patterns are a profile through a successional sequence is widespread: it has been described for peatlands (e.g. Dansereau and Segadas-Vianna 1952) and small marshes along lakes (e.g. Pearsall 1920; Spence 1982). In all these circumstances, organic matter produced by the wetland, combined in some cases with sediment trapped by the vegetation, gradually increases the elevation of the substrate, turning shallow water into marsh, and marsh into land.

This view – zonation being succession – goes back at least to the early 1800s (Gorham 1953). J. A. De Luc's book, *Geologic Travels,* published in 1810, recognized six discrete stages in the transformation of a lake into a peaty meadowland. Further, De Luc proposed that the rate of succession is greatest on shallow shores; on steep shores the vegetation zones are narrow and the process of change through time nearly non-existent. Walker (1970) also draws attention to Gough's description in 1793 of how lakes are converted to dry land by the accumulation of organic matter, so that "the margin of the pond will be progressively advanced" and the land thereby produced "will, in time, be covered with a bed of vegetable earth," the upper limit of which is set by dry periods because exposure to air will allow decomposition. Such observations were systematized as a successional sequence called a hydrosere by Tansley (1939). As the concept of ecological succession was

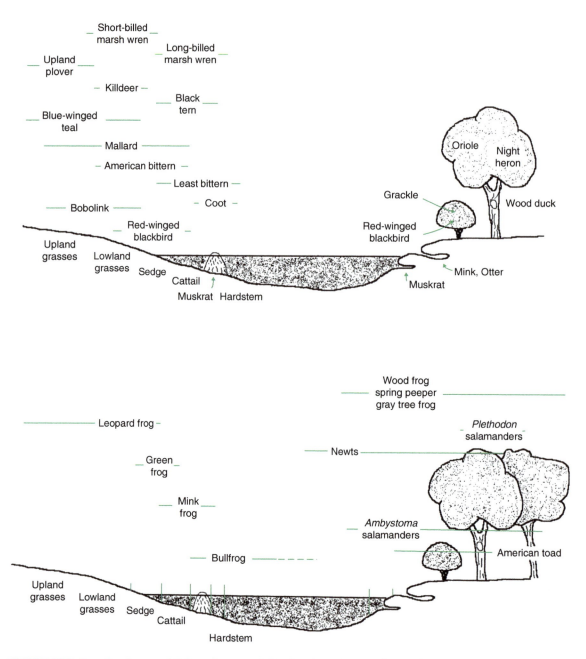

FIGURE 10.3 Zonation in some birds and mammals (top) and amphibians (bottom) in relation to water level and vegetation. (After Weller 1994a.)

popularized with the growth of ecology in the mid-1900s, "pond zonation" was frequently presented as "pond succession" in introductory ecology texts.

Zonation and succession may be closely linked in circumstances such as small ponds and peatlands, where organic matter accumulates, but even De Luc apparently understood that his generalization did not apply to the steep shores of lakes. With the explosion of ecological studies in the later 1900s, it became clearer that there are many natural forces that delay or even restart such successional sequences. As the effects of fires, floods, storms, and droughts were better documented, many "temporal" successional sequences could perhaps be better understood as dynamic balances between succession and disturbance (e.g. Pickett and White 1985). Simultaneously, population biologists were placing increasing emphasis on the mechanistic interactions among species, leading Horn (1976) to suggest that succession was best understood as a "statistical result of a plant-by-plant replacement process." The importance of disturbance, and the complexity of responses to it, has challenged many of the standard ideas about succession, stability, and predictability in nature (Botkin 1990).

One definitive study examined no fewer than 159 transitions in vegetation types from a series of 20 sediment cores (Walker 1970). In these cores one could find pollen from different vegetation types along a successional path from open water (1) through reeds (5) to peat bog (11). If succession was straightforward and unidirectional, then all 159 transitions should have shown change in the same direction. In fact, there were many exceptions (Figure 10.4, top). Seventeen percent were outright reversals in direction, although these, according to Walker, could well be caused by short-term changes in water level or climate. All successional changes had to pass through a marsh stage dominated by reeds (vegetation type 5 in the table and figure). And, in the end, nearly all ended up in bog (Figure 10.4, bottom). (Note that in Walker's study, mixed marsh was number 12, and simply represented an uncommon and early stage in sucession – I have kept his numbering in case you wish to read his original paper.) Hence, we have to accept, at the very least, that even in cases where succession is in progress, many factors, including fires and beaver dams and muskrat grazing, can reverse the direction of change, at least temporarily.

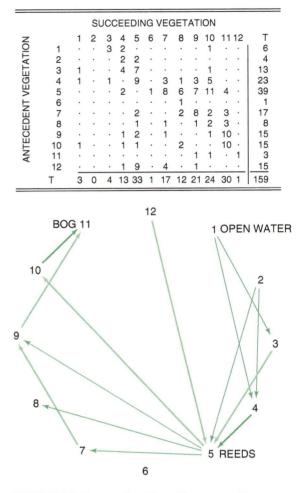

	\multicolumn{13}{c}{SUCCEEDING VEGETATION}
ANTECEDENT VEGETATION	1	2	3	4	5	6	7	8	9	10	11	12	T
1	·	·	3	2	·	·	·	·	·	1	·	·	6
2	·	·	·	2	2	·	·	·	·	·	·	·	4
3	1	·	·	4	7	·	·	·	·	1	·	·	13
4	1	·	1	·	9	·	3	1	3	5	·	·	23
5	·	·	·	2	·	1	8	6	7	11	4	·	39
6	·	·	·	·	·	·	·	1	·	·	·	·	1
7	·	·	·	·	2	·	·	2	8	2	3	·	17
8	·	·	·	·	1	·	1	·	1	2	3	·	8
9	·	·	1	2	·	1	·	·	·	1	10	·	15
10	1	·	·	1	1	·	·	2	·	·	10	·	15
11	·	·	·	·	·	·	·	·	1	1	·	1	3
12	·	·	·	1	9	·	4	·	1	·	·	·	15
T	3	0	4	13	33	1	17	12	21	24	30	1	159

FIGURE 10.4 Frequencies of transition among 12 vegetation stages, ranging from open water (1) through reed swamp (5) to bog (11) to mixed marsh (12), in 20 pollen cores from a range of wetlands including small lakes, valley bottoms, and coastal lagoons in the British Isles. Top, tabulated frequencies; bottom, transition diagram (line thickness shows relative frequency). (After Walker 1970.)

Another source of data that has challenged the succession view is the ubiquity of buried reserves of seeds (Table 4.1). We now understand that disturbance will trigger the re-emergence of species from pools of their buried seeds. Charles Darwin himself had commented on the remarkable number of seedlings that emerged from a spoonful of mud, and increasingly, ponds and potholes were found to be vast repositories of buried seeds (e.g. Salisbury

1970; van der Valk and Davis 1976, 1978). This led van der Valk to propose that many zonation patterns were not successional sequences, but rather represented short-term responses of plant communities to local changes in the environment.

There has therefore been a progression of views on zonation, the past ones emphasizing long-term unidirectional succession, the later ones emphasizing the short-term responses of organisms to changing environmental conditions. Two specific examples nicely illustrate this shift in emphasis. In 1952, Dansereau and Segadas-Vianna could draw zonation profiles of peat bogs in eastern North America (Figure 7.9), and confidently relate them to succession diagrams ending in climax vegetation of *Picea mariana* or *Acer saccharinum* (these being named the Pictum marianae and Aceratum saccharophori associations). The many other vegetation types they named were considered to belong to one of three stages of bog succession: pioneer, consolidation, and subclimax, all leading, by means of peat accumulation, from open water to woodland. In 1996 Yu *et al.* described zonation through a single shoreline swamp at Rice Lake (just north of Lake Ontario), with a zonation sequence not unlike that discussed by Dansereau and Segadas-Vianna. Aided by sediment cores, and by studies of pollen and plant macrofossils, Yu *et al.* found two main stages in the vegetation history. An open marsh stage with sedge genera such as *Carex* and *Eleocharis* persisted for some 2700 years with no successional change, a situation they explain by fluctuating water levels. Then, about 8300 years BP, there was a transition to perennials associated with wet meadows (e.g. *Verbena hastata, Lycopus americanus*, and *Carex* spp.) and by about 7500 years BP a transition to cedar (*Thuja occidentalis*) swamp. This change coincided with a regional period of warm and dry climate. The adjoining lake levels dropped and the swamp went dry about 1000 years later. During a cooler and wetter period, lake levels rose and the cedar swamp reappeared. Yu *et al.* conclude: "Paleoecological data for the past 11000 years show that there were no significant successional changes

of marsh communities for about 2700 years ... When change did occur, it was ultimately controlled by allogenic [external] factors such as climate and water level changes." Further, when the climate changed, "The herbaceous marsh converted directly to cedar swamp without the shrub-marsh and(or) alder-thicket stages."

These two studies illustrate the change in perspective that has occurred over the last 50 years. It would be far too easy, however, merely to conclude (as is often done) that a correct view (dynamics) has replaced a wrong one (succession). Even Dansereau and Segadas-Vianna noted that fluctuating water levels could control vegetation succession, and that fire could cause vegetation to regress. And Yu *et al.* would have to concede that, at Rice Lake, trees are now growing in accumulations of 2 meters of peat and several more of organic silt, thereby elevating the swamp forest above what would otherwise be open water. Whether one therefore focuses upon succession or on short-term dynamics would appear to be somewhat a matter of emphasis and perspective: general patterns as opposed to site histories, large-scale processes as opposed to small-scale dynamics, and classification as opposed to process.

These developments leave us with two questions about zonation. What purpose or advantage is there in relating zonation to succession? If there is some value, then in what circumstances is this a correct parallel to draw? For the purposes of this book, I assume that viewing zonation as succession may be useful in habitats such as peatlands, where unidirectional change driven by the accumulation of peat is a powerful and useful generalization. Even progressive changes in peat accumulation may, however, occasionally reverse themselves (Figure 10.4). In other cases, such as the shores of large lakes or rivers, the connection between zonation and succession is weak, and if anything, confuses rather than clarifies the causes of patterns seen in the vegetation (Figure 2.27). In these cases, it may be best to view the shoreline as a dynamic response to changes in water level, with short-term successional trends (or perhaps just competition) repeatedly interrupted by flood, drawdowns, ice scour, and fire. Overall, I suggest that succession is a useful concept to keep in our vocabulary, but we should be careful about when and where we use the concept.

10.3.2 Physical factors

The direct effects of physical factors have also been offered as an explanation for zonation on shorelines and for the distribution patterns of most plants. Pearsall (1920) studied plant patterns in wetlands around English lakes, and concluded (p. 181) "sediments become finer as water deepens; since sediments are zoned along lake shores and since they differ in chemical composition, we are justified in assuming that zonation of vegetation is a result of differences in soil conditions." He placed particular emphasis upon soil organic matter, and silt and clay content. Spence's review (1982) added in some extra factors, such as lower light levels in deeper water, but still assumed as a first approximation, at least, that physical factors themselves produced the different distributions of species.

Elsewhere, Myers (1935) described the kinds of zonation he encountered along watercourses in northeastern South America, and offered the explanation of physical factors as controls upon the different kinds of shoreline vegetation. Near the sea, he said, the zonation consisted of mangroves such as *Rhizophora mangle* which mixed with and then, as the water freshened, gradually gave way to *Pterocarpus draco*. "The distance to which the mangrove zone extends upstream is doubtless determined by the influence of brackish water, and this, in its turn, in these uniformly sluggish streams ... depends chiefly on the size of the river." The sequence from the ocean inland went as follows: (i) *Rhizophora*, (ii) *Pterocarpus* (often mixed with *Pachira aquatica*), (iii) mixed bank vegetation "smothered by a dense curtain of creepers," (iv) swamp forest with no differentiated bank fringe, (v) tall rainforests with no differentiated bank fringe. Myers was of the opinion that the kind of zonation he saw could be explained by three main causes: the width of the stream, the character of the water, and distance from the sea.

Since then, there has been increased sophistication in the study of plant response to flooding. As we have already seen (Chapter 1), flooding is associated with low soil oxygen levels. Aerenchyma provides one means of avoiding this stress, but in the absence of transported oxygen, the aerobic metabolism of the plant is superseded by the glycolytic pathway, and the products of anaerobic metabolism accumulate (Crawford 1982). These problems are compounded when plants are flooded by saline rather than fresh water.

When you compare species from different habitats, there are certainly metabolic differences among species, as illustrated by the degree to which plants accumulate alcohol dehyrdrogenase when flooded (Figure 10.5). It is tempting to assume therefore, that the distributions of species in zoned wetlands (whether freshwater or saltwater) are directly a consequence of their abilities to cope with physical constraints imposed by flooding and salinity. Like the view of zonation as succession, it provides a useful one-size-fits-all view of wetlands. But is it correct or useful? One way to explore the importance of physiology is to use field experiments where one explores the possibility of biological interactions. If one can show that factors like competition are producing zonation, then physiological differences alone may not account for the patterns seen in nature.

10.3.3 Biological interactions can cause zonation

So what evidence do we have for biological factors producing zonation? There are fewer examples for us to draw upon, because these sorts of studies require properly designed experiments and often need to run for several years.

Let us begin with an example from salt marshes. In Alaskan salt marshes, the zonation of vegetation is closely connected to flooding (Jefferies 1977; Vince and Snow 1984). Four zones can be delineated with

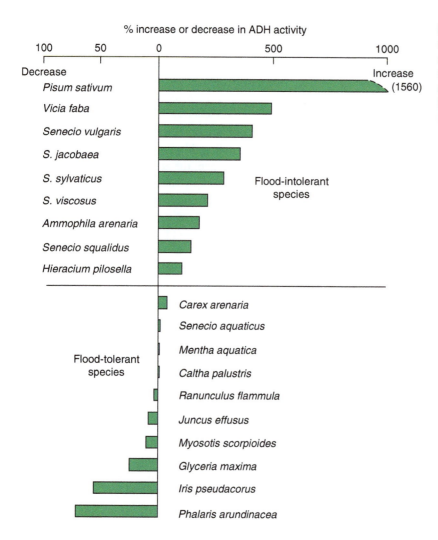

FIGURE 10.5 Alcohol dehydrogenase (ADH) levels in an array of species including flood-tolerant plants (bottom) and flood-intolerant plants (top). (From Crawford and McManmon 1968.)

increasing elevation: outer mud flat (*Puccinellia nutkaensis*), inner mud flat (*Triglochin maritimum*), outer sedge marsh (*Carex ramenski*), and inner sedge marsh (*Carex lyngbyaei*). At one extreme, the outer with *P. nutkaensis* is flooded some 15 times per summer for periods of 2–5 days each, leading to a soil water salinity of some 15–35%. The inner sedge marsh with *C. lyngbyaei* is flooded only twice per summer, when a new or full moon coincides with the perigee (although this single flood may last more than 5 days) and soil salinity is only 6–11%, slightly below the 12% for flooding seawater.

Reciprocal transplant experiments across these four zones (plus a fifth, *Poa eminens*, which grows on riverbank levees), showed that all species could grow in zones when neighboring plants were removed (Snow and Vince 1984). Further, the *P. nutkaensis* from the outer mud flat grew nearly four times larger when transplanted upslope to the inner mud flat than when transplanted to its own zone. The two species from the highest elevations (*C. lyngbyaei* and *P. eminens*) did, however, show reduced growth when transplanted downslope to the outer mud flat. When the same five species were grown at different salinities in pots, all grew best in waterlogged but low-salinity conditions. Thus, in spite of conspicuous zonation, the limited distributions of these species cannot be accounted for simply by tolerances to salinity or flooding. Zonation therefore must be partly produced by biological interactions; in general, Snow and Vince (1984) suggest, "species occurring in zones along a physical gradient are often limited by physiological tolerance toward one end of the gradient, and by competitive ability towards the other."

A similar set of experiments were applied to study zonation in New England salt marshes (Bertness and Ellison 1987). Although the species were different (*Spartina alterniflora, S. patens, Distichlis spicata, Salicornia europea),* the conclusions were similar: "the performance of each species was lowest in the low marsh and highest on the terrestrial border of the marsh" (p. 142).

Other studies in salt marshes report similar results. For example, on the east coast of North America, the woody species *Iva frutescens* (marsh elder) occurs at higher elevations in marshes. Bertness *et al.* (1992) found that, when these shrubs were transplanted to elevations lower than those they normally occupied, all died within 1 year. Since death occurred in both cleared and uncleared plots, the lower limit of *I. frutescens* is apparently set by physiological constraints rather than competition.

Similar results have been found in freshwater marshes. Grace and Wetzel (1981) studied two common and widespread species of cattails (*Typha latifolia* and *T. angustifolia*); together these species comprised 95% of the biomass at their study site, a small experimental pond in the American Midwest. While both species are relatively tall and spread from extensive mats of rhizomes, the taller of the two, *T. angustifolia*, usually occupies the lower areas of shoreline in the deeper water. Is this just because each species grows exactly where it is best suited by physiology? Both species were transplanted to pots and grown without neighbors at a range of elevations from 15 cm above the waterline to 100 cm below it. The transplants of one species grew well over a greater range of elevations than the natural population,

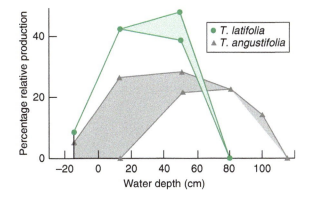

FIGURE 10.6 The growth of two species of *Typha* as a function of water depth; the shaded regions show reduction caused by the presence of the other species. (After Grace and Wetzel 1981.)

suggesting the interaction was strongly one-sided (Figure 10.6). The *T. latifolia* was only marginally affected by *T. angustifolia,* whereas *T. angustifolia* which naturally occurred in the deeper water was apparently excluded from higher elevations by *T. latifolia.* Here is evidence that zonation can be attributed to competition, and that a dominant competitor can exclude a weaker neighbor forcing it into a zone that is physiologically suboptimal.

Another widespread feature of zonation patterns in wetlands is the presence of woody plants at higher elevations (Figure 10.7, left). This produces the characteristic zonation pattern encountered throughout, for example, the northern temperate zone including North America (Keddy 1983), northern Europe (Spence 1964; Bernatowicz and Zachwieja 1966), and Asia (Yabe and Onimaru 1997). Is each species simply responding to the flooding regime, or are biological factors such as competition contributing to these patterns? Experimentally removing these shrubs from many selected areas of shoreline showed that the number of shoreline plants at this elevation increased (Figure 10.7, right).

It is therefore clear that at least some of the herbaceous plants found in flooded conditions can actually grow under considerably drier conditions. This has two possible explanations. It may be that the species that spread up the shore are merely spilling

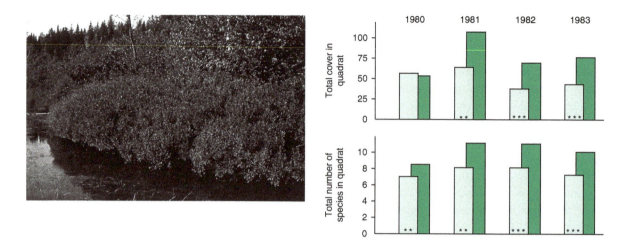

FIGURE 10.7 Shrubs occupy higher elevations in many wetlands (left). Experimentally removing the shrubs increases the cover and number of species of herbaceous wetland plants (right). (From Keddy 1989b.) (See also color plate.)

over from their preferred habitat into marginal conditions created by removing shrubs. It is also possible that these plants are moving to higher elevations which are not marginal, but which actually are better for growth than the lower elevations. Returning to Figure 10.6, *Typha angustifolia* actually can grow better near the water line (where it is naturally absent) than it can in 100 cm of water (where it is naturally present). In nature it apparently occupies a habitat that is less suitable than adjoining drier habitats occupied by neighboring species.

In conclusion, early studies on zonation made the simple assumption that each species grows to the limits permitted by its own physiology. The importance of competition from neighbors in controlling species distributions has since been implied in studies from a wide range of habitats and species (Miller 1967; Mueller-Dombois and Ellenberg 1974; Colwell and Fuentes 1975; Keddy 1989a). Recent experiments demonstrate that neighbors can exert a significant influence upon distributions. That is to say, zonation is an ecological, not just a physiological, phenomenon. Further exploration

of the mechanisms requires the introduction of some new terminology.

10.3.4 Ecological and physiological response curves in zonation

The terminology of ecological and physiological response curves (Mueller-Dombois and Ellenberg 1974) or, equally, the terms realized and fundamental niches (Pianka 1981) clarify the biological and physiological interactions that produce zonation. The **ecological response curve** (realized niche) is the distribution pattern of a species in the field with neighbors present. Zonation patterns such as those in Figure 10.1 show only ecological response curves. In contrast, the **physiological response curve** is the distribution of a species when neighbors are removed, in which case the distribution is presumably explained by the direct effect of physical factors. In the majority of cases studied, the distribution of organisms expands when neighbors are removed – the physiological response curve is usually greater than the ecological response curve. The greater the difference between the two, the

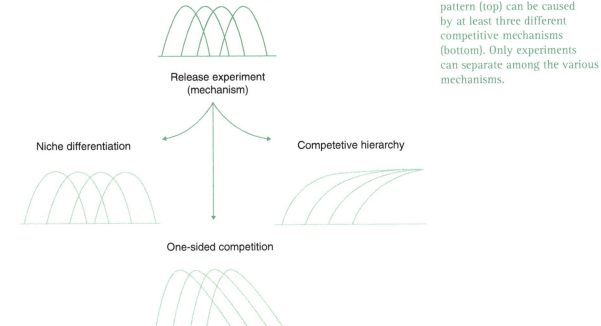

Resource partitioning

Release experiment
(mechanism)

Niche differentiation

Competetive hierarchy

One-sided competition

FIGURE 10.8 A zonation pattern (top) can be caused by at least three different competitive mechanisms (bottom). Only experiments can separate among the various mechanisms.

greater the effects of competition from neighbors in producing zonation. (Note that if there are commensal or mutualistic relationships, the removal of neighbors may lead to narrower physiological response curves [e.g. Bertness and Leonard 1997].)

In the zoological literature, zonation and ecological response curves are often referred to as "resource partitioning" (Schoener 1974), and it is generally assumed that ecological and physiological response curves (or, equally, realized and fundamental niches) are very similar. However, in the absence of field experiments, this is pure speculation (Keddy 1989a; Wisheu 1998). When appropriate experiments on partitioning are carried out, two extreme situations are possible. In one case (Figure 10.8, left) the physiological curves remain nearly identical to the ecological (top). In such circumstances, competition plays a minor role in producing zonation patterns. In the other case (Figure 10.8, right), the physiological response curves shift and nest one within another, a situation termed **inclusive niches** or **shared**

preference. In such circumstances, competition plays a major role in producing field distributions. Here is a situation where we need fewer ecologists drawing zonation patterns or writing about "ecotones," and more conducting field experiments.

It may be possible to connect these ideas to the strategy concepts developed by Grime (1977, 1979) and Southwood (1977, 1988). Using their terminology, one group of species can be classified as stress tolerators. Stress tolerators occupy habitats that are chronically unproductive, and they occupy those sites not because they are better competitors, but simply because they can tolerate the extremely undesirable conditions better than other species. There appear to be many examples of wetland species occupying marginal habitats that are beyond the physiological tolerance limits of most other species, including *Zostera* (eelgrass) in salt marshes, and umbrids (mudminnows) in low-pH bog ponds.

Perhaps, then, many emergent and submersed plants are stress tolerators. That is to say, they are excluded by competition to a marginal habitat that is unsuitable for other species. Although they tolerate flooded habitats, they actually grow better under less stressful conditions. In order to tolerate the extreme conditions, they must reduce rates of photosynthesis or divert photosynthate away from foraging, growth, and reproduction into those adaptations crucial to tolerating the stress. Deeply buried rhizomes, aerenchyma, and reduction in leaf surface area could all be interpreted as costs imposed by conditions. A further cost of such traits could be inherently low growth rates – recall that aquatic plants have inordinately low assimilation rates, usually less than 10 mol CO_2/m^2 per second (Sand-Jensen and Krause-Jensen 1997).

It may seem to be outrageous to suggest that wetland plants would generally grow better in drier areas. But there is a long list of costs associated with flooding. The biomass invested in petioles increases steadily with depth in all floating-leaved plants that are rooted; this biomass could instead be allocated to leaves or seeds if the plants were growing in shallower water or on mud flats. There are lesser but surely measurable costs associated with the production of aerenchyma; even if aerenchyma could be produced nearly without costs, the presence of aerenchyma confirms the metabolic constraints imposed by flooded soils. One could therefore postulate a scenario in which wetland plants tolerate extremes of flooding but do not physiologically require them. In this scenario, flooding has the primary role of killing the terrestrial plants that would otherwise invade the site and exclude the wetland species. That is, the requirement for flooding may be as much ecological as physiological.

The assumption that organisms are best adapted to the sites they occupy still is often automatic, particularly in physiological studies, but there is growing evidence that many species occupy habitats that are physiologically suboptimal in order to escape the higher costs of occupying habitats where better competitors are already established. We have already seen data suggesting that wetland plant species would grow better under less flooded conditions than those in which they are naturally found (e.g. Figures 10.6,

10.7). And, while competition is an important and pervasive force in wetlands (e.g. Keddy 1990a; Gopal and Goel 1993), a number of recent experiments suggest that competition is relatively less important in areas that are permanently flooded (e.g. McCreary et al. 1983; Wilson and Keddy 1991), leading Grace (1990) to conclude independently that deep water offers a refuge for weaker competitors. Postulating that wetland plants would all have shared preference for mud flats or wet meadows may be an unrealistic extreme, but a third alternative is possible, one-sided competition (Figure 10.8, bottom). Here each species' physiological response curve is shifted in the same direction relative to its ecological response curve. In the case of wetland zonation, one may postulate that, in the absence of neighbors, each species would extend landward of its field distribution. Were this to be the case, wetland plants might be sorted into competitive hierarchies where the best competitors have excluded other species into progressively deeper water, forcing such species to adopt increasingly costly adaptations to tolerate flooding.

The problem with exploring such issues is the size and scale of the field experiments needed to study them. Studies with single species are helpful, but we never know how far we can generalize. To surmount this problem we recently grew ten different wetland plant species representing a wide array of growth forms along an elevation gradient in the absence of any neighboring species. That is, we removed competition (or mutualism) as a source of zonation. The species included widespread wetland grasses (*Panicum hemitomon*), emergents (*Peltandra virginica, Pontederia cordata*), and sedges (*Cladium jamaicense, Schoenoplectus americanus*). Over 3 years, these wetland species all grew better in areas with little flooding (Figure 10.9). Now there are minor differences among species – it appears that *Acorus calamus* grew better at lower elevations than *Sagittaria lancifolia*, but overall the pattern appears clear: most of these species show preference for moist soils, all are damaged by prolonged flooding, and if flooded for more than half the growing season, they die. Hence, other factors, such as differential

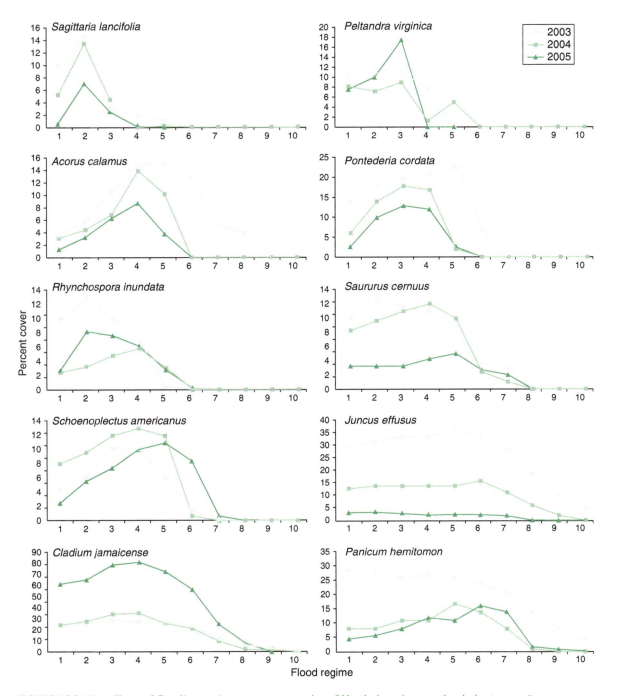

FIGURE 10.9 The effects of flooding regime upon ten species of North American wetland plants over 3 years (2003–2005). All plants were grown without any other species present. The flooding regime ranged from never flooded (left) to continually flooded (right) in an experimental pond in Louisiana. (P. A. Keddy, unpublished data.)

tolerances to competition or grazing, need to be invoked to explain their distributions.

10.3.5 Zonation in arid zone salt marshes

The controls on salt marsh zonation may be quite different in more arid climates. Here, high rates of evapotranspiration produce a salinity gradient that increases with elevation. Hence flooding and salinity are uncoupled as controlling factors. It appears that in Mediterranean-type salt marshes, it is less likely that there is an elevation gradient with one end that is benign and one end that is stressful. Consider an example from southern California, for example, where three zones can be recognized: a low zone with *Salicornia virginica*, a middle zone with *Arthrocnemum subterminale,* and an upper hypersaline salt flat. Transplant experiments using *S. virginica* and *A. subterminale* showed that the intermediate elevations were the most suitable for growth of both species, presumably because lower flooding combined favorably with lower salinity (Pennings and Callaway 1992). The two species were therefore crowded into one region favorable to both: since the border between *Salicornia* and *Arthrocnemum* occurs in prime habitat for both, the competitive interactions were not one-sided but rather represented a stand-off: each species excluded the other from the portion of the superior habitat in which it was the dominant competitor. These marshes therefore differ from the examples we saw earlier, in that the intermediate zone was the less stressful. However, the example also shows that there may be one elevation for which there is a physiological shared preference, with biological interactions therefore producing the final zonation pattern.

10.3.6 Positive interactions also affect zonation in salt marshes

Positive interactions may also influence zonation. Here are three examples. The anoxic soil conditions at low elevations may be alleviated by oxygen transported by aerenchyma, stimulating the growth of neighbors (Bertness and Ellison 1987; Bertness and Shumway 1993). High soil salinities may be ameliorated by neighbors, allowing seedlings of species such as *Iva frutescens* to establish (Bertness and Hacker 1994). *Juncus gerardi* both shades and aerates intertidal soils, stimulating the growth of neighboring species (Hacker and Bertness 1999). Such positive effects can lead to higher biological diversity on shorelines (Hacker and Gaines 1997). Overall, then, the zonation found in salt marshes appears to result from both positive and negative interactions (Figure 10.10).

When you remove species experimentally to test for competition, you are in fact able to test simultaneously for mutualism. Recall that if a species grows better in cleared plots, this provides evidence of competition; equally, if it grows worse in cleared plots (relative to appropriate controls, of course) then there is evidence for mutualism. If you look back to the competition experiment in Figure 5.9, and look in the top panel at total competition intensity along the gradient, you will see a group of three points with negative competition intensity. These may indicate plots where the effects of neighbors were in fact beneficial – which might make sense in a stressed sandy site that is exposed to waves. Hence, removal experiments allow us to test for biological factors in general. Only when individuals with and without neighbors have identical performance are you justified to assume that biological interactions are negligible. But note that this neutrality is something that you have to demonstrate with an experiment. The assumption that biological factors are negligible – that organisms are only reacting to the physical environment – is no longer acceptable as a starting point in wetland ecology.

10.3.7 Experimental evaluation of zonation and fertility

Zonation patterns may be modified by fertility. The striking changes in plant zonation with changing soil

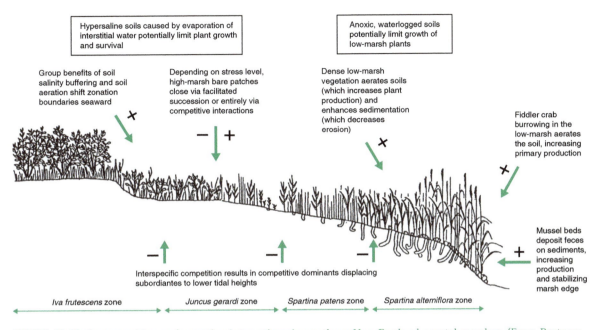

FIGURE 10.10 Some positive and negative interactions in southern New England coastal marshes. (From Bertness and Leonard 1997.)

fertility have been best documented on freshwater shorelines (e.g. Pearsall 1920; Keddy 1983), but the best experimental test comes from coastal marshes. Levine *et al.* (1998) fertilized a series of competition experiments involving typical salt marsh plants: *Spartina alterniflora, S. patens, Juncus gerardi*, and *Distichlis spicata*. The competitive interactions in fertilized treatments were the reverse of those in the controls. It appeared that *S. alterniflora*, which normally occupied the low elevation zone closest to the ocean, was able, when fertilized, to invade higher areas of the shoreline to exclude both *S. patens* and *J. gerardi*.

10.3.8 Plant species richness and resource specialization

It has long been believed that, all other things being equal (which, of course, they rarely are), higher numbers of species can coexist if they each use a narrower range of resources (e.g. MacArthur 1972; Schoener 1974; Pianka 1981). Certainly, when you

look at a zonation pattern, it seems reasonable: does it not seem probable that more kinds of plants or animals could coexist in a wetland if each occupied a narrower zone of water depths? The test seems simple: measure the range of elevations occupied by each species, and the number of species, and test for a relationship over a large number of sites. This has been done, using a lake in Nova Scotia with an exceptionally rich flora and large numbers of rare species. Some gravel shorelines are spectacular in their species richness (Figure 1.7*b*), while others are rather deficient. Yet, when you measure the mean width occupied by the species, there is no evidence for greater specialization of species on the shorelines with the most species (Figure 10.11). Indeed, the evidence seems to be that the shorelines with large numbers of species have gentle slopes made of a unusual glacial till, and regular disturbance from waves. Similar results were found in Keddy (1983). Such results suggest that coexistence in plants is likely to be explained by factors other than specializations along water depth gradients.

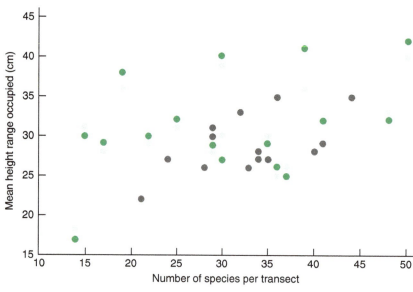

FIGURE 10.11 The mean elevation range occupied by a plant species plotted against species richness in 30 lakeshore transects. Light dots include all lakeshore species; dark dots are shoreline species alone; gray dots indicate both species groups. (From Keddy 1984.)

10.4   Zonation and changing sea level

Sea levels rise and fall through time. The amount of water locked in continental glaciers is one of the most important factors affecting sea level. Over the past century, we have been experiencing rising sea levels, at the rate of 1.8 mm/yr (Figure 7.19). If global temperatures rise enough to melt the Greenland ice cap, this could cause a change of 6.5 meters (Table 10.2). There is debate not only about how likely this event is, but how fast it will happen (Dowdeswell 2006; Kerr 2006). Recall that thresholds are events where a small change in a causal factor (say mean global temperature) produces a large change in a response variable (say glacier size). Recall too that the transition from ice to water is a classic threshold, since it takes only a small change to produce the phase transition from solid to liquid, or vice versa. While we should always be cognizant of how much sea levels have changed in the past, the data assembled by Douglas (shown in Figure 7.19) make it clear that we are currently in an era of rising sea levels. A good source of evidence is the location of mooring rings in old harbors – once well above sea level, many are now submerged (Figure 10.12). And no, it is not that the land is sinking, since many of these sites occur in areas that were once glaciated and are still rising in a process known as post-glacial rebound. The sea is simply rising faster than the land.

In the past, shorelines were free to migrate inland when sea levels rose. An added problem in interpreting the effects of rising sea levels for coastlines is the presence of human cities, farms, or roads inland from marshes. A thousand years ago, the marsh would have slowly moved inland, and its area would have remained more or less constant. Now many marshes are pinned between rising oceans and human infrastructure, so as sea levels rise, the wetland slowly disappears.

Where there is natural landscape along the coast, a characteristic zonation pattern occurs. This is typified by a zone of dead forest. A forest does not move inland (like Birnam Wood did in Shakespeare's play *Macbeth*). Rather, the individuals nearest the sea die. Hence, the zone of dead trees is one of the obvious features along receding coasts (Figure 10.13). The marsh then slowly moves inland as herbaceous

Table 10.2 **The estimated potential sea level rise that would be caused by melting of present-day glaciers and ice sheets**

Location	Volume (km³)	Potential sea level rise (m)
East Antarctic ice sheet	26 039 200	64.80
West Antarctic ice sheet	3 262 000	8.06
Arctic peninsula	227 100	0.46
Greenland	2 620 000	6.55
All other ice caps, ice fields, and valley glaciers	180 000	0.45
Total	32 328 300	80.32

Source: U.S. Geological Survey (2000).

FIGURE 10.12 Construction of the fortress of Louisbourg (left, photo by A. Fennell of painting by L. Parker, from Johnston 1983) was begun in 1719; (right) this old mooring ring was above high tide then – and now it is well below (Taylor *et al.* 2000).

species spread under the dead trees. The exact profile of the shoreline, and the depth of peat, will depend upon a set of factors including rate of rising sea level, rate of primary production, rates of decomposition, rate of herbivory, and frequency of pulses such as hurricanes. A shoreline may not retreat gradually but leap inland with each major storm.

Although low coastal areas like Louisiana and Bangladesh are receiving the most attention, the steady rise of sea level is an issue in many other places. In northeastern North America (Nova Scotia and New Brunswick), sea levels are rising in the range of 30 to 40 cm per century (Begin *et al.* 1989), thereby causing a regression of forest, and sometimes also creating areas of wetland between the forest and the ocean. Along the coast of New Brunswick, for example, sand dunes are moving upland with rising sea levels, and burying peatlands and spruce forests.

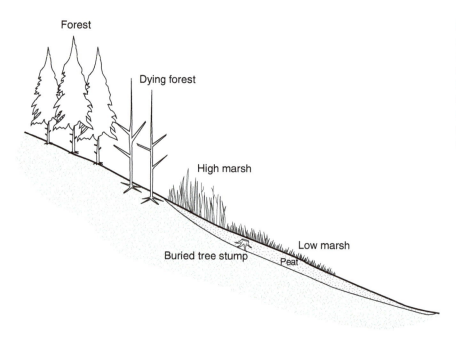

Forest

Dying forest

High marsh

Low marsh

Buried tree stump   Peat

FIGURE 10.13 As sea levels rise, coastal marshes slowly migrate landward, leaving a trail of peat behind them in deeper water. Dead trees on the edge of the upper marsh are the most obvious clue that this process is occurring.

Between the forest and dunes there are frequently areas of shallow water or marsh; this flooding reduces tree growth rates and regeneration. As sea levels continue to rise, these trees in turn are killed and buried by the migrating dunes. Depending upon topography and drainage, the area of marsh changes with time. A complex system of forest, peat bog, sand dunes, and freshwater lagoons therefore occurs, with the dunes and lagoons revealing their origin through the still rooted stumps and standing dead trees emergent amidst them. The presence of conifer stumps in a coastal wetland, like mooring rings under water, is rather obvious evidence that coastlines are changing.

Overall, we have three choices for adapting to these events. Planned retreat recognizes the inevitable, and involves abandoning areas closest to the shoreline. Accommodation involves constructing human features to minimize risk. Ports could be built on shorelines, but human dwellings might be restricted to higher elevations inland. There is also the protection option, reinforcing the shoreline with sea walls or artificially enhanced dunes or wetlands (Nicholls and Mimura 1998; Vasseur and Catto 2008).

What does this mean for zonation? On one hand, we need to view zonation as a biological phenomenon largely driven by competition, as you have seen from the experiments above. On the other hand, we need to realize that when water levels change, these affect the biological interactions. We have already seen in Chapter 2 how zonation patterns change in the Great Lakes with fluctuations in water levels. It appears that many coastal marshes will appear like Figure 10.13, as biological interactions like competition rebalance in the face of rising sea levels. Although Figure 10.13 is a good starting point, the outcome and shape of our coasts will be influenced by a combination of factors depending upon rates of rise, rates of sedimentation, rates of peat formation, and frequency of storms, producing an array of potential zonation patterns and shoreline profiles (Brinson *et al.* 1995).

10.5   Statistical studies of zonation

Although there are vast numbers of papers with sketches of species distributions along gradients, virtually none has taken the next logical step: the quantitative study of zonation and its control by environmental factors. Such studies are even rarer than experiments. There are at least four reasons for the statistical properties of zonation. (i) Although there are many pictures and a vast literature describing zonation, there is no way to compare such studies without measurable properties. (ii) The zoological literature abounds with theories of resource use (e.g. Miller 1967; MacArthur 1972; Pianka 1981), and zoned communities provide an exquisite opportunity to test hypotheses about such phenomena. (iii) The issue of whether ecological communities are continuous or discrete has raged on for decades without resolution, and there is no way to slay this dragon except to actually measure the manner in which communities change along gradients. (iv) Science requires measurable properties. Without actually measuring species distributions along gradients, we can only tell entertaining tales about them.

What properties might we measure on zonation? Here are four, with a brief rationale for each.

(i) The degree to which species distributional limits are clustered ("boundary clustering"). At one extreme (Figure 10.14, left) they may be overdispersed, like the shingles on a roof; at the other extreme (Figure 10.14, right) they may be clustered (Pielou 1975; Underwood 1978). The middle case is a random distribution. Since one can analyze landward and waterward (or upper and lower) distributional limits independently, there are actually two properties here.

(ii) The range of elevation that each species occupies in a transect. This is a crude measure of realized niche width for a species; averaged over all species, one obtains a measure of mean niche width on that gradient.

(iii) Species richness. Some shorelines have many species on them, others have very few. By counting the number of species in transects of standard width, one can relate species richness to other properties.

(iv) Exposure. It has been widely observed that zonation patterns change with exposure to waves (e.g. Pearsall 1920; Bernatowicz and Zachwieja 1966; Hutchinson 1975). By measuring the position of transects along gradients of exposure to waves, one can determine how properties (i) to (iii) are affected by waves and ice scouring.

Given the great theoretical interest in the effects of disturbance upon ecological communities (e.g. Connell 1978; Grime 1979; Huston 1979), it seems remarkable that more studies have not made use of these circumstances.

We now have at least four quantitaive properties that we can measure along gradients: boundary clustering, niche width, species richness, and exposure. The next step is to explore some relationships among them.

The first example, Pielou and Routledge (1976), examined data on species distributions in five sets of salt marshes at different latitudes in eastern North America. In many of the transects, species boundaries were significantly clustered, that is, there were zones

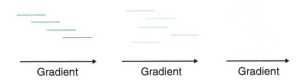

| Gradient | Gradient | Gradient |

FIGURE 10.14 Species may be distributed along gradients in a manner that is overdispersed (left) like shingles on a roof, random (middle), or underdispersed (right) like pages of a book. Underdispersed boundaries are usually called clustered boundaries. Statistical tests can distinguish among these possibilities.

composed of sets of species with similar distributional limits. Salt marsh zonation, therefore, looks similar to the right side of Figure 10.14. Moreover, the upper limits were more clustered than the lower limits, irrespective of latitude (Figure 10.15). This pioneering study showed that with proper sampling methods and appropriate null models, it was possible to find measurable patterns in zoned communities.

The causes of such patterns cannot be deduced solely from statistical analyses. None the less, Pielou and Routledge did find evidence that biological interactions were responsible for some of the species distributions. Their logic was as follows. If these patterns were solely the result of physiological responses to salinity and inundation, then distributional limits of species would be independent. If, however, one species set the limits of another through competition, then there would be a tendency for distributional limits to coincide. That is, species distributional limits would tend to abut one another.

In terms of physiological and ecological response curves, Pielou and Routledge (1976, pp. 102–6) suggest that physiological and ecological factors will create different kinds of zonation patterns. Using a set of 40 transects near Halifax, Nova Scotia, they found that distributional limits tended to coincide ($p < 0.001$). Therefore, they concluded that competition produces some of the observed clustering of zonation in salt marshes. Regrettably, the test was too crude to test for changes in the intensity of competition among latitudes.

A subsequent attempt to explore patterns among these properties used data on zonation from a small sandy lake typical of many near the Great Lakes. This lake had an array of zonation patterns including those associated with open sand beaches, sheltered fertile bays, and floating bog margins (Keddy 1981, 1983). The flora of this lake, and the array of vegetation types, appear in many ways typical of the northern temperate zone. The following patterns were found:

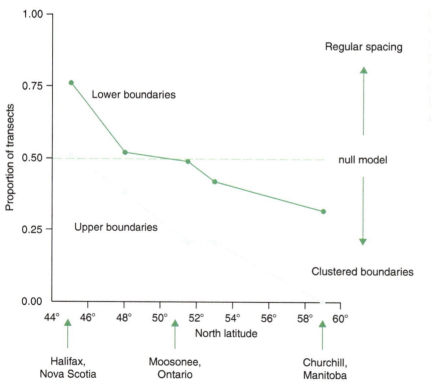

FIGURE 10.15 The clustering of species distributions in salt marshes plotted against latitude. Notice that the lower the measure of clustering, the more species distributional limits coincide. (After Pielou and Routledge 1976.)

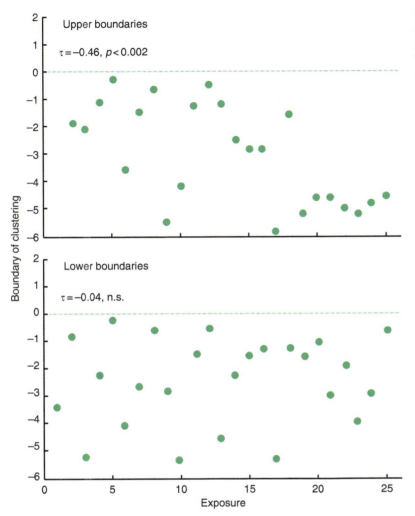

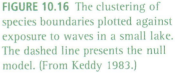

FIGURE 10.16 The clustering of species boundaries plotted against exposure to waves in a small lake. The dashed line presents the null model. (From Keddy 1983.)

(i) Both the upper and lower boundaries of species were clustered. That is, just as Pielou and Routledge (1976) showed, there were certain elevations where more species reached their distributional limits than would be expected by chance alone. This is shown in Figure 10.16 where the measures of boundary of clustering for each of 25 transects fall below zero.

(ii) The degree to which species distributions were clustered (that is, the intensity of the zonation on a shoreline) increased with exposure to waves. This occurred because exposure to waves increased the clustering of upper boundaries (Figure 10.16, top); lower boundaries were unaffected (Figure 10.16, bottom).

(iii) Species distributions were pushed up the shoreline as exposure increased. Figure 10.17 shows how aquatics such as *Lobelia dortmanna* moved up the shoreline as exposure to waves increased. This pattern also showed up in the joint distribution of species as a landward shift in distributional limits (Figure 10.18).

(iv) Mean niche width did not significantly increase as the number of species in a transect increased.

That is to say, more species were not packed in by increased specialization of each species in the community. However, while the mean may be the same, exposed shores have significantly greater variation in niche widths. That is, some species have very narrow distributions, and others have much broader distributions, than in sheltered bays.

The above patterns occurred in a lake in Ontario. How general are they? As a first test for biogeographic generality, the same questions were posed for a lake in Nova Scotia, a lake in a different biographic region, with a substantially different flora and a different type of bedrock (Keddy 1984). Similar patterns were found (Table 10.3), except that the intensity of clustering did not increase with exposure. These patterns, and their relative consistency across eastern North America, suggest that it may be possible to group zoned wetlands into categories having specified patterns. Further, some of these properties may be related to broader debates over the kinds of communities that occur in nature, and the manner in which species are packed into them. Several more recent studies have added to both the empirical data base and its conceptual interpretation, so let us continue with the theme of statistical investigations of zonation patterns.

We have just seen that it is possible to measure different properties of zonation, and to test whether these measured values are different from those which would arise by chance. Measurement is an important

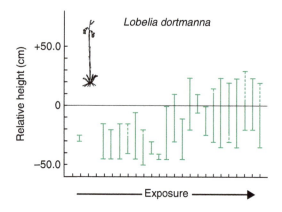

FIGURE 10.17 The relative height occupied by a shoreline plant as a function of exposure to waves; zero marks the August water line. (After Keddy 1983.)

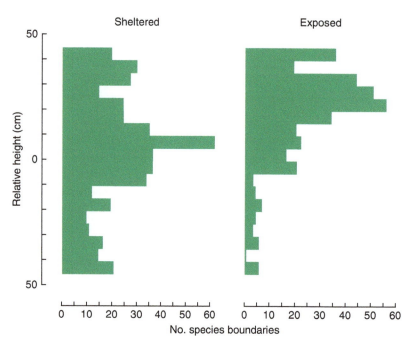

FIGURE 10.18 The relative height (see Figure 10.17) of species distributional limits (upper and lower boundaries combined) for ten sheltered transects (left) and ten exposed transects (right) at Axe Lake. (From Keddy 1983.)

Table 10.3 **Clustering of species boundaries on a lakeshore in eastern North America. Data consisted of 30 transects with 117 species on the shoreline of Gillfillan Lake (Lat. 43° 57′, Long. 65° 48′) in the Tusket River valley of Nova Scotia.**

Boundary	Are boundaries clustered?	Does intensity of clustering change with exposure?	Does location shift with exposure?
Upper	yes ($t=-9.12$, $p<0.001$)	no ($t=0.0$, $p=1.00$)	landward 40 cm
Lower	yes ($t=-3.16$, $p<0.01$)	no ($t=0.06$, $p=0.64$)	landward 20 cm

Source: Data collection and analysis as in Keddy (1983.)

first step in science. Measurement discloses that there are non-random patterns in zonation. Further, we have seen that the degree of non-randomness (or, if you prefer, the intensity of the patterns) sometimes changes along environmental gradients. These empirical relationships provide tools for the quantitative exploration of zonation patterns.

Such measurements and relationships are of far greater significance if they can be related to broader theoretical issues, or to general models for how ecological communities are assembled. One of the most persistent themes of enquiry in community ecology over the last century has revolved around the existence of communities. The first question has been rather general: (i) do ecological communities exist? The second has been more empirical: (ii) what non-random patterns occur in assemblages of species? In practice, these two questions are often mixed together, the assumption being that non-random patterns prove the existence of communities. The general question has therefore been: are living organisms organized into discrete communities as opposed to random assemblages (e.g. Whittaker 1967; Connor and Simberloff 1979; McIntosh 1985)?

There have been two basic approaches to search for evidence of communities. The first has used rigorously defined null models for species composition and compared observed composition to that which would occur randomly (e.g. Connor and Simberloff 1979). In some cases, non-random composition of communities has indeed been detected (Harvey *et al.* 1983; Weiher and Keddy 1995). The second approach, and this is the one more relevant to zonation, has created null models for species distributions along gradients and compared real communities against these null models (Pielou 1975). A vast majority of the published studies on the existence of communities examines island data (Harvey *et al.* 1983), and very few have followed Pielou's suggestion to exploit the power of null models for zonation patterns, although, conveniently for us, most of the latter have been done in wetlands. Let us therefore consider the use of zonation patterns in more depth.

The debate concerning the nature of community organization has continued sporadically for more than 70 years. Colinvaux (1978) provides an entertaining introduction to this controversy, and Whittaker (1962) a more technical view. A convenient starting point is Clements (1916), who proposed that there are relatively discrete ecological units, called communities, that tend to repeat across landscapes. His view, also called the "community unit concept" (Whittaker 1975) was accepted by the majority of ecologists during the first part of the last century. Gleason (1926, 1939) argued, instead, that each organism is distributed individually, and that communities are not discrete, but rather intergrade. His view came to predominate, in part, because the description of zonation patterns

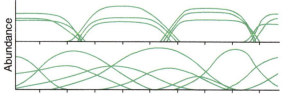

Community unit hypothesis
(Clementsian)

Individualisitic hypothesis
(Gleasonian)

FIGURE 10.19 The individualistic and community unit
hypotheses recast into a
testable form. (After Shipley
and Keddy 1987.)

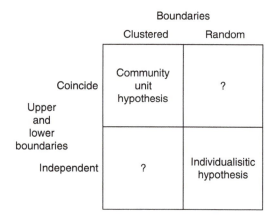

appeared to show patterns of species replacement that were inconsistent with the patterns predicted by Clements (McIntosh 1967; Whittaker 1967). However, all such studies suffered from the problem of using subjective methods of analysing the observed patterns; they failed to employ inferential statistics to compare empirical data to the proposed models. The relative merits of the individualistic as opposed to community unit views therefore remained to be statistically evaluated.

It is possible to test between these alternatives by casting them into testable form using species distributions patterns (Shipley and Keddy 1987). The "community unit" concept proposes that, when species distributions are plotted along some gradient or gradient-complex whose rate of change is constant, there exist groups of species, "communities," which replace themselves along the chosen gradient (Whittaker 1975). Within each grouping, most species have similar distributions, and the end of one group coincides with the beginning of another. The individualistic concept, in contrast, proposes that "centres and boundaries of species distributions are scattered along the environmental gradient" (Whittaker 1975). No distinct groups of species are predicted to exist. These alternatives are illustrated in the top part of Figure 10.19.

Following Pielou (1975, 1977), explicit hypotheses of these two concepts can be formulated using upper and lower boundaries of species along gradients.

The *community unit hypothesis* states that:

(i) there should be significantly more boundaries (both upper and lower) in some intervals of the gradient than in others, i.e. boundaries are clustered;
(ii) the number of upper and lower boundaries per interval should increase and decrease together along the gradient.

The *individualistic hypothesis* states that:

(i) the average number of boundaries (both upper and lower) in each interval of the gradient should be equal except for random variation about the mean;

(ii) the number of upper boundaries per interval of the gradient should be independent of the number of lower boundaries.

The patterns generated by these hypotheses are shown in Figure 10.19. Note that the 2 × 2 table suggests at least two other possibilities for patterns along a gradient, as pointed out by Whittaker (1975). Shipley and Keddy (1987) collected data on species boundaries from 13 transects located in a freshwater riverine marsh. As with the example from Axe Lake, the distribution of species boundaries was tabulated for 5-cm increments of elevation. Along this gradient the dominant species changed from *Carex crinita* to *Acorus calamus* to *Typha angustifolia*. These data were analyzed using analysis of deviance, which is analogous to analysis of variance, but does not assume normality in the error structure of the model. They found that both upper and lower boundaries (Figure 10.20) were clustered. This was clearly contrary to the individualistic concept, but they also found that the pattern of clustering was different between upper and lower boundaries, a result inconsistent with their formulation of the community unit concept. They therefore concluded that, rather than a simple dichotomy between two models, the data suggested the need to erect multiple models for the kinds of communities that exist in nature. In other words, more than 50 years of debate about pattern had dragged on, in part, because the patterns were not expressed in clear testable form. This example illustrates the power of zonation patterns as a research tool in ecology.

This study, however, also had two significant weaknesses. First, it tested a broad general model with data from a single wetland. Second, it used only data on the distributional limits of species. Hoagland and Collins (1997a) have tried to rectify these deficiencies. First, they collected data from 42

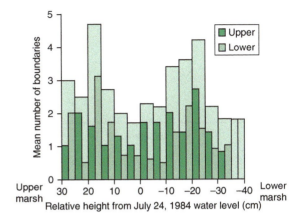

FIGURE 10.20 Zonation in a riverine marsh. The mean number of species boundaries in each 5-cm height interval is plotted against relative height. Within each height interval the mean number of upper boundaries (dark), lower boundaries (medium), and total boundaries (light) are shown. (From Shipley and Keddy 1987.)

wetland sites. Second, they measured three attributes of zonation patterns: (i) boundaries of species distributions, (ii) modes of species response curves, and (iii) nested structure. The use of the three properties not only provides a more powerful way to test among competing models, but it also allows the creation of new kinds of community models. Hoagland and Collins trace the origins of four contrasting models of zoned communities:

(i) The highly deterministic community unit model of Clements (1936) could be interpreted to imply that plant communities are comprised of distinguishable associations of species with little overlap in species distributions among associations. This model can be portrayed as a series of species response curves in which the starting and ending points of species distributions are clustered (Figure 10.21a).

(ii) Other interpretations of this community unit model are possible. Clements (1936) described the occurrence of "predominants," species that were dominant and spanned one or more associations. Figure 10.21b shows a model in which boundaries and modes of response

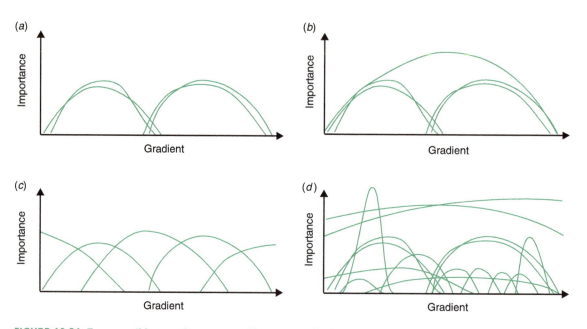

FIGURE 10.21 Four possible zonation patterns. The top pair (*a*, *b*) represent the community model, whereas the lower two (*c*, *d*) represent the continuum model. The right-hand pair (*b*, *d*) possess the additional feature of being nested. (From Hoagland and Collins 1997a).

curves are clustered yet some species response curves are nested within the curves of other, more dominant species.

(iii) The individualistic distribution of species (Gleason 1926) and the continuum concept of vegetation (Whittaker 1967) are represented in Figure 10.21*c* as a series of broadly overlapping species response curves with randomly distributed starting and stopping boundaries, and modes, along an environmental gradient.

(iv) Dominant species may be regularly spaced and encompass several curves of subordinant species; the hierarchical continuum model predicts that modes and boundaries of species response curves are random, but because distributions are hierarchical, this model predicts that species distributions are nested (Figure 10.21*d*).

Three test statistics were used to discriminate among these models in the 42 wetland sites. The three test statistics were as follows: Morisita's index

(Hurlbert 1990) was used to determine whether or not species boundaries were clustered:

$$I = Q \sum_{i=1}^{Q} \left(\frac{n_i}{N} \right) \left(\frac{n_i - 1}{N - 1} \right)$$

where Q is the number of quadrats, n_i is the number of starting and stopping boundaries in the ith quadrat, and N is the total number of boundaries.

The degree of aggregation (P) of species modes was determined using the sample variance of distance between modes (Poole and Rathcke 1979):

$$P = \frac{1}{k+1} \times \sum_{i=0}^{k} \{ y_{i+1} - y_i - [1/(k+1)] \}^2$$

where k is the number of species, $y_{i+1} - y_i$ is the distance between modes, and $1/(k+1)$ is the mean of $y_{i+1} - y_i$. If $P = 1$, modes are randomly distributed, if $P < 1$, modes are regularly distributed, and if $P > 1$, modes are aggregated.

Table 10.4 **Summary of models of distribution along gradients (based on distribution of boundaries of species response curves, modes of species response curves, and degree of nestedness of species distributions) and the prevalences of these models in a set of 42 transects from Minnesota and Oklahoma wetlands**

	Boundaries clustered	Modes clustered	Distributions nested	Examples found
Community unit	yes	yes	no	0
Nested community unit	yes	yes	yes	3
Alternative model a	yes	no	yes	7
Alternative model b	no	yes	yes	16
Continuum	no	no	no	0
Nested continuum	no	no	yes	16

Source: After Hoagland and Collins (1997a).

Nestedness was determined by using the index of Wright and Reeves (1992):

$$N_C = \sum_{i=1}^{K-1} \sum_{m=i-1}^{K} \sum_{j=1}^{S} X_{ij} X_{mj}$$

where S is the total number of species, K is the number of quadrats, and $X_{ij} = 1$ if species j is present at quadrat 1 and 0 if it is absent. This index counts the number of times that a species' presence in a quadrat correctly predicts that species' presence in quadrats that are more species rich.

The value of N_C was then used to calculate a relative nestedness index:

$$C = \frac{N_C - E\{N_C\}}{\max\{N_C\} - E\{N_C\}}$$

where $E\{N_C\}$ is the expected value and $\max\{N_C\}$ is the value of N_C for a perfectly nested matrix. C ranges from 0 (complete independence) to 1 (perfect nestedness). Cochran's Q was used to test for significance of nested species distributions.

All 42 transects were nested (Table 10.4). This is an important generalization; Hoagland and Collins interpret this as evidence for "hierarchical" community structure. Given the many uses of the word hierarchy, it may be more useful to simply use the descriptive result: nested patterns are the rule in zoned vegetation.

Clustering of boundaries occurred in only 10/42 transects; thus the continuum model is more prevalent than indicated by Pielou and Routledge (1976), Keddy (1981), or Shipley and Keddy (1987). Unfortunately, the use of Morisita's index rather than previously used indices raises the possibility that the prevalence of the continuum model in Hoagland and Collins (1997a) data may be an artefact of the test used. Such problems emphasize the need for methodological consistency.

More than half of the transects did not fit into any of the four main models (Table 10.4). Seven had clustered boundaries but unclustered modes, whereas 16 had clustered modes but unclustered boundaries. This work shows the merit of applying a battery of tests to zonation patterns. The differences among the transects, and among published studies, suggest that ecologists need to use a number of different models to describe the kinds of zonation patterns in nature.

10.6   General lessons from analysis of zonation

Here is a situation where wetland ecology can contribute to an understanding of all ecological communities. Do communities exist? There is perhaps a general lesson emerging from the above statistical studies. The continuum hypothesis of Gleason is now generally regarded as correct; Colinvaux's entertaining review (1978) states that Clements was wrong because Whittaker's data show that "zone boundaries could not be found. Instead the data showed clearly that individual species of plants came and went with gentle gradualness as one ascended a mountain, that there was that endless blending of species that should result if each kind of plant did its own free thing, without benefit of social organization" (p. 71). Remarkably, this important conclusion was reached based on two sources of evidence. The first was ordination of plant communities (e.g. McIntosh 1967; Whittaker 1967) (sometimes called "indirect gradient analysis"), a technique that by its very nature assumes the continuum hypothesis. The second source was the visual inspection of species distributions along real environmental gradients (e.g. Whittaker 1956, 1967), an approach that was carried out without creating null models, and without using techniques developed by Pielou (1975, 1977). An important unifying theme in ecology was therefore evaluated with inadequate (or even inappropriate) techniques, leading to a conclusion that now appears to be just wrong.

For whatever the general zonation patterns in forests may be, the few herbaceous zonation patterns that have been carefully analyzed and tested against null models (e.g. Pielou and Routledge 1976; Keddy 1983; Shipley and Keddy 1987; Hoagland and Collins 1997a) do seem to show that species boundaries occur in clusters. The interpretation of these clustered boundaries is still unclear. It may be that there is some discontinuity in the underlying gradient, such as a sudden transition from aerobic to anaerobic conditions, or the upper limit of ice scour on a shoreline.

It may also be that a competitive dominant sets the distributional limits for a group of weaker competitors. Or perhaps a few dominant species are distributed as Gleason postulated, each dominant having a group of subordinates and commensals associated with it. The cluster of upper boundaries observed at Axe Lake (Figure 10.17) occurred where shrubs began to occur, suggesting that one of the latter two explanations may account for the patterns there. But, even if the last explanation – a dominant with subordinates and commensals – were the mechanistic explanation for clustered boundaries, is this not more in accord with Clements than Gleason (Figure 10.21, top)? Zoned wetland communities indeed may have important lessons for the entire discipline of community ecology.

A first step in any scientific discipline, or in a single study, is to find pattern. Zonation makes pattern obvious, and therefore provides a powerful tool for the investigation of wetland communities. While many explanations for the pattern have been offered, it is only recently that experiments have begun to unravel the many factors that cause them. Competition and mutualism are two biological forces involved. Fertility and disturbance also are important. Hence, the causes of zonation require that we combine our understanding of physical factors like flooding with biological factors like competition. It is no longer acceptable to assume that zonation is simply a physical phenomenon.

Of course, one does not always need to understand every detail of cause and effect to uncover broad generalizations in science. A toolbox of statistical methods for examining the patterns in zonation has yielded significant new evidence on the nature of communities. Here is a case where wetlands provide some general insight into many other types of plant communities. If were are looking for a general lesson from this chapter, it might come from Pielou (1975), who was of the opinion that instead of seeking mythical uniform habitats, we would be better off to look for and study gradients.

Chapter contents

11 Services and functions

In the first chapter we encountered the concept of wetlands providing services such as food production and climate regulation. How much are they worth? One estimate is $14 785/ha per year for interior wetlands and $22 832/ha per year for coastal estuaries (Costanza *et al.* 1997). That is, a hectare of wetland produces services that are roughly the value of a small car or a year of university tuition, each year. Another estimate gives the global value of $1.8 billion per year (Schuyt and Brander 2004). Where do such numbers come from? In this chapter we shall look at some examples of services provided by wetlands, focusing on three areas: production of food, regulation of the atmosphere, and culture/recreation. Efforts to quantify these services are not without their critics. There are those who resist putting dollar values on nature, since not everything that humans value has a price. None the less, the use of human currency to evaluate natural services is a growing field in economics (e.g. Costanza *et al.* 1997). Even if you have reservations about the approach, you need to understand how it is done.

11.1   Wetlands have high production

The capture of solar energy by plants is the foundation of virtually all life on Earth. The enormous production of human food in wetlands including rice, fish, amphibians, crustaceans, and mammals testifies to the rate of production in wetlands. The rate of organic production in wetlands is one of the highest in the world, matched nearly by tropical forest. In this section we will discuss the factors that make wetlands such important sites of production.

11.1.1 Wetlands are sites of high primary production

Figure 11.1 shows that swamps and marshes are some of the most productive ecosystems on Earth; they rival both rainforest and cultivated land. But, unlike agricultural fields, primary production in wild wetlands occurs with no fossil fuel inputs in the form of gasoline and fertilizer, no tending by humans, no artificial irrigation, and no heavy machinery. Wetlands can therefore be regarded as factories in the landscape that mass produce both organic matter and oxygen to support surrounding ecosystems. Draining such wetlands may therefore be compared to systematically smashing the factories that support life on Earth.

11.1.2 Wetlands have high secondary production

High rates of primary production provide raw materials for the construction of other life forms. The production of animal biomass in wetlands is some 9.0 g/m^2 per year, 3.5 times the value for terrestrial ecosystems (Turner 1982). This production has both direct economic values (e.g. fisheries, trapping, hunting) and values that are more difficult to measure (e.g. carbon flow, recreation, support of endangered species).

Let us begin with the obvious – some wetland-dwelling animals eat plants. Look at the stomach contents of turtles (Table 6.3) and waterfowl (Table 6.4). One could construct similar tables for

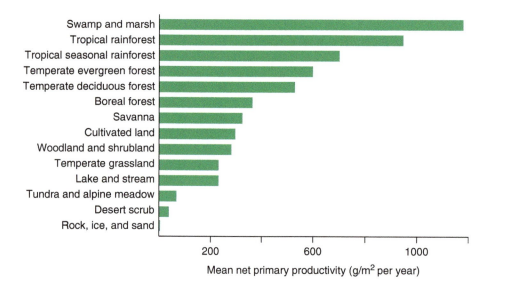

Mean net primary productivity (g/m^2 per year)

FIGURE 11.1 Mean net primary productivity of wetlands (top) compared with other ecosystems. (From data in Whittaker and Likens 1973.)

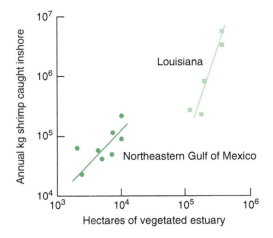

FIGURE 11.2 The relationship between the mean annual yield of shrimp caught inshore and the area of vegetated estuary. (From Turner 1977.)

nearly every animal in a wetland. Many wetland animals do not feed only on plants but on other secondary producers: the turtles in Table 6.3 feed also upon fish and mollusks. And turtles are in turn consumed by predators such as otters and alligators.

In some cases, the area of secondary production is distant from the area of primary production. Shrimp harvests in estuaries of the Gulf of Mexico are strikingly correlated with the area of salt marsh (Figure 11.2). Similarly, Welcomme (1976, 1979, 1986) has found that the area of floodplain in African rivers predicts the fish catch from these rivers. A production of 40–60 kg/ha for the maximum flooded area is typical for tropical floodplains throughout the world. Further, on a worldwide basis, there is a quantitative relationship:

$$catch(kg) = 5.46 \times floodplain\ area(ha).$$

11.1.3 Much of the energy passes through a decomposer-based food web

In spite of such examples above, little of the primary production of world ecosystems is directly consumed by wildlife. This statement may seem remarkable. There is a great deal of production in wetlands, and

many animals in wetlands, and we spent all of Chapter 6 looking at herbivores. The point, which you may recall from Chapter 6, is that most of the primary production passes directly to decomposers (Kurihara and Kikkawa 1986). That is, in most cases, wetland animals feed on other secondary producers that have fed on decomposers (Figure 11.3).

To put this in context, in a mixed deciduous forest, herbivores consume only 1% of primary production while in grassland, herbivores consume about 8%. Similar low figures are found in wetlands. Herbivores consumed only some 10% of primary production in both peatlands (Miller and Watson 1983) and salt marshes (Wiegert et al. 1981), although Lodge (1991) reports higher values for grazing on aquatic macrophytes. In salt marshes, decomposers are the base of a food chain that supports estuarine and oceanic fisheries (Turner 1977; Montague and Wiegert 1990), and a similar process appears to occur in rivers bordered by large floodplains (Welcomme 1976, 1986). In peatlands, the constant high water table and the acidic substrate reduce the activities of decomposers, so a substantial proportion of the plant debris accumulates as peat (Gorham 1957; Miller and Watson 1983).

At the risk of being repetitive, although the exact number varies among types of wetlands, overall, the preponderance of energy flow bypasses grazers (Figure 11.3). The processing of this ca. 90% of the energy requires the activity of decomposers. Kurihara and Kikkawa (1986) conclude: "For most ecosystems, the concept of secondary production must incorporate the ... role of decomposers in making the energy of primary production available to animals." The efficiency of decomposers in consuming primary production is illustrated by measurements showing that over 90% of the carbon fixed annually in peatlands is re-released as carbon dioxide (Silvola et al. 1996). Further explorations of decomposer activity can be found in Polunin (1984), Heal et al. (1978), Good et al. (1978), Dickinson (1983), and Brinson et al. (1981). If you look carefully at the cover of this book, you will see that some

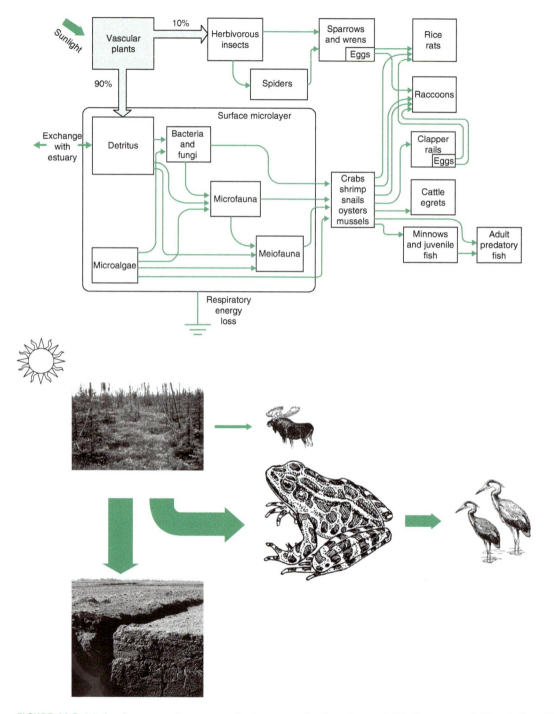

FIGURE 11.3 Wetlands are a major source of primary production. Some of this is consumed directly by wildlife, but a majority of the biomass is first processed by decomposers including insects and bacteria. The top figure shows a detailed analysis of energy flow in a coastal marsh, where no peat is accumulating (after Montague and Wiegert 1990). The bottom diagram shows a simplified version for a wetland where peat is accumulating (bog, peat, courtesy C. Rubec; moose, frog, heron courtesy B. Hines, U.S. Fish and Wildlife Service).

attempt has been made to include the often unseen invertebrates that process primary production, although, of course, many of them are microscopic bacteria.

In the end, the primary production that is not consumed directly by herbivores, nor processed by decomposers, accumulates as peat (Figure 11.3, bottom).

11.1.4 Wetlands may be used only seasonally

Many animals use wetlands for only part of the year. Consider, for example, the immense herds of grazing animals found on the East African plains that we covered in Section 6.3.2. Here let us add from two complementary sources for the story – Denny (1993a) for the botanist's perspective, and Sinclair and Fryxell (1985) for the zoologist's. To appreciate the processes, we must understand that water availability in this region changes at two timescales: annual cycles driven by rainy seasons, and longer fluctuations driven by variation in mean annual rainfall (Sinclair and Fryxell 1985). In semi-arid areas, the dry season forces grazing animals to converge on, and remain within, a 20-km radius of permanent water supplies such as rivers and swamps. In southern Sudan, for example, there are large areas of seasonally flooded and permanently flooded grasslands at the headwaters of the Nile (Denny 1993a). The deeper water areas may have the emergent *Cyperus papyrus* but the shallower areas have "lush, nutritious grasses much favoured by herbivorous browsers." Some 800 000 white-eared kob, a species of antelope, occur here. Each year when the rains stop, animals migrate from shorter grass areas into ephemeral wetlands. Even elephants use these wetlands (Mosepele *et al.* 2009). Overall, it appears that wetlands allow animal herds to move between wet lands and dry lands over the year, thereby allowing a landscape to support much larger mammal populations than would otherwise be possible.

11.1.5 There are exceptions

Having emphasized the high productivity of wetlands, we should note that aquatic plants do not appear to fit the above generalization, having relatively low production when compared to terrestrial plants (Figure 11.1). Three explanations have been offered for this observation: terrestrial plants have complex canopies with many leaf layers to intercept sunlight, their leaves can acclimate to high or low irradiance, and there is both rapid diffusion of gases and a large reservoir of carbon dioxide in the air (Sand-Jensen and Krause-Jensen 1997). These explanations, however, apply only to differences between aquatic communities and terrestrial communities. What about differences among types of wetlands? Low rates of production in aquatic wetlands are likely a consequence of limited supplies of carbon dioxide and light for submersed leaves.

Peatlands also have relatively low production, probably as a consequence of low nutrient levels and short growing seasons. The vast accumulations of peat found in northern wetlands like the West Siberian Lowland and the Hudson Bay Lowland have taken thousands of years to accumulate.

11.1.6 Some historical context

These basic patterns of primary production have only recently been determined. Leith (1975) recounts how photosynthesis itself was only discovered in the period from 1772 to 1779, and how in 1804 de Saussure gave the correct equation for photosynthesis. In 1919, Schroeder provided an estimate of dry matter production on land, 28×10^9 t. Future work required better mapping of world vegetation types, and better data on oceanic production. By 1960, Müller was able to estimate 10.3×10^9 t of carbon produced on land and 25×10^9 t in the sea.

The creation of the International Biological Program (IBP) in the early 1960s co-ordinated attempts to estimate primary production better in different ecosystems, and to incorporate these data into ecosystem and global models (Leith and Whittaker 1975). Detailed analyses of primary production and its use by different consumers were documented for coastal wetlands as well as other ecosystem types (Odum 1971; Leith and Whittaker 1975). I will not describe the different methods for measuring energy flow in wetlands; you can read about it books like Leith and Whittaker. What we are interested in is the results – the data from studies of energy flow provided the foundation for compiling Figure 11.1. Later work tried to put such measurements into large energy-flow models for ecosystems (Leith and Whittaker 1975). While the value of these systems models is doubted by some scientists (McIntosh 1985), they are still prominent in many publications on wetlands (e.g. Good *et al.* 1978; Patten 1990).

11.2 Wetlands regulate climate

Wetlands play an important role in regulating the climate through carbon storage, the production of methane, and their historical role in producing coal.

11.2.1 Carbon storage

The amount of carbon dioxide in the atmosphere is one factor that controls the Earth's temperature. Carbon dioxide is transparent to sunlight, but reflects heat back to Earth. This is the basic mechanism of a greenhouse, and hence the origin of the term greenhouse effect. Since the Industrial Revolution, the concentration of carbon dioxide in the atmosphere has been rising (Figure 11.4). This is thought to be an important cause of projected changes in climate.

Since swamps and marshes are ecosystems in which plants rapidly extract carbon dioxide from the atmosphere (roughly 1 kilogram for every square meter), it is reasonable to conclude that these wetlands are particularly important in removing carbon dioxide from the atmosphere and cooling the Earth. Of course, this also depends upon how much of the organic matter is consumed by other organisms, in which case the carbon dioxide may be rapidly cycled back into the atmosphere (Figure 11.3). Peatlands are one notable exception. Here the rate of decomposition is far lower than the rate of production, with the consequence that carbon remains stored in partially decayed plant material. Some 500 million hectares (nearly 4% of the Earth's ice-free land area) now consists of peatlands (Gorham 1990). These peatlands store carbon that would otherwise be released to the atmosphere as carbon dioxide. One estimate suggests that 500 billion metric tons of carbon would be released into the atmosphere if all the peatlands on Earth were destroyed (Dugan 1993). This means that the world's large peatlands may have an enormous importance in protecting the Earth from higher temperatures. The world's largest peatlands are in central Russia (the West Siberian Lowland), northern Canada (Hudson Bay Lowland, Mackenzie Valley Lowland), and southern South America (Magellanic moorlands). Many other smaller peatlands in Europe and Asia also store carbon.

The rate of carbon storage can be disrupted by human activities. Drainage of these wetlands can increase rates of decomposition, releasing carbon dioxide into the atmosphere (Silvola *et al.* 1996). Drainage can also increase fire frequencies, increasing carbon dioxide production (Gorham 1991; Hogg *et al.* 1992). Burning peat for electricity will have the same effects. Some countries with peatlands have few trees, in which case humans have learned to cut and dry peat for heating their homes (recall Figure 4.14).

There is concern that rising temperatures themselves may be sufficient to increase rates of decomposition, in which case we can expect significant climatic consequences (Gorham 1991; Woodwell *et al.* 1995), chiefly a further increase

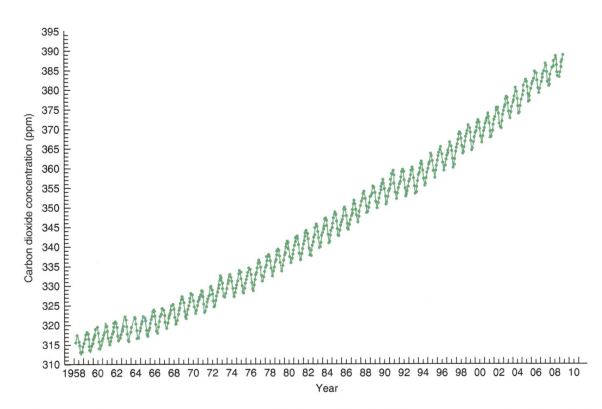

FIGURE 11.4 The concentration of carbon dioxide in the atmosphere (measured at the Mauna Loa observatory) is increasing with time. Note too that there is a cycle – each summer growing plants in the northern hemisphere reduce carbon dioxide levels by about 5 ppm. Decay returns this carbon dioxide to the atmosphere in the winter. Wetlands store carbon dioxide as peat and reduce the rate of increase. (From Keeling and Whorf 2005 and Tans 2009.)

in mean global temperature. This is not just speculation: Silvola *et al.* (1996) have shown that carbon dioxide production increases with higher temperature or with a lower water table. Warmer and drier summers may therefore speed up the rate of release of carbon dioxide from storage in peatlands, enhancing the greenhouse effect.

11.2.2 Methane production

Methane (CH_4) is a very simple molecule. It is also the most abundant organic chemical in the Earth's atmosphere, although its concentration is measured only in parts per billion (ppb). Because it absorbs infrared light, it is also an important greenhouse gas (Cicerone and Ormland 1988; Forster *et al.* 2007). Indeed, one molecule of methane generates as much

greenhouse effect as 23 molecules of carbon dioxide, although methane degrades more rapidly, with a half-life of about 7 years (House and Brovkin 2005).

Over the past 650 000 years, methane has cycled between 400 ppb during glacial periods to about 700 ppb during interglacial periods. Air samples extracted from dated ice cores suggest that methane concentrations have slowly increased from ca. 700 to 1000 ppb over the last two millennia, with more rapid increases recently in the 1970s and 1980s (Figure 11.5). The level found in 2005 – 1774 ppb – is therefore more than twice the level recorded from other interglacial periods. Although methane levels continue to increase, the rate of increase appears to have slowed over the past few decades; the reasons are unclear (Forster *et al.* 2007).

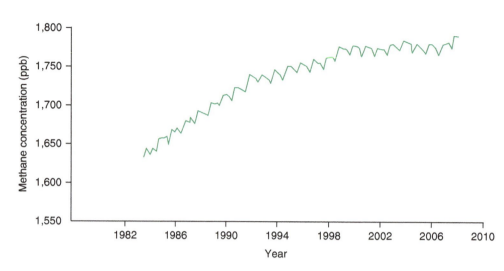

FIGURE 11.5 The concentration of methane in the atmosphere is increasing with time. Wetlands play an important, but poorly understood, role in regulating atmospheric methane levels. (Data from U.S. National Oceanographic and Atmospheric Administration.)

Natural wetlands contribute from one-third to one-half of the methane released to the atmosphere each year (Cicerone and Ormland 1988; Whiting and Chanton 1993; House and Brovkin 2005). This amounts to more than 100 Tg of methane (a Teragram $= 10^{12}$ g); 25% of this comes from tropical and subtropical swamps and marshes, whereas 60% is released from high-latitude peatlands (Matthews and Fung 1987). There is still considerable uncertainty on the figure of 100 Tg – the Millenium Ecosystem Assessment (House and Brovkin 2005) puts it between 92 and 237 Tg per year, while Whalen (2005) narrows it down to 145 Tg per year.

Human agriculture is certainly the other major source, also about one-third of the global total, and it comes largely from ruminant animals and rice paddies. Rice paddies contribute in the order of 100 Tg of methane (Aselman and Crutzen 1989). Rice paddies have higher emission rates on a m^2 basis, 300–1000 mg CH_4/m^2 per day, than natural wetlands (Table 11.1).

Part of the difficulty with making this kind of generalization is the inherent variation. Methane production varies among wetland types, among locations in wetlands, and with both temperature and flooding, making it difficult to generalize (Whalen

2005). So let us turn from global averages to look more at the processes involved in this service. We are particularly interested in the organisms that make methane and that consume methane, and how methane moves from the wetland to the atmosphere.

Methane is produced by a group of decomposers known as methanogenic archaebacteria, an ancient group of microorganisms that are strict anaerobes and live in highly reduced conditions. They do not break down organic matter themselves, but rather use the carbon dioxide generated by other decomposers as a substrate, and combine it with hydrogen: $4H_2 + CO^2 = CH_4 + 2H_2O$. One ATP is produced for each methane molecule produced. It also appears that other organic molecules such as acetate (CH_3COOH) can be used in this process (Valentine 2002).

Methane is consumed by other microorganisms. In anoxic conditions, methane oxidation apparently requires no fewer than three organisms, two different groups of archaebacteria existing in "consortia" with sulfate-reducing bacteria (Valentine 2002).

The emissions of methane from a wetland therefore depend ultimately upon how the local environment affects the relative abundance and activity of the above groups of microorganisms. Methane production will vary enormously with local

Table 11.1 Global wetland methane emissions extrapolated from measured emission rates in field experiments

Wetland type	Emission rate (mg CH_4/m^2 per day)	Area (10^{12} m^2)	Mean prod. period (days)	Emission (Tg/yr)
Lakes	43	0.12	365	2
Bogs	15	1.87	178	5
Floodplains	100	0.82	122	10
Marshes	253	0.27	249	17
Fens	80	1.48	169	20
Swamps	84	1.13	274	26
Rice fields[a]	310+	1.31	130	145
Total		7.00		100–300

[a] Rice fields have a second temperature-dependent term that leads to ranges from 300 to 1000 CH_4/m^2 per day.
Source: After Aselman and Crutzen (1989).

conditions. Roots of higher plants can reduce methane production by releasing oxygen and suppressing methane production, whereas root decay and root exudates can accelerate methane production (Segers 1998). It is likely that the oxidized upper levels of the wetland remove significant amounts of the methane produced in deeper layers (Segers 1998; Whalen 2005).

In some cases, the aerenchyma in plants provides a route for the diffusion of methane into the atmosphere. In one peatland, Shannon *et al.* (1996) found that a majority (64–90%) of the methane produced in an ombrotrophic peatland was emitted by one herbaceous plant, *Scheuchzeria palustris*. The aerenchyma of the plant transported the methane produced by methanogenic bacteria from below the soil surface into the atmosphere. Other plants such as *Carex* spp., *Peltandra virginiana*, and *Typha* are also known to emit methane.

Now back to the atmosphere (Figure 11.5). Once methane reaches the atmosphere, it is removed by reaction with the hydroxyl free radical (OH) which is produced photochemically in the atmosphere (Forster *et al.* 2007). A dramatic drop in growth of atmospheric concentrations occurred in 1992. It is thought that the Mt. Pinatubo volcanic eruption in July 1991 injected enough material

into the low stratosphere of the tropics to shift photochemistry and accelerate removal of CH_4 by atmospheric OH.

11.2.3 And then there is coal

On a larger timescale, consider the degree to which our civilization is based upon another wetland product: coal. The ability to mine coal was a trigger of the Industrial Revolution, and by the 1980s we consumed in the order of 3 billion tons per year (Manfred 1982). Even highly industrialized countries such as the United States still depend upon coal for roughly one-fourth of their energy consumption (Manfred 1982). Emerging economies in India and China will increase the rate at which coal is mined and burned. Coal comes from swamps that existed long in the past (Figure 11.6). By burning the coal, humans are releasing carbon dioxide that was once extracted from the atmosphere by wetland plants – this is why coal is called a fossil fuel. The burning of coal is the most obvious (but not the only) cause of the rising trend in carbon dioxide levels in the atmosphere. To the degree that they remove carbon dioxide from the air and store it, wetlands provide a counterbalance. Coal mines also emit methane.

FIGURE 11.6 Coal was produced in vast wetlands such as this Carboniferous coal swamp. (© The Field Museum, #GE085637c.) When coal is burned, the stored carbon returns to the atmosphere as carbon dioxide. Stored nutrients such as nitrogen are also released. (See also color plate.)

11.3   Wetlands regulate the global nitrogen cycle

In Chapter 3 we learned about the effects of nitrogen availability on the distribution and abundance of plants and animals. Here we will learn about the significant role wetlands play in the nitrogen cycle.

11.3.1 Nitrogen is abundant in the air but scarce in organisms

We take it for granted that the atmosphere is 78% nitrogen and 21% oxygen with only trace amounts of carbon dioxide and methane. But why is the atmosphere the way it is? In his 1789 *Treatise on Chemistry,* published only a few years before he went to the guillotine, Lavoisier addressed in one of his first sections the composition of the atmosphere:

We have already seen that the atmospheric air is composed of two gases ... one of which is capable, by respiration of contributing to animal life ... the other, on the contrary, is endowed with directly opposite qualities; it cannot be breathed by animals, neither will it admit of the combustion of inflammable bodies, nor of the calcination of metals.

The former we call oxygen, the latter nitrogen (although Lavoisier preferred the term azote). We now know some important further features of this azotic gas. First, the Earth's atmosphere differs from those of both neighboring planets (Venus and Mars) in having this gas predominant in its atmosphere. Second, nitrogen is essential for the construction of amino acids, the building blocks of proteins and life –

each has a nitrogen molecule in its structure. Third, only a few organisms can remove nitrogen from the atmosphere, so that both plant growth and animal growth is limited by the availability of nitrogen (e.g. Raven *et al.* 1992; White 1993). Finally, the enzyme that catalyzes the conversion of atmospheric nitrogen to biologically usable forms, nitrogenase, functions only under anoxic conditions, presumably because it originated early in the Earth's history when the atmosphere was still anoxic. Therefore, when cyanophytes reduce atmospheric nitrogen to a biologically usable form, they do so in special thick-walled cells called heterocysts in which the enzyme is protected from oxygen.

Overall, we can say that the shortage of nitrogen for making proteins is one of the central and unifying themes of plant and animal ecology. This is all the more strange given the abundance of nitrogen in the atmosphere.

11.3.2 Wetlands allow chemical transformation of nitrogen

Wetlands are an important part of the cycling of nitrogen because the hypoxic or anaerobic conditions allow chemical transformations of nitrogen. Moreover, since the water level changes "wetlands maintain the widest range of oxidation–reduction reactions of any ecosystem on the landscape. This allows them to function as effective transformers of nutrients and metals . . ." (Faulkner and Richardson 1989, p. 63). That is, wetlands are sites where elements are transformed among an array of chemical states (Rosswall 1983; Armentano and Verhoeven 1990; Patten 1990). The complex biogeochemical cycle of nitrogen involves multiple biotic and abiotic transformations involving seven valency states ($+5$ to -3). In wetlands, most nitrogen is stored in organic sediments. There are two scales at which nitrogen movement and transformation can be studied. At the within-wetland scale, the principal flows occur among three components: organic matter, the oxidized surface layer, and deeper anoxic layers. At a landscape scale, there are flows

among three other components: the surrounding terrestrial landscape, the wetland, and the atmosphere. Since we have already seen how nitrogen moves in soils (Figure 1.14), let us consider the larger scale here.

At larger scales, inputs of nitrogen to wetlands include fixation, runoff, and precipitation. Outputs include runoff and gaseous nitrogen produced by denitrification.

Wetlands provide two services. They can increase or decrease nitrogen levels in the water.

Whether a wetland is a source or sink for nitrogen depends upon the relative rates of fixation and denitrification in turn (Table 11.2). Recall that these processes are largely dependent upon the proximity of the surface oxidized layer to the anoxic regions deeper in the wetland (Faulkner and Richardson 1989).

11.3.3 Increasing nitrogen levels through fixation

In areas where nitrogen is scarce, cyanobacteria can fix nitrogen and increase local productivity. This is an important process in rice paddies, and also in natural nutrient-limited systems like the Everglades.

During nitrogen fixation, bacteria reduce atmospheric nitrogen (N_2) to ammonium (NH_4^+), providing a continual flow of nitrogen from the atmosphere to the soil. Rates of fixation in wetlands are, however, usually rather low (from 1.0 to 3.5 g/m^2 per year) (Table 11.2). Exceptions may include rice fields, floodplains, and wetlands such as the Everglades where cyanobacteria fix nitrogen. Some published estimates are considerably higher than those in Table 11.2; Whitney *et al.* (1981) estimated nearly 15 g/m^2 per year for salt marshes in eastern North America.

The principal organisms involved in nitrogen fixation in wetlands are cyanobacteria such as *Nostoc*. Better known are the bacteria such as *Azotobacter* and *Clostridium* which form nodules on

Table 11.2 Nitrogen fixation and denitrification in wetlands

	N fixation		Denitrification	
Wetland type	Mean rate (g/m^2 per year)	Total (Tg/yr)	Mean rate (g/m^2 per year)	Total (Tg/yr)
Temperate				
Peat mires	1.0	3.0	0.4	1.2
Floodplains	2.0	6.0	1.0	3.0
Tropical				
Peat mires	1.0	0.5	0.4	0.2
Swamp forest	3.5	7.8	1.0	2.2
Floodplains	3.5	5.2	1.0	1.5
Rice fields	3.5	5.0	7.5	10.8
Total		27.5		18.9
Total terrestrial		139		43–390

Source: From Armentano and Verhoeven (1990).

the roots of legumes, but legumes are relatively uncommon in most wetlands. A group of filamentous bacteria known as actinomycetes forms nodules on the roots of some trees aud shrubs associated with wetlands, notably the alders (*Alnus*) and wax myrtles (*Myrica*). *Rhizobium* is also associated with a family found in wetlands, the Ulmaceae. Finally, the cyanobacterium *Anabaena* often occurs in association with the floating water fern *Azolla,* and plays an important role in fixing nitrogen for rice paddies.

11.3.4 Lowering nitrogen levels through denitrification

Wetlands can reduce the nitrogen in water by capturing it in plant tissue, storing it in organic sediments, or converting it back to atmosphereic nitrogen. This service is of particular value in those cases where nitrogen is locally abundant and produces unwanted plant growth such as algal blooms. The importance of wetlands for denitrification has likely increased since industrial fixation of nitrogen (using the Haber process) has caused nitrogen enrichment (eutrophication) of both rivers and precipitation.

Denitrification is carried out by microorganisms living in anaerobic conditions, as we saw in Chapters 1 and 3. In this process, NO^{-3}, the biologically useful state, is converted back to N_2 or N_2O. These diffuse upward through the soil back into the atmosphere. Appreciable amounts are actually transported upward by aerenchyma in rooted plants (Faulkner and Richardson 1989). In general, denitrification rates are slightly lower than fixation rates. As a first, very rough approximation, nitrogen fixation is from 1–3 g/m^2 per year, while denitrification is about 1 g/m^2 per year (Table 11.2). Rice fields are an exception. The attempt to measure these processes accurately at the global scale (e.g. Lavelle *et al.* 2005) is a challenge, in part because the relative rates of nitrogen fixation and denitrificaton vary in so many ways. Not only do the rates vary among types of wetlands, but they vary spatially in wetlands – and then there is temporal variation on top of that, depending upon season and amount of flooding. Consider a few more examples. Bowden (1987) reported denitrification rates nearly an order of magnitude higher (30 g/m^2 per year), which would mean the wetlands are efficiently transforming organic nitrogen to atmospheric nitrogen. You can read more about biogeochemical cycling of nitrogen in sources such as Faulkner and

Richardson (1989), Armentano and Verhoeven (1990), and Lavelle *et al.* (2005).

In general, it appears that the rates of denitrification exceed rates of fixation, so that wetlands can be thought of as sites where organic nitrogen arrives in runoff and detritus, and is then returned to the atmosphere.

11.3.5 Treatment wetlands

Since nitrogen and phosphorus are significant causes of eutrophication, there is considerable interest in the use of wetlands to process wastewater and runoff. Here we have to recall the principal difference between nitrogen and phosphorus cycles, as introduced in Chapters 1 and 3. Nitrogen has a gaseous phase in its cycle, and it is possible to use artificial wetlands for denitrification, which returns nitrogen to the atmosphere as N_2 gas. Both nitrogen and phosphorus are necessary for construction of plant tissue. Hence plants can remove both of these nutrients from water. Of course, if the plants fall back into the water and decay, there was only temporary storage and the nutrients are returned to the water. If, however, the plants are harvested, or if they are eaten by herbivores that leave the site, then it is possible for nutrients to be removed from the location. Otherwise, nutrients

accumulate in the wetland, which, as we say in Chapter 3, can have deleterious effects upon some of the species therein. Nutrient removal is worth re-emphasizing: if you burn a wetland, some nitrogen is lost to the atmosphere through volatilization, but the rest falls in place as ash. Hence, burning will be of limited use in controlling eutrophication – and note that you now know enough to predict it may be helpful with eutrophication by nitrogen, but will likely have minimal impact on eutrophication by phosphorus. Mowing and harvesting, as practiced in traditional cultures, actually removes the nutrients from the wetland and transports them elsewhere. Finally, both nitrogen and phosphorus can be stored in sediment. The only problem with storage in sediment is that this means that sediment (or possibly peat) is accumulating, in which case the wetland is slowly filling in.

Overall, then, wetlands can offer an important service by improving water quality. The service is greatly affected by how the wetland is managed, and may, if care is not taken, eventually lead to the loss of the wetland.

Many communities are finding that artificially constructed treatment wetlands are a useful way to treat wastewater (Figure 11.7), particularly surface runoff, and there is now an entire industry building around treatment wetlands (Hammer 1989; Knight

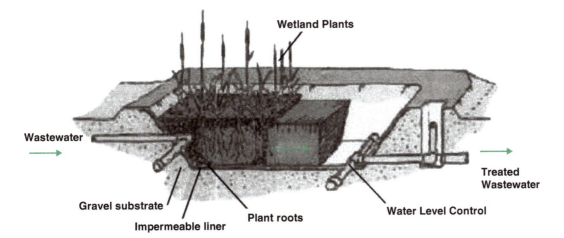

FIGURE 11.7 Treatment wetlands are constructed to reduce concentrations of nitrogen and phosphorus in wastewater. (From U.S. Environmental Protection Agency 2004.)

and Kadlec 2004). In coastal areas, constructed wetlands may provide both nutrients and fresh water. Several huge treatment wetlands are being built to try to reduce nutrient inputs to the Everglades (Sklar *et al.* 2005). Whether treatment wetlands will work at this scale is unknown, particularly as these treatment wetlands will have to deliver water with extremely low nutrient levels if they are to prevent cattail expansion in the Everglades.

11.4 Wetlands support biological diversity

The ability of wetlands to support large numbers of species enables them to perform an important service – wetlands act as storehouses of natural diversity. In this section we will discuss biodiversity as a service and the number of species that wetlands support.

11.4.1 Biodiversity storage is a service

We have already explored some of the factors that control biological diversity in wetlands in Chapter 9. When we talk about biodiversity as a service, we are describing just how many species the wetland supports. That is, we treat a wetland as a sort of warehouse of biological materials or of genetic diversity. Many species also provide other services that we explicitly measure in separate categories. For example, the presence of a particular species of cyanophyte would be one unit of the biodiversity of a wetland. The services of that cyanophyte might appear in several other categories: primary production, nitrogen fixation, food for an endangered species, carbon storage ... it is entirely possible for one species to provide multiple services.

When we describe biodiversity as a service, particular value is given to species that are regionally or globally rare. This is because rare species represent a section of biodiversity that could be lost, and, generally, the fewer the individuals present, the greater the probability that they will disappear. I have tried to incorporate some examples of such species in this book, including the gopher frog (Figure 2.5*b*), furbish lousewort (Figure 2.5*e*) and Plymouth gentian (Figure 2.5*f*), Venus fly-trap and prairie white-fringed orchid (Figure 3.4), and bog turtle (Figure 5.13), as well as rhinoceros (Section 6.3.4), Bengal tigers

(Section 8.5), and snail kites (Section 13.2.2). There are many, many more. Increasingly, every region, state, province, and nation has lists of significant species and their status. The usual three status levels are "species of concern" through "threatened species" to "endangered species." Species of concern are normally on a watch list of species that appear to be declining, while endangered species are normally at imminent risk of disappearance. Great care is taken before assigning these status levels, and they are frequently adjusted as new information becomes available. Different regions of the world often use different terms for describing status, although there is a steady convergence of terminology. The ultimate world authority is the IUCN *Red List*, created in 1963. The *Red List* classifies species using status levels ranging from "least concern" to "critically endangered" (http://www.iucnredlist.org/). The list also includes the many species thought to be already extinct.

11.4.2 Services can be measured for whole wetlands or individual species

In principle, we can think about services in two ways. There is the service provided by a wetland as a whole, and the services provided by each individual or species. In this chapter, the focus has been on the services of whole wetlands. This is partly because it is usually this information that government agencies need to know for conservation planning.

In a general way, the service performed by a wetland is the total of the services provided by all the species. If we knew all the services performed by each individual in each species, and summed them all, we would have one estimate of the service performed by the wetland. Of course, the problem is that we do not know the services provided by many species, nor do we know how many individuals there are. Sometimes, their services may even cancel each other out – for example denitrifying bacteria may cancel out the effects of nitrogen-fixing bacteria. As a further complication, services like water storage and carbon storage in peat are clearly the consequence of many species together, some of which may have been dead for centuries. Hence, for studying services it is probably better to take a top–down approach, that is, to ask about the service of the whole wetland without first worrying about which species is providing which service. We may be able to measure oxygen production, methane production, water storage, fish production, or bird production, even if we do not yet understand all the different species in the wetland that contribute to that service.

All the same, some services may be provided by a small number of species. Sphagnum mosses store organic carbon. Cyanophytes fix atmospheric nitrogen. Fish provide human food. To illustrate, Table 11.3 shows some services provided by selected species. In most cases, we do not know what services, if any, a species performs. A wetland that stores biodiversity therefore stores an unknown number of services, often provided by an unknown number of species. It is likely that some species will provide enormous services, while others may provide minor services. The point is that we often do not yet know. As but one example, most people dislike mosquitoes; few know that if we somehow eliminated all the mosquitoes from a set of wetlands, we would not only take away a food supply for many other insects, fish, and birds (including species consumed by humans), but we would even prevent pollination of local forest orchids (Table 11.3). At the other extreme, rice is a staple food. Of course, when a wetland is turned into a rice paddy, many of the species that occur there naturally disappear, so the biodiversity service is reduced.

As science progresses, we will gain a better understanding of wetland services provided by individual species. In the interim, the mere presence of these species is itself a value. Indeed, as we shall see below, sometimes the cultural and recreational value of a selected species far outweighs any other known service.

11.4.3 Wetlands provide habitat for some 100 000 species of animals

Wetlands not only support large numbers of individual species, but they support many different kinds of species. Some 100 000 animal species alone require freshwater habitats (Lévêque *et al.* 2005). Of these, some 50 000 are insects; there are 21 000 vertebrate species, 10 000 crustacean species, and 5000 mollusk species. Among the vertebrates, amphibians occur solely in fresh water, with ca. 5500 species. To this list one would need to add species using coastal wetlands for a global total.

In Chapter 9 we saw what kinds of environmental factors determine the number and kind of species found in wetlands. Under the topic of services, let us add that wetlands support diversity in several ways. First, there are species that are obligately dependent upon wetlands. Amphibians are a typical example. Many other species, however, use wetlands only occasionally as a source of water, food, and shelter. The herds of African mammals are a typical example. Finally, since wetlands (like mountain ranges) are often among the last wild places in landscapes, those large carnivores that need large areas of habitat may find wetlands to be the last wild places for refuge – examples include the Bengal tiger in the Sundarbans, the Florida panther in the Everglades, and the Iberian lynx (the world's most endangered feline) in the Doñana wetlands of southern Spain.

11.4.4 Management for biodiversity

One of the great emerging challenges for biologists is the management of wetlands to maintain, or even enhance, biological diversity. At one time, biologists were expected to maximize production of a few species, like muskrats or ducks. In the history of Louisiana, for example, enormous areas of coastal

Table 11.3 Selected examples of ecological services provided by wetland species

Service	Example
Food	(a) Rice is a staple food for a large proportion of the human population. According to the FAO (2009), 600 million tons were grown in 2007, of which 220 million tons were consumed in India and China alone (IRRI 2009).
	(b) Fish provide food for many human populations, and are particularly important as a source of protein in poorer nations.
	(c) Vegetables that come from wetlands include Chinese water chestnut (the tuber on *Eleocharis dulcis*), wetland taro (*Colocasia esculenta*), and lotus root (*Nelumbo nucifera*).
	(d) Fruits from temperate wetlands include cranberries (*Vaccinium*) and elderberries (*Sambucus*). Fruits from tropical wetlands include Acai berries (*Euterpe oleracea*) and ungurahua fruits (*Oenocarpus bataua*), both of which are species of palm trees.
	(e) Wild rice (genus *Zizania*) requires little cultivation, and is of some importance to aboriginal North Americans, who increasingly collect the rice for sale as a natural food product.
Artistic inspiration and appreciation	(a) Claude Monet, the French impressionist, produced four water lily paintings. One, called *Le Bassin aux Nymphéas*, painted in 1919, sold for $78.8 million in London in 2008.
	(b) Dragonflies, frogs, and turtles have all inspired artists to create work of beauty. Their representations can be found in many cultures, both ancient and modern.
Medicinal plants/Artistic inspiration	*Acorus calamus* has long been considered an aphrodisiac. It is also hallucinogenic. Walt Whitman's folio of poems *Leaves of Grass* has, in the third edition, a section called the "Calamus" poems.
Medicine	Aronia berries (*Aronia melanocarpa*) have high concentrations of antioxidants and are used in many herbal treatments.
Lumber	Cypress trees provide attractive and decay-resistant wood.
Pollination	*Aedes* mosquitoes carry pollinia for some *Platanthera* orchids.
Fertilization	Cyanophytes such as *Nostoc* and *Anabaena* enhance the fertility of rice paddies by fixing atmospheric nitrogen.
Clothing	Fur has provided humans with warm clothing for millennia. Fur can also be processed to make felt. (The author has a hat made in Argentina from nutria felt.)
Paper	The word paper actually comes from the plant papyrus (*Cyperus papyrus*), which is harvested from Egyptian wetlands and has been used to make paper for millennia. Other local uses include baskets, hats, fish traps, trays, floor mats, roofs, and rope. Reeds are collected as raw material for paper in China.
Construction material	Reeds are harvested for thatching on houses in Europe and for constructing boats and houses in Iraq.

marsh were burned, ditched, and impounded simply to increase the abundance of muskrats to produce more pelts (O'Neil 1949), and often with little consideration for impacts on other species or the long-term survival of the marshes themselves. Increasingly, biologists are being charged with managing wetlands for the benefit of all the species they contain. This is far more of a challenge than single-species management. It is however the way of the future. All of Chapter 9 was therefore devoted to biodiversity. If you skipped that chapter, it might be a good time to go back and read it.

11.5 Wetlands provide recreation and cultural services

There is no easy, and certainly no single, way to measure the value of recreation and culture. Civilized societies have always had museums and art galleries and theaters, but how do you assess their value? Do the Louvre or the Smithsonian Institution or the Great Wall of China have a cash value? Let's look at some methods of measuring economic value and their application to wetlands.

11.5.1 Three approaches to measuring economic value

Some philosophers would argue that trying to put an economic value on culture and recreation debases them. None the less, there are others who do believe it is possible to assign cash values even to culture and recreation. And even if these cash values are imperfect, they are better than nothing, so the argument goes. In order to fit culture and recreation into economic decision-making, we simply have to use the standard currency for measuring value: dollars, pounds, euros, yen, or roubles. There are many methods for attempting to put economic values on systems (Costanza *et al.* 1997; Daily 1997; Heal 2000; Krieger 2001), and there is a good deal of disagreement. For simplicity, consider three main options: hedonic price indices, replacement cost, and travel costs.

Hedonic price indices To put a value on views, you find the difference in sale prices of similar homes, one set with good views and one set without. This could be applied in some case to wetlands, such as comparing the value of homes with and without access to wetlands or coastline.

Replacement cost The value of good soil might be calculated by replacement cost. We might ask how much it would take to grow the equivalent amount of food using hydroponics. Or how much would it cost to buy fish that a wetland is currently producing. In a

real example, New York was faced with securing its future water supply. A new water treatment plant would have cost them $9 billion, including operating costs. Protecting 80 000 acres of land in the Catskills that provides clean water cost, instead, $1.5 billion. Thus, there was a clear advantage to making use of a natural service. But as Heal (2000) observes, what then is the value of the water: $1.5 billion, $9 billion (replacement cost), or the difference between the two? And what if the land is also providing, as it certainly does, other ecological services such as oxygen production or recreation?

Travel costs When people have choices on how to spend their money, the amount that they allocate to travel to natural areas, or museums, or theaters, says something about the value they put on that activity. Since actual entry to many wetlands and parks is usually available at low cost (unlike say, opera tickets) the travel costs are a major component of a user's willingness to pay for an experience.

11.5.2 Two large examples

While none of these methods is perfect, we shall start with the travel costs, and see how that story develops. I will illustrate the process using two recent studies that have tried to put an economic value on nature and natural areas – a Canadian study on the value of nature based on a national poll of 87 000 people (Environment Canada 2000) and an American study into the economic value of wildlife refuges (Carver and Caudill 2007). These have the advantage of being large in scope; the disadvantage is that wetlands are not separated from other wild places.

Number of visitors

Those guest books you see in museums have a purpose – they allow the staff to count how many people enter, and thereby justify their budgets.

So always sign guest books. If there are gates where entry fees are paid, direct counts of visits to specific locations can been made. Here are some numbers from the United States in 2006:

National Parks	272.6 million visits
Bureau of Land Management	55 million visitors
National Wildlife Refuges	34.7 million visitors

While such figures show that people value wild areas, they say nothing about the economic return of such activity.

Expenditures

One obvious method is to measure the travel costs that a visitor pays in order to reach a site. This can include vehicle mileage, boat rental, or airline tickets (Carvalho 2007).

Travel costs, are however, insufficient for measuring expenditures. The Canadian study (Environment Canada 2000) found that travel was only about one-fourth of the expenditure associated with enjoyment of nature:

Equipment	28.4%
Transportation	23.5%
Food	18.4%
Accommodation	12.7%
Other items (e.g. entry fees)	5.8%

Equipment was the biggest expense: cameras and binoculars for the birdwatchers, guns and ammunition for hunters, rods and boats for fishermen, tents and canoes for the explorers. If you have priced a good set of binoculars or a good canoe, you can see how much people will spend to see a bird, shoot a deer, hook a shad, or travel a wild river. The total expenditure for 1 year, 1996, was $11 billion.

Multiplier effects

Expenditures alone do not include the multiplier effects or ripple effects of these expenditures in the economy as a whole. When you buy gas on the way to a wild area, or hire a guide, or stay in a lodge, the money you spend cycles through the economy. Again, there is no single way to measure these effects. The Canadian study produced five measures intended to reflect these multiplier effects. For every dollar spent on nature-related activities, almost $1.50 of gross business production was generated. Although the idea of multiplying the expenses by 1.5 gives some sense of multiplier effects, increasingly complex economic models are employed. These economic measures were determined:

Gross business production	$16.3 billion
Gross domestic product	$11.4 billion
Government revenue from taxes	$5.1 billion
Personal income	$5.5 billion
Number of jobs sustained	201 400

The American study used economic modeling to include effects on the economy including car repairs, shoes, and alcohol. They concluded that visitors to Wildlife Refuges contributed $1.7 billion to the economy and contributed 26 800 jobs.

Willingness to pay

Another method is to measure the willingness to pay. In the case of the Upper Paraná River floodplain, the interviewed tourists were asked how much they would be willing to contribute to a foundation dedicated to protecting the natural values of the area (Carvalho 2007). This is questionable since the user does not actually have to pay the funds, nor are they faced with alternative scenarios for use of the money.

Associated with willingness to pay you will often see "surplus value" being calculated. Surplus value reflects how much more people are willing to pay for a service above what it actually costs them. In the Canadian study, respondents reported that they would have been willing to pay an extra $2 billion before limiting their outdoor activity. Again, however, there is real difficulty with measuring surplus value, since it depends upon people's best guess of how much they would pay before ceasing their activity. They might, however, switch from a long visit to a shorter visit, from a distant site to a nearer one, or simply economize with cheaper binoculars. Anyone who knows a devoted fly fisherman or deer hunter or birdwatcher knows too that these activities have such a high value that they would not easily be given up. Asking such people how much more they would pay seems like an exercise in futility. None the less, it is done.

11.5.3 Estimates of economic value of wetlands for recreation

Since the above examples addressed the recreational value of nature rather than wetlands, you might wonder about values for wetlands alone. Here are a few examples that are specific to wetlands.

Floodplain in Brazil One undammed fragment of the Upper Paraná River floodplain in Brazil, 230 km in length, is a popular destination for tourists. By applying a combination of the methods above to tourists, Carvalho (2007) calculated an estimated value of $533.00 per hectare. The total value was $356.5 million per year.

Marshes in the Great Lakes Two wetland areas on the north shore of Lake Erie have been studied

(Kreutzwiser 1981, pers. comm.) In 1978, 17 000 people used the Long Point marshes for recreation, and derived an estimated $213 000 of recreational value. Assuming 1460 ha of marshes, this yields $146/ha annually (in 1978 Canadian dollars). Similar studies in Point Pelee National Park produced higher values of $1425/ha annually. The higher figures for Point Pelee partly reflect the higher travel costs, since visitors tend to travel longer distances to reach Pelee. This likely reflects its international reputation, including special events such as spring bird migration.

Wetlands at the global scale Costanza *et al.* (1997) estimated the following values in $/ha per year for wetlands, using in most cases willingness to pay (WTP) approaches. I have also included coastal estuaries given their close association with tidal marshes and mangroves.

Recreational (e.g. ecotourism, sport fishing):

Tidal marsh/mangroves	658
Swamps/floodplains	491
Estuaries	381

Cultural (esthetic, educational, spiritual):

Tidal marsh/mangroves	(no information)
Swamps/floodplains	1761
Estuaries	29

11.6 Wetlands reduce flood peaks

Water levels in rivers change with time (Chapter 2). In temperate zones, high-water periods are caused by the melting of snow; in tropical areas, high-water periods are often associated with rainy seasons. Most wetland organisms can tolerate flooding, and many benefit from or depend upon it. From their perspective, flooding is necessary, and their life cycles are timed to exploit the flood peak. In this section we will look at how wetlands help to reduce flood peaks.

11.6.1 Flooding is natural and inevitable

When humans build on floodplains, flooding becomes a problem. What people call a river's "banks" are, after all, usually the river's edge during a seasonal low. Water levels that rise above those banks are inevitable. Yet too many people who live in floodplains seem surprised when the river rises. Many hectares of farms, factories, and cities are flooded every time the river enters a higher phase (recall Figure 2.1). Of course, as *The Epic of Gilgamesh* (Sanders 1972) reminds us, so long as people have built on floodplains, they have complained about floods.

11.6.2 Levees and flood walls often make the situation worse

The natural response to seeing a river in flood is to build a wall along the river bank to stop the "flood." These flood walls, artificial levees, dikes, impoundments, and so on, now line and confine rivers throughout the world (recall Figures 2.25, 7.8). All have many unfortunate consequences.

- Artificial levees end the natural link between the river and the floodplain, with negative effects on the organisms in both the floodplain and the river. The wetlands begin to desiccate, and growth slows from lack of nutrients; riverine fish are denied access to wetlands for feeding and rearing their young.
- Artificial levees encourage more people to move onto the floodplain, so the number of people at risk increases with time.
- Artificial levees prevent the floodplain from absorbing and storing water, which makes the floods even higher – particularly for people downstream.
- Artificial levees cause the land inside the levee to subside, so the land becomes even lower than the river, and even more prone to flooding.

As a consequence, human development of watersheds often leads to steadily increasing losses from floods. Whether you talk about the Mississippi River, the Rhine River, or the Yangtze, the story is more or less the same. This is not a new problem (Kelly 1975). When settlers moved into the deciduous forests of eastern North America, they first cleared forests in the soils most immediately useful for planting. Small wet patches could then be drained with ditches, and, as technology for drainage improved with the use of buried tiles, increasingly large areas of swamps could be undertaken. In southern Ontario, large areas of swamps were under-drained with tiles in the 1860s, thereby creating farmland described as "first class lands ... fit to produce any kind of crop." But almost immediately these projects generated flooding in adjacent lower lands, and by 1873 a county council had petitioned the provincial legislature to set up a system of arbitration to settle disputes about flood damage (Kelly 1975)!

We now know that wetlands provide the service of floodwater retention: water may be stored within the substrate (as in peatlands) or above the soil surface in the entire basin. Floodplain wetlands therefore reduce flooding downstream by allowing flows to spread out over larger areas of landscape, thereby reducing both the velocity and the depth of discharge.

11.6.3 You can estimate the value of flood protection

Thibodeau and Ostro (1981) attempted to put an economic value upon development of 8500 acres of marsh and wooded swamp in the Charles River basin in Massachusetts (Table 11.4). The benefits from these wetlands were divided into categories including flood control, water supply, increases in nearby land value, pollution reduction, and recreation and esthetics. Flood control values were estimated by forecasting flood damage that would have occurred without wetlands. In one case, during a 1995 storm, the U.S. Army Corps of Engineers estimated that the wetlands of the Charles River reduced peak river flows by 65% and delayed flooding over a period of 3 days after the actual storm. What property damage would have occurred if these wetlands had not been present? Thibodeau and Ostro estimate projected annual flood damage of nearly $18 million, which translates into a value of about $2000 per acre of wetland (Table 11.4). An asset that yields $2000 in perpetuity has a present economic value of more than $33 000 per acre.

Of course, a single private owner cannot capture most of these benefits. They are largely external benefits.

Table 11.4 **Summary of the benefits of 1 acre of Charles River wetland in New England**

Service	Estimate of value	
	Low	High
Increases in land value		
Flood prevention	$33 370	$33 370
Local amenity	$150	$480
Pollution reduction		
Nutrients and BOD	$16 960	$16 960
Toxic substances	+	+
Water supply	$100 730	$100 730
Recreation and esthetics		
Recreation	$2145	$38 469
Subtotal	$153 000	$190 009
Preservation and research	+	+
Vicarious consumption and option demand	+	+
Undiscovered benefits	+	+
Total including visual–cultural benefits	$153 535+	$190 009+

Source: From Thibodeau and Ostro (1981).

Table 11.5 **The economic value of 1 hectare of wetland, as estimated from the median value of 89 sites**

Service	Value (US$ per hectare per year in 2000)
Flood control	464
Recreational fishing	374
Amenity/recreation	492
Water filtering	288
Biodiversity	214
Habitat nursery	201
Recreational hunting	123
Water supply	45
Materials	45
Fuelwood	14

Source: From Schuyt and Brander (2004).

It may well be to his economic advantage to fill the land, reaping its development value. When this happens, it is the town, the watershed, and the region which suffer the loss.

Thibodeau and Ostro (1981) are describing the "tragedy of the commons" (Hardin and Baden 1977), which, as Hardin (1968) first presented it for grazing communities, leads each citizen to make apparently rational decisions in their best short-term interest. Yet, when each individual in the community goes through the same decision-making process, and acts in this apparently rational manner, the result is destruction for the entire community. The property owner filling in the acre of wetland, the multinational logging executive felling the next tract of tropical forest, and the herdsman deciding to graze an additional animal upon the communal pasture, all are making a decision that produces short-term economic benefits to the individual or corporation, but which ultimately damages the larger community.

11.6.4 Adapting to life on floodplains

In short, losses from flooding are inevitable once floodplains are settled. When wetlands are drained, and levees built, it gets worse. As I write this, a flood peak is rolling down the Mississippi River in Missouri. Cedar Rapids and Des Moines have water flowing through their streets. No doubt, as you are reading this, a flood peak is rolling down some other river in the world. One can read about flood storage, and see lines in tables (e.g. Tables 11.4 and 11.5) that put a value on wetlands, but often we still miss the simple message. As a personal example, which does offer some psychological insight into human attitudes, my father bought a home overlooking a floodplain. I grew up there. Every spring he complains to me about how high the water is. I used to try to explain that that is what happens to a floodplain, and encourage him to enjoy the wood ducks and the great blue herons. Now I just save my breath. At some instinctive level it seems to offend his sense of order that the river should flow at a level other than its typical July level. Period. However deeply ingrained such views are in our fellow human beings, our professional challenge is to build systems which take advantage of wetlands yet remove people from risk.

The quite remarkable story about the service of flood storage is how the construction of artificial levees has caused flooding, even though the levees are supposed to protect from floods. When a levee breaks, and the flood waters re-enter what was an old piece of floodplain, the flood peak immediately falls. If several levees upstream break, the polders (the areas that were once floodplain and wetland) often are able to absorb most of the floodwaters and end the flooding. Hence, people downstream find themselves hoping that the levees upstream will break before the flood peak arrives at their own doorsteps! What this shows very clearly is that if the floodplains upstream had been left undeveloped, they would be performing their flood control service by absorbing the floodwaters, and there would have been no dangerous flood downstream in the first place. In his book *The Control of Nature* John McPhee (1989) describes how The Great Flood of 1927 in the Mississippi River "tore the valley apart" (p. 42). Yet it was nowhere near a record flood, it was not even a 100-year flood. It was a consequence of levees that left the water confined into a narrow channel. It was not an act of God, he says, it was an act of engineers.

The commonsense approach is to ensure that valuable infrastructure is built at higher elevations, and that structures at lower elevations either be elevated on pilings, or be expendable (Nicholls and Mimura 1998; Keller and Day 2007; Vasseur and Catto 2008). Many regions now have floodplain maps that restrict development within frequently flooded areas. This is a basic principle of land use planning, and can be found in older, although classic, books such as *Design with Nature* (McHarg 1969).

Of course, private landowners often complain that they cannot build on their property because it is zoned floodplain and demand compensation. They obstruct zoning and planning. Of course, had they been allowed to build on the floodplain, the same people would be demanding government compensation when their house or factory was damaged by a flood. Given that some people have to complain about something, it is generally easier and cheaper to allow them to complain about not being able to build than to complain about having their house destroyed. Over time, the message sinks in that land on floodplains should be left as land.

Of course, there are always going to be a few people who avoid rational discussion. Barbara Tuchman has written about such people in *The March of Folly* (1984). I doubt, however, that any of those people are reading this book.

11.6.5 There is money to be made from engineered disasters

Continuing on that theme, Mark Twain once noted, roughly, "there is no point trying to convince someone to believe something when he will profit from not believing it." Hence, we should not expect everyone to accept the need to make commonsense planning decisions. When I was in Louisiana, private landowners were demanding the right to do whatever they wanted with their land, even turning land below sea level into subdivisions, while at the same time they were insisting that the federal government step in and protect their land with levees and restore their wetlands, too, free, all while keeping taxes low. There is, apparently, no federal statute that says landowners have to be logically consistent.

It is unfortunate that bad decisions by one community force other communities to make the same bad decision. *A community that builds taller levees and impounds bigger areas exports its flooding to neighbors.* Levee building pits one community against another, each building its levees higher, in the hope that it will be a neighboring community that floods instead of them. There is no end to the cycle.

Thus one begins an expensive and never-ending vicious cycle of levee construction up and down the river valley. It is likely to be far more economical to buy wetlands and leave them for flood storage in the first place, instead of building enormous levees downstream to handle the flood.

There is an enormous industry that benefits from money spent on flood control. Indeed, some have said that in Louisiana, levee construction has less to do with flood control than with obtaining federal money (Houck 2006). Buying and restoring wetlands upstream to provide long-term flood storage is an obvious solution to recurring flooding, as is restricting building in the most flood-prone areas. The more levees we build along rivers, the higher the floods

will become. Hence, it is time to plan adaptively for life on floodplains.

- Protect existing wetlands for flood storage
- Reduce the area of land protected by levees to enhance flood storage
- Move critical infrastructure to higher land
- Elevate critical infrastructure that cannot be moved.

Given the enormous value of the services of flood control, and recreation, wetlands should increasingly become part of land use planning in watersheds. It is happening, and levees are being removed in parts of North America, Europe, and Asia. You will see some examples in the next chapter.

11.7   Wetlands record history

Plant and animal debris often accumulates in wetlands owing to the low oxygen levels, and the resulting layers of peat and sediment can record the sequence of plant species that occupied a site over millennia. Since we know what environmental conditions these plants required, one can reconstruct how the environment has changed. Peatlands are particularly important and well studied. One frequently finds that the accumulations of organic matter provide a nearly complete record of the plant associations that occurred on the site over thousands, or tens of thousands, of years. This record most commonly takes the form of pollen and plant fragments, but can be supplemented by insect parts, charcoal fragments, archeological artefacts, and even rooted trees that have been buried over the years (e.g. Watts and Winter 1966; Walker 1970; Moore 1973; Godwin 1981; Delcourt and Delcourt 1988, 1991). They can also record contaminants such as lead and show us how deposition rates changed with time. (Exceptions include alluvial flood plains, where the sediments are constantly reworked by meandering rivers, so that the sedimentary record is lost [e.g. Nanson and Beach 1977; Salo *et al.* 1986]).

Let us take Ireland as an example. Figure 11.8 shows the types of pollen recovered from a peat bog near Tipperary. More than 8 meters of peat now cover the original soil surface. Some 10 000 years ago the site was open tundra, as indicated by the abundant birch and sedge pollen. Pine woods developed some 8000 years ago, to be replaced by elm–oak woodland some 6000 years ago. This suggests a steady amelioration of climate. About 3000 years ago, *Ulmus* (elm) pollen declines and herb pollen increases; this appears to reflect woodland clearance by Neolithic farmers. About 1800 years ago the clearances become more extensive, apparently due to the arrival of Bronze Age farmers. At many sites, wooden trackways constructed from branches or split logs were apparently constructed to cross bogs and link farming communities (Godwin 1981). At about AD 300, there was a reduction in intensity of farming, but since then there has been a steady increase in amounts of grass and herb pollen, indicating greater human impacts upon the Irish landscape.

Such records provide important opportunities to study long-term changes in vegetation and climate, the impacts of human cultures upon

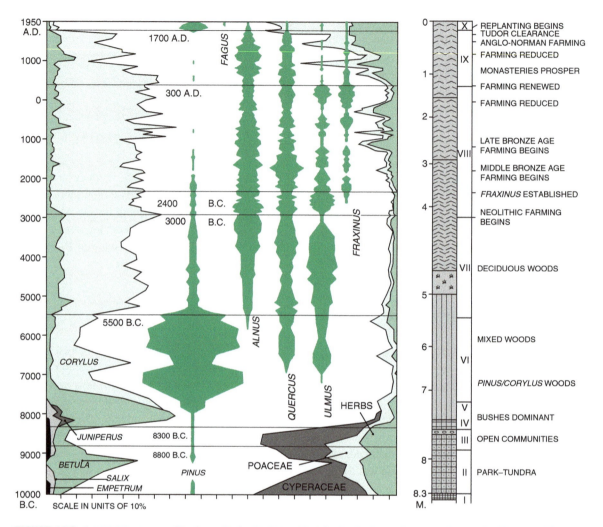

FIGURE 11.8 A 10 000-year profile through the Littleton Bog, Ireland, shows how tundra gradually turned into deciduous forest, and then how humans stripped the land of its forests. (After Mitchell 1965, from Taylor 1983.)

vegetation, and natural processes such as succession in wetlands. In many cases peatlands can be considered to be archives for adjoining regions of the Earth's surface (Godwin 1981). Changes in vegetation and land use are not the only records stored in bogs. A Danish almanac of 1837 records: "There is a strange power in bog water which prevents decay. Bodies have been found which must have lain in bogs for more than a thousand years, but which, though admittedly somewhat shrunken and brown, are in other respects unchanged." More

than 690 human bodies have been recovered from peat bogs. The most famous are perhaps Lindow Man and Tollund Man. The bodies are distributed across Germany, Denmark, Holland, England, Scotland, Ireland, Norway, and Sweden (Stead *et al.* 1986; Coles and Coles 1989). Most are from the period between 100 BC and AD 500. Men, women, and children have been found, the outstanding feature being that they are so well preserved that they are sometimes first assumed to be the result of a recent murder. Some, such as the Tollund

Man, were apparently strangled, with the plaited skin noose still attached to the neck; others appear to have been pegged down while still alive (Glob 1969). The bodies give the appearance of having been tanned, a process now attributed to a polysaccharide (sphagnan) produced by *Sphagnum* (Painter 1991).

Many studies of wetland services do not explicitly include the role of wetlands in preserving archeological and climatological data. Growing concerns about human impacts on climate, and about rates of deposition of atmosphere comtaminants like lead and mercury, are likely to further increase the value of such records.

11.8 Adding up the services: WWF and MEA evaluate wetland services

The World Wildlife Fund undertook a review and meta-analysis of 89 wetland evaluation studies (Schuyt and Brander 2004). Their objective was to better quantify the global value of wetlands, particularly in light of the criticisms of the Constanza *et al.* (1997) studies, and the lack of detail on the types of wetlands. The task, is of course, complicated by the many services that wetlands perform, combined with the many different types of wetlands and the many geographical regions in which they occur.

To combine the 89 existing studies, they divided wetlands into five types and found the economic value (in US dollars in the year 2000) for each. Their first example, the Pantanal, was shown in Table 1.8. The median values were:

Unvegetated sediment	$374/ha
Freshwater wood	$206/ha
Salt/brackish marsh	$165/ha
Freshwater marsh	$145/ha
Mangrove	$120/ha

The high value of unvegetated sediments is unexpected, and is partly explained by the value in storm protection and as nursery grounds for commercial fisheries in areas like the Wadden Sea in the Netherlands and the Rufiji delta in Tanzania. Migratory waterbirds also feed in mud flats, and invertebrate populations may be higher that in the nearby vegetated areas (Peterson *et al.* 1989). The low value of mangroves, in contrast, may reflect the predominance of their use for fuelwood in areas of low income.

Using these data, WWF next extrapolated to the rest of the world using a database on 3800 wetlands representing about 63 million hectares, yielding a value of $1.8 billion per year. Wetlands in Asia had particularly high values, likely a reflection of the high population density of this part of the world.

These values are conservative. First, as the list of services in Table 11.5 shows, some services were not included, such as water supply (extractive use by industry), erosion control, climatic stabilization, carbon sequestration, maintenance of ecosystem stability, medicinal resources, and genetic resources. Second, the figure of 63 million hectares is on the low side. Other estimates are 10 or even 20 times higher. If you use the Ramsar estimate (12.8 million km^2), the total economic value of the world's wetlands, based on the services examined in the WWF report (and therefore not all services) could be around $70 billion per year. This larger figure would be consistent with the study valuing the services of the Pantanal alone at $15 billion per year (Table 1.8).

The Millenium Ecosystem Assessment (2005) provided a comprehensive overview of human impacts on the biosphere. This assessment tabulated a list of 17 services provided by ecosystems in general. These services were assigned to one of four categories: provisioning, regulating, cultural and supporting. The MEA then assigned relative values for each of these services for inland wetlands (Figure 11.9) and coastal wetlands (Figure 11.10). Compare these figures to Table 1.7.

It appears that we have been significantly undervaluing wetlands. As knowledge of services increases, the value of wetlands is likely to increase further.

Inland Wetlands

Services	Comments and Examples	Permanent and Temporary Rivers and Streams	Permanent Lakes, Reservoirs	Seasonal Lakes, Marshes, and Swamps, including Floodplains	Forested Wetlands, Marshes, and Swamps, Including Floodplains	Alpine and Tundra Wetlands	Springs and Oases	Geothermal Wetlands	Underground Wetlands, Including Caves and Groundwater systems
Provisioning									
Food	production of fish, wild game, fruits, grains, and so on	high	high	high	high	low	low		
Fresh water	storage and retention of water; provision of water for irrigation and for drinking	high	high	medium	low	low	low		high
Fiber and fuel	production of timber, fuelwood, peat, fodder, aggregates	low	medium	low	high	medium		low	
Biochemical products	extraction of materials from biota	low	low	?	?	?	?	?	?
Genetic materials	medicine, genes for resistance to plant pathogens, ornamental species, and so on	low	low	?	low	?	?	?	?
Regulating									
Climate regulation	regulation of greenhouse gases, temperature, precipitation, and other climatic processes; chemical composition of the atmosphere	low	high	low	high	low	low	low	low
Hydrological regimes	groundwater recharge and discharge; storage of water for agriculture or industry	high	high	low	medium	low	low		low
Pollution control and detoxification	retention, recovery, and removal of excess nutrients and pollutants	high	medium	low	medium	low			high
Erosion protection	retention of soils and prevention of structural change (such as coastal erosion, bank slumping, and so on)	high	low	low	medium	?	low		low
Natural hazards	flood control; storm protection	low	high	high	medium	low	medium		low
Cultural									
Spiritual and inspirational	personal feelings and well-being; religious significance	high	high	low	medium	low	high	low	low
Recreational	opportunities for tourism and recreational activities	high	high	low	low	low	medium		
Aesthetic	appreciation of natural features	low	medium	low	medium	low	medium		
Educational	opportunities for formal and informal education and training	high	high	medium	low	low	medium		
Supporting									
Biodiversity	habitats for resident or transient species	high	high	high	medium	low	low	low	low
Soil formation	sediment retention and accumulation of organic matter	high	low	low	high	low	?	?	
Nutrient cycling	storage, recycling, processing, and acquisition of nutrients	high	high	high	high	low	low	?	low
Pollination	support for pollinators	low	low	low	high	low	low		

FIGURE 11.9 The relative magnitude (per unit area) of ecosystem services provided by inland wetlands: low (small dot), medium (intermediate dot), high (large dot), ? = unknown; blank cells indicate that the service is not considered applicable to inland wetlands. The figure shows the global average pattern according to expert opinion. (From Millennium Ecosystem Assessment 2005.)

Coastal Wetlands

Services	Comments and Examples	Estuaries and Marshes	Mangroves	Lagons, Including Salt Ponds	Intertidal Flats, Beaches, and Dunes	Kelp	Rock and Shell Reefs	Seagrass Beds	Coral Reefs
Provisioning									
Food	production of fish, algae, and invertebrates	●	●	·	◐	·	◐	·	●
Fresh water	storage and retention of water; provision of water for irrigation and for drinking	·			·				
Fiber, timber, fuel	production of timber, fuelwood, peat, fodder, aggregates	●	●	◐					
Biochemical products	extraction of materials from biota	·	·				·		·
Genetic materials	medicine; genes for resistance to plant pathogens, ornamental species, and so on	·	·	·		●			
Regulating									
Climate regulation	regulation of greenhouse gases, temperature, precipitation, and other climatic processess; chemical composition of the atmosphere	◐	◐	◐	·		·	·	◐
Biological regulation	resistance of species invasions; regulating interactions between different trophic levels; preserving functional diversity and interactions	◐	●	◐	·				·
Hydrological regimes	groundwater recharge/discharge; storage of water for agriculture or industry	·			·				
Pollution control and detoxification	retention, recovery, and removal of excess nutrients and pollutants	●	●	◐		?	·	·	·
Erosion protection	retention of soils	·	●	·	·				
Natural hazards	flood control; storm protection	●	●	·	·	·	◐	◐	●
Cultural									
Spiritual and inspirational	personal feelings and well-being	◐	·	◐	●	·	·	·	●
Recreational	opportunities for tourism and recreational activities	◐	·	·	●	·			●
Aesthetic	appreciation of natural features	·	·	◐	◐				●
Educational	opportunities for formal and informal education and training	·	·	·	·		·		·
Supporting									
Biodiversity	habitats for resident or transient species	◐	·	·	●	·	●	·	●
Soil formation	sediment retention and accumulation of organic matter	◐	◐	·	·				
Nutrient cycling	storage, recycling, processing and acquisition of nutrients	◐	◐	◐	·	·	·		◐

FIGURE 11.10 The relative magnitude (per unit area) of ecosystem services provided by coastal wetlands: low (small dot), medium (intermediate dot), high (large dot), ? = unknown; blank cells indicate that the service is not considered applicable to coastal wetlands. The figure shows the global average pattern according to expert opinion. (From Millennium Ecosystem Assessment 2005.)

CONCLUSION

We began with the challenge of measuring ecological services. We have now examined some of the principal services provided by wetlands. Some, like the value of fish, are easy to measure. Others, like regulation of climate are equally important, but much harder to measure. And others still, like the value of wetlands to culture, seem immeasurable. Of course, when a painting like Claude Monet's *Le Bassin aux Nymphéas* sells for $78.8 million, this neatly translates art into dollars.

Here are two more examples.

When the young Polish novelist Józef Konrad Korzeniowski took the aging *Roi des Belges* up the Congo River in 1899, who would have guessed that it would give us Joseph Conrad (a new name) and the darkly famous novella *Heart of Darkness* (Figure 11.11, top)? And who could have guessed then that an entirely

FIGURE 11.11 Wetlands have played a prominent role in the world's literature. Top: Joseph Conrad (1857–1924) sailed up the Congo River in 1899 in the *Roi des Belges* (built 1887, only this ancient photo survives; from en.wikipedia.org), inspiring his book *Heart of Darkness* (1902). Bottom: Mark Twain (1835–1910) (courtesy Library of Congress, P&P) worked as a riverboat pilot and wrote several books based upon his experience, including *Life on the Mississippi* (1883).

new medium, color film, would be used to tell stories, and that *Heart of Darkness* would metamorphose into *Apocalypse Now*?

And then there was the young typesetter Samuel Clemens who decided, in 1856, to give up a journalistic assignment from the Keokuk *Saturday Post* for a series of comic letters about travel in South America, and instead become a riverboat pilot on the Mississippi River. Who would have guessed that this event would eventually give us Mark Twain (another new name) and legacies like *Life on the Mississippi* (1883) (Figure 11.9, bottom) and, only a year later, *The Adventures of Huckleberry Finn*?

There are just two of many famous artists whose lives were inextricably bound up with wetlands. In this chapter I have tried to lay out the fundamentals of putting economic values on wetlands. It is an issue that is likely to grow in importance and sophistication. And, at the same time, Claude Monet, Joseph Conrad, and Mark Twain are just three people who illustrate the power of wetlands to influence human creativity in ways that are hard to predict and even harder to measure.

Chapter contents

12 Research: paths forward

A book, particularly a "textbook" can easily create the impression that it has all the facts and nothing more needs to be learned. Science, however, is a process, and knowledge continues to grow. In principle, scientists should have a short and clear set of questions that need to be answered, and familiarity with the tools that will help answer those questions. Going out and studying the first thing that catches our eye, or measuring everything we can think of, is not advisable. It happens too often. Wetland ecology, more than most, would benefit from a stronger grounding in the methods and tools of science. Here I would like you to think about how wetland ecology fits into the last 100 years of scientific progress, and how we can take it forward for everyone's benefit. Everyone from new graduate students to seasoned and graying professors can benefit from taking a little time to reflect on the big picture. So let us start with the age of exploration and the search for ... the source of the Nile ... and penguin eggs.

12.1   Some context: the great age of explorers

There was a time when exploring the world's geography was a part of science in general, and a part of wetland ecology. Wallace, co-discoverer of evolution, began his scientific career with an expedition to the Amazon. Darwin made his epic voyage to the Galápagos. Von Humboldt set a world elevation record climbing a peak in the Andes. Each discovery generated new questions. One that remained was the source of the Nile River. Another was the nature of the South Pole. Let us use these as examples and leap back a century to this challenge of physical exploration.

It was only a little over 100 years ago, September 16, 1864, to be precise, when the British Association for the Advancement of Science met in Bath, England, and among the celebrities were the two most controversial figures of African exploration, Richard Burton and John Hanning Speke. *The Times* called their impending formal confrontation a gladiatorial exhibition. The topic of debate? A wetland. More specifically, the source of the Nile (Morris 1973).

Consider the challenges they faced. A joint expedition to Africa in 1858, arrival at Lake Tanganyika with Speke nearly blind from trachoma and Burton half-paralyzed by malaria, and then Speke's solitary reconnaissance trip, which 25 days later brought him to the shore of Lake Victoria. On Livingstone's last and greatest adventure, still on the hunt for the Nile headwaters, he was "delayed by tribal wars, constantly sick, losing his teeth one by one" when he reached the Arab slaver's village of Ujiji and languished near death. On November 10, 1871 he was discovered by Henry Stanley of the *New York Herald*, and greeted with the now famous "Dr Livingstone, I presume?"

The era of global exploration ended, in one way, not with the Nile but with the final voyage to the South Pole (Jones 2003). Even then, there were questions as to whether the trip was more of a voyage for national honor than for scientific discovery,

although the British Expedition led by Captain Scott made an effort to include exploration, even to man-hauling many pounds of rock samples back on the already heavy sledges.

It is worth reading more about those times, if only to refine your own thoughts on what the modern role of science should be. Consider. When Captain Scott and his companions reached the South Pole (January 17, 1912) they found a flag already there – left by the Norwegian Roald Amundsen a month earlier. They now faced a 1400-km (850-mile) journey across Antarctic ice to reach their base camp. On the trek back, Petty Officer Edgar Evans collapsed in the snow and died. Captain Lawrence Oates, crippled by frostbite, and fearing that his slow pace would cause the death of his companions, walked into the snow on March 17 and did not return. On March 19, the three survivors pitched their tents in the snow, their food and fuel exhausted, but knowing it was only 18 km from a depot with fresh supplies. This was where their bodies were found a year later by a rescue expedition. Reading the accounts of the suffering, one wonders whether the effort was worth it.

Skeptical questions about the motives and the risks do need to be asked, but when we become cynical, it is worth reminding ourselves that on this same trip, three of the team (Wilson, Bowers, and Cherry-Garrard) (Figure 12.1) made an epic journey to collect eggs of the Emperor penguin, then thought to be the most primitive species of bird on Earth. They wanted embryos to answer questions about the origin of birds and their relationship to other vertebrates. Hence, they sledged for 2 weeks in the continual darkness of an Antarctic winter, dragging their supplies through a succession of blizzards, through temperatures as low as −60 °C (−77 °F), to reach Cape Crozier and its penguin rookery. Collecting five unhatched eggs, they then had to retrace their steps for another 2 weeks of the same, just to regain contact with the rest of the expedition. Three eggs survived (and are now in the Natural History Museum in

FIGURE 12.1 Exploration! The Cape Crozier party leaves for a 4-week night journey in the Antarctic winter to collect Emperor penguin eggs in 1911. Left to right: Bowers, Henry Robertson, 1883–1912; Wilson, Edward A., 1872–1912; Cherry-Garrard, Apsley, 1886–1959. (Courtesy National Library of Australia.)

London). The account of this trip, titled *The Worst Journey in the World* (Cherry-Garrard 1922), "remains one of the classic narratives of exploration" according to Jones (2003, p. 264). Still, the age of heroic exploration did, in many ways, die with Scott and his team, since their failures received more attention that the scientific successes. Moreover, the following years of the First World War began to make people think more skeptically about science. The outbreak of the First World War saw technology and science used in unprecedented ways, from machine guns to airplanes to tanks to poison gas. It raised, and still raises, troubling questions about just what it is that scientists are trying to achieve, and whether it will benefit or harm humankind.

Setting aside the bigger question of the potential harm caused by science, let us return to the small one. Is there still a role for exploration? The good news is that some exploration will continue to be necessary. We still need accurate species lists for many wetlands. New wetland species undoubtedly remain to be named. Some wetlands like the Congo River basin, in spite of their global significance, are still imperfectly explored (Campbell 2005; Keddy *et al.* 2009b). There does seem to be something in our human nature that enjoys search and discovery. Every student has the capacity to find something new, whether it is a new species of wetland plant for your county flora, or a new species of dragonfly in a national park. To me, the thrill of finding a new location for a rare plant or animal is part of the pleasure of working as a scientist.

Yet, overall, we are now entering a new era, an era where the essential challenges to the scientist require not the discovery of the headwaters of the Nile, or the enumeration of the palm trees along the Amazon, or the collection of Emperor penguin eggs, but something more difficult. Our new task is the discovery of things that are essentially unseen and unseeable. They are (1) the essential **processes** that occur in wetlands, and (2) the **relationships** among environmental factors and life forms. You cannot preserve a process in a bottle of formaldehyde, nor can you photograph a relationship with a high-tech camera. Processes and relationships are the hidden laws or rules that are under, or behind, or inside (none of these words is quite right) the biological reality around us. Our current task is to find these, to describe them, to quantify them, and to subject them to rigorous experiment without ever seeing them. The closest we will come to actually seeing them is when we write a report and prepare a graph or figure that exemplifies our ideas.

The closest analogies might be early years in chemistry, going back to the era when scholars first became interested in the composition of the

atmosphere, nitrogen fixation by legumes, or carbon storage in wood, when even the periodic table had yet to be drawn.

While there remain new geographical discoveries to be made, particularly in poorly known groups such as the arthropods and microorganisms, and perhaps in regions under the oceans, the great period of explorers in sailing ships and steamers has passed. We are now in an era of new challenges. Our challenge is to pursue these with the same devotion as Speke and Scott, as Wallace and Darwin. Perhaps, chastened by a century of warfare, of poison gas and nuclear weapons and engineered diseases, we could also add a new requirement. Our efforts should focus on knowledge that will be of benefit to other living beings, not on knowledge that will be used to harm them.

12.2   Four basic types of information

We can identify four basic steps in gaining knowledge about wetlands. We will first consider these types before we move on to cover more sophisticated analyses.

12.2.1 Species accounts

One way of looking at the world is to study individual species. This has the advantage of simplifying the process. Find a species. Find a biologist. Let one study the other. Thus, the book cover has both a snapping turtle and a great egret, rather conspicuous wetland species that have been studied a good deal. People who work with insects and plants in particular find this highly unsatisfactory, because there are far more species than there are biologists interested in them. Perhaps countries like China and India, each with more than a billion people, can afford to have one biologist assigned to each plant and animal species, but even if this were the case, we can argue that it is not a very efficient way to do science. This is not to say that we should not learn the names of wild

species – indeed, I have included many species names in the figures.

There are certain costs to the species-oriented approach. First, species that are not popular get overlooked. When I teach, I tend to meet students who want to study whales and lions and moose. Another group wants to study ducks and deer and trout. I rarely meet ones who want to study mud snails, algae, or methanogens. As a result, our understanding of the natural world is warped. We know a great deal about life forms with backbones and fur. Or feathers. Or gills and scales. We know relatively little about others. Imagine yourself newly arrived on Earth, and interested in wetlands: what species would you choose to study based on the criterion of importance? And how would you decide to measure importance?

Although our knowledge of the natural world is growing, my students are always surprised to find the limitations of information on line. Here are three tests. (1) Try to find a list of the frogs found in one of the world's biodiversity hotspots, the mountains of southwest China. If you succeed, select one and try to find its range map and diet. And the type of wetland in which it occurs. (2) Birds are particularly well studied. Find a list of the birds nesting in the Congo River delta. Which species of migratory birds use that delta? Which ones nest there, and when? (3) The Hudson Bay Lowland is one of the world's largest wetlands. Try to find an estimate of carbon storage and methane production in that specific wetland. Diamond mines are being dug in that wetland – which plant species occur in the vicinity of those mines, and what is happening to the local water table? The point I am trying to emphasize is that enormous gaps in our knowledge exist. We should plan future work to fill those gaps. Our knowledge of wetlands must extend beyond large charismatic species.

12.2.2 Delineation

We need maps of wetlands. Mapping is one of the most basic parts of geology and biology. If you read the travels of early biologists, you know that much of it was driven by simple questions like "Where does this river go? How big is this forest? How high is this mountain?" These are legitimate questions, and our knowledge of the world now, with an atlas in every library, and satellite images available on line, is truly remarkable. In spite of this, there are important gaps. We still lack good maps for some of the world's largest wetlands. And satellite imagery, while it might be able to differentiate between flooded and non-flooded forest, is a poor substitute for having biologists on the ground.

To produce a map of a wetland, you need criteria for recognizing when wetland stops and upland begins. In the United States, there is a formal process of wetland delineation, and an official technical manual done by the U.S. Army Corps of Engineers (1987). Using criteria like soil type and the presence of wetland plants, biologists are employed to map wetlands at regional scales (U.S. Army Corps of Engineers 1987, Tiner 1999). These wetlands are

then protected by certain legislation and regulations, and government agencies must issue permits for any activities that could alter the wetland.

Plants are a useful guide to the presence of wetlands. The U.S. Fish and Wildlife Service has therefore sorted native plants into several categories of official wetland indicator status, including **obligate wetland plants** and **facultative wetland plants** (www.plants.usda.gov/wetland.html). Obligate wetland plants are entirely dependent upon water, while facultative wetland plants usually occur in wetlands but are occasionally found elsewhere. Some obligate wetland species you have encountered in this book include *Platanthera leucophaea* (Figure 3.4), *Sabatia kennedyana* (Figure 2.5f), *Sagittara lancifolia* (source of data in Figure 8.6), as well as *Nuphar lutea* and *Pontederia cordata* on the cover itself. The obligate list also includes many trees including cypress (*Taxodium* spp.), tupelo (*Nyssa* spp.), and mangrove (*Laguncularia racemosa*, *Rhizophora* spp.). Such lists provide an important tool for locating and delineating wetlands.

Each country tends to have its own procedures, and these are often modified by state or provincial regulations, so we will leave it as an exercise for you to find out the laws and policies that protect wetlands where you live. To use a Canadian example, all the major wetlands around my home have now been mapped (Figure 12.2). Can you find something similar for your county?

12.2.3 Inventory

Once a wetland is mapped or legally "delineated," it is natural to ask "What lives there?" Indeed, one of the most basic questions in biology is: what is here? Although young scientists today will find it hard to match Wallace canoeing up the Amazon to ask "What is here?" or Darwin sailing to the Galápagos to ask "What is here?" or Scott sledging to the South Pole to ask "What is there?", this none the less remains an important question at more local scales.

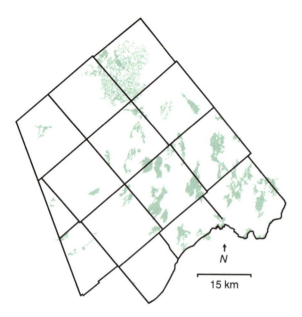

FIGURE 12.2 The vast majority of wetlands in southern Ontario have been mapped, investigated, and evaluated for protection. Here are the wetlands of provincial significance in Lanark County (Ontario, Canada) where the author resides. (Courtesy Ontario Ministry of Natural Resources.)

Many local wetlands still do not have complete inventories. It can be a very pleasant pastime to select a poorly known wetland, and then try to complete a list of all the creatures that live there. It is also an excellent way to hone your skills as a biologist, and contribute to scientific knowledge at the same time. Pick a wetland and go to work. While you are at it, you may discover a new species for your county, or state, or even nation.

Inventories are also done professionally. When an area is designated a protected area in some way (say a park, an ecological reserve, a special management area) it is normal to have a team of biologists explore the area and publish a report. Some of you may find work as a consulting biologist doing exactly this. Of course, once the report is done, the real work begins. The early reports try to describe the area as well as possible. But often it is local biologists and naturalists who take the time to do further exploration and find species that the first report missed.

12.2.4 Evaluation

Once a wetland is mapped and delineated, it is still necessary to measure its ecological significance. So long as cities are growing, and land is being cleared for agriculture, there has to be some way to decide how valuable each wetland is. We saw some approaches to measuring the services provided by wetlands in Chapter 11, but there has to be a simpler system that can be applied systematically to each and every wetland in a region.

In Ontario, Canada, a wetland evaluation system has been used to assess more than 2300 wetlands. The evaluation system has four components: biological, social, hydrological, and special features (Table 12.1). Once each wetland is evaluated, it is then assigned a score. Each category can have up to 250 points, for a total out of 1000. Any wetland that receives more than 600 points in total, or in which the biological or special features component reaches 250, is designated a Provincially Significant Wetland (PSW). Groups of wetlands can be evaluated together as a wetland complex if they meet certain criteria of interconnectedness.

Provincially Significant Wetlands have many kinds of protection. I, for example, am writing this book on the edge of a wetland complex (the Scotch Corners Wetland Complex) that has been evaluated as a PSW. It has rare plants (*Peltandra virginica*, *Galearis spectabilis*) and significant birds (nesting osprey, nesting herons), many mammals (fishers, otters) and at least six kinds of frogs.

Although some people are still unhappy that their farm has designated wetlands, most people now accept maps like Figure 12.2 as a part of our rural heritage. Some people, like me, even buy land because they like knowing that the land will be protected from further development. Developers tend to avoid wetlands because they know that they will encounter expensive delays by trying to build in areas with demonstrated levels of natural value. Increasingly, landowners like having wetlands, because if your wetland is mapped and evaluated as significant, you pay low taxes on the wetland acreage.

Table 12.1 **Evaluation criteria for assessing wetland significance in the province of Ontario, Canada. Wetlands scoring a total of at least 600 or scoring 250 for the Biological or Special Feature components are determined to be provincially significant wetlands (see Figure 12.2)**

Component	Primary criterion (*secondary criterion examples*)	Maximum possible score	
		Primary criterion	Component[a]
Biological	Productivity (*growing degree days, wetland/site type*)	50	
	Biodiversity (*wetland types, vegetation communities, surrounding habitat diversity, interspersion, open water type*)	150	250
	Size (*biodiversity–area index*)	50	
	Economically valuable products (*wood, rice, fish, furbearers*)	50	
	Recreational activities (*number and intensity*)	80	
	Landscape esthetics (*distinctness, human disturbance*)	10	
Social	Education and public awareness (*education, research*)	40	250
	Proximity to areas of human settlement	40	
	Ownership	10	
	Size	20	
	Aboriginal/social values	30	
	Flood attenuation	100	
	Water quality improvement (*short and long term, groundwater discharge*)	100	
Hydrological	Shoreline erosion control	15	250
	Groundwater recharge	60	
	Carbon sink	5	
	Rarity (*wetland types, number of species and relative significance*)	[b]	
Special Features	Significant features or habitat (*colonial birds, winter cover, waterfowl breeding/staging/molting, fish habitat*)	625	250
	Ecosystem age	25	
	Great Lakes coastal wetlands	75	
Total			1000

[a] 250 per component assigned for criteria total ≥250.
[b] No limit to criterion score.
Source: From Ontario Ministry of Natural Resources (1993).

12.3   Limitations to species-based research

The above four steps will provide a great deal of information for conservation. But they are unlikely to provide good grounds for making predictions about how wetlands as a whole will change in response to perturbations. Although species-based work is appealing, it may not be a particularly useful approach to understanding the behavior of communities and ecosystems. This is because wetlands have so many species. Here is the problem, in the words of Rigler (1982), who wrote about the failure of species-based models in limnology

A temperate lake may support 1000 species. If each species interacted with every other species we would have $(1000 \times 999)/2$ or 0.5×10^6 potential interactions to investigate. Each potential interaction must be demonstrated to be insignificant or quantified. If we estimate one man-year per potential interaction it would take half a million years to gather the data required for one systems analysis model.

Indeed, you can divide scientific problems into three categories, small-, medium-, and large-number systems (Weinberg 1975). My own education did not address the importance of general systems theory in research, and so I suspect that most readers will have the same limitations.

Small-number systems These have very few components and few interactions, and are amenable to precise mathematical description. Population ecology is an example. We can predict exponential growth from a few measurements of species biology. Of course, these sorts of models have their own problems. Small-number systems are an artificial construct. They are created by artificially removing populations from the many connections they have with other populations. Hence, the small-number approach may seem appealing, in part because it fits with species-based views of nature, but it succeeds only by ignoring most of the system.

Large-number systems These have so many similar components that the average behavior becomes a useful description of the system. The ideal gas law in physics provides one example. The position and velocity of a particular gas molecule are not of interest, but the properties of volume, temperature, and pressure are. Hence, some people think that we can borrow the approaches of physicists to studying nature. However, as one of my students once told me, a frog is not a billiard ball. What he meant was that many models of large number systems treat each particle as a billiard ball. Ecological systems, however, have components that are very different from one another. My student could also have said a diatom is not a wood stork, or a beaver is not a sedge. It is therefore doubtful that we can treat communities and ecosystems as if they were large number systems.

Medium-number systems The problem in ecology according to Lane (1985) is that ecosystems are neither large- nor small-number systems. They are **medium-number** systems. They are the worst situation. They contain too many components to be treated analytically with species-based models, and too few components (with major difference among them) for statistical analysis.

So what are we to do? There is no easy answer. But to pretend that the problem does not exist is probably the worst option of all. Working with medium-number systems may be as much an art as a science.

I will suggest three approaches that may have value: empirical ecology, assembly rules, and simplification. We will explore these alternative approaches in detail over the next three sections.

12.4   Empirical ecology

The first alternative for dealing with medium-number systems does not have a widely used name. We could call it empirical ecology, or predictive ecology, following Rigler (1982) and Rigler and Peters (1995). This approach to simplification focuses on predictive relationships among a few key state variables. The challenge here is to measure the most important properties of a system, and seek measurable predictive relationships among them. The main challenge is to find what those important properties are. In physics they could include temperature and pressure. It is less clear what the equivalents are in ecology.

12.4.1 Measurement of state variables – choose carefully

There are many properties of wetlands that you can measure. Area. Water level. Seasonal variation in water level. Nitrogen and phosphorus levels in the water. Seasonal variation in the foregoing. Rate of primary production. Seasonal and spatial variation in rates of primary production. Rate of secondary production. Seasonal and spatial variation in rate of secondary production. Number of bird species. Number of nesting bird species. Number of frog species. Number of tadpoles. Rates of survival of tadpoles and adults. Number of turtle species. Rates of egg production. Distance from water to nests. Rates of predation on eggs by skunks and raccoons. Number of species of orchids. Number of species of ferns. Number of species of sedges. Number of species of invasive plants. Biomass of plants. Ratio of above-ground biomass and below-ground biomass. Nitrogen and phosphorus content of shoots. Number of seeds buried in mud. Spatial variation in seed density. Number of species of algae. Biomass of algae. Primary production of algae. Seasonal and spatial variation in the foregoing. Number of species of macroinvertebrates. Seasonal and spatial variation in the foregoing. Emergence time for each species of odonate. Amount of coarse woody debris in the wetland. Rectal temperature of turtles. Nutrient inputs from surface flow. Inputs from groundwater. Inputs from rainfall. Inputs from bird defecation. Rates of methane production. Role of ruminants in methane production. Seasonal and spatial variation in methane production. To name but a few possibilities.

The point is that there are an enormous number of state variables that can be measured. There are a few field workers who still seem to take pride in how many different things they can measure. Only recently I was at a high-level meeting about an

important wetland and the assembled scientists could only seem to agree that they should measure everything possible just to be on the safe side. Of course, if you put all your budget into measuring everything possible, it is entirely likely that you will have only one site. In the end, having only one site with lots of measurements is like having only one species with lots of measurements. Neither allows any sort of generalization.

The real questions you have to ask are:

- What is the question you are trying to answer by your study?
- Which state variables to you need to measure to answer the question?

12.4.2 Relationships are essential to the advance of science

What question should you ask?

What state variable should you measure?

Wetland ecology is currently at the point where neither answer is obvious. I personally have a particular soft spot for species including American alligators, Blanding's turtles, and pitcher plants. But this is no justification whatsoever for claiming that the study of them is important to wetland ecology. It might be. Or they might be trivial. How do we tell? If you were in physics, you would know that there is agreement that certain state variables like temperature and mass have importance for a wide range of phenomena. It is less clear in ecology in general, and wetland ecology in particular. Too often people end up measuring certain state variables simply because that is what they learned to do in graduate school. Or simply because they like the species. (As for me, in the end, I chose to study wetland habitats because I thought that the best way to protect species was to protect the habitat. Besides, there were no alligators in Canada, and Blanding's turtles were hard to find.)

One way to think about the problem rationally is to look for examples where we have already found relationships. The vegetation types of peatlands are

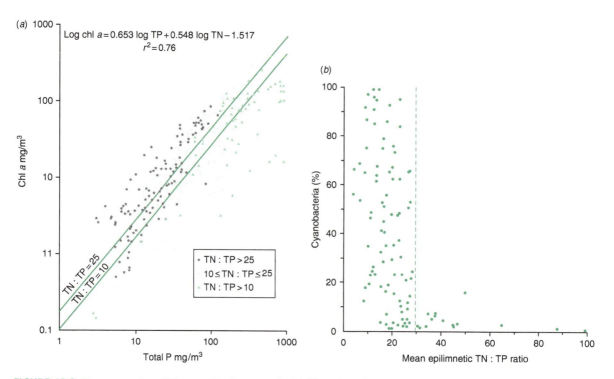

FIGURE 12.3 Two examples of the empirical approach. (*a*) There is a close predictive relationship between the concentration of phosphorus in water and the abundance of algae (as measure by chlorophyll *a* concentrations. As the ratio of N : P increases, the intercept of the line increases. (From Smith 1982.) (*b*) The proportion of the algae that are cyanobacteria has a strong threshold at just below a total N : total P ratio of 30. (From Smith 1983.)

arranged along gradients of calcium concentration and pH (Figure 3.15). Nitrate levels in rivers are related to human population in the river basin (Figure 3.8). Competition intensity increases with plant biomass (Figure 5.9). The biomass of mammals decreases with distance from wetlands (Figure 6.6). The biomass of herbivores increases with total net productivity (Figure 6.14). The number of species decreases with increasing road density (Figure 8.12) The number of plant species decreases with salinity (Figure 8.7). The number of species is positively related to wetland area (Figure 9.3).

Lakes provide an example – the biomass of algae is related to phosphorus levels (Figure 12.3*a*). The ratio of N to P determines the type of algae that occur (Figure 12.3*b*). Science is built up from the study of such basic relationships among state variables. As we

find more examples of such simple relationships, we can make wetland science increasingly rigorous. Sometimes it is useful to think about an example well outside one's own field – consider here the Hertzsprung–Russell star chart as a fine example of one figure that includes an enormous amount of information about stars (Figure 12.4). What are the equivalents in wetland ecology?

There is even a measure of our success at finding such relationships among state variables. It is the percent of variance that the independent variable predicts. There are standard statistical tools in multiple regression analysis that allow us to determine how tightly the pair of state variables are related. Increasingly, tools like multiple regression analysis allow us to explore how a set of variables can account for one state variable, providing useful

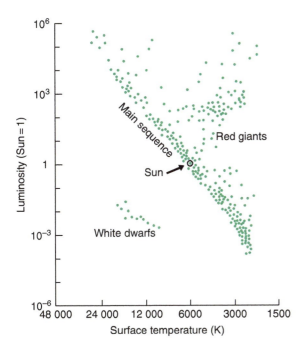

FIGURE 12.4 The Hertzsprung–Russell diagram summarizes fundamental relationships among stars, providing an example of how large amounts of information can be summarized along only two axes. (From Keddy 1994.)

information on correlations and causation (Shipley 2000). In Figure 8.13, for example, you saw how an entire set of independent variables each contributed to the number of plant species found in a wetland.

Once you have found a relationship between a pair of state variables you can use it to make useful predictions. One could argue that the ability to make predictions is the only legitimate way to measure scientific progress. As Peters (1980a, b) observed so many times, to justify a study as "increasing understanding" merely says that the study will affect the psychological state of the scientist.

In general, then, the predictive approach encourages us to measure a few important variables in a large number of systems. This means that when you go out to a wetland, you could measure a few simple properties and see how the wetland fits into the natural variation. This is a standard approach in limnology, as you can see from Figure 12.3. From this perspective, the worst research strategy is to pick one species or one wetland and measure as many things as possible.

12.5 Assembly rules driven by key factors

The second alternative approach to working with medium-number systems is the framework provided by assembly rules (Weiher and Keddy 1995). Assembly rules draw attention to a relatively small number of environmental factors that organize communities. In this book, we began with hydrology and fertility as key organizing factors. From this perspective, nature can perhaps be cleaved with a few sharp cuts into meaningful patterns. Hydrology, fertility, salinity, and a few other factors provide the sword to cut apart the complexity of wetlands. Experiments can then manipulate these factors to sort out causal relationships, and managers can manipulate these same factors to produce the desired characteristics of wetlands.

12.5.1 A few key factors select from the species pool

The raw material for a wetland is the pool of species available to colonize the site; the pool of species is the product of long-term processes such as evolution and extinction (Figure 12.5). The objective of assembly rules, then, is to predict which subset of this species pool for a given region will occur in a specified habitat (Keddy 1992a; Weiher and Keddy 1999). It basically is a problem of deleting those species unsuited to a specified set of environmental conditions. A first objective would be simply to predict the presence or absence of species in a habitat. The second objective would be to predict abundance as well as presence.

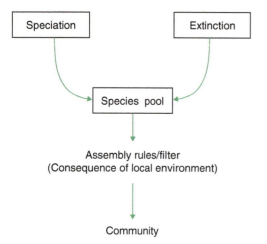

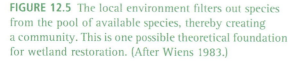

FIGURE 12.5 The local environment filters out species from the pool of available species, thereby creating a community. This is one possible theoretical foundation for wetland restoration. (After Wiens 1983.)

The process of constructing communities from species pools is therefore in many ways analogous to the processes of evolution through natural selection. In natural selection, habitats serve as filters for genotypes, with the least-suited genotypes being filtered out, and the best-suited surviving to reproduce. In the case of assembly rules, habitats again serve as filters and eliminate those sets of traits that are unsuitable to that environment. The species that comprise the community are those with the traits that survive the filter. We have systematically explored the important wetland filters in this book (Table 12.2)

Given the list of environmental factors that act as filters in wetlands, two biological data sets for ecological communities are needed: species pool and matrix of the traits of species in this pool. "Assembly rules" then specify which particular subset of traits (and therefore species possessing them) will be filtered out. More precisely, in the situation where we have knowledge of traits for each species in the pool, we are looking for a procedure to specify whether or not a trait (or sets of them) will permit species to persist under a defined set of environmental conditions. The exact procedures for doing this most effectively need further work. The following examples illustrate some of the potential.

Table 12.2 The estimated relative importance of environmental factors that determine the properties of wetlands. These can be considered the key filters for assembling wetlands from species pools

Environmental factor	Relative importance (%)
Hydrology (Chapter 2)	50
Fertility (Chapter 3)	15
Salinity (Chapter 8)	15
Disturbance (Chapter 4)	15
Competition (Chapter 5)	<5
Grazing (Chapter 6)	<5
Burial (Chapter 7)	<5

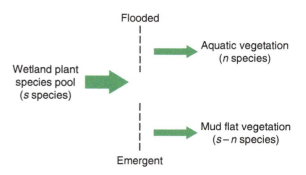

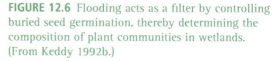

FIGURE 12.6 Flooding acts as a filter by controlling buried seed germination, thereby determining the composition of plant communities in wetlands. (From Keddy 1992b.)

12.5.2 Prairie wetlands: hydrology as a filter

Species in prairie wetlands must periodically regenerate from buried seeds (recall Table 2.2 and Figure 8.3). The problem is to predict species composition in these wetlands after a specified change in water level. Only one trait is necessary to predict regeneration: whether or not a species could germinate under water (van der Valk 1981). By measuring only this one trait for all species, one can predict which part of the species pool will occur (Figure 12.6).

In later work, van der Valk (1988) asked whether the densities of buried seeds of four emergent plants predict the densities of adult shoots after a reduction in water level. The results were slightly less satisfying – but of course, the study was asking a species-level question. All four species were large graminoids, which might be expected to have rather similar traits (*Scolochloa festucacea, Scirpus lacustris, Typha* × *glauca, Phragmites australis*). While assembly rules might be useful for predicting whether one has mud flat annuals or large monocots, it may be asking any model to predict which mud flat annual or which graminoid will appear. The use of such similar species to test assembly rules based upon traits perhaps illustrates the tendency of ecologists to think in terms of species rather than functional groups.

12.5.3 Fish in lakes: oxygen and pH as filters

We have already seen the importance of hypoxia in controlling fish distributions and life history in floodplains. The lowest concentration of oxygen in the water can then be considered to be a filter, which selectively removes different portions of the fish fauna. The ability to tolerate this filter can he determined for each fish species, whether by screening *(sensu* Grime and Hunt 1975) as in Junk (1984), or by reference to other traits.

Let us look at an example with fewer species. In central North America, Magnuson and his co-workers (e.g. Tonn and Magnuson 1982; Magnuson *et al.* 1989) have studied the distributions of fish in lakes in the lake district of Wisconsin and Michigan. One county alone, Vilas County, has over 1300 lakes. Typical fish range from mudminnows and redbelly dace to large predators such as northern pike and largemouth bass.

Overall, the lakes can be divided into those without and with large predators: *Umbra*-cyprinid and centrarchid-*Esox* lakes. Low oxygen levels in winter are the key filter. The lakes with large predators can be divided into two types depending on whether bass or pike is the dominant predator (Tonn *et al.* 1983).

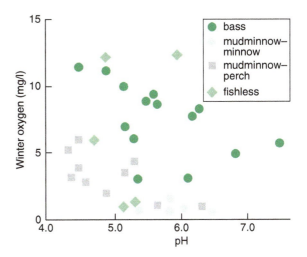

FIGURE 12.7 Winter oxygen levels and pH act as filters to create different fish communities. (From Magnuson *et al.* 1989.)

The *Umbra*-cyprinid lakes also can be sorted into two groups: mudminnow–minnow lakes, and mudminnow–perch lakes (Magnuson *et al.* 1989). Winter oxygen levels and pH largely distinguish these later two groups (Figure 12.7).

If low pH and low oxygen act as filters, this can explain why fish with high oxygen and high pH requirements do not inhabit shallow lakes with low pH. But it does not explain the reverse. Why do minnows and mudminnows not inhabit the lakes with higher oxygen and pH? Apparently, smaller fish are excluded to lakes from which predators are absent (Magnuson *et al.* 1989).

Sketching this as a series of filters (Figure 12.8), we begin with the pool of fish available to these lakes on the left. Low oxygen and low pH eliminate centrarchid fish from small and shallow lakes. Predation eliminates minnows and mudminnows from the larger lakes.

12.5.4 Coastal wetlands: salinity and frost as a filters

Coastal wetlands nicely illustrate the principles of pools and filters. We have already seen how salinity is a strong filter, and how it controls the number of

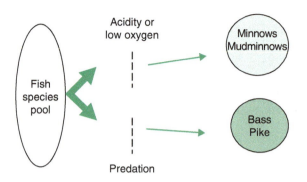

FIGURE 12.8 Different filters create different fish communities from a common pool.

species in coastal wetlands (Section 8.1). In general, higher salinity means fewer species (Figure 8.7). Brief periods of low salinity from spring rain, or spring flooding, may be necessary for many coastal species to germinate and establish at all (Figure 4.23)

Superimposed upon salinity is the factor of cold. We have also seen in Chapter 4 that freezing weather can turn mangrove swamp into salt marsh. Along the northern and southern boundary of mangroves, therefore, a single filter – tolerance to freezing weather – is an important plant trait, and cold weather an important filter (Figure 4.19). But note that it is not the mean temperature that matters. It takes only one northern weather system in a winter to keep coastlines as herbaceous wetlands.

12.5.5 Restoration in coastal wetlands: manipulating salinity and elevation

Many coastal areas are experiencing signs of stress such as loss in land area, conversion of wetland to open water, and declining wildlife production as a consequence. Restoration requires reversing these processes (Lewis 1982; Turner and Streever 2002). You could approach coastal restoration from the point of view of filters and traits. Although the next chapter is devoted to restoration, let us leap ahead a little and look at coastal restoration from the perspective of pools and filters. From this perspective, most coastal problems arise from two factors: increasing salinity and decreasing elevation.

Hence, restoration involves altering these two factors by decreasing salinity and increasing elevation. The most basic restoration techniques will increase inputs of fresh water and silt. Often this involves little more than allowing natural processes, such as spring flooding, to resume. Gaps can be built into the levees to allow fresh water to escape and spread over the marsh surface. Ideally, the control structure should allow both water and sediment to enter.

However, many coastal areas have additional problems, particularly networks of canals. These have arisen from past logging (Figure 4.16), from oil and gas exploration, and from shipping routes. Canals have multiple consequences: the spoil banks from the dredged material obstruct water flow, and tend to develop woody vegetation, often including many exotic species. The dredged canal interferes with movement of fresh water and may allow saline water easy access inland during storms. These canals need to be backfilled to allow normal transport of fresh water and sediment. Figure 12.9 illustrates how canals can be filled to restore normal elevations and allow fresh water to move more naturally through a delta.

Many coastal areas, from Bangladesh to Louisiana, have received both sources of damage: levees and canals. The result has been rapid loss of wetlands and erosion of natural deltas. In extreme cases, where natural forces cannot be harnessed, sediment can be pumped to fill in depressions, or new terraces can be constructed to ensure that marsh plants are not inundated too frequently. In these cases, the research challenge consists of fine-tuning the procedures so that they are as effective as possible in re-establishing wetlands at relatively low cost.

12.5.6 Experimental studies of filters and pools

The application of different filters should allow one to construct many different types of communities from one species pool. It should also allow one to rank filters in order of importance.

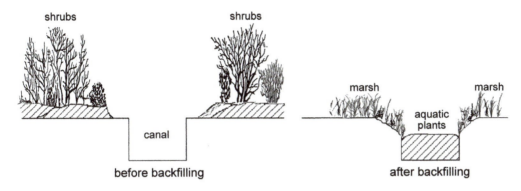

FIGURE 12.9 Canals (left) alter elevation and salinity in coastal wetlands and contribute to loss of these wetlands. Backfilling canals can create more normal elevations and allow flow patterns to re-establish. (After Turner and Streever 2002.)

In one experiment, a standard pool of 20 wetland plant species was sown into 120 containers representing 24 wetland environments (Weiher and Keddy 1995; Weiher *et al.* 1996). The environmental conditions manipulated included most of the major variables thought to influence wetlands: (i) water depth, (ii) timing and duration of flooding, (iii) leaf litter, (iv) soil surface texture, (v) sowing date, and (vi) presence or absence of *Typha*. Each of these factors was repeated at high and low fertility. Species composition was then measured for five growing seasons. Each environmental factor had a significant effect upon species composition but water level and fertility were the most important filters. The 24 possible sets of conditions yielded four types of wetland communities (Figure 12.10).

The relative importance of filters can be assayed by exposing species to different filters alone and in combination. In one such study (Geho *et al.* 2007), 16 species of wetland plants were exposed to three different filters alone and in combination: herbivores, competition, and elevation (as added sediments). Herbivores had the largest effect on reducing plant biomass, although it affected only two species significantly. One was bald cypress (*Taxodium distichum*), and the other was cattail (*Typha domingensis*). Without properly designed experiments, the importance of herbivory and competition would not have been obvious. Since the establishment of

coastal cypress forests is an important conservation issue, their sensitivity to herbivores is noteworthy (see also Myers *et al.* 1995). And since *T. domingensis* is able to produce large monospecific stands, the fact that it was apparently limited by herbivores may have important implications for controlling the abundance of *Typha* elsewhere. On a species-by-species basis, however, four of the species – twice as many – were affected by competition. *Pontederia cordata* (one of the species on the book cover) seemed to be the weakest competitor, and it was indeed not present in the natural vegetation. So while we have just made the point that salinity is an overriding factor in coastal wetlands, in this experiment, in which salinity was not modified, competition and herbivory emerged as the two critical factors.

These kinds of experiments are a reminder of the necessity of care in designing experiments. A critic could say that an experiment will usually find what it looks for. If you fertilized, you should not be surprised to find fertility effects. If you manipulate neighbors, you should not be surprised to find competition. If you manipulate salinity, you will likely find that it too has effects. The challenge is to design experiments that combine these in a sensible and meaningful way in order to sort out the relative importance in natural systems. Which, conveniently, brings us to the next topic: how do you simplify nature without losing important information?

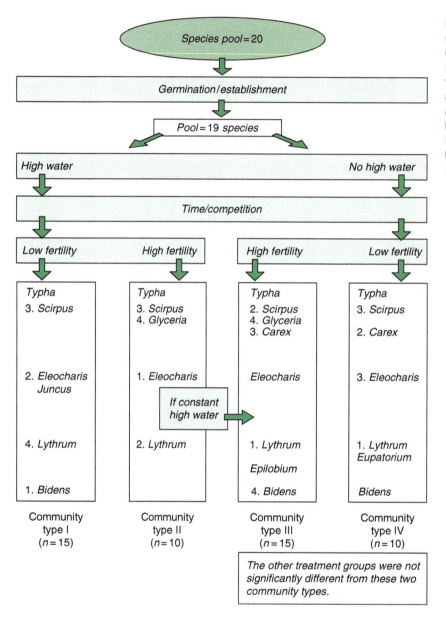

FIGURE 12.10 Twenty-four different environmental conditions, each replicated five times, produced four basic wetland vegetation types from a common species pool. It appears that five filters (colored boxes) can account for the observed patterns. (From Weiher and Keddy 1995.)

12.5.7 Biotic factors as filters

The foregoing examples mostly involve the direct effects of abiotic factors acting as filters. Biotic factors do, of course, have the same potential effects.

Herbivory can be a strong filter, as you saw in Chapter 6. Although coastal marshes are normally viewed as resulting from salinity and burial, there is a growing body of evidence that grazers such as snails, geese, and mammals can have important effects as filters (Silliman et al. 2009). This has further consequences. If grazers can act as filters, then the predators that feed on grazers, say crabs eating snails, or alligators eating nutria, become important. Predation is certainly a strong filter in ponds

(Wilbur 1984; Carpenter *et al.* 1987), which is why ponds without fish are critical for many species of amphibians. Alligators may also have effects on wetlands through controlling the abundance of other prey species such as fish and turtles (Bondavalli and Ulanowicz 1999).

Competition may be an important filter in the sense that weak competitors are excluded from large areas of wetlands. Established plants may also prevent other common species from colonizing apparently appropriate habitat (Figure 5.1). You can think of natural disturbances, or periods of grazing, as factors that temporarily reduce the importance of this filter and allow new species to occupy a wetland.

Finally, if filters like anoxia or salinity are controlling the wetland, then neighboring plants may also facilitate establishment or survival by reducing the constraining effects of physical factors (Bertness and Hacker 1994; Castellanos *et al.* 1994; Bertness and Leonard 1997).

Other biotic effects, sometimes termed examples of "ecological engineering" (Jones *et al.* 1994) may be less obvious, but just as important in some wetlands. Beavers, alligators, and elephants are conspicuous examples of species that can engineer habitats. In practice there are many more examples. Even oysters and mussels can act as engineers by shaping the physical conditions of estuaries (Thomas and Nygard 2007), so when humans over-harvest oysters they are in fact reversing this engineering (Kirby 2004). From this perspective, humans are pervasive engineers, with dams, levees, canals, and roads all changing the naturally operating filters in wetlands.

In principle, then, each of these biotic factors could be treated as a separate filter itself – say, elephants as a filter in the Okavanga delta (Mosepele *et al.* 2008), or geese as a filter on the Hudson Bay coastline (Henry and Jeffries 2009).

12.6   Simplification through aggregation into groups

Another approach to dealing with middle-number systems does not have a formal name, but it can be called **simplification**. Instead of trying to deal with a large number of species and their enormous number of interactions, we reduce the number of species to a small number of functional groups. These groups have different names, depending upon the taxa. Zoologists often use the term "guilds," but the more general term, **functional types**, is more widely used.

12.6.1 What does it mean to simplify? The middle way

Starfield and Bleloch (1991) have written elegantly about the simplification approach, and they admit that learning to compromise is the first step toward building pragmatic models.

Many people, they say, approach ecological modeling in terms of diagrams such as Figure 12.11a. "Their preconception is that ecosystems are made up of components that interact in a complex way and that models should be built to represent their complexity" (p. 14). You can see many such figures in books on wetland ecology. The description of energy flow in coastal wetlands in the preceding chapter (Figure 11.3, top) is an example of how complex studies can become. Consider how much effort is required in measuring each species' individual contribution. Now consider how each of the species effects may change with location or climate. The task rapidly becomes overwhelming.

But while nature is indeed complex, as Rigler reminded us above, making enormously complex models that represent every species is not feasible, since the number of interactions (not to mention

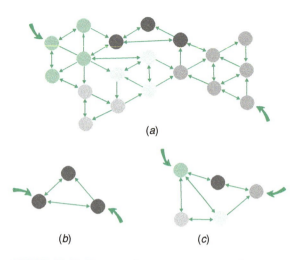

(a)

(b)   (c)

FIGURE 12.11 Representing an ecosystem at three different levels of complexity: (a) a detailed system model, (b) isolating a part of the system, and (c) a less detailed ("lumped") system model. (From Starfield and Bleloch 1991.)

higher-order interactions) rises as the square of the number of species. Starfield and Bleloch (1991) note, politely, that "often the usefulness of such models, once they have been built, is disappointing." Our first compromise, they conclude, is simplification. The way to accomplish this is to start with the management problem itself, rather than with a mental picture of the ecosystem. One then searches for the simplification that is most appropriate to solve the problem.

The most obvious approach is to cut out one piece of the system (Figure 12.11b) and treat it in isolation. That is, you make a smaller-number system. You have seen many examples earlier in the book of one or a few species that were studied in depth. These help us understand how species respond to filters, and to each other. But the small piece that has been cut out is artificial. The other factors and species cannot be ignored entirely. As but one example, recall how *Sagittaria lancifolia* was not harmed by flooding or salinity or grazing, in isolation, but it was harmed when they were combined (Figure 8.6).

In some cases, it may be possible to treat the rest of the system as an artificial driving force (thick

arrows). One can think of dealing with wading birds in the Everglades, or frogs in ponds, or mud flat annuals in potholes, where "the rest of the world" might be simplified into a few key factors such as duration of flooding.

An alternative is to combine components that are similar to one another, as indicated by the similarities in shading in Figure 12.11. The most reasonable grounds for combining them would be similarities in function. One then ends up with a complete representation of the system, but one that has been simplified (Figure 12.11c). In fact, this was a decision made by the scientists who produced the energy flow diagram – they chose to combine all the vascular plants into one category labeled "vascular plants" at the upper left of Figure 11.3 (top). Had they tried to measure primary production from each photosynthetic species, and the flow from each of those species to each herbivore and decomposer, the task would have been impossible. So the figure simplifies. On one hand, these sorts of decisions are necessary. On the other hand, they also may hide critical factors – perhaps the distinction between rushes and grasses is critical in this system. Or perhaps diatoms should have been included. The bottom of Figure 11.3 is even more simplified, with energy flow reduced to just five categories. Simplification should always be done as carefully and sensibly as possible. But there are no guarantees. Somewhere between the extremes of measuring everything imaginable and measuring just one thing there is some sort of intermediate. Choosing the appropriate level of simplification is thus "a pragmatic compromise between the complexity of ecosystems on one hand, and the need to solve a problem, with limited data and in a reasonable amount of time on the other" (Starfield and Bleloch 1991, p. 15.)

A further advantage to simplification into functional groups is that it enhances communication among scientists and managers. Taxonomic classification exists to represent the evolutionary relationships of organisms, and the degree to which different kinds interbreed with each other. It did not originate as a tool to serve the needs of ecologists. When trying to communicate with scientists from other parts of the world, the nomenclature is often an obstacle to exchange of ideas; a different fauna or flora is like a different language. This problem is particularly severe for botanists and entomologists because of the large number of plant and insect species.

Functional groups, therefore, have the dual benefit of providing a naturally simplified approach to wetlands and enhanced communication among ecologists. A third benefit may be that the emphasis upon function provides a natural bridge to those scientists, managers, administrators, and politicians who think in terms of ecological services rather than wetland ecology.

12.6.2 Functional classification for ecological prediction

How do we sort species into types? Let us first remind ourselves of our goals: we want to be able to make predictions about the future states of wetland ecosystems, and particularly to predict changes in services that may result from various human activities. A major obstacle to being able to make such predictions is the large number of species that have to be included in community models. We therefore need to put species into groups.

Classification into groups could have two objectives: (i) forming groups with similar evolutionary histories in order to reconstruct phylogenies, or (ii) forming groups with similar ecological traits for predictive ecology. The former approach has had a major impact upon the historical development of ecology: many of the most high-profile research questions in ecology dealing with diversity (e.g. Hutchinson 1959; May 1986; Connell 1987) can be traced back to the phylogenetic basis of species taxonomy. The recent proliferation of molecular approaches to systematics has greatly reinforced this view of nature, sometimes to the detriment of functional thinking. If we begin with phylogenetic species classifications, we naturally fall

into a certain line of inquiry. The logic appears to go in the following manner. Since there is a large number of species (e.g. May 1988), how did so many species arise? Darwin provided an answer, and stimulated a century of research into the mechanisms and consequences of evolution through natural selection. This led to the second major question: how do all these species coexist (May 1986)? The coexistence of many different species is the great question bequeathed by Darwin. Coexistence has been a central theme of ecology at least since Hutchinson's 1959 paper entitled "Homage to Santa Rosalia" (Jackson 1981; May 1986), but it may have rather little to do with practical questions of ecosystem management.

If, however, we begin with functional classifications, the path of inquiry has a different logic. While there is of course enormous species diversity of the biosphere, there is also obvious repetition of certain themes. Most wetlands have groups of mud flat annuals, floating-leaved aquatics, wading birds, and predatory insects, but the names of the species change with geography. From the functional point of view, the important questions include: (i) What are these major convergent groups and how many are there? (ii) How many do we need for a sufficient level of precision in our models? Growing out of this are other questions. What are the traits which they share? How do we use a knowledge of these traits to predict how a particular functional group will change after an external perturbation? How can we use a knowledge of these traits to predict the group of species that will be present in a specified environment?

Nearly every group of organisms has been explored in this way. Let us look at a few examples.

Birds These are perhaps the easiest to work with because food supply places strong selective pressure upon bill form, and provides a convenient means to sort species into basic feeding groups (Figure 12.12). At the finer scale, bills can vary in other attributes such as densities of comb-like lamellae used for filtering food particles from debris. Other attributes

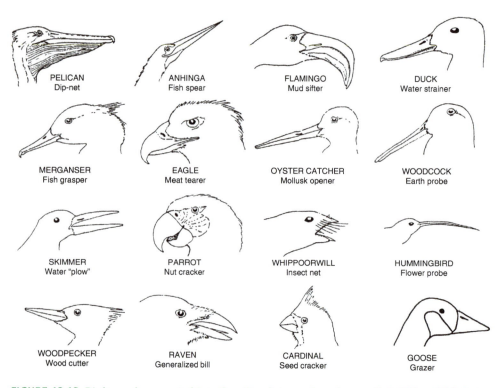

FIGURE 12.12 Birds can be arranged into functional groups based upon their bills, which in turn reflect their food sources. (After Welty 1982.)

such as foraging habitat, nesting habitat, and migration can be used to recognize functional groups (Weller 1999).

Fish Fish too can be classified by feeding strategy (Figure 12.13), with food type being reflected in the characteristics of the feeding apparatus. A still simpler classification, offered by Hoover and Killgore (1998), uses body shape to sort fish into one of four categories (accelerator, station holder, cruiser, and maneuverer), along a morphological gradient running from fusiform and elongated (cigar-shaped) to broad and laterally compressed bodies. Other attributes such as foraging habitat, spawning habitat, and oxygen demands can be used to expand the classification. Diet and body morphology can also be used (Lowe-McConnell 1975; Wikramanayake 1990; Winemiller 1991).

Insects These are frequently classified by their feeding system (Cummins 1973; Cummins and Klug 1979), considering both the dominant food type and the means by which they process it (Figure 12.14). Habitat, dispersal, life cycle, and size can be used to expand the system.

Mammals Mammals can be divided into functional groups based upon size, diet (which can often be inferred from dentition), and habitat type (Figure 12.15). There are 30 types of mammals in North America, according to Severinghaus (1981).

Plants The many types of plants are often classified by growth form (Raunkiaer 1937; Dansereau 1959) with particular emphasis upon woodiness, leaf size, leaf texture, and location of meristems. Life history, propagule type, competitive ability, and seed

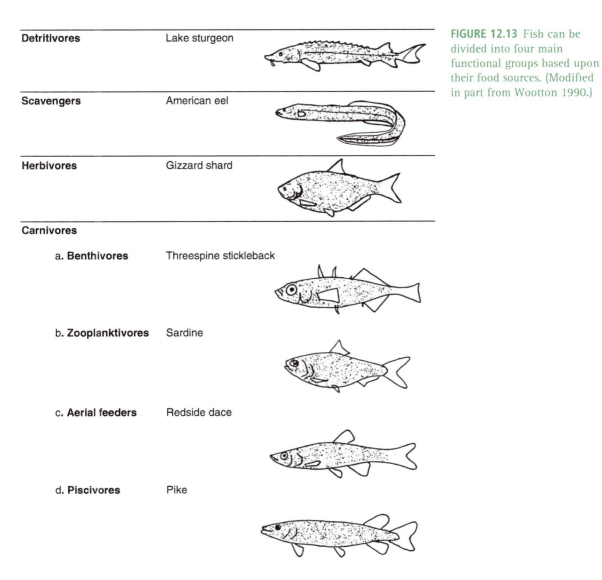

Detritivores	Lake sturgeon	
Scavengers	American eel	
Herbivores	Gizzard shard	
Carnivores		
a. **Benthivores**	Threespine stickleback	
b. **Zooplanktivores**	Sardine	
c. **Aerial feeders**	Redside dace	
d. **Piscivores**	Pike	

FIGURE 12.13 Fish can be divided into four main functional groups based upon their food sources. (Modified in part from Wootton 1990.)

germination requirements can be used to expand the system (Grime 1979; Weiher *et al.* 1999).

12.6.3 Problems and prospects

Particular functional groups likely have shared sensitivity to particular kinds of environmental stresses (Severinghaus 1981). In his words (using the word functional group rather than guild):

Once the impact on any one species in a functional group is determined, the impact on every other species in that functional group is known. Furthermore, this information can be applied to any ecosystem within which that functional group is found. If an endangered species is contained in a functional group, it is possible to predict the impact on that species without studying it specifically, which for most endangered species is virtually impossible to do anyway. Economically, the potential cost-savings are tremendous, since only a few species per functional group need to be studied to establish the resulting impacts on all members of the functional group.

Functional Group	Dominant Food	Feeding Mechanism	Example of Order	
Shredders	Living tissue	Herbivore	Lepidoptera 	
	Decomposing tissue	Detritivore	Plecoptera 	
	Wood	Gouger	Coleoptera 	
Collectors	Decomposing organic matter	Detritivore	Collembola 	
Scrapers	Periphyton	Herbivore	Coleoptera 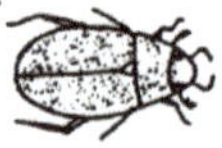	
Macrophyte piercers	Living tissue	Herbivore	Neuroptera 	
Predators	Living tissue	Engulfer	Megaloptera 	
		Piercer	Neuroptera 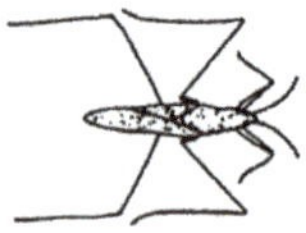	
Parasites	Living tissue	Internal and external parasite	Hymenoptera 	

FIGURE 12.14 There are enormous numbers of insect species, and they process a large portion of the biomass in wetlands. Yet they can be divided into only six functional groups based upon their dominant feeding mechanism. (Modified in part from Merritt and Cummins 1984.)

While there will always, of course, be differences among species within functional groups, this none the less clearly states the potential value of simplification.

The existence of functional groups and their value to science and management is increasingly recognized (e.g. Southwood 1977; Severinghaus 1981; Terborgh and Robinson 1986; Simberloff and Dayan 1991). Still, there is a problem – each group of organisms often has its own nomenclature. Functional groups in birds and mammals are sometimes called "guilds" (Root 1967; Severinghaus 1981), in fish "ecomorphological types" (Winemiller 1991), and in insects "functional feeding groups" (Cummins and Klug 1979). Most animal studies begin with food as the basic resource, and then group species that use a similar food. Terms such as "water strainer" (Figure 12.12), "zooplanktivore" (Figure 12.13), or "macrophyte piercer" (Figure 12.14) clearly delineate groups using the type of resource being consumed. However, such studies retain a taxonomic bias, since the bird that is a "water strainer" may be feeding on the same copepod species as a fish that is a "zooplanktivore."

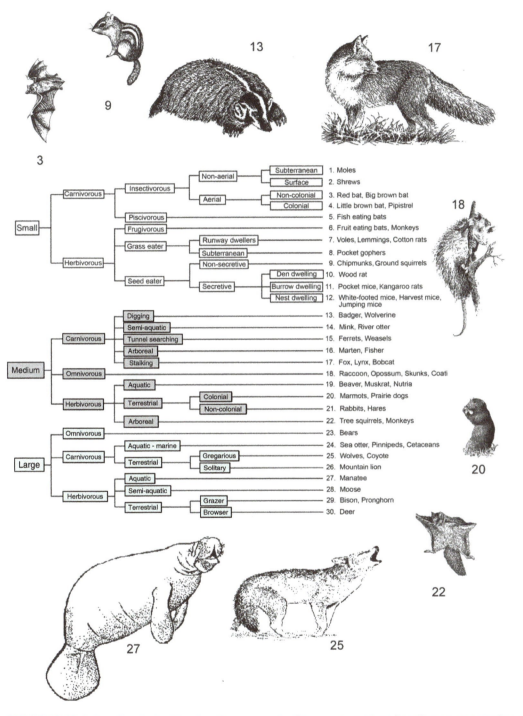

FIGURE 12.15 A functional classification for mammals of temperate regions based upon non-marine mammals inhabiting the continental U.S.A. (From Severinghaus 1981; sketches by R. Savannah, U.S. Fish and Wildlife Service.)

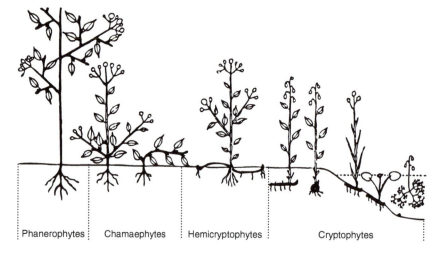

FIGURE 12.16 The Raunkiaer system classifies plants on the basis of location and protection of their meristems. (From Goldsmith and Harrison 1976.)

Phanerophytes   Chamaephytes   Hemicryptophytes   Cryptophytes

Parts of the plant that die in the unfavorable season are unshaded; persistent axes with surviving buds are black

12.6.4 More on functional classification of wetland plants

There are three reasons for saying more about plants. First, they are particularly difficult to assign to groups. We have seen that animals are often classified by the resources they consume, but plants use so few resources (largely CO_2, water, N, P, K). Second, because plants provide habitat for everything else, nearly everyone, even zoologists, has to learn something about plant functional types. Third, we can use them to look in more detail at the costs and benefits of making functional groups overall.

One of the most ubiquitous methods of plant classification was proposed by Raunkiaer (1937). His basic theme, paraphrased, is that life is not easy for plants. Unlike animals, they must remain rooted in a site as the environment changes around them. Raunkiaer focused on the most important challenge faced by plants: protecting their meristems during unfavorable periods. Recall that unlike animals, plants have indeterminate growth, directed by defined areas of cell multiplication called the meristems. If these are killed, the plant can neither

grow nor reproduce. Raunkiaer focused our attention on how plants protect their meristems, and erected the categories shown in Figure 12.16.

Raunkiaer's system is excellent for coarse-scale comparison, say for comparing marshes to swamps. It is less useful for more fine-scale work. In a set of marshes, all of the plants may be in only two functional groups: cryptophytes or therophytes (annuals). A finer level of classification may be needed. We must understand that this does not mean there is something wrong with Raunkiaer. Rather, the point is that we need different models to describe or predict at different scales. At the coarse scale, Raunkiaer is excellent. At finer scales, we need more information about the organisms.

Dansereau (1959) developed a more complicated system that uses categories of traits to describe vegetation. His categories were life form, stratification (height), coverage, function (evergreenness), leaf shape, and leaf texture. Any vegetation type can be placed in a reduced number of functional groups.

But here we encounter a new problem: as we reduce scale, the number of groups proliferates. Let us take aquatic plants as a convenient example, in part because we have some large monographs on

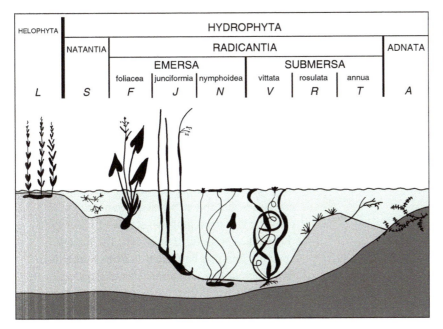

HELOPHYTA	HYDROPHYTA							
	NATANTIA	RADICANTIA						ADNATA
		EMERSA			SUBMERSA			
		foliacea	junciformia	nymphoidea	vittata	rosulata	annua	
L	S	F	J	N	V	R	T	A

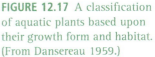

FIGURE 12.17 A classification of aquatic plants based upon their growth form and habitat. (From Dansereau 1959.)

this group (e.g. Sculthorpe 1967; Hutchinson 1975). Dansereau has nine life forms of aquatic plants (Figure 12.17). The principal traits are whether or not the plants are rooted, their relationship with the water surface, and the nature of their leaves (Figure 12.17). Hutchinson (1975) has 22 to 26 groups depending upon how you count them. It is also possible to classify by propagule type (Dansereau 1959). Hence, without caution, trying to simplify the plants into functional groups generates its own styles of confusion. In most cases, the objective is to find the minimum number of groups that allow one to answer the question being asked.

12.6.5 A general procedure for constructing functional groups

There is one general procedure for constructing such functional groups (Figure 12.18). Often, it is done subjectively, but objective approaches can be used too. A key part is the trait matrix. Most traits considered in the above classifications are traits that can be determined by eye, such as life form, lifespan, method of vegetative propagation, and position of over-wintering shoots. However, it may be preferable to include ecological and physiological properties such as nutrient uptake, competition, and interaction with agents of disturbance or stress. Traits related to these properties may not be obvious upon inspection, but may be none the less closely related to the function of the plant in a community.

Since many of these traits are not obvious upon inspection, we need to apply the process of screening as developed by Grime and Hunt (1975) and Grime et al. (1981). The objective of screening is to develop a simple bioassay for a particular attribute, and then apply it systematically to an entire set of species. Shipley et al. (1989) created a matrix examining seven juvenile and 13 adult plant traits. The objectives were to explore quantitative relationships among traits to (i) test whether juvenile and adult traits were independent and (ii) explore relationships among the traits. In juveniles, the important traits were variation in seed size, which was inversely correlated with germination rate in light (axis 1), and higher growth rates with reduced germination at constant temperatures (axis 2). More than half the variation in seedling life history traits was accounted

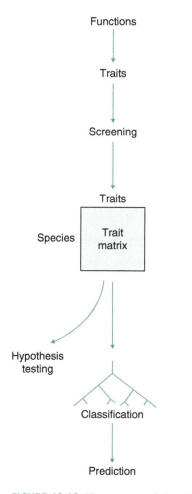

Functions

Traits

Screening

Traits

Species | Trait matrix

Hypothesis testing

Classification

Prediction

FIGURE 12.18 The process of classifying functional groups based upon a matrix of traits. (From Boutin and Keddy 1993.)

for by these two axes alone. Germination is known to be highly influenced by both light and fluctuating temperatures (Grime 1979; Grime *et al.* 1981) and it appears that wetland plants differ in their response to these two key environmental factors. Since the presence of established plants (shading) is likely to reduce the survival rates of seedlings, seedlings must either be able to escape adult plants by finding gaps, or else resist suppression. These first axes may be interpreted as two evolutionary solutions to this problem: seeds that are large and slow-growing and seeds that are small but rapidly growing. The two key axes in adult plants were the width of the canopy

(axis 1) and the height of the plants (axis 2). This can be interpreted as the importance of holding space and denying it to neighbors.

Perhaps the biggest surprise in the above work was the discovery that juvenile and adult traits were uncoupled. That is to say, the correlation matrices for adult traits showed no association with the correlation matrices for juvenile traits. Perhaps the traits required for regeneration in gaps are fundamentally different from the traits required to hold space as adults. This would mean that two categories, fugitive or stress-tolerant, could be constructed for each of two stages of life history (Figure 12.19). In turn, these four life history combinations can be related to three properties: frequency of gap formation, size of gaps, and soil fertility.

The thought that juveniles are in different functional groups from adults may be unexpected for plants, but there are many examples in the animal kingdom. Young fish may begin as zooplanktivores, but be piscivores as adults. These changes with age are a significant further complication in trying to use species-based approaches to communites and ecosystems. They are also an obstacle to simplification.

12.6.6 Example of functional groups in marsh plants

Another study used a matrix of 43 species by 27 traits. The species were selected to represent wetland habitats and diverse groups from across eastern North America. Species included rare or endangered taxa from infertile lake shores (*Coreopsis rosea, Panicum longifolium*), annuals typical of mud flats (*Bidens cernua, Cyperus aristatus*), large perennials (*Phalaris arundinacea, Typha × glauca*), reeds from river banks (*Scirpus acutus, Eleocharis calva*), and an array of other species which represented other life forms and habitats. Traits included: (i) relative growth rate (RGR), which is known to be correlated with rates of resource acquisition (e.g. Grime and Hunt 1975) and seedling stress tolerance (Shipley

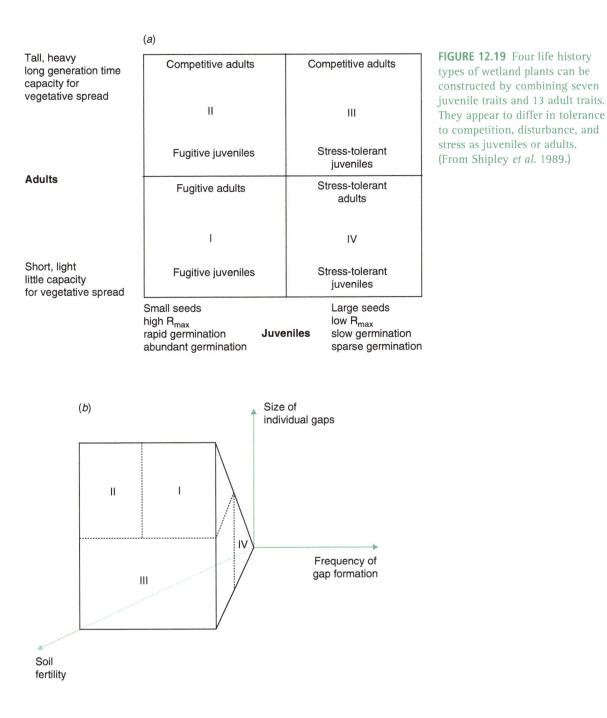

FIGURE 12.19 Four life history types of wetland plants can be constructed by combining seven juvenile traits and 13 adult traits. They appear to differ in tolerance to competition, disturbance, and stress as juveniles or adults. (From Shipley *et al.* 1989.)

and Keddy 1987), (ii) height of juveniles, height of adults, and rates of shoot extension; height is associated with competitive ability for light (e.g. Givnish 1982; Gaudet and Keddy 1988), (iii) above-

and below-ground biomass allocation, as well as photosynthetic area, which are believed to be associated with foraging for different light to nutrient ratios (e.g. Tilman 1982, 1986), and

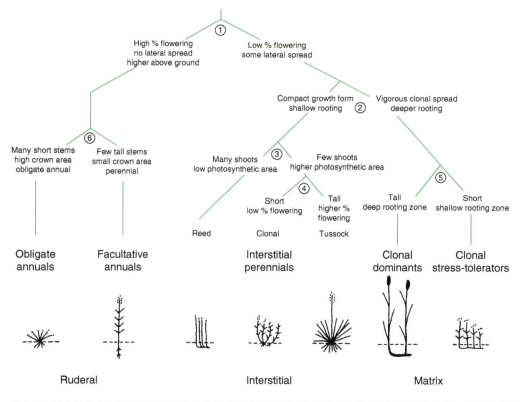

FIGURE 12.20 A dendrogram showing functional types derived through agglomerative clustering of 43 wetland plant species. (From Boutin and Keddy 1993.)

(iv) morphological traits such as shortest and longest distance between aerial shoots as measures of the way in which species held space; such traits are important if, as seems to be the case, plant communities are largely under dominance control (Yodzis 1986).

Figure 12.20 summarizes the results, with the addition of key traits. One main group (left side) had a high percentage of individuals and species flowering in their first growing season, and no lateral spreading of their vegetative growth. In contrast, the other group (right) did not flower much in their first year of growth but they expanded the vegetative parts, especially the below-ground system. These two groups apparently reflect the distinction between "ruderal" (*sensu* Grime 1979) and "perennial" strategies.

The "ruderals" consisted of two further groups. Plants in both groups flowered in the first year, but

one subgroup died at the end of the growing season ("obligate annuals") whereas the other remained alive ("facultative annuals").

Within the "perennials," there was a clear distinction between species that spread clonally and species with a more compact growth form. These two types can be considered "matrix" species and "interstitial" species (*sensu* Grubb 1986).

At a finer scale, the "matrix" species were further composed of two groups. "Clonal dominants" were tall and robust species with vigorous lateral spread that frequently produce monospecific stands in fertile habitats (e.g. *Typha* × *glauca*). "Clonal stress-tolerators" were much smaller and were more often found on infertile sand and gravel shorelines (e.g. *Scirpus torreyi*).

If such a classification has value, we would expect other traits to be predicted from knowledge of species membership in these different functional types. Shipley and Parent (1991) tested this by examining three germination attributes: time to germination, maximum germination rate, and proportion of seeds germinating for 64 wetland plant species. Dividing the species into three functional groups (annual, facultative annual, and obligate perennial), they found that the obligate perennials took significantly longer to begin germination, and had significantly smaller maximum germination rates.

12.6.7 Expert systems

The procedure outlined above has the merits of using functional traits that may actually be important to the ecology of the species. Height is related to competitive ability. Relative growth rate is related to stress tolerance. Evergreenness is related to nutrient requirements, and so on. But such work is also extremely labor intensive, since it requires measuring large numbers of traits on large numbers of species, and then combining them all in some meaningful way. That is why simpler systems like the Raunkiaer (Figure 12.16), Dansereau (Figure 12.17), and Hutchinson systems (Table 12.3) continue to be used.

An alternative approach might use the combined expertise of botanists to assign species to groups. Thus, for example, we saw above (Section 12.2.2) that North American plant species have an official wetland indicator status that has been assigned for use in wetland delineation. This is useful for recognizing wetlands and mapping wetland boundaries, but there are not enough groups to discriminate among types of wetlands. Another approach assigns each species an index of conservatism, C (Swink and Wilhelm 1994; Nichols 1999; Herman *et al.* 2001), which is intended to indicate how dependent the species is upon natural vegetation types with minimal human alteration. This allows plants to be typically assigned to ten categories. Widespread and common wetland species such as *Phragmites australis* and *Typha*

Table 12.3 A comparison of three schemes of life form classification for aquatic plants

Hutchinson	Fassett-Wilson	Dansereau
A. Natant (Planophyta)		
I. At surface (Pleuston *s.s.* or Acropleustophyta)	Type 5	Natantia (S)
a. Lemnids		
b. Salviniids		
c. Hydrocharids		
d. Eichhorniids		
e. Stratiotids		
II. At mid-depth (Megaloplankton or Mesopleustophyta)	Type 5	Natantia (S)
a. Wolffiellids		
b. Utricularids		
c. Ceratophyllids		
B. Rooted in sediment (Rhizophyta)		
I. Part of vegetative structure above water (Hyperhydates)	Type 4	Junciformia (J)
a. Graminids		
b. Herbids		
c. Ipomeids		
d. Decodontids		
e. Aeschynomenids		
f. Sagittariids		Foliacea (F)
g. Nelumbids		Foliacea (F)
II. Leaves mostly floating, not regularly above surface (Ephydates)	Type 3	Nymphoidea (N)
a. Nymphaeids		
b. Natopotamids		
c. Marsileids		
d. Batrachids		
e. Trapids		
III. Leaves entirely submerged or almost so (Hyphydates)		
a. Vittate, with long stem	Type 1	Vittata (V)
1. Magnopotamids		
2. Parvopotamids		
3. Myriophyllids		

Table 12.3 (cont.)

Hutchinson	Fassett-Wilson	Dansereau
b. Rosulate, stem very short	Type 2	Rosulata (R)
1. Vallisneriids		
2. Otteliids		
3. Isoetids		

Source: From Hutchinson (1975).

latifolia receive a score of 1, while species that depend upon small fragments of undisturbed habitat like *Platanthera leucophaea* (Figure 3.4) or *Primula mistassinica* receive a score of 10. We will return to this topic under wetland indicators (Section 14.8). In Europe, Ellenberg has assigned plants to categories based upon the fertility of their habitats (Figure 3.14).

We can conclude that expert systems work well for describing, delineating, and evaluating wetlands. They therefore have great value for planning and conservation. They do not, however, answer the question of why certain plants behave in similar ways, and why certain species are rare or occupy narrowly restricted sets of conditions. The study of traits and groups of traits may eventually provide the answer and provide more natural functional groups.

12.7   Six tactical guidelines

Money spent on the wrong kind of research is like money spent on buying the wrong kind of habitat – resources that could have been wisely allocated to conservation are lost. We must plan our research with the same dedication and effort as generals like Montgomery or Patton planned their military campaigns. Six guidelines may be of assistance.

12.7.1 Generality

First and foremost, scientific advice must be applicable to a variety of circumstances. Species-specific and site-specific studies are not in themselves a viable approach to managing a global or national system of protected areas. For example, there are over 2000 significant wetlands that have already been identified in just one part of Ontario (Ontario Ministry of Natural Resources 2007). Assume as a first approximation, that each supports 1000 species. If we expect to understand how to manage such wetlands by studying each species, and allocate one year per species, we must allocate 1000 person years per wetland. If we consider the interactions between the organisms (and we must), then 1000 species yields roughly half a million interactions, which translates into a half million person years per wetland (see also Rigler 1982). It is therefore not possible to study each interaction or even each species to provide management plans for natural areas.

The only way to manage a large collection of wetlands is to look for general principles that apply to numerous sites, or to combine species into groups based on similar ecological properties. Such principles and general models can be applied to many specific sites or species, and refined if necessary. The continuum from general to site-specific models can be represented as a nested hierarchy of models, with the general principles at the top, and the specific site at the bottom (Figure 12.21). One can start at the top and work down to any site, but it is far more difficult to start at the bottom and then extrapolate to the rest of the world.

12.7.2 Explicit constraints

Now let us appear to contradict the first principle. When general principles are established and applied, it is necessary to be aware of constraints to the

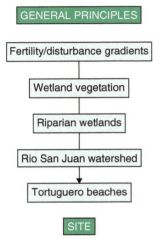

FIGURE 12.21 General principles (top) organize more specific information (bottom) in a hierarchical fashion.

generality. Consider, for example, the seed bank model that was developed for prairie potholes (van der Valk 1981). It now seems that some managers believe that all wetlands must be managed by fluctuating water levels and allowing regeneration from buried seeds. Certainly this model applies to lakeshores (Keddy and Reznicek 1982, 1986) and some ponds (Salisbury 1970; McCarthy 1987). It may apply to many relatively fertile sites with a history of natural disturbance. Other wetland vegetation types, such as bogs and fens, do not rapidly regenerate from seed after periodic disturbance. Such vegetation types could be degraded or destroyed by application of the prairie pothole model. We therefore need guidelines for determining which ecosystem types require which type of management.

This requires careful balance. We cannot, and should not try to, build a new model for every wetland we encounter. Science and management are based upon generalities, upon recurring patterns, upon general principles. Hence, we should start with the broad general principles described in this book, but be prepared when necessary to add constraints. Nutrients may be the overriding factor in the Everglades, while salinity may be the overriding factor in river deltas, while fire may be the overriding factor in other habitats. Our models, and our indicators, need to specify the habitats to which they apply.

12.7.3 First things first

When we build a house, we normally begin with the major features (foundation, walls) and only then work on the minor ones (door handles, light fixtures). Unfortunately, this perfectly commonsense approach to house building does not seem to carry over into ecology. Sometimes our scholarly journals lead one to believe that some ecologists would pick out door knobs and then be puzzled that they have neither a door nor a house in which to install them. At the risk of restating the obvious, we should start with the most important factors and variables, and then and only then move to the finer ones. To start this discussion, I suggest that (at least in the areas I know) some 50% of the variation in wetland communities is attributable to hydrology. Fertility and salinity probably account for something like a further 15% each. All other factors (e.g. grazing, fire) address only residual variance (recall Table 12.2). We might therefore anticipate that the number one priority of wetland ecologists has been and would be the development of quantitative models linking wetland community structure to hydrological variables.

12.7.4 Description and prediction

Protecting wetlands by zoning or acquisition is only the first step which prevents the obvious threats. Management plans are then required. Management plans require prediction – forecasting the possible effects of human impacts from surrounding activities in the landscape, as well as the consequences of different kinds of management. For example, a management plan will have to consider threats from eutrophication. We have previously seen that the construction of dams produces predictable

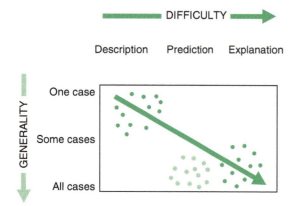

FIGURE 12.22 Descriptive studies of single situations are much easier to do than predictive or explanatory models that apply to many cases or sites. (After Leary 1985.)

consequences for wetlands downstream, as illustrated by the Peace–Athabasca delta. Equally, eutrophication has predictable negative consequences, as we have seen in both the New Jersey Pine Barrens and the Everglades.

No one should therefore build a dam or put nutrients into groundwater without knowing what the result will be. Still, prediction is often far more difficult than description. In his study of kinds of research, Leary (1985) concludes that generality and explanation (Figure 12.22, lower right) are the most difficult, even if they are the most important. They therefore require the most incentive, since all other things being equal, it is tempting to try to solve easy problems. In the case of conservation, it is probably true that we need prediction more than explanation (light dots). Yet it still seems that there is far more scientific activity in description (Figure 12.22, upper left) than in prediction and understanding (Figure 12.22, lower right). This may be fine in the inventory stages of wetland protection, but long-term survival of natural systems requires a change in emphasis toward general predictive models and carefully designed field experiments to unravel the network of causation that produces ecological patterns.

12.7.5 Attitudinal inertia

Good research addresses important problems in new ways. Traditionally, biologists have focused activities on selected species, particularly those big animals that are favored by hunters. This "moose–goose syndrome" (Keddy 1989a) still colors wetland research and conservation activities. Consider, for example, the effort put into mapping deer habitat as opposed to the effort in mapping turtle nesting beaches, or the number of biologists studying ducks as opposed to invertebrates or plants. This produces inertia in the scientific response to conservation problems. This problem of attitudinal inertia is one of the most expensive and dangerous problems we currently face, since it means that money invested to protect wetlands and wild places is diverted to investigations that are not a priority.

12.7.6 Inner and outer obstacles

A majority of wetland management problems arise because of human actions that have harmed wetlands. One can do the highest quality of science to solve problems, and find it is ignored because people have other priorities. It is not even clear if humans have the ability to make rational decisions about management of their own natural resources. Some examples suggest that humans are very poor judges of the threats posed by their behavior (Tuchman 1984; Slovic 1987). Others suggest that greed and denial lead inevitably to the collapse of civilizations (Diamond 1994, 2005; Wright 2004). This is beyond the scope of this book – except to observe that human psychology has to be considered as an integral part of policy-making (Slovic 1987). In the end, managing wetlands may require considerable attention to managing people, a topic to which we will briefly return in the final chapter.

CONCLUSION

We might begin research in wetland ecology by collecting data on a particular species found in wetlands, or we might begin by picking a wetland and then documenting all the species that are found there. Many people who become wetland ecologists may have started with a favorite species of frog or turtle, or a favorite local wetland. More systematic data from large numbers of species and wetlands allow us to evaluate wetlands for conservation purposes. The Ontario wetland evaluation system provides a useful example that could be extended to other regions of the world with modest effort.

But collecting data on single species and single wetlands can take us only so far. In this chapter, I have addressed the broader issue of how we carry out question-based science and how we build predictive models for wetlands. We will also have to include variables like the key factors that organized this book (hydrology, fertility, disturbance, etc.). In the next chapter we will add the daunting task of adding ecological services to our list of wetland attributes. This adds a whole new class of measurable aspects of wetlands.

Overall, it is safe to conclude that wetland ecology demands a more systematic and thoughtful approach, and a familiarity with an array of scientific methods. Hence this chapter. Species-based approaches are insufficient. There are too many species, too little knowledge about the rest of the system. The alternative, picking one wetland and measuring everything possible, has equal problems. There is no replication, and there are too many variables to measure. This led us to consider three approaches that may have merit for building up general models: (1) empirical ecology, (2) assembly rules based upon filters and traits, or (3) simplification through functional groups. We can think of these as toolboxes that we can draw upon in future studies.

Overall, we need scientists to provide us with more manuals and toolboxes – imagine the difficult task of automobile mechanics if there were no shop manuals and every tool had to be built before they could begin to fix a car. Often, ecologists find themselves in just about this position. In most of the chapters in the book I try provide such a manual and mention the tools that are available, but in this chapter we have had to admit that better manuals and better tools are needed. But again, rather than start from scratch, we could borrow and adapt: the Ontario wetland evaluation system, the U.S. wetland delineation system, and even the Hertzsprung–Russell star chart could guide us.

In conclusion, it is relatively easy to visit a wetland and measure something: it is much harder to ask thoughtful questions and answer them in a way that will be generally useful to others.

Chapter contents

13 | Restoration

It is really quite easy to make a wetland. In many parts of the world, if you dig a depression below the water table, or build a small dam across a drainage ditch, in short order, you have a wetland. Within several years, it may even have a good deal of biological diversity. I have both dug ponds and dammed ditches myself, with satisfactory results, creating habitat for everything from yellow water lilies to otters to snapping turtles. So why, someone practical might ask, is wetland restoration such a big deal? Why bother to study it at all – why not just buy a back hoe and get to work? Why are there conferences, and symposia, and workshops, and books, and book chapters (like this one) addressing wetland restoration? In this chapter we will approach the topic of restoration in the following steps. We will begin looking at some simple examples of wetland restoration. Then we will consider just what the word restoration really means, and the issue of why these simple wetlands are often insufficient. We will then look at another set of examples. We will then look at some common problems that cause restoration to fail. Finally, we will look at some conceptual issues that provide a scientific framework for the task of restoration.

13.1   The importance of understanding wetland restoration

Discussing wetland restoration is important for three main reasons.

First, even though it may seem easy, it really is not. In one study, only two out of 34 restoration projects succeeded in creating the desired ecological community (Lockwood and Pimm 1999)! What about wetlands in particular? One study of 22 wetlands in Virginia found that the created wetlands had fewer kinds of birds and fewer individuals than nearby natural wetlands – and that it was wetland-dependent species that were particularly poor (Desrochers *et al.* 2008). In their words, "Created wetlands that we surveyed failed to completely replicate the bird and plant communities that we observed in nearby natural reference salt marshes . . . ." A larger data set consists of the more than 6800 ha (17 000 acres) lost each year in the United States from 1993 to 2000. These losses are permitted by the U.S. Army Corps of Engineers under section 404 – with the understanding that there will be 1.78 hectares of mitigation (that is, new wetlands created) for every lost hectare. In fact, the permitted projects attained only 0.69 ha, a success rate of well under 50% – for students, this would be the same as a course grade of 39%. At the finer scale, an examination of 70 sites in Massachusetts showed that all the replacement wetlands contained fewer species than reference wetlands. Hence, not only are areas of wetland not being re-created according to targets, but those that are created do not contain the full array of species. Whether this is because of lack of effort, corruption, and ignorance, or inherent difficulties of restoration, is harder to say. It is entirely possible that some types of damage to wetlands are simply irreversible (Zedler and Kercher 2005). One lesson seems clear. The restoration of wetlands is not as easy as it seems. Hence, it is necessary to look at some simple techniques that are used to create wetlands, and possible problems that can arise.

Second, and probably by far the most important, is the distinction between making a wetland and making a specific type of wetland. Some wetlands are easy to make – say a cattail patch with red-winged blackbirds nesting. These sorts of wetlands are often even made unintentionally when humans block drainage with highways or subdivisions. Other types of wetlands are very hard to make – say species-rich fens, vernal pools, and peat bogs. Often a wetland is valued for the biota it contains. Overall, it is easy to make habitat for painted turtles, hard to make habitat for spotted turtles. Easy to make habitat for red-winged blackbirds and Canada geese, hard to make habitat for Everglades snail kites and wood storks. Easy to make habitat for cattails and rushes, hard to make habitat for *Calopogon* orchids and Venus fly-traps. Hence, we could say that the real difficulty in making wetlands is making those specific kinds of wetlands that are most biologically useful. The difficulty lies in predicting how actions taken now will determine the species composition and ecological services provided by the constructed wetland, and, further, in ensuring that these persist through time. This added element – persistence through time – is an important one, since at least in the case of plants, one can buy many types of plants from nurseries, and plant them at a site, but if all but a few kinds die, then the restoration would hardly be judged a success. In summary, then, at its simplest, wetland restoration requires *the creation of a specified composition that will persist through time.*

Third, we should not forget that it is human nature to try to inflate the importance of one's work, and one way to inflate its importance is to pretend that it is very hard to do. Scientists would soon be out of work if they admitted that some of their work really is not that difficult. So they have to invent difficulty. Indeed, says Paul Ehrlich, "The National Academy of Sciences would be unable to give a unanimous decision if asked whether the sun would rise tomorrow."

Actually, the topic is complicated somewhat by multiple meanings of the word restoration.

Or, perhaps, careless use of the term when it is not really appropriate.

13.2   Three examples

Let us begin by considering three simple examples of wetland restoration: plugging drainage ditches, the restoration of the Everglades, and removing levees on the Danube River.

13.2.1 Plugging drainage ditches: the author's own property in Canada

Many areas of wetland have been drained by ditches. Therefore, probably the easiest way to make a wetland is to plug one or more of those drainage ditches. Or, one can wait for a beaver to do it. This is remarkably efficient. Figure 13.1 shows aerial photographs of my own property in Canada. I have put my money where my mouth is and bought a wetland complex to protect it. The left-hand image, taken in 1946, shows only one pond, at the upper left. Much of the land has been deforested entirely, and the low wet areas are being used to produce marsh hay. Over the next 60 years, as the farms were abandoned, beaver populations recovered. More

than ten ponds now occur in the same landscape. These ponds have a rich array of wetland plants (e.g. *Nuphar lutea*, *Sagittaria rigida*, *Pontederia cordata*, *Zizania aquatica*), many kinds of frogs (bullfrogs, green frogs, leopard frogs, gray tree frogs), nesting waterbirds (e.g. great blue herons, blue-winged teal, kingfishers), and mammals (muskrats, otters, beavers).

So this all seems like good news. One of the problems with such restoration lies in the details. For example, small areas of seepage and floodplain do not show up obviously on the photos, so the relative lack of change in these wetlands could be overlooked. The oblong depression at the lower right was already wetland in 1946 – a wet meadow. The flooding by beavers has changed it from a type of wetland that is relatively significant to one that is relatively common. Indeed, one might argue that beavers are not only able to turn old farmland into shallow water, they are also very good at turning seepage

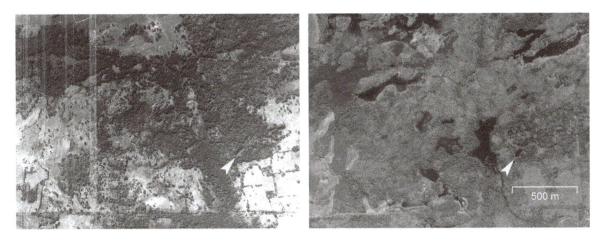

FIGURE 13.1 Aerial images of the author's property in 1946 (left) and 1991 (right) showing how beavers have restored wetlands to one landscape. Arrows show wet meadow (1946) converted to pond (1991).

FIGURE 13.2 Four stages of restoration in one of the author's wetlands: former wetland dried out by drainage ditches (upper left), replacing old beaver dam and filling ditches with earth (upper right), first year (lower left), second year (lower right). The wetland is now a breeding site for wood frogs, leopard frogs, mink frogs, spring peepers, American toads, gray tree frogs, green frogs, and bullfrogs. (See also color plate.)

areas, wet meadows, and small fens into shallow water.

In some cases where wetlands have been degraded, it may be impractical to wait for beavers. Or the food supply may be insufficient to support beavers. In this case, one can use an earth dam to accomplish the same task. One of the ponds in Figure 13.1 had been abandoned by the beavers, turned into wet meadow with species of *Eleocharis*, *Scirpus*, and *Sparganium*, and then began to dry out further through old drainage ditches (Figure 13.2, upper left). If we had waited long enough, the beavers would undoubtedly have rebuilt the dam, but our management objective

was to maintain the diversity of animals and plants near our home. Therefore, over the main drainage ditch we built a small earth dam (Figure 13.2, upper right) which created a typical shallow water flora and fauna (Figure 13.2, lower left) surrounded by large areas of wet meadow. Within a single year the site had revegetated (Figure 13.2, lower right) and now has breeding populations of all the frogs known to occur in this wetland complex. This accomplished my management objectives, which included providing wet meadow for breeding frogs so we could hear native frogs calling at night, and for viewing waterbirds and turtles from my office.

As you learned in Chapter 2, water level fluctuations are an important part of maintaining wetland diversity, and wet meadows are particularly high in diversity. A solid and permanent dam might allow water levels to fall enough to create wet meadows. Our plan is to fluctuate the water levels over a 5-year cycle. Occasional low-water periods will ensure that we maintain wet meadows around the edge of the pond to maintain plant diversity, and to increase wildlife habitat. Even the lowest low will, however, have a nucleus of standing water to ensure that frogs and turtles have some habitat in which to hibernate.

I include this example first partly to show that I have practical experience in this topic, and partly to show how easy it is. At the same time, there are subtleties here, that require knowledge of wetland ecology. Too often, people use a bulldozer to dig a deep pond with steep sides and then have mowed lawn to the water edge. Instead, we have made at least five science-based modifications to maximize plant and animal diversity: (1) native vegetation surrounds the pond, (2) water levels will fluctuate among years to ensure that wet meadows remain, and (3) a nucleus of deeper water will remain even during the low-water year to ensure the survival of truly aquatic species. Moreover, (4) we left the gentle natural contours, so that small changes in water level will create large areas of wet meadows. Finally, (5) stumps and logs have been left where they lay to provide coarse woody debris.

13.2.2 Everglades

Now let us leap to the other extreme – the vast, and vastly expensive – effort to restore the Everglades. The Everglades, the famous "river of grass" (Figure 13.3), are one of the most intensively studied wetlands in North America. They are also part of one of the most expensive restoration programs yet undertaken – the Comprehensive Everglades Restoration Plan (CERP) – priced at more than $8 billion. The Everglades were once a vast rain-fed wetland, with extremely low nutrient levels, and steady flow from north to south, producing a distinctive sedge-dominated vegetation type adapted to wet infertile conditions (Loveless 1959; Davis and Ogden 1994; Sklar *et al.* 2005). They were, in the words of Grunwald (2006, p. 9) "not quite land and not quite water but a soggy confusion of the two." The slow but steady flow of water, combined with extremely low nutrients, appears to have been a defining ecological feature in controlling the vegetation. Superimposed upon this were dry periods which controlled fire regimes (recall Figure 4.6).

Phosphorus concentrations across most of the Everglades were likely as low as 4 to 10 µg/l and loading rates averaged less than 0.1 g P/m^2 per year. The Everglades thus illustrate the characteristics of the type of low-fertility wetlands described in Chapter 3. These extremely low nutrient levels produced distinctive periphyton. The main groups of periphyton are diatoms, cyanobacteria, and green algae, which grow attached to plants, on the soil, or in the water. These begin a distinctive food web, as well as providing oxygen for shallow-water species. Recall from Chapter 2 that this food web supports many wading birds including great egrets, white ibis, wood storks, and roseate spoonbills. Nesting is timed to coincide with seasonal low-water periods which force prey species to concentrate in the remaining few wet areas. Another well-known bird in the Everglades is the snail kite (*Rostrhamus sociabilis*) which feeds almost exclusively on apple snails (*Pomacea paludosa*) which are themselves controlled by the nutrient levels and water regime.

The Everglades have now been heavily impacted by humans (Ingebritsen *et al.* 1999; Sklar *et al.* 2005). Drainage began in the 1880s, and now enormous canals have been constructed, both with the intention of draining the Everglades, and with the intention of moving water for rapidly growing cities (Figure 13.4). At the same time, the sugar industry began to exploit the northern Everglades, and increasing amounts of nutrient-rich water poured south out of the cane fields, fertilizing the Everglades. Plume hunters

1 Everglade kite,
  Rostrhamus sociabilis
2 Pileated woodpecker,
  Phloeceastes pileatus
3 Prothonotary warbler,
  Protonotaria citrea
4 Rough green snake,
  Opheodrys aestivus
5 Limpikin,
  Aramus guarauna
6 Raccoon, *Procyon lotor*
7 Flamingo,
  Phoenicopterus ruber
8 Mississippi alligator,
  Alligator mississippiensis
9 Roseate spoonbill,
  Ajaia ajaja
10 Eastern fox squirrel,
  Sciurus niger
11 Snail,
  Isognomon melina alata
12 Green tree frog,
  Hyla cinerea
13 Green anolis,
  Anolis carolinensis
14 Zebra butterfly,
  Heliconius charitonius
15 Purple gallinule,
  Porphyrula martinica
16 Snail, *Pomacea flagellata*
17 Swamp rabbit,
  Sylvilagus sp.
18 Oxeye tarpon,
  Megalops cyprinoides
19 Cottonmouth moccasin,
  Ancistrodon piscivorus

FIGURE 13.3 A scene from the Everglades. The Comprehensive Everglades Restoration Plan aims to protect and restore the conditions that maintain the native biota of the Everglades. (From Dugan 2005.) (See also color plate.)

deliberately targeted wading birds for their feathers. Finally, there were deliberate attempts to modify the vegetation by introducing exotic species.

The changes are measurable in many ways: reduction in the area of wetlands, lower water levels, increased frequency of droughts, a 90% decline in wading birds, increasing populations of exotic species, and even reduction in landscape features like the characteristic tree islands. A multibillion-dollar program is now attempting to restore the Everglades while maintaining water flow to adjoining urban areas. One objective is to reduce nutrient concentrations in the water to below 10 µg/l phosphorus. This has required the building of enormous (18 000 ha) treatment wetlands

(stormwater treatment areas) to reduce nutrient loads in runoff before this water enters the Everglades (Sklar *et al.* 2005; Chimney and Goforth 2006). Another proposed objective is the restoration of the annual drying periods that support nestlings of wading birds (Brosnan *et al.* 2007). Some would argue that these are irreconcilable objectives – that you cannot continue to modify water quality, flow regime, and availability of water for humans without large-scale detrimental effects on other species. Others believe otherwise.

The Comprehensive Everglades Restoration Plan, which aims to reconcile these conflicting needs, is a work in progress which students will need to follow. A good beginning for the bigger picture is

FIGURE 13.4 Enormous canals have altered the natural hydrology of the Everglades, and provided a conduit for nutrient enriched water to enter the wetlands. (See also color plate.)

The Swamp (Grunwald 2006), which led one reviewer to conclude:

Half the original Everglades has disappeared, the remainder is slowly dying and the pressures of population growth and development in Florida continue unabated. (The sugar fields may one day give way to something even worse: condominiums.) Good intentions, and lots of government money, may not be enough. (Grimes 2006)

13.2.3 Removing levees: the Danube River

Although natural levees occur along many rivers, humans have often built much higher artificial levees to prevent spring flooding. Well-known examples include levees along the Danube River in Europe and

the Mississippi River in North America (Figure 2.25). One way to restore habitat along these rivers is simply remove, or breach, the levees (Schiemer *et al.* 1999; Roni *et al.* 2005). Remove the levee, and when floodwaters return, wetlands re-establish. Let us look at an example from the Danube River, where levee removal has begun. Marius Condac, a wildlife warden, witnessed one levee being opened: "It was spring, the water was very high," he said. "So as soon as the machine had dug a hole, the water broke through with great power. We all cheered. The river was winning back its land." (Simons 1997)

Some geographical context. The Danube River flows from west to east across Europe, from the Black Forest of Germany to the Danube delta at the Black Sea. It crosses through ten countries, and drains more than 800 000 km² in its course. Like most rivers (Dynesius and Nilsson 1994), it has been heavily altered by humans – over 700 dams and

FIGURE 13.5 Removing artificial levees will also restore wetlands. (left) Prior to dike removal. (right) After removing some 6 km of dikes, natural flood regimes were restored and in 2004 the Danube River flowed freely over Tataru Island. (Courtesy World Wildlife Fund.) (See also color plate.)

weirs have been built along the river and its tributaries. As a consequence, the floodplain wetlands have shrunk from more than 40 000 to less than 8000 km^2 – a loss in excess of 80%.

The Danube delta in the Black Sea, nearly 800 000 ha, is the largest in Europe, and it supports 176 species of breeding birds and 45 species of freshwater fish (Gastescu 1993; Schiemer *et al.* 1999). It lies largely in Romania, with about one-fifth being in Ukraine. Like many other wetlands, it too has been crisscrossed with dredged canals (1750 km of them) and surrounded by embankments and levees. As but one example, dikes were built around Tataru Island in Ukraine "in order to drain around half the 738 ha island for forestry and horticulture. Under strict forestry laws, the local forestry service had to sell 1000 m^3 of wood, 3 tons of meat, 700 kg of honey, 3000 muskrats, and 0.5 tons of medicinal plants to the state every year. Pigs, sheep, horses, and other domestic animals were kept on the island . . ." (WWF 2003).

Now some political context. Although Tataru Island is in Ukraine, much of the delta lies in adjoining Romania, once ruled by the Communist

dictator, Nicolae Ceausescu, who, in the mid 1980s, had decreed that large areas of the delta should be transformed into agricultural land (Simons 1997). He sent 6000 men to build dikes, pump the land dry, and convert it into grain fields. Readers will be relieved to know that he was executed by a firing squad in 1989.

In fall 2003, restoration began in the delta. On Tataru Island, in adjoining Ukraine, some 6 km of dikes that surrounded that island were removed, restoring natural flooding. In 2004 the Danube flowed freely over the island (Figure 13.5). A guest house has been built to accommodate visitors, so you can one day visit this site for yourself. In 1994 and 1996, dikes were also opened in two former agricultural polders, Babina (2100 ha) and Cernovca (1560 ha), in Romania (Schneider *et al.* 2008). Monitoring has documented the recovery of a wide range of wetland species, as well as increased retention of nitrogen and phosphorus from the river. Seventeen major floodplain restoration sites have been identified along the Danube, as part of a larger plan to re-create a green corridor along the river (World Wildlife Fund 1999).

13.3   More on principles of restoration

Now that we have explored three examples of wetland restoration let us take a step back and look more closely at the underlying principles.

13.3.1 What does the word restoration really mean?

The word restoration is often carelessly used to mean many different things. A word that means too many things often seems to end up meaning nothing. Hence, let us use the word precisely, guided by Figure 13.6. We start at the upper left, with the original state of the system, which could also be termed a pre-perturbed system, or in some circumstances, a natural or pristine system. One or more forces has damaged (rapid change) or degraded (gradual change) the site (first solid line) so that the present state is different from this original state. So starting from the present state, what are the options? There are four. The most obvious is that the system could degrade further (second solid line). Should humans intervene, they have three options shown by the dashed lines:

(1) Convert the site to an alternative ecosystem
(2) Repair certain selected attributes of the system
(3) Restore the site to its original state.

Hence, the term **restoration** means the action of returning an area of landscape to a specified previously occurring ecological state. Note the components. First, restoration has a specified target state, and second, there is evidence that this state existed in the past. Since there are so many terms used to describe human activities in wetlands, here are a few related to conservation and restoration, with restoration first for comparison.

Restoration Returning an area of landscape to a specified previously occurring ecological state. (Example: removing embankments to allow a river to annually flood a former wetland with the objective of recreating a wet prairie.)

Mitigation Purchasing or creating wetlands to compensate for damage being done elsewhere. (Example: paying for restoration of one cypress swamp to compensate for building a subdivision on another.) A legal rather than scientific term that is most commonly used in the United States of America.

Rehabilitation Making specified changes to an existing wetland in order to improve one or more services. (Example: a group such as Ducks Unlimited removes patches of cattails to create pools of open water for ducks and wading birds.)

Preservation Maintaining an existing highly valued wetland in its valued state. (Example: a group such as The Nature Conservancy purchases a set of vernal pools with the intention of keeping populations of endangered species at their current level.)

Creation Making a new wetland in an area where it was not previously present. (Example: making a pond in a city to attract wildlife. This could be called

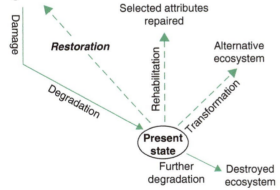

FIGURE 13.6 The present state of this system is degraded from its original state. There are several future states possible, and only one process should be called restoration. (After Magnuson *et al.* 1980; Cairns 1989; SER (2004) terminology.)

restoration if there are historical records of similar ponds there before the city was built.)

Conservation A general term that implies a wetland will be retained more or less green and wet but without specifying exactly how it will be managed. Often a group of stakeholders will be allowed to choose the future state. (Example: the Atchafalaya Swamp is still being heavily altered by humans but with the general agreement that it will remain a wetland.)

The more precise the restoration target or desired ecological state, the better. Thus, the goal "to create a nice wetland" is insufficient. A better goal would be "to create a wetland dominated by specific plant species to provide habitat for specific animal species." For example, in the Everglades, one could specify the goal of creating "a cypress prairie wetland with sheet flow of water through shallow ponds dominated by muhly grass (*Muhlenbergia capillaris*) and saw grass (*Cladium jamaicense*), and containing reproducing populations of apple snails (*Pomacea paludosa)* to support snail kites (*Rostrhamus sociabilis*)."

Although this is better, it is still vague. Consider. What will the rate of sheet flow be, and how will this vary among seasons? What will be the nutrient quality of the water? How many other plant species will coexist with the two dominant ones mentioned? Which ones will be planted and which ones will be expected to regenerate naturally? How many apple snails will be produced per year per hectare? Will there be suitable nesting habitat nearby for snail kites?

According to the definition above, restoring a site requires us to know what it was once like. We know that all systems change with time, even without human interference – specific examples you have already seen include the Great Lakes (Figure 2.4), peatlands (Figures 7.9, 7.11), the Everglades (Figure 4.6), and the Mississippi River delta (Figure 7.18). Humans are not the only cause of change, although human impacts are certainly

increasing. We can learn about earlier states of wetlands from a variety of sources. There may be older scientific studies that we can use for reference, there may be information from pollen or sediment analyses, or there may be relatively pristine sites nearby. All of these may need to be used for evidence in order to decide what the original state of the system was.

Consider the Great Lakes again. Some 25 000 years ago the Great Lakes were filled with glaciers. The original state of the Great Lakes, for restoration purposes, is therefore usually considered to be the period before European humans arrived and began extensive changes to the environment through commercial fishing, dam construction, and deforestation. That would be roughly the 1600s. This of course, raises the legitimate question of to what extent the local ecosystems had already been modified by the earlier wave of immigrants across the Bering Strait – aboriginals also cleared land, burned forests, hunted, and fished. Overall, their impacts seem to have been much smaller. If, as seems to be the case, they also caused the extinction of much of North America's original megafauna (Figures 6.11, 6.12), their impacts may have been more widespread and significant (Janzen and Martin 1982). Hence, in asking which time one should choose for a restoration, there is no single entirely right answer. However, whenever you are involved in restoration, you should be aware of the available background information on the ecological history of the site, and at least show that you have considered these issues in choosing the restoration target. (If you have not, and there is a public hearing, someone will likely ask you to justify your choice, and thoroughly embarrass you if you have been too lazy to think it through first.)

In some, indeed, perhaps many, cases, there is doubt that one can restore a site. Key species that once occupied the site may be extinct. Since some Great Lakes fish species are now extinct (Christie 1974), food webs are bound to be different in restored wetlands. Other key factors that produced wetlands, like pulse flooding, sheet flow, herds of bison, or fire, may no longer be possible because of adjoining urban areas. In this case, we should use a word that does not imply the idea of re-creating the original system. Rehabilitation might be the appropriate word for such cases. Let us move from the Great Lakes to the Louisiana coastline. While working in Louisiana, I was surprised at how many people would talk about restoring the wetlands in the most vague way, apparently unaware that a restored wetland should have bison (now restricted to sites much further west), red wolves (now restricted to a few sites much further east), large alligators (now heavily hunted, with altered population size and size-class structure), no nutria (which were introduced in the 1930s), and enormous spring floods (now controlled by the presence of levees along the river). True restoration may be very difficult. That is not to say it is not desirable – there is no reason why a large-scale restoration could not occur. It is simply that real restoration would require changes including (1) reintroduction of bison and red wolves, (2) larger alligator populations, (3) extirpation of nutria, (4) large flood pulses, (5) filling canals and leveling spoil banks, and (6) allowing natural changes in river channels.

There is a third possibility shown in Figure 13.6. One may have to admit that restoration cannot be achieved, and even rehabilitation is doubtfully possible. Here, the best one can do is create an alternative ecosystem that is admittedly artificial. This system may have elements of the original natural system, such as selected plant and bird species, but could not be considered natural. Examples might include ponds on golf courses, cypress swamps used for treatment of freshwater sewage, or stormwater treatment ponds in subdivisions. This is not to downplay the importance of such sites in the landscape – the challenge is to make them useful to as many species as possible. But it is misleading to call them restoration.

Before one begins a restoration project, one has to know whether one is restoring, rehabilitating,

or simply building a wet spot to treat sewage or store stormwater. They all have their place. But they should not be confused with one another. And in each case there should be specific goals stated in advance – as well as monitoring to ensure they are attained. Which brings us naturally to the topic of monitoring.

13.3.2 Monitoring

Monitoring consists of making predetermined measurements of selected physical or biological factors at regular intervals. Common factors to measure include water depth, dissolved nutrients, and number of calling amphibians or birds. The challenge in monitoring is to choose the minimum number of variables that will produce the maximum amount of information. It is actually a real scientific challenge to choose the correct variables. In physics, for example, we know that the essential variables for a system will usually include mass, pressure, volume, and temperature. We do not yet have a predetermined set of essential variables in ecology, but consensus is being reached on which factors it is useful to monitor – a topic we will return to in Section 14.8. Let us restrict ourselves here to the purpose of monitoring.

The basic objective of a monitoring program is to determine whether the objective of a project has been met. Is there a wetland? Does it have the desired composition? Without monitoring, it is impossible to decide whether or not restoration has occurred.

The second basic objective of a monitoring program is to provide an opportunity to correct emerging problems, that is, for adaptive environmental assessment (Holling 1978, Walters 1997). However well a project as been designed and thought out, problems happen. It may not even be related to the design of the project – perhaps the climate is changing or new invasive species are present. Adaptive environmental assessment allows one to change the restoration project while it is in progress to respond to unexpected events.

Table 13.1 Five questions for monitoring and adaptive management

(1) What are the ecological properties/indicators that should be measured to assess the integrity of the ecosystem? (Water quality? Primary production? Abundance of selected species?)

(2) What is the best way to measure these properties/indicators? (Size of sample units? Number of sample units? Distribution of sample units in space and time? Stratification procedures?)

(3) How will the data be collected, stored, analyzed, and shared? (Agency responsible? Instruments? Software? Backups? Type of analysis?)

(4) What are the acceptable ranges for each property/indicator? (Are there warning values that indicate unacceptable high or low levels? Are there long-term climate cycles or fire frequencies that must be taken into account?)

(5) What is the adaptive action if a property reaches a specified unacceptable level? (Who is responsible for making the decision? Who is responsible for carrying out the management?)

The ideal monitoring program, therefore, continues through time.

As a manager of a specific wetland, you may find that three of your most important duties are (1) monitoring, (2) interpreting the results, and (3) making adaptive changes to your management plan. Table 13.1 provides a list of the questions you need to ask yourself in designing an adaptive management plan. In Chapter 14 we shall look at some potential indicators.

13.3.3 When does restoration succeed?

It is easy to throw out the word success. It is quite another to define it clearly and measure it properly. Here is where some basic theory will help us think clearly about the situation. Returning to the definition of restoration above, one way to think about restoration is to ask what the composition of the original system was, and how it has been perturbed. There are good quantitative tools for doing so. A useful way to think about this draws upon the quantitative ecological technique of ordination (Bloom 1980). From this perspective, the original state, or the target state, can be defined by a set of samples described by a centroid and 95% confidence envelope. A perturbation is then defined quite specifically as a change that pushes the composition of the system outside of the envelope; restoration consists of changes that push it back inside this envelope. In Figure 13.7 the original composition is defined by the boxes and a centroid (dark dot).

Another approach that accomplishes the same goal is to use reference wetlands. These would be wetlands that have a long history of protection, perhaps wetlands surrounded by native vegetation and with a minimal history of human disturbance. The composition of the communities in these reference wetlands then illustrates the target area for restoration, the area inside the box in Figure 13.7. Indeed, one of the reasons for having a protected areas system is to provide natural areas that represent the original state of ecosystems to provide reference points for understanding the impacts humans are having upon the rest of the landscape. Maintaining such reference wetlands within a landscape requires a properly designed reserve system (Section 14.4).

Overall, restoration is an enormous challenge. There is much to learn. As we saw in Section 13.1, some restoration projects fail to even create wetlands! As we shall see in Section 14.4.1, even when wetlands are created, they continue to rank below natural wetlands when measured quantitatively (Mushet et al. 2002).

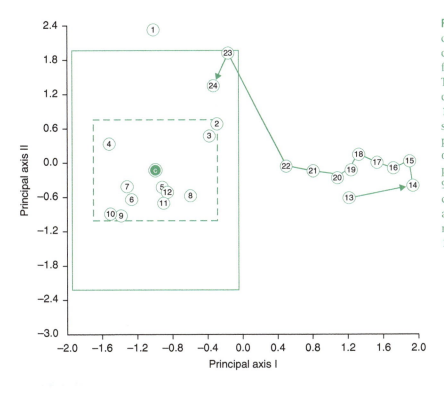

FIGURE 13.7 Defining and charting the recovery of a community after perturbation from a multivariate perspective. The data are from a benthic community, with sample units 1–12 before perturbation and sample units 13–24 after perturbation. The solid and dashed boxes represent two procedures for calculating a 95% polygon around the centroid (c) using parametric and non-parametric methods, respectively. (From Bloom 1980.)

13.4   More examples

We started with the proposition that it was easy to make a wetland. We then saw that it is not as easy at it seems, particularly if one has specific targets for the type of wetland community. This, of course, takes us back to the earlier chapters in the book where we saw how small differences in water level, nutrient status, or grazing can have a major impact upon species composition. This led us through the topics of monitoring and adaptive management, keeping a certain amount of flexibility so one can refine the management to help achieve the desired targets. Let us look at three larger examples of restoration where the challenges are rather more daunting. The first is restoring wetlands along a river in an area that has been densely populated for centuries. The second is restoring wetlands in a delta that has been degraded by multiple human impacts. The third is rebuilding wetlands where the original system has been entirely removed.

13.4.1 Yangtze River

The Yangtze is the third largest river in the world, being 6300 km long and draining an area of 1.8 million km². The headwaters arise in the Himalayas of Tibet at an elevation of more than 5 km above sea level, and the river flows eastward to empty into the East China Sea at Shanghai (Figure 13.8). The headwaters have one of the world's largest high-altitude wetlands, Ruoergai, on the eastern edge of the Tibetan plateau, with 600 000 hectares of peat bogs, marshes, and meadows. One the way to the sea, the river passes through China's two largest freshwater lakes. And at the sea it has built a large delta with coastal marshes.

The Yangtze makes an interesting and important case history of how to reconcile human activity with wetland restoration. Consider. More than 400 million people live in this drainage basin, more than the

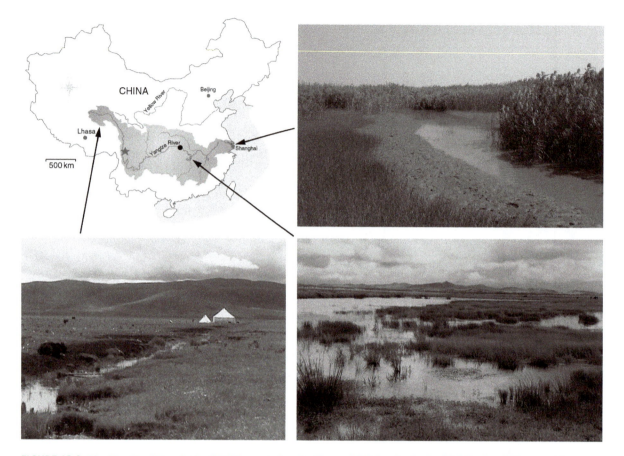

FIGURE 13.8 The Yangtze River is the third longest river in the world. It begins in the highlands of Tibet, amidst some of the world's largest high-altitude peatlands (Ruoergai peatland, bottom left; courtesy Wetlands International). Here it also flows through mountains which comprise one of the world's biodiversity hotspots, the mountains of Southwest China (star, top left). Further east it passes through large lakes such as Dongting Lake (lower right; from www.hbj. hunan.gov.cn/dongT1/default.aspx). Where it enters the sea there are large deltaic wetlands (top right; courtesy M. Zhijun). The world's largest dam, the Three Gorges Dam (Fig. 2.21), is indicated by the black dot (top left). (See also color plate.)

entire population of the United States of America. The basin has also supported human populations for millennia. There was conversion of wetlands for agriculture as early as the "Southern Song" dynasty (AD 420–479). But in the Communist era reclamation reached unprecedented levels. From 1950 to 1980, 12 000 km² of lakes and wetlands were impoldered along the Yangtze (China Development Brief 2004). The basin contains the two largest freshwater lakes in China, Dongting Lake and Poyang Lake. And, like the rest of the world, the Yangtze faces problems created by megaprojects like the Three Gorges Dam.

Let us look in particular at the two freshwater lakes. The value of these wetlands is illustrated by their rich biodiversity – 300 bird species, 200 fish species, 90 reptile species, and 60 amphibian species. A few noteworthy examples include Yangtze dolphin (*Lipotes vexillifer*), Yangtze alligator (*Alligator sinensis*), Chinese sturgeon (*Acipenser sinensis*), and white-naped crane (*Grus vipio*). Water levels in the

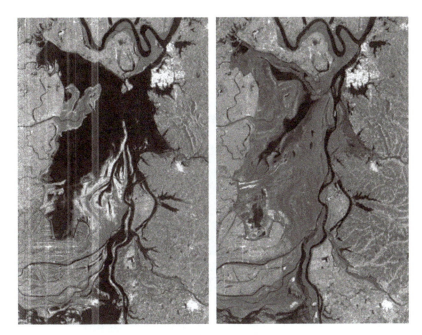

FIGURE 13.9 The water levels in Dongting Lake, the second largest freshwater lake in China, change from high (left, July 2006) to low (right, October 2006) depending upon inputs from the Yangtze River. (Courtesy Institute of Space and Information Science, Chinese University of Hong Kong.)

lakes fluctuate (Figure 13.9). During summer flood period, the marshes become open water with villages occurring on islands; flood levels are highest during El Niño events. Large areas of wetland around both lakes have been converted to agriculture (a process termed impoldering: Zhao and Fang 2004). Since impoldering reduces the capacity of the lake to accommodate floodwaters, the result has been increased flood levels, with catastrophic flooding in 1998 (Shankman *et al.* 2006). In Dongting Lake, the rate of conversion to agriculture was high between 1920 and 1970 (Zhao and Fang 2004). Hence, as one of its conservation priorities, the World Wildlife Fund has set the specific target of restoring the wetlands of Dongting Lake to the 4350 km² extent they occupied in the 1950s. Note the date, here. Earlier in the chapter, we addressed the issue of what time in the past should be the reference point. The 1950s may provide a practical target, but clearly one that is far from the original state of this landscape.

Consider the example of the Quinshan Polder, built on the edge of Dongting Lake in 1975 (China Development Brief 2004). This polder required 30 000 laborers in Hunan Province to invest around

1 million working days shoveling earth and rubble to create a system of dikes to turn 11 km² of lake into agricultural land. Although the soil in the polder was composed of fertile silts, the labor costs to maintain the embankments were so high that agricultural return from crops such as rice was in fact marginal. In 2003 the dikes were opened to reflood the land. This required relocating 5700 people, some of whom farm in other polders or now fish in the newly flooded area. The area has also been included within the Muping Hu Nature Reserve. Thousands of waterbirds have now returned.

13.4.2 Breeching levees with engineered control structures: Louisiana

The next example comes from Louisiana. As with the Danube River, the Mississippi River has been bordered by many levees to control flooding. These levees also prevent water from flowing overland, and thereby prevent spring flood pulses from carrying fresh water, sediment, and nutrients into adjoining swamps and marshes. Simultaneously, the wetlands along the river, particularly in the delta, have been

FIGURE 13.10 The Caernarvon Diversion structure on the Mississippi River allows floodwaters to pass through an artificial levee and enter the wetlands of Breton Sound in the distance. (Courtesy J. Day.) (See also color plate.)

crisscrossed by canals built for shipping, logging, and the oil and gas industry. As a consequence, vast areas of swamp and marsh are slowly becoming open water.

The problems caused by levee construction are exhaustively documented, but owing to human fears of flooding, few levees have been removed. The Caernarvon Freshwater Diversion Project was an early attempt to breach the levee to allow floodwater to pass into marshes of Breton Sound, while at the same time maintain complete human control over the water (Figure 13.10). Here is a summary of the project

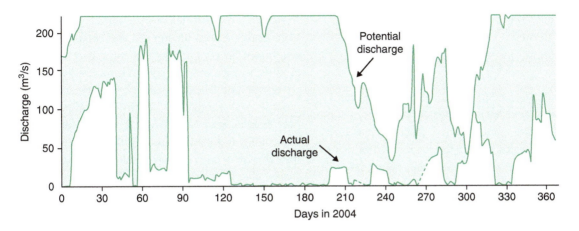

FIGURE 13.11 Actual discharge and potential discharge through the Caernarvon Freshwater Diversion Project in 2004. (Courtesy J. Lopez.)

from a website maintained by the Louisiana government.

The project consists of a diversion structure containing five 15-foot square gated culverts and inflow and outflow channels. The design discharge is 8,000 cubic feet per second; however, the actual amount of diverted flow depends on a detailed operational plan. The Corps of Engineers constructed the project and the Louisiana Department of Natural Resources is responsible for its operation. The Caernarvon Interagency Advisory Group consisting of 14 representatives of federal and state agencies, fisheries, and landowners provides overall operational oversight. Construction was completed in February 1991 at a cost of $26.1 million. The federal share was 75% of the costs and the State of Louisiana's share was 25%. (www.lacoast.gov/programs/Caernarvon/factsheet.htm)

Although this project was far more expensive than the Tataru Island project, and far more technologically sophisticated, it seems to have accomplished, at best, more or the less the same objective of breaching a levee to allow spring flood pulses from a river to rejuvenate adjoining marshes.

Remarkably, large construction projects have another problem – they are subjected to human interference. Far from allowing normal flood pulses, continual political interference actually has greatly restricted the flow of spring floodwaters from the Mississippi River through the Caernarvon Diversion. Indeed, at a recent meeting I attended, it was clear that the flow regime was not only much below capacity, but when pulses did occur, they were often at entirely the wrong season. Naturally I enquired why such a thing would be allowed, and was told that a mélange of complaints from hunters, fisherman, boaters, and local landowners had produced this highly artificial flow regime. Figure 13.11 shows the flow regime encountered in 2004; superimposed upon this is the flow regime that would have resulted if the structure were operated wide open. Thus, from the point of view of the wetland, the expensive control structures had actually produced a less desirable result than if the levee had simply been gapped by a bulldozer.

Problems such as these raise many questions about the value of highly engineered solutions to wetland restoration. Since so much money is being invested in building, running and monitoring such projects, the U.S. Environmental Protection Agency hired a scientific committee to review their utility. After reviewing projects around the United States, they submitted their report in 1998. Their conclusions? The first two (Sanzone and McElroy 1998, p. iii) were:

The collective experience around the country has shown that unintended, unanticipated, and sometimes undesirable effects have resulted from structural management of marsh hydrology. Although marsh management practices have evolved over the years to include more sophisticated structures and management approaches for controlling water levels, there is insufficient information at present to determine whether these new structural approaches are inherently better than those used in the past.

More generally, they concluded (p. 42), a structure

generally restricts the supply of mineral sediments needed to accrete soil, does not seem to protect wetlands, and may even hasten their demise. There may be a better case for the application of SMM [Structures in Marsh Management] in protecting tidal freshwater wetlands with highly organic or even floating soils. However, critical scientific appraisals of the effectiveness of SMM in such environments have yet to be performed.

So, we have started with the idea that it is easy to create a wetland, and ended with the conclusions that in many cases, high-profile technological solutions have not been demonstrated to work effectively. Why should such a simple process end in ambiguity? One is reminded of the Scottish poet Robert Burns, who wrote in 1785 a poem titled "To a Mouse": "The best laid schemes o'mice an' men, Gang aft a-gley" (that is, the best laid plans frequently fail). Or, the more recent Murphy's law – if something can go wrong, it will.

13.4.3 Prairie potholes

An extreme case of the challenge posed by restoration is re-establishment of prairie pothole wetlands in areas that have been drained and sown to row crops for at least 25 years. Galatowitsch and van der Valk (1996) examined the success of an entire set of such restoration projects. From a total of 62

restoration projects, ten were selected on hydric soils that had been tile drained and completely cultivated for corn and soybeans for 25–75 years. That is, in each of these sites, restoration involved re-creation of a wetland where it had been absent for decades and where there was little reason to expect any residual seed bank. Given the importance of hydrology as a controlling factor or filter in the establishment of wetland communities, it might seem reasonable, at least as a first approximation, to assume that appropriate hydrology alone would re-establish wetlands. Perhaps steps as simple as plugging drainage ditches or removing tiles would suffice. In a comparison of ten "restored" wetlands to ten adjacent natural wetlands, the natural wetlands had a mean of 46 species compared to a mean of only 27 for the restored wetlands. Further, there were differences among functional groups; the restored sites had more species of submersed aquatics, but fewer species of sedge meadows. The seed banks of the communities also differed; natural sites had nearly twice as many species (15 vs. 8) and more than twice as high a density of buried seeds ($7300/m^2$ vs. $3000/m^2$). Submersed aquatics, wet prairie and wet meadow species were all absent from the seed banks of the restored wetlands. Even the zonation patterns of individual species differed between the restored and natural sites. Galatowitsch and van der Valk propose the term "efficient-community hypothesis" for the view that vegetation will re-establish itself rapidly after hydrology has been restored, and reject this hypothesis as a reasonable basis for restoration in prairie potholes. Part of the explanation may lie with rates of loss of wetland seeds; both seed densities and species richness decline with the duration a wetland has been drained. After 50 years, seed densities are $<1000/m^2$ (compared with $3000-7000/m^2$ in natural sites) and species richness is three species (compared with 12 in natural sites) (van der Valk *et al.* 1992).

There is also evidence that aquatic invertebrates are under-represented in restored wetlands (Galatowitsch and van der Valk 1994). Species with poor dispersal capabilities will likely have to be reintroduced during restoration in order to re-establish the original ecological communities.

13.5   One big problem: invasive species

While the example is fresh in our mind, let us use the Everglades to introduce this widespread problem, a problem that increasingly is likely to obstruct the best intentions of restoration ecologists.

The invasion of exotic species is a global problem. In the book *Ecological Imperialism* (Crosby 1993, p. 7) we read:

On the pampa, Iberian horses and cattle have driven back the guanaco and rhea; in North America, speakers of Indo-European languages have overwhelmed speakers of Algonkin and Muskhogean and other Amerindian languages; in the antipodes, the dandelions and house cats of the Old World have marched forward, and kangaroo grass and kiwis have retreated. Why?

Why? is the all important question. While it seems obvious that some species possess traits that allow them to invade other areas successfully, we are still unraveling what these traits might be. Meanwhile the list of exotic invasive species continues to grow. Wetlands provide many examples. In North America, the list of exotic invasive species impacting wetlands includes plants (purple loosestrife, *Lythrum salicaria*; water hyacinth, *Eichhornia crassipes*), mammals (nutria, *Myocastor coypus*; wild boar, *Sus scrofa*), invertebrates (zebra mussels, *Dreissena polymorpha*; quagga mussels, *Dreissena rostriformis*; Charru mussels, *Mytella charruana*), fish (northern snakehead, *Channa argus*; common carp, *Cyprinus carpio*; bighead carp, *Hypophthalmichthys nobilis*), toads (cane toads, *Bufo marinus*), and even snakes (Burmese python, *Python molurus*).

For restoration purposes, it is important to distinguish between two similar definitions, an exotic species and an invasive species.

An **exotic species** is one that did not naturally occur in a specified geographical area. Historical records often allow us to document which species naturally occurred in an area, and which arrived after Europeans began to alter the landscape, and this is noted in many identification manuals. Archeological investigations can provide good evidence on which species were present, or at least being harvested, hundreds of years ago.

Note the phrase "specified geographical area." A species might be exotic in all of North America (e.g. the melaleuca tree, introduced to Florida, but native to Asia). Or a species might be native in one state or biogeographical region, but exotic nearby. In general, it is best to try to always obtain locally grown restoration material from local seed sources to avoid such problems.

An **invasive species** is one that has the potential to rapidly spread and replace native species. Many of the most dangerous invasive species are also exotic. However, some apparently native species have the capacity to dominate wetlands. Examples include *Typha* species, *Phalaris arundinacea*, and *Phragmites australis* (Zedler and Kercher 2004). The most invasive cattail, however, is a hybrid known as *Typha* × *glauca*. If you are planning a restoration project, you must consider not only the possibility of exotic species dominating the site, but also the possibility that unwanted native species may quickly invade and dominate the project.

Invasive species, exotic or native, may already be present in the landscape as buried seeds, waiting to invade a newly created wetland. They may arrive on machinery used in building the wetland. They may arrive with nursery stock used in planting. They may arrive attached to visitors or their boats. They are already a problem in many wetlands, and they promise to be an ever larger problem in the future. Let us continue to use the Everglades as the study system.

Melaleuca (*Melaleuca quinquenervia*) is an evergreen subtropical tree that is both exotic and invasive in the Everglades; it was intentionally introduced to Florida (Ewel 1986). Melaleuca is native to coastal lowlands in Australia, New Caledonia, and New Guinea where it forms open nearly monospecific stands that burn regularly. It was introduced to Florida on multiple occasions, and seeds were even spread from airplanes as part of a deliberate attempt to afforest the Everglades (Dray *et al.* 2006)! One of the early proponents of its introduction (although not the first) was Dr. John Gifford, the first American to hold a doctorate in forestry:

As a bank official, nurseryman, and land-development company entrepreneur, Gifford quickly joined the drainage movement to reclaim the Everglades. His primary interest was experimentation with introduced trees that would absorb water and dry up the south Florida wetlands. In 1906, Gifford introduced the cajupet melaleuca, an Australian native, to Florida, planting seeds at his home on Biscayne Bay and at a nursery in Davie, Broward County. (http://everglades.fiu.edu/reclaim/bios/gifford.htm)

Once established, melaleuca tolerates extended flooding, moderate drought, and some salinity on almost any soil in South Florida. By 1920 it had begun to spread. Melaleuca has flaky outer bark and oil-laden foliage which burn readily, and within weeks of a fire can flower and produce serotinous capsules each with about 250 tiny seeds. A single burned melaleuca can produce millions of seeds.

To explore its potential as an invasive species, Myers (1983) introduced some 22 000 000 seeds into six mature communities and two disturbed communities, finding that germination was only 0.01% in mature communities, but an order of magnitude greater at 0.14% in disturbed communities. If one bypassed the germination phase using out-planted seedlings, melaleuca also had much higher survival in disturbed communities (ca. 90% survival) as opposed to native communities

(ca. 25% survival). Disturbance seems to be an important prerequisite for establishment. This need not seem surprising, since disturbance is also essential for many native species to flourish, creating the gaps in which seedlings can establish (Section 4.4). Everything from digging ditches to building impoundments may create ideal conditions for invasive species to establish. Even simple features like access roads can be dangerous to the native flora.

In habitats where disturbances are natural, invasive species may have regular opportunities for invasion. Both fire and fluctuating water levels provide disturbance essential for the maintenance of plant diversity in southern Florida (Figure 4.6), and this may provide added invasion opportunities for species such as melaleuca. There is much ongoing study of control methods for melaleuca (e.g. Ewel 1986; Mazzotti *et al.* 1997; Rayamajhi *et al.* 2002; Serbesoff-King 2003). But the species now occurs some 200 000 ha (500 000 acres) of South Florida. In other areas, the species may still be absent because of low seed mobility. Therefore, Ewel (1986) suggests that resource managers might be well advised to concentrate on eliminating seed sources nearest the pine–cypress ecotones into which melaleuca is pre-adapted to spread. Once the species is well established, such as in areas of the Everglades, both fire and herbicide can be used to control melaleuca. Prescribed burns remove the trees from a large area, but a potential problem is that melaleuca debris produces hot fires that may damage organic soils (Mazzotti *et al.* 1997) and stands can re-establish from seeds or sprouts (Turner *et al.* 1998). Herbicide is particularly effective at more local scales, although costs are in the order of $400/ha ($1000/acre). Since 1995, the South Florida Water Management District alone has spent more than $2 million a year on melaleuca control (Laroche and Baker 2001). Biological control by insects is also being explored. Likely a combination of all of these will be necessary to obtain control (Turner *et al.* 1998). It is not yet clear whether we can reasonably hope for melaleuca removal (its extermination from wild areas) or merely control (keeping it at relatively low levels through repeated intervention).

There are new species arriving continually. *Lygodium microphyllum* (Old World climbing fern) began spreading in the 1960s. This species can create a leafy covering up tree trunks and into the canopy – changing the shading regime, smothering trees, and most importantly, increasing the frequency and intensity of fire (Pemberton *et al.* 2002; Wu *et al.* 2006). Moreover, it can spread long distances by microscopic spores to colonize newly disturbed sites.

Not all invasive species are exotic species. Several species of cattails (*Typha* spp.) are native to North America, although there is still some debate about their origins. They have been historically absent from many types of wetlands. As a consequence of recent changes in the environment of the Everglades, *Typha* has now been able to invade and replace the native *Cladium jamaicense* (saw grass). From the air one can see how plumes of invading cattail now appear to track where nutrients flow into the Everglades from agricultural areas. There are several hypotheses that might account for this invasion. Nutrients are the most likely cause, but there have also been significant changes in hydrology over the years. Perhaps there is some interaction of factors, say increased standing water combined with increased nutrient levels. Nor is the list limited to these two factors, since other factors such as changes in fire frequency might also be contributing to this invasion. Hence, this is a perfect example of the need to consider multiple hypotheses that might explain an observed change, and then devise tests among them (e.g. Newman *et al.* 1996, 1998). One can then respond intelligently. In the northern Everglades, for example, it appears that increased phosphorus is the first factor, and then

changes in hydrology or fire come next, depending upon the area studied (Newman *et al.* 1998). Current work in the Everglades strongly suggests a predominant role for nutrients as the cause, and time will tell whether the planned reduction in phosphorus loading to the Everglades will be sufficient for saw grass to displace the cattails. The possibility that herbicides or fire might accelerate the conversion back to saw grass is also being explored.

The role of cattails is complex. As well as being a visible invasive species, cattails are also an indicator of changes in many other species, particularly in the distinctive periphyton (comprising more than 100 species of diatoms, cyanophytes, and green algae) and other species dependent upon this unusual Everglades trophic group such as roseate spoonbills and wood storks (Gottlieb *et al.* 2006). Hence, one has to think about this problem carefully: when we talk about cattail invasion, are we referring simply to the presence of a single unwanted species, or are we referring to the complex ecosystem changes that are occurring as indicated by the presence of this species?

The case of cattails in the Everglades illustrates a more general problem with cattail invasion elsewhere. As we saw in the chapter on competition (Chapter 5), clonal species with dense canopies can exclude many other native species from wetlands, and the centrifugal model (recall Figure 5.11) illustrates the catastrophic effects this can have on plant diversity, and upon organisms that require open conditions. The impacts of invasive species – including everything from trees like melaleuca to floating plants like water hyacinth (Figure 13.12) – will continue to complicate attempts at restoring natural habitats and protecting threatened species.

13.6   A brief history of restoration

Ecosystem restoration is the process of re-creating an ecological community (e.g. Cairns 1980; Jordan *et al.* 1987; Dahm *et al.* 1995). It is "an emerging

profession within the science of ecology" (Bonnicksen 1988). It is attracting billions of dollars and producing an enormous stream of published

FIGURE 13.12 Invasive aquatic plants, like water hyacinth (*Eichhornia crassipes*, bottom; courtesy Center for Aquatic and Invasive Plants, University of Florida), are notorious for their ability to invade and to dominate wet places (top; W. Durden, U.S. Department of Agriculture, Agricultural Research Service). They can reduce both biological diversity and ecological services. Such invasives pose a significant risk to restored wetlands as well as to natural wetlands. (See also color plate.)

papers. While it is true that the field is growing rapidly, we should not fall into the trap of saying that restoration is somehow entirely "new." Bonnicksen, like many other writers in this field, only traces the roots of restoration ecology back as far as Aldo Leopold in 1949.

More than a decade earlier, however, Clements (1935) wrote an essay titled "Experimental ecology in the public service" in which he described the applications of ecology to a wide range of applied problems. He referred to the need for "natural landscaping" (p. 359) and laid out its basic rules:

The chief of these is that nature is to be followed as closely as possible and hence native materials alone are to be employed, preferably from the outset but invariably in the final composition . . . The process of succession by which nature reclothes bare areas is to be utilized as the chief tool of landscaping, but the process is often to be hastened or telescoped to secure more rapid and varied results. (p. 360)

Clements even noted the need for indicators:

a necessary adjunct is the use of indicators to record existing conditions and their gradual change into grazing communities of the desired composition and yield. (p. 353)

The history of restoration pre-dates Clements, too. Half a century before Clements, in 1883, Phipps wrote a book on the restoration of forests, and Larson (1996) has described what appears to be one of the earliest practical restoration projects in North America, the replanting of a forest in a gravel pit near the University of Guelph by Professor William Brown, an arboriculturalist from Scotland. In Beard's classic book on the vegetation of the Caribbean islands (Beard 1949), there is also a discussion of forest restoration activities in the early 1900s. In wetlands, the use of *Spartina angelica* for "reclamation" of coastal mud flats was also of interest early in the last century (Chung 1982). In the 1930s, the British blocked drainage ditches and used portable pumps to raise water levels in the Woodwalton Fen (Sheail and Wells 1983).

There is no need for us pretend that restoration is something entirely new to human thinking. We should know something about the historical origins of our scientific discipline. Indeed, it is vital that we learn from past mistakes. What may be new is the scope of the projects and the number of people involved in them.

Currently, restoration ecology has one important potential benefit to the history and development of ecology. This is the potential to bring together a wide range of scientific activities. It challenges conservationists, applied ecologists, and theoreticians in different ways. Conservationists are challenged to shift some energy from protecting remnant fragments of habitat toward the longer-term goal of restoring and reconnecting entire landscapes. The Wild Earth proposal for North America (Wild Earth 1992) is one example. There is now the Society for Ecological Restoration International too. Applied ecologists are being challenged to move from manipulating single species, such as a few species of fish or waterbirds, to the reconstruction of entire ecosystems. Theoretical ecologists are challenged to develop practical tools to guide restoration and monitor its success with indicators.

CONCLUSION

We have covered a lot of ground in this chapter – from the author's own property in Canada to the Everglades to the Danube River to the Yangtze. All of these projects do have certain principles in common. You have seen, for example, that modifying hydrology and fertility can have enormous impacts, positive and negative. If you are going to be involved in restoration yourself, these examples also remind you of the importance of having *clear goals, realistic methods, measurable indicators, and feedback mechanisms (adaptive management).* Let us close this chapter by dealing with each of these in turn. We will spend more time on each in the final chapter.

If restoration is to succeed, it must first have a clear **goal**. This goal is most likely to be obvious if it can be shown as a single map illustrating the desired outcome of the project. Restoration cannot proceed without such a clearly articulated goal. One still sees too many maps of methods, rather than goals.

Maps of ditches, embankments, culverts, and so on are nothing more than a map of expenditures and methods. The map of outcomes shows predicted habitats accompanied by a list of desirable outcomes. If you have the task of evaluating a restoration proposal, looking for a clear statement of the goal is likely to tell you a great deal about the rest of the project. In the author's project (Figure 13.2) an explicit goal is to maintain the number of native species of breeding frogs. In the Everglades (Figure 13.3) an explicit goal is to increase the number of individuals and species of wading birds, both of which require creating wetlands with specific types of plant communities such as wet meadows.

There are many reasons to be careful to state our goals explicitly. First, it keeps us honest: what is it that we are trying to do? It is easy to throw around the word "restoration" without being clear about one's plans. Choosing the right plan requires us to know something about the natural world, and to approach restoration with an attitude of respect and modesty. How do we know if we are on the right track? "A thing is right when it tends to preserve the integrity, stability and beauty of the biotic community. It is wrong when it tends otherwise." This statement by Aldo Leopold (*A Sand County Almanac*, 1949) could be a useful topic of contemplation while planning a restoration project. Being explicit about our goals forces us to think about whether what we are proposing to do is right – *sensu* Leopold.

A good restoration plan also has clearly laid out **methods** that we believe will enable us to achieve our targets. The tools of restoration (ditches, embankments, fires, planting) come into play only once we have set out the goal. Each tool should be aimed to achieve a specific outcome. Each stage of the restoration plan should address which causal factors are being manipulated, and what the projected outcomes are, based upon our best scientific knowledge. However, as noted above, often managers leap to methods before specifying targets. Targets must come first. Once we have decided, say, to reduce salinity in coastal wetlands in Louisiana, large freshwater diversions (Figure 13.10) are one of the methods we can apply. In advance of construction we must decide whether we want fresh water alone, or fresh water with sediment, and whether we will let the river dictate flow volumes or whether we wish to control flow volumes. Costs vary greatly among these methods. Often it may be much cheaper and more effective to simply remove levees as was done along the Danube (Figure 13.5).

To know whether we are making progress toward our goals we need measurable **indicators** and their target values. Thus, I have a list of expected species of frogs in my own wetland, and they will be monitored by listening for different mating calls. In the Everglades, a much more expensive monitoring program will track the abundance of wading birds. If certain frogs or birds do not appear, then something has gone wrong. If we set a target, and fail to meet it, we know something is wrong, and we can set about trying to fix it. We will therefore return to the topic of indicators in Chapter 14 to introduce some specific tools that you might use.

Once we have been explicit about our goals, objectives, methods, and indicators, we can proceed. If later experience shows that we have failed to meet our objectives, we can modify our methods, or even go back and question the validity of our targets. This is the period in which monitoring the indicators allows us to modify our management – **adaptive management**. In adaptive environmental management we anticipate that there are likely to be certain failures, and we have back-up plans to address them (Holling 1978; Walters 1997). There is a risk that adaptive management will be used to cover up ignorance and poor planning, of course – Holling himself was very clear that adaptive management did not give a license for simply messing around. But we also, as scientists, have to admit to failure – our knowledge of nature is imperfect. We must do the very best possible job under the circumstances, then modestly admit that failure is still possible – and be prepared for it.

Chapter contents

14 Conservation and management

We have now more or less completed our journey through wetland ecology. We began in Chapter 1 with definitions of wetlands, and then worked through the factors that create different types of wetlands. We have seen how major properties of wetlands like zonation, and the services they provide, are shaped by these causal factors. We have considered how to conduct research and how to restore wetlands. It is now time to conclude. We are left with only a few issues.

First, we need to put the whole topic back together, looking at the current state of wetlands and humans and their interactions. Given that we know the current situation, we can then ask what next: what are our objectives for the coming decades and even centuries? In other words, where are we now, and where do we wish to go from here? That is the focus of this last chapter. It would, however, be careless and misleading to ask these questions without knowing where we have been.

14.1   Humans have greatly changed wetlands

Our current situation has arisen out of past trends. Let us therefore begin by looking at a few selected examples of wetland changes over time. When we look at familiar examples, we are inclined to think that we already understand them. Therefore, I have also chosen examples that will be less familiar and may well provide some useful insights for the future.

14.1.1 Mesopotamia

Let us now return to the ancient tale of Gilgamesh with which we opened Chapter 2. This takes us back to the pre-scientific era when people were living on floodplains, and harvesting resources, but where science and mythology had not separated. Several important books have suggested that humans have rarely been wise enough to manage their resources sustainably (Tuchman 1984; Wright 2004; Diamond 2005). So, with this in mind, let us return to *The Epic of Gilgamesh* (Sanders 1972) from Chapter 2, a flood story that appears to both pre-date, but also influence, the flood story in the Bible. It may be significant that in an early part of the epic, Gilgamesh and his companion Enkidu travel to a mysterious cedar forest (probably in north Syria or southwest Persia [now Iran]): "They gazed at the mountain of cedars, the dwelling-place of the gods . . . The hugeness of the cedar rose in front of the mountain, its shade was beautiful, full of comfort . . ." (p. 77). They encounter a monstrous guardian of the forest, Humbaba, whom they kill with their swords. "They attacked the cedars, the seven splendours of Humbaba were extinguished" (p. 83). *The Epic of Gilgamesh* therefore records an early episode of deforestation. Those of us familiar with the role of forests in wetlands will not consider it coincidental that four chapters later the gods, including Ninurta, the god of wells and canals, are "cowering like curs" as a flood sweeps downstream.

Thousands of years later humans are still interacting with wetlands in this area. The area, once the land of Gilgamesh and King (Chapter 2) was known for many years as Mesopotamia. The enormous Tigris–Euphrates river system in Iraq and Iran supports several enormous marshes, collectively called the Mesopotamian marshlands (Partow 2001) (Figure 14.1). The wetlands are dominated by enormous stands of reeds (*Phragmites australis*), with cattails (*Typha angustifolia*) at the margins. Seasonally flooded zones are often saline, and have typical wetland genera including *Carex*, *Scirpus*, and *Juncus*. At least 134 bird species have been recorded, and 18 of these are globally threatened. Three species, the Iraq babbler, Basra reed warbler, and gray hypocolius, breed here almost exclusively. Wading birds included the sacred ibis and the Goliath heron. The native lions have been exterminated but gray wolves still occur. There are also indigenous human populations, the Ma'dan or marsh Arabs, who live in reed huts.

These wetlands are now being disrupted by many forces acting simultaneously. Over the last century 32 enormous dams have been constructed, with eight more under construction and 13 more planned (Partow 2001; Lawler 2005). One of the largest dams is Turkey's Ataturk Dam. The cumulative effect of these dams allows storage of five times the volume of the entire flow of the Euphrates. The consequences for downstream wetlands include those you would expect from earlier chapters in this book: a loss of spring flood peaks, reduced flow, increased salinity, and decreased sediment. The marsh area in 1973 to 1976 was between 8926 km^2 (about the original size of the Everglades), but had shrunk to 1296 km^2 in 2000. Up to this point, the story is one typical of many riverine wetlands described in Chapter 2: widespread destruction attributable mainly to altered flow regimes.

An added problem for these marshes was the effects of the brutal war fought between Iraq and Iran from 1980 to 1988. Since the marsh Arabs were viewed as potential allies of the Iranians, Saddam

FIGURE 14.1 The Mesopotamian marshes (top; © Nature Iraq) have been affected by humans for thousands of years, most recently by drainage, dam construction, and warfare (bottom; from Lawler 2005). *Phragmites* reeds are the mainstay of marsh culture, being used as housing material, woven into mats, and fed to water buffalo. (See also color plate.)

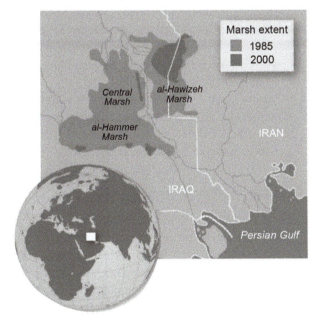

Hussein began to deliberately drain the marshes to force the marsh Arabs to leave the border area. Pearce (1993) describes how as part of this activity, in 1993 Saddam's engineers diverted almost the entire flow of the Euphrates into a 560-km long drainage canal (known as the Third River). Construction was often carried out in a brutal manner: "artillery initially bombards a district where engineering works are planned, so as to clear the local population; troops move in, to secure the district ... Once a section has been completed, mines are laid to protect the embankments from attack."

As a consequence of the new dams and the deliberate drainage, the vast Central Marsh which covered 3000 km^2 in 1973 had shrunk by 97%. As the marsh area fell, there were catastrophic effects upon other species. A subspecies of otter, the bandicoot rat, and an endemic bat became extinct (Lawler 2005). Some half million marsh Arabs became environmental refugees and many ended up in refugee camps (Partow 2001).

When Saddam Hussein was overthrown in 2003, "local residents jubilantly broke open the dikes and dams, reflooding nearly half of the marshes" (Lawler 2005). The degree to which the marsh will recover from Saddam Hussein's actions is still unclear. There is now the enormously increased capacity of dams constructed upstream. As well, some of the marsh Arabs have become accustomed to agriculture involving sheep, wheat, and cattle, and may object to restoration. And the boundary between Iraq and Iran continues to be a site of political tensions. Will it be possible to protect and restore these wetlands, or will they succumb to the combined effects of deforestation, dams, levees, roads, and warfare?

14.1.2 The Roman Empire and the Tiber River

The Roman Empire was one of the greatest empires the world has seen – and the Romans had problems with wetlands. The Roman civilization originated with the Etruscans, who "reclaimed Tuscany from forest and swamp" and built drainage tunnels to take the overflow from lakes (Durant 1944). The early history of Rome is little known, in part because the Gauls burned the city in 390 BC, presumably destroying most historical records. Although Rome was built on seven hills, it was not a healthy location: "rains, floods and springs fed malarial marshes in the surrounding plain and even in the lower levels of the city" (Durant 1944, p.12) but Etruscan engineers built walls and sewers for Rome, and "turned it from a swamp into a protected and civilized capital." One of the main sewers, the Cloaca Maxima, was large enough that wagons loaded with hay could pass

beneath its arches; the city's refuse and rainwater passed through openings in the streets into these drains and then into the Tiber, "whose pollution was a lasting problem in Roman life" (p. 81). Meanwhile, deforestation occurred apace to provide building materials and fuel. It is unlikely to be a coincidence that the Tiber "was perpetually silting its mouth and blocking Rome's port at Ostia; two hundred vessels foundered there in one gale … About 200 BC vessels began to put in at Puteoli, 150 miles south of Rome, and ship their goods overland to the capital."

The deforestation of the Mediterranean hills led to changes in forests, hillsides, streams, springs, valleys, and wetlands (Thirgood 1981). Some 100 years later Julius Caesar had great plans "to free Rome from malaria by draining Lake Fucinus and the Pontine marshes, and reclaiming these acres for tillage. He proposed to raise dykes to control the Tiber's floods; by diverting the course of that stream he hoped to improve the harbour at Ostia, periodically ruined by the river's silt" (p. 193). These plans were cut short when he was assassinated by a group of conspirators in 44 BC who saw in these and other ambitions the seeds of a potential monarch.

The problems of sedimentation in harbors continue 1000 years later – how much silt and burial is needed to maintain deltas and coastlines, particularly in an era which seems to include rising sea levels?

14.1.3 The Rhine and the Low Countries

The Low Countries of the Rhine delta also illustrate the long history of human interference with wetlands in Europe. The Netherlands are the delta of the Rhine river, which like most European rivers, once had extensive floodplain forests dominated by woody species such as *Acer pseudoplatanus*, *Fraxinus excelsior*, *Populus alba*, and *Quercus robur*. Altogether there may be some 40 tree species, depending upon flooding frequency and soil type (Szczepanski 1990; Wiegers 1990). Higher frequencies of flooding produce *Alnus* or *Salix* thickets. The long history of human activity such as agriculture, logging, drainage, and diking have

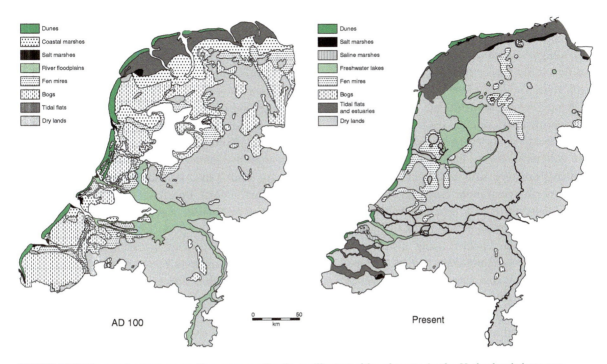

FIGURE 14.2 Human impacts upon European wetlands, as illustrated by changes in the Netherlands between AD 100 and the present. (From Wolff 1993, after Zagwijn 1986.)

eliminated most floodplain forests; in Poland, for example, only 1–2% of the landscape can be considered forested wetlands (Szczepanski 1990).

After the last Ice Age, levels of the North Sea rose rapidly, and about 6000 BP a system of barrier beaches formed along the coast (Figure 14.2). Sediments from the Rhine gradually filled the tidal basin behind the barrier coast, allowing marsh vegetation to develop. These marshes gradually changed into ombrotrophic raised bogs. In areas with higher tidal fluctuations, or less sediment, estuarine conditions persisted, and salt and brackish marshes formed, with fresh marshes and peat bogs developing at the landward. Closer to the Rhine and the Meuse, swamp forests and freshwater tidal areas formed.

Around AD 1000 years ago colonists were attracted here to build dikes and polders and reclaim bogs. In the coastal region, dikes were built first to defend farmland from flooding and then to extend the area of arable land. The Frisians in particular specialized in such work, followed by the Flemings

and Hollanders, who extended their practices inland to the Elbe plain in Germany. The system consisted of digging drainage ditches to lower the water table, at first for cattle grazing and then for arable farming. Colonists were given permission to cut drainage ditches as far back from common watercourse as they wished. Thus by the twelfth and thirteenth centuries, a large area of peat bog plains was converted for agriculture. At the same time, water boards were established to co-ordinate building of dikes (van de Kieft 1991).

Drainage of peatlands is followed by subsidence, particularly if the peatlands are also burned to provide extra nutrients for agriculture. This necessitated the constriction of dams and dikes. Eventually, as sediment was deposited along watercourses, and subsidence continued, the river channels increased in elevation relative to the land behind the embankments (Wolff 1993). In the fourteenth and fifteenth centuries, large areas of agricultural land were lost to flooding (e.g. the

Dollard estuary: 150 km² inundated in the fourteenth to fifteenth century; the Biesbosch freshwater tidal area: 300 km² inundated in 1421; the Reimerswaal tidal flats in the Oosterschelde estuary: 100 km² in 1530). Thus, over 50% of the land area in the present Dutch province of Noord-Holland changed into lakes or disappeared back into the sea between the tenth and fourteenth centuries. This process was reversed again with technological improvements in the seventeenth century, with drainage of coastal areas reaching a maximum in the twentieth century. The present landscape reflects these extensive changes in hydrology and vegetation (Figure 14.2). There are now several hundred polders along this coast. Many occur on peatlands along rivers and are drained by pumps; others are now raised above sea level by siltation and are drained by sluice gates at ebb tide. The Zuiderzee, originally an estuary of the Rhine River, was divided in half in 1932 by a barrier dam, and the inner sections turned into four large polders fed with fresh water by the IJssel River.

During the First World War, Belgian engineers deliberately flooded parts of nearby Belgium in the Yser district by sea water in order to slow the advance of the German army. In his treatise, *Animal Ecology*, Elton (1927) summarizes work by Massart from ca. 1920:

The sea-water killed off practically every single plant in this district, and all available places were very soon colonised by marine animals and plants … When the country was drained again at the end of the war, … the bare sea bottom was colonised by a flora of salt-marsh plants, but these gave way gradually to an almost normal vegetation until in many places the only traces of the advance and retreat of the sea were the skeletons of barnacles (*Balanus*) and mussels (*Mytilus*) on fences and notice-boards, and the presence of prawns (*Palaemonetes varians*) left behind in some of the shell holes. (pp. 24–25)

In 1970 the Haringvliet area was separated from the North Sea by a dam with 17 sluices, and, as a consequence, the daily water table fluctuations declined from ca. 150 to 30 cm. Salt marsh and brackish marsh communities disappeared within a few years. The current vegetation is largely controlled by grazing and flooding regimes, with *Phragmites* and *Scirpus* still present in wetter areas and *Agrostis stolonifera* in heavily grazed areas (van der Rijt *et al.* 1996).

The Wadden Sea, an estuarine environment that forms the northern coastline of the Netherlands, is incompletely separated from the North Sea by barrier islands. Some 1200 km² was designated for nature protection in 1982. De Groot (1992) has applied his system of wetland services to the Wadden Sea, of which 45% is in this protected area. Regulation services include moderating the climate and increasing precipitation on the adjoining land, primary production, and storage and recycling of nutrients. Production services include the yields of crustaceans and shellfish for human consumption, as well as sand and shells for construction. Estimating (de Groot 1992, p. 215) that all services together give goods and services in excess of US$6000/ha per year, he concludes that many tidal areas in the Netherlands have been carelessly damaged, and "Although the Dutch Wadden Sea, compared to other wetlands, is relatively well-protected and managed, it to is still threatened by many development plans and ongoing harmful human activities such as pollution and military training." (p. 218)

Overall, then, thousands of square kilometers of peatlands, salt marshes, and shallow lakes have been lost. Further nutrients and contaminants are carried into the area by the Rhine River. The remaining wetlands, however, occupy a key position on the West Palearctic flyway, and some 16% of the Netherlands is still classified as internationally important wetland (Best *et al.* 1993; Wolff 1993). These reserves "occur as small isolated patches in a matrix of agricultural land or as complexes formed by peat dredging, diking of oxbow lakes, etc." (Verhoeven *et al.* 1993, p. 33). In such small landscapes, hydrology is carefully controlled for the purpose of optimizing agricultural production in adjoining fields. Further, the remnant wetlands are being enriched with nutrients from four sources

(Verhoeven *et al.* 1993): atmospheric deposition, surface water flow from heavily fertilized agricultural areas, inputs from eutrophic river water, and infiltration of contaminated groundwater. The multiple factors of drainage, hydrological stabilization, eutrophication, grazing, and pollution pose a major challenge to conservation managers.

When Goethe (1831, p. 222) introduced Faust, the alchemist who sells his soul to the devil, he allows Faust to repent and aspire to carry out good works:

Below the hills, a marshy plain
infects what I so long have been retrieving:
that stagnant pool likewise to drain
were now my latest and my best achieving.

The Netherlands are of some interest because they illustrate land use changes in Europe as a whole, because they represent a delta of a major European river, and because they are well studied. At the other end of Europe, Greek wetlands face similar threats: 63% of wetlands have been lost and surveys report that more than half of all wetlands (and 100% of deltas) have experienced declines in water quality (Zalidis *et al.* 1997). Many others have been altered by changes in the water regime or loss of area. The extensive number of published papers on wetlands in the Low Countries (and even this section of the book) could be quite misleading: it should be borne in mind that the Netherlands comprise only 0.3% of the total area of Europe, and only 0.02% of the land area of the world (Wolff 1993). In spite of these facts, the number of papers on the Netherlands appears to outnumber the attention paid to the Pantanal, the Amazon, and the Niger.

These few examples from the history of human impacts upon wetlands suggest that little has changed from the Tiber and Rhine of antiquity to the Parana (Chapter 1) and Amazon (Chapter 4) of modernity. But there are two possible sources of cautious optimism. First, while Europeans have badly damaged their own wetlands through several millennia of landscape modification, there is no essential reason to slavishly repeat these steps elsewhere. One can hope that other regions can learn from, rather than carelessly emulate, the European experience. Second, the scientific understanding of wetlands, while still incomplete, is vastly greater than it was in the days of the Etruscans. Whether human attitudes can change and science can advance to the point where we can avoid past mistakes is one of the unanswered questions of the new millennium. It certainly extends well beyond the specific problems facing wetlands.

14.2 Wetlands have changed with time

Although humans have been a principal cause of change, particularly in the last century with expanding population and technology, we are not the only cause of change. Wetlands have existed for millions of years. If nothing else, they have changed as the fauna and flora of Earth evolved. Coal swamps dominated by *Lepidodendron* trees (Figure 11.6) no longer exist. But even these coal swamps were exposed to prolonged wet and dry periods (Figure 14.3).

When we look at a reconstruction of a coal swamp like Figure 11.6, it may seem foreign. Perhaps we feel like a peatland ecologist encountering a mangrove swamp. But if we were to look more carefully, we would probably discover that the same processes we have seen in this book were occurring then. Water level fluctuations. Fertility gradients. Disturbance. Herbivory. Primary production. Decomposition. Carbon storage. Methane production. In many ways, then, these wetlands were very similar to those of today. We must learn to seek the similarities in process at the same time as we appreciate their differences; without this, we will slide into geographic, taxonomic, and methodological Balkanization.

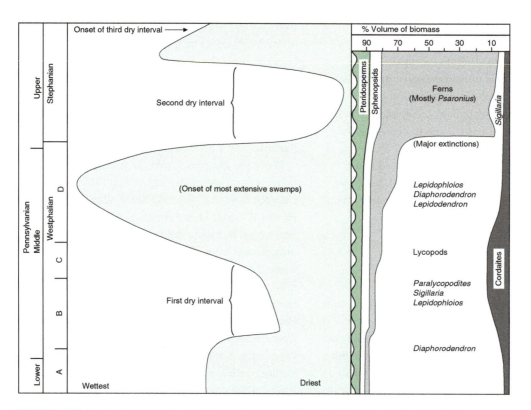

FIGURE 14.3 Wetlands have changed through time, as illustrated by the origin and disappearance of coal swamps and their associated flora and fauna. (From Stewart and Rothwell 1993.)

One need not look back millions of years to find the ebb and flow of waters. Over merely the last 30 000 years, the world has seen the formation of great pluvial lakes in Africa, southwestern North America and Australia (Figure 14.4). Most of these are now gone, although remnants persist, like Great Salt Lake in Utah and Lake Mackay in Australia. In Africa pluvial lakes reached their maximum extent around 9000 BP; in North America, between 24 000 and 12 000 BP, and in Australia earlier still, perhaps 30 000 to 26 000 BP (Flint 1971; Street and Grove 1979). Imagine the extensive areas of wetlands, and the clouds of migratory waterfowl, that must have once occupied areas of the Earth that are now sand flats or remnant saline lakes. Our own millennium appears to be one of the most arid in the late Quaternary (Figure 14.5). If at times we despair about the impacts of our own species upon wetlands,

perhaps Figures 14.4 and 14.5 can put it somewhat in a larger perspective.

Wetlands change at shorter timescales too, timescales that can be easily measured in human generations. Figure 11.8 showed the changes in a European wetland as human civilization developed there. Figure 14.6 shows the estimated impacts of aboriginal civilizations on their landscape in the Americas. Figure 14.7 shows us change on a shorter timescale still – the time over which Europeans arrived and modified wetlands in eastern North America.

Humans often fear change, and so we stabilize lake water levels, build dams to stop spring flooding, channelize rivers, and put riprap along eroding river banks. As wetland ecologists we need to overcome these fears and learn to work with change. This does not mean that we must accept that all changes

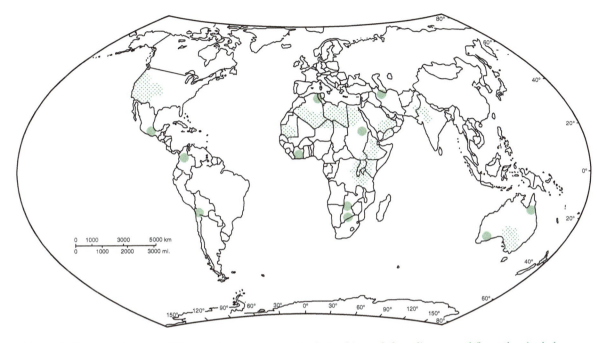

FIGURE 14.4 Over the last 30 000 years pluvial lakes have formed in and then disappeared from the shaded regions of the Earth. Well-known examples include Great Salt Lake in North America and Lake Mackay in Australia. Dots show isolated lakes. (After Street and Grove 1979.)

wrought by humans are desirable, or even acceptable. But as Botkin (1990) reminds us, and as Figures 14.2–14.7 show, working with naturally dynamic systems is the situation with which we must contend.

We need to learn to work with, not against, change in wetlands and other wild places. The third principle of wetland ecology that I introduced in Chapter 1 is *the multiple factors that produce a community or ecosystem will change through time.* Change in wetlands is nothing new. Many examples of change have been presented in this book: Amazonian wetlands responding to river erosion and deposition (Figure 4.5), the Florida Everglades responding to natural fires and droughts (Figure 4.6), Californian salt marshes changing with salinity and rainfall (Figure 4.23), deltas changing shape with changes in river channels and hurricanes (Figure 4.18). Practicing science and conservation in the light of ecosystem change has been discussed at

greater length in *Discordant Harmonies* (Botkin 1990). The basic conclusion is that there are no easy answers. Humans can damage ecosystems by suppressing natural dynamics, just as much as they can by causing change by damming rivers, diking salt marshes, and draining peatlands. This is one reason why natural area systems need to be large enough for us to allow natural process such as flooding, erosion, and fire to continue without interruption.

Of course, one of the difficult problems in conservation and management is to decide which changes are acceptable and which are not. Allowing meander systems to evolve in a floodplain would seem acceptable; allowing exotic species such as purple loosestrife, water hyacinth, or nutria to spread is unacceptable. One allows a natural process to continue, the other causes a rapid change that is not intrinsic to particular wetlands. The difference will not always be so clear.

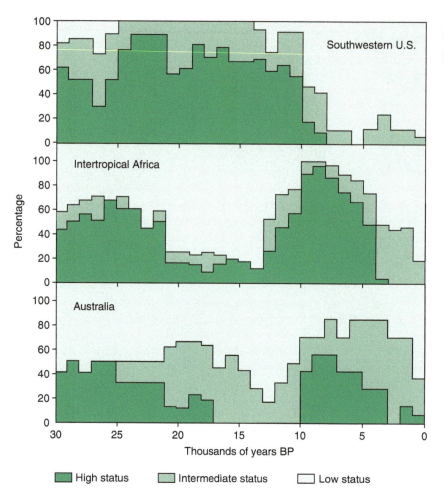

FIGURE 14.5 Lake levels for the past 30 000 years in three parts of the world. (After Street and Grove 1979.)

14.3   Two views on conservation objectives

In order for wetlands to continue to provide services to humans, we must keep wetlands in our landscape. Let us see how this is being done, and what more might be done in future. Overall, we could say that there are two perspectives on conservation of wetlands. They start from different views, but in practice tend to arrive at more or less similar results.

One view puts the focus on services. That is, we could think of wetlands as little more than living factors that provide services to humans. From this

view, our task is to maintain the services. These might include flood control, water purification, muskrat or duck production, recreation, and so on. So long as these services are performed, we have achieved our management goal. The fact that they are bogs, fens, and swamps, with different plant and animal species, and different rates of disturbance and fertility, may be less important.

The other view puts the focus on more intrinsic values, as natural communities of living organisms. In order to protect them, we strive to maintain the

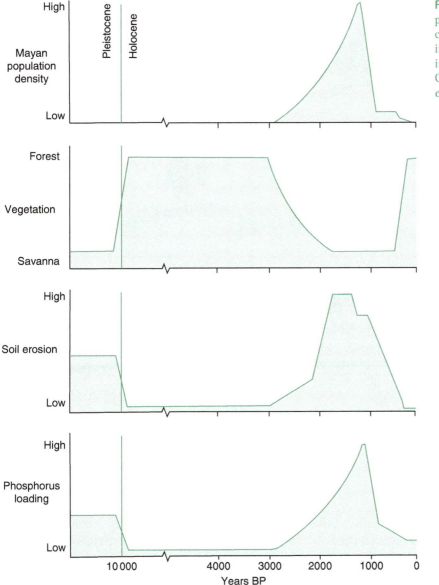

FIGURE 14.6 Aboriginal populations in America caused significant increases in erosion, as illustrated by impacts of the Mayans in Guatemala. (After Binford *et al.* 1987.)

patterns and processes within individual wetlands. One might even argue that they have a right to exist, just as our own species does. So long as we protect the full array of bogs, fens, and swamps with their normal complement of species, we argue, one may also assume that they are providing the needed services.

Both views can work together. Most wetlands, of course, have multiple services: a single wetland will have a role in controlling hydrology, yielding wildlife, producing methane, fixing nitrogen, and supplying human recreation. Since wetlands do perform multiple services, one of the most thorny problems of management is ensuring that

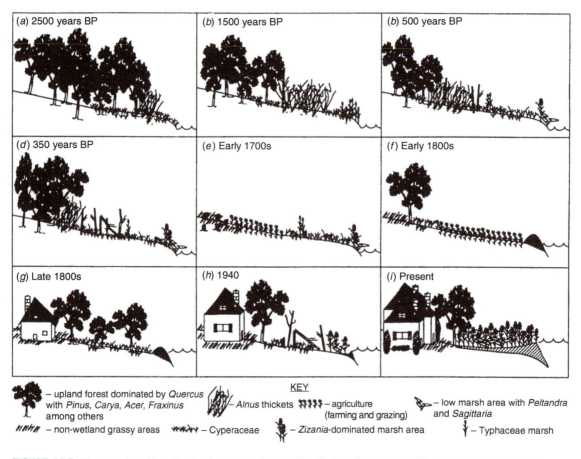

KEY

– upland forest dominated by *Quercus* with *Pinus, Carya, Acer, Fraxinus* among others

– *Alnus* thickets

– agriculture (farming and grazing)

– low marsh area with *Peltandra* and *Sagittaria*

– non-wetland grassy areas

– Cyperaceae

– *Zizania*-dominated marsh area

– Typhaceae marsh

FIGURE 14.7 Changes in a New England salt marsh associated with the arrival of Europeans. (From Orson *et al.* 1992.)

management for one service or goal does not cause loss of other equally important services. Humans being what they are, it is all to easy to focus upon a single problem, a single service, or a single species, and ignore everything else.

Given the high rates of endangerment and extinction (Figure 9.25) let us look at maintaining biodiversity. Maintaining biodiversity is a service that we explored in Chapter 9. Moreover, the very presence of specific plant and animal groups can be treated as an indicator that other services are continuing to occur.

There is a further urgent reason to focus on maintaining diversity. Ehrlich and Ehrlich (1981) describe the loss of species from communities as being analogous to the loss of rivets from the wings of an aeroplane. A certain number of rivets can be lost without the wings falling off because there is some redundancy of function, but eventually if too many are lost, the function declines. As a first approximation, we may assume that most ecological services of wetlands are carried out by more than one species; this is why species fall naturally into functional groups. If one species is lost, another may perform its role. But if too many are lost, that service is no longer performed. The degree of redundancy, and hence the safety margin, is still an unknown.

14.4   Protection: creating reserve systems

Our first challenge is to ensure that significant areas of wetland are protected from further degradation. Once these areas are protected, the next generation of managers will have to grapple with their wise management; the first task in setting up reserve systems is to make their future jobs as easy as possible. In this section we will take a closer look at the creation and maintenance of reserve systems.

14.4.1 A reserve system includes core and buffer areas

One of the most important steps is finding the core areas that will provide the foundation for the reserve system (Table 14.1). The next task is to ensure that each is shielded by an appropriate buffer zone (Figure 14.8). The design of reserves, and of reserve systems, is a topic which itself deserves an entire book (e.g. Shrader-Frechette and McCoy 1993; Noss and Cooperrider 1994). Here is a brief introduction, based largely on Noss (1995).

Beginning with the **core protected areas**, the size of each protected wetland should be large enough to retain the diversity of wetland types and full array of species present. The well-documented relationship between species and area (Chapter 9) shows that in general, the bigger the site, the more species that are likely to be protected. Big areas have two particular merits. Big areas are important to maintain large predators that have large territories and are highly mobile (Weber and Rabinowitz 1996). As well, the bigger the site, the greater the possibility that natural processes can continue to generate habitat diversity. An alluvial wetland reserve, for example, ought in principle to be large enough to allow for flooding and bank erosion to continue unabated. If these processes are missing, it may be impossible to retain the biological characteristics of the reserve, and it certainly will compound the difficulties and costs of management.

Table 14.1 **Some factors to guide the selection and prioritizing of wetlands for conservation**

Factor	Comments
Size	Most ecological services increase with area
Naturalness	Minimal alteration to natural patterns and processes
Representation	An example of one or more important ecosystem types
Significance	Relative regional or global importance
Rare species	Significant species present
Diversity	Many native species present
Productivity	Production of commercial species
Hydrological services	Flood reduction, groundwater recharge, springs
Social services	Ongoing use in education, tourism, recreation
Carrier services	Contribution to global life-support system: oxygen production, nitrogen fixation, carbon storage
Food services	Harvesting for human consumption
Special services	Spawning, breeding, or nesting area; migratory stopover
Potential	Suitability for restoration
Prospects	Probability of long-term survival: future threats, buffer zones, possibilities for expansion, patrons, supporting organizations
Corridors	Existing connections to other protected areas; site itself is a corridor
Science services	Published work on site, existing use by scientists, existing research station, potential for future research

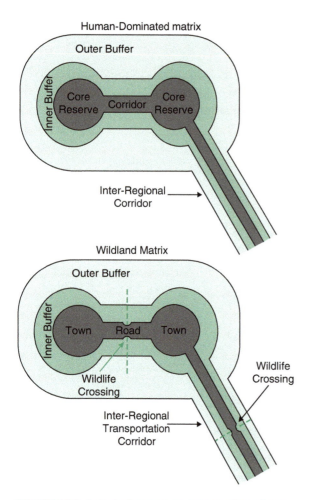

FIGURE 14.8 A typical reserve system consists of core areas surrounded by buffers and linked by corridors (top). In wilder parts of the world, the cities themselves may be surrounded by buffers with a matrix of wild lands (bottom). (From Noss 1995.)

Many other factors can be used to select core protected areas including naturalness, significance, rare species, ecological services, and value for research (Table 14.1).

The protected wetlands should **represent** habitat types than are of significance at the local, regional, or global scale. They may represent common wetland types or rare wetland types. Protection of both kinds of wetlands are complementary objectives for setting up reserve systems. At this scale, each wetland needs to be considered in the context of surrounding wetlands: are there examples of similar quality already protected? Are there more important wetland types that are not yet protected? Answers to these questions are often found through **gap analysis**, a process of identifying gaps in wetland type representation in a reserve system. Algorithms now exist to evaluate different reserve scenarios in order to maximize the value of a reserve system (Pressey *et al.* 1993). The objective is to define the smallest number of areas needed to achieve certain goals, such as providing one, two, or three protected examples of each species, or each community type.

Each core area needs to be surrounded by a **buffer zone** where land use practices are regulated to higher standards than elsewhere in order to ensure that nutrients, pollution, or exotic species are not carried into the protected site from immediately adjoining areas. Biosphere reserves (regions recognized internationally by UNESCO) provide an example of such an arrangement with protected core areas such as a national park surrounded by larger landscapes in which human use includes consideration for the viability of the core area.

Although we usually view reserves as cores surrounded by buffers, in some wild places, we may wish to turn the model inside out. That is, we may wish to treat our settlements as isolated units, and put a buffer around each settlement to ensure that the remaining landscape stays wild (Figure 14.8, bottom). We could also look at this as a longer-term model for landscape restoration, where cities and farms fit into a matrix, surrounded by wild places and supported by the services they provide.

14.4.2 Reserves are linked by corridors

The reserves must be connected with corridors so that dispersal can occur from one reserve to the next. As reserves become increasingly smaller and more isolated from one another, dispersal becomes increasingly constrained and species become increasingly broken into metapopulations with the dynamics typical of island species (MacArthur and Wilson 1967; Hanski and Gilpin 1991; Hanski 1994).

Table 14.2 The international classification for protected areas developed by IUCN

Category I: Strict Nature Reserve/Wilderness Protection Area An area of land and/or sea possessing some outstanding or representative ecosystems, geological, or physiological features and/or species, which is protected and managed to preserve its natural condition.

Category II: National Park Natural area of land and/or sea designated to (a) protect the ecological integrity of one or more ecosystems for present and future generations, (b) exclude exploitation or occupation inimical to the purposes of designation of the area, and (c) provide a foundation for spiritual, scientific, educational, recreational, and visitor opportunities, all of which must be environmentally and culturally compatible.

Category III: Natural Monument Area containing specific natural or natural/cultural feature(s) of outstanding or unique value because of their inherent rarity, representativeness, or esthetic qualities or cultural significance.

Category IV: Habitat/Species Management Area Area of land and/or sea subject to active intervention for management purposes so as to ensure the maintenance of habitats to meet the requirements of specific species.

Category V: Protected Landscape/Seascape Area of land, with coast or sea as appropriate, where the interaction of people and nature over time has produced an area of distinct character with significant esthetic, ecological, and/or cultural value. Safeguarding the integrity of this traditional interaction is vital to the protection, maintenance, and evolution of such an area.

Category VI: Managed Resource Protected Area Protected area managed mainly for the sustainable use of natural resources – area containing predominantly unmodified natural systems, managed to ensure long-term protection and maintenance of biological diversity, while also providing a sustainable flow of natural products and services to meet community needs.

Source: Adapted from Anonymous (1994). *Guidelines for Protected Area Management Categories.* Gland, Switzerland and Cambridge, UK: IUCN and the World Conservation Monitoring Centre. www.iucn.org/themes/wcpa/wpc2003/pdfs/outputs/pascat/pascatrev_info3.pdfhow. For data on different countries, consult Earthtrends at http://earthtrends.wri.org.

While local extinction from small areas of wetland might be entirely normal given the natural dynamics of wetlands, once reserves become isolated fragments within a landscape, there may be no local populations available to recolonize the site. Species with limited dispersal may be expected to disappear slowly from the entire reserve system. Since many wetlands are linked naturally by rivers, restoring riparian corridors may be a natural means for linking core areas.

14.4.3 Different kinds of reserves comprise the system

Most nations now have systems of protected areas. The names given to areas incorporated vary across regions and also change with management objectives. Designations can include wildlife management areas,

national parks, and ecological reserves. Each kind of protected area has its own set of rules. Some rules provide strict protection, others allow many means of exploitation. To provide a way of comparing how areas are managed, the IUCN (International Union for the Conservation of Nature) has recognized six categories, I through VI, that range from strictly protected areas (I) to sustainably used areas (VI) (Table 14.2).

For wetlands in particular, there is an added category of protection – recognition under the Ramsar Convention on Wetlands (Figure 14.9). Ramsar, by the way, is not an acronym. It is the name of the city in Iran where this important international agreement on wetland conservation was signed in 1971. Since then, more than 1800 wetlands totaling more than 180 million hectares have been designated as wetlands of international importance. The Convention has three objectives: working toward

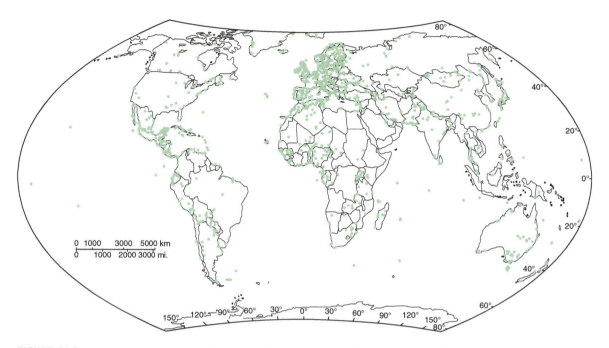

FIGURE 14.9 Ramsar sites designated as of May 2009 according to Wetlands International maps (http://ramsar.wetlands.org/GISMaps/WebGIS/tabid/809/Default.aspx) updated using the Ramsar List of Wetlands of International Importance (www.ramsar.org/sitelist.pdf).

wise use of wetlands, expanding a global ecological network of wetlands, and promoting cooperation across nations and cultures.

Wetlands in western Europe are over-represented under the Ramsar Convention, yet this is the part of the world, where, in general, wetlands are both small and degraded by human activity. We need a shopping list to set future priorities for protected wetlands, and where better to start than with the world's ten largest wetlands (Table 1.3)? Part of the reason for focusing on the largest wetlands was to encourage wetland ecologists to take the largest possible global perspective in planning their conservation strategies. From the global perspective, we must be cautious about spending too much money on the precise management of tiny fragments of wetlands in heavily populated areas if this means that resources are being directed away from globally significant wetlands such as the Amazon or the Pantanal or the Congo.

Setting up reserve systems literally is a race against time. There are growing reasons for optimism at the same time as one is discouraged by the ongoing rates of wetland destruction. Of course, it is possible to acquire degraded habitats and restore them, but this is a poor alternative to protecting areas that are still relatively pristine or that still provide important services.

14.4.4 Protected areas have economic value

One of the major obstacles to protection is the view that protecting ecosystems means withdrawing them from human use and thereby reducing human economic welfare. As we saw in Chapter 11, these areas in fact provide many valuable services. Shrimp and fish production, are, for example, dependent upon salt marshes and floodplains (Welcomme 1976; Turner 1977). For many wetlands, the issue of services may provide economic arguments for preservation. Even if these services are ignored, however, there is a further merit to protected areas; contrary to expectation, it appears that they actually stimulate economic activity (Rasker and Hackman 1996). At the local scale, most homeowners will know that owning a home near or adjoining green space increases the home's value. But let us look at a much larger example. Owing to the importance of this point, it is necessary to spend some time on this example.

Large carnivores such as lions, wolves, and tigers are some of the most difficult species to protect, because they need large areas of habitat. Too often, protection is seen as something that will damage the economy – one is given the rather bleak choices between environment and economy (Rasker and Hackman 1996). That is, there is "a belief that, however, appealing, carnivore conservation is a luxury we cannot afford because the opportunity cost in terms of jobs and resources forgone is too high." This is a commonly heard argument around the world; what may be surprising is the paucity of data for or against it. Rasker and Hackman set out to test this proposition by comparing economic indicators for two regions in northwest Montana. Four counties with large protected areas (Flathead, Lewis & Clark, Teton, Powell) are compared to three resource-extractive counties (Lincoln, Sanders, Mineral). The wilderness counties total some 3.4 million ha (839 000 protected) whereas the resource-extractive counties totaled nearly 2 million ha (33 000 protected). The latter resource-extractive counties were chosen because the conflicts between jobs and environment are intense, and because lumber harvesting and hard rock mining have traditionally played an important part in their economies. Although these are only counties, they are the size of nations in many other parts of the globe. If, indeed, "locking up" land in reserves causes economic hardship, then the counties with protected areas should show reduced economic performance relative to the counties with few protected lands. Figure 14.10 shows the striking results. A range of economic indicators including employment growth and personal income growth were above the U.S.A. and

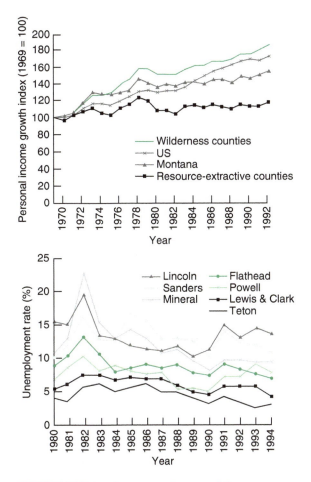

FIGURE 14.10 Employment and personal income growth in four regions: wilderness counties (green), U.S.A., Montana, and resource-extractive counties. (After Rasker and Hackman 1996.)

Montana averages and even more above the means for the resource-extractive counties. "From 1969 to 1992 wilderness counties added new jobs and income in every non-agricultural sector of the economy. The resource-extractive counties lost more than 1300 jobs in the construction, transportation, and public utilities sectors." The resource-extractive counties also suffered from higher unemployment rates. Rasker and Hackman (p. 996) conclude:

The bulk of growth in Greater Yellowstone was in industries that do not rely on natural resources extracted from the ecosystem. From 1969 to 1992 more than 99% of all the new jobs and personal income (and 88% of existing jobs) came from industries other than mining, logging, and ranching or farming ... Research on the economy of the Greater Yellowstone has uncovered a new paradigm for economic development in the West: protection of the wild and scenic character of the landscape and the quality of life in local communities serves as a magnet to retain local people and their businesses. These qualities are a vital part of the economic well-being of local residents...

While neither of these examples is exclusively wetland, they illustrate the possibilities of progress toward protecting large reserve systems that are more than a series of islands in an agricultural landscape. Even if we focus only upon wetlands, intact watersheds are essential to maintaining hydrology and water quality; in a sense, then, any protected wetland really forces managers to focus upon the entire watershed with which the wetland interacts.

Once reserve systems have been organized, there are two further steps: (1) management plans are needed for each site and for the system as a whole, and (2) indicators are needed to provide a method for monitoring whether the management plans are achieving their goals. The next sections deal with the management of protected areas and systems of protected areas. In section 14.8, we will return to the role of indicators.

14.4.5 Maintaining reserve systems

A reserve system is set up to protect the full array of ecosystems, communities, and species that occur in a landscape. If there is systematic change within the reserve system, an entire section of the representativity may be lost. Exactly such a trend has been occurring in wetlands over the last century. Recall that hydrology and fertility are the two key factors that determine the kinds of wetland that occur in a landscape. The variation in hydrology in wetlands has been steadily declining, from factors as

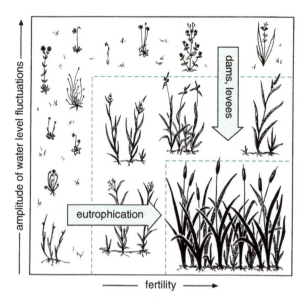

FIGURE 14.11 Human activities have compressed wetlands onto an increasingly narrow array of flooding and fertility regimes, leading to a loss of many wetland types.

diverse as drainage ditches that permanently lower the water table, to levees that prevent floodwaters from spilling onto alluvial marshes, to dams that hold back spring floods. The full array of hydrological regimes on Earth may therefore be converging upon increased stability and reduced variation. In an analogous way, there are systematic trends in fertility: a steady increase driven by eutrophication from sources including sewage from large cities, artificial production of fertilizers, burning of coal, runoff from agricultural landscapes, and atmospheric deposition. There is no need to repeat here the many examples we have seen of these processes, except to note that they are global in extent. Since the wetlands that arise in landscapes are produced by particular sets of hydrology and fertility, and since entire sets of conditions including high flooding levels and low fertility are vanishing from the landscape, we may assume that the corresponding wetland types are vanishing as well (Figure 14.11) That is to say, the array of wetland types within a landscape is being increasingly squeezed into the bottom right of the figure: eutrophic wetlands with relatively stable water levels. The invasion of woody plants into marshes, the disappearance of *Erica* heathlands, the replacement of wet meadows by *Typha* marshes, and the replacement of native species by exotics in infertile wetlands are all special cases of this widespread process of community convergence. Moreover, this change is being driven by two processes that continue largely unabated: the construction of dams, and the deposition of nutrients, as indicated by the large arrows, continue to squeeze wetlands into a progressively narrower region of possibilities. One of the high priorities for management is to reverse this process and re-establish sets of environmental conditions that represent the fuller array of possibilities in a landscape.

All too often, each problem is seen as a special case in a specific wetland. The significance is then misunderstood. For example, in the 1265-page compendium *Freshwater Wetlands and Wildlife* (Sharitz and Gibbons 1989), there are no index entries under fertility, nutrients, eutrophication, nitrogen, or phosphorus. Hence, the broad general risk to wetlands from enrichment is easily overlooked. Another example is the widespread problem of woody plant invasion, which is sometimes explained away as natural succession (Larson *et al.* 1980; Golet and Parkhurst 1981), rather than being seen as a response to degradation in hydrology.

Yet another way of viewing this problem is to envisage it as the removal of certain filters that once produced the structure in communities. Consider the plants first. Removing long periods of flooding removes the filter that kept woody plants at bay, allowing them to invade herbaceous meadows. Removing the filter of infertility allows rapidly growing plants with dense canopies to invade herbaceous meadows. We can already predict the endangered wetland plants of the future; rosette plants (e.g. *Parnassia, Saxifraga, Lobelia*), evergreen plants (e.g. *Erica, Eriocaulon, Lilaeopsis*), carnivorous plants (e.g. *Drosera, Dionaea,*

Utricularia), plants of infertile sands (e.g. *Castilleja, Cacalia, Gratiola*) or eroding shorelines (e.g. *Senecio, Pedicularis, Sabatia*), as well as species that require unusual nutrient ratios, recurring fire, intense flooding, or high grazing pressure. What impact will this have upon animals? Presumably species that forage in wet meadows (like bog turtles, Section 5.9), species that require the above plants to complete their life cycles, insects specialized upon plants with low tissue nutrient levels, reptile species that nest in freshly deposited sands and silts, migratory birds that feed on mud flats around lakes, and, in general, any functional group that tolerates extreme flooding and unusual fertility conditions will be most at risk. Near where I am writing, spotted turtles and wood turtles, which occupy shoreline fens and sandy floodplains, are at risk, as opposed to red-winged blackbirds and Canada geese that nest in cattails and shallow water.

It is likely that so much anthropogenic wetland change has occurred that none of us has ever seen the full array of wetland types that our landscape once possessed. That is to say, our frame of reference – the landscape we grew up with – may already be so altered that it is not a useful reference point for designing and managing reserve systems. Peripheral types of wetlands (as in Figures 5.11 and 5.12) may have already disappeared. This, of course, opens a broad range of possibilities: just what is the array of wetland types we want to protect with a reserve system? Do we aim for the landscape of our childhood, the landscape of the mid nineteenth century, or the landscape that may have occurred before humans appeared upon the scene?

There is no easy answer to such questions (Leopold 1949; Botkin 1990), but one approach might be to consider the array of environmental factors that would have occurred in the landscape before humans modified it. Hydrological and sedimentation models would allow us to determine a mean and standard deviation for both flooding regimes and fertility regimes in a landscape without human impacts. Whether or not managers could ever re-create such landscapes, it would provide a realistic point of reference for management. Imagine such a model for the Rhine River valley; what was the delta once like, and what has this to say about intensive management of remaining wetland fragments? To what extent could large floodplains be removed from human use so that natural flooding regimes could be allowed to re-establish? How would the apparent costs of this balance against the cost of building dams, repairing levees, and repairing the inevitable flood damage? The Rhine or the Mississippi may be too large to start with, but are there watersheds where this process could be started on a more regional scale?

Two challenges facing managers are therefore very clear. The first is to reduce the magnitude of the forces that are still driving wetlands into convergence, that is (1) to maintain the hydrological variation of wetlands and (2) to reduce rates of eutrophication. The second is to reverse the process by re-establishing the type of habitat at the upper left of Figure 14.11; this will require re-establishing infertile conditions and high flood regimes. Re-establishing the full array of wetlands types within a landscape leads naturally to the process of wetland restoration.

14.4.6 Maintaining services in reserve systems

If a landscape contains a full array of wetland types, from raised bog to floodplain forest, it is reasonable to assume, at least as a first approximation, that most services are being performed. The actual rate of performance of each service could be calculated by determining the service on a square-meter basis, and then multiplying by the area of that wetland type in the landscape, a process we saw in many of the examples in Chapter 11. The first principle introduced in Chapter 1 could therefore be rephrased to state: "The services provided by any wetland are controlled by multiple environmental factors acting simultaneously." Determining such quantitative relationships is an important priority in wetland ecology; far too many studies report these services for a single wetland rather than seeking general empirical relationships between basic properties and level of service.

Table 14.3 Some stressors potentially affecting wetlands

enrichment/eutrophication
organic loading and reduced dissolved oxygen
contaminant toxicity
acidification
salinization
sedimentation/burial
turbidity/shade
vegetation removal
thermal alteration
dehydration
inundation
fragmentation of habitat
road-related mortality
over-harvesting
invasive species
coarse woody debris removal

Source: Adapted from Adamus (1992).

One way of summarizing human impacts on services provided by wetland ecosystems is to apply the framework of stressors and responses (e.g. Odum 1985; Freedman 1995). In the preceding chapters we have seen many environmental factors that can change the ecological services or species composition of wetlands. These have ranged from alterations in hydrology through eutrophication to over-hunting of alligators. Each of these human alterations can be considered a stressor, that is, "an environmental influence that causes measurable ecological detriment or change" (Freedman 1995). For each stressor (Table 14.3) we could list the expected changes in wetland service or structure. For example, increasing fertility will lead to increases in wetland production and biomass, but a probable reduction in species diversity.

In conclusion, even if important wetlands receive legal protection, they must still be managed appropriately to retain the services that they perform. This requires action by two quite different groups of people: regulators and managers. Sometimes it appears that scientists are "too conservative in speech and action," leading to confusion among regulators about the true risks of action versus non-action (Maguire 1991). Indeed, "more research" can become a substitute for action. Managers may be even more dangerous than scientists and regulators; where regulators may fail to act, managers may fail to restrain their action. Over my short career as a biologist, I have seen fens diked and flooded for enhancing waterfowl production, rare wetland plant communities flooded to maintain stocks of exotic sport fish, and infertile watersheds fertilized in order to enhance waterfowl production. These are examples of the misapplication of ecological principles, and we shall have to remain on guard for them continually.

14.5 Problems and prospects of reserve systems

The importance of large areas, and interconnected reserve systems, is reinforced by the problems that face managers in trying to protect isolated fragments of habitat. These problems are particularly severe for Europeans, where there has been a long history of human modification of the landscape. This example will likely be unfamiliar to North American readers, but this makes it all the more valuable, since, as population growth continues in North America, the pressures on the landscape will be similar to those in Europe.

Let us consider the fens of eastern England, adjacent to The Wash along the coast with the North Sea (Sheail and Wells 1983). These wetlands extend inland some 60 km from the ocean. The coastal areas are tidal marsh. In uplands, the depth and character of the peat reflects differences in local drainage. In between, along the River Nene, there are more alkaline conditions, and series of lakes created by the meandering river. The largest lake is Whittlesea Mere, which in 1697 was said to be 3 miles (5 km) broad and 6 miles (10 km) long; most of this is less than 2 m deep. The number and area of lakes may have declined since the medieval period onward, and in 1826, Whittlesea Mere dried up completely during one dry summer.

The Domesday survey carried out in 1086 outlined the various rights or privileges on fen lakes, and later documents also drew attention to value for fish production and hunting for waterfowl. Records from the manorial court at Upwood in the 1600s reveal attempts to regulate land use, including rights of grazing in the fen and of excavating turf for fuel. Farmers were forbidden from digging over "10 000 cesses of turf from the fen in one year." Proposals to drain these fens were led by "Adventurers" who in the early 1600s were granted royal charters for ambitious drainage projects; in return for their investment, they received a portion (usually about one-third) of the drained land (Fraser 1973). The fen-dwellers disapproved. Their indigenous culture included fishing, hunting, and communal grazing. Some even objected to drainage in principle, "Fens were made to be fens and must ever continue such" (Sheail and Wells 1983, p. 53). As work proceeded, there were "ugly scenes of riot and physical protest." On one occasion "a crowd of men and women armed with scythes and pitchforks uttered fierce threats against anyone who tried to drive their cattle off the fens" (p. 54). In 1637, a local resident of Ely named Oliver Cromwell became a spokesman on behalf of the fen-dwellers. (Years later, after winning the Civil War, and being declared Lord Protector of England, Cromwell was still mocked by some of his enemies as "Lord of the Fens" [Fraser 1973].)

By the 1700s the number and variety of species had begun to fall. Waterfowl were perhaps over-hunted, distinctive butterflies may have been over-collected, but habitat destruction was probably most important. In 1844 an Act of Parliament combined the drainage of the Huntingdonshire fen with the improvement of watercourses further downstream. It was not until 1850 that the last of the meres, Whittlesea Mere, could be drained. Both windmills and steam scoop wheels were used for further draining fens, and in 1851 it was the first site in England where a centrifugal pump from the Netherlands was used. In the 1890s, according to Sheail and Wells (1983), an observer remarked "all is gone – reeds, sedges, the glittering water, the butterflies, the gypsies, the bitterns, the wild fowl, and in its place ... a dreary flat of black arable land, with hardly a jack snipe to give it a charm and characteristic attraction."

The first attempt at preservation was made in 1910, with the purchase of 137 ha of the Woodwalton Fen. The water table was falling, in part from peat cutting. Woody plants began to invade the fen; some trees had established on the nature reserve as early as the 1860s, and by 1931 most of the reserve was covered by "dense impenetrable thickets of sallow bushes." Hence, drainage ditches were partially blocked to maintain water levels during times of drought, and in 1935 a portable pump was used to raise water from neighboring drains into the reserve during dry weather. It would, of course, be possible to cut out the invading woody plants, but what would be the point if the fen was dried out? Drainage ditches were deepened further after the Second World War, and in 1972 a clay-cored bank was constructed on the northern and western perimeter of the reserve so as to reduce the amount of water percolating out of the reserve into drainage ditches. A photograph in Sheail and Wells (1983) shows a small rectangular plot of land, largely wooded, forlornly surrounded by drainage ditches and agricultural land. The Holme Fen National Nature Reserve, 256 ha set aside in 1952, is some 3 km away. It has some species associated with undrained fenland such as *Calluna vulgaris*, *Erica tetralix*, and *Cladium mariscus*, but it too is being invaded by scrub and trees as the water table falls.

Some 100 km to the east, a similar discouraging history of habitat loss has been described for the Norfolk Broadlands (Moss 1983, 1984). Some 46 shallow lakes, or broads, were created by peat cutting between the ninth and fourteenth centuries AD. Drainage by wind pumps in the late eighteenth and early nineteenth centuries, combined with intensification of agriculture and sewage disposal in the twentieth century, reduced wetland area and caused both the rapid growth of emergent macrophytes and loss of aquatic plants. The Norfolk Broads developed some of the highest total phosphorus concentrations recorded for freshwater lakes in the world (Moss 1983). Further, the coypu (called nutria in the United States, *Myocastor coypus*), a large South American rodent, was introduced for fur farming about 1929; some escaped and by the 1960s there were estimated to be 200 000 wild animals. The inevitable results of these factors has been decreased numbers of species and habitats remaining in the landscape (Figure 14.12).

These fen examples illustrate how very difficult it is to mantain isolated reserves in landscapes with large human populations. Other examples from this book have included the drainage of prairie potholes combined with falling water tables from irrigation, the construction of large dams on rivers, the impacts of grazing and canals in the Pantanal, phosphorus-laden water entering the Everglades, atmospheric deposition of nitrogen in western European heathlands, removal of annual flooding with levees along the Danube and Mississippi, possible changes in fire frequency in peatlands with global warming, and changes associated with rising sea levels. Such examples serve to re-emphasize the need for large reserves, with buffer strips, as part of an interconnected system.

In the longer run, we could restore habitat around existing core areas by re-establishing natural causal factors. Returning to eastern England, the two remnant fens near Cambridge – Holme Fen and Woodwalton Fen – will now become core areas within a 3000-ha restored wetland (Figure 14.13). This will not only add buffers around these reserves, but a corridor linking them, and a larger area of habitat. Traditional uses such as reed-cutting will continue.

Since the area of wildlife habitat is still in decline at the global scale – as illustrated by the rising numbers of species on the IUCN *Red List* (Figure 9.25), the

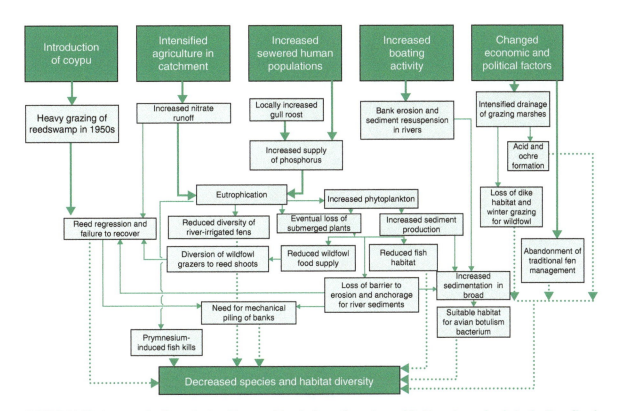

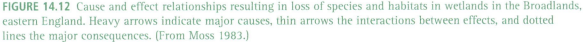

FIGURE 14.12 Cause and effect relationships resulting in loss of species and habitats in wetlands in the Broadlands, eastern England. Heavy arrows indicate major causes, thin arrows the interactions between effects, and dotted lines the major consequences. (From Moss 1983.)

challenge for conservationists and managers is not only to set up reserve systems, but to ensure that within each system, natural habitats continue to be renewed. This requires sufficiently large reserves for natural dynamics to occur, or else increasingly expensive intervention by managers to attempt to simulate these processes. Fortunately, fire and flooding provide two powerful tools for constructing landscapes and generating new patches of habitat. Indeed, these forces might allow us to begin to rebuild wilderness in fragmented landscapes east of the Mississippi River in North America (Figure 14.14).

A modest goal might be protection of 12% of the landscape within reserves (World Commission on Environment and Development 1987). This is, of course, not a definitive number – it was derived by assuming that since 4% of the landscape was reserved at the time, a goal of three times this amount might

be reasonable. "There is a danger that such an ad hoc number will become a standard before we have any evidence that it is sufficient to protect biodiversity" (Sinclair *et al.* 1995). Noss (1995) therefore suggests that after the first steps (mapping out a preliminary reserve network with core reserves, buffer zones, and continuity), one should identify the species with the largest area requirements still extant in the region, and estimate the area needed to provide for both short-term and long-term viable populations of that species. A next step would be to identify the extirpated native species with the largest area requirements that could reasonably be reintroduced, and again estimate area for short-term and long-term survival. If the reserve system is not sufficient to maintain long-term viable populations of these species, plans must be made to enlarge the network or enhance connectivity within the system or to

FIGURE 14.13 The fens of eastern England have been drained at least since the reign of Charles I in the early 1600s. Over 99% have been lost. The Great Fen Project plans to restore 3000 hectares around two core remnants, Holme Fen and Woodwalton Fen (top). (Courtesy The Wildlife Trust, Cambridge.) (See also color plate.)

adjoining regions. Tools like gap analysis allow scientists to survey reserve systems and seek out landscapes that should be added to the system.

The need to re-create habitats, particularly when only isolated fragments remain, is the topic of the next section. The situation in the English fens – or the Everglades, or the Pine Barrens, or the Mississippi delta, or the Sundarbans – illustrate the challenges to be faced in the coming decades.

14.6   More on restoration

Designing a reserve system and managing it appropriately is a challenging mixture of basic and applied science. In Chapter 1, the second principle stated: *to understand and manage wetlands we must determine the quantitative relationships between environmental factors and the properties of wetlands.* Since *wetlands are the product of many environmental factors acting simultaneously,* it follows that we manipulate wetlands by changing one or more of these factors – by changing flooding regimes, by reducing phosphorus in the water

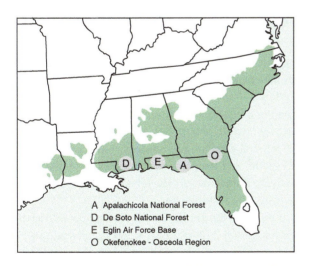

A Apalachicola National Forest
D De Soto National Forest
E Eglin Air Force Base
O Okefenokee - Osceola Region

FIGURE 14.14 Four regions east of the Mississippi River have core areas which could, with restoration, each eventually provide large areas of wetland where flooding and fire occur with minimal human intervention. Such sites would also provide habitat for reintroduction of large carnivores such as red wolves and panthers. The shaded area indicates the natural distribution of longleaf pine (*Pinus palustris*) ecosystems. (From Keddy 2009.)

entering the wetlands, by reintroducing natural grazers, or allowing fire. Each modification of an environmental factor is an act of management. Any management program should be undertaken only with a specific goal in mind, and with an understanding of the known quantitative linkages that allow one to forecast the results of the manipulation. All management should have a clearly articulated goal, because it is only when the goal is articulated that we can later determine whether or not the management has been successful. And what should the goal be? Here we can re-emphasize Leopold's (1949) essay on land ethics with which Noss (1995) begins: "A thing is right when it tends to preserve the integrity, stability, and beauty of the biotic community. It is wrong when it tends otherwise."

Leopold did not explain what he meant by integrity, and although the word is increasingly used by managers, it is still poorly defined (e.g. Woodley *et al.* 1993; Noss 1995; Higgs 1997). Noss is of the opinion that the difficulty in defining integrity does not reduce its value – other terms like justice, freedom, love, and democracy are also vague and slippery, and this has not kept scientists, philosophers, and policy-makers from thinking about them and being guided by their intent (Rolston 1994). Rather than enter this discussion here, let us adopt the view that integrity has three essential components: (1) maintaining biological diversity, (2) ensuring ecosystem persistence through time, and (3) maintaining performance of ecological services. These are all relatively measurable, even if the term integrity is not. All three are also interrelated, in that if diversity declines, services will naturally be impaired. Similarly, the continued performance of services is probably essential for persistence. The proliferation of terms for wise management should not distract us from setting clear goals and ensuring that the best possible science is brought to bear for achievement of those goals.

Managers will rarely inherit a watershed with entirely intact and pristine wetland ecosystems; in most cases there already will have been considerable loss in wetland area, reductions in services, and declines in biological diversity. Two of the principal challenges facing mangers will therefore be (1) deciding to what degree it is possible to reverse these undesirable changes and (2) implementing the programs to make these reversals. In Chapter 13 we saw some of the tools that are available, and some examples of progress.

A principal distinction between North American and European perspectives on restoration and ecosystem management is their different biological reference points: there is a tendency for Europeans to set the goal of maintaining a familiar historical landscape created by humans (e.g. species-rich meadows typical of the eighteenth and nineteenth centuries), whereas the North American tendency is to set the goal of re-creating the ecosystems judged to have been present before humans of European ancestry altered the landscape. Further, Europeans accept intensive management (e.g. cattle grazing, peat-cutting, mowing) whereas North Americans tend to prefer natural controlling factors (erosion, fire, and flooding). One can hope for increasing overlap between these two views of management; in densely populated areas of Asia and North America, there may have to be increasing use of European management experience in order to maintain small examples of desired ecosystem types. Equally, Europeans may begin to value the possibility of managing larger areas of landscape for their original composition rather than for their cultural familiarity.

14.7   So what shall we create with restoration?

Restoration is a growing field of applied ecology. In the United States of America there is a "no-net-loss" policy for wetlands; damage to wetlands is to be avoided, but if damage is necessary, it must be mitigated, which means that compensatory wetlands must be constructed to equal or exceed the services that were performed by the damaged site. More precisely, mitigation is defined as "the avoidance, minimization, rectification, and reduction or elimination of negative impacts or compensation by replacement or substitution" (Office of Technology Assessment, in Zedler 1996). Successful mitigation means "providing a habitat that is functionally equivalent to the one that will be lost" (Zedler 1996), and assumes that ecosystems can be made to order.

The first step is to ensure that replacement wetlands are hydrologically equivalent to the lost wetlands, since hydrology provides the template for the development of the wetland on a site. "Any attempt to replace wetlands with ecologically or hydrologically equivalent types must be based on an understanding of the relationship of individual wetlands to the landscape" (Bedford 1996). The three key hydrological variables, she asserts, are: (1) relative importance of various water sources, (2) mineral element and nutrient content, and (3) spatial and temporal dynamics. This comes close to the first three factors used in this book: hydrology, fertility, and disturbance.

Surveys of the kinds of wetlands being constructed for mitigation (Figure 14.15) suggest that shallow-water wetlands along rivers are relatively easy to create, whereas wet meadows (lacustrine fringe, riverine fringe) are not. Mitigation, while well intended, is therefore actually changing the nature of wetlands in the landscape. This problem is not necessarily restricted to mitigation: restoration could equally lead to such problems if the original distribution of wetland types and controlling factors in the landscape is not used as a reference point

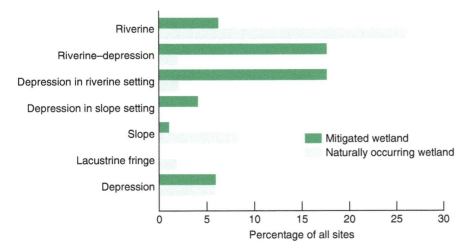

FIGURE 14.15 The relative frequency of seven types of wetland in naturally occurring as opposed to mitigated wetlands. Note that the mitigated wetlands have an over-representation of two types of wetlands, "riverine–depression" and "depression in riverine setting." Other wetland types, such as "slope" wetlands and "lacustrine fringe" wetlands, are rarely re-created. (Data from the northwestern United States; courtesy M. Kentula and U.S. Environmental Protection Agency.)

against which to set the targets and judge the results of individual projects.

Our task at hand is therefore clear: increased protection for wetland habitats around the world, better scientific management of them, and restoration of wetlands in areas where they have been lost. Two further tasks remain. The first is identifying indicators to measure our performance, the second is the systematic application of scientific principles in order to solve practical problems. Consider them in turn.

14.8   Indicators: setting goals and measuring performance

In seeking to re-create, restore, or simply manipulate natural wetlands, we need some procedure to measure success. This procedure must be based upon credible scientific criteria. The number of acres managed, or the amount of money spent, means nothing if the wetlands involved have been damaged by our management.

This is where indicators are helpful, indeed essential (e.g. Keddy 1991a; Adamus 1992, 1996; McKenzie *et al.* 1992; Woodley *et al.* 1993; Tiner 1999). Indicators provide an instrument panel for wetland management. As Tansley said in 1914 (long before the advent of computer controlled recording devices): "The mere taking of an instrument in the field and recording of observations ... is no guarantee of scientific results." At present, we have difficulty in choosing indicators because ecology is not well enough developed as a science to tell us what the essential properties of wetlands are. We can, however, divide the task into three steps: selecting the appropriate state variables for use as indicators, setting critical limits to them, and then testing the indicators in monitoring programs.

14.8.1 Selecting state variables

What properties of communities should we measure to guide our decision-making? In the past, indicators have been developed haphazardly, often reflecting the interests of specific user groups and value systems, rather than according to more broad-scale ecological criteria. This history is reflected in the kinds of databases we currently have. The following criteria might guide our efforts to select indicators.

(1) Ecologically meaningful: closely related to maintenance of essential environmental processes (e.g. water level fluctuations) and ecosystem services (e.g. primary production).
(2) Large scale: measuring the state of entire systems or key processes rather than small pieces or selected species.
(3) Pragmatic: guided by measurable or empirical attributes of systems rather than conceptual or theoretical concepts and notions.
(4) Sensitive: quick response to stresses and perturbations, to minimize lag and give maximum response times for decision-makers.
(5) Simple: easy to measure, therefore inexpensive.

With these criteria in mind, there are at least three categories of indicators (Table 14.4).

Abiotic factors

We might measure abiotic environmental factors that maintain and control the community type. Obvious factors include duration of flooding, water nutrient concentrations, salinity, or road density. We know that factors like these are important in controlling the composition of wetlands and the services they provide. At one time, physical factors alone were monitored. Cairns *et al.* (1992) recall that in 1948, "most pollution assessment was carried out by what were then called sanitary engineers (waste treatment specialists) and chemists. The accepted procedure was that if certain limited chemical/physical conditions were met . . . there was little or no need to examine the biota" (p. ix). Physical factors are likely to be of continued use, particularly in systems where one or only a few physical factors really have an overwhelming importance. Thus, the concentration of phosphorus in lakes (Figure 12.3), or in water crossing the Everglades (Section 13.2.2), is so important that we can learn a great deal by simply monitoring this single factor. The same is likely true of salinity in major deltas like the Mississippi River delta (Figure 8.8).

Table 14.4 Some potential indicators for monitoring wetland management

Abiotic factors
 duration of flooding
 nutrient levels in water (particularly N, P, Ca)
 pH
 dissolved oxygen
 suspended sediment
Biotic factors
 number of species
 number of rare, significant, or threatened species
 selected indicator species
 indices of floristic quality
 indices of biotic integrity
Services
 fish production
 waterbird production
 fur production
 reed production
 water storage

Biotic factors

Measuring biotic factors can have advantages. First, species can integrate the effects of many physical factors, so monitoring the presence of a species or group of species may tell you more than the same effort invested in physical factors. At its most simplistic level this approach uses indicators species, selected species that are particularly sensitive to certain factors thought to be of interest. Carnivorous plants, for example, are indicators of infertile conditions (Section 3.2). Or, looking at Figure 8.18, the presence of forest cover – indicated by green – tells you a good deal about the situation in the Ganges delta. Indeed, forest cover is often an important factor for water quality (Figure 7.17) and wetland quality (Figure 8.13).

Rather than focus on individual indicator species, in many cases it may be useful to assess wetland status or monitor management performance by combining observations on many species. If we measure the sensitivity of plants to an environmental factor (e.g. nutrient levels), pooling the species results for a wetland should provide an indicator of the

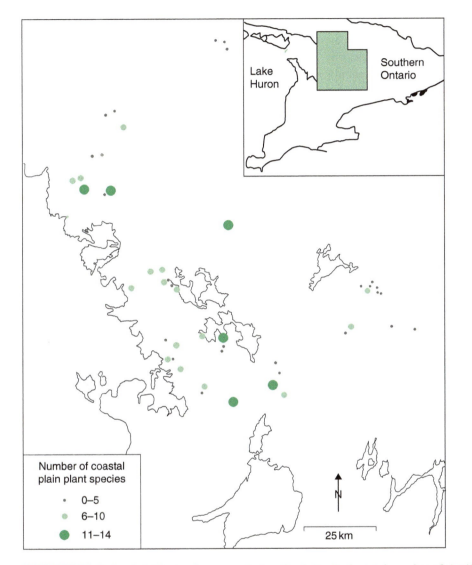

FIGURE 14.16 A simple indicator for comparing wetland sites is the total number of significant species they contain, as in this set of 49 lakeshore wetlands near Georgian Bay, Canada. (From Keddy and Sharp 1994.)

factor's significance for the wetland itself. For example, by adding up the number of significant plant species in lakes, one can rank lakes in terms of the significance of their shoreline wetlands (Figure 14.16). Adding measures of species abundance or global conservation status would provide more information still.

The index of conservatism (Section 12.6.7) is a good example of using information for many species

simultaneously. In this system, you will recall, an expert panel assigns every native plant species a score for how dependent the species is upon natural vegetation types with minimal human alteration. Widespread and common wetland species such as *Phragmites australis* and *Typha latifolia* receive a score of 1, while species that depend upon small fragments of undisturbed habitat like *Platanthera leucophaea* receive a score of 10. To obtain a score for a entire wetland, one makes a complete list of the n species present, and obtains the coefficient of conservatism, C, for each from a reference table. One can then calculate two values. The first, C, is simply the mean coefficient of conservatism: $\overline{C} = (\Sigma C)/n$. The second, the floristic quality index, FQI, is $(\Sigma C)/\sqrt{n}$. These scores provide an objective tool for comparing sites based upon how sensitive the species are to human perturbations, or how likely the site is to represent a system that is relatively unaffected by human perturbations. This is an improvement upon data such as Figure 14.16, since it not only shows how many species are in a site, but how significant they are. In practice, there is likely to be a strong relationship between rare species and those with high degrees of conservatism, at least in regions with highly disturbed landscapes. However, in principle, a species can be highly indicative of pristine conditions without being rare or threatened.

Consider three examples.

In Wisconsin 554 lakes were assessed using C values assigned to 128 emergent and aquatic plants (Nichols 1999). Scores for species ranged from 1 (e.g. *Phragmites australis, Typha latifolia*) to 10 (e.g. *Littorella uniflora, Myriophyllum tenellum, Gratiola aurea*). Over all lakes, the median number of species was 13 (range 1–44), the mean coefficient of conservatism was 6 (range 2–9.5), while the mean FQI was 22.2 (range 3.0 to 44.6). Thus, any specific lake can be ranked relative to other lakes based upon its FQI, and further, with monitoring, changes in the FQI can be tracked through time.

In North Dakota FQI values were used to compare a natural wetland complex with three restored wetlands (Mushet *et al.* 2002). In addition, however, the study used data from 204 wetlands in the region to assist in the evaluation. These wetlands included natural wetlands within native prairie, drained wetlands, and restored wetlands. Restored wetlands generally had lower FQI indices (usually less than 20) than natural wetlands (usually greater than 22), but of course, both were well above highly degraded wetlands. An additional feature of thus study was a comparison of the expert systems approach (using opinions of expert botanists) and with indices of conservatism calculated from the 204 regional wetlands. Both were used to independently calculate measures of conservatism and FQI. The results were so similar that the use of expert opinions alone appears justified in future FQI studies.

More generally, Swink and Wilhelm (1994) suggest that a wetland restoration effort is a success if it can achieve a C of 3.0–3.5 and an FQI value of 25–35 after 5 years. These values, are, however relatively low, since their lower criterion for a significant terrestrial site is 35. In nearby Michigan, areas with FQI higher than 35 are considered significant, while areas above 50 "are extremely rare and represent a significant component of Michigan's native biodiversity and natural landscapes" (Herman *et al.* 2001).

Other state variables

Some of the services that wetlands provide can also be useful indicators. The abundance of commercially valuable species, or harvest yields, can provide information on the status of wetlands. Many have the added advantage of having good historical records. Fish harvests, waterfowl harvests, and oyster harvests are three such examples.

In certain cases, it may be useful to find specific measures of the stress a system is under (Woodwell and Whittaker 1968; Rapport 1989; Odum 1985; Rapport *et al.* 1985; Schindler 1987; Freedman 1995). Ecosystems that are under stress appear to display certain similar responses. These include increased community respiration, increased nutrient loss, decreased diversity of native species, and increased presence of invasive species. In wetlands, indicators of stress might include a decline in the number of obligate wetland species, or increasing abundance of species such as *Typha* or *Phragmites*. In rivers it might be high sediment loads (Figure 7.2) or high nitrate concentrations (Figure 3.8). In lakes it might be a high N : P ratio, or an abundance of algae (Figure 12.3).

Combining indicators

Many wetland evaluation systems combine a series of indicators. The Ontario system introduced in Table 12.1 includes biological, social, and hydrological factors, as well as species features such as rare species and colonial bird nesting sites. In this system, the combined total score allows us to rank wetlands in terms of their significance and quality, up to a total score of 1000.

Let us look at another example, from a part of the world where rare types of wetlands are colliding with urbanization: New Jersey. Here one encounters wetlands that have low fertility, large numbers of significant species including carnivorous plants, and rapid intensification of human land use. What factors might be used as indicators of habitat quality?

To put the data into context, the New Jersey Pine Barrens have arisen on the east coast of North America on top of a vast sand and gravel deposit produced by coastal events dating back through hundreds of millions of years, including deposition by ancient versions of the Hudson River (Gibson *et al.* 1999). About a half million hectares was once dominated by pine–oak forest with patches of ericaceous shrubs and grasslands, as well as pools, bogs, and wet meadows. Fire and flooding played important roles in producing, and maintaining, this vegetation mosaic. Humans have not only altered the system in obvious ways such as logging and urban sprawl, but in far more complex ways, through changing the fire regime, altering hydrology, increasing nutrient levels in the water, drawing down the water table, and constructing roads. Hence, there are multiple factors causing the degradation of wetlands in the Pine Barrens. To explore the effects of humans on the wetlands might require more than one indicator. Thus, as part of an ecological integrity assessment, Zampella *et al.* (2006) combined two physical factors (specific conductance and pH) with measurements of composition including stream vegetation, fish, and frogs. These were collected from 88 locations in the Mullica River basin, and analyzed with multivariate methods. Not surprisingly, the most important factor controlling all of these was the degree of perturbation by humans

(Figure 14.17). As the effects of humans intensify, the number of Pine Barrens species declines, and the number of non-native species increases. The Pinelands typify the conflicts that arise between growing human populations and wild places, and the current status of Pinelands National Reserve could be seen as an uneasy and still-evolving compromise with an unknown future.

14.8.2 Setting critical limits

Once indicators are selected, an added useful step is to set acceptable and desirable levels for them. For each indicator, there would be a range of values specified, one limit being the tolerable level and the other being the desirable. The purpose is to identify a threshold beyond which it is clear that degradation is proceeding. If the system moved outside this specified range, managers would know that remedial action was needed to restore integrity. For example, one might set a goal of zero exotics as desirable for a rare wetland vegetation type, and two exotics as being tolerable. If more exotics than this invaded the site, one would investigate the reasons for the invasion, and then take the appropriate remedial action. Or, as in the Everglades, one might set the upper limit of 10 µg/l phosphorus in the water (Section 13.2.2). The FQI provides another way of accomplishing this with upper values of 50 being highly significant, and lower values of 25 being marginal (Section 14.8.1). In wet meadows, one might specify that biomass values should remain below 200 g/0.25 m^2 (Section 9.4).

In the long run, managers need a handbook that (1) lists major wetland types, and (2) specifies for each the appropriate indicators with their desirable and acceptable levels. Some indicators (e.g. exotics) might have similar levels for all wetland types, whereas others (e.g. amphibian biomass) might have different critical limits for each wetland or habitat type.

14.8.3 Monitoring

Selecting indicators and setting critical limits is obviously part of an evolutionary process. As

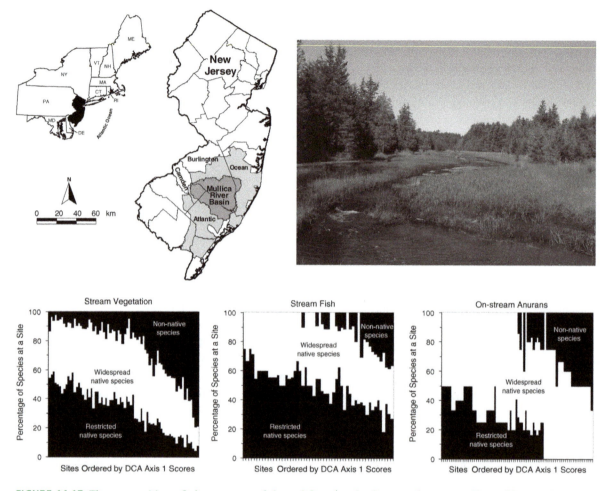

FIGURE 14.17 The composition of plants, stream fish, and frogs/toads changes along a gradient of human impact. These 88 sites from the Mullica River basin in New Jersey are ordered by scores obtained from detrended correspondence analysis (DCA) from least impacted by humans (left) to most impacted by humans (right). (From Zampella *et al.* 2006; photo of Tulpehocken Creek courtesy J. F. Bunnell.) (See also color plate.)

scientific knowledge of community ecology and experience with ecosystem management increase, we need to remain open to changing both indicators and critical limits. Indicators would therefore evolve to reflect our constantly improving knowledge. It is therefore essential to monitor as projects occur, and then to use the information from monitoring to revise criteria for future projects (e.g. Holling 1978; Beanland and Duinker 1983; Noss 1995; Rosenberg *et al.* 1995).

In many cases, of course, the restoration ecologist inherits a perturbed site. In such a case, it is up to the recovery team to decide what the desired composition is, and what indicator levels are intended. That is, the restoration needs explicit targets. These could be based upon historical data from the site, published data from other sites that provide the desired end point, or new data from other less-perturbed sites. One might even choose a different ecological

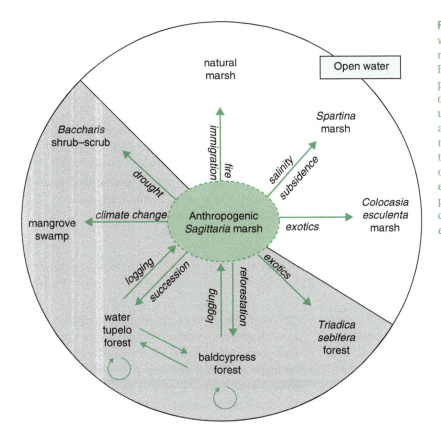

FIGURE 14.18 A perturbed wetland (such as a *Sagittaria* marsh created by logging, Figures 4.16, 6.15; see also color plate) can change into many different future states depending upon the environmental factors affected by human activity. It may be possible to restore the site to cypress swamp (bottom), but other possibilities have to be evaluated and considered, particularly if sea level or river channels change. (From Keddy *et al.* 2007.)

state, perhaps one that is disappearing from the landscape. It is not always clear which target is appropriate.

Consider an example from coastal Louisiana, an area of degraded wetland which was once cypress swamp, and is now herbaceous wetland (Figure 14.18). The current state is a human created (anthropogenic) *Sagittaria* marsh, with multiple drainage ditches. One possible target is to restore the wetland to cypress swamp (bottom). This could require steps such as increasing the input of fresh water and nutrients, controlling herbivory from nutria, and backfilling drainage ditches. It might also require artificial planting or control of invasive exotics. Returning the area to cypress is probably the most desirable option. But there are other

possibilities – a simple one-way reversal to cypress swamp is not the only option. Other options exist and may even be imposed by circumstances. Invasive exotic species such as *Colocasia esculenta* and *Triadica sebifera* may establish their own vegetation types (right). If, for example, rising sea levels will increase salinity, and the construction of new levees will decrease flooding, then another ecological state may have to be accepted, such as brackish marsh, or *Spartina* marsh. If nothing is done, the site may revert to open water (upper right). Depending upon climate, it might even be possible to convert the area to mangroves (left).

Any management program should begin with a thorough understanding of the history of the system, and the possible scenarios for future states. Once the decision is made – that is, once the recovery state is defined – the task of the wetland ecologist is to move the community from the current damaged state back into the desired region. Again, one has to be realistic about what is possible: there is little point, say, in promising freshwater cypress swamp in an area exposed to rising sea levels and expanded levee systems.

Overall, then, we could end up with a shopping list:

(1) Protect representative wetlands in a systematic way.
(2) Plan reserve systems to maintain ecological services.
(3) Provide buffer zones to protect the cores areas.
(4) Provide corridors to link the core areas.
(5) Maintain natural forces that create the wetlands and their surrounding landscape.
(6) Carry out gap analysis to ensure that the system is complete.
(7) Monitor the system and adjust and expand it to ensure continued survival of the species, the wetland types and the ecological services.
(8) Build a body of scientific understanding to allow items (1)–(7) to occur as efficiently and effectively as possible.

14.9 Humans as the biggest problem

Wetlands continue to be damaged by human activities, even in areas that are well recognized as national and international priorities – the Mississippi River delta and the Everglades being but two North American examples. Every part of the world has its own problems. The Yangtze River delta is now being harmed by the Three Gorges Dam, just as the Peace River delta was disrupted some 40 years ago by the Bennett Dam, and new dams are planned for major rivers including the Congo and the Amazon. Such problems rarely arise because of scientific limitations (that is, from a lack of understanding of the external world). Nor do they arise from lack of money. It seems that most wetlands are threatened, in the end, by human attitudes (that is, the inner realm of human thoughts and feelings). Greed and denial are powerful emotional states that we encounter. As scientists we are trained to dissect and analyze living systems with exquisite care, but we can blunder into human interactions like drunken elephants in a minefield.

Our biggest challenge may be managing greed and cronyism. There are good evolutionary reasons why humans always crave more, and why we prefer to work with members of our own tribe, but these two motives in combination may produce disaster (Wright 2004; Diamond 2005). At very least, let us remember that many of the obstacles to wetland research and conservation do not exist in the field where we can measure them with our instruments, but inside the heads of fellow citizens. Wetland management therefore has two separate components (Figure 14.19). If we ignore the left-hand one, we are like a general who will not admit that a minefield or mountain range is an obstacle to his campaign.

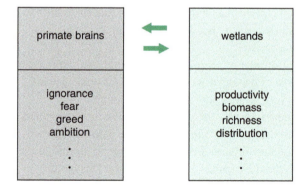

FIGURE 14.19 Wetland conservation and management require not only an understanding of wetlands (right), but an appreciation of human perceptions and motivations (left). There is considerable evidence that humans are incapable of making rational decisions regarding the sustainable use of their own landscapes.

CONCLUSION

We are at a difficult point in human history. Wetlands are increasingly threatened by the activities of our own species. Even if we doubt the likelihood of the most gloomy scenarios such as nuclear war and nuclear winter, or desertification and mass starvation, we cannot doubt the accumulating insidious effects of many less dramatic effects such as deforestation, desertification, soil erosion, drainage of wetlands, and rising rates of extinction. Or the threat of rapid climate change, the melting of the Greenland ice sheet, and the flooding of coastal communities. In this sense, ecologists are like the legendary thin red line of British soldiers; we are a minority who stand between our civilization and the ecosystems upon which we all depend. These ecosystems are mute. We alone provide them with voices. This is a heavy responsibility to bear, and one may wish that instead of being a biologist, one had instead become a lawyer, a small-town doctor, or a store manager.

One may wish that instead of this book one had read a murder mystery or a romance. But given knowledge, we now have the duty to act. We could seek counsel from another professional organization where responsibility, duty, and the exercise of power are valued, the military.

It is an honor to serve in the armed forces ... It is also a duty of our citizens to serve in the armed forces, as volunteers or in accordance with our nation's laws, and to perform the military missions that this service may require. If the day should come when a large proportion of our citizens regard this service as less than an honor, and less than an obligation of citizenship, our proud nation will have begun the descent to lie beside other peoples who were unable or unwilling to fight for their principles or for the retention of their freedoms. (Crocker 1990, p. 31.)

Action has several components. With respect to our own activities, there is the responsibility to work on significant problems rather than allowing our minds to flit about and occupy us with each autecological curiosity that catches our attention. We can avoid conducting research that is simply haphazardly selected problems in haphazardly selected sites of attractive species with no consideration of the literature outside of one's own geographic region and taxonomic group. There is also the responsibility to speak clearly and act with integrity in defense of the world's ecosystems. To remain silent in the face of folly is irresponsible. Of course, there are costs. You may wish to read *Death in the Everglades* (McIver 2003) about Guy Bradley, who was hired by the Audubon Society to help protect some of the last egret rookeries in Florida from poachers. On July 8, 1905, Bradley approached Walter Smith who, with his son and a friend, were killing egrets at Oyster Keys rookery. Bradley was shot and killed. He was buried on a shell ridge at Cape Sable overlooking Florida Bay. The grave was later washed away in a storm.

Before putting the book down, we must ask ourselves where we go from here. Figure 14.20 reminds us that fundamentally our path is straightforward.

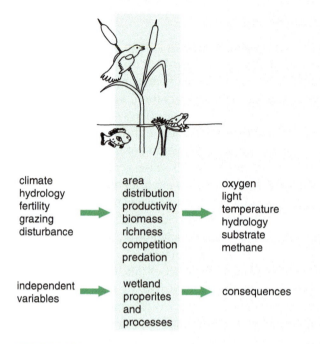

climate   area   oxygen
hydrology   distribution   light
fertility   productivity   temperature
grazing   biomass   hydrology
disturbance   richness   substrate
                 competition   methane
                 predation

independent   wetland   consequences
variables   properites
                 and
                 processes

FIGURE 14.20 A general framework for wetland ecology. Wetland ecology is the study of the independent or causal factors (left) that determine wetland properties and processes (center), as well as the measurement and evaluation of consequences arising from these properties and processes (right).

There is a set of causal factors that create wetlands. These produce measurable properties in wetlands. In turn, wetlands provide services that extend well beyond their own borders. Our responsibility is to determine the relationships and convey them clearly and effectively to those around us in order to ensure that wetlands are conserved and managed wisely. Certainly, as Guy Bradley made the leap of faith that if he protected the egrets from extinction during his lifetime, people in the future would carry on protecting wild birds and wild places with the same dedication. The future will certainly require continued efforts in both research and conservation if we are to succeed in understanding and protecting the world's wetlands.

References

Abraham, K. F. and Keddy, C. J. (2005). The Hudson
Bay Lowland. In *The World's Largest Wetlands:
Ecology and Conservation*, eds. L. H. Fraser and
P. A. Keddy, pp. 118–48. Cambridge, UK: Cambridge
University Press.

Adam, P. (1990). *Saltmarsh Ecology*. Cambridge, UK:
Cambridge University Press.

Adams, G. D. (1988). Wetlands of the prairies of Canada.
In *Wetlands of Canada*, National Wetlands Working
Group, Ecological Land Classification Series No. 24,
pp. 158–98. Montreal, QC: Polyscience Publications
for Sustainable Development Branch, Environment
Canada.

Adamus, P. R. (1992). Choices in monitoring wetlands.
In *Ecological Indicators*, eds. D. H. McKenzie,
D. E. Hyatt, and V. J. McDonald, pp. 571–92. London:
Elsevier.

Adamus, P. R. (1996). *Bioindicators for Assessing
Ecological Integrity of Prairie Wetlands*, EPA/600/
R-96/082. Corvallis, OR: U.S. Environmental
Protection Agency, National Health and
Environmental Effects Research Laboratory,
Western Ecology Division.

Adamus, P. R. and Stockwell, L. T. (1983). *A Method
for Wetland Functional Assessment*, Vol. 1 *Critical
Review and Evaluation Concepts*, Report No.
FHA-PI-82-23, and Vol. 2 *Federal Highway
Administration Assessment Method*, Report No.
FHA-PI-82-24. Springfield, VA: National Technical
Information Service.

Adamus, P. R., ARA Inc., Clairain, E. J., Smith, R. D., and
Young, R. E. (1987). *Wetland Evaluation Technique
(WET)*, Vol. 2, *Methodology*. Vicksburg, MS: U.S.
Army Corps of Engineers.

Aerts, R. and Berendse, F. (1988). The effect of increased
nutrient availability on vegetation dynamics in wet
heathlands. *Vegetatio*, **76**, 63–9.

Agrawala, S., Ota, T., Ahmed, A. U., Smith, J., and
van Aalst, M. (2003). *Development and Climate
Change in Bangladesh: Focus on Coastal Flooding
and The Sundarbans*. Paris: Environment Directorate,
OECD.

Agren, G. I. and Fagerstrom, T. (1984). Limiting
dissimilarity in plants: randomness prevents
exclusion of species with similar competitive
abilities. *Oikos*, **43**, 369–75.

Alestalio, J. and J. Haikio. (1979). Forms created by the
thermal movement of lake ice in Finland in winter
1972–73. *Fennia*, **157**, 51–92.

Alho, C. J. R. (2005). The Pantanal. In *The World's
Largest Wetlands: Ecology and Conservation*,
eds. L. H. Fraser and P. A. Keddy, pp. 271–303.
Cambridge, UK: Cambridge University Press.

Alho, C. J. R., Lacher, T. E., Jr., and Goncalves, H. C.
(1988). Environmental degradation in the Pantanal
ecosystem. *BioScience*, **38**, 164–71.

Allison, M. A. (1998). Historical changes in the
Ganges–Brahmaputra delta front. *Journal of Coastal
Research*, **14**, 1269–75.

Allison, S. K. (1995). Recovery from small-scale
anthropogenic disturbances by northern California
salt marsh plant assemblages. *Ecological
Applications*, **5**, 693–702.

Anderson, R. C., Liberta, A. E., and Dickman, L. A. (1984).
Interaction of vascular plants and vesicular-
arbuscular mycorrhizal fungi across a soil moisture-
nutrient gradient. *Oecologia*, **64**, 111–17.

Anthoni, J. F. (2006). The chemical composition of
seawater. www.seafriends.org.nz/oceano/seawater.
htm (accessed June 4, 2008)

Archibold, O. W. (1995). *Ecology of World Vegetation*.
London: Chapman and Hall.

Aresco, M. J. (2004). Highway mortality of turtles and
other herpetofauna at Lake Jackson, Florida, USA,
and the efficacy of a temporary fence/culvert
system to reduce roadkills. In *Proceedings of the
2003 International Conference on Ecology and
Transportation*, eds. C. L. Irwin, P. Garrett, and
K. P. McDevmott, pp. 433–49. Raleigh, NC: Center
for Transportation and the Environment, North
Carolina State University.

Armentano, T. V. and Verhoeven, J. T. A. (1990).
Biogeochemical cycles: global. In *Wetlands and
Shallow Continental Water Bodies*, Vol. 1, *Natural*

and Human Relationships, ed. B. C. Patten, pp. 281–311. The Hague, the Netherlands: SPB Academic Publishing.

Armstrong, W., Armstrong, J., Beckett, P. M. and Justin, S. H. F. W. (1991). Convective gas-flows in wetland plant aeration. In *Plant Life under Oxygen Deprivation*, eds. M. B. Jackson, D. D. Davies, and H. Lambers, pp. 283–302. The Hague, the Netherlands: SPB Academic Publishing.

Armstrong, J., W. Armstrong and P. M. Beckett. (1992). *Phragmites australis:* Venturi- and humidity-induced pressure flows enhance rhizome aeration and rhizosphere oxidation. *New Phytologist*, 120, 197–207.

Arnold, S. J. (1972). Species densities of predators and their prey. *The American Naturalist*, 106, 220–35.

Arnold, T. W. and Frytzell, E. K. (1990). Habitat use by male mink in relation to wetland characteristics and avian prey abundances. *Canadian Journal of Zoology*, 68, 2205–8.

Arrhenius, O. (1921). Species and area. *Journal of Ecology*, 9, 95–9.

Arroyo, M. T. K., Pliscoff, P., Mihoc, M., and Arroyo-Kalin, M. (2005). The Magellanic moorland. In *The World's Largest Wetlands*, eds. L. H. Fraser and P. A. Keddy, pp. 424–45. Cambridge, UK: Cambridge University Press.

Aselman, I. and Crutzen, P. J. (1989). Global distribution of natural freshwater wetlands and rice paddies, their net primary productivity, seasonality and possible methane emissions. *Journal of Atmospheric Chemistry*, 8, 307–58.

Atwood, E. L. (1950). Life history studies of the nutria, or coypu, in coastal Louisiana. *Journal of Wildlife Management*, 14, 249–65.

Auclair, A. N. D., Bouchard, A. and Pajaczkowski, J. (1976a). Plant standing crop and productivity relations in a *Scirpus–Equisetum* wetland. *Ecology*, 57, 941–52.

Auclair, A. N. D., Bouchard, A. and Pajaczkowski, J. (1976b). Productivity relations in a *Carex*-dominated ecosystem. *Oecologia*, 26, 9–31.

Austin, M. P. (1982). Use of a relative physiological performance value in the prediction of performance in multispecies mixtures from monoculture performance. *Journal of Ecology*, 70, 559–70.

Austin, M. P., Pausas, J. G., and Nicholls, A. O. (1996). Patterns of tree species richness in relation to

environment in southeastern New South Wales, Australia. *Australian Journal of Ecology*, 21, 154–64.

Bacon, P. R. (1978). *Flora and Fauna of the Caribbean*. Trinidad: Key Caribbean Publications.

Baedke, S. J. and T. A. Thompson. (2000). A 4700-year record of lake level and isostasy for Lake Michigan. *Journal of Great Lakes Research*, 26, 416–26.

Bakker, J. P. (1985). The impact of grazing on plant communities, plant populations and soil conditions on salt marshes. *Vegetatio*, 62, 391–8.

Bakker, S. A., Jasperse, C. and Verhoeven, J. T. A. (1997). Accumulation rates of organic matter associated with different successional stages from open water to carr forest in former turbaries. *Plant Ecology*, 129, 113–20.

Baldwin, A. H. and Mendelssohn, I. A. (1998a). Response of two oligohaline marsh communities to lethal and nonlethal disturbance. *Oecologia*, 116, 543–555.

Baldwin, A. H. and Mendelssohn, I. A. (1998b). Effects of salinity and water level on coastal marshes: an experimental test of disturbance as a catalyst for vegetation change. *Aquatic Botany*, 61, 255–68.

Baldwin, A. H., McKee, K. L., and Mendelssohn, I. A. (1996). The influence of vegetation, salinity and inundation of seedbanks of oligohaline coastal marshes. *American Journal of Botany*, 83, 470–9.

Ball, P. J. and Nudds, T. D. (1989). Mallard habitat selection: an experiment and implications for management. In *Freshwater Wetlands and Wildlife*, eds. R. R. Sharitz, and J. W. Gibbons, pp. 659–71. US Department of Energy. Proceedings of a Symposium held at Charleston, South Carolina, March 24–27, 1986. Washington, DC: U.S. Department of Energy.

Barbour, C. D. and Brown, J. H. (1974). Fish species diversity in lakes. *The American Naturalist*, 108, 473–89.

Bardecki, M. J., Bond, W. K., and Manning, E. W. (1989). Assessing Greenock Swamp: functions benefits and values. In *Wetlands: Inertia or Momentum?*, pp. 235–44. Conference Proceedings, Oct 21–22. Toronto, ON: Federation of Ontario Naturalists.

Barko, J. W. and Smart, R. M. (1978). The growth and biomass distribution of two emergent freshwater plants, *Cyperus esculentus* and *Scirpus validus*, on different sediments. *Aquatic Botany*, 5, 109–17.

Barko, J. W. and Smart, R. M. (1979). The nutritional ecology of *Cyperus esculentus*, an emergent aquatic plant, grown on different sediments. *Aquatic Botany*, 6, 13–28.

Barko, J. W. and Smart, R. M. (1980). Mobilization of sediment phosphorus by submersed freshwater macrophytes. *Freshwater Biology*, 10, 229–38.

Barnard, J. R. (1978). Externalities from urban growth: the case of increased storm runoff and flooding. *Land Economics*, 54, 298–315.

Barry, J. M. (1997). *Rising Tide: The Great Mississippi Flood of 1927 and How It Changed America*. New York: Simon and Schuster.

Barthelemy, A. (1874). De la respiration et de la circulation des gaz dans les végétaux. *Annales des Sciences Naturelles Botaniques*, 19, 131–75.

Bartram, W. (1791). *Travels through North & South Carolina, Georgia, East & West Florida, the Cherokee Country, the Extensive Territories of the Muscogulges, or Creek Confederacy, and the Country of the Chactaws: Containing an Account of the Soil and Natural Productions of These Regions, Together with Observations on the Manners of the Indians*. Philadelphia, PA: James and Johnson. (Digital edition, 2001, in *Documenting the South*, Chapel Hill, NC: University of North Carolina.)

Batt, B. D. J., Anderson, M. G., Anderson, C. D., and Caswell, F. D. (1989). The use of prairie potholes by North American ducks. In *Northern Prairie Wetlands*, ed. A. G. van der Valk, pp. 204–27. Ames, IA: Iowa State University Press.

Bauder, E. T. (1989). Drought stress and competition effects on the local distribution of *Pogogyne abramsii*. *Ecology*, 70, 1083–9.

Bazely, D. R. and Jefferies, R. L. (1989). Lesser snow geese and the nitrogen economy of a grazed salt marsh. *Journal of Ecology*, 77, 24–34.

Bazilevich, N. I., Rodin, L. Y., and Rozov, N. N. (1971). Geophysical aspects of biological productivity. *Soviet Geography, Review and Translations*, 12, 293–317.

Beanland, G. E. and Duinker, P. N. (1983). *An Ecological Framework for Environmental Impact Assessment in Canada*. Halifax, NS: Institute for Resource and Environmental Studies, Dalhousie University, and Federal Environmental Assessment Review Office.

Beard, J. S. (1949). *The Natural Vegetation of the Windward and Leeward Islands*. Oxford, UK: Clarendon Press.

Bedford, B. L. (1996). The need to define hydrologic equivalence at the landscape scale for freshwater wetland mitigation. *Ecological Applications*, 6, 57–68.

Bedford, B. L. and Preston, E. M. (1988). Developing the scientific basis for assessing cumulative effects of wetland loss and degradation on landscape functions: status, perspectives and prospects. *Environmental Management*, 12, 751–71.

Beebee, T. J. C. (1996). *Ecology and Conservation of Amphibians*. London: Chapman and Hall.

Beeftink, W. G. (1977). The coastal salt marshes of western and northern Europe: an ecological and phytosociological approach. In *Wet Coastal Ecosystems*, ed. V. J. Chapman, pp. 109–55. Amsterdam, the Netherlands: Elsevier.

Begin, Y., Arseneault, S., and Lavoie, J. (1989). Dynamique d'une bordure forestière par suite de la hausse récente du niveau marin, rive sud-ouest du Golfe du Saint-Laurent, Nouveau-Brunswick. *Géographie physique et Quaternaire*, 43, 355–66.

Belanger L. and Bedard, J. (1994). Role of ice scouring and goose grubbing in marsh plant dynamics. *Journal of Ecology*, 82, 437–45.

Belkin, D. A. (1963). Anoxia: tolerance in reptiles. *Science*, 139, 492–3.

Bender, E. A, Case, T. J., and Gilpin, M. E. (1984). Perturbation experiments in community ecology: theory and practice. *Ecology*, 65, 1–13.

Benson, L. (1959). *Plant Classification*. Lanham, MD: Lexington Books.

Berenbaum, M. R. (1991). Coumarins. In *Herbivores: Their Interactions with Secondary Plant Metabolites*, eds. G. A. Rosenthal and M. R. Berenbaum, pp. 221–49. San Diego, CA: Academic Press.

Berendse, F. and Aerts, R. (1987). Nitrogen-use efficiency: a biologically meaningful definition? *Functional Ecology*, 1, 293–6.

Bernatowicz, S. and Zachwieja, J. (1966). Types of littoral found in the lakes of the Masurian and Suwalki Lakelands. *Komitet Ekolgiezny-Polska Akademia Nauk*, 14, 519–45.

Bertness, M. D. (1991). Interspecific interactions among high marsh perennials in a New England salt marsh. *Ecology*, 72, 125–37.

Bertness, M. D. and Ellison, A. E. (1987). Determinants of pattern in a New England salt marsh plant community. *Ecological Monographs*, 57, 12–147.

Bertness, M. D. and Hacker, S. D. (1994). Physical stress and positive associations among marsh plants. *The American Naturalist*, **144**, 363–72.

Bertness, M. D. and Leonard, G. H. (1997). The role of positive interactions in communities: lessons from intertidal habitats. *Ecology*, **78**, 1976–89.

Bertness, M. D. and Shumway, S. W. (1993). Competition and facilitation in marsh plants. *The American Naturalist*, **142**, 718–34.

Bertness, M. D. and Yeh, S. M. (1994). Cooperative and competitive interactions in the recruitment of marsh elders. *Ecology*, **75**, 2416–29.

Bertness, M. D., Gough, L., and Shumway, S. W. (1992a). Salt tolerances and the distribution of fugitive salt marsh plants. *Ecology*, **73**, 1842–51.

Bertness, M. D., Wikler, K., and Chatkupt, T. (1992b). Flood tolerance and the distribution of *Iva frutescens* across New England salt marshes. *Oecologia*, **91**, 171–8.

Best, E. P. H., Verhoeven, J. T. A., and Wolff, W. J. (1993). The ecology of The Netherlands wetlands: characteristics, threats, prospects and perspectives for ecological research. *Hydrobiologia*, **265**, 305–20.

Bethke, R. W. and Nudds, T. D. (1993). Variation in the diversity of ducks along a gradient of environmental variability. *Oecologia*, **93**, 242–50.

Biesterfeldt, J. M., Petranka, J. W., and Sherbondy, S. (1993). Prevalence of chemical interference competition in natural populations of wood frogs, *Rana sylvatica. Copeia*, **3**, 688–95.

Bilby, R. E., and Ward, J. (1991). Characteristics and function of large woody debris in streams draining old-growth, clear-cut, and 2nd-growth forests in southwestern Washington. *Canadian Journal of Fisheries and Aquatic Sciences*, **48**, 2499–508.

Binford, M. W., Brenner, M., Whitmore, T. J., Higuera-Gundy, A., Deevey, E. S., and Leyden, B. (1987). Ecosystems, paleoecology and human disturbance in subtropical and tropical America. *Quaternary Scientific Review*, **6**, 115–28.

Bliss, L. C. and Gold, W. G. (1994). The patterning of plant communities and edaphic factors along a high arctic coastline: implications for succession. *Canadian Journal of Botany*, **72**, 1095–107.

Blizard, D. (1993). *The Normandy Landings D-Day: The Invasion of Europe 6 June 1944*. London: Reed International.

Bloom, S. A. (1980). Multivariate quantification of community recovery. In *The Recovery Process in Damaged Ecosystems*, ed. J. Cairns, pp. 141–51. Ann Arbor, MI: Ann Arbor Science Publishers.

Bodsworth, F. (1963). *Last of the Curlews*. Toronto, ON: McClelland and Stewart.

Boers, A. M., Veltman, R. L. D., and Zedler, J. B. (2007) *Typha × glauca* dominance and extended hydroperiod constrain restoration of wetland diversity. *Ecological Engineering*, **29**, 232–44.

Boesch, D. F., Josselyn, M. N., Mehta, A. J., Morris, J. T., Nuttle, W. K., Simenstad, C. A., and Swift, D. P. J. (1994). Scientific assessment of coastal wetland loss, restoration and management in Louisiana. *Journal of Coastal Research*, Special Issue No. **20**.

Bogan, A. E. (1996). *Margaritifera hembeli*. In: IUCN (2007). *2007 IUCN Red List of Threatened Species*. www.iucnredlist.org (accessed June 30, 2008)

Bolen, E. G., Smith, L. M., and Schramm, H. L., Jr. (1989). Playa lakes: prairie wetlands of the southern High Plains. *BioScience*, **39**, 615–23.

Bond, G. (1963). In *Plant Physiology*, eds. F. B. Salisbury and C. W. Ross (1985), 3rd edn, p. 254, Figure 13.3. Belmont, CA: Wadsworth.

Bondavalli, C. and Ulanowicz, R. E. (1999). Unexpected effects of predators upon their prey: the case of the American Alligator. *Ecosystems*, **2**, 49–63.

Bonetto, A. A. (1986). The Parana River system. In *The Ecology of River Systems*, eds. B. R. Davies and K. F. Walker, pp. 541–55. Dordrecht, the Netherlands: Dr. W. Junk Publishers.

Bonnicksen, T. M. (1988). Restoration ecology: philosophy, goals and ethics. *The Environmental Professional*, **10**, 25–35.

Bormann, E. H. and Likens, G. E. (1981). *Patterns and Process in a Forested Ecosystem*. New York: Springer-Verlag.

Boston, H. L. (1986). A discussion of the adaptation for carbon acquisition in relation to the growth strategy of aquatic isoetids. *Aquatic Botany*, **26**, 259–70.

Boston, H. L. and Adams, M. S. (1986). The contribution of crassulacean acid metabolism to the annual productivity of two aquatic vascular plants. *Oecologia*, **68**, 615–22.

Botch, M. S. and Masing, V. V. (1983). Mire ecosystems in the USSR. In *Ecosystems of the World*, Vol. 4B, *Mires: Swamp, Bog, Fen and Moor – Regional Studies*, ed. A. J. P. Gore, pp. 95–152. Amsterdam, the Netherlands: Elsevier.

Botkin, D. B. (1990). *Discordant Harmonies. A New Ecology for the Twenty-first Century.* New York: Oxford University Press.

Boucher, D. H. (1985). *The Biology of Mutualism: Ecology and Evolution.* New York: Oxford University Press.

Boutin, C. and Keddy, P. A. (1993). A functional classification of wetland plants. *Journal of Vegetation Science*, **4**, 591–600.

Bowden, W. B. (1987). The biogeochemistry of nitrogen in freshwater wetlands. *Biogeochemistry*, **4**, 313–48.

Bowers, M. D. (1991). Iridoid glycosides. In *Herbivores: Their Interactions with Secondary Plant Metabolites*, eds. G. A. Rosenthal and M. R. Berenbaum, pp. 297–325. San Diego, CA: Academic Press.

Boyd, C. E. (1978). Chemical composition of wetland plants. In *Freshwater Wetlands: Ecological Processes and Management Potential*, eds. R. E. Good, D. F. Whigham, and R. L. Simpson, pp. 155–68. New York: Academic Press.

Boyd, R. and Penland, S. (1988). A geomorphologic model for Mississippi River Delta evolution, *Transactions Gulf Coast Association of Geological Societies*, **38**, 443–52.

Bradley, C. E. and Smith, D. G. (1986). Plains cottonwood recruitment and survival on a prairie meandering river floodplain, Milk River, southern Alberta and northern Montana. *Canadian Journal of Botany*, **64**, 1433–42.

Brandle, R. A. (1991). Flooding resistance of rhizomatous amphibious plants. In *Plant Life under Oxygen Deprivation*, eds. M. B. Jackson, D. D. Davis, and H. Lambers, pp. 35–46. The Hague, the Netherlands: SPB Academic Publishing.

Brasher, S. and Perkins, D. F. (1978). The grazing intensity and productivity of sheep in the grassland ecosystem. In *Production Ecology of British Moors and Montane Grasslands*, Ecological Studies Vol. 27, eds. O. W. Heal and D. F. Perkins, pp. 354–74. Berlin, Germany: Springer-Verlag.

Brewer, J. S. and Grace, J. B. (1990). Plant community structure in an oligohaline tidal marsh. *Vegetatio*, **90**, 93–107.

Bridgham, S. D., Pastor, J., Janssens, J. A., Chapin, C., and Malterer, T. J. (1996). Multiple limiting gradients in peatlands: a call for a new paradigm. *Wetlands*, **16**, 45–65.

Brinkman, R. and Van Diepen, C. A. (1990). Mineral soils. In *Wetlands and Shallow Continental Water Bodies*, Vol. 1, *Natural and Human Relationships*, ed. B. C. Patten, pp. 37–59. The Hague, the Netherlands: SPB Academic Publishing.

Brinson, M. M. (1993a). Changes in the functioning of wetlands along environmental gradients. *Wetlands*, **13**, 65–74.

Brinson, M. M. (1993b). *A Hydrogeomorphic Classification for Wetlands*, Technical Report No. WRP-DE-4. Washington, DC: U.S. Army Corps of Engineers.

Brinson, M. M. (1995). Functional classifications of wetlands to facilitate watershed planning. In *Wetlands and Watershed Management: Science Applications and Public Policy*, eds. J. A. Kusler, D. E. Willard, and H. C. Hull Jr., pp. 65–71. A collection of papers from a national symposium and several workshops at Tampa, FL, Apr 23–26. Berne, NY: Association of State Wetland Managers.

Brinson, M. M., Lugo, A. E. and Brown, S. (1981). Primary productivity, decomposition and consumer activity in freshwater wetlands. *Annual Review of Ecology and Systematics*, **12**, 123–61.

Brinson, M. M., Christian, R. R. and Blum, L. K. (1995). Multiple states in the sealevel induced transition from terrestrial forest to estuary. *Estuaries*, **18**, 648–59.

Bronmark, C. (1985). Interactions between macrophytes, epiphytes and herbivores: an experimental approach. *Oikos*, **45**, 26–30.

Bronmark, C. (1990). How do herbivorous freshwater snails affect macrophytes? – a comment. *Ecology*, **71**, 1213–15.

Brosnan, D., Courtney, S., Sztukowski, L., Bedford, B., Burkett, V., Collopy, M., Derrickson, S., Elphick, C., Hunt, R., Potter, K., Sedinger, J. and Walters, J. (2007). *Everglades Multi-Species Avian Ecology and Restoration Review: Final Report.* Portland, OR: Sustainable Ecology Institute.

Brown, J. F. (1997). Effects of experimental burial on survival, growth, and resource allocation of three species of dune plants. *Journal of Ecology*, **85**, 151–8.

Brown, L. R. (2001). *Paving the Planet: Cars and Crops Competing for Land.* Washington, DC: Earth Policy Institute.

Brown, S., Brinson, M. M., and Lugo, A. E. (1979). Structure and function of riparian wetlands. In *Strategies for Protection and Management of Floodplain Wetlands and Other Riparian Ecosystems*, Gen. Tech. Rep. No. WO-12, tech. coord. R. R. Johnson and J. F. McCormick, pp. 17–31. Washington, DC: U.S. Department of Agriculture, Forest Service.

Bruland, G. L. and Richardson, C. J. (2005). Hydrologic, edaphic, and vegetative responses to microtopographic reestablishment in a restored wetland. *Restoration Ecology*, **13**, 515–23.

Brunton, D. F. and Di Labio, B. M. (1989). Diversity and ecological characteristics of emergent beach flora along the Ottawa River in the Ottawa–Hull region, Quebec and Ontario. *Naturaliste Canadien*, **116**, 179–91.

Brutsaert, W. (2005). *Hydrology: An Introduction*. Cambridge, UK: Cambridge University Press.

Bubier, J. L. (1995). The relationship of vegetation to methane emission and hydrochemical gradients in northern peatlands. *Journal of Ecology*, **83**, 403–20.

Bucher, E. H., Bonetto, A., Boyle, T. P., Canevari, P., Castro, G., Huszar, P., and Stone, T. (1993). *Hidrovia: An Initial Environmental Examination of the Paraguay–Paraná Waterway*. Manomet, MA and Buenos Aires, Argentina: Wetlands for the Americas.

Bump, S. R. (1986). Yellow-headed blackbird nest defense: aggressive responses to marsh wrens. *The Condor*, **88**, 328–35.

Burger, J., Shisler, J., and Lesser, F. H. (1982). Avian utilization on six salt marshes in New Jersey. *Biological Conservation*, **23**, 187–212.

Burnett, J. H. (1964). The study of Scottish vegetation. In *The Vegetation of Scotland*, ed. J. H. Burnett, pp. 1–11. Edinburgh, UK: Oliver and Boyd.

Bury, B. R. (1979). Population ecology of freshwater turtles. In *Turtles: Perspectives and Research*, eds. M. Harless and H. Morlock, pp. 571–602. New York: John Wiley.

Cade, B. S. and Noon, B. R. (2003). A gentle introduction to quantile regression for ecologists. *Frontiers in Ecology and the Environment*, **1**, 412–20.

Cade, B. S., Terrell, J. W., and Schroeder, R. L. (1999). Estimating effects of limiting factors with regression quantiles. *Ecology*, **80**, 311–23.

Cairns, J. (ed.) (1980). *The Recovery Process in Damaged Ecosystems*. Ann Arbor, MI: Ann Arbor Science Publishers.

Cairns, J. (ed.) (1988). *Rehabilitating Damaged Ecosystems,* Vols. 1 and 2. Boca Raton, FL: CRC Press.

Cairns, J. (1989). Restoring damaged ecosystems: is predisturbance condition a viable option? *The Environmental Professional*, **11**, 152–9.

Cairns, J., Jr., Niederlehner, B. R., and Orvos, D. R. (1992). *Predicting Ecosystem Risk*. Princeton, NJ: Princeton Scientific Publishing.

Callaway, R. M. and King, L. (1996). Temperature-driven variation in substrate oxygenation and the balance of competition and facilitation. *Ecology*, **77**, 1189–95.

Campbell, D. (2005). The Congo River basin. In *The World's Largest Wetlands: Ecology and Conservation*, eds. L. H. Fraser and P. A. Keddy, pp. 149–65. Cambridge, UK: Cambridge University Press.

Campbell, D. R. and Rochefort, L. (2003). Germination and seedling growth of bog plants in relation to the recolonization of milled peatlands. *Plant Ecology*, **169**, 71–84.

Canadian Hydrographic Service. (2009). *Historical water level data*. www.waterlevels.gc.ca/C&A/historical_e. html (accessed May 4, 2009)

Canny, M. J. (1998). Transporting water in plants. *American Scientist*, **86**, 152–9.

Carignan, R. and Kalff, J. (1980). Phosphorus sources for aquatic weeds: water or sediments? *Science*, **207**, 987–9.

Carpenter, S. R. and Kitchell, J. F. (1988). Consumer control of lake productivity. *BioScience*, **38**, 764–9.

Carpenter, S. R. and Lodge, D. M. (1986). Effects of submersed macrophytes on ecosystem processes. *Aquatic Botany*, **26**, 341–70.

Carpenter, S. R., Kitchell, J. F., Hodgson, J. R., Cochran, P. A., Elser, J. J., Elser, M. M., Lodge, D. M., Kretchmer, D., He, X., and von Ende, C. N. (1987). Regulation of lake primary productivity by food web structure. *Ecology*, **68**, 1863–76.

Carpenter, S. R., Chisholm, S. W., Krebs, C. J., Schindler, D. W., and Wright, R. F. (1995). Ecosystem experiments. *Science*, **269**, 324–7.

Carvalho, A. R. (2007). An ecological economics approach to estimate the value of a fragmented wetland in Brazil (Mato Grosso do Sul state). *Brazilian Journal of Biology*, **67**, 663–71.

Carver, E. and Caudill, J. (2007). *Banking on Nature: The Economic Benefits to Local Communites of National Wildlife Refuge Visitation*. Washington, DC: U.S. Fish and Wildlife Service.

Castellanos, E. M., Figueroa, M. E., and Davy, A. J. (1994). Nucleation and facilitation in saltmarsh succession: interactions between *Spartina maritima* and *Arthrocnemum perenne*. *Journal of Ecology*, 82, 239–48.

Catling, P. M., Spicer, K. W., and Lefkovitch, L. P. (1988). Effects of the introduced floating vascular aquatic, *Hydrocharis morsus-ranae* (Hydrocharitaceae), on some North American aquatic macrophytes. *Naturaliste Canadien*, 115, 131–7.

Cavalieri, A. J. and Huang, A. H. C. (1979). Evaluation of proline accumulation in the adaptation of diverse species of marsh halophytes to the saline environment. *American Journal of Botany*, 66, 307–12.

Cazenave, A. and Nerem, R. (2004). Present-day sea level change: observations and causes. *Reviews of Geophysics*, 42, 139–50.

Chaneton, E. J. and Facelli, J. M. (1991). Disturbance effects on plant community diversity: spatial scales and dominance hierarchies. *Vegetatio*, 93, 143–56.

Chapin, F. S., III. (1980). The mineral nutrition of wild plants. *Annual Review of Ecology and Systematics*, 11, 233–60.

Chapman, V. J. (1940). The functions of the pneumatophores of *Avicennia nitida* Jacq. *Proceedings of the Linnean Society of London*, 152, 228–33.

Chapman, V. J. (1974). *Salt Marshes and Salt Deserts of the World*. Lehre, Germany: J. Cramer.

Chapman, V. J. (ed.) (1977). *Wet Coastal Ecosystems*. Amsterdam, the Netherlands: Elsevier.

Charlton, D. L. and Hilts, S. (1989). Quantitative evaluation of fen ecosystems on the Bruce Peninsula. In *Ontario Wetlands: Inertia or Momentum*, eds. M. J. Bardecki and N. Patterson, pp. 339–54. Proceedings of Conference, Ryerson Polytechnical Institute, Toronto, Oct 21–22, 1988. Toronto, ON: Federation of Ontario Naturalists.

Cherry-Garrard, A. (1922). *The Worst Journey in the World*. London: Constable.

Chesson, P. L. and Warner, R. R. (1981). Environmental variability promotes coexistence in lottery competitive systems. *The American Naturalist*, 117, 923–43.

Chimney, M. and Goforth, G. (2006). History and description of the Everglades Nutrient Removal Project. *Ecological Engineering*, 27, 268–78.

China Development Brief. (2004). Ploughshares into fishing nets. www.chinadevelopmentbrief.com/node/204 (accessed Dec 3, 2007)

Christensen, N. L. (1999). Vegetation of the Coastal Plain of the southeastern United States. In *Vegetation of North America*, 2nd edn, eds. M. Barbour and W. D. Billings, pp. 397–448. Cambridge, UK: Cambridge University Press.

Christensen, N. L., Burchell, R. B., Liggett, A., and Simms, E. L. (1981). The structure and development of pocosin vegetation. In *Pocosin Wetlands: An Integrated Analysis of Coastal Plain Freshwater Bogs in North Carolina*, ed. C. J. Richardson, pp. 43–61. Stroudsburg, PA: Hutchinson Ross.

Christensen, N. L., Bartuska, A. M., Brown, J. H., Carpenter, S., D'Antonio, C., Francis, R., Franklin, J. F., MacMahon, J. A., Noss, R. F., Parsons, D. J., Peterson, C. H., Turner, M. G., and Woodmansee, R. G. (1996). The report of the Ecological Society of America Committee on the Scientific Basis for Ecosystem Management. *Ecological Applications*, 6, 665–91.

Christie, W. J. (1974). Changes in the fish species composition of the Great Lakes. *Journal of the Fisheries Research Board of Canada*, 31, 827–54.

Chung, C. (1982). Low marshes, China. In *Creation and Restoration of Coastal Plant Communities*, ed. R. R. Lewis III, pp. 131–45. Boca Raton, FL: CRC Press.

Cicerone, R. J. and Ormland, R. S. (1988). Biogeochemical aspects of atmospheric methane. *Global Biogeochemical Cycles*, 2, 299–327.

Clapham, W. B., Jr. (1973). *Natural Ecosystems*. New York: Macmillan.

Clark, M. A., Siegrist, J., and Keddy, P. A. (2008). Patterns of frequency in species-rich vegetation in pine savannas: effects of soil moisture and scale. *Ecoscience*, 15, 529–35.

Clarke, L. D. and Hannon, N. J. (1967). The mangrove swamp and salt marsh communities of the Sydney district. I. Vegetation, soils and climate. *Journal of Ecology*, 55, 753–71.

Clarke, L. D. and Hannon, N. J. (1969). The mangrove swamp and salt marsh communities of the Sydney district. II. The holocoenotic complex with particular reference to physiography. *Journal of Ecology*, **57**, 213–34.

Clegg, J. (1986). *Pond Life*. London: Frederick Warne.

Clements, F. E. (1916). *Plant Succession: An Analysis of the Development of Vegetation*. Washington, DC: Carnegie Institution of Washington.

Clements, F. E. (1935). Experimental ecology in the public service. *Ecology*, **16**, 342–63.

Clements, F. E. (1936). Nature and structure of climax. *Journal of Ecology*, **24**, 254–82.

Clements, F. E., Weaver, J. E., and Hanson, H. C. (1929). *Plant Competition*. Washington, DC: Carnegie Institution of Washington.

Clymo, R. S. and Duckett, J. G. (1986). Regeneration of *Sphagnum*. *New Phytologist*, **102**, 589–614.

Clymo, R. S. and Hayward, P. M. (1982). The ecology of *Sphagnum*. In *Bryophyte Ecology*, ed. A. J. E. Smith, pp. 229–89. London: Chapman and Hall.

Cobbaert, D, Rochefort, L., and Price, J. S. (2004). Experimental restoration of a fen plant community after peat mining. *Applied Vegetation Science*, **7**, 209–20.

Coleman, J. M., Roberts, H. H., and Stone, G. W. (1998). Mississippi River Delta: an overview. *Journal of Coastal Research*, **14**, 698–716.

Coles, B. and Coles, J. (1989). *People of the Wetlands: Bogs, Bodies and Lake-Dwellers*. London: Thames and Hudson.

Coley, P. D. (1983). Herbivory and defense characteristics of tree species in a lowland tropical forest. *Ecological Monographs*, **53**, 209–33.

Colinvaux, P. (1978). *Why Big Fierce Animals Are Rare: An Ecologist's Perspective*. Princeton, NJ: Princeton University Press.

Colwell, R. K. and Fuentes, E. R. (1975). Experimental studies of the niche. *Annual Review of Ecology and Systematics*, **6**, 281–309.

Committee on Characterization of Wetlands. (1995). *Wetlands: Characteristics and Boundaries*. Washington, DC: National Academy of Sciences Press.

Committee on Ecological Land Classification. (1988). *Wetlands of Canada, Ecological Land Classification Series No. 24*. Ottawa, ON: National Wetlands Working Group, Environment Canada.

Conant, R. and Collins, J. T. (1998). *A Field Guide to Reptiles and Amphibians, Eastern/Central North America*, 3rd edn. New York: Houghton Mifflin.

Connell, J. H. (1978). Diversity in tropical rain forests and coral reefs. *Science*, **199**, 1302–10.

Connell, J. H. (1980). Diversity and the coevolution of competitors, or the ghost of competition past. *Oikos*, **35**, 131–8.

Connell, J. H. (1987). Maintenance of species diversity in biotic communities. In *Evolution and Coadaptation in Biotic Communities*, eds. S. Kawano, J. H. Connell, and T. Hidaka, pp. 208–18. Tokyo: University of Tokyo Press.

Connell, J. H. and Orias, E. (1964). The ecological regulation of species diversity. *The American Naturalist*, **98**, 399–414.

Conner, W. H. and Buford, M. A. (1998). Southern deepwater swamps. In *Southern Forested Wetlands: Ecology and Management*, eds. M. G. Messina and W. H. Conner, pp. 261–87. Boca Raton, FL: Lewis Publishers.

Conner, W. H., Day, J. W., Jr., Baumann, R. H., and Randall, J. M. (1989). Influence of hurricanes on coastal ecosystems along the northern Gulf of Mexico. *Wetlands Ecology and Management*, **1**, 45–56.

Connor, E. F. and McCoy, E. D. (1979). The statistics and biology of the species–area relationship. *The American Naturalist*, **113**, 791–833.

Connor, E. F. and Simberloff, D. (1979). The assembly of species communities: chance or competition? *Ecology*, **69**, 1132–40.

Cordone, A. J. and Kelley, D. W. (1961). The influences of inorganic sediment on the aquatic life of streams. *California Fish and Game*, **47**, 189–228.

Cornwell, W. K., Bedford, B. L., and Chapin, C. T. (2001). Occurrence of arbuscular mycorrhizal fungi in a phosphorus-poor wetland and mycorrhizal response to phosphorus fertilization. *American Journal of Botany*, **88**, 1824–9.

Costanza, R., Cumberland, J., Daly, H., Goodland, R., and Norgaard, R. (1997). *An Introduction to Ecological Economics*. Boca Raton, FL: St. Lucie Press.

Cowardin, L. M. and Golet, F. C. (1995). US Fish and Wildlife Service 1979 wetland classification: a review. *Vegetatio*, **118**, 139–52.

Cowardin, L. M., Carter, V., Golet, F. C., and LaRoe, E. T. (1979). *Classification of Wetlands and Deepwater Habitats of the United States*, FWS/OBS-79/31. Washington, DC: U.S. Department of the Interior Fish and Wildlife Service.

Cowling, R. M., Rundel, P. W., Lamont, B. B., Arroyo, M. K., and Arianoutsou, M. (1996a). Plant diversity in Mediterranean-climate regions. *Trends in Ecology and Evolution*, **11**, 362–6.

Cowling, R. M., MacDonald, I. A. W., and Simmons, M. T. (1996b). The Cape Peninsula, South Africa: physiographical, biological and historical background to an extraordinary hot-spot of biodiversity. *Biodiversity and Conservation*, **5**, 527–50.

Craft, C. B., Vymazal, J., and Richardson, C. J. (1995). Response of everglades plant communities to nitrogen and phosphorus additions. *Wetlands*, **15**, 258–71.

Craighead, F. C., Sr. (1968). The role of the alligator in shaping plant communities and maintaining wildlife in the southern Everglades. *The Florida Naturalist*, **41**, 2–7, 69–74.

Crawford, R. M. M. (1982). Physiological response to flooding. In *Encyclopedia of Plant Physiology*, new series Vol. 12B, *Physiological Plant Ecology II*, eds. O. L. Large, P. S. Nobel, C. B. Osmond, and H. Ziegler, pp. 453–77. Berlin, Germany: Springer-Verlag.

Crawford, R. M. M. and Braendle, R. (1996). Oxygen deprivation stress in a changing environment. *Journal of Experimental Botany*, **47**, 145–59.

Crawford, R. M. M. and McManmon, M (1968). Inductive responses of alcohol and malic acid dehydrogenases in relation to flooding tolerance in roots. *Journal of Experimental Botany*, **19**, 435–41.

Crawley, M. J. (1983). *Herbivory: The Dynamics of Plant/Animal Interactions*. Oxford, UK: Blackwell Scientific Publications.

Crocker, L. P. (1990). *Army Officer's Guide*, 45th edn. Harrisburg, PA: Stackpole Books.

Crook, D. A. and Robertson, A. I. (1999). Relationships between riverine fish and woody debris: implications for lowland rivers. *Marine and Freshwater Research*, **50**, 941–53.

Crosby, A.W. (1993). *Economic Imperialism: The Biological Expansion of Europe 900–1900*. Cambridge, UK: Cambridge University Press.

Crow, G. E. (1993). Species diversity in aquatic angiosperms: latitudinal patterns. *Aquatic Botany*, **44**, 229–58.

Crowder, A. A. and Bristow, J. M. (1988). Report: the future of waterfowl habitats in the Canadian lower Great Lakes wetlands. *Journal of Great Lakes Research*, **14**, 115–27.

Cummins, K. W. (1973). Trophic relationships of aquatic insects. *Annual Review of Entomology*, **18**, 83–206.

Cummins, K. W. and Klug, M. J. (1979). Feeding ecology of stream invertebrates. *Annual Review of Ecology and Systematics*, **10**, 147–72.

Currie, D. J. (1991). Energy and large-scale patterns of animal- and plant-species richness. *The American Naturalist*, **137**, 27–49.

Cyr, H. and Pace, M. L. (1993). Magnitude and patterns of herbivory in aquatic and terrestrial ecosystems. *Nature*, **361**, 148–50.

Czaya, E. (1983). *Rivers of the World*. Cambridge, UK: Cambridge University Press.

Dacey, J. W. H. (1980). Internal winds in water lillies: an adaptation for life in anaerobic sediments. *Science*, **210**, 1017–19.

Dacey, J. W. H. (1981). Pressurized ventilation in the yellow water lily. *Ecology*, **62**, 1137–47.

Dacey, J. W. H. (1988). In *Plant Physiology*, 3rd edn, eds. F. B. Salisbury and C. W. Ross, pp. 68–70. Belmont, CA: Wadsworth.

Dahm, C. N., Cummins, K. W., Valett, H. M., and Coleman, R. L. (1995). An ecosystem view of the restoration of the Kissimmee River. *Restoration Ecology*, **3**, 225–38.

Daily, G. C. (1997). *Nature's Services: Societal Dependence Upon Natural Ecosystems*. Washington, DC: Island Press.

Damman, A. W. H. (1986). Hydrology, development, and biogeochemistry of ombrogenous bogs with special reference to nutrient relocation in a western Newfoundland bog. *Canadian Journal of Botany*, **64**, 384–94.

Damman, A. and Dowhan, J. (1981). Vegetation and habitat conditions in Western Head Bog, a southern Nova Scotian plateau bog. *Canadian Journal of Botany*, **59**, 1343–59.

Dansereau, P. (1959). Vascular aquatic plant communities of southern Quebec: a preliminary analysis. *Transactions of the Northeast Wildlife Conference*, **10**, 27–54.

Dansereau, P. and Segadas-Vianna, F. (1952). Ecological study of the peat bogs of eastern North America. *Canadian Journal of Botany*, **30**, 490–520.

Darlington, P. J. (1957). *Zoogeography: The Geographical Distribution of Animals*. New York: John Wiley.

Davis, D. W. (2000). Historical perspective on crevasses, levees, and the Mississippi River. In *Transforming New Orleans and Its Environs: Centuries of Change*, ed. C. E. Colten, pp. 84–108. Pittsburgh, PA: University of Pittsburgh Press.

Davis, S. M. and Ogden, J. C. (eds.) (1994). *Everglades: The Ecosystem and its Restoration*. Delray Beach, FL: St. Lucie Press.

Day, J. W., Jr., Boesch, D. F., Clairain, E. J., Kemp, G. P., Laska, S. B., Mitsch, W. J., Orth, K., Mashriqui, H., Reed, D. J., Shabman, L., Simenstad, C. A., Streever, B. J., Twilley, R. R., Watson, C. C., Wells, J. T., and Whigham, D. F. (2007). Restoration of the Mississippi Delta: lessons from Hurricanes Katrina and Rita. *Science*, 315, 1679–84.

Day, R. T., Keddy, P. A., McNeill, J., and Carleton, T. (1988). Fertility and disturbance gradients: a summary model for riverine marsh vegetation. *Ecology*, 69, 1044–54.

Day, W. (1984). *Genesis on Planet Earth*, 2nd edn. New Haven, CT: Yale University Press.

Dayton, P. K. (1979). Ecology: a science and a religion. In *Ecological Processes in Coastal and Marine Systems*, ed. R. J. Livingston, pp. 3–18. New York: Plenum Press.

DeBenedictis, P. A. (1974). Interspecific competition between tadpoles of *Rana pipiens* and *Rana sylvatica*: an experimental field study. *Ecological Monographs*, 44, 129–51.

de Groot, R. S. (1992). *Functions of Nature*. Groningen, the Netherlands: Wolters-Noordhoff.

Delany, S. N. and Scott, D. A. (2006). *Waterbird Population Estimates*, 4th edn. Wageningen, the Netherlands: Wetlands International.

Delcourt, H. R. and Delcourt, P. A. (1988). Quaternary landscape ecology: relevant scales in space and time. *Landscape Ecology*, 2, 23–44.

Delcourt, H. R. and Delcourt, P. A. (1991). *Quaternary Ecology: A Paleoecological Perspective*. London: Chapman and Hall.

del Moral R., Titus, J. H., and Cook, A. M. (1995). Early primary succession on Mount St. Helens, Washington, USA. *Journal of Vegetation Science*, 6, 107–20.

De Luc, J. A. (1810). Geologic travels. In Gorham, E. (1953). Some early ideas concerning the nature, origin and development of peat lands. *Journal of Ecology*, 41, 257–74.

Denny, P. (1972). Sites of nutrient absorption in aquatic macrophytes. *Journal of Ecology*, 60, 819–29.

Denny, P. (1985). *The Ecology and Management of African Wetland Vegetation*. Dordrecht, the Netherlands: Dr. W. Junk Publishers.

Denny, P. (1993a).Wetlands of Africa: Introduction. In *Wetlands of the World*, Vol. 1, eds. D. F. Whigham, D. Dykyjova, and S. Hejny, pp. 1–31. Dordrecht, the Netherlands: Kluwer.

Denny, P. (1993b). Eastern Africa. In *Wetlands of the World*, Vol. 1, ed. D. F. Whigham, D. Dykyjova, and S. Hejny, pp. 32–46. Dordrecht, the Netherlands: Kluwer.

Denny, P. (1995). Benefits and priorities for wetland conservation: the case for national conservation strategies. In *Wetlands. Archaeology and Nature Conservation*, eds. M. Cox, V. Straker, and D. Taylor, pp. 249–74. London: HMSO.

Desmukh, I. (1986). *Ecology and Tropical Biology*. Palo Alto, CA: Blackwell Scientific Publications.

Desrochers, D. W., Keagy, J. C., and Cristol, D. A. (2008). Created versus natural wetlands: avian communities in Virgina salt marshes. *Ecoscience*, 15, 36–43.

Diamond, J. M. (1975). Assembly of species communities. In *Ecology and Evolution of Communities*, eds. M. L. Cody and J. M. Diamond, pp. 342–444. Cambridge, MA: Belknap Press of Harvard University Press.

Diamond, J. M. (1983). Laboratory, field and natural experiments. *Nature*, 304, 586–7.

Diamond, J. (1994). Ecological collapses of past civilisations. *Proceedings of the American Philosophical Society*, 138, 363–70.

Diamond, J. (2005). *Collapse: How Societies Choose to Fail or Succeed*. New York: Penguin Books.

Dickinson, C. H. (1983). Micro-organisms in peatlands. In *Ecosystems of the World* Vol. 4A, *Mires: Swamp, Bog, Fen and Moor-General Studies*, ed. A. J. P. Gore, pp. 225–45. Amsterdam, the Netherlands: Elsevier.

Digby, P. G. N. and Kempton, R. A. (1987). *Multivariate Analysis of Ecological Communities*. London: Chapman and Hall.

Dinerstein, E. (1991). Seed dispersal by greater one-horned rhinoceros (*Rhinoceros unicornis*) and the flora of *Rhinoceros* latrines. *Mammalia*, 55, 355–62.

Dinerstein, E. (1992). Effects of *Rhinoceros unicornis* on riverine forest structure in lowland Nepal. *Ecology*, 73, 701–4.

Dittmar, L. A. and Neely, R. K. (1999). Wetland seed bank response to sedimentation varying in loading rate and texture. *Wetlands*, **19**, 341–51.

Douglas, B. C. (1997). Global sea rise: a redetermination. *Surveys in Geophysics*, **18**, 279–92.

Dowdeswell, J. A. (2006). The Greenland ice sheet and global sea-level rise. *Science*, **311**, 963–4.

Doyle, T. W., Garrett, F. G., and Books, M. A. (2003). Modeling mangrove forest migration along the southwest coast of Florida under climate change. In *Integrated Assessment of the Climate Change Impacts on the Gulf Coast Region*, eds. Z. H. Ning, R. E. Tumer, T. Doyle, and K. K. Abdollahi, pp. 211–21. Baton Rouge, LA: Gulf Coast Climate Change Assessment Council (GCRCC) and Louisiana State University (LSU) Graphic Services.

Dray, F. A., Jr, Bennett, B. C., and Center, T. D. (2006). Invasion history of *Melaleuca quinquenervia* (Cav.) S. T. Blake in Florida. *Castanea*, **71**, 210–25.

Dugan, P. (ed.) (1993). *Wetlands in Danger*. New York: Oxford University Press.

Dugan, P. (ed.) (2005). *Guide to Wetlands*. Buffalo, NY: Firefly Books.

Dumortier, M., Verlinden, A., Beeckman H., and van der Mijnsbrugge, K. (1996). Effects of harvesting dates and frequencies on above- and below-ground dynamics in Belgian wet grasslands. *Ecoscience*, **3**, 190–8.

Duncan, R. P. (1993). Flood disturbance and the coexistence of species in a lowland podocarp forest, south Westland, New Zealand. *Journal of Ecology*, **81**, 403–16.

Durant, W. (1944). *The Story of Civilization III: Caesar and Christ*. New York: Simon and Schuster.

du Rietz, G. E. (1931). *Life-Forms of Terrestrial Flowering Plants*. Uppsala, Sweden: Almqvist & Wiksell.

Dynesius, M. and Nilsson, C. (1994). Fragmentation and flow regulation of river systems in the northern third of the world. *Science*, **266**, 753–62.

Edmonds, J. (ed.) (1997). *Oxford Atlas of Exploration*. New York: Oxford University Press.

Ehrenfeld, J. G. (1983). The effects of changes in land-use on swamps of the New Jersey pine barrens. *Biological Conservation*, **25**, 353–75.

Ehrlich, A. and Ehrlich, P. (1981). *Extinction: The Causes and Consequences of the Disappearance of Species*. New York: Random House.

Elakovich, S. D. and Wootten, J. W. (1989). Allelopathic potential of sixteen aquatic and wetland plants. *Journal of Aquatic Plant Management*, **27**, 78–84.

Ellenberg, H. (1985). Veranderungen der Flora Mitteleuropas unter dem Einflus von Dungung und Immissionen. *Schweizerische Zeitschrift für Forstwesen*, **136**, 19–39.

Ellenberg, H. (1988). Floristic changes due to nitrogen deposition in central Europe. In *Critical Loads for Sulfur and Nitrogen*, eds. J. Nilsson and P. Grennfelt, pp. 375–83. Report from a workshop held at Skokloster, Sweden, Mar 19–24, 1988. Copenhagen: Nordic Council of Ministers.

Ellenberg, H. (1989). Eutrophierung: das gravierendste Problem im Naturschutz? *Norddeutsche Naturschutzakademie*, **2**, 9–12.

Ellery, W. N., Ellery, K., Rogers, K. H., McCarthy, T. S., and Walker, B. H. (1993). Vegetation, hydrology and sedimentation processes as determinants of channel form and dynamics in the northeastern Okavango Delta, Botswana. *African Journal of Ecology*, **31**, 10–25.

Ellison, A. M. and Farnsworth, E. J. (1996). Spatial and temporal variability in growth of *Rhizophora mangle* saplings on coral cays: links with variation in insolation, herbivory, and local sedimentation rate. *Journal of Ecology*, **84**, 717–31.

Elton, C. (1927). *Animal Ecology*. London: Sidgwick and Jackson.

Elveland, J. (1978). *Management of Rich Fens in Northern Sweden: Studies of Various Factors Influencing the Vegetational Dynamics*, Statens naturvardsverk PM 1007. Solna, Sweden: Forskningsnamnden.

Elveland, J. (1979). *Irrigated and Naturally Flooded Hay-Meadows in North Sweden: A Nature Conservancy Problem*, Statens naturvardsverk PM 1174. Solna, Sweden: Forskningssekretariatet.

Elveland, J. and Sjoberg, K. (1982). *Some Effects of Scything and Other Management Procedures on the Plant and Animal Life of N. Swedish Wetlands Formerly Mown for Hay*, Statens naturvardsverket PM 1516. Solna, Sweden: Forskningssekretariatet.

Encyclopaedia Britannica. (1991). Vol. 16, p. 481. Chicago, IL: Encyclopaedia Britannica Inc.

Environment Canada. (1976). *Marine Environmental Data Service, Ocean and Aquatic Sciences: Monthly and Yearly Mean Water Levels*, Vol. 1, *Inland*. Ottawa, ON: Department of Environment.

Environment Canada. (2000). *The Importance of Nature to Canadians: The Economic Significance of Nature-Related Activities*. Ottawa, ON: Environment Canada.

Eriksson, O. (1993). The species-pool hypothesis and plant community diversity. *Oikos*, **68**, 371–4.

Essame, H. (1974). *Patton: A Study in Command*. New York: Charles Scribner's Sons.

Ewel, J. J. (1986). Invasibility: lessons from south Florida. In *Ecology of Biological Invasions of North America and Hawaii*, eds. H. A. Mooney and J. A. Drake, pp. 214–30. New York: Springer-Verlag.

Facelli, J. M., Leon, R. J. C., and Deregibus, V. A. (1989). Community structure in grazed and ungrazed grassland sites in the flooding Pampa, Argentina. *American Midland Naturalist*, **121**, 125–33.

Faith, D. P., Minchin, P. R. and Belbin, L. (1987). Compositional dissimilarity as a robust measure of ecological distance. *Vegetatio*, **69**, 57–68.

Farney, R. A. and Bookhout, T. A. (1982). Vegetation changes in a Lake Erie marsh (Winous Point, Ottawa County, Ohio) during high water years. *Ohio Journal of Science*, **82**, 103–7.

Faulkner, S. P. and Richardson, C. J. (1989). Physical and chemical characteristics of freshwater wetland soils. In *Constructed Wetlands for Wastewater Treatment*, ed. D. A. Hammer, pp. 41–72. Chelsea, MI: Lewis Publishers.

Fernandez-Armesto, F. (1989). *The Spanish Armada: The Experience of War in 1588*. Oxford, UK: Oxford University Press.

Field, R., Stuzeski, E. J., Masters, H. E., and Tafuri, A. N. (1974). Water pollution and associated effects from street salting. *Journal of Environmental Engineering Division*, **100**, 459–77.

Findlay, S. C. and Houlahan, J. (1997). Anthropogenic correlates of biodiversity in southeastern Ontario wetlands. *Conservation Biology*, **11**, 1000–9.

Finney, B. P. and Johnson, T. C. (1991). Sedimentation in Lake Malawi (East Africa) during the past 10,000 years: a continuous paleoclimatic record from the southern tropics. *Palaeogeography, Palaeoclimatology, Palaeoecology*, **85**, 351–66.

Fitter, A. and Hay, R. (2002). *Environmental Physiology of Plants*, 3rd edn. San Diego, CA: Academic Press.

Flint, R. F. (1971). *Glacial and Quaternary Geology*. New York: John Wiley.

Flores, D. L. (ed.) (1984). *Jefferson and Southwestern Exploration: The Freeman and Custis Accounts of the Red River Expedition of 1806*. Norman, OK: University of Oklahoma Press.

Food and Agriculture Organization of the United Nations (FAO). (2009). *Commodities by Country*. http://faostat.fao.org/site/339/default.aspx (accessed Dec 4, 2009)

Forman, A. T. and Alexander, L. E. (1998). Roads and their ecological effects. *Annual Review of Ecology and Systematics*, **29**, 207–31.

Forman, R. T. T. (ed.) (1998). *Pine Barrens: Ecosystem and Landscape*. Rutgers, NJ: Rutgers University Press.

Forman, R. T. T., Sperling, D., Bissonette, J., Clevenger, A. P., Cutshall, C. D., Dale, V. H., Fahrig, L., France, R., Goldman, C. R., Heanue, K., Jones, J. A., Swanson, F. J., Turrentine, T., and Winter, T. C. (2002). *Road Ecology: Science and Solutions*. Washington, DC: Island Press.

Forster, P., Ramaswamy, V., Artaxo, P., Berntsen, T., Betts, R., Fahey, D. W., Haywood, J., Lean, J., Lowe, D. C., Myhre, G., Nganga, J., Prinn, R., Raga, G., Schulz, M., and Van Dorland, R. (2007). Changes in atmospheric constituents and in radiative forcing. In *Climate Change 2007: The Physical Science Basis. Contribution of Working Group I to the Fourth Assessment Report of the Intergovernmental Panel on Climate Change*, eds. S. Solomon, D. Qin, M. Manning, Z. Chen, M. Marquis, K. B. Averyt, M. M. B. Tignor and H. L. Miller, pp. 129–234. Cambridge, UK: Cambridge University Press.

Foster, D. R. and Glaser, P. H. (1986). The raised bogs of south-eastern Labrador, Canada: classification, distribution, vegetation and recent dynamics. *Journal of Ecology*, **74**, 47–71.

Foster, D. R. and Wright, H. E., Jr. (1990). Role of ecosystem development and climate change in bog formation in central Sweden. *Ecology*, **71**, 450–63.

Foster, D. R., King, G. A., Glaser, P. H., and Wright, H. E., Jr. (1983). Origin of string patterns in boreal peatlands. *Nature*, **306**, 256–7.

Fox, A. D. and Kahlert, J. (1999). Adjustments to nitrogen metabolism during wing moult in Greylag Geese, *Anser anser*. *Functional Ecology*, **13**, 661–9.

Fragoso, J. M. V. (1998). Home range and movement patterns of white-lipped Peccary (*Tayassu pecari*) herds in the northern Brazilian Amazon. *Biotropica*, 30, 458–69.

Francis, T. B. and Schindler, D. E. (2006). Degradation of littoral habitats by residential development: woody debris in lakes of the Pacific Northwest and Midwest, United States. *AMBIO: A Journal of the Human Environment*, 35, 274–80.

Fraser, A. (1973). *Cromwell: The Lord Protector*. New York: Konecky and Konecky.

Fraser, L. H. and Keddy, P. A. (eds.) (2005). *The World's Largest Wetlands: Ecology and Conservation*. Cambridge, UK: Cambridge University Press.

Freedman, B. (1995). *Environmental Ecology*, 2nd edn. San Diego, CA: Academic Press.

Fremlin, G. (ed. in chief) (1974). *The National Atlas of Canada*, 4th edn, revd. Toronto, ON: Macmillan.

Frenzel, B. (1983). Mires: repositories of climatic information or self-perpetuating ecosystems? In *Ecosystems of the World* Vol. 4A, *Mires: Swamp, Bog, Fen and Moor – General Studies*, ed. A. J. P. Gore, pp. 35–65. Amsterdam, the Netherlands: Elsevier.

Fretwell, S. D. (1977). The regulation of plant communities by food chains exploiting them. *Perspectives in Biology and Medicine*, 20, 169–85.

Frey, R. W. and Basan, P. B. (1978). Coastal salt marshes. In *Coastal Sedimentary Environments*, ed. R. A. Davis, pp. 101–69. New York: Springer-Verlag.

Fritzell, E. K. (1989). Mammals in prairie wetlands. In *Northern Prairie Wetlands*, ed. A. van der Valk, pp. 268–301. Ames, IA: Iowa State University Press.

Galatowitsch, S. M. and van der Valk, A. G. (1994). *Restoring Prairie Wetlands: An Ecological Approach*. Ames, IA: Iowa State University Press.

Galatowitsch, S. M. and van der Valk, A. G. (1996). The vegetation of restored and natural prairie wetlands. *Ecological Applications*, 6, 102–12.

Galinato, M. and van der Valk, A. (1986). Seed germination of annuals and emergents recruited during drawdowns in the Delta Marsh, Manitoba, Canada. *Aquatic Botany*, 26, 89–102.

Garcia, L. V., Maranon, T., Moreno, A., and Clemente, L. (1993). Above-ground biomass and species richness in a Mediterranean salt marsh. *Journal of Vegetation Science*, 4, 417–24.

Gastescu, P. (1993). The Danube Delta: geographical characteristics and ecological recovery. *Earth and Environmental Science*, 29, 57–67.

Gaston, K. J. (2000). Global patterns in biodiversity. *Nature*, 405, 220–7.

Gaston, K. J., Williams, P. H., Eggleton, P., and Humphries, C. J. (1995). Large scale patterns of biodiversity: spatial variation in family richness. *Proceedings of the Royal Society of London Series B*, 260, 149–54.

Gaudet, C. L. and Keddy, P. A. (1988). A comparative approach to predicting competitive ability from plant traits. *Nature*, 334, 242–3.

Gaudet, C. L. and Keddy, P. A. (1995). Competitive performance and species distribution in shoreline plant communities: a comparative approach. *Ecology*, 76, 280–91.

Geho, E. M., Campbell, D., and Keddy, P. A. (2007). Quantifying ecological filters: the relative impact of herbivory, neighbours, and sediment on an oligohaline marsh. *Oikos*, 116, 1006–16.

Geis, J. W. (1985). Environmental influences on the distribution and composition of wetlands in the Great Lakes basin. In *Coastal Wetlands*, eds. H. H. Prince and F. M. D'Itri, pp. 15–31. Chelsea, MI: Lewis Publishers.

Gentry, A. H. (1988). Changes in plant community diversity and floristic composition on environmental and geographical gradients. *Annals of the Missouri Botanical Garden*, 75, 1–34.

German Advisory Council on Global Change. (2006). *The Future Oceans: Warming Up, Rising High, Turning Sour*, Special Report. Berlin, Germany: German Advisory Council on Global Change.

Gibson, D. J., Zampella, R. A., and Windisch, A. G. (1999). New Jersey Pine Plains: the "true barrens" of the New Jersey Pine Barrens. In *Savannas, Barrens, and Rock Outcrop Communities of North America*, eds. R. C. Anderson. J. S. Fralish, and J. M. Bastin, pp. 52–66. Cambridge, UK: Cambridge University Press.

Gignac, L. D. and Vitt, D. H. (1990). Habitat limitations of *Sphagnum* along climatic, chemical, and physical gradients in mires of western Canada. *The Bryologist*, 93, 7–22.

Gilbert, J. J. (1988). Suppression of rotifer populations by *Daphnia*: a review of the evidence, the mechanisms, and the effects on zooplankton community structure. *Limnology and Oceanography*, **33**, 1286–303.

Gilbert, J. J. (1990). Differential effects of *Anabaena affinis* on cladoceran and rotifers: mechanisms and implications. *Ecology*, **71**, 1727–40.

Gilbert, R. and Glew, J. R. (1986). A wind-driven ice-push event in eastern Lake Ontario. *Journal of Great Lakes Research*, **12**, 326–31.

Gill, D. (1973). Modification of northern alluvial habitats by river development. *The Canadian Geographer*, **17**, 138–53.

Giller, K. E. and Wheeler, B. D. (1986). Past peat cutting and present vegetation patterns in an undrained fen in the Norfolk Broadland. *Journal of Ecology*, **74**, 219–47.

Givnish, T. J. (1982). On the adaptive significance of leaf height in forest herbs. *The American Naturalist*, **120**, 353–81.

Givnish, T. J. (1988). Ecology and evolution of carnivorous plants. In *Plant–Animal Interactions*, ed. W. B. Abrahamson, pp. 243–90. New York: McGraw-Hill.

Gladwell, M. (2002). *The Tipping Point: How Little Things Can Make a Big Difference*. New York: Little, Brown.

Glaser, P. H. (1992). Raised bogs in eastern North America: regional controls for species richness and floristic assemblages. *Journal of Ecology*, **80**, 535–54.

Glaser, P. H., Janssens, J. A., and Siegel, D. I. (1990). The response of vegetation to chemical and hydrological gradients in the Lost River peatland, northern Minnesota. *Journal of Ecology*, **78**, 1021–48.

Gleason, H. A. (1926). The individualistic concept of the plant association. *Bulletin of the Torrey Botanical Club*, **53**, 7–26.

Gleason, H. A. (1939). The individualistic concept of the plant association. *American Midland Naturalist*, **21**, 92–110.

Glob, P. V. (1969). *The Bog People. Iron-Age Man Preserved*, translated from the Danish by R. Bruce-Mitford. Ithaca, NY: Cornell University Press.

Glooschenko, W. A. (1980). Coastal ecosystems of the James/Hudson Bay area of Ontario, Canada. *Zeitschrift für Geomorphologie, NF*, **34**, 214–24.

Godfrey, W. E. (1966). *The Birds of Canada*. Ottawa, ON: Information Canada.

Godwin, Sir H. (1981). *The Archives of the Peat Bogs*. Cambridge, UK: Cambridge University Press.

Godwin, K. S., Shallenberger, J., Leopold, D. J., and Bedford, B. L. (2002). Linking landscape properties to local hydrogeologic gradients and plant species occurrence in New York fens: a hydrogeologic setting (HGS) framework. *Wetlands*, **22**, 722–37.

Goethe, J. W. (1831). *Goethe's Faust, Part 2*, translated by B. Taylor, revised and edited by S. Atkins, 1962. New York: Collier Books.

Goin, C. J. and Goin, O. B. (1971). *Introduction to Herpetology*, 2nd edn. San Francisco, CA: W. H. Freeman.

Goldsmith, F. B. (1973). The vegetation of exposed sea cliffs at South Stack, Anglesey. II. Experimental studies. *Journal of Ecology*, **61**, 819–29,

Goldsmith, F. B. (ed.) (1991). *Monitoring for Conservation and Ecology*. London: Chapman and Hall.

Goldsmith, F. B. and Harrison, C. M. (1976). Description and analysis of vegetation. In *Methods in Plant Ecology*, ed. S. B. Chapman, pp. 85–155. Oxford, UK: Blackwell Scientific Publications.

Golet, F. C. and Parkhurst, J. A. (1981). Freshwater wetland dynamics in South Kingston, Rhode Island, 1939–1972. *Environmental Management*, **5**, 245–51.

Good, R. E., Whigham, D. F., and Simpson, R. L (eds.) (1978). *Freshwater Wetlands: Ecological Processes and Management Potential*. New York: Academic Press.

Gopal, B. (1990). Nutrient dynamics of aquatic plant communities. In *Ecology and Management of Aquatic Vegetation in the Indian Subcontinent*, ed. B. Gopal, pp. 177–97. Dordrecht, the Netherlands: Kluwer.

Gopal, B. and Goel, U. (1993). Competition and allelopathy in aquatic plant communities. *Botanical Review*, **59**, 155–210.

Gopal, B., Kvet, J., Loffler, H., Masing, V. and Patten, B. (1990). Definition and classification. In *Wetlands and Shallow Continental Water Bodies*, Vol. 1, *Natural and Human Relationships*, ed. B. C. Patten, pp. 9–15. The Hague, the Netherlands: SPB Academic Publishing.

Gore, A. J. P. (ed.) (1983). *Ecosystems of the World*, Vol. 4A, *Mires: Swamp, Bog, Fen and Moor – General Studies*. Amsterdam, the Netherlands: Elsevier.

Gore, A. J. P. (1983). Introduction. In *Ecosystems of the World*, Vol. 4A, *Mires: Swamp, Bog, Fen and*

Moor – General Studies, ed. A. J. P. Gore. Amsterdam, the Netherlands: Elsevier.

Gorham, E. (1953). Some early ideas concerning the nature, origin and development of peat lands. *Journal of Ecology*, **41**, 257–74.

Gorham, E. (1957). The development of peatlands. *Quarterly Review of Biology*, **32**, 145–66.

Gorham, E. (1961). Water, ash, nitrogen and acidity of some bog peats and other organic soils. *Journal of Ecology*, **49**, 103–6.

Gorham, E. (1990). Biotic impoverishment in northern peatlands. In *The Earth in Transition*, ed. G. M. Woodwell, pp. 65–98. Cambridge, UK: Cambridge University Press.

Gorham, E. (1991). Northern peatlands role in the carbon cycle and probable responses to climatic warming. *Ecological Applications*, **1**, 182–95.

Gosselink, J. G. and Turner, R. E. (1978). The role of hydrology in freshwater wetland ecosystems. In *Freshwater Wetlands: Ecological Processes and Management Potential*, eds. R. E. Good, D. F. Whigham, and R. L. Simpson, pp. 63–79. New York: Academic Press.

Gottlieb, A. D., Richards, J. H., and Gaiser, E. E. (2006). Comparative study of periphyton community structure in long and short hydroperiod Everglades marshes. *Hydrobiologia*, **569**, 195–207.

Gough, J. (1793). Reasons for supposing that lakes have been more numerous than they are at present; with an attempt to assign the causes whereby they have been defaced. *Memoirs of the Literary and Philosophical Society of Manchester*, 4, 1–19. In Walker, D. (1970). *Direction and Rate in Some British Post-Glacial Hydroseres*. In *Studies in the Vegetational History of the British Isles*, eds. D. Walker and R. G. West, pp. 117–39. Cambridge, UK: Cambridge University Press.

Gough, L. G., Grace, J. B., and Taylor, K. L. (1994). The relationship between species richness and community biomass: the importance of environmental variables. *Oikos*, **70**, 271–9.

Goulding, M. (1980). *The Fishes and the Forest: Explorations in Amazonian Natural History*. Berkeley, CA: University of California Press.

Grace, J. B. (1990). On the relationship between plant traits and competitive ability. In *Perspectives on Plant Competition*, eds. J. B. Grace and D. Tilman, pp. 51–65. San Diego, CA: Academic Press.

Grace, J. B. (1999). The factors controlling species density in herbaceous plant communities: an assessment. *Perspectives in Plant Ecology, Evolution and Systematics*, **2**, 1–28.

Grace, J. B. and Ford, M. A. (1996). The potential impact of herbivores on the susceptibility of the marsh plant *Sagittaria lancifolia* to saltwater intrusion in coastal wetlands. *Estuaries*, **19**, 13–20.

Grace, J. B. and Wetzel, R. G. (1981). Habitat partitioning and competitive displacement in cattails (*Typha*): experimental field studies. *The American Naturalist*, **118**, 463–74.

Graf, D. L. and Cummings, K. S. (2007). Review of the systematics and global diversity of freshwater mussel species (Bivalvia: Unionoida). *Journal of Molluscan Studies*, **73**, 291–314.

Graham, J. B. (1997). *Air Breathing Fishes*. San Diego, CA: Academic Press.

Greening, H. (1995). Resource-based watershed management in Tampa Bay. In *Wetlands and Watershed Management: Science Applications and Public Policy*, eds. J. A. Kusler, D. E. Willard, and H. C. Hull Jr., pp. 172–81. A collection of papers from a national symposium and several workshops at Tampa, FL, Apr 23–26. Berne, NY: Association of State Wetland Managers.

Griffiths, R. A., Denton, J., and Wong, A. L. (1993). The effect of food level on competition in tadpoles: interference mediated by prototheca algae? *Journal of Animal Ecology*, **62**, 274–9.

Grime, J. P. (1973). Competitive exclusion in herbaceous vegetation. *Nature*, **242**, 344–7.

Grime, J. P. (1974). Vegetation classification by reference to strategies. *Nature*, **250**, 26–31.

Grime, J. P. (1977). Evidence for the existence of three primary strategies in plants and its relevance to ecological and evolutionary theory. *The American Naturalist*, **111**, 1169–94.

Grime, J. P. (1979). *Plant Strategies and Vegetation Processes*. Chichester, UK: John Wiley.

Grime, J. P. and Hunt, R. (1975). Relative growth-rate: its range and adaptive significance in a local flora. *Journal of Ecology*, **63**, 393–422.

Grime, J. P., Mason, G., Curtis, A. V., Rodman, J., Band, S. R., Mowforth, M. A. G., Neal, A. M., and Shaw, S.

(1981). A comparative study of germination characteristics in a local flora. *Journal of Ecology*, **69**, 1017–59.

Grimes, W. (2006). Visionaries and rascals in Florida's wetlands: review of *The Swamp: The Everglades, Florida and the Politics of Paradise*. *The Washington Post*, Mar 8, 2006.

Grishin, S. Y., del Moral, R., Krestov, P. V., and Verkholat, V. P. (1996). Succession following the catastrophic eruption of Ksudach volcano (Kamchatka, 1907). *Vegetatio*, **127**, 129–53.

Groombridge, B. (ed.) (1992). *Global Biodiversity: Status of the Earth's Living Resources*, a report compiled by the World Conservation Monitoring Centre. London: Chapman and Hall.

Grootjans, A. P., van Diggelen, R., Everts, H. F., Schipper, P. C., Streefkerk, J., de Vries, N. P., and Wierda, A. (1993). Linking ecological patterns to hydrological conditions on various spatial scales: a case study of small stream valleys. In *Landscape Ecology of a Stressed Environment*, eds. C. C. Vos and P. Opdam, pp. 60–99. London: Chapman and Hall.

Grosse, W., Buchel, H. B., and Tiebel, H. (1991). Pressurized ventilation in wetland plants. *Aquatic Botany*, **39**, 89–98.

Grover, A. M. and Baldassarre, G. A. (1995). Bird species richness within beaver ponds in south-central New York. *Wetlands*, **15**, 108–18.

Grubb, P. J. (1977). The maintenance of species-richness in plant communities: the importance of the regeneration niche. *Biological Review*, **52**, 107–45.

Grubb, P. J. (1985). Plant populations and vegetation in relation to habitat disturbance and competition: problems of generalizations. In *The Population Structure of Vegetation*, ed. J. White, pp. 595–621. Dordrecht, the Netherlands: Dr. W. Junk Publishers.

Grubb, P. J. (1986). Problems posed by sparse and patchily distributed species in species-rich plant communities. In *Community Ecology*, eds. J. M. Diamond and T. J. Case, pp. 207–25. New York: Harper and Row.

Grubb, P. J. (1987). Global trends in species-richness in terrestrial vegetation: a view from the northern hemisphere. In *Organization of Communities Past and Present*, eds. J. H. R. Gee and P. S. Giller, pp. 99–118. 27th Symposium of the British Ecological Society, Aberystwyth. Oxford, UK: Blackwell Scientific Publications.

Grumbine, R. E. (1994). What is ecosystem management? *Conservation Biology*, **8**, 27–38.

Grumbine, R. E. (1997). Reflections on 'What is ecosystem management?' *Conservation Biology*, **11**, 41–7.

Grunwald, M. (2006). *The Swamp: The Everglades, Florida and the Politics of Paradise*. New York: Simon and Schuster.

Gurevitch, J., Morrow, L., Wallace, A., and Walsh, A. (1992). A meta-analysis of competition in field experiments. *The American Naturalist*, **140**, 539–72.

Guy, H. P. (1973). Sediment problems in urban areas. In *Focus on Environmental Geology*, ed. R. W. Tank, pp. 186–92. New York: Oxford University Press.

Guyer, C. and Bailey, M. A. (1993). Amphibians and reptiles of longleaf pine communities. In *The Longleaf Pine Ecosystem: Ecology, Restoration and Management*, ed. S. M. Hermann, pp. 139–58. Proceedings of the Tall Timbers Fire Ecology Conference No. 18. Tallahassee, FL: Tall Timbers Research Station.

Hacker, S. D. and Bertness, M. D. (1999). Experimental evidence for factors maintaining plant species diversity in a New England salt marsh. *Ecology*, **80**, 2064–73.

Hacker, S. D. and Gaines, S. D. (1997). Some implications of direct positive interactions for community species diversity. *Ecology*, **78**, 1990–2003.

Haeuber, R. and Franklin, J. (eds.) (1996). Perspectives on ecosystem management. *Ecological Applications*, **6**, 692–747.

Hairston, N. G., Smith, F. E., and Slobodkin, L. B. (1960). Community structure, population control, and competition. *The American Naturalist*, **94**, 421–5.

Haith, D. A. and Shoemaker, L. L. (1987). Generalized watershed loading functions for stream-flow nutrients. *Water Resources Bulletin*, **23**, 471–8.

Hamilton, S. K., Sipel, S. J., and Melack, J. M. (1996). Inundation patterns in the Pantanal wetland of South America determined from passive microwave remote sensing. *Archiv für Hydrobiologie*, **137**, 1–23.

Hammer, D. A. (1969). Parameters of a marsh snapping turtle population Lacreek refuge, South Dakota. *Journal of Wildlife Management*, **33**, 995–1005.

Hammer, D. A. (ed.) (1989). *Constructed Wetlands for Wastewater Treatment: Municipal, Industrial and Agricultural*. Chelsea, MI: Lewis Publishers.

Hanski, I. (1994). Patch-occupancy dynamics in fragmented landscapes. *Trends in Ecology and Evolution*, 9, 131–5.

Hanski, I. and Gilpin, M. (1991). Metapopulation dynamics: a brief history and conceptual domain. *Biological Journal of the Linnean Society*, 42, 3–16.

Hardin, G. (1968). The tragedy of the commons. *Science*, 162, 1243–8.

Hardin, G. and Baden, J. (1977). *Managing the Commons*. San Francisco, CA: W. H. Freeman.

Harington, C. R. (1996). Giant beaver. (Reproduced courtesy of the Canadian Museum of Nature, Ottawa). www.beringia.com/02/02maina6.html (accessed July 28, 2008)

Harmon, M. E., Franklin, J. F., Swanson, F. J., Sollins, P., Gregory, S. V., Lattin, J. D., Anderson, N. H., and Cline, S. P. (1986). Ecology of coarse woody debris in temperate ecosystems. *Advances in Ecological Research*, 15, 133–302.

Harper, J. L. (1977). *Population Biology of Plants*. London: Academic Press.

Harper, J. L., Williams, J. T., and Sagar, G. R. (1965). The behavior of seeds in soil. I. The heterogeneity of soil surfaces and its role in determining the establishment of plants from seed. *Journal of Ecology*, 53, 273–86.

Harris, R. R., Fox, C. A., and Risser, R. (1987). Impact of hydroelectric development on riparian vegetation in the Sierra Nevada region, California, USA. *Environmental Management*, 11, 519–27.

Harris, S. W. and Marshall, W. H. (1963). Ecology of water-level manipulations on a northern marsh. *Ecology*, 44, 331–43.

Hart, D. D. (1983). The importance of competitive interactions within stream populations and communities. In *Stream Ecology: Application and Testing of General Ecological Theory*, eds. J. R. Barnes and G. W. Minshall, pp. 99–136. New York: Plenum Press.

Hartman, J. M. (1988). Recolonization of small disturbance patches in a New England salt marsh. *American Journal of Botany*, 75, 1625–31.

Harvey, P. H., Colwell, R. K., Silvertown, J. W., and May, R. M. (1983). Null models in ecology. *Annual Review of Ecology and Systematics*, 14, 189–211.

Haukos, D. A. and Smith, L. M. (1993). Seed-bank composition and predictive ability of field vegetation in playa lakes. *Wetlands*, 13, 32–40.

Haukos, D. A. and Smith, L. M. (1994). Composition of seed banks along an elevational gradient in playa wetlands. *Wetlands*, 14, 301–7.

Hayati, A. A. and Proctor, M. C. F. (1991). Limiting nutrients in acid-mire vegetation: peat and plant analyses and experiments on plant responses to added nutrients. *Journal of Ecology*, 79, 75–95.

Heal, G. (2000). Valuing ecosystem services. *Ecosystems*, 3, 24–30.

Heal, O. W., Latter, P. M., and Howson, G. (1978). A study of the rates of decomposition of organic matter. In *Production Ecology of British Moors and Montane Grasslands*, eds. O. W. Heal and D. F. Perkins, pp. 136–59. Berlin, Germany: Springer-Verlag.

Hellquist, C. B. and Crow, G. E. (1984). *Aquatic Vascular Plants of New England*, Part 7, *Cabombaceae, Nymphaeaceae, Nelumbonaceae, and Ceratophyllaceae*, Station Bulletin No. 527. Durham, NH: University of New Hampshire.

Helsinki Commission. (2003). *The Baltic Marine Environment 1999–2002*, Baltic Sea Environment Proceedings No. 87. Helsinki: Helsinki Commission.

Hemphill, N. and Cooper, S. D. (1983). The effect of physical disturbance on the relative abundances of two filter-feeding insects in a small stream. *Oecologia*, 58, 378–82.

Henry, H. A. L. and Jeffries, R. L. (2009). Opportunist herbivores, migratory connectivity and catastrophic shifts in arctic coastal systems. In *Human Impacts on Salt Marshes: A Global Perspective*, eds. B. R. Silliman, E. D. Grosholz, and M. D. Bertness, pp. 85–102. Berkeley, CA: University of California Press.

Herman, K. D., Masters, L. A., Penskar, M. R., Reznicek, A. A., Wilhelm, G. S., Brodovich, W. W., and Gardiner, K. P. (2001). *Floristic Quality Assessment with Wetland Categories and Examples of Computer Applications for the State of Michigan*, revd 2nd edn. Lansing, MI: Natural Heritage Program, Michigan Department of Natural Resources.

Higgs, E. S. (1997). What is good ecological restoration? *Conservation Biology*, 11, 338–48.

Hik, D. S., Jefferies, R. L., and Sinclair, A. R. E. (1992). Foraging by geese, isostatic uplift and asymmetry in the development of salt-marsh plant communities. *Journal of Ecology*, 80, 395–406.

Hill, N. M. and Keddy, P. A. (1992). Prediction of rarities from habitat variables: coastal plain plants on Nova Scotian lakeshores. *Ecology*, **73**, 1852–9.

Hill, N. M., Keddy, P. A., and Wisheu, I. C. (1998). A hydrological model for predicting the effects of dams on the shoreline vegetation of lakes and reservoirs. *Environmental Management*, **22**, 723–36.

Hoagland, B. W. and Collins, S. L. (1997a). Gradient models, gradient analysis, and hierarchical structure in plant communities. *Oikos*, **78**, 23–30.

Hoagland, B. W. and Collins, S. L. (1997b). Heterogeneity in shortgrass prairie vegetation: the role of playa lakes. *Journal of Vegetation Science*, **8**, 277–86.

Hochachka, P. W., Fields, J., and Mustafa, T. (1973). Animal life without oxygen: basic biochemical mechanisms. *American Zoology*, **13**, 543–55.

Hogenbirk, J. C. and Wein, R. W. (1991). Fire and drought experiments in northern wetlands: a climate change analogue. *Canadian Journal of Botany*, **69**, 1991–7.

Hogg, E. H., Lieffers, V. J., and Wein, R. W. (1992). Potential carbon losses from peat profiles: effects of temperature, drought cycles, and fire. *Ecological Applications*, **2**, 298–306.

Holling, C. S. (ed.) (1978). *Adaptive Environmental Assessment and Management*. Chichester, UK: John Wiley.

Hook, D. D. (1984). Adaptations to flooding with fresh water. In *Flooding and Plant Growth*, ed. T. T. Kozlowski, pp. 265–94. Orlando, FL: Academic Press.

Hook, D. D., McKee, W. H., Jr., Smith, H., Gregory, J., Burrell, V. J., Jr., DeVoe, W. R., Sojka, R. E., Gilbert, S., Banks, R., Stolzy, L. H., Brooks, C., Matthews, T. D., and Shear, T. H. (eds.) (1988). *The Ecology and Management of Wetlands*, Vol. 1, *Ecology of Wetlands*. Portland, OR: Timber Press.

Hoover, J. J. and Killgore, K. J. (1998). Fish communities. In *Southern Forested Wetlands: Ecology and Management*, eds. M. G. Messina and W. H. Conner, pp. 237–60. Boca Raton, FL: Lewis Publishers.

Horn, H. (1976). Succession. In *Theoretical Ecology: Principles and Applications*, ed. R. M. May, pp. 187–204. Philadelphia, PA: W.B. Saunders.

Hou, H.-Y. (1983). Vegetation of China with reference to its geographical distribution. *Annals of the Missouri Botanical Garden*, **70**, 509–48.

Houck, O. (2006). Can we save New Orleans? *Tulane Environmental Law Journal*, **19**, 1–68.

Houlahan, J., Keddy, P., Makkey, K., and Findlay, C. S. (2006). The effects of adjacent land-use on wetland plant species richness and community composition. *Wetlands*, **26**, 79–96.

House, J. and Brovkin, V. (eds.) (2005). Climate and air quality. In *Ecosystems and Human Well-Being: Current State and Trends – Findings of the Condition and Trends Working Group of the Millennium Ecosystem Assessment*, eds. R. Hassan, R. Scholes, and N. Ash, pp. 355–90. Washington, DC: Island Press.

Howard, R. T. and Mendelssohn, I. A. (1999). Salinity as a constraint on growth of oligohaline marsh macrophytes. I. Species variation in stress tolerance. *American Journal of Botany*, **86**, 785–94.

Howard-Williams, C. and Thompson, K. (1985). The conservation and management of African wetlands. In *The Ecology and Management of African Wetland Vegetation*, ed. P. Denny, pp. 203–30. Dordrecht, the Netherlands: Dr. W. Junk Publishers.

Howarth, R. W., Fruci, J. R., and Sherman, D. (1991). Inputs of sediment and carbon to an estuarine ecosystem: influence of land use. *Ecological Applications*, **1**, 27–39.

Hubbell, S. P. and Foster, R. B. (1986). Biology, chance, and the history and structure of tropical rain forest tree communities. In *Community Ecology*, eds. J. Diamond and T. J. Case, pp. 314–29. New York: Harper and Row.

Huber, O. (1982). Significance of savanna vegetation in the Amazon Territory of Venezuela. In *Biological Diversification in the Tropics*, ed. G. T. Prance, pp. 221–44. New York: Columbia University Press.

Hughes, J. D. and Thirgood, J. V. (1982). Deforestation, erosion and forest management in ancient Greece and Rome. *Journal of Forestry*, **26**, 60–75.

Hunter, M. D. and Price, P. W. (1992). Playing chutes and ladders: heterogeneity and the relative roles of bottom-up and top-down forces in natural communities. *Ecology*, **73**, 724–32.

Hurlbert, S. H. (1984). Pseudoreplication and the design of ecological field experiments. *Ecological Monographs*, **54**, 187–211.

Hurlbert, S. H. (1990). Spatial distribution of the montane unicorn. *Oikos*, **58**, 257–71.

Huston, M. (1979). A general hypothesis of species diversity. *The American Naturalist*, 113, 81–101.

Huston, M. (1994). *Biological Diversity: The Coexistence of Species on Changing Landscapes*. Cambridge, UK: Cambridge University Press.

Hutchinson, G. E. (1959). Homage to Santa Rosalia or why are there so many kinds of animals? *The American Naturalist*, 93, 145–9.

Hutchinson, G. E. (1975). *A Treatise on Limnology*, Vol. 3, *Limnological Botany*. New York: John Wiley.

Ingebritsen, S. E., McVoy, C., Glaz, B., and Park, W. (1999). Florida Everglades: subsidence threatens agriculture and complicates ecosystem restoration. In *Land Subsidence in the United States*, U.S. Geological Survey Circular No. 1182, eds. D. Galloway, D. R. Jones, and S. E. Ingebritsen, pp. 95–106. Reston, VA: U.S. Geological Survey.

Ingram, H. A. P. (1982). Size and shape in raised mire ecosystems: a geophysical model. *Nature*, 297, 300–3.

Ingram, H. A. P. (1983). Hydrology. In *Ecosystems of the World*, Vol. 4A, *Mires: Swamp, Bog, Fen and Moor – General Studies*, ed. A. J. P. Gore, pp. 67–158. Amsterdam, the Netherlands: Elsevier.

International Joint Commission. (1980). *Pollution in the Great Lakes Basin from Land Use Activities*. Detroit, MI and Windsor, ON: International Joint Commission.

International Rice Research Institute (IRRI). (2009). Rough rice consumption, by country and geographical region: USA. http://beta.irri.org/solutions/index.php? (accessed Dec 4, 2009)

Irion, G. M., Müller, J., de Mello, J. N., and Junk, W. J. (1995). Quaternary geology of the Amazon lowland. *Geo-Marine Letters*, 15, 172–8.

Isabelle, P. S., Fooks, L. J., Keddy, P. A., and Wilson, S. D. (1987). Effects of roadside snowmelt on wetland vegetation: an experimental study. *Journal of Environmental Management*, 25, 57–60.

IUCN. (2008) *Red List*. www.iucnredlist.org

Jackson, J. B. C. (1981). Interspecific competition and species distributions: the ghosts of theories and data past. *American Zoologist*, 21, 889–901.

Jackson, M. B. and Drew, M. C. (1984). Effects of flooding on growth and metabolism of herbaceous plants. In *Flooding and Plant Growth*, ed. T. T. Kozlowski, pp. 47–128. Orlando, FL: Academic Press.

Janis, C. (1976). The evolutionary strategy of the Equidae and the origins of rumen and cecal digestion. *Evolution*, 30, 757–74.

Janzen, D. H. and Martin, P. S. (1982). Neotropical anachronisms: the fruits the gomphotheres ate. *Science*, 215, 19–27.

Jean, M. and Bouchard, A. (1991). Temporal changes in wetland landscapes of a section of the St. Lawrence River, Canada. *Environmental Management*, 15, 241–50.

Jefferies, R. L. (1977). The vegetation of salt marshes at some coastal sites in arctic North America. *Journal of Ecology*, 65, 661–72.

Jefferies, R. L. (1988a). Pattern and process in Arctic coastal vegetation in response to foraging by lesser snow geese. In *Plant Form and Vegetation Structure*, eds. M. J. A. Werger, P. J. M. van der Aart, H. J. During, and J. T. A. Verhoeven, pp. 281–300. The Hague, the Netherlands: SPB Academic Publishing.

Jefferies, R. L. (1988b). Vegetational mosaics, plant-animal interactions and resources for plant growth. In *Plant Evolutionary Biology*, eds. L. Gottlieb and S. K. Jain, pp. 341–69. London: Chapman and Hall.

Jeglum, J. K. and He, F. (1995). Pattern and vegetation-environment relationships in a boreal forested wetland in northeastern Ontario, *Canadian Journal of Botany*, 73, 629–37.

Jenkins, S. H. (1975). Food selection by beavers. *Oecologia*, 21, 157–73.

Jenkins, S. H. (1979). Seasonal and year to year differences in food selection by beavers. *Oecologia*, 44, 112–16.

Jenkins, S. H. (1980). A size–distance relation in food selection by beavers. *Ecology*, 61, 740–6.

Jochimsen, D. M. (2006). Factors influencing the road mortality of snakes on the Upper Snake River Plain, Idaho. In *Proceedings of the 2005 International Conference on Ecology and Transportation*, eds. C. L. Irwin, P. Garrett, and K. P. McDermott, pp. 351–65. Raleigh, NC: Center for Transportation and the Environment, North Carolina State University.

Johnsgard, P. A. (1980). Where have all the curlews gone? *Natural History*, 89(8), 30–3. Reprinted in *Papers in Ornithology*, http://digitalcommons.unl.edu/Gioscioenithology/23

Johnson, D. L., Lynch, W. E., Jr., and Morrison, T. W. (1997). Fish communities in a diked Lake Erie wetland and an adjacent undiked area. *Wetlands*, 17, 43–54.

Johnson, M. G., Leach, J. H., Minns, C. K., and Oliver, C. H. (1977). Limnological characteristics of Ontario lakes in relation to associations of walleye (*Stizostedion vitreum*), northern pike (*Esox lucius*), lake trout (*Salvelinus namaycush*) and smallmouth bass (*Micropterus dolomieui*). *Journal of the Fisheries Research Board of Canada*, 34, 1592–601.

Johnson, P. D. and Brown, K. M. (1998). Intraspecific life history variation in the threatened Louisiana pearlshell mussel, *Margaritifera hembeli. Freshwater Biology*, 40, 317–29.

Johnson, W. B., Sasser, C. E., and Gosselink, J. G. (1985). Succession of vegetation in an evolving river delta, Atchafalaya Bay, Louisiana. *Journal of Ecology*, 73, 973–86.

Johnson, W. C. (1994). Woodland expansion in the Platte River, Nebraska: patterns and causes. *Ecological Monographs*, 64, 45–84.

Johnson, W. C., Burgess, R. L., and Keammerer, W. R. (1976). Forest overstory vegetation and environment on the Missouri River floodplain in North Dakota. *Ecological Monographs*, 46, 59–84.

Johnston, A. J. B. (1983). *The Summer of 1744: A Portrait of Life in 18th-Century Louisbourg.* Hull, QC: Parks Canada.

Johnston, C. A. and Naiman, R. J. (1990). Aquatic patch creation in relation to beaver population trends. *Ecology*, 71, 1617–21.

Johnston, J. W., Thompson, T. A., Wilcox, D. A., and Baedke, S. J. (2007). Geomorphic and sedimentologic evidence for the separation of Lake Superior from Lake Michigan and Huron. *Journal of Paleolimnology*, 37, 349–64.

Jones, C. G., Lawton, J. H., and Shachak, M. (1994). Organisms as ecosystem engineers. *Oikos*, 69, 373–86.

Jones, M. (2003). *The Last Great Quest: Captain Scott's Antarctic Sacrifice.* New York: Oxford University Press.

Jones, R. H., Sharitz, R. R., Dixon, P. M., Segal, D. S., and Schneider, R. L. (1994). Woody plant regeneration in four floodplain forests. *Ecological Monographs*, 64, 345–67.

Jordan, W. R., III, Gilpin, M. E., and Aber, J. D. (1987). *Restoration Ecology: Synthetic Approach to Ecological Research.* Cambridge, UK: Cambridge University Press.

Judson, S. (1968). Erosion of the land, or what's happening to our continents? *American Scientist*, 56, 356–74.

Junk, W. J. (1983). Ecology of swamps on the Middle Amazon. In *Ecosystems of the World*, Vol. 4B, *Mires: Swamp, Bog, Fen and Moor – Regional Studies*, ed. A. J. P. Gore, pp. 98–126. Amsterdam, the Netherlands: Elsevier.

Junk, W. J. (1984). Ecology of the várzea, floodplain of Amazonian white-water rivers. In *The Amazon: Limnology and Landscape Ecology of a Mighty Tropical River and its Basin*, ed. H. Sioli, pp. 215–43. Dordrecht, the Netherlands: Dr. W. Junk Publishers.

Junk, W. J. (1986). Aquatic plants of the Amazon system. In *The Ecology of River Systems*, eds. B. R. Davies and K. F. Walker, pp. 319–37. Dordrecht, the Netherlands: Dr. W. Junk Publishers.

Junk, W. J. (1993). Wetlands of tropical South America. In *Wetlands of the World*, Vol. 1, eds. D. F. Whigham, D. Dykyjova and S. Hejny, pp. 679–739. Dordrecht, the Netherlands: Kluwer.

Junk, W. J. and Piedade, M. T. F. (1994). Species diversity and distribution of herbaceous plants in the floodplain of the middle Amazon. *Verhandlungen Internationale Vereinigung für theoretische und angewandte Limnologie*, 25, 1862–5.

Junk, W. J. and Piedade, M. T. F. (1997). Plant life in the floodplain with special reference to herbaceous plants. In *The Central Amazon Floodplain*, ed. W. J. Junk, pp. 147–85. Berlin, Germany: Springer-Verlag.

Junk, W. J. and Welcomme, R. L. (1990). Floodplains. In *Wetlands and Shallow Continental Water Bodies*, Vol. 1, *Natural and Human Relationships*, ed. B. C. Patten, pp. 491–524. The Hague, the Netherlands: SPB Academic Publishing.

Junk, W. J., Bayley, P. B., and Sparks, R. E. (1989). The flood pulse concept in riverfloodplain systems. In *Proceedings of the International Large River Symposium*, ed. D. P. Dodge, pp. 110–27. *Canadian Journal of Fisheries and Aquatic Sciences*, Special Publication No. 106.

Junk, W. J., Soares, M. G. M., and Saint-Paul, U. (1997). The fish. In *The Central Amazon Floodplain*, ed. W. J. Junk, pp. 385–408. Berlin, Germany: Springer-Verlag.

Junk, W. J., Brown, M., Campbell, I. C., Finlayson, M., Gopal, B., Ramberg, L., and Warner, B. G. (2006). The comparative biodiversity of seven globally important wetlands: a synthesis. *Aquatic Sciences*, **68**, 400–14.

Jurik, T. M., Wang, S., and van der Valk, A. G. (1994). Effects of sediment load on seedling emergence from wetland seed banks. *Wetlands*, **14**, 159–65.

Justin, S. H. F. W. and Armstrong, W. (1987). The anatomical characteristics of roots and plant response to soil flooding. *New Phytologist*, **106**, 465–95.

Kajak, Z. (1993). The Vistula River and its riparian zones. *Hydrobiologia*, **251**, 149–57.

Kalamees, K. (1982). The composition and seasonal dynamics of fungal cover on peat soils. In *Peatland Ecosystems: Researches into the Plant Cover of Estonian Bogs and Their Productivity*, ed. V. Masing, pp. 12–29. Tallinn, Estonia: Academy of Sciences of the Estonian S. S. R.

Kalliola, R., Salo, J., Puhakka, M., and Rajasilta, M. (1991). New site formation and colonizing vegetation in primary succession on the Western Amazon floodplains. *Journal of Ecology*, **79**, 877–901.

Kaminski, R. M. and Prince, H. H. (1981). Dabbling duck and aquatic macroinvertebrate responses to manipulated wetland habitat. *Journal of Wildlife Management*, **45**, 1–15.

Kaminski, R. M., Murkin, H. M., and Smith, C. E. (1985). Control of cattail and bulrush by cutting and flooding. In *Coastal Wetlands*, eds. H. H. Prince and F. M. D'Itri, pp. 253–62. Chelsea, MI: Lewis Publishers.

Kantrud, H. A., Millar, J. B., and van der Valk, A. G. (1989). Vegetation of the wetlands of the prairie pothole region. In *Northern Prairie Wetlands*, ed. A. G. van der Valk, pp. 132–87. Ames, IA: Iowa State University Press.

Karrow, P. F. and P. E. Calkin (eds.) (1985). *Quaternary Evolution of the Great Lakes*, Special Paper No. 30. St John's, Nfld: Geological Association of Canada.

Keddy, C. J. and McCrae, T. (1989). *Environmental Databases for State of the Environment Reporting*, Technical Report No. 19. Ottawa, ON: State of the Environment Reporting Branch, Environment Canada.

Keddy, C. J. and Sharp, M. J. (1994). A protocol to identify and prioritize significant coastal plain plant assemblages for conservation. *Biological Conservation*, **68**, 269–74.

Keddy, P. A. (1976). Lakes as islands: the distributional ecology of two aquatic plants, *Lemna minor* L. and *L. trisulca* L. *Ecology*, **57**, 353–9.

Keddy, P. A. (1981). Vegetation with coastal plain affinities in Axe Lake, near Georgian Bay, Ontario. *Canadian Field Naturalist*, **95**, 241–8.

Keddy, P. A. (1982). Quantifying within lake gradients of wave energy, substrate particle size and shoreline plants in Axe Lake, Ontario. *Aquatic Botany*, **14**, 41–58.

Keddy, P. A. (1983). Shoreline vegetation in Axe Lake, Ontario: effects of exposure on zonation patterns. *Ecology*, **64**, 331–44.

Keddy, P. A. (1984). Plant zonation on lakeshores in Nova Scotia: a test of the resource specialization hypothesis. *Journal of Ecology*, **72**, 797–808.

Keddy, P. A. (1985a). Lakeshores in the Tusket River Valley, Nova Scotia: distribution and status of some rare species, including *Coreopsis rosea* Nutt. and *Sabtia kennedyana* Fern. *Rhodora*, **87**, 309–20.

Keddy, P. A. (1985b). Wave disturbance on lakeshores and the within-lake distribution of Ontario's Atlantic coastal plain flora. *Canadian Journal of Botany*, **63**, 656–60.

Keddy, P. A. (1989a). *Competition*. London: Chapman and Hall.

Keddy, P. A. (1989b). Effects of competition from shrubs on herbaceous wetland plants: a 4-year field experiment. *Canadian Journal of Botany*, **67**, 708–16.

Keddy, P. A. (1990a). Competitive hierarchies and centrifugal organization in plant communities. In *Perspectives on Plant Competition*, eds. J. B. Grace and D. Tilman, pp. 265–90. San Diego, CA: Academic Press.

Keddy, P. A. (1990b). Is mutualism really irrelevant to ecology? *Bulletin of the Ecological Society of America*, **71**(2), 101–2.

Keddy, P. A. (1991a). Biological monitoring and ecological prediction: from nature reserve management to national state of environment indicators. In *Biological Monitoring for Conservation*, ed. F. B. Goldsmith, pp. 249–67. London: Chapman and Hall.

Keddy, P. A. (1991b). Water level fluctuations and wetland conservation. In *Wetlands of the Great*

Lakes, eds. J. Kusler and R. Smardon, pp. 79–91. Proceedings of an International Symposium, Niagara Falls, NY, May 16–18, 1990. Berne, NY: Association of State Wetland Managers.

Keddy, P. A. (1991c). Reviewing a festschrift: what are we doing with our scientific lives? *Journal of Vegetation Science*, 2, 419–24.

Keddy, P. A. (1992a). Assembly and response rules: two goals for predictive community ecology. *Journal of Vegetation Science*, 3, 157–64.

Keddy, P. A. (1992b). A pragmatic approach to functional ecology. *Functional Ecology*, 6, 621–6.

Keddy, P. A. (1994). Applications of the Hertzsprung–Russell star chart to ecology: reflections on the 21st birthday of Geographical Ecology. *Trends in Ecology and Evolution*, 9, 231–4.

Keddy, P. A. (2001). *Competition*, 2nd edn. Dordrecht, the Netherlands: Kluwer.

Keddy, P. A. (2007). *Plants and Vegetation: Origins, Processes, Consequences*. Cambridge, UK: Cambridge University Press.

Keddy, P. A. (2009). Thinking big: a conservation vision for the Southeastern Coastal Plain of North America. *Southeastern Naturalist*, 7, 213–26.

Keddy, P. A. and Constabel, P. (1986). Germination of ten shoreline plants in relation to seed size, soil particle size and water level: an experimental study. *Journal of Ecology*, 74, 122–41.

Keddy, P. A. and Fraser, L. H. (2000). Four general principles for the management and conservation of wetlands in large lakes: the role of water levels, nutrients, competitive hierarchies and centrifugal organization. *Lakes and Reservoirs: Research and Management*, 5, 177–85.

Keddy, P. A. and Fraser, L. H. (2002). The management of wetlands for biological diversity: four principles. In *Modern Trends in Applied Aquatic Ecology*, eds. R. S. Ambasht and N. K. Ambasht, pp. 21–42. New York: Kluwer.

Keddy, P. A. and MacLellan, P. (1990). Centrifugal organization in forests. *Oikos*, 59, 75–84.

Keddy, P. A. and Reznicek, A. A. (1982). The role of seed banks in the persistence of Ontario's coastal plain flora. *American Journal of Botany*, 69, 13–22.

Keddy, P. A. and Reznicek, A. A. (1986). Great Lakes vegetation dynamics: the role of fluctuating water levels and buried seeds. *Journal of Great Lakes Research*, 12, 25–36.

Keddy, P. A. and Shipley, B. (1989). Competitive hierarchies in herbaceous plant communities. *Oikos*, 54, 234–41.

Keddy, P. A. and Wisheu, I. C. (1989). Ecology, biogeography, and conservation of coastal plain plants: some general principles from the study of Nova Scotian wetlands. *Rhodora*, 91, 72–94.

Keddy, P. A., Lee, H. T., and Wisheu, I. C. (1993). Choosing indicators of ecosystem integrity: wetlands as a model system. In *Ecological Integrity and the Management of Ecosystems*, eds. S. Woodley, J. Kay, and G. Francis, pp. 61–79. Delray Beach, FL: St. Lucie Press.

Keddy, P. A., Twolan-Strutt, L., and Wisheu, I. C. (1994). Competitive effect and response rankings in 20 wetland plants: are they consistent across three environments? *Journal of Ecology*, 82, 635–43.

Keddy, P. A., Fraser, L. H., and Wisheu, I. C. (1998). A comparative approach to examine competitive responses of 48 wetland plant species. *Journal of Vegetation Science*, 9, 777–86.

Keddy, P. A., Campbell, D., McFalls T., Shaffer, G., Moreau, R., Dranguet, C., and Heleniak, R. (2007). The wetlands of lakes Pontchartrain and Maurepas: past, present and future. *Environmental Reviews*, 15, 1–35.

Keddy, P. A., Gough, L., Nyman, J. A., McFalls, T., Carter, J., and Siegnist, J. (2009a). Alligator hunters, pelt traders, and runaway consumption of Gulf coast marshes: a trophic cascade perspective on coastal wetland losses. In *Human Impacts on Salt Marshes: A Global Perspective*, eds. B. R. Silliman, E. D. Grosholz, and M. D. Bertness, pp. 115–33. Berkeley, CA: University of California Press.

Keddy, P. A., Fraser, L. H., Solomeshch, A. I., Junk, W. J., Campbell, D. R., Arroyo, M. T. K., and Alho, C. J. R. (2009b). Wet and wonderful: the world's largest wetlands are conservation priorities. *BioScience*, 59, 39–51.

Keeley, J. E., DeMason, D. A., Gonzalez, R., and Markham, K. R. (1994). Sediment based carbon nutrition in tropical alpine Isoetes. In *Tropical Alpine Environments Plant Form and Function*, eds. P. W. Rundel, A. P. Smith, and F. C. Meinzer, pp. 167–94. Cambridge, UK: Cambridge University Press.

Keeling, C. D. and Whorf, T. P. (2005). Atmospheric CO_2 records from sites in the SIO air sampling network. In *Trends: A Compendium of Data on Global Change* eds. T.A. Boden *et al.*, pp. 16–26. Oak Ridge, TN: Carbon Dioxide Information Analysis Center, Oak Ridge National Laboratory, U.S. Department of Energy.

Keller, E. A. and Day, J. W. (2007). Untrammeled growth as an environmental "March of Folly". *Ecological Engineering*, 30, 206–14.

Kelly, K. (1975). The artificial drainage of land in nineteenth-century southern Ontario. *Canadian Geographer*, 4, 279–98.

Kendall, R. L. (1969). An ecological history of the Lake Victoria Basin. *Ecological Monographs*, 39, 121–76.

Kenrick, P. and Crane, P. R. (1997). *The Origin and Early Diversification of Land Plants: A Cladistic Study.* Washington, DC: Smithsonian Institution Press.

Keogh, T. M., Keddy, P. A., and Fraser, L. H. (1998). Patterns of tree species richness in forested wetlands. *Wetlands*, 19, 639–47.

Kercher, S. M., Carpenter, Q. J., and Zedler, J. B. (2004). Interrelationships of hydrologic disturbance, reed canary grass (*Phalaris arundinacea* L.), and native plants in Wisconsin wet meadows. *Natural Areas Journal*, 24, 316–25.

Kerr, R. A. (2006). A worrying trend of less ice, higher seas. *Science*, 311, 1698–701.

Kershaw, K. A. (1962). Quantitative ecological studies from Landmannahellir, Iceland. *Journal of Ecology*, 50, 171–9.

Kershner, J. L. (1997). Setting riparian/aquatic restoration objectives within a watershed context. *Restoration Ecology*, 5, 15–24.

Kirby, M. X. (2004). Fishing down the coast: historical expansion and collapse of oyster fisheries along continental margins. *Proceedings of the National Academy of Sciences of the USA*, 101, 13 096–99.

Kirk, K. L. and Gilbert, J. J. (1990). Suspended clay and the population dynamics of planktonic rotifers and cladocerans. *Ecology*, 71, 1741–55.

Klimas, C. V. (1988). River regulation effects on floodplain hydrology and ecology. In *The Ecology and Management of Wetlands*, Vol. 1, *Ecology of Wetlands*, eds. D. D. Hook, W. H. McKee, Jr., H. K. Smith, J. Gregory, V. G. Burrell, Jr., M. R. DeVoe, R. E. Sojka, S. Gilbert, R. Banks, L. H. Stolzy, C. Brooks,

T. D. Matthews, and T. H. Shear, pp. 40–9. Portland, OR: Timber Press.

Knight, R. L. and Kadlec, R. H. (2004). *Treatment Wetlands*. Boca Raton, FL: Lewis Publishers.

Koerselman, W. and Verhoeven, J. T. A. (1995). Eutrophication of fen ecosystems: external and internal nutrient sources and restoration strategies. In *Restoration of Temperate Wetlands*, eds. S. Wheeler, S. Shaw, W. Fojt, and R. Robertson, pp. 91–112. Chichester, UK: John Wiley.

Kozlowski, T. T. (ed.) (1984a). *Flooding and Plant Growth*. Orlando, FL: Academic Press.

Kozlowski, T. T. (1984b). Responses of woody plants to flooding. In *Flooding and Plant Growth*, ed. T. T. Kozlowski, pp. 129–63. Orlando, FL: Academic Press.

Kozlowski, T. T. and Pallardy, S. G. (1984). Effect of flooding on water, carbohydrate, and mineral relations. In *Flooding and Plant Growth*, ed. T. T. Kozlowski, pp. 165–93. Orlando, FL: Academic Press.

Kramer, D. L., Lindsay, C. C., Moodie, G. E. E., and Stevens, E. D. (1978). The fishes and the aquatic environment of the Central Amazon basin, with particular reference to respiratory patterns. *Canadian Journal of Zoology*, 56, 717–29.

Krieger, J. (2001). *The Economic Value of Forest Ecosystem Services: A Review*. Washington, DC: The Wilderness Society.

Kreutzwiser, R. D. (1981). The economic significance of the Long Point marsh, Lake Erie, as a recreational resource. *Journal of Great Lakes Research*, 7, 105–10.

Kuhry, P. (1994). The role of fire in the development of *Sphagnum*-dominated peatlands in western boreal Canada. *Journal of Ecology*, 82, 899–910.

Kuhry, P., Nicholson, B. J., Gignac, L. D., Vitt, D. H., and Bayley, S. E. (1993). Development of *Sphagnum*-dominated peatlands in boreal continental Canada. *Canadian Journal of Botany*, 71, 10–22.

Kurihara, Y. and Kikkawa, J. (1986). Trophic relations of decomposers. In *Community Ecology: Pattern and Process*, eds. J. Kikkawa and D. J. Anderson, pp. 127–60. Melbourne, Vic: Blackwell Scientific Publications.

Kurimo, H. (1984). Simultaneous groundwater table fluctuation in different parts of the Virgin Pine Mires. *Silva Fennica*, 18, 151–86.

Kurtén, B. and Anderson, E. (1980). *Pleistocene Mammals of North America*. New York: Columbia University Press.

Kusler, J. A. and Kentula, M. E. (eds.) (1990). *Wetland Creation and Restoration: Status of the Science*. Washington, DC: Island Press.

Kusler, J. A., Willard, D. E., and Hull, H. C., Jr. (eds.) (1995). *Wetlands and Watershed Management: Science Applications and Public Policy*. A collection of papers from a national symposium and several workshops at Tampa, FL, Apr 23–26. Berne, NY: Association of State Wetland Managers.

LaBaugh, J. W. (1989). Chemical characteristics of water in northern prairie wetlands. In *Northern Prairie Wetlands*, ed. A. G. van der Valk, pp. 56–90. Ames, IA: Iowa State University Press.

Laing, H. E. (1940). Respiration of the rhizomes of *Nuphar advenum* and other water plants. *American Journal of Botany*, 27, 574–81.

Laing, H. E. (1941). Effect of concentration of oxygen and pressure of water upon growth of rhizomes of semi-submerged water plants. *Botanical Gazette*, 102, 712–24.

Lane, P. A. (1985). A food web approach to mutualism in lake communities. In *The Biology of Mutualism: Ecology and Evolution*, ed. D. H. Boucher, pp. 344–74. New York: Oxford University Press.

Larcher, W. (1995). *Physiological Plant Ecology: Ecophysiology and Stress Physiology of Functional Groups*, 3rd edn. New York: Springer-Verlag.

Laroche, F. B. and Baker, G. E. (2001). Vegetation management within the Everglades protection area. In *2001 Everglades Consolidated Report*, Appendix 14. Miami, FL: South Florida Water Management District.

Larson, D. W. (1996). Brown's Woods: an early gravel pit forest restoration project, Ontario, Canada. *Restoration Ecology*, 4, 11–18.

Larson, J. S. (1988). Wetland creation and restoration: an outline of the scientific perspective. In *Increasing our Wetland Resources*, eds. J. Zelazny and J. S. Feierabend, pp. 73–9. Proceedings of a conference in Washington, DC, Oct 4–7, 1987. Reston, VA: National Wildlife Federation–Corporate Conservation Council.

Larson, J. S. (1990). Wetland value assessment. In *Wetlands and Shallow Continental Water Bodies*, Vol. 1, *Natural and Human Relationships*, ed.

B. C. Patten, pp. 389–400. The Hague, the Netherlands: SPB Academic Publishing.

Larson, J. S., Mueller, A. J., and MacConnell, W. P. (1980). A model of natural and man-induced changes in open freshwater wetlands on the Massachusetts coastal plain. *Journal of Applied Ecology*, 17, 667–73.

Latham, P. J., Pearlstine, L. G., and Kitchens, W. M. (1994). Species association changes across a gradient of freshwater, oligohaline, and mesohaline tidal marshes along the lower Savannah River. *Wetlands*, 14, 174–83.

Latham, R. E. and Ricklefs, R. E. (1993). Continental comparisons of temperatezone tree species diversity. In *Species Diversity in Ecological Communities: Historical and Geographical Perspectives*, eds. R. E. Ricklefs and D. Schluter, pp. 294–314. Chicago, IL: University of Chicago Press.

Laubhan, M. K. (1995). Effects of prescribed fire on moist-soil vegetation and soil macronutrients. *Wetlands*, 15, 159–66.

Lavelle, P., Dugdale, R., and Scholes, R. (eds.) (2005). Nutrient cycling. In *Ecosystems and Human Well-being: Current State and Trends – Findings of the Condition and Trends Working Group of the Millennium Ecosystem Assessment*, eds. R. Hassan, R. Scholes, and N. Ash, pp. 331–53. Washington, DC: Island Press.

Lavoisier, A. (1789). *Elements of Chemistry. In Great Books of the Western World*, 2nd edn, 1990, ed. chief M. J. Adler, pp. 1–33. Chicago, IL: Encyclopaedia Britannica Inc.

Lawler, A. (2005). Reviving Iraq's wetlands. *Science*, 307, 1186–9.

Leary, R. A. (1985). A framework for assessing and rewarding a scientist's research productivity. *Scientometrics*, 7, 29–38.

Leck, M. A. and Graveline, K. J. (1979). The seed bank of a freshwater tidal marsh. *American Journal of Botany*, 66, 1006–15.

Leck, M. A., Parker, V. T., and Simpson, R. L. (eds.) (1989). *Ecology of Soil Seed Banks*. San Diego, CA: Academic Press.

Lee, R. (1980). *Forest Hydrology*. New York: Columbia University Press.

Legendre, L. and Legendre, P. (1983). *Numerical Ecology*. Amsterdam, the Netherlands: Elsevier.

Leitch, J. A. (1989). Politicoeconomic overview of prairie potholes. In *Northern Prairie Wetlands*, ed. A. van der Valk, pp. 2–14. Ames, IA: Iowa State University Press.

Leith, H. (1975). Historical survey of primary productivity research. In *Primary Productivity of the Biosphere*, eds. H. Leith and R. H. Whittaker, pp. 7–16. New York: Springer-Verlag.

Lemly, A. D. (1982). Modification of benthic insect communities in polluted streams: combined effects of sedimentation and nutrient enrichment. *Hydrobiologia*, **87**, 229–45.

Lent, R. M., Weiskel, P. K., Lyford, F. P., and Armstrong, D. S. (1997). Hydrologic indices for nontidal wetlands. *Wetlands*, **17**, 19–30.

Leonard, M. L. and Picman, J. (1986). Why are nesting marsh wrens and yellow-headed blackbirds spatially segregated? *Auk*, **103**,135–40.

Leopold, A. (1949). *A Sand County Almanac*. New York: Oxford University Press.

Le Page, C. and Keddy, P. A. (1998). Reserves of buried seeds in beaver ponds. *Wetlands*, **18**, 242–8.

Lévêque, C., Balian, E. V., and Martens, K. (2005). An assessment of animal species diversity in continental waters. *Hydrobiologia*, **542**, 39–67.

Levin, H. L. (1992). *The Earth Through Time*, 4th edn. Forth Worth, TX: Saunders College Publishing.

Levine, J., Brewer, J. S., and Bertness, M. D. (1998). Nutrients, competition and plant zonation in a New England salt marsh. *Journal of Ecology*, **86**, 285–92.

Levitt, J. (1977). The nature of stress injury and resistance. In *Responses of Plants to Environmental Stresses*, ed. J. Levitt, pp. 11–21. New York: Academic Press.

Levitt, J. (1980). *Responses of Plants to Environmental Stresses*, Vols. 1 and 2, 2nd edn. New York: Academic Press.

Lewis, D. H. (1987). Evolutionary aspects of mutualistic associations between fungi and photosynthetic organisms. In *Evolutionary Biology of Fungi*, eds. A. D. M. Rayner, C. M. Brasier, and D. Moore, pp. 161–78. Cambridge, UK: Cambridge University Press.

Lewis, R. R., III (ed.) (1982). *Creation and Restoration of Coastal Plant Communities*. Boca Raton, FL: CRC Press.

Lieffers, V. J. (1984). Emergent plant communities of oxbow lakes in northeastern Alberta: salinity, water-level fluctuation, and succession. *Canadian Journal of Botany*, **62**, 310–16.

Liu, K. and Fearn, M. L. (2000). Holocene history of catastrophic hurricane landfalls along the Gulf of Mexico coast reconstructed from coastal lake and marsh sediments. In *Current Stresses and Potential Vulnerabilities: Implications of Global Change for the Gulf Coast Region of the United States*, eds. Z. H. Ning and K. K. Abdollhai, pp. 38–47. Baton Rouge, LA: Franklin Press for Gulf Coast Regional Climate Change Council.

Llewellyn, D. W., Shaffer, G. P., Craig, N. J., Creasman, L., Pashley, D., Swan, M., and Brown, C. (1996). A decision-support system for prioritizing restoration sites on the Mississippi River alluvial plain. *Conservation Biology*, **10**, 1446–55.

Lockwood, J. L and Pimm, S. L. (1999). When does restoration succeed? In *Ecological Assembly Rules: Perspectives, Advances, Retreats*, eds. E. Weiher and P. Keddy, pp. 363–92. Cambridge, UK: Cambridge University Press.

Lodge, D. M. (1991). Herbivory on freshwater macrophytes. *Aquatic Botany*, **41**, 195–224.

Loffler, H. and Malkhazova, S. (1990). Impacts of wetlands on man. In *Wetlands and Shallow Continental Water Bodies*, Vol. 1, *Natural and Human Relationships*, ed. B. C. Patten, pp. 347–62. The Hague, the Netherlands: SPB Academic Publishing.

Loope, L., Duever, M., Herndon, A., Snyder, J., and Jansen, D. (1994). Hurricane impact on uplands and freshwater swamp forest. *BioScience*, **44**, 238–46.

Louda, S. and Mole, S. (1991). Glucosinolates: chemistry and ecology. In *Herbivores: Their Interactions with Secondary Plant Metabolites*, eds. G. A. Rosenthal and M. R. Berenbaum, pp. 124–64. San Diego, CA: Academic Press.

Louda, S. M., Keeler, K. H., and Holt, R. D. (1990). Herbivore influences on plant performance and competitive interactions. In *Perspectives in Plant Competition*, eds. J.B. Grace and D. Tilman, pp. 413–44. New York: Academic Press.

Loveless, C. M. (1959). A study of the vegetation in the Florida everglades. *Ecology*, **40**, 1–9.

Lowe-McConnell, R. H. (1975). *Fish Communities in Tropical Freshwaters: Their Distribution, Ecology and Evolution*. London: Longman.

Lowe-McConnell, R. H. (1987). Fish of the Amazon System. In *The Ecology of River Systems*, eds. B. R. Davies and K. F. Walker, pp. 339–51. Dordrecht, the Netherlands: Dr. W. Junk Publishers.

Lowery, G. H. (1974). *The Mammals of Louisiana and its Adjacent Waters*. Baton Rouge, LA: Louisiana State University Press.

Lu, J. (1995). Ecological significance and classification of Chinese wetlands. *Vegetatio*, **118**, 49–56.

Lugo, A. E. and Brown, S. (1988). The wetlands of Caribbean islands. *Acta Científica*, **2**, 48–61.

Lugo, A. E. and Snedaker, S. C. (1974). The ecology of mangroves. *Annual Review of Ecology and Systematics*, 5, 39–64.

Lugo, A. E., Brown, S., and Brinson, M. M. (1988). Forested wetlands in freshwater and saltwater environments. *Limnology and Oceanography*, 33, 849–909.

Lugo, A. E., Brinson, M. and Brown, S. (eds.) (1990). *Forested Wetlands*. Amsterdam, the Netherlands: Elsevier.

Lutman, J. (1978). The role of slugs in an *Agrostis-Festuca* grassland. In *Production Ecology of British Moors and Montane Grasslands*, eds. O. W. Heal and D. F. Perkins, pp. 332–47. Berlin, Germany: Springer-Verlag.

Lynch, J. A., Grimm, J. W., and Bowersox, V. C. (1995). Trends in precipitation chemistry in the United States: a national perspective, 1980–1992. *Atmospheric Environment*, 29, 1231–46.

MacArthur, R. H. (1972). *Geographical Ecology*. New York: Harper and Row.

MacArthur, R. H. and MacArthur, J. (1961). On bird species diversity. *Ecology*, 42, 594–8.

MacArthur, R. and Wilson, E. O. (1967). *The Theory of Island Biogeography*. Princeton, NJ: Princeton University Press.

MacRoberts, D. T., MacRoberts, B. R., and MacRoberts, M. H. (1997). *A Floristic and Ecological Interpretation of the Freeman and Custis Red River Expedition of 1806*. Shreveport, LA: Louisiana State University Press.

Magnuson, J. J., Regier, H. A., Christie, W. J., and Sonzongi, W. C. (1980). To rehabilitate and restore Great Lake ecosystems. In *The Recovery Process in Damaged Ecosystems*, ed. J. Cairns, Jr., pp. 95–112. Ann Arbor, MI: Ann Arbor Science Publishers.

Magnuson, J. J., Paszkowski, C. A., Rahel, F. J., and Tonn, W. M. (1989). Fish ecology in severe environments of small isolated lakes in northern Wisconsin. In *Freshwater Wetlands and Wildlife*, eds. R. Sharitz and J. W. Gibbons, pp. 487–515. Conf-8603101, DOE Symposium Series No. 61. Oak Ridge, TN: Office of Scientific and Technical Information, U.S. Department of the Environment.

Maguire, L. A. (1991). Risk analysis for conservation biologists. *Conservation Biology*, 5, 123–5.

Malmer, N. (1986). Vegetational gradients in relation to environmental conditions in northwestern European mires. *Canadian Journal of Botany*, 64, 375–83.

Maltby, E. and Turner, R. E. (1983). Wetlands of the world. *Geographical Magazine*, 55, 12–17.

Maltby, E., Legg, C. J., and Proctor, C. F. (1990). The ecology of severe moorland fire on the North York Moors: effects of the 1976 fires, and subsequent surface and vegetation development. *Journal of Ecology*, 78, 490–518.

Mandossian, A. and McIntosh, R. P. (1960). Vegetation zonation on the shore of a small lake. *American Midland Naturalist*, 64, 301–8.

Mancil, E. (1980). Pullboat logging. *Journal of Forest History*, 24, 135–41.

Manfred, G. (1982). *World Energy Supply*. Berlin, Germany: Walter de Gruyter.

Mark, A. F., Johnson, P. N., Dickinson, K. J. M., and McGlone, M. S. (1995). Southern hemisphere pattered mires, with emphasis on southern New Zealand. *Journal of the Royal Society of New Zealand*, 25, 23–54.

Marquis, R. J. (1991). Evolution of resistance in plants to herbivores. *Evolutionary Trends in Plants*, 5, 23–9.

Marschner, H. (1995). *Mineral Nutrition of Higher Plants*, 2nd edn. London: Academic Press.

Martin, P. S. and Klein, R. J. (1984). *Quaternary Extinctions: A Prehistoric Revolution*. Tucson, AZ: University of Arizona Press.

Martini, I. P. (1982). Introduction to scientific studies in Hudson and James Bay. *Naturaliste Canadien*, 109, 301–5.

Maseuth, J. D. (1995). *Botany: An Introduction to Plant Biology*, 2nd edn. Philadelphia, PA: Saunders College Publishing.

Matthews, E. and Fung, I. (1987). Methane emission from natural wetlands: global distribution, area, and environmental characteristics of sources. *Global Biogeochemical Cycles*, 1, 61–86.

Matthews, W. J. (1998). *Patterns in Freshwater Fish Ecology*. New York: Chapman and Hall.

Maun, M. A. and Lapierre, J. (1986). Effects of burial by sand on seed germination and seedling emergence of four dune species. *American Journal of Botany*, 73, 450–5.

May, R. M. (1981). Patterns in multi-species communities. In *Theoretical Ecology*, ed. R. M. May, pp. 197–227. Oxford, UK: Blackwell Scientific Publications.

May, R. M. (1986). The search for patterns in the balance of nature: advances and retreats. *Ecology*, 67, 1115–26.

May, R. M. (1988). How many species are there on Earth? *Science*, 241, 1441–9.

Mayewski, P. A., Lyons, W. B., Spencer, M. J., Twickler, M. S., Buck, C. F., and Whitlow, S. (1990). An ice-core record of atmospheric response to anthropogenic sulphate and nitrate. *Nature*, 346, 554–6.

Mayr, E. (1982). *The Growth of Biological Thought: Diversity, Evolution, and Inheritance*, Cambridge, MA: Belknap Press of Harvard University Press.

Mazzotti, F. J., Center, T. D., Dray, F. A. and Thayer, D. (1997). *Ecological Consequences of Invasion by* Melaleuca quinquenervia *in Southern Florida Wetlands: Paradise Damaged, Not Lost*. Gainesville, FL: University of Florida, Institute of Food and Agricultural Sciences.

McAuliffe, J. R. (1984). Competition for space, disturbance, and the structure of a benthic stream community. *Ecology*, 65, 894–908.

McCanny, S. J., Keddy, P. A., Arnason, T. J., Gaudet, C. L., Moore, D. R. J., and Shipley, B. (1990). Fertility and the food quality of wetland plants: a test of the resource availability hypothesis. *Oikos*, 59, 373–81.

McCarthy, K. A. (1987). Spatial and temporal distributions of species in two intermittent ponds in Atlantic County, NJ. M.Sc. thesis, Rutgers University, Rutgers, NJ.

McClure, J. W. (1970). Secondary constituents of aquatic angiosperms. In *Phytochemical Phylogeny*, ed. J. B. Harborne, pp. 233–65. New York: Academic Press.

McDougall, D. (2008). Global warning's front line. *Guardian Weekly*, Apr 11, p. 42.

McGeoch, M. A. and Gaston, K. J. (2002). Occupancy frequency distributions: patterns, artifacts and mechanism. *Biological Reviews*, 77, 311–31.

McHarg, I. L. (1969). *Design with Nature*. Garden City, NJ: Natural History Press for American Museum of Natural History.

McIntosh, R. P. (1967). The continuum concept of vegetation. *Botanical Review*, 33, 130–87.

McIntosh, R. P. (1985). *The Background of Ecology: Concept and Theory*. Cambridge, UK: Cambridge University Press.

McIver, S. B. (2003). *Death in the Everglades: The Murder of Guy Bradley, America's First Martyr to Environmentalism*. Gainesville, FL: University of Florida Press.

McJannet, C. L., Keddy, P. A., and Pick, F. R. (1995). Nitrogen and phosphorus tissue concentrations in 41 wetland plants: a comparison across habitats and functional groups. *Functional Ecology*, 9, 231–8.

McKee, K. L. and Mendelssohn, I. A. (1989). Response of a freshwater marsh plant community to increased salinity and increased water level. *Aquatic Botany*, 34, 301–16.

McKenzie, D. H., Hyatt, D. E., and McDonald, V. J. (1992). *Ecological Indicators*, Vols. 1 and 2. London: Elsevier.

McMillan, M. (2006). Bog turtles make new friends: landowners and livestock. *Environmental Defense Fund, Center for Conservation Incentives*. www.edf. org. May 27, 2004, updated: Sep 13, 2006. (accessed July 17, 2008)

McNaughton, S. J., Russ, R. W., and Seagle, S. W. (1988). Large mammals and process dynamics in African ecosystems. *BioScience*, 38, 794–800.

McPhee, J. (1989). *The Control of Nature*. New York: Farrar Straus Giroux.

McWilliams, R. G. (transl. and ed.) (1981). *Iberville's Gulf Journals*. Tuscaloosa, AL: University of Alabama Press.

Mead, K. (2003). *Dragonflies of the North Woods*. Duluth, MN: Kollath-Stensaas.

Meadows, D. H., Meadows, D. L., Randers, J., and Behrens, W. W., III (1974). *The Limits to Growth: A Report for the Club of Rome's Project on the Predicament of Mankind*, 2nd edn. New York: New American Library.

Meave, J. and Kellman, M. (1994). Maintenance of rain forest diversity in riparian forests of tropical savannas: implications for species conservation during Pleistocene drought. *Journal of Biogeography*, 21, 121–35.

Meave, J., Kellman, M., MacDougall, A., and Rosales, J. (1991). Riparian habitats as tropical refugia. *Global Ecology and Biogeography Letters*, 1, 69–76.

Mendelssohn, I. A. and McKee, K. L. (1988). *Spartina alterniflora* die-back in Louisiana: time-course investigation of soil waterlogging effects. *Journal of Ecology*, 76, 509–21.

Menges, E. S. and Gawler, S. C. (1986). Fourth-year changes in population size of the endemic Furbish's Lousewort: implications for endangerment and management. *Natural Areas Journal*, 6, 6–17.

Merritt, R. W. and Cummins, K. W. (eds.) (1984). *An Introduction to the Aquatic Insects of North America*, 2nd edn. Dubuque, IA: Kendall/Hunt Publishing.

Messina, M. G. and Conner, W. H. (eds.) (1998). *Southern Forested Wetlands: Ecology and Management*. Boca Raton, FL: Lewis Publishers.

Michener, W. K., Blood, E. R., Bildstein, K. L., Brinson, M. M., and Gardner, L. R. (1997). Climate change, hurricanes and tropical storms, and rising sea level in coastal wetlands. *Ecological Applications*, 7, 770–801.

Middleton, B. A. (ed.) (2002). *Flood Pulsing in Wetlands: Restoring the Natural Hydrological Balance*. New York: John Wiley.

Millennium Ecosystem Assessment. (2005). *Ecosystems and Human Well-Being: Wetlands and Water Synthesis*. Washington, DC: World Resources Institute.

Miller, G. R. and Watson, A. (1978). Heather productivity and its relevance to the regulation of red grouse populations. In *Production Ecology of British Moors and Montane Grasslands*, eds. O. W. Heal and D. F. Perkins, pp. 278–85. Berlin, Germany: Springer-Verlag.

Miller, G. R. and Watson, A. (1983). Heather moorland in northern Britain. In *Conservation in Perspective*, eds. A. Warren and F. B. Goldsmith, pp. 101–17. Chichester, UK: John Wiley.

Miller, M. W. and Nudds, T. D. (1996). Prairie landscape change and flooding in the Mississippi River valley. *Conservation Biology*, 10, 847–53.

Miller, R. M., Smith, C. I., Jastrow, J. D., and Bever, J. D. (2001). Mycorrhizal status of the genus *Carex* (Cyperaceae). *American Journal of Botany*, 86, 547–53.

Miller, R. S. (1967). Pattern and process in competition. *Advances in Ecological Research*, 4, 1–74.

Miller, R. S. (1968). Conditions of competition between redwings and yellowheaded blackbirds. *Journal of Animal Ecology*, 37, 43–62.

Milliman, J. D. and Meade, R. H. (1983). World-wide delivery of river sediment to the oceans. *Journal of Geology*, 91, 1–21.

Mitchell, G. F. (1965). Littleton Bog, Tipperary: an Irish vegetational record. *Geological Society of America, Special Paper*, 84, 1–16.

Mitsch, W. J. and Gosselink, J. G. (1986). *Wetlands*. New York: Van Nostrand Reinhold.

Mitsch, W. J. and Wu, X. (1994). Wetlands and global change. In *Advances in Soil Science: Global Carbon Sequestration*, eds. B. A. Stewart, R. Lal, and J. M. Kimble, pp. 205–30. Chelsea, MI: Lewis Publishers.

Mitsch, W. J., Day, J. W., Jr., Gilliam J. W., Groffman P. M., Hey, D. L., Randall, G. W., and Wang, N. (2001). Reducing nitrogen loading to the Gulf of Mexico from the Mississippi River Basin: strategies to counter a persistent ecological problem. *BioScience*, 51, 373–88.

Moeller, R. E. (1978). Carbon-uptake by the submerged hydrophyte *Utricularia purpurea*. *Aquatic Botany*, 5, 209–16.

Monda, M. J., Ratti, J. T., and McCabe, T. R. (1994). Reproductive ecology of tundra swans on the arctic national wildlife refuge, Alaska. *Journal of Wildlife Management*, 58, 757–73.

Montague, C. L. and Wiegert, R. G. (1990). Salt marshes. In *Ecosystems of Florida*, eds. R. L. Myers and J. J. Ewel, pp. 481–516. Orlando, FL: University of Central Florida Press.

Montgomery, K. G. (1958). *The Memoirs of Field-Marshal the Viscount Montgomery of Alamein*. London: Collins.

Moore, D. R. J. (1998). The ecological component of ecological risk assessment: lessons from a field experiment. *Human and Ecological Risk Assessment*, 4, 1103–23.

Moore, D. R. J. and Keddy, P. A. (1989). The relationship between species richness and standing crop in wetlands: the importance of scale. *Vegetatio*, 79, 99–106.

Moore, D. R. J. and Wein, R. W. (1977). Viable seed populations by soil depth and potential site recolonization after disturbance. *Canadian Journal of Botany*, 55, 2408–12.

Moore, D. R. J., Keddy, P. A., Gaudet, C. L., and Wisheu, I. C. (1989). Conservation of wetlands: do infertile wetlands deserve a higher priority? *Biological Conservation*, **47**, 203–17.

Moore, P. D. (1973). The influence of prehistoric cultures upon the initiation and spread of blanket bog in upland Wales. *Nature*, **241**, 350–3.

Moorhead, K. K. and Reddy, K. R. (1988). Oxygen transport through selected aquatic macrophytes. *Journal of Environmental Quality*, **17**, 138–42.

Morgan, M. D. and Philipp, K. R. (1986). The effect of agricultural and residential development on aquatic macrophytes in the New Jersey Pine Barrens. *Biological Conservation*, **35**, 143–58.

Morowitz, H. J. (1968). *Energy Flow in Biology*. New York: Academic Press.

Morris, J. (1973). *Pax Britannica*, 3 Vols. London: Faber and Faber. Reprinted 1992 by Folio Society, London.

Mosepele, K., Moyle, P. B., Merron, G. S., Purkey, D. R., and Mosepele B. (2009). Fish, floods and ecosystem engineers: aquatic conservation in the Okavango Delta, Botswana. *BioScience*, **59**, 53–64.

Moss, B. (1983). The Norfolk Broadland: experiments in the restoration of a complex wetland. *Biological Reviews of the Cambridge Philosophical Society*, **58**, 521–61.

Moss, B. (1984). Medieval man-made lakes: progeny and casualties of English social history, patients of twentieth century ecology. *Transactions of the Royal Society of South Africa*, **45**, 115–28.

Mountford, J. O., Lakhani, K. H., and Kirkham, F. W. (1993). Experimental assessment of the effects of nitrogen addition under hay-cutting and aftermath grazing on the vegetation of meadows on a Somerset peat moor. *Journal of Applied Ecology*, **30**, 321–32.

Mueller-Dombois, D. and Ellenberg, H. (1974). *Aims and Methods of Vegetation Ecology*. New York: John Wiley.

Müller, J., Rosenthal, G., and Uchtmann, H. (1992). Vegetationsveränderungen und Ökologie nordwestdeutscher Feuchtgrünlandbrachen. *Tuexenia*, **12**, 223–44.

Müller, J., Irion, G., de Mello, J. N., and Junk, W. J. (1995). Hydrological changes of the Amazon during the last glacial–interglacial cycle in Central Amazonia (Brazil). *Naturwissenschaften*, **82**, 232–5.

Murkin, H. R. (1989). The basis for food chains in prairie wetlands. In *Northern Prairie Wetlands*, ed. A. G. van der Valk, pp. 316–38. Ames, IA: Iowa State University Press.

Mushet, D. M., Euliss, N. H., Jr., and Shaffer, T. L. (2002). Floristic quality assessment of one natural and three restored wetland complexes in North Dakota, USA. *Wetlands*, **22**, 126–38.

Myers, J. G. (1935). Zonation of vegetation along river courses. *Journal of Ecology*, **3**, 356–60.

Myers, N., Mittermeier, R. A., Mittermeier, C. G., da Fonseca, G. A. B., and Kent, J. (2000). Biodiversity hotspots for conservation priorities. *Nature*, **403**, 853–8.

Myers, R. K. and van Lear, D. H. (1998). Hurricane–fire interactions in coastal forests of the south: a review and hypothesis. *Forest Ecology and Management*, **103**, 265–76.

Myers, R. L. (1983). Site susceptibility to invasion by the exotic tree *Melaleuca quinquenervia* in southern Florida. *Journal of Applied Ecology*, **20**, 645–58.

Myers, R. S., Shaffer, G. P., and Llewellyn, D. W. (1995). Baldcypress (*Taxodium distichum* (L.) Rich.) restoration in southeastern Louisiana: the relative effects of herbivory, flooding, competition and macronutrients. *Wetlands*, **15**, 141–8.

Naiman, R. J., Johnston, C. A., and Kelley, J. C. (1988). Alteration of North American streams by beaver. *BioScience*, **38**, 753–62.

Nanson, G. C. and Beach, H. F. (1977). Forest succession and sedimentation on a meandering-river floodplain, northeast British Columbia, Canada. *Journal of Biogeography*, **4**, 229–51.

Navid, D. (1988). Developments under the Ramsar Convention. In *The Ecology and Management of Wetlands*, Vol. 2, *Management, Use and Value of Wetlands*, eds. D. D. Hook, W. H. McKee, Jr., H. K. Smith, J. Gregory, V. G. Burrell, Jr., M. R. DeVoe, R. E. Sojka, S. Gilbert, R. Banks, L. H. Stolzy, C. Brooks, T. D. Matthews, and T. H. Shear, pp. 21–7. Portland, OR: Timber Press.

Neiff, J. J. (1986). Aquatic plants of the Parana system. In *The Ecology of River Systems*, eds. B. R. Davies and K. F. Walker pp. 557–71. Dordrecht, the Netherlands: Dr. W. Junk Publishers.

Neill, W. T. (1950). An estivating bowfin. *Copeia*, **3**, 240.

Newman, S., Grace, J. B., and Koebel, J. W. (1996). The effects of nutrients and hydroperiod on mixtures of *Typha domingensis*, *Cladium jamaicense*, and *Eleocharis interstincta*: implications for Everglades restoration. *Ecological Applications*, 6, 774–83.

Newman, S., Schuette, J., Grace, J. B., Rutchey, K., Fontaine, T., Reddy, K. R., and Pietrucha, M. (1998). Factors influencing cattail abundance in the northern Everglades. *Aquatic Botany*, 60, 265–80.

New York Natural Heritage Program. (2008). *Online Conservation Guide for* Glyptemys muhlenbergii. www.acris.nynhp.org/guide.php?id=7507. (accessed July 27, 2008)

Nicholls, R. J. and Mimura, N. (1998). Regional issues raised by sea-level rise and their policy implications. *Climate Research*, 11, 5–18.

Nichols, S. A. (1999). Floristic quality assessment of Wisconsin lake plant communities with example applications. *Journal of Lake and Reservoir Management*, 15, 133–41.

Niering, W. A. and Warren, R. S. (1980). Vegetation patterns and processes in New England salt marshes. *BioScience*, 30, 301–7.

Nilsson, C. (1981). Dynamics of the shore vegetation of a north Swedish hydroelectric reservoir during a 5-year period. *Acta Phytogeographica Suecica*, 69, 1–96.

Nilsson, C. and Jansson, R. (1995). Floristic differences between riparian corridors of regulated and free-flowing boreal rivers. *Regulated Rivers: Research and Management*, 11, 55–66.

Nilsson, C. and Keddy, P. A. (1988). Predictability of change in shoreline vegetation in a hydroelectric reservoir, northern Sweden. *Canadian Journal of Fisheries and Aquatic Sciences*, 45, 1896–904.

Nilsson, C. and Wilson, S. D. (1991). Convergence in plant community structure along disparate gradients: are lakeshores inverted mountainsides? *The American Naturalist*, 137, 774–90.

Nilsson, C., Grelsson, G., Johansson, M., and Sperens, U. (1989). Patterns of plant species richness along riverbanks. *Ecology*, 70, 77–84.

Nilsson, C., Grelsson, G., Dynesius, M., Johansson, M. E., and Sperens, U. (1991). Small rivers behave like large rivers: effects of postglacial history on plant species richness along riverbanks. *Journal of Biogeography*, 18, 533–41.

Norgress, R. E. (1947). The history of the cypress lumber industry in Louisiana. *Louisiana Historical Quarterly*, 30, 979–1059.

Noss, R. (1995). *Maintaining Ecological Integrity in Representative Reserve Networks*, A World Wildlife Fund Canada/World Wildlife Fund United States Discussion Paper. Washington, DC: WWF.

Noss, R. F. and Cooperrider, A. (1994). *Saving Nature's Legacy: Protecting and Restoring Biodiversity*. Washington, DC: Defenders of Wildlife and Island Press.

Novacek, J. M. (1989). The water and the wetland resources of the Nebraska sandhills. In *Northern Prairie Wetlands*, ed. A. G. van der Valk, pp. 340–84. Ames, IA: Iowa State University Press.

Noy-Meir, I. (1975). Stability of grazing systems: an application of predator–prey graphs. *Journal of Ecology*, 63, 459–81.

Nudds, T. D., Sjoberg, K., and Lundberg, P. (1994). Ecomorphological relationships among Palearctic dabbling ducks on Baltic coastal wetlands and a comparison with the Nearctic. *Oikos*, 69, 295–303.

Nuttle, W. K., Brinson, M. M., Cahoon, D., Callaway, J. C., Christian, R. R., Chmura, G. L., Conner, W. H., Day, R. H., Ford, M., Grace, J., Lynch, J. C., Orson, R. A., Parkinson, R. W., Reed, D., Rybczyk, J. M., Smith, T. J., III, Stumpf, R. P., and Williams, K. (1997). The Working Group on Sea Level Rise and Wetland Systems: conserving coastal wetlands despite sea level rise. *Eos*, 78, 257–62.

Odum, E. P. (1971). *Principles of Ecology*. Philadelphia, PA: W. B. Saunders.

Odum, E. P. (1985). Trends expected in stressed ecosystems. *BioScience*, 35, 419–22.

Odum, W. E. and McIvor, C. C. (1990). Mangroves. In *Ecosystems of Florida*, eds. R. L. Myers and J. J. Ewel, pp. 517–48. Orlando, FL: University of Central Florida Press.

Oksanen, L. (1990). Predation, herbivory, and plant strategies along gradients of primary production. In *Perspectives on Plant Competition*, eds. J. B. Grace and D. Tilman, pp. 445–74. New York: Academic Press.

Oksanen, L., Fretwell, S. D., Arruda, J., and Niemela, P. (1981). Exploitation ecosystems in gradients of primary productivity. *The American Naturalist*, 118, 240–261.

O'Neil, T. (1949). *The Muskrat in the Louisiana Coastal Marshes*. New Orleans, LA: Louisiana Department of Wildlife and Fisheries.

Ontario Ministry of Natural Resources. (1993). *Ontario Wetland Evaluation System: Southern Manual*, 3rd edn, revised 2002. Toronto, ON: Ontario Ministry of Natural Resources.

Ontario Ministry of Natural Resources. (2007). *Significant Wetlands and the Ontario Wetland Evaluation System*. Peterborough, ON: Ontario Ministry of Natural Resources.

Oomes, M. J. M and Elberse, W. T. (1976). Germination of six grassland herbs in microsites with different water contents. *Journal of Ecology*, 64, 745–55.

Orson, R. A., Simpson, R. L., and Good, R. E. (1990). Rates of sediment accumulation in a tidal freshwater marsh. *Journal of Sedimentary Petrology*, 60, 859–69.

Orson, R. A., Simpson, R. L., and Good, R. E. (1992). The paleoecological development of a late Holocene, tidal freshwater marsh of the Upper Delaware River estuary. *Estuaries*, 15, 130–46.

Osborne, P. L. and Polunin, N. V. C. (1986). From swamp to lake: recent changes in a lowland tropical swamp. *Journal of Ecology*, 74, 197–210.

Ostrofsky, M. L. and Zettler, E. R. (1986). Chemical defenses in aquatic plants. *Journal of Ecology*, 74, 279–87.

Padgett, D. J. and Crow, G. E. (1993). A comparison of floristic composition and species richness within and between created and natural wetlands of southeastern New Hampshire. In *Proceedings of the 20th Annual Conference on Wetlands Restoration and Creation*, ed. F. J. Webb, Jr., pp. 171–86. Tampa, FL: Hillsborough Community College.

Padgett, D. J. and Crow, G. E. (1994). Foreign plant stock: concerns for wetland mitigation. *Restoration and Management Notes*, 12, 168–71.

Painter, S. and Keddy, P. A. (1992). *Effects of Water Level Regulation on Shoreline Marshes: A Predictive Model Applied to the Great Lakes*. Burlington, ON: Environment Canada, National Water Research Institute.

Painter, T. J. (1991). Lindow Man, Tollund Man, and other peat-bog bodies: the preservative and antimicrobial action of sphagnan, a reactive glycuronoglycan with tanning and sequestering properties. *Carbohydrate Polymers*, 15, 123–42.

Palczynski, A. (1984). Natural differentiation of plant communities in relation to hydrological conditions of the Biebrza valley. *Polish Ecological Studies*, 10, 347–85.

Parmalee, P. W. and Graham, R. W. (2002). Additional records of the Giant Beaver, *Castoroides*, from the mid-South: Alabama, Tennessee, and South Carolina. *Smithsonian Contributions to Paleobiology*, 93, 65–71.

Partow, H. (2001). *The Mesopotamian Marshlands: Demise of an Ecosystem*, Early Warning and Assessment Technical Report. Nairobi, Kenya: United Nations Environment Programme.

Partridge, T. R. and Wilson, J. B. (1987). Salt tolerance of salt marsh plants of Otago, New Zealand. *New Zealand Journal of Botany*, 25, 559–66.

Patrick, W. H., Jr. and Reddy, C. N. (1978). Chemical changes in rice soils. In *Soils and Rice*, pp. 361–79. Los Baños, Philippines: International Rice Research Institute.

Patten, B. C. (ed.) (1990). *Wetlands and Shallow Continental Water Bodies*, Vol. 1, *Natural and Human Relationships*. The Hague, the Netherlands: SPB Academic Publishing.

Patten, D. T. (1998). Riparian ecosystems of semi-arid North America: diversity and human impacts. *Wetlands*, 18, 498–512.

Peace–Athabasca Delta Implementation Committee. (1987). *Peace–Athabasca Delta Water Management Works Evaluation: Final Report*. Ottawa, ON: Environment Canada, Alberta Environment and Saskatchewan Water Corporation.

Peace–Athabasca Delta Project Group. (1972). *The Peace–Athabasca Delta Summary Report, 1972*. Ottawa, ON: Department of the Environment.

Peach, M. and Zedler, J. B. (2006). How tussocks structure sedge meadow vegetation. *Wetlands*, 26, 322–35.

Pearce, F. (1991). The rivers that won't be tamed. *New Scientist*, 1764, 38–41.

Pearce, F. (1993). Draining life from Iraq's marshes. *New Scientist*, 1869, 11–12.

Pearman, P. B. (1997). Correlates of amphibian diversity in an altered landscape of Amazonian Ecuador. *Conservation Biology*, 11, 1211–25.

Pearsall, W. H. (1920). The aquatic vegetation of the English Lakes. *Journal of Ecology*, 8, 163–201.

Pearse, P. H., Bertrand, F. X., and MacLaren, J. W. (1985). *Currents of Change, Final Report*. Ottawa, ON: Inquiry on Federal Water Policy.

Peat, H. J. and Fitter, A. H. (1993). The distribution of arbuscular mycorrhizae in the British flora. *New Phytologist*, **125**, 845–54.

Pechmann, J. H. K., Scott, D. E., Gibbons, J. W., and Semlitsch, R. D. (1989). Influence of wetland hydroperiod on diversity and abundance of metamorphosing juvenile amphibians. *Wetlands Ecology and Management*, **1**, 3–11.

Pedersen, O., Sand-Jensen, K., and Revsbech, N. P. (1995). Diel pulses of O_2 and CO_2 in sandy lake sediments inhabited by *Lobelia dortmanna*. *Ecology*, **76**, 1536–45.

Peet, R. K. (1974). The measurement of species diversity. *Annual Review of Ecology and Systematics*, **5**, 285–307.

Peet, R. K. and Allard, D. J. (1993). Longleaf pine vegetation of the southern Atlantic and eastern Gulf Coast regions: a preliminary classification. In *The Longleaf Pine Ecosystem: Ecology, Restoration and Management*, ed. S. M. Hermann, pp. 45–81. Tallahassee, FL: Tall Timbers Research Station.

Pehek, E. L. (1995). Competition, pH, and the ecology of larval *Hyla andersonii*. *Ecology*, **76**, 1786–93.

Pemberton, R. W., Goolsby, J. A., and Wright, T. (2002). Old world climbing fern. In *Biological Control of Invasive Plants in the Eastern United States*, Publication No. FHTET-2002-04, eds. R. Van Driesche, S. Lyon, B. Blossey, M. Hoddle, and R. Reardon, pp. 139–47. Morgantown, WV: U.S. Department of Agriculture Forest Service.

Pengelly, J. W., Tinkler, K. J., Parkins, W. G., and McCarthy, F. M. (1997). 12 600 years of lake level changes, changing sills, ephemeral lakes and Niagara gorge erosion in the Niagara Peninsula and Eastern Lake Erie basin. *Journal of Paleolimnology*, **17**, 377–402.

Penland, S., Boyd, R., and Suter, J. R. (1988). The transgressive depositional systems of the Mississippi delta plain: a model for barrier shoreline and shelf sand development. *Journal of Sedimentary Petrology*, **58**, 932–49.

Pennings, S. C. and Callaway, R. M. (1992). Salt marsh zonation: the relative importance of competition and physical factors. *Ecology*, **73**, 681–90.

Pennings, S. C., Carefoot, T. H., Siska, E. L., Chase, M. E., and Page, T. A. (1998). Feeding preferences of a generalist salt-marsh crab: relative importance of multiple plant traits. *Ecology*, **79**, 1968–79.

Perkins, D. F. (1978). Snowdonia grassland: introduction, vegetation and climate. In *Production Ecology of British Moors and Montane Grasslands*, eds. O. W. Heal and D. F. Perkins, pp. 290–6. Berlin, Germany: Springer-Verlag.

Peters, R. H. (1980a). From natural history to ecology. *Perspectives in Biology and Medicine*, **23**, 191–203.

Peters, R. H. (1980b). Useful concepts for predictive ecology. In *Conceptual Issues in Ecology*, ed. E. Saarinen, pp. 63–99. Dordrecht, the Netherlands: D. Reidel.

Peterson, L. P., Murkin, H. R., and Wrubleski, D. A. (1989). Waterfowl predation on benthic macroinvertebrates during fall drawdown of a northern prairie marsh. In *Freshwater Wetlands and Wildlife*, eds. R. R. Sharitz and J. W. Gibbons, pp. 661–96. Washington, DC: U.S. Department of Energy.

Petr, T. (1986). The Volta River system. In *The Ecology of River Systems*, eds. B. R. Davies and K. F. Walker, pp. 163–83. Dordrecht, the Netherlands: Dr. W. Junk Publishers.

Pezeshki, S. R., Delaune, R. D., and Patrick, W. H., Jr. (1987a). Effects of flooding and salinity on photosynthesis of *Sagittaria Lancifolia*. *Marine Ecology Progress Series*, **41**, 87–91.

Pezeshki, S. R., Delaune, R. D., and Patrick, W. H., Jr. (1987b). Response of the freshwater marsh species *Panicum hemitomon* Schult. to increased salinity. *Freshwater Biology*, **1**, 195–200.

Pfadenhauer, J. and Klotzli, F. (1996). Restoration experiments in middle European wet terrestrial ecosystems: an overview. *Vegetatio*, **126**, 101–15.

Phillips, G. L., Eminson, D., and Moss, B. (1978). A mechanism to account for macrophyte decline in progressively eutrophicated fresh-waters. *Aquatic Botany*, **4**, 103–26.

Phipps, R. W. (1883). *On the Necessity of Preserving and Replanting Forests*. Toronto, ON: Blackett and Robinson.

Pianka, E. R. (1981). Competition and niche theory. In *Theoretical Ecology*, ed. R. M. May, pp. 114–41. Oxford, UK: Blackwell Scientific Publications.

Pickett, S. T. A. (1980). Non-equilibrium coexistence of plants. *Bulletin of the Torrey Botanical Club*, **107**, 238–48.

Pickett, S. T. A. and White, P. S. (1985). *The Ecology of Natural Disturbance and Patch Dynamics*. Orlando, FL: Academic Press.

Picman, J. (1984). Experimental study on the role of intra- and inter-specific behaviour in marsh wrens. *Canadian Journal of Zoology*, 62, 2353–6.

Pieczynska, E. (1986). Littoral communities and lake eutrophication. In *Land Use Impacts on Aquatic Ecosystems*, eds. J. Lauga, H. Decamps, and M. M. Holland, Proceedings of the Toulouse Workshop organized by MAB-UNESCO and PIREN-CNRS, pp. 191–201 Paris: UNESCO.

Pielou, E. C. (1975). *Ecological Diversity*. New York: John Wiley.

Pielou, E. C. (1977). *Mathematical Ecology*. New York: John Wiley.

Pielou, E. C. and Routledge, R. D. (1976). Salt marsh vegetation: latitudinal gradients in the zonation patterns. *Oecologia*, 24, 311–21.

Pietropaolo, J. and Pietropaolo, P. (1986). *Carnivorous Plants of the World*. Portland, OR: Timber Press.

Pimental, D., Hurd, L. E., Bellotti, A. C., Forster, M. J., Oka, I., Sholes, O. D., and Whitman, W. J. (1973). Food production and the energy crisis. *Science*, 182, 443–9.

Poiana, K. A. and Johnson, W. C. (1993). A spatial simulation model of hydrology and vegetation dynamics in semi-permanent prairie wetlands. *Ecological Applications*, 3, 279–93.

Polunin, N. V. C. (1984). The decomposition of emergent macrophytes in fresh water. *Advances in Ecological Research*, 14, 115–66.

Pomeroy, L. R. and Wiegert, R. J. (eds.) (1981). *The Ecology of a Salt Marsh*. Berlin, Germany: Springer-Verlag.

Ponnamperuma, F. N. (1972). The chemistry of submerged soils. *Advances in Agronomy*, 24, 29–96.

Ponnamperuma, F. N. (1984). Effects of flooding on soils. In *Flooding and Plant Growth*, ed. T. T. Kozlowski, pp. 9–45. Orlando, FL: Academic Press.

Poole, R. W. and Rathcke, B. J. (1979). Regularity, randomness, and aggregation in flowering phenologies. *Science*, 203, 470–1.

Power, M. E. (1992). Top-down and bottom-up forces in food webs: do plants have primacy? *Ecology*, 73, 733–46.

Prance, G. T. and Schaller, J. B. (1982). Preliminary study of some vegetation types of the Pantanal, Mato Grosso, Brazil. *Brittonia*, 34, 228–51.

Pressey, R. L., Humphries, C. J., Margules, C. R., Vane-Wright, R. I., and Williams, P. H. (1993). Beyond opportunism: key principles for systematic reserve selection. *Trends in Ecology and Evolution*, 8, 124–8.

Preston, F. W. (1962a). The canonical distribution of commonness and rarity: Part I. *Ecology*, 43, 185–215.

Preston, F. W. (1962b). The canonical distribution of commonness and rarity: Part II. *Ecology*, 43, 410–32.

Price, M. V. (1980). On the significance of test form in benthic salt-marsh foraminifera. *Journal of Foraminiferal Research*, 10, 129–35.

Prince, H. H. and D'Itri, F. M. (eds.) (1985). *Coastal Wetlands*. Chelsea, MI: Lewis Publishers.

Prince, H. H. and Flegel, C. S. (1995). Breeding avifauna of Lake Huron. In *The Lake Huron Ecosytem: Ecology, Fisheries and Management*, eds. M. Munawar, T. Edsall, and J. Leach, pp. 247–72. Amsterdam, the Netherlands: SPB Academic Publishing.

Prince, H. H., Padding, P. I., and Knapton, R. W. (1992). Waterfowl use of the Laurentian Great Lakes. *Journal of Great Lakes Research*, 18, 673–99.

Prowse, T. D. and Culp, J. M. (2003). Ice breakup: a neglected factor in river ecology. *Canadian Journal of Civil Engineering*, 30, 128–44.

Radford, A. E., Ahles H. E., and Bell, C. R. (1968). *Manual of the Vascular Flora of the Carolinas*. Chapel Hill, NC:University of North Carolina Press.

Rapport, D. J. (1989). What constitutes ecosystem health? *Perspectives in Biology and Medicine*, 33, 120–32.

Rapport, D. J., Thorpe, C., and Hutchinson, T. C. (1985). Ecosystem behaviour under stress. *The American Naturalist*, 125, 617–40.

Rasker, R. and Hackman, A. (1996). Economic development and the conservation of large carnivores. *Conservation Biology*, 10, 991–1002.

Raunkiaer, C. (1908). The statistics of life forms as a basis for biological plant geography. In *The Life Forms of Plants and Statistical Plant Geography: Being the Collected Papers of Raunkiaer*, pp. 111–47. Oxford, UK: Clarendon Press.

Raunkiaer, C. (1937). *Plant Life Forms*, translated by H. Gilbert-Cater. Oxford, UK: Clarendon Press.

Raup, H. M. (1975). Species versatility in shore habitats. *Journal of the Arnold Arboretum*, 56, 126–63.

Raven, P. H., Evert, R. F., and Eichhorn, S. E. (1992). *Biology of Plants*, 5th edn. New York: Worth Publishers.

Ravera, O. (1989). Lake ecosystem degradation and recovery studied by the enclosure method. In *Ecological Assessment of Environmental Degradation, Pollution and Recovery*, ed. O. Ravera. Amsterdam, the Netherlands: Elsevier.

Rawes, M. and Heal, O. W. (1978). The blanket bog as part of a Pennine moorland. In *Production Ecology of British Moors and Montane Grasslands*, eds. O. W. Heal and D. F. Perkins, pp. 224–43. Berlin, Germany: Springer-Verlag.

Rayamajhi, M. B., Purcell, M. F., Van, T. K., Center, T. D., Pratt, P. D., and Buckingham, G. R. (2002). Australian paperbark tree (*Melaleuca*). In *Biological Control of Invasive Plants in the Eastern United States*, Publication No. FHTET-2002–04, eds. R. Van Driesche, S. Lyon, B. Blossey, M. Hoddle, and R. Reardon, pp. 117–30. Morgantown, WV: U.S. Department of Agriculture Forest Service.

Read, D. J., Koucheki, H. K., and Hodgson, J. (1976). Vesicular–arbuscular mycorrhizae in natural vegetation systems. I. The occurrence of infection. *New Phytologist*, **77**, 641–53.

Read, D. J., Francis, R., and Finlay, R. D. (1985). Mycorrhizal mycelia and nutrient cycling in plant communities. In *Ecological Interactions in Soil*, ed. A. H. Fitter, pp. 193–217. Oxford: Blackwell Scientific Publications.

Reddoch, J. and Reddoch, A. (1997). The orchids in the Ottawa district. *Canadian Field-Naturalist*, **111**, 1–185.

Reddy, K. R. and Patrick, W. H. (1984). Nitrogen transformations and loss in flooded soils and sediments. *CRC Critical Reviews in Environmental Control*, **13**, 273–309.

Reid, D. M. and Bradford, K. J. (1984). Effect of flooding on hormone relations. In *Flooding and Plant Growth*, ed. T. W. Kozlowski, pp. 195–219. Orlando, FL: Academic Press.

Reid, W. V., McNeely, J. A., Tunstall, J. B., Bryant, D. A., and Winograd, M. (1993). *Biodiversity Indicators for Policymakers*. Washington, DC: World Resources Institute.

Rejmankova, E., Pope, K. O., Pohl, M. D., and Rey-Benayas, J. M. (1995). Freshwater wetland plant communities of northern Belize: implications for paleoecological studies of Maya wetland agriculture. *Biotropica*, **27**, 28–36.

Reuss, M. (1998). *Designing the Bayous: The Control of Water in the Atchafalaya Basin 1800–1995*. Alexandria, VA: U.S. Army Corps of Engineers Office of History.

Reynoldson, T. B. and Zarull, M. A. (1993). An approach to the development of biological sediment guidelines. In *Ecological Integrity and the Management of Ecosystems*, eds. S. Woodley, J. Kay, and G. Francis, pp. 177–200. Delray Beach, FL: St. Lucie Press.

Reznicek, A. A. and Catling, P. M. (1989). Flora of Long Point. *Michigan Botanist*, **28**, 99–175.

Richardson, C. J. (ed.) (1981). *Pocosin Wetlands: An Integrated Analysis of Coastal Plain Freshwater Bogs in North Carolina*. Stroudsburg, PA: Hutchinson Ross.

Richardson, C. J. (1985). Mechanisms controlling phosphorus retention capacity in freshwater wetlands. *Science*, **228**, 1424–7.

Richardson, C. J. (1989). Freshwater wetlands: transformers, filters, or sinks? In *Freshwater Wetlands and Wildlife*, eds. R. R. Sharitz and J. W. Gibbons, pp. 25–46. Proceedings of a symposium held at Charleston, South Carolina, Mar 24–27, 1986. Washington, DC: U.S. Department of Energy.

Richardson, C. J. (1991). Pocosins: an ecological perspective. *Wetlands*, **11**, 335–54.

Richardson, C. J. (1995). Wetlands ecology. In *Encyclopedia of Environmental Biology*, Vol. 3, ed. W. A. Nierenberg, pp. 535–50. San Diego, CA: Academic Press.

Richardson, C. J. and Gibbons, J. W. (1993). Pocosins, Carolina bays and mountain bogs. In *Biodiversity of the Southeastern United States*, eds. W. H. Martin, S. G. Boyce, and A. C. Echternacht, pp. 257–310. New York: John Wiley.

Richey, J. E., Meade, R. H., Salati, E., Devol, A. H., Nordin, C. F., and dos Santos, U. (1986). Water discharge and suspended sediment concentrations in the Amazon River: 1982–1984. *Water Resources Research*, **23**, 756–64.

Richter, B. D., Braun, D. P., Mendelson, M. A., and Master, L. L. (1997). Threats to imperiled freshwater fauna. *Conservation Biology*, **11**, 1081–93.

Richter, K. O. and Azous, A. L. (1995). Amphibian occurrence and wetland characteristics in the Puget Sound Basin. *Wetlands*, **15**, 305–12.

Richter, S. C. and Seigel, R. A. (2002). Annual variation in the population ecology of the endangered gopher frog, *Rana sevosa* Goin and Netting. *Copeia*, 2002, 962–72.

Richter, S. C, Young, J. E., Seigel, R. A., and Johnson, G. N. (2001). Postbreeding movements of the dark gopher frog, *Rana sevosa* Goin and Netting: implications for conservation and management. *Journal of Herpetology,* 35, 316–21.

Richter, S. C., Young, J. E., Johnson, G. N., and Seigel, R. A. (2003). Stochastic variation in reproductive success of a rare frog, *Rana sevosa*: implications for conservation and for monitoring amphibian populations. *Biological Conservation*, 111, 171–7.

Rickerl, D. H., Sancho, F. O., and Ananth, S. (1994). Vesicular–arbuscular endomycorrhizal colonization of wetland plants. *Journal of Environmental Quality*, 23, 913–16.

Ricklefs, R. E. (1987). Community diversity: relative roles of local and regional processes. *Science*, 235, 167–71.

Rigler, F. H. (1982). Recognition of the possible: an advantage of empiricism in ecology. *Canadian Journal of Fisheries and Aquatic Sciences*, 39, 1323–31.

Rigler, F. H. and Peters, R. H. (1995). *Science and Limnology*. Oldendorf/Lutie, Germany: Ecology Institute.

Riley, J. L. (1982). Hudson Bay lowland floristic inventory, wetlands catalogue and conservation strategy. *Naturaliste Canadien*, 109, 543–55.

Riley, J. L. (1989). Southern Ontario bogs and fens off the Canadian Shield. In *Wetlands: Inertia or Momentum?* Conference Proceedings, Oct 21–22, pp. 355–67. Toronto, ON: Federation of Ontario Naturalists.

Riley, T. Z. and Bookhout, T. A. (1990). Responses of aquatic macroinvertebrates to early-spring drawdown in nodding smartweed marshes. *Wetlands*, 10, 173–85.

Ritchie, J. C. (1987). *Postglacial Vegetation of Canada*. New York: Cambridge University Press.

Roberts, J. and Ludwig, J. A. (1991). Riparian vegetation along current-exposure gradients in floodplain wetlands of the River Murray, Australia. *Journal of Ecology*, 79, 117–27.

Robertson, P. A., Weaver, G. T., and Cavanaugh, J. A. (1978). Vegetation and tree species patterns near the northern terminus of the southern floodplain forest. *Ecological Monographs*, 48, 249–67.

Robertson, R. J. (1972). Optimal niche space of the redwinged blackbird (*Agelaius phoeniceus*).

I. Nesting success in marsh and upland habitat. *Canadian Journal of Zoology*, 50, 247–63.

Robins, R. H. (n.d.). Walking catfish. www.flmnh.ufl. edu/fish/Gallery/Descript/WalkingCatfish/ WalkingCatfish.html (accessed June 1, 2008)

Robinson, A. R. (1973). Sediment, our greatest pollutant? In *Focus on Environmental Geology*, ed. R. W. Tank, pp. 186–92. London: Oxford University Press.

Rogers, D. R., Rogers, B. D., and Herke, W. H. (1992). Effects of a marsh management plan on fishery communities in coastal Louisiana. *Wetlands*, 12, 53–62.

Rolston, H. (1994). Foreword. In *An Environmental Proposal for Ethics: The Principle of Integrity*, ed. L. Westra, pp. xi–xiii. Lanham, MD: Rowman and Littlefield. In Noss, R. (1995). *Maintaining Ecological Integrity in Representative Reserve Networks*, A World Wildlife Fund Canada/World Wildlife Fund United States Discussion Paper. Washington, DC: WWF.

Roni, P., Hanson, K., Beechie, T., Pess, G., Pollock, M., and Bartley, D. M. (2005). *Habitat Rehabilitation for Inland Fisheries: Global Review of Effectiveness and Guidance for Rehabilitation of Freshwater Ecosystems*, FAO Fisheries Technical Paper No. 484. Rome, Italy: Food and Agriculture Organization.

Rood, S. B. and Mahoney, J. M. (1990). Collapse of riparian poplar forests downstream from dams in western prairies: probable causes and prospects for mitigation. *Environmental Management*, 14, 451–64.

Root, R. (1967). The niche exploitation pattern of the blue-grey gnatcatcher. *Ecological Monographs*, 37, 317–50.

Rørslett, B. (1984). Environmental factors and aquatic macrophyte response in regulated lakes: a statistical approach. *Aquatic Botany*, 19, 199–220.

Rørslett, B. (1985). Regulation impact on submerged macrophytes in the oligotrophic lakes of Setesdal, South Norway. *International Association for Theoretical and Applied Limnology*, 22, 2927–36.

Rosen, B. H., Gray, S., and Flaig, E. (1995). Implementation of Lake Okeechobee watershed management strategies to control phosphorus load. In *Wetlands and Watershed Management: Science Applications and Public Policy*, eds. J. A. Kusler, D. E. Willard, and H. C. Hull, Jr., pp. 199–207.

A collection of papers from a national symposium and several workshops at Tampa, FL, Apr 23–26. Berne, NY: Association of State Wetland Managers.

Rosenberg, D. M. and Barton, D. R. (1986). The Mackenzie river system. In *The Ecology of River Systems*, eds. B. R. Davies and K. F. Walker, pp. 425–33. Dordrecht, the Netherlands: Dr. W. Junk Publishers.

Rosenberg, D. M., Bodaly, R. A., and Usher, P. J. (1995). Environmental and social impacts of large scale hydro-electric development: who is listening? *Global Environmental Change*, 5, 127–48.

Rosenthal, G. A. and Berenbaum, M. R. (eds.) (1991). *Herbivores: Their Interactions with Secondary Plant Metabolites*. San Diego, CA: Academic Press.

Rosenzweig, M. L. (1995). *Species Diversity in Space and Time*. Cambridge, UK: Cambridge University Press.

Rosgen, D. L. (1994). A classification of natural rivers. *Catena*, 22, 169–99.

Rosgen, D. L. (1995). River restoration utilizing natural stability concepts. In *Wetlands and Watershed Management: Science Applications and Public Policy*, eds. J. A. Kusler, D. E. Willard, and H. C. Hull, Jr., pp. 55–62. A collection of papers from a national symposium and several workshops at Tampa, FL, Apr 23–26. Berne, NY: Association of State Wetland Managers.

Rosswall, T. (1983). The nitrogen cycle. In *The Major Biogeochemical Cycles and Their Interactions*, SCOPE Report No. 21, eds. B. Bolin and R. B. Cook, pp. 46–50. Chichester, UK: John Wiley.

Rothhaupt, K. O. (1990). Resource competition of herbivorous zooplankton: a review of approaches and perspectives. *Archives in Hydrobiology*, 118, 1–29.

Rowe, C. L. and W. A. Dunson. (1995). Impacts of hydroperiod on growth and survival of larval amphibians in temporary ponds of Central Pennsylvania, USA. *Oecologia*, 102, 397–403.

Rozan, T. F., Hunter, K. S., and Benoit, G. (1994). Industrialization as recorded in floodplain deposits of the Quinnipiac River, Connecticut. *Marine Pollution Bulletin*, 28, 564–9.

Ryan, P. A. (1991). Environmental effects of sediment on New Zealand streams: a review. *New Zealand Journal of Marine and Freshwater Research*, 25, 207–21.

Rybicki, N. B. and Carter, V. (1986). Effect of sediment depth and sediment type on the survival of *Vallisneria americana* Michx. grown from tubers. *Aquatic Botany*, 24, 233–40.

Salisbury, F. B. and Ross, C. W. (1988). *Plant Physiology*, 3rd edn. Belmont, CA: Wadsworth.

Salisbury, S. E. (1970). The pioneer vegetation of exposed muds and its biological features. *Philosophical Transactions of the Royal Society of London Series B*, 259, 207–55.

Salo, J., Kalliola, R., Hakkinen, I., Makinen, Y., Niemela, P., Puhakka, M., and Coley, P. D. (1986). River dynamics and the diversity of Amazon lowland forest. *Nature*, 322, 254–8.

Sanders, N. K. (1972). *The Epic of Gilgamesh*, an English version with an introduction by N. K. Sanders, rev edn. London: Penguin Books.

Sand-Jensen, K. and Krause-Jensen, D. (1997). Broad-scale comparison of photosynthesis in terrestrial and aquatic plant communities. *Oikos*, 80, 203–8.

Sansen, U. and Koedam, N. (1996). Use of sod cutting for restoration of wet heathlands: revegetation and establishment of typical species in relation to soil conditions. *Journal of Vegetation Science*, 7, 483–6.

Santelmann, M. V. (1991). Influences on the distribution of *Carex exilis*: an experimental approach. *Ecology*, 72, 2025–37.

Sanzone, S. and McElroy, A. (eds.) (1998). *Ecological Impacts and Evaluation Criteria for the Use of Structures in Marsh Management*, EPA-SAB-EPEC-98-003. Washington, DC: U.S. Environmental Protection Agency Science Advisory Board.

Sather, J. H. and Smith, R. D. (1984). *An Overview of Major Wetland Functions*, FWS/OBS-84/18. Washington, DC: U.S. Fish and Wildlife Service.

Sather, J. H., Smith, R. D., and Larson, J. S. (1990). Natural values of wetlands. In *Wetlands and Shallow Continental Water Bodies*, Vol. 1, *Natural and Human Relationships*, ed. B. C. Patten, pp. 373–87. The Hague, the Netherlands: SPB Academic Publishing.

Saucier, R. T. (1963). *Recent Geomorphic History of the Pontchartrain Basin*. Baton Rouge, LA: Louisiana State University Press.

Saunders, D. A., Hobbs, R. J., and Ehrlich, P. R. (eds.) (1993). *Nature Conservation 3: Reconstruction of Fragmented Ecosystems Global and Regional Perspectives*. Chipping Norton, NSW: Surrey Beatty.

Savile, D.B.O. (1956). Known dispersal rates and migratory potentials as clues to the origin of the North American biota. *American Midland Naturalist*, **56**, 434–53.

Scagel, R.F., Bandoni, R.J., Rouse, G.E., Schofield, W.B., Stein, J.R., and Taylor, T.M.C. (1966). *Plant Diversity: An Evolutionary Approach*. Belmont, CA: Wadsworth.

Scharf, F.S., Juanes, F., and Sutherland, M. (1998). Inferring ecological relationships from the edges of scatter diagrams: comparison of regression techniques. *Ecology*, **79**, 448–60.

Schiemer, F., Baumgartner, C., and Tockner, K. (1999). Restoration of floodplain rivers: the 'Danube Restoration Project'. *Regulated Rivers: Research and Management*, **15**, 231–44.

Schindler, D.W. (1977). Evolution of phosphorus limitation in lakes. *Science*, **195**, 260–2.

Schindler, D.W. (1987). Detecting ecosystem responses to anthropogenic stress. *Canadian Journal of Fisheries and Aquatic Sciences*, **44**, 6–25.

Schneider, E., Tudor, M., and Staras, M, M. (eds.) (2008). *Evolution of Babina Polder after Restoration Works: Agricultural Polder Babina, A Pilot Project of Ecological Restoration*. Frankfurt am Main, Germany: WWF Germany, and Tulcea, Romania: Danube Delta National Institute for Research and Development.

Schneider, R. (1994). The role of hydrologic regime in maintaining rare plant communities of New York's coastal plain pondshores. *Biological Conservation*, **68**, 253–60.

Schnitzler A. (1995). Successional status of trees in gallery forest along the river Rhine. *Journal of Vegetation Science*, **6**, 479–86.

Schoener, T.W. (1974). Resource partitioning in ecological communities. *Science*, **185**, 27–39.

Schoener, T.W. (1985). Some comments on Connell's and my reviews of field experiments on interspecific competition. *The American Naturalist*, **125**, 730–40.

Scholander, P.F., Hammel, H.T., Bradstreet, E.D., and Hemmingsen, E.A. (1965). Sap pressure in vascular plants. *Science*, **148**, 339–46.

Schröder, H.K., Andersen, H.E., Kiehl, K., and Kenkel, N. (2005). Rejecting the mean: estimating the response of fen plant species to environmental factors by non-linear quantile regression. *Journal of Vegetation Science*, **16**, 373–82.

Schubel, J.R., Shen, H., and Park, M. (1986). Comparative analysis of estuaries bordering the Yellow Sea. In *Estuarine Variability*, ed. D.A. Wolfe, pp. 43–62. San Diego, CA: Academic Press.

Schuyt, K. and Brander, L. (2004). *Living Waters: Conserving the Source of Life – The Economic Values of the World's Wetlands*. Amsterdam, the Netherlands: European Union, and Gland, Switzerland: World Wildlife Fund.

Scott, W.S. and Wylie, N.P. (1980). The environmental effects of snow dumping: a literature review. *Journal of Environmental Management*, **10**, 219–40.

Sculthorpe, C.D. (1967). *The Biology of Aquatic Vascular Plants*. Reprinted 1985 Edward Arnold, by London.

Segers, R. (1998). Methane production and methane consumption: a review of processes underlying wetland methane fluxes. *Biogeochemistry*, **41**, 23–51.

Seidl, A.F. and Moraes, A.S. (2000). Global valuation of ecosystem services: application to the Pantanal da Nhecolandia, Brazil. *Ecological Economics*, **33**, 1–6.

Serbesoff-King, K. (2003). Melaleuca in Florida: a literature review on the taxonomy, distribution, biology, ecology, economic importance and control measures. *Journal of Aquatic Plant Management*, **41**, 98–112.

Severinghaus, W.D. (1981). Guild theory development as a mechanism for assessing environmental impact. *Environmental Management*, **5**, 187–90.

Seward, A.C. (1931). *Plant Life Through the Ages*. London: Cambridge University Press.

Shaffer, G.P., Sasser, C.E., Gosselink, J.G., and Rejmanek, M. (1992). Vegetation dynamics in the emerging Atchafalaya Delta, Louisiana, USA. *Journal of Ecology*, **80**, 677–87.

Shankman, D., Keim, B.D., and Song, J. (2006). Flood frequency in China's Poyang Lake region: trends and teleconnections. *International Journal of Climatology*, **26**, 1255–66.

Shannon, R.D., White, J.R., Lawson, J.E., and Gilmour, B.S. (1996). Methane efflux from emergent vegetation in peatlands. *Journal of Ecology*, **84**, 239–46.

Sharitz, R.R. and McCormick, J.F. (1973). Population dynamics of two competing annual plant species. *Ecology*, **54**, 723–40.

Sharitz, R.R. and Gibbons, J.W. (eds.) (1989). *Freshwater Wetlands and Wildlife*. Proceedings of a symposium held at Charleston, South Carolina, Mar 24–27, 1986. Washington, DC: U.S. Department of Energy.

Sharitz, R. R. and Mitsch, W. J. (1993). Southern floodplain forests. In *Biodiversity of the Southeast United States/Lowland Terrestrial Communities*, eds. W. H. Martin, S. G. Boyce, and A. C. Echternacht, pp. 311–71. New York: John Wiley.

Sharp, M. J. and Keddy, P. A. (1985). Biomass accumulation by *Rhexia virginica* and *Triadenum fraseri* along two lakeshore gradients: a field experiment. *Canadian Journal of Botany*, 63, 1806–10.

Shay, J. M. and Shay, C. T. (1986). Prairie marshes in western Canada, with specific reference to the ecology of five emergent macrophytes. *Canadian Journal of Botany*, 64, 443–54.

Sheail, J. and Wells, T. C. E. (1983). The Fenlands of Huntingdonshire, England: a case study in catastrophic change. In *Ecosystems of the World*, Vol. 4B, *Mires: Swamp, Bog, Fen and Moor – Regional Studies*, ed. A. J. P. Gore, pp. 375–93. Amsterdam, the Netherlands: Elsevier.

Sheldon, S. P. (1987). The effects of herbivorous snails on submerged macrophyte communities in Minnesota lakes. *Ecology*, 68, 1920–31.

Sheldon, S. P. (1990). More on freshwater snail herbivory: a reply to Bronmark. *Ecology*, 71, 1215–16.

Shimwell, D. W. (1971). *The Description and Classification of Vegetation*. Seattle, WA: University of Washington Press.

Shipley, B. (2000). *Cause and Correlation in Biology*. Cambridge, UK: Cambridge University Press.

Shipley, B. and Keddy, P. A. (1987). The individualistic and community-unit concepts as falsifiable hypotheses. *Vegetatio*, 69, 47–55.

Shipley, B. and Keddy, P. A. (1994). Evaluating the evidence for competitive hierarchies in plant communities. *Oikos*, 69, 340–5.

Shipley, B. and Parent, M. (1991). Germination responses of 64 wetland species in relation to seed size, minimum time to reproduction and seedling relative growth rate. *Functional Ecology*, 5, 111–18.

Shipley, B. and Peters, R. H. (1990). A test of the Tilman model of plant strategies: relative growth rate and biomass partitioning. *The American Naturalist*, 136, 139–53.

Shipley, B., Keddy, P. A., Moore, D. R. J., and Lemky, K. (1989). Regeneration and establishment strategies of emergent macrophytes. *Journal of Ecology*, 77, 1093–110.

Shipley, B., Keddy, P. A., Gaudet, C., and Moore, D. R. J. (1991a). A model of species density in shoreline vegetation. *Ecology*, 72, 1658–67.

Shipley, B., Keddy, P. A., and Lefkovitch, L. P. (1991b). Mechanisms producing plant zonation along a water depth gradient: a comparison with the exposure gradient. *Canadian Journal of Botany*, 69, 1420–4.

Shrader-Frechette, K. S. and McCoy, E. D. (1993). *Methods in Ecology: Strategies for Conservation*. Cambridge, UK: Cambridge University Press.

Siegel, S. (1956). *Nonparametric Statistics for the Behavioral Sciences*. New York: McGraw-Hill.

Silander, J. A. and Antonovics, J. (1982). Analysis of interspecific interactions in a coastal plant community: a perturbation approach. *Nature*, 298, 557–60.

Silliman, B. R. and Zieman, J. C. (2001). Top-down control of *Spartina alterniflora* production by periwinkle grazing in a Virginia salt marsh. *Ecology*, 82, 2830–845.

Silliman, B. R., Grosholz, E. D., and Bertness, M. D. (eds.) (2009). *Human Impacts on Salt Marshes: A Global Perspective*. Berkeley, CA: University of California Press.

Silvola, J., Alm, J., Ahlholm, U., Nykanen, H., and Martikainen, P. J. (1996). CO_2 fluxes from peat in boreal mires under varying temperature and moisture conditions. *Journal of Ecology*, 84, 219–28.

Simberloff, D. and Dayan, T. (1991). The guild concept and the structure of ecological communities. *Annual Review of Ecology and Systematics*, 22, 115–43.

Simons, M. (1997). Big, bold effort revives the Danube wetlands. *The New York Times*, Oct 19, 1997, pp. 1, 8.

Sinclair, A. R. E. (1983). The adaptations of African ungulates and their effects on community function. In *Tropical Savannas*, ed. F. Boulière, pp. 401–22. Amsterdam, the Netherlands: Elsevier.

Sinclair, A. R. E. and Fryxell, J. M. (1985). The Sahel of Africa: ecology of a disaster. *Canadian Journal of Zoology*, 63, 987–94.

Sinclair, A. R. E, Hik, D. S., Schmitz, O. J., Scudder, G. G. E., Turpin, D. H., and Larter, N. C. (1995).

Biodiversity and the need for habitat renewal. *Ecological Applications*, **5**, 579–87.

Sioli, H. (1964). General features of the limnology of Amazonia. *Verhandlungen Internationale Vereinigung für theoretische und angewandte Limnologie*, **15**, 1053–8.

Sioli, H. (1986). Tropical continental aquatic habitats. In *Conservation Biology: The Science of Scarcity and Diversity*, ed. M. E. Soulé, pp. 383–93. Sunderland, MA: Sinauer Associates.

Sippel, S. J., Hamilton, S. K., Melack, J. M., and Novo, E. M. M. (1998). Passive microwave observations of inundation area and the area/stage relation in the Amazon River floodplain. *International Journal of Remote Sensing*, **19**, 3055–74.

Skellam, J. G. (1951). Random dispersal in theoretical populations. *Biometrika*, **38**, 196–218.

Sklar, F. H. and van der Valk, A. G. (eds.) (2002). *Tree Islands of the Everglades*. Dordrecht, the Netherlands: Kluwer.

Sklar, F. H., Chimney, M. J., Newman, S., McCormick, P., Gawlick, D., Miao, S., McVoy, C., Said, W., Newman, J., Coronado, C., Crozier, G., Korvela, M., and Rutchey, K. (2005). The ecological–societal underpinnings of Everglades restoration. *Frontiers in Ecology and Environment*, **3**, 161–9.

Slack, N. G., Vitt, D. H., and Horton, D. G. (1980). Vegetation gradients of minerotrophically rich fens in western Alberta. *Canadian Journal of Botany*, **58**, 330–50.

Slovic, P. (1987). Perception of risk. *Science*, **236**, 280–5.

Smart, R. M. and Barko, J. W. (1978). Influence of sediment salinity and nutrients on the physiological ecology of selected salt marsh plants. *Estuarine and Coastal Marine Science*, **7**, 487–95.

Smith, D. C. and Douglas, A. E. (1987). *The Biology of Symbiosis*. London: Edward Arnold.

Smith, D. W. and Cooper, S. D. (1982). Competition among Cladocera. *Ecology*, **63**, 1004–15.

Smith, E. K. (2006). *Bog Turtle* (Clemmys muhlenbergii), *Fish and Wildlife Habitat Management Leaflet No. 44*. Natural Resources Conservation Service, Washington, D.C. and Wildlife Habitat Council, Silver Spring. MD. ftp-fc.sc.egov.usda.gov/WHMI/WEB/pdf/TechnicalLeaflets/bog_turtle_Oct%2023.pdf

Smith, L. M. (2003). *Playas of the Great Plains*. Austin, TX: University of Texas Press.

Smith, L. M. and Kadlec, J. A. (1983). Seed banks and their role during the drawdown of a North American marsh. *Journal of Applied Ecology*, **20**, 673–84.

Smith, L. M. and Kadlec, J. A. (1985a). Fire and herbivory in a Great Salt Lake marsh. *Ecology*, **66**, 259–65.

Smith, L. M. and Kadlec, J. A. (1985b). Comparisons of prescribed burning and cutting of Utah marsh plants. *Great Basin Naturalist*, **45**, 463–6.

Smith, P. G. R., Glooschenko, V., and Hagen, D. A. (1991). Coastal wetlands of three Canadian Great Lakes: inventory, current conservation initiatives, and patterns of variation. *Canadian Journal of Fisheries and Aquatic Sciences*, **48**, 1581–94.

Smith, V. H. (1982). The nitrogen and phosphorus dependence of algal biomass in lakes: an empirical and theoretical analysis. *Limnology and Oceanography*, **27**, 1101–12.

Smith, V. H. (1983). Low nitrogen to phosphorus ratios favor dominance by bluegreen algae in lake phytoplankton. *Science*, **221**, 669–71.

Snodgrass, J. W., Komoroski, M. J., Bryan, A. L., Jr., and Burger, J. (2000). Relationships among isolated wetland size, hydroperiod, and amphibian species richness: implications for wetland regulations. *Conservation Biology*, **14**, 414–19.

Snow, A. A. and Vince, S. W. (1984). Plant zonation in an Alaskan salt marsh. II. An experimental study of the role of edaphic conditions. *Journal of Ecology*, **72**, 669–84.

Society for Ecological Restoration International Science and Policy Working Group (SER). (2004). *The SER International Primer on Ecological Restoration*. Tucson, AZ: Society for Ecological Restoration. www.ser.org

Sousa, W. P. (1984). The role of disturbance in natural communities. *Annual Review of Ecology and Systematics*, **15**, 353–91.

Southwood, T. R. E. (1977). Habitat, the templet for ecological strategies? *Journal of Animal Ecology*, **46**, 337–65.

Southwood, T. R. E. (1988). Tactics, strategies, and templets. *Oikos*, **52**, 3–18.

Specht, A. and Specht, R. L. (1993). Species richness and canopy productivity of Australian plant communities. *Biodiversity and Conservation*, **2**, 152–67.

Spence, D. H. N. (1964). The macrophytic vegetation of freshwater lochs, swamps and associated fens.

In *The Vegetation of Scotland*, ed. J. H. Burnett, pp. 306–425. Edinburgh, UK: Oliver and Boyd.

Spence, D. H. N. (1982). The zonation of plants in freshwater lakes. *Advances in Ecological Research*, **12**, 37–125.

Spencer, D. F. and Ksander, G. G. (1997). Influence of anoxia on sprouting of vegetative propagules of three species of aquatic plants. *Wetlands*, **17**, 55–64.

Springuel, I. (1990). Riverain vegetation in the Nile valley in Upper Egypt. *Journal of Vegetation Science*, **1**, 595–8.

Starfield, A. M. and Bleloch, A. L. (1991). *Building Models for Conservation and Wildlife Management*, 2nd edn. Edina, MN: Burgers International Group.

Stead, I. M., Bourke, J. B., and Brothwell, D. (1986). *Lindow Man: The Body in the Bog*. London: British Museum Publications.

Steedman, R. J. (1988). Modification and assessment of an index of biotic integrity to quantify stream quality in southern Ontario. *Canadian Journal of Fisheries and Aquatic Sciences*, **45**, 492–501.

Stevens, P. W., Fox, S. L., and Montague, C. L. (2006). The interplay between mangroves and saltmarshes at the transition between temperate and subtropical climate in Florida. *Wetlands Ecology and Management*, **14**, 435–44.

Stevenson, J. C., Ward, L. G., and Kearney, M. S. (1986). Vertical accretion in marshes with varying rates of sea level rise. In *Estuarine Variability*, ed. D. A. Wolfe, pp. 241–59. San Diego, CA: Academic Press.

Stewart, R. E. and Kantrud, H. A. (1971). *Classification of Natural Ponds and Lakes in the Glaciated Prairie Region*, Resource Publication No. 92. Washington, DC: U.S. Fish and Wildlife Service.

Stewart, W. N. and Rothwell, G. W. (1993). *Paleobotany and the Evolution of Plants*, 2nd edn. New York: Cambridge University Press.

Strahler, A. N. (1971). *The Earth Sciences*, 2nd edn. New York: Harper and Row.

Street, F. A. and Grove, A. T. (1979). Global maps of lake-level fluctuations since 30 000 yrs B.P. *Quaternary Research*, **12**, 83–118.

Stuart, S. A., Choat, B., Martin, K. C., Holbrook, N. M., and Ball, M. C. (2007). The role of freezing in setting the latitudinal limits of mangrove forests. *New Phytologist*, **173**, 576–83.

Stuckey, R. L. (1975). A floristic analysis of the vascular plants of a marsh at Perry's Victory Monument, Lake Erie. *Michigan Botanist*, **14**, 144–66.

Sutter, R. D. and Kral, R. (1994). The ecology, status, and conservation of two nonalluvial wetland communities in the south Atlantic and eastern Gulf coastal plain, USA. *Biological Conservation*, **68**, 235–43.

Swink, F. and Wilhelm, G. (1994). *Plants of the Chicago Region* 4th edn. Indianapolis, IN: Indiana Academy of Science.

Szalay, F. A. de and Resh, V. H. (1997). Responses of wetland invertebrates and plants important in waterfowl diets to burning and mowing of emergent vegetation. *Wetlands*, **17**, 149–56.

Szczepanski, A. J. (1990). Forested wetlands of Poland. In *Forested Wetlands*, ed. A. E. Lugo, M. Brinson and S. Brown, pp. 437–46. Amsterdam, the Netherlands: Elsevier.

Taiz, L. and Zeiger, E. (1991). *Plant Physiology*. Menlo Park, CA: Benjamin Cummings.

Talling, J. F. (1992). Environmental regulation in African shallow lakes and wetlands. *Revue d'Hydrobiologie Tropicale*, **25**, 87–144.

Tallis, J. H. (1983). Changes in wetland communities. In *Ecosystems of the World*, Vol. 4A, *Mires: Swamp, Bog, Fen and Moor – General Studies*, ed. A. J. P. Gore, pp. 311–47. Amsterdam, the Netherlands: Elsevier.

Tans, P. (2009). Recent monthly mean CO_2 at Mauna Loa. www.esol.noaa.gov/gmd/ccgg/trends (accessed May 7, 2009)

Tansley, A. G. (1939). *The British Islands and Their Vegetation*. Cambridge, UK: Cambridge University Press.

Tansley, A. G. and Adamson, R. S. (1925). Studies of the vegetation of the English chalk. III. The chalk grasslands of the Hampshire–Sussex border. *Journal of Ecology*, **13**, 177–223.

Tarr, T. L., Baber, M. J., and Babbitt, K. J. (2005). Invertebrate community structure across a wetland hydroperiod gradient in southern New Hampshire, USA. *Wetlands Ecology and Management*, **13**, 321–34.

Taylor, D. R., Aarssen, L. W., and Loehle, C. (1990). On the relationship between r/K selection and environmental carrying capacity: a new habitat templet for plant life history strategies. *Oikos*, 58, 239–50.

Taylor, J. A. (1983). The peatlands of Great Britain and Ireland. In *Ecosystems of the World*, Vol. 4B, *Mires: Swamp, Bog, Fen and Moor – Regional Studies*, ed. A. J. P. Gore, pp. 1–46. Amsterdam, the Netherlands: Elsevier.

Taylor, K. L. and Grace, J. B. (1995). The effects of vertebrate herbivory on plant community structure in the coastal marshes of the Pearl River, Louisiana, USA. *Wetlands*, 15, 68–73.

Taylor, R. B., Josenhans, H., Balcom, B. A., and Johnston, A. J. B. (2000). *Louisbourg Harbour through Time, Geological Survey of Canada Open File Report* 3896. Ottawa, ON: Geological Survey of Canada.

Teller, J. T. (1988). Lake Agassiz and its contribution to flow through the Ottawa–St. Lawrence system. In *The Late Quaternary Development of the Champlain Sea Basin*, Geological Association of Canada Special Paper No. 35, ed. N. R. Gadd, pp. 281–9. St. John's, Nfld: Geological Association of Canada.

Teller, J. T. (2003). Controls, history, outbursts and impact of large late-Quaternary proglacial lakes in North America. In *The Quaternary Period in the United States*, eds. A. Gilespie, S. Porter, and B. Atwater, pp. 45–61. Amsterdam, the Netherlands: Elsevier.

Terborgh, J. and Robinson, S. (1986). Guilds and their utility in ecology. In *Community Ecology: Pattern and Process*, eds. J. Kikkawa and D. J. Anderson, pp. 65–90. Melbourne, Vic: Blackwell Scientific Publications.

Thibodeau, F. R. and Ostro, B. D. (1981). An economic analysis of wetland protection. *Journal of Environmental Management*, 12, 19–30.

Thirgood, J. V. (1981). *Man and the Mediterranean Forest: A History of Resource Depletion*. London: Academic Press.

Thomas, J. D. (1982). Chemical ecology of the snail hosts of Schistosomiasis: snail–snail and snail–plant interactions. *Malacologia*, 22, 81–91.

Thomas, J. and Nygard, J. (eds.) (2007). *The Importance of Habitat Created by Molluscan Shellfish to Managed Species along the Atlantic Coast of the United States*, Habitat Management Series No. 8. Washington, DC: Atlantic States Marine Fisheries Commission.

Thompson, D. J. and Shay, J. M. (1988). First-year response of a *Phragmites* marsh community to seasonal burning. *Canadian Journal of Botany*, 67, 1448–55.

Thompson, K. (1985). Emergent plants of the permanent and seasonally-flooded wetlands. In *The Ecology and Management of African Wetland Vegetation*, ed. P. Denny, pp. 43–107. Dordrecht, the Netherlands: Dr. W. Junk Publishers.

Thompson, K. and Hamilton, A. C. (1983). Peatlands and swamps of the African continent. In *Ecosystems of the World*, Vol. 4B, *Mires: Swamp, Bog, Fen and Moor – Regional Studies*, ed. A. J. P. Gore, pp. 331–73. Amsterdam, the Netherlands: Elsevier.

Thoreau, H. D. (1854). Republished 1965 as *Walden and Civil Disobedience*. New York: Airmont.

Tilman, D. (1982). *Resource Competition and Community Structure*. Princeton, NJ: Princeton University Press.

Tilman, D. (1986). Evolution and differentiation in terrestrial plant communities: the importance of the soil resource: light gradient. In *Community Ecology*, eds. J. Diamond and T. J. Case, pp. 359–80. New York: Harper and Row.

Tilman, D. (1988). *Plant Strategies and the Dynamics and Structure of Plant Communities*. Princeton, NJ: Princeton University Press.

Tiner, R. W. (1999). *Wetland Indicators: A Guide to Wetland Identification, Delineation, Classification and Mapping*. Boca Raton, FL: CRC Press.

Tinkle, W. J. (1939). *Fundamentals of Zoology*. Grand Rapids, MI: Zondervan.

Todd, T. N. and Davis, B. M. (1995). Effects of fish density and relative abundance on competition between larval lake herring and lake whitefish for zooplankton. *Archiv für Hydrobiologie, Special Issues in Advanced Limnology*, 46, 163–71.

Tomlinson, P. B. (1986). *The Botany of Mangroves*. Cambridge, UK: Cambridge University Press.

Toner, M. and Keddy, P. A. (1997). River hydrology and riparian wetlands: a predictive model for ecological assembly. *Ecological Applications*, 7, 236–46.

Tonn, W. M. and Magnuson, J. J. (1982). Patterns in the species composition and richness of fish assemblages in northern Wisconsin lakes. *Ecology*, 63, 1149–66.

Tonn, W. M., Magnuson, J. J., and Forbes, A. M. (1983). Community analysis in fishery management:

an application with northern Wisconsin lakes. *Transactions of the American Fisheries Society,* **112**, 368–77.

Toth, L. A. (1993). The ecological basis of the Kissimmee River restoration plan. *Florida Scientist,* **1**, 25–51.

Townsend, A. R., Braswell, B. H., Holland, E. A., and Penner, J. E. (1996). Spatial and temporal patterns in terrestrial carbon storage due to deposition of fossil fuel nitrogen. *Ecological Applications,* **6**, 806–14.

Townsend, G. H. (1984). *Simulating the Effect of Water Regime Restoration Measures on Wildlife Populations and Habitat within the Peace–Athabasca Delta,* Technical report No. 13. Saskatoon, Sask.: Western and Northern Region, Canadian Wildlife Service.

Trombulak, S. C. and Frissell, C. A. (2000). Review of ecological effects of roads on terrestrial and aquatic communities. *Conservation Biology,* **14**, 18–30.

Tsuyuzaki, S. and Tsujii, T. (1990). Preliminary study on grassy marshland vegetation, western part of Sichuan Province, China, in relation to yak-grazing. *Ecological Research,* **5**, 271–6.

Tsuyuzaki, S., Urano, S., and Tsujii, T. (1990). Vegetation of alpine marshland and its neighboring areas, northern part of Sichuan Province, China.*Vegetatio,* **88**, 79–86.

Tuchman, B. (1984). *The March of Folly.* New York: Ballantine Books.

Turner, C. E., Center, T. D., Burrows, D. W., and Buckingham, G. R. (1998). Ecology and management of *Melaleuca quinquenervia*, an invader of wetlands in Florida, U.S.A. *Wetlands Ecology and Management,* **5**, 165–78.

Turner, R. E. (1977). Intertidal vegetation and commercial yields of penaeid shrimp. *Transactions of the American Fisheries Society,* **106**, 411–16.

Turner, R. E. (1982). Protein yields from wetlands. In *Wetlands: Ecology and Management,* Proceedings of the First International Wetlands Conference, New Delhi, India, Sept 10–17, 1980.

Turner, R. E. and Rabelais, N. N. (2003). Linking landscape and water quality in the Mississippi River Basin for 200 years. *BioScience,* **53**, 563–72.

Turner, R. E. and Streever, B. (2002). *Approaches to Coastal Wetland Restoration: Northern Gulf of Mexico.* The Hague, the Netherlands: SPB Academic Publishing.

Turner, R. E., Baustian, J. J., Swenson, E. M., and Spicer, J. S. (2006). Wetland sedimentation from hurricanes Katrina and Rita. *Science,* **314**, 449–52.

Turner, R. M. and Karpiscak, M. M. (1980). *Recent Vegetation Changes along the Colorado River between Glen Canyon Dam and Lake Mead, Arizona,* Geological Survey Professional Paper No. 1132. Washington, DC: U.S. Government Printing Office.

Tyler, G. (1971). Hydrology and salinity of Baltic sea-shore meadows: studies in the ecology of Baltic sea-shore meadows III. *Oikos,* **22**, 1–20.

Twolan-Strutt, L. and Keddy, P. A. (1996). Above- and below-ground competition intensity in two contrasting wetland plant communities. *Ecology,* **77**, 259–70.

Underwood, A. J. (1978). The detection of non-random patterns of distribution of species along a gradient. *Oecologia,* **36**, 317–26.

Underwood, A. J. (1986). The analysis of competition by field experiments. In *Community Ecology: Pattern and Process,* eds. J. Kikkawa and D. J. Anderson, pp. 240–68. Melbourne, Vic: Blackwell Scientific Publications.

Urban, D. L. and Shugart H. H. (1992). Individual based models of forest succession. In *Plant Succession,* eds. D. C. Glenn-Lewin, R. K. Peet, and T. T. Veblen, pp. 249–92. London: Chapman and Hall.

U.S. Army Coastal Engineering Research Centre. (1977). *Shore Protection Manual,* Vol. 1, 3rd edn. Washington, DC: U.S. Government Printing Office.

U.S. Army Corps of Engineers. (1987). *Corps of Engineers Wetlands Delineation Manual,* Technical Report No. Y-87-1. Vicksburg, MS: Department of the Army, Waterways Experiment Station.

U.S. Army Corps of Engineers. (2004). *The Mississippi River and Tributaries Project.* U.S. ACE, New Orleans District. www.mvn.usace.army.mil/pao/bro/misstrib.htm (accessed Apr 7, 2009)

U.S. Environmental Protection Agency. (2004). *Constructed Treatment Wetlands,* EPA 843-F-03-013. Washington, DC: U.S. Government Printing Office.

U. S. Fish and Wildlife Service. (1989). *Louisiana Pearlshell* (Margaritifera hembeli) *Recovery Plan.* Jackson, MS: U.S. Fish and Wildlife Service.

U.S. Fish and Wildlife Service. (2001). *Bog Turtle* (Clemmys muhlenbergii), *Northern Population,*

Recovery Plan. Hadley, MA: U.S. Fish and Wildlife Service.

U.S. Geological Survey. (1996). http://earthshots.usgs.gov/Knife/Knife. (accessed June 15, 2009)

U.S. Geological Survey. (2000). *Sea Level and Climate*, U.S.G.S. Fact Sheet No. 002-00. Reston, VA: U.S. Department of the Interior.

Valiela, I., Foreman, K., LaMontagne, M., Hersh, D., Costa, J., D'Avanzo, C., Babione, M., Sham, C., Brawley, J., Peckol, P., DeMeo-Anderson, B., and Lajtha, K. (1992). Couplings of watersheds and coastal waters: sources and consequences of nutrient enrichment in Waquoit Bay, Massachusetts. *Estuaries*, **15**, 443-57.

Valentine, D. L. (2002). Biogeochemistry and microbial ecology of methane oxidation in anoxic environments: a review. *Journal Antonie van Leeuwenhoek*, **81**, 271-82.

Vallentyne, J. R. (1974). *The Algal Bowl: Lakes and Man*, Miscellaneous Special Publication No. 22. Ottawa, ON: Department of the Environment, Fisheries and Marine Service.

van Breeman, N. (1995). How *Sphagnum* bogs down [sic] other plants. *Trends in Ecology and Evolution*, **10**, 270-5.

van de Kieft, C. (1991). The Low Countries. In *The New Encyclopedia Britannica*, 15th edn, Vol. **23**, 314-25. Chicago, IL: Encyclopedia Britannica Inc.

van de Rijt, C. W. C. J., Hazelhoff, L., and Blom, C. W. P. M. (1996). Vegetation zonation in a former tidal area: a vegetation-type response model based on DCA and logistic regression using GIS. *Journal of Vegetation Science*, **7**, 505-18.

van der Leeden, F., Troise, F., and Tood, D. K. (eds.) (1990). *The Water Encyclopedia*, 2nd edn. Chelsea, MI: Lewis Publishers.

van der Pijl, L. (1972). *Principles of Dispersal in Higher Plants*. New York: Springer-Verlag.

van der Toorn, J., Verhoeven, J. T. A., and Simpson, R. L. (1990). Fresh water marshes. In *Wetlands and Shallow Continental Water Bodies*, Vol. 1, ed. B. C. Patten, pp. 445-65. The Hague, the Netherlands: SPB Academic Publishing.

van der Valk, A. G. (1981). Succession in wetlands: a Gleasonian approach. *Ecology*, **62**, 688-96.

van der Valk, A. G. (1988). From community ecology to vegetation management: providing a scientific basis for management. In *Transactions of the 53 North American Wildlife and Natural Resources Conference*, pp. 463-70. Washington, DC: Wildlife Management Institute.

van der Valk, A. G. (1989). *Northern Prairie Wetlands*. Ames, IA: Iowa State University Press.

van der Valk, A. G. and Davis, C. B. (1976). The seed banks of prairie glacial marshes. *Canadian Journal of Botany*, **54**, 1832-8.

van der Valk, A. G. and Davis, C. B. (1978). The role of seed banks in the vegetation dynamics of prairie glacial marshes. *Ecology*, **59**, 322-35.

van der Valk, A. G., Swanson, S. D., and Nuss, R. F. (1983). The response of plant species to burial in three types of Alaskan wetlands. *Canadian Journal of Botany*, **61**, 1150-64.

van der Valk, A. G., Pederson, R. L., and Davis, C. B. (1992). Restoration and creation of freshwater wetlands using seed banks. *Wetlands Ecology and Management*, **1**, 191-7.

Van Wijck, C. and de Groot, C. J. (1993). The impact of desiccation of a freshwater marsh (Garcines Nord, Camargue, France) on sediment-water-vegetation interactions. *Hydrobiologia*, **252**, 95-103.

Vasseur, L. and Catto, N. R. (2008). Atlantic Canada. In *From Impacts to Adaptation: Canada in a Changing Climate 2007*, eds. D. S. Lemmen, F. J. Warren, J. Lacroic, and E. Bush, pp. 119-70. Ottawa, ON: Government of Canada.

Verhoeven, J. T. A. and Liefveld, W. M. (1997). The ecological significance of organochemical compounds in *Sphagnum*. *Acta Botanica Neerlandica*, **46**, 117-30.

Verhoeven, J. T. A., Kemmers, R. H. and Koerselman, W. (1993). Nutrient enrichment of freshwater wetlands. In *Landscape Ecology of a Stressed Environment*, eds. C. C. Vos and P. Opdam, pp. 33-59. London: Chapman and Hall.

Verhoeven, J. T. A., Koerselman, W., and Meuleman, A. F. M. (1996). Nitrogen- or phosphorus-limited growth in herbaceous, wet vegetation: relations with atmospheric inputs and management regimes. *Trends in Ecology and Evolution*, **11**, 493-7.

Verry, E. S. 1989. Selection and management of shallow water impoundments for wildlife. In *Freshwater Wetlands and Wildlife*, eds. R. R. Sharitz and J. W. Gibbons, pp. 1177-94. Washington, DC: U.S. Department of Energy.

Vesey-FitzGerald, D. F. (1960). Grazing succession among East African game animals. *Journal of Mammalogy*, **41**, 161–72.

Vijayakumar, S. P., Vasudevan, K., and Ishwar, N. M. (2001). Herpetofaunal mortality on roads in the Anamalai Hills, Southern Western Ghats. *Hamadryad*, **26**, 265–72.

Vince, S. W. and Snow, A. A. (1984). Plant zonation in an Alaskan salt marsh. I. Distribution, abundance, and environmental factors. *Journal of Ecology*, **72**, 651–67.

Vitousek, P. M. (1982). Nutrient cycling and nitrogen use efficiency. *The American Naturalist*, **119**, 553–72.

Vitousek, P. M., Aber, J., Howarth, R. W., Likens, G. E., Matson, P. A., Schindler, D. W., Schlesinger, W. H., and Tilman, G. D. (1997). *Human Alteration of Global Nitrogen Cycle: Causes and Consequences*, Issues in Ecology No. 1, Washington, DC: Ecological Society of America.

Vitt, D. H. (1990). Growth and production dynamics of boreal mosses over climatic, chemical and topographic gradients. *Botanical Journal of the Linnean Society*, **104**, 35–59.

Vitt, D. H. (1994). An overview of factors that influence the development of Canadian peatlands. *Memoirs of the Entomological Society of Canada*, **169**, 7–20.

Vitt, D. H. and Chee, W. (1990). The relationships of vegetation to surface water chemistry and peat chemistry in fens of Alberta, Canada. *Vegetatio*, **89**, 87–106.

Vitt, D. H. and Slack, N. G. (1975). An analysis of the vegetation of *Sphagnum*-dominated kettle-hole bogs in relation to environmental gradients. *Canadian Journal of Botany*, **53**, 332–59.

Vitt, D. H. and Slack, N. G. (1984). Niche diversification of *Sphagnum* relative to environmental factors in northern Minnesota peatlands. *Canadian Journal of Botany*, **62**, 1409–30.

Vitt, D. H., Yenhung, L., and Belland, R. J. (1995). Patterns of bryophyte diversity in peatlands of continental western Canada. *The Bryologist*, **98**, 218–27.

Vivian-Smith, G. (1997). Microtopographic heterogeneity and floristic diversity in experimental wetland communities. *Journal of Ecology*, **85**, 71–82.

Vogl, R. (1969). One hundred and thirty years of plant succession in a southeastern Wisconsin lowland. *Ecology*, **50**, 248–55.

Vogl, R. (1973). Effects of fire on the plants and animals of a Florida wetland. *American Midland Naturalist*, **89**, 334–47.

Vörösmarty, C. J., Fekete, B., and Tucker, B. A. (1996). *River Discharge Database*, Version 1.0, vols. 0–6. Paris: UNESCO.

Walker, B. H. and Wehrhahn, C. F. (1971). Relationships between derived vegetation gradients and measured environmental variables in Saskatchewan wetlands. *Ecology*, **52**, 85–95.

Walker, D. (1970). Direction and rate in some British post-glacial hydroseres. In *Studies in the Vegetational History of the British Isles*, eds. D. Walker and R. G. West, pp. 117–39. Cambridge, UK: Cambridge University Press.

Walters, C. (1997). Challenges in adaptive management of ripanian and coastal ecosystems. *Conservation Ecology*, **1**(2), www.consecol.org/vol1/iss2/art1/ (accessed June 15, 2008)

Wang, S., Jurik, T. M., and van der Valk, A. G. (1994). Effects of sediment load on various stages in the life and death of cattail (*Typha* × *glauca*). *Wetlands*, **14**, 166–73.

Ward, A. and S. W. Trimble. (2004). *Environmental Hydrology*, 2nd edn. Boca Raton, FL: CRC Press.

Wassen, M. J., Barendregt, A., Palczynski, A., de Smidt, J. T., and de Mars, H. (1990). The relationship between fen vegetation gradients, groundwater flow and flooding in undrained valley mire at Biebrza, Poland. *Journal of Ecology*, **78**, 1106–22.

Waterkeyn, A., Grillas, P., Vanschoenwinkel, B., and Brendonck, L. (2008). Invertebrate community patterns in Mediterranean temporary wetlands along hydroperiod and salinity gradients. *Freshwater Biology*, **53**, 1808–22.

Waters, T. F. (1995). *Sediment in Streams: Sources, Biological Effects, and Control*, American Fisheries Society Monograph No. 7. Nashville, TN: American Fisheries Society.

Watts, W. A. and Winter, T. C. (1966). Plant macrofossils from Kirchner Marsh, Minnesota: a paleoecological study. *Geological Society of America Bulletin* **77**, 1339–60.

Weaver, J. E. and Clements, F. E. (1938). *Plant Ecology*, 2nd edn. New York: McGraw-Hill.

Weber, W. and Rabinowitz, A. (1996). A global perspective on large carnivore conservation. *Conservation Biology*, **10**, 1046–54.

Weddle, R. S. (1991). *The French Thorn: Rival Explorers in the Spanish Sea, 1682-1762*. College Station, TX: Texas A&M University Press.

Weiher, E. (1999). The combined effects of scale and productivity on species richness. *Journal of Ecology*, **87**, 1005-11.

Weiher, E. and Boylen, C. W. (1994). Patterns and prediction of a and b diversity of aquatic plants in Adirondack (New York) lakes. *Canadian Journal of Botany*, **72**, 1797-804.

Weiher, E. and Keddy, P. A. (1995). The assembly of experimental wetland plant communities. *Oikos*, **73**, 323-35.

Weiher, E. and Keddy, P. A. (eds.) (1999). *Assembly Rules in Ecological Communities: Perspectives, Advances, Retreats*. Cambridge, UK: Cambridge University Press.

Weiher, E., Wisheu, I. C., Keddy, P. A., and Moore, D. R. J. (1996). Establishment, persistence, and management implications of experimental wetland plant communities. *Wetlands*, **16**, 208-18.

Weiher, E., Clarke, G. D. P., and Keddy, P. A. (1998). Community assembly rules, morphological dispersion, and the coexistence of plant species. *Oikos*, **81**, 309-22.

Weiher, E., van der Werf, A., Thompson, K., Roderick, M., Garnier E., and Eriksson, O. (1999). Challenging Theophrastus: a common core list of plant traits for functional ecology. *Journal of Vegetation Science*, **10**, 609-20.

Wein, R. W. (1983). Fire behaviour and ecological effects in organic terrain. In *The Role of Fire in Northern Circumpolar Ecosystems*, eds. R. W. Wein and D. A. Maclean, pp. 81-95. New York: John Wiley.

Weinberg, G. M. (1975). *An Introduction to General Systems Thinking*. New York: John Wiley.

Weisner, S. E. B. (1990). *Emergent Vegetation in Eutrophic Lakes: Distributional Patterns and Ecophysiological Constraints*. Lund, Sweden: Grahns Boktryckeri.

Welcomme, R. L. (1976). Some general and theoretical considerations on the fish yield of African rivers. *Journal of Fish Biology*, **8**, 351-64.

Welcomme, R. L. (1979). *Fisheries Ecology of Floodplain Rivers*. London: Longman.

Welcomme, R. L. (1986). Fish of the Niger system. In *The Ecology of River Systems*, eds. B. R. Davies and K. F. Walker, pp. 25-48. Dordrecht, the Netherlands: Dr. W. Junk Publishers.

Weller, M. W. (1978). Management of freshwater marshes for wildlife. In *Freshwater Wetlands: Ecological Processes and Management Potential*, eds. R. E. Good, D. F. Whigham, and R. L. Simpson, pp. 267-84. New York: Academic Press.

Weller, M. W. (1994a). *Freshwater Marshes: Ecology and Wildlife Management*, 3rd edn. Minneapolis, MN: University of Minnesota Press.

Weller, M. W. (1994b). Bird-habitat relationships in a Texas estuarine marsh during summer. *Wetlands*, **14**, 293-300.

Weller, M. W. (1999). *Wetland Birds: Habitat Resources and Conservation Implications*. Cambridge, UK: Cambridge University Press.

Welty, J. C. (1982). *The Life of Birds*, 3rd edn. New York: Saunders College Publishing.

Werner, E. E. (1984). The mechanisms of species interactions and community organization in fish. In *Ecological Communities: Conceptual Issues and the Evidence*, eds. D. R. Strong, Jr., D. Simberloff, L. G. Abele, and A. B. Thistle, pp. 360-82. Princeton, NJ: Princeton University Press.

Werner, E. E. and Hall, D. J. (1976). Niche shifts in sunfishes: experimental evidence and significance. *Science*, **191**, 404-6.

Werner, E. E. and Hall, D. J. (1977). Competition and habitat shift in two sunfishes (Centrarchidae). *Ecology*, **58**, 869-76.

Werner, E. E. and Hall, D. J. (1979). Foraging efficiency and habitat switching in competing sunfishes. *Ecology*, **60**, 256-64.

Werner, E. E., Skelly, D. K., Relyea R. A., and Yurewicz, K. L. (2007). Amphibian species richness across environmental gradients. *Oikos*, **116**, 1697-712.

Werner, K. J. and Zedler, J. B. (1997). Microtopographic heterogeneity and floristic diversity in experimental wetland communities. *Journal of Ecology*, **85**, 71-82.

Western, D. (1975). Water availability and its influence on the structure and dynamics of a savannah large mammal community. *African Wildlife Journal*, **13**, 265-86.

Westhoff, V. and Van der Maarel, E. (1973). The Braun-Blanquet approach. In *Ordination and Classification of Communities*, ed. R. H. Whittaker, pp. 617-726. The Hague, the Netherlands: Dr. W. Junk Publishers.

Wetzel, R. G. (1975). *Limnology*. Philadelphia, PA: W. B. Saunders.

Wetzel, R. G. (1989). Wetland and littoral interfaces of lakes: productivity and nutrient regulation in the Lawrence Lake ecosystem. In *Freshwater Wetlands and Wildlife*, eds. R. R. Sharitz and J. W. Gibbons, pp. 283–302. Proceedings of a Symposium held at Charleston, South Carolina, Mar 24–27, 1986. Washington, DC: U.S. Department of Energy.

Whalen, S. C. (2005). Biogeochemistry of methane exchange between natural wetlands and the atmosphere. *Environmental Engineering Science*, 22, 73–94.

Wheeler, B. D. and Giller, K. E. (1982). Species richness of herbaceous fen vegetation in Broadland, Norfolk in relation to the quantity of above-ground plant material. *Journal of Ecology*, 70, 179–200.

Wheeler, B. D. and Proctor, M. C. F. (2000). Ecological gradients, subdivisions and terminology of north-west European mires. *Journal of Ecology*, 88, 187–203.

Wheeler, B. D. and Shaw, S. C. (1991). Above-ground crop mass and species richness of the principal types of herbaceous rich-fen vegetation of lowland England and Wales. *Journal of Ecology*, 79, 285–301.

Whigham, D. F., Dykyjova, D., and Hejny, S. (eds.) (1992). *Wetlands of the World*, Vol. 1. Dordrecht, the Netherlands: Kluwer.

White, P. S. (1979). Pattern, process and natural disturbance in vegetation. *Botanical Review*, 45, 229–99.

White, P. S. (1994). Synthesis: vegetation pattern and process in the Everglades ecosystem. In *Everglades: The Ecosystem and its Restoration*, eds. S. Davis and J. Ogden, pp. 445–60. DelRay Beach, FL: St. Lucie Press.

White, P. S., Wilds, S. P., and Thunhorst, G. A. (1998). Southeast. In *Status and Trends of the Nation's Biological Resources*, eds. M. J. Mac, P. A. Opler, C. E. Puckett Haecker, and P. D. Doran, pp. 255–314. Reston, VA: U.S. Department of the Interior, U.S. Geological Survey.

White, T. C. R. (1993). *The Inadequate Environment*. Berlin, Germany: Springer-Verlag.

Whiting, G. J. and Chanton, J. P. (1993). Primary production control of methane emission from wetlands. *Nature*, 364, 794–5.

Whitney, D. M., Chalmers, A. G., Haines, E. B., Hanson, R. B., Pomeroy, L. R., and Sherr, B. (1981). The cycles of nitrogen and phosphorus. In *The Ecology of a Salt Marsh*, eds. L. R. Pomeroy and R. G. Wiegert, pp. 161–78. New York: Springer-Verlag.

Whittaker, R. H. (1956). Vegetation of the Great Smoky Mountains. *Ecological Monographs*, 26, 1–80.

Whittaker, R. H. (1962). Classification of natural communities. *Botanical Review*, 28, 1–160.

Whittaker, R. H. (1967). Gradient analysis of vegetation. *Biological Reviews*, 42, 207–64.

Whittaker, R. H. (1975). *Communities and Ecosystems*. New York: Macmillan.

Whittaker, R. H. and Likens, G. E. (1973). Carbon in the biota. In *Carbon in the Biosphere*, eds. G. M. Woodwell and E. R. Peacan, pp. 281–302. Springfield, VA: National Technical Information Service.

Wickware, G. M. and Rubec, C. D. A. (1989). *Ecoregions of Ontario*, Ecological Land Classification Series No. 26. Ottawa, ON: Environment Canada, Sustainable Development Branch.

Wiegers, J. (1990). Forested wetlands in western Europe. In *Forested Wetlands*, eds. A. E. Lugo, M. Brinson, and S. Brown, pp. 407–36. Amsterdam, the Netherlands: Elsevier.

Wiegert, R. G. L., Pomeroy, R., and Wiebe, W. J. (1981). Ecology of salt marshes: an introduction. In *The Ecology of a Salt Marsh*, eds. L. R. Pomeroy and R. G. Wiegert, pp. 3–20. New York: Springer-Verlag.

Wiens, J. A. (1965). Behavioral interactions of red-winged blackbirds and common grackles on a common breeding ground. *The Auk*, 82, 356–74.

Wiens, J. A. (1983). Avian community ecology: an iconoclastic view. In *Perspectives in Ornithology*, essays presented for the centennial of the American Ornithologists' Union, eds. A. H. Brush and G. A. Clark, Jr., pp. 355–403. Cambridge, UK: Cambridge University Press.

Wikramanayake, E. D. (1990). Ecomorphology and biogeography of a tropical stream fish assemblage: evolution of assemblage structure. *Ecology*, 71, 1756–64.

Wilbur, H. M. (1972). Competition, predation and the structure of the *Ambystoma–Rana sylvatica* community. *Ecology*, 53, 3–21.

Wilbur, H. M. (1984). Complex life cycles and community organization in amphibians. In *A New*

Ecology: Novel Approaches to Interactive Systems, eds. P. W. Price, C. N. Slobodchikoff, and W. S. Gaud, pp. 195–225. New York: John Wiley.

Wilcox, D. A. and Meeker, J. E. (1991). Disturbance effects on aquatic vegetation in regulated and unregulated lakes in northern Minnesota. *Canadian Journal of Botany*, **69**, 1542–51.

Wilcox, D. A. and Simonin, H. A. (1987). A chronosequence of aquatic macrophyte communities in dune ponds. *Aquatic Botany*, **28**, 227–42.

Wilcox, D. A. and Xie, Y. (2007). Predicting wetland plant responses to proposed water-level-regulation plans for Lake Ontario: GIS-based modeling. *Journal of Great Lakes Research*, **33**, 751–73.

Wilcox, D. A., Kowalski, K. P, Hoare, H. L., Carlson, M. L., and Morgan, H. N. (2008) Cattail invasion of sedge/grass meadows in Lake Ontario: photointerpretation analysis of sixteen wetlands over five decades. *Journal of Great Lakes Research*, **34**, 301–23.

Wild Earth. (1992). *The Wildlands Project*, Special Issue. Richmond, VT: Wild Earth.

Williams, C. B. (1964). *Patterns in the Balance of Nature*. London: Academic Press.

Williams, M. (1989). The lumberman's assault on the southern forest, 1880–1920. In *Americans and Their Forests: A Historical Geography*, ed. M. Williams, pp. 238–88. Cambridge, UK: Cambridge University Press.

Williamson, G. B. (1990). Allelopathy, Koch's postulates and the neck riddle. In *Perspectives on Plant Competition*, eds. J. B. Grace and D. Tilman, pp. 143–62. San Diego, CA: Academic Press.

Willis, A. J. (1963). Braunton Burrows: the effects on the vegetation of the addition of mineral nutrients to the dune soils. *Journal of Ecology*, **51**, 353–74.

Wilsey, B. J, Chabreck, R. H., and Linscombe, R. G. (1991). Variation in nutria diets in selected freshwater forested wetlands of Louisiana. *Wetlands*, **11**, 263–78.

Wilson, E. O. (1993). *The Diversity of Life*. New York: W.W. Norton.

Wilson, E. O. and Bossert, W. H. (1971). *A Primer of Population Biology*. Sunderland, MA: Sinauer Associates.

Wilson, J. A. (1972). *Principles of Animal Physiology*. New York: Macmillan.

Wilson, J. B., Wells, T. C. E., Trueman, I. C., Jones, G., Atkinson, M. D., Crawley, M. J., Dodds, M. E., and Silvertown, J. (1996). Are there assembly rules for plant species abundance? An investigation in relation to soil resources and successional trends. *Journal of Ecology*, **84**, 527–38.

Wilson, S. D. and Keddy, P. A. (1985). Plant zonation on a shoreline gradient: physiological response curves of component species. *Journal of Ecology*, **73**, 851–60.

Wilson, S. D. and Keddy, P. A. (1986a). Species competitive ability and position along a natural stress/disturbance gradient. *Ecology*, **67**, 1236–42.

Wilson, S. D. and Keddy, P. A. (1986b). Measuring diffuse competition along an environmental gradient: results from a shoreline plant community. *The American Naturalist*, **127**, 862–9.

Wilson, S. D. and Keddy, P. A. (1988). Species richness, survivorship, and biomass accumulation along an environmental gradient. *Oikos*, **53**, 375–80.

Wilson, S. D. and Keddy, P. A. (1991). Competition, survivorship and growth in macrophyte communities. *Freshwater Biology*, **25**, 331–7.

Winemiller, K. O. (1991). Ecomorphological diversification in lowland freshwater fish assemblages from five biotic regions. *Ecological Monographs*, **61**, 343–65.

Winter, T. C. and Rosenberry, D. O. (1995). The interaction of ground water with prairie pothole wetlands in the Cottonwood Lake area, east-central North Dakota, 1979–1990. *Wetlands*, **15**, 193–211.

Wisheu, I. C. (1998). How organisms partition habitats: different types of community organization can produce identical patterns. *Oikos*, **83**, 246–58.

Wisheu, I. C. and Keddy, P. A. (1989a). Species richness – standing crop relationships along four lakeshore gradients: constraints on the general model. *Canadian Journal of Botany*, **67**, 1609–17.

Wisheu, I. C. and Keddy, P. A. (1989b). The conservation and management of a threatened coastal plain plant community in eastern North America (Nova Scotia, Canada). *Biological Conservation*, **48**, 229–38.

Wisheu, I. C. and Keddy, P. A. (1991). Seed banks of a rare wetland plant community: distribution patterns and effects of human-induced disturbance. *Journal of Vegetation Science*, **2**, 181–8.

Wisheu, I. C. and Keddy, P. A. (1992). Competition and centrifugal organization of plant communities:

theory and tests. *Journal of Vegetation Science*, 3, 147–56.

Wisheu, I. C. and Keddy, P. A. (1996). Three competing models for predicting the size of species pools: a test using eastern North American wetlands. *Oikos*, 76, 253–8.

Wisheu, I. C., Keddy, P. A., Moore, D. J., McCanny, S. J., and Gaudet, C. L. (1990). Effects of eutrophication on wetland vegetation. In *Wetlands of the Great Lakes*, eds. J. Kusler and R. Smardon, pp. 112–21. Berne, NY: Association of State Wetland Managers.

Wium-Anderson, S. (1971). Photosynthetic uptake of free CO_2 by the roots of *Lobelia dortmanna*. *Plantarum*, 25, 245–8.

Wolff, W. J. (1993). Netherlands wetlands. *Hydrobiologia*, 265, 1–14.

Woo, M., Rowsell, R. D., and Clark, R. G. (1993). *Hydrological Classification of Canadian Prairie Wetlands and Prediction of Wetland Inundation in Response to Climatic Variability*, Occasional Paper No. 79. Ottawa, ON: Canadian Wildlife Service.

Woodley, S., Kay, J., and Francis, G. (eds.) (1993). *Ecological Integrity and the Management of Ecosystems*. Delray Beach, FL: St. Lucie Press.

Woodward, F. I. and Kelly, C. K. (1997). Plant functional types: towards a definition by environmental constraints. In *Plant Functional Types*, eds. T. M. Smith, H. H. Shugart, and F. I. Woodward, pp. 47–65. Cambridge, UK: Cambridge University Press.

Woodwell, G. M. and Whittaker, R. H. (1968). Effects of chronic gamma radiation on plant communities. *Quarterly Review of Biology*, 43, 42–55.

Woodwell, G. M., Mackenzie, F. T., Houghton, R. A., Apps, A. J., Gorham, E., and Davidson, E. A. (1995). Will the warming speed the warming? In *Biotic Feedbacks in the Global Climatic System*, eds. G. M. Woodwell and F. T. Mackenzie, pp. 393–411. New York: Oxford University Press.

Wootton, R. J. (1990). Biotic interaction. II. Competition and mutualism. In *Ecology of Teleost Fishes*, ed. R. J. Wootton, pp. 216–37. London: Chapman and Hall.

World Commission on Environment and Development. (1987). *Our Common Future*. Oxford, UK: Oxford University Press.

World Conservation Monitoring Centre. (1992). *Global Biodiversity: Status of the Earth's Living Resources*. London: Chapman and Hall.

World Resources Institute. (1992). *World Resources 1992–1993*. Oxford, UK: Oxford University Press.

World Wildlife Fund (WWF). (1999). *Evaluation of Wetlands and Floodplain Areas in the Danube River Basin: Final Report*. Sofia, Bulgaria: WWF Danube–Carpathian Programme, and Rastatt, Germany: WWF Auen-Institut.

World Wildlife Fund (WWF). (2003). Dikes bulldozed in Danube Delta, news release Oct 30, 2003. assets.panda.org/downloads/danube_delta_fact sheet_en.pdf

Wright, H. E. and Bent, A. M. (1968). Vegetation bands around Dead Man Lake, Chuska Mountain, New Mexico. *American Midland Naturalist*, 79, 8–30.

Wright, R. A. (2004). *A Short History of Progress*. Toronto, ON: Anansi Press.

Wu, Y., Rutchey, K., Wang, N., and Godin, J. (2006). The spatial pattern and dispersion of *Lygodium microphyllum* in the Everglades wetland ecosystem. *Biological Invasions*, 8, 1483–93.

Yabe, K. (1993). Wetlands of Hokkaido. In *Biodiversity and Ecology in the Northernmost Japan*, eds. S. Higashi, A. Osawa, and K. Kanagawa, pp. 38–49. Hokkaido, Japan: Hokkaido University Press.

Yabe, K. and Numata, M. (1984). Ecological studies of the Mobawa–Yatsumi marsh: main physical and chemical factors controlling the marsh ecosystem. *Japanese Journal of Ecology*, 34, 173–86.

Yabe, K. and Onimaru, K. (1997). Key variables controlling the vegetation of a cool–temperate mire in northern Japan. *Journal of Vegetation Science*, 8, 29–36.

Yang, S. L., Belkin, I. M., Belkina, A. I., Zhao, Q. Y., Zhu, J., and Ding, P. X. (2003). Delta response to decline in sediment supply from the Yangtze River: evidence of the recent four decades and expectations for the next half-century. *Estuarine, Coastal and Shelf Science*, 57, 689–99.

Yodzis, P. (1986). Competition, mortality, and community structure. In *Community Ecology*, eds. J. Diamond and T. J. Case, pp. 480–92. New York: Harper and Row.

Yodzis, P. (1989). *Introduction to Theoretical Ecology*. New York: Harper and Row.

Yu, Z., McAndrews, J. H., and Siddiqi, D. (1996). Influences of Holocene climate and water levels on vegetation dynamics of a lakeside wetland. *Canadian Journal of Botany*, **74**, 1602–15.

Zagwijn, W. H. (1986). *Geologie van Nederland*, Vol. 1, *Nederland in het Holoceen*. Haarlem, the Netherlands: Staatssuitgeverij, and The Hague: Rijks Geologische Dienst.

Zalidis, G. C., Mantzavelas, A. L., and Gourvelou, E. (1997). Environmental impacts on Greek wetlands. *Wetlands*, **17**, 339–45.

Zampella, R. A., Bunnell, J. F., Laidig, K. J., and Procopio, N. A. (2006). Using multiple indicators to evaluate the ecological integrity of a coastal plain stream system. *Ecological Indicators*, **6**, 644–63.

Zedler, J. B. (1988). Why it's so difficult to replace wetland functions. In *Increasing our Wetland Resources*, eds. J. Zelazny and J. S. Feierabend. Proceedings of a conference in Washington, DC, Oct 4–7, 1987. Reston, VA: National Wildlife Federation–Corporate Conservation Council.

Zedler, J. B. (1996). Ecological issues in wetland mitigation: an introduction to the forum. *Ecological Applications*, **6**, 33–7.

Zedler, J. B. and Beare, P. A. (1986). Temporal variability of salt marsh vegetation: the role of low-salinity gaps and environmental stress. In *Estuarine Variability*, ed. D. A. Wolfe, pp. 295–306. San Diego, CA: Academic Press.

Zedler, J. B. and Kercher, S. (2004). Causes and consequences of invasive plants in wetlands: opportunities, opportunists, and outcomes. *Critical Reviews in Plant Sciences*, **23**, 431–52.

Zedler, J. B. and Kercher, S. (2005). Wetland resources: status, ecosystem services, degradation, and restorability. *Annual Review of Environment and Resources*, **30**, 39–74.

Zedler, J. B. and Onuf, C. P. (1984). Biological and physical filtering in arid-region estuaries: seasonality, extreme events, and effects of watershed modification. In *The Estuary as a Filter*, ed. V. S. Kennedy, pp. 415–32. New York: Academic Press.

Zedler, J. B., Paling, E., and McComb, A. (1990). Differential responses to salinity help explain the replacement of native *Juncus kraussii* by *Typha orientalis* in Western Australian salt marshes. *Australian Journal of Ecology*, **15**, 57–72.

Zelazny, J. and Feierabend, J. S. (eds.) (1988). *Increasing our Wetland Resources*. Proceedings of a conference in Washington, DC Oct 4–7, 1987. Reston, VA: National Wildlife Federation–Corporate Conservation Council.

Zhao, S. and Fang, J. (2004). Impact of impoldening and lake restoration on land-cover changes in Dongting Lake area, Central Yangtze. *Amtio*, **33**, 311–15.

Zhulidov, A. V., Headley, J. V., Roberts, R. D., Nikanorov, A. M., and Ischenko, A. A. (1997). *Atlas of Russian Wetlands*, eds. M. J. Branned, translated by Y.V. Flingeffman and O.V. Zhulidov. Saskatoon, Sask.: Environment Canada, National Hydrology Research Institute.

Zobel, M. (1988). Autogenic succession in boreal mires: a review. *Folia Geobotanica & Phytotaxonomica*, **23**, 417–45.

Index

Locators in **bold** refer to major content
Locators in *italics* refer to figures/tables
Locators for headings with subheadings refer to general aspects of that topic only

CPSIA information can be obtained
at www.ICGtesting.com
Printed in the USA
LVHW011115171121
703569LV00002B/24